Judaism and Environmental Ethics

A Reader

Edited by Martin D. Yaffe

LEXINGTON BOOKS

Lanham • Boulder • New York • Oxford

LEXINGTON BOOKS

A division of Rowman & Littlefield Publishers, Inc.
A wholly owned subsidary of The Rowman & Littlefield Publishing Group, Inc.
4501 Forbes Boulevard, Suite 200
Lanham, MD 20706

Estover Road
Plymouth PL6 7PY
United Kingdom

British Library Cataloguing in Publication Information Available

Library of Congress Cataloging-in-Publication Data

Judaism and environmental ethics : a reader / edited by Martin D. Yaffe.
    p. cm.
    Includes bibliographical references (p.) and index.
    ISBN 0-7391-0117-X (cloth : alk. paper)—ISBN 0-7391-0118-8 (pbk. : alk. paper)
        1. Human ecology—Religious aspects—Judaism. 2. Nature—Religious aspects—Judaism.
    3. Environmental ethics. 4. Human ecology—Philosophy. I. Yaffe, Martin D.

    BM538.H85 J86 2001
    297.3'8—dc21

                                                                    00-067819

Printed in the United States of America

♾™ The paper used in this publication meets the minimum requirements of
American National Standard for Information Sciences—Permanence of Paper
for Printed Library Materials, ANSI/NISO Z39.48-1992.

To the students and teachers of the Dallas Jewish community

Contents

Part II: The Ethical Question

Part III: The Philosophical Question

Preface

If discussions of the relationships among ecology, Judaism, and philosophy were an art, or insofar as they are, this anthology might be described as the state-of-the-art concerning the interface among those three different disciplines. I have tried, at any rate, to gather the most thoughtful and probing of the current discussions and to place them in a single volume for handy reference and further reflection. By way of an introduction, I have added my own analysis and appraisal of the essays I have chosen. The introduction is meant to indicate how one might begin to understand those essays, faithfully and truthfully, for the purpose of making mutual comparisons, as well as of making further progress in thinking through the three-sided issues involved in questions of Judaism and environmental ethics. The starting-point of this reader, in other words, is that discussions of the urgency of our current environmental crisis lead to larger discussions about both Judaism and philosophy, so that the latter discussions come to share in the urgency of the former.

Among the virtues of the anthologized contributors to this volume is that each sees something of that threefold urgency.

Gratitude for help in the preparation of this volume goes first of all to my Department Chairman, and Director of the Center for Environmental Philosophy at University of North Texas, Gene Hargrove. He is "father of the *logos*" (Plato, *Symposium* 177d) for suggesting that, as a service to the budding discipline of environmental ethics within philosophy and religion departments, I collect a useful sample of philosophical assessments of Judaism's role in our coming to grips with the current ecological crisis. He hoped from the start that, as a comparative newcomer to the discussion,

I would find it philosophically instructive. I have meanwhile found it instructive from a Jewish point of view as well.

My departmental colleague Baird Callicott has been steadfastly encouraging in our frequent discussions concerning this volume, and unhesitatingly generous in supplying me with resources from his personal library.

Other friends too, not all of whom happen to be professional academics, have pressed me to clarify or modify my argument here and there in the introduction. I am thankful for their comments and criticisms, even where I did not always see to following things through their way: Ken Green, George Greene, Reid Heller, Josh Parens, Richard Ruderman, Alan Udoff, and especially Eric Rosenblum.

In addition, I have benefited from the routine and not-so-routine kindnesses of Murray Baumgarten, Tim Beale, Jeremy Benstein, Laurence Berns, Keith Brown, Joe Cohen, Jan Dickson, Manfred Gerstenfeld, David Gilner, John Grim and Mary Evelyn Tucker, Mrs. Elinor Jonas, David Mize, Ellis Rivkin, Bob Sacks, Bernard Scharfstein, Steve Shaw, and Stuart Warner.

Being pressed for technical advice and assistance, I looked to the customary competence and geniality of Judy Evans, Becky Hughes, Joann Lucksich, Patricia Smith, Kathy Stamm, and especially Derlly Boutwell. Many thanks.

Subvention needs for this volume were met thanks to the extraordinary generosity of The Nancy C. and Jeffrey A. Marcus Foundation of Dallas, and a number of private persons in the Dallas Jewish community who wish to remain anonymous.

This list would not be complete without mention of my editor at Lexington Books, Serena Leigh, who saw the possible merit of this volume from its infancy and helped nurture it to maturity.

Finally, there is the ongoing, loving support of my wife, Connie.

The readings in this volume originally appeared in the following publications and are reprinted here with minor revisions. Permission to reprint is gratefully acknowledged:

Allen, E. L., "The Hebrew View of Nature," *Journal of Jewish Studies* 2 (1951): 100–104.
Artson, Bradley Shavit, "Our Covenant with Stones: A Jewish Ecology of Earth," *Conservative Judaism* 44 (1991–92): 25–35.
Benstein, Jeremy, "'One, Walking and Studying . . .': Nature vs. Torah," *Judaism: A Quarterly Journal* 44 (1995): 146–68.
Bleich, J. David, *Contemporary Halakhic Problems, Volume III* (New York: Ktav Publishing House and Yeshiva University Press, 1989).
Blidstein, Gerald, "Man and Nature in the Sabbatical Year," *Tradition: A Journal of Orthodox Thought* 8 (1966): 48–55.
Cohen, Jeremy, "On Classical Judaism and Environmental Crisis," *Tikkun* 5, no. 2 (March/April 1990): 74–77.

Ehrenfeld, David, and Philip J. Bentley, "Judaism and the Practice of Stewardship," *Judaism: A Quarterly Journal* 34 (1985): 301–11.

Ehrenfeld, David, and Joan G. Ehrenfeld, "Some Thoughts on Nature and Judaism," *Environmental Ethics* 7 (1985): 93–95.

Jonas, Hans, "Contemporary Problems in Ethics from a Jewish Perspective," *CCAR Journal* 15 (January 1968): 27–39.

Kass, Leon R., *The Hungry Soul: Eating and the Perfecting of Our Nature* (New York: Free Press, 1994).

Katz, Eric, "Nature's Healing Power, the Holocaust, and the Environmental Crisis," *Judaism: A Quarterly Journal* 46 (1997): 79–89.

Kay, Jeanne, "Comments on the Unnatural Jew," *Environmental Ethics* 7 (1985): 189–91.

Kay, Jeanne, "Concepts of Nature in the Hebrew Bible," *Environmental Ethics* 10 (1988): 309–27.

Leopold, Aldo, "The Forestry of the Prophets," *The Forester* 18 (1920): 412–19.

Levy, Ze'ev, "Ethical Issues of Animal Welfare in Jewish Thought," *Judaism: A Quarterly Journal* 45 (1996): 47–57.

Sacks, Robert D., *Commentary on the Book of Genesis* (Lewiston, N.Y.: Edwin Mellen Press, 1990).

Schaffer, Arthur, "The Agricultural and Ecological Symbolism of the Four Species of *Sukkot*," *Tradition: A Journal of Orthodox Thought* 20 (1982): 128–40.

Schwartz, Eilon, "*Bal Tashchit*: A Jewish Environmental Precept," *Environmental Ethics* 19 (1997): 355–74.

Schwartz, Eilon, "Judaism and Nature: Theological and Moral Issues to Consider While Renegotiating a Jewish Relationship to the Natural World," *Judaism: A Quarterly Journal* 44 (1995): 437–47.

Schwarzschild, Steven S., "The Unnatural Jew," *Environmental Ethics* 6 (1984): 347–62.

Troster, Lawrence, "Created in the Image of God: Humanity and Divinity in an Age of Environmentalism," *Conservative Judaism* 44 (1991–92): 14–24.

Wyschogrod, Michael, "Judaism and the Sanctification of Nature," *The Melton Journal* 24 (spring 1991): 5–7.

Introduction

... even if the prophets were ignorant of
science, they were wise in the ways of men.

—Aldo Leopold

WHAT THIS READER IS ABOUT

The selections that fill this philosophical reader on Judaism and environmental ethics have been brought together for the following, pressing reasons:

1. Each reading is, or serves as, a thoughtful response to the current widespread but dubious opinion that Judaism, and especially the Hebrew
   Bible, are somehow responsible for our current environmental crisis,
   the large-scale spoiling of our natural surroundings caused especially
   by the careless and wasteful use of modern technology.
2. Each reading has moral recommendations, or else philosophical implications, for how Jews and others ought to face that crisis in the light of
   traditional Jewish teachings.
3. Each reading recognizes that science, religion, and philosophy approach the environmental crisis from different starting points. So each
   takes into account, to a greater or lesser extent, that any attempt to
   bring together scientific ecology, Judaism, and philosophy calls for
   some reflection on the scope and limits of what each discipline has to
   say separately.

In my introductory survey and assessment of the readings I have chosen, I
will touch on these reasons more fully.

1

Three Interrelated Questions

To say all this in another way, the selected readings represent the current state of the discussion concerning Judaism and environmental ethics. Each reading raises three separate but interrelated questions:

> *The Historical Question*: Does the Hebrew Bible, or subsequent Jewish tradition, teach environmental responsibility or not?
> *The Ethical Question*: What Jewish teachings, if any, appropriately address today's environmental crisis?
> *The Philosophical Question*: How do ecology, Judaism, and philosophy fit together, or perhaps fail to fit, in attempting to face the current crisis?

I have divided the readings into three groups, according to their emphasis on one or another of these questions.

A PRIOR QUESTION: WHY IS THIS SUBJECT INTERDISCIPLINARY?

To assess the virtues and possible shortcomings of our readings, we should begin by asking why Judaism is pertinent to environmental ethics, and why the answer to this question is unavoidably interdisciplinary. Otherwise the further questions these readings raise are apt to be dismissed as special pleading, or idiosyncratic bias in favor of either Judaism or philosophy, by those whose acquaintance with today's environmental crisis is mostly practical or technical. Admittedly, Judaism and philosophy are not exactly technical disciplines. One might easily infer, therefore, that they have little role in helping us respond properly to today's crisis, except to follow the lead of ecologists in calling attention to the crisis. Indeed, among the technically minded who find themselves on or near the front lines of our defense against environmental deterioration, neither Judaism nor philosophy seems at first glance to deserve much more respect than we usually accord camp followers. So we must ask, Why are questions about whether or not Judaism is environmentally sound *not* just technical ones, to be answered by the authoritative findings of ecologists?

Aldo Leopold versus the Bible

In replying to this question, I must step aside from the present readings for a moment, and look at an argument by one of the past century's most eloquent spokesmen on behalf of the need for environmental protection, Aldo Leopold.[1] Leopold, for one, finds it necessary to go beyond his own technical discipline, forest ecology, in order to show that environmental protection is not simply a matter to be left to experts, but a pressing moral concern for human beings and citizens in general. In his effort to explain why he considers the need for environmental protection so pressing, he goes so far as to criticize the ethical principles he claims to find in the Hebrew Bible, in contrast to alternative principles he considers more favorable to ecology nowadays. And yet, as the readings gathered in this volume will make abundantly clear, Leopold's all-too-hasty critique of what he takes to be the biblical view is highly selective and dubious.

About the Bible, or at any rate about Abraham, the model patriarch to whom the biblical text looks in narrating the background for the theological and political legislation we have since come to call biblical morality, Leopold at the beginning of his justly celebrated *A Sand County Almanac* writes as follows:

> Conservation is getting nowhere because it is incompatible with our Abrahamic concept of land. We abuse land because we regard it as a commodity belonging to us. When we see land as a community to which we belong, we may begin to use it with love and respect. There is no other way for land to survive the impact of mechanized man, nor for us to reap from it the esthetic harvest it is capable, under science, of contributing to culture.[2]

Leopold charges, peremptorily and without any further consideration of the biblical text, that Abraham and his descendants deserve contempt for viewing the land as a "commodity" that they are entitled to use or abuse at their own unrestrained convenience.[3] Leopold's proposed alternative, the only one he considers appropriate for meeting the land's urgent need to resist the encroachments of today's "mechanized man," is to view the land instead as a living part of the human community, or rather as itself a community to which humans in turn belong. Only so, he insists, will humans ever come to treat the land with proper love and respect.

Later in *A Sand County Almanac*, Leopold again contrasts the ethical principles he attributes to Abraham with his own. This time, he does so even more insistently and with less elaboration, and not without a touch of sarcasm: "Abraham knew exactly what the land was for: it was to drip milk and honey into Abraham's mouth. At the present moment, the assurance with which we regard this assumption is inverse to the degree of our education."[4] Leopold's Abraham, it seems, is positively reprehensible for seeking to consume the nourishing and sweet fruits of the land without having to take into account the inherent needs and purposes of the land. Leopold insinuates that Abraham is a kind of inverse role model for educated persons nowadays. If Leopold's insinuation were correct, then the biblical Abraham might well deserve the sneer that accompanies it. Yet the insinuation is not well informed, especially given the standard of educated awareness which it invokes. It shows little or no acquaintance with the relevant textual evidence concerning

Abraham and his descendants which happens to fall outside Leopold's immediate expertise—including, as we shall see, the Bible's insistence on God's ownership of the land, its prohibitions against wanton destruction and cruelty to animals, and the institutions of the sabbatical and jubilee years.[5] For just that reason, Leopold cannot help leaving himself exposed to the serious countercharge that his glib assessment of the ethical implications of the biblical chapters to which he alludes (Gen. 12–24) tends to weaken his overall argument about the need for environmental protection, instead of strengthening it. The practical lesson I glean from this circumstance is that for anyone who, like Leopold, must venture beyond the limits of his own field in order to consider its ethical implications for today's environmental crisis, some independent consideration of the appropriate ethical principles seems needed as well. This last, for all practical purposes, means an educated person's openness to either the Bible or philosophy or, in the final analysis, both.

Aldo Leopold versus Homer's *Odyssey*

Yet because Leopold says too little about the Bible for us to see this last point in sufficient detail, let us turn for illustrative purposes to what he says in a parallel way about another ancient source for our educated understanding of ethical principles, Homer's *Odyssey*. At the beginning of his chapter on "The Land Ethic" in *A Sand County Almanac*, Leopold writes as follows:

> When god-like Odysseus returned from the wars in Troy, he hanged all on one rope a dozen slave-girls of his household whom he suspected of misbehavior during his absence.
> This hanging involved no question of propriety. The girls were property. The disposal of property was then, as now, a matter of expediency, not of right and wrong.[6]

Leopold's point in citing the slave-girls episode in Homer's *Odyssey*, and construing its significance as he does, is to suggest a progressive widening of the sphere of ethical obligation since ancient times, so as to prepare us in our own day to include our natural habitat as something we might see ourselves duty-bound to protect and foster:

> Concepts of right and wrong were not lacking from Odysseus' Greece: witness the fidelity of his wife through the long years before at last his black-prowed galleys clove the wine-dark seas for home. The ethical structure of that day covered wives, but had not yet been extended to human chattels. During the three thousand years which have since elapsed, ethical criteria have been extended to many fields of conduct, with corresponding shrinkages in those judged by expediency only.[7]

Accordingly, as post-Homeric generations came to abhor in principle any putatively expedient mistreatment of slaves as ethically improper, so too—

if Leopold's argument moves us in the direction he evidently intends it to—
we must consider abhorring in principle any putatively expedient mistreatment of our natural habitat as ethically improper.

What are we to make of Leopold's argument here, which I have quoted
more or less in its entirety? As much as we might admire it for its moral urgency, we cannot help noticing that it rests on a number of erroneous claims
about Homer's epic. Despite what Leopold mistakenly suggests, the execution of the girls, though extremely violent and obviously mishandled, was
hardly a mere consequence of their being human chattels. The incident was
entirely bound up with the all-embracing questions of right and wrong—
domestic, political, and theological—which, *pace* Leopold, are central to the
theme of Homer's *Odyssey*.[8]

First and foremost, Odysseus was not just another householder, but king
of Ithaca—and reportedly had been a just and gentle king.[9] The twelve girls
had been sleeping illicitly with a dozen or more of the hundred and eight
suitors who were occupying—and despoiling—Odysseus' estate for the last
three years of his almost twenty-year absence during the Trojan War and its
aftermath. Odysseus could remove and punish the suitors only by killing
them all at once in a surprise inside-attack, as he and his son Telemachus and
two loyal servants had just succeeded in doing with the goddess Athena's
help. At any rate, the suitors' crimes, and the girls' complicity in those crimes,
were tantamount to treason, arguably a capital offense. Nor was the girls'
consorting with the suitors merely a matter of suspicion. Not only did
Odysseus note the girls' irregular comings and goings firsthand; in addition,
the irregularities were duly reported to him by his most experienced, loyal,
and trustworthy woman-slave, who had been his and Telemachus's wet-
nurse in their infancies.[10] Finally, according to Homer, Odysseus himself did
not hang the girls; Telemachus did. Overreacting to Odysseus' orders,[11]
Telemachus ignored Odysseus' stipulation that the girls be executed by
quick beheadings, rather than by hangings, so as to spare them the additional agony of a lingering death.

We need not ask here whether a better grasp of Homer might have led
Leopold to modify the ethical views at which he arrived prior to consulting
Homer.[12] Our immediate question is, rather, Why does an otherwise consci-
entious scholar like Leopold, highly observant and prudent within the limits
of his own field, venture outside his field so carelessly?

One possibility is that Leopold is simply presumptuous in extending,
uncritically or unreflectively, habits of thought appropriate to one area
of study headlong into other areas. Or it may be that the reverse is true,
that is to say, that Leopold fails to extend his scholarly habits of thought
as an ecologist *far enough* into his examination of texts like those of
Homer and the Bible. Leopold's *A Sand County Almanac* exhibits a
remarkable brilliance in understanding endangered species, especially
birds and land-animals, in their own terms. But Leopold is not nearly so

successful in understanding Homer's *Odyssey* or the Bible on their own terms, before drawing his unsupported inferences about their allegedly unsatisfactory ethical standards when measured against today's environmental crisis. Worse, he does not even appear to have tried very hard. He does come close to suggesting the possible dubiousness of his accusation against the Bible, at least, in an early published piece of his, "The Forestry of the Prophets"—which we have included among our readings—where he praises the practical ecological wisdom of the biblical prophets. Yet *A Sand County Almanac* shows him to have been of a considerably less informative and more intransigent state of mind.

Of course, it may be that Leopold is simply blinded by moral fervor—specifically, by the urge to pity and protect the innocent who are otherwise vulnerable and defenseless, as ancient slave-girls may be thought to be, and as Leopold understands our modern natural habitat to be. For present purposes, however, it is not necessary to decide between moral blindness and scholarly presumptuousness. It is enough to see that Leopold's argument in favor of environmental protection requires an ethical component that his technical expertise as an ecologist cannot by itself supply.

Lynn White Jr. and Arnold Toynbee versus Genesis 1:28

Were Leopold an isolated instance of the scholarly shortcoming I have just described, it might not have been worth our while going so far afield before approaching the readings in this volume. Unfortunately, however, Leopold is not alone. The same dubious charge that the Bible is ecologically unfriendly has often been repeated by others—most famously, by historians Lynn White Jr. and Arnold Toynbee.[13] White and Toynbee differ from Leopold in that their purported prooftext is not the account of Abraham in Genesis 12–24, but rather Genesis 1:26–28:

> And God said, Let us make man in our own image after our own likeness; let them have dominion over the fish of the sea, the fowl of the sky, the beast and all the creeping things that creepeth on the earth.
> And God created man in His own image, in the image of God He created him; male and female he created them.
> God blessed them and said to them, be fruitful and multiply; fill the earth and master it; have dominion over the fish of the sea and the fowl of the sky and all the living things that creepeth on the earth.

White infers from these verses that "God planned all of [creation] for man's benefit and rule: no item in the physical creation had any purpose save to serve man's purposes."[14] Toynbee adds that, especially nowadays, this passage "reads like a license for the population explosion, and like both a license and an incentive for mechanization and pollution."[15] But like Leopold, neither White nor Toynbee offers adequate scholarly evidence to support his far-reaching insinuations about the Bible's complicity in today's crisis. Let us look at the arguments, brief as they are, of each in turn.

White argues that the modern notion that humans ought to treat nature as an object for conquest is distinctively Western. Practically speaking, modern science and technology are said to have originated in the Middle Ages, under the influence and encouragement of Latin Christianity. Christianity had long displaced the pre-Christian, animistic view of nature, which attributed guardian spirits to particular trees, springs, streams, and hills. As a result, humans' "effective monopoly on spirit in this world was confirmed, and the old inhibitions to the exploitation of nature crumbled."[16] New mechanical inventions, including the heavy plow, further changed humans' relation to their natural landscape. "Formerly man had been part of nature; now he was the exploiter of nature."[17] Europe's Latin Christianity differed from Byzantium's Greek Christianity, moreover, in maintaining that human sin was to be atoned for morally, by right conduct, rather than intellectually, by new insight. Hence nature was to be conceived not so much "as a symbolic system" through which God provides sermonic lessons for our edification, but as a clue to the workings of God's mind for our "discovering how his creation operates."[18] Europe thereby became receptive to "an implicit faith in perpetual progress which was unknown either in Greco-Roman antiquity or to the Orient."[19] Late-medieval Europeans, according to White, found the first authoritative statement of that faith in Genesis 1:28.

Jeremy Cohen, whom we shall look at more directly in a moment, finds two overriding difficulties in White's argument.[20] First, White nowhere documents his claim that medieval theologians—or, for that matter, biblical writers or postbiblical authorities—ever thought of Genesis 1:28 as he says they did, that is, as authorizing technological mastery over nature. Second, White elsewhere says that St. Francis of Assisi—whom he here proposes as "a patron saint for ecologists" for his having returned to the pre-biblical animistic view of nature[21]—has by virtue of having introduced into medieval theology "the new idea that natural phenomena are important in themselves . . . opened a door to objective examination of nature and partly explains the enthusiasm for experimental science in the Franciscan order at that time."[22] If, as Cohen indicates, White not only lacks direct evidence to corroborate the role he attaches to Genesis 1:28, but also recognizes in St. Francis's unbiblical animism a competing source for the notion of technological mastery over nature, then how trustworthy is White's overall contention that the Bible is to be blamed for supposedly originating that notion?

Toynbee, like White, calls attention to European Christianity's having displaced paganism's animistic views of nature. The older view, Toynbee observes, survives nowadays only in the nonmonotheistic societies of the East, or else as the religious backdrop for the literature we in the West have inherited from ancient Greece and Rome. In either case, the contrast between the older views and the modern one suggests to Toynbee "the startling and disturbing truth that monotheism, as enunciated in the Book of Genesis, has removed the age-old restraint that was once placed on man's greed by his awe."[23] What Toynbee calls "the monotheistic disrespect for nature" has outlasted even the decline of monotheistic religion in the West. His explanation is as follows: The founders of the Royal Society, the organized promoters of modern science and technology in seventeenth-century Britain, saw its program as a way to distract Europe from sectarian religious wars. They did not wish to abolish biblical religion as such, but only to dissipate its heritage of sectarian divisiveness. Hence they promulgated a nonsectarian, technology-friendly understanding of Genesis 1:28's "fill the earth and master it,"[24] which seemed to license humans to do whatever they liked with nature. To that verse, they juxtaposed Genesis 3:19's "In the sweat of thy face shalt thou eat bread," which seemed to supply the motive for humans to act in accord with that license. Given the large-scale environmental distress that has since accompanied the success of the Royal Society's program, however, Toynbee urges us to revoke Genesis 1:28's license altogether. Since the original license was granted under religious auspices, he concludes, the only remedy lies in a religious reversion to premonotheistic animism.

Toynbee's argument only partly escapes the difficulties we have already noticed in White's argument. Unlike White, Toynbee does cite direct evidence—in the writings of the Royal Society, at least—that Genesis 1:28 has been taken to authorize technological mastery of nature. Yet like White, Toynbee does not bother to fit that evidence, such as it is, with the further possibility that the Royal Society was seeking to promote technological mastery of nature anyway and simply used, or rather abused, Genesis 1:28 as a rhetorical instrument for its own purposes. That is to say, neither Toynbee nor White asks whether the promoters of modern science and technology were historically accurate, or merely rhetorically opportunistic, in ascribing to Genesis 1:28 or the biblical tradition the morally dubious meaning they attached to it. Rather than raising that question, with all its implications for the ecological credentials of the Bible and biblical morality, both Toynbee and White manage to suppress it. Like Leopold, they abandon scholarly inquiry as they reach the edge of their specialized field, where far-reaching ethical questions await, and substitute their own barely-argued moralizing instead. Hence, like Leopold, they too remain vulnerable to charges of moral shortsightedness and intellectual irresponsibility.

Unlike the three narrowly focused authors whom we have just considered, the readings in the present volume recognize that how Genesis 1:28 (and its Jewish setting) bears on our contemporary environmental crisis is, first and last, an interdisciplinary question. Let us therefore turn to what they have to say about it from the standpoint, to begin with, of what I have called *the historical question*.

THE HISTORICAL QUESTION: DOES THE BIBLE SPOIL THINGS?

The following readings supply considerable counterevidence against the claims of White, Toynbee, and others to the effect that, given its ongoing deference to Genesis 1:28, Judaism is environmentally indifferent or worse. Jeremy Cohen's "On Classical Judaism and Environmental Crisis" examines what Genesis 1:28 has meant historically by surveying what its pre-modern interpreters thought it meant. E. L. Allen's "The Hebrew View of Nature" and Jeanne Kay's "Concepts of Nature in the Hebrew Bible" each consider the implicit meaning of "nature" within the biblical text itself. Aldo Leopold's aforementioned "The Forestry of the Prophets" praises the Bible's practical ecological wisdom. Arthur Schaffer's "The Agricultural and Ecological Symbolism of the Four Species of *Sukkot*" traces the ecological overtones of the Bible's fall harvest festival. David Ehrenfeld and Philip J. Bentley's "Judaism and the Practice of Stewardship" summarizes the biblical and postbiblical heritage of environmental conscientiousness. Gerald Blidstein's "Man and Nature in the Sabbatical Year" looks at the postbiblical practice of the biblical institution of the sabbatical year in particular. Finally, Robert D. Sacks examines the meaning of Genesis 1:28 in passing, in the context of his commentary on the Book of Genesis as a whole. To see whether the charges of White, Toynbee, et al. are historically correct, therefore, let us start by considering each of these readings in turn.

Jeremy Cohen: Historical Methodology

Jeremy Cohen's "On Classical Judaism and Environmental Crisis" is an apt place to begin looking at what I have called *the historical question* about Judaism and ecology. Cohen explicitly addresses the claims of White, Toynbee, and other historians who construe the expression "fill the earth and master it" (Gen. 1:28) in particular as unfriendly to modern ecological concerns. He attacks their line of argument at its weak point. He speaks of their "flawed methodology" in "link[ing] the verse directly to specific social and scientific tendencies of our own day." Such interpretations are anachronistic. By ignoring the question of what the verse meant to the religious traditions to which the Bible gives rise in the first place, White and Toynbee have no way of knowing whether the meaning they ascribe to it is historically correct or not. Instead they invite the suspicion that their interpretations—or, rather, misinterpretations—are clouded by a preoccupation with the contemporary crisis in which they, as historians, find themselves before they start to investigate. They are, in short, unhistorical.

Cohen proceeds more circumspectly. Following a hermeneutical suggestion by the contemporary philosopher Hans-Georg Gadamer, he seeks to "measure the impact of [Genesis 1:28] in terms of its societal function and its interpretation over time."[25] In other words, he gauges the text's meaning by asking what its Jewish and Christian audiences in fact thought it meant. The results of Cohen's survey throw his rival historians' allegations into doubt.

Limiting himself largely to the postbiblical and medieval period, Cohen discerns two exegetical tendencies. In the first place, he maintains, Jewish and Christian commentators alike tended to draw from the divine injunction to "fill the earth and master it" the implication that humans are both godlike in their ability to exercise mastery over the earth and animal-like in their need to procreate. The resulting mix of divinity with sexuality in humans, far from offering a clear warrant for considering them superior to nature, was found to be puzzling, since it indicates humans' in-between character, their ongoing need to reconcile angelic and beastly traits in themselves so as to temper the one and ennoble the other. In the second place, Jews and Christians also puzzled over the apparent contradiction between God's granting the blessing of mastery, etc., to all humanity, and His granting it exclusively to Israel—or to Christians as the new Israel. "[T]heologians, jurists, preachers, mystics, and poets" struggled to resolve the latter tension, as well as the former, without ever achieving unanimity on whether the verse in question allows humans a free hand over their environment or not. Even among commentators who did reach that conclusion, "one never senses a dispensation for noxious exploitation or destruction," about which today's environmentally conscious historians are worried.

For understanding rabbinic Judaism's practical approach to environmental questions, on the other hand, Cohen rightly directs historians away from homiletical speculation on the creation account, and toward the legal prohibition of Deuteronomy 20:19–20:

> When in your war against a city you have to besiege it a long time in order to capture it, you must not destroy [*lo tashchit*] its trees, wielding an ax against them. You may eat of them, but you must not cut them down. Are the trees of the field human to withdraw before you under siege?
>
> Only trees which you know do not yield food may be destroyed; you may cut them down from constructing siegeworks against the city that is waging war on you, until it has been reduced.

Rabbinic law expands these verses, which restrict cutting down trees even during wartime, into a prohibition against any wanton destruction, as Cohen notes. Later on, we shall look in more detail at this prohibition, called by the rabbis *bal tashchit*.[26] Meanwhile, we must point out a difficulty that Cohen himself leaves unresolved.

Cohen's historicist approach—that is, his working premise that the meaning of a text is how it appears within the putative limits of a given historical period—is an effective rhetorical weapon against his immediate opponents. Assuming that White and Toynbee would not fault his historicism, as seems to be the case, Cohen can proceed with confidence to embarrass them for overlooking the considerable body of evidence during the period between biblical and modern times which fails to support, and even goes against, their contentions. A difficulty remains, however. In identifying the meaning of the biblical text with its subsequent glosses, Cohen's method does not answer the more basic question of what Genesis 1:28 means in its own terms.[27] Cohen looks vulnerable to the following counterargument, which his opponents might have mounted in full force had they cared to. Perhaps the Bible's "fill the earth and master it" is only an imperfect expression of the project to master nature as it developed after the interlude of the Middle Ages, notably in the seventeenth-century philosophical and scientific writings of Francis Bacon,[28] René Descartes,[29] and others among the founders of modern science, whom the biblical text may be said to have encouraged or inspired. If so, wouldn't the biblical text turn out to bear some onus for the excesses of modern technology after all?

E. L. Allen, and Jeanne Kay: Surveying the Biblical Text

What is needed, it seems, is to look at the biblical text directly, with a view to discovering whether or not it teaches something other than unfettered mastery of nature. Such is the task E. L. Allen's "The Hebrew View of Nature" and Jeanne Kay's "Concepts of Nature in the Hebrew Bible" each set for themselves. Because these two essays seem variants of a single argument—with, moreover, a shared difficulty—we shall consider them side by side.

Allen notices a difficulty in bringing to light the Bible's attitude toward nature. Nature in the Bible, as he says, "is never seen in abstraction." In contrast with modern notions, it is not simply a "neutral" material for humans to work upon. Nor is it to be worshiped, say, as a source of aesthetic inspiration. Even less is it a depository of magical powers to be invoked by means of ritual acts, as in the ancient Canaanite fertility cults. It is instead "one of the spheres in which God meets man personally and in which he is called upon to exercise responsibility." It is "ethically conditioned." Man's divinely appointed dominion over it is "a trust which he receives." "He rules therefore by a delegated authority and not by his own caprice." Humans in general, and the Israelites in particular, are in turn accountable for any mistreatment of the land, as of their fellow humans, under threat of divine retribution. "That even the earth has its rights," for example, is evident in the institution of the sabbatical year (Lev. 25), during which all farmwork ceases, the soil regenerates, and the humans and animals who live on it rest. Divine retribution—in the Israelites' case, endemic diseases, environmental desolation, and, ultimately, political exile (see, e.g., Lev. 26:14–45)—is "a personal response of God to the conduct of the people to whom he has given the land of Israel as their place of responsibility." In other words, nature is a living instrument of divine providence, an organic component of God's "moral universe."

Agreeing implicitly with Allen that the Bible presents nature in entirely moral terms, Kay aims to shift the controversy over Genesis 1:28 to new ground. Instead of dwelling solely on the narrower topic of whether the Bible countenances environmental indifference or worse, she explores the biblical appreciation for nature as such. However the Bible's moralizing may differ from modern environmentalism's, Kay reasons, it may prove a viable alternative, or at least a valuable supplement. So she proposes to examine what the biblical books as a whole say about nature "synchronically" (or without regard to historical differences among the biblical authors) and "geosophically" (or as typical of their historical time and place). Proceeding in that way, she considers in passing the Bible's likeness to other ancient religions, its solutions to its own ecological problems, and its "currently unfashionable retribution theology," so as to rebut prevalent suspicions nowadays that the pagan nature-worship the Bible opposes may be more ecologically sound than the Bible.

Her arguments are thus polemical. Against those who claim that nature as divinely created is only spiritless matter, Kay points out that the Hebrew terms *nefesh* and *ruach* (both translated by her as "spirit") apply to animals and plants as well as to humans, that animals are explicitly subject to divine commandments and participate in divine covenants, and that nature too is said both to praise and fear God and to await a millennium when it will no longer suffer for humans' wrongdoings. Against those who oversimplify the Bible's granting humans dominance over nature, Kay answers that biblical writers describe few egalitarian relationships among humans either, that God's care for nature is for other than utilitarian reasons, and that nature in turn is depicted not only as mocking humans in their efforts to know or tame it, but also as empathizing with them in their joy or sadness, and of course as cooperating with God in exacting retribution for their sins, when plants and animals are given dominance over humans instead—though, conversely, animals can sometimes be benign toward "righteous" humans depending on "their wholeheartedness toward God." Finally, against those who still insist that Genesis 1:28 gives humans a license for wanton destruction, Kay cites biblical examples of "premeditated decimation of nature" to show that this is "not man's prerogative, but God's."

Subsequently, she defends the Bible's moralizing from broader ecological allegations as well. Isn't nature in the Bible, one might ask, an innocent victim of the environmental deterioration by which God promises to punish sinful humans? Yes, Kay admits; but here as elsewhere, the Bible means to alert potential wrongdoers to the damage they might do, so as to encourage their repentance. Then isn't biblical monotheism ecologically short-sighted in condemning animism and nature-worship, despite their environmental salutariness? Well, she replies, the Bible objects only to worshiping the spirits housed in natural objects, not to associating sacredness with this or that natural setting; on the contrary, God Himself is shown in natural settings—as the bringer of rainfall, earthquakes, volcanoes, etc. Even so, if the Bible thus sanctifies nature in part, why doesn't it endorse nature-worship altogether? Kay answers that the Bible's practical alternative to nature-worship is its injunction to "choose life" (Deut. 30:15–20), to which she gives a quasi-Darwinian gloss. It means, she says, not only choosing the preconditions for one's personal or communal survival vis-à-vis nature's immediate life-threats, but also fostering the environmental preconditions for the lives of future generations, i.e., for immortality via one's offspring.

Nevertheless Kay's and Allen's arguments fall short in facing the historical difficulty touched on earlier by Allen, namely, that nature in the Bible is "never seen in abstraction." We learn only by suggestion from Allen, and not at all from Kay, that there is in fact no biblical word or concept exactly equivalent to "nature." The term "nature" thus seems to have been imposed on the biblical text, rather than simply found in it. That both Allen and Kay provide elegant historical accounts of something that, strictly speaking, does not exist, is somewhat unsettling. Let us retrace our steps through Kay's argument in particular, to see whether this difficulty is only minor or has further repercussions.

Kay, like Allen, starts from the premise, asserted rather than proved, that the Bible considers nature exclusively within its own moral horizon. In other words, Kay supposes that the Bible looks at nature from the purview of the divinely revealed law only. Yet does this not mean that, contra Kay and Allen, the complaints of White, Toynbee, et al. may be correct in that, for overriding theological reasons, the Bible is not necessarily open to an ecologically sound scientific understanding of nature as such—for which, after all, it does not even have a name?

In support of her detailed defense of the Bible's ecologically sound moralizing, Kay cites a large number of biblical incidents. These are impressive, but their numbers alone do not decide the issue. Kay adduces them on the assumption that they conform as well to her basic premise that (to state it in yet another way) the Bible's ecological moralizing and the ecologically competent scientific study of nature are altogether compatible from the Bible's own point of view. For example, to buttress her detailed argument, alluded to above, that "a few righteous people gain ascendancy over animals by virtue of their wholeheartedness toward God," Kay mentions the following:

> The "beasts of the field" are not to multiply against the Israelites under Joshua. The shepherd David overcomes the lion, ravens feed Elijah, King Solomon gains unprecedented knowledge of nature [sic] and its ways (I Sam. 17:34–46, I Kings 5:13, 17:6). In contrast, Balaam's ass prevents him from cursing the Israelites, and bears come out of the forest to kill Elisha's tormentors (Num. 22:23–33; II Kings 2:24). The great fish swallows the errant Jonah, but delivers the prophet safely to shore when he repents.

This list—Joshua's indirectly limiting beast population growth, David's killing a sheep-stalking lion, Elijah's being fed by ravens, Solomon's acquiring natural science, Baalam's being restrained by his she-ass, Elisha's being protected by bears, and Jonah's being swallowed and later spewed out by a fish—is more problematic than it looks at first glance. Consider only the most pertinent incident here. Solomon's wholeheartedness toward God, which according to Kay's argument enabled him to acquire natural science, nevertheless was not lifelong.[30] To accommodate his many foreign wives and mistresses, Solomon soon paganized Jerusalem with temples to their gods in addition to the biblical God's own Temple, and the city's unprecedented building and facelifting costs provoked a tax revolt and civil war after his death which led to splitting the country into two. If Kay's argument were simply correct, Solomon's scientific activities ought to have shrunk as his heart strayed. But the Bible makes no such suggestion. Considering the context in which Solomon's natural science is mentioned (1 Kings 5:13), the biblical narrator implies instead that it is of a piece with the morally dubious cosmopolitanism of his later years, and not just with his wholeheartedness early on. If so, then might not the politically disastrous consequences of Solomon's cosmopolitanism also be meant to show, from the Bible's own point of view, something of the vulnerability of the Israelites' God-given moral (or divinely mandated legal) order, and not simply God's favoring the wholehearted? But then, would not Solomon's natural science—again, from the Bible's own point of view—be morally suspect for its indifference (or, perhaps, contribution) to that politically and theologically problematic cosmopolitanism?

Kay's (and Allen's) inadvertently suppressing such questions—about the possible clash between biblical morality and natural science—seems the result of her aforementioned "synchronic" and "geosophic" way of interpreting the biblical text. Such an approach unavoidably blurs contextual differences. To look only for what incidents like those Kay cites share with one another is to disregard whether the biblical text may be designed as well to suggest the deeper and more far-reaching theological and political implications of each incident when understood in its proper context.

We shall continue to face the foregoing difficulty and others surrounding the question of how the Bible as a whole sees, or fails to see, nature. Meanwhile, it is necessary to consider whether the Bible's ecological soundness can be defended more persuasively, if more modestly, by looking instead at the practical environmental awareness of biblical and postbiblical Judaism. Three areas seem well documented: the practical ecological wisdom of the biblical prophets (Leopold's "The Forestry of the Prophets"); the ecological overtones of *Sukkot* (Schaffer's "The Agricultural and Ecological Symbolism of the Four Species of *Sukkot*"); and the biblical and postbiblical heritage of environmental conscientiousness (Ehrenfeld and Bentley's "Judaism and the Practice of Stewardship" and Blidstein's "Man and Nature in the Sabbatical Year"). Let us consider each in turn.

Aldo Leopold: The Ecological Wisdom of the Prophets

Leopold's good-humored praise of the forestry of the biblical prophets is rather tongue-in-cheek. He does not credit them with technical knowledge so much as with an admirable range and depth of practical experience. He finds them surprisingly well acquainted with such matters as forest fires, forest utilization, and silviculture: Joel's comparison of the ravaging effects of divine punishment to that of a wildfire (Joel 1:19–2:11), for example, is "one of the most graphic descriptions of fire ever written;" Isaiah, Jeremiah, Ezekiel, and Song of Songs all speak knowingly of cedar as a commercially desirable wood, and Isaiah even muses that, with the impending fall of Babylon, the trees will rejoice at the resulting depression of the cedar market (Is. 14:7); also, both Solomon and Isaiah speak about planned cultivation—Solomon of large-scale vineyards, orchards, gardens, and parks (Eccles. 2:4–6), and Isaiah of a carpenter's utilitarian planting of a single fir (Is. 41:9). Leopold himself refers condescendingly to the Bible's "habit of thinking of natural phenomena as acts of God instead of as cause and effect." He seems oblivious to the deeper question of the problematic relation between natural science and biblical morality as we have already seen it arise within the biblical text itself. At the same time, he finds Ezekiel's practical wisdom about ecology highly credible: "Seemeth it a small thing unto you to have fed upon the good pasture, but ye must tread down with your feet the residue of your pasture? And to have drunk of the clear waters, but ye must foul the residue with your feet?" (Ezek. 24:18).

In these words of Ezekiel, says Leopold to his twentieth-century reader, "the doctrine of conservation, from its subjective side, [is] as aptly put as by any forester of this generation."

Arthur Schaffer: The Ecological Overtones of *Sukkot*

Schaffer asks why the Bible, uncharacteristically, fails to supply an explanation for the symbolism of the four species of plants to be displayed during the annual fall-harvest festival of *Sukkot* ("Booths" or "Tabernacles"). The plant samples include a willow branch, an unopened date-palm leaf, a myrtle twig, and a citron (Lev. 23:40). Rabbinic authorities, he observes, tend to offer little more than homilies on the possible allegorical meaning of these four species. An exception is Maimonides, who infers that the species are meant to commemorate the Israelites' experience of the fruitfulness of their land on entering it for the first time, after their forty years of desert wandering en route from Egypt. All four species, Maimonides adds, are ritually useful inasmuch as they stay plentiful, look attractive, and keep fresh during the week-long festival. Even Maimonides, however, is silent about why the biblical text mentions just those four and no others. Schaffer ascribes the commentators' silence to their lack of familiarity with Israel's indigenous flora and plant ecology, since most of them lived in the diaspora. He learns instead from a suggestion by the contemporary Israeli botanist Nogah Hareuveni, who in turn was led by Maimonides's remarks to observe that each species represents one of Israel's four environmental regions, with which the biblical author would be familiar as a matter of course: date palms flourish in the desert, willows by the Jordan River, myrtle in the forests, and citron in the cultivated areas.

Schaffer elaborates and deepens Hareuveni's suggestion. He calls attention to biblical Israel's annual climatological cycle. Six months of cool, intermittent rains alternated with six months of almost rainless heat. The long rainy season allowed for three plantings and harvests per year, and eliminated the need for irrigation. At the same time, it strengthened the Israelites's dependence on God, as provider of the rains. *Sukkot*, then, was also a rain festival, as is evident from its sacrificial water libations and ritual water pourings (in addition to the usual wine pourings) along the sides of the Temple altar, to which willow branches were also ceremonially affixed. Like the willows, Schaffer notes, the other three species too were symbols of an abundance of water—in Israel's riverine wetlands (willow), desert oases (palm), stream-lined forest elevations (myrtle), and farmlands (citron). Hence, "the four species uniquely and specifically represent water, in a manner that bears uncontestable evidence to our ancestors' intimate familiarity with the native flora and ecology of Israel."

In passing, Schaffer makes a theological point that bears on the mastery-of-nature controversy instigated by White and Toynbee:

> The near total dependence of Israel on rain allows only limited mastery and dominion over agriculture. The inhabitants of the land are not governed by their "own labors" but by divine providence—"the rain of heaven" [Deut. 11:11]. In the holy land the watchful eye of God, His nurturing care and concern, permits agricultural success; man's labors alone are not sufficient.

Schaffer's point concerns the Bible's own contrast between rain dependent Israel and irrigation dependent Egypt (see Deut. 11:10–12). The contrast is not merely agricultural. The Israelites' reliance on a rain-providing God, who watches and nurtures from heaven, set limits to any thought of exercising mastery over the earth on their own. Climatological dependence meant being theologically beholden to fulfilling their covenant with that God. Of course, Schaffer's point still leaves us room to wonder whether the details of their covenant, or the biblical law, mandated sound environmental practices as well which the Israelites actually followed. That they did in fact follow such practices is the argument of Ehrenfeld and Bentley, and also Blidstein, in the readings that follow.

David Ehrenfeld and Philip J. Bentley: Environmental Stewardship

Ehrenfeld and Bentley's way of showing that biblical law in fact promoted sound environmental practices is to adduce the corresponding practices mandated by rabbinic law, or else documented in other postbiblical evidence. Before doing so, however, they find it necessary to challenge some prevalent misconceptions that prevent us from understanding those practices adequately.

One such misconception is that the only way to avoid harming the environment is through strict self-denial. (Jainist monks, for example, abstain from meat eating, fast often to conserve plant life, walk barefoot to avoid crushing small creatures, and breathe though gauze masks so as not to inhale tiny airborne organisms.) The rabbis say instead that humans are stewards, or caretakers, of the earth. Ehrenfeld and Bentley admit that this notion can be distorted nowadays to mean that humans may treat their environment however they wish, on the assumption that nonhuman surroundings are simply there to be subjugated. But this, they maintain, is a distortion to which rabbinic teachings are staunchly opposed.

Another misconception is that rabbinic law would have to address modern issues such as global pollution, environmental destruction, and others directly. It does not, Ehrenfeld and Bentley concede. It does offer ethical guidance on environmental matters indirectly, however. So we must adduce and apply rabbinic principles judiciously, if we are not to confuse them with our own, possibly less satisfactory notions. One principle Ehrenfeld and Bentley adduce is that when humans do evil, nature reacts (cf. Deut. 11:13–17). Another is that each created thing has its divinely ordained purpose. A third is that, ethically speaking, nothing comes from nothing (as, e.g., even Adam had to tend the Garden of Eden before being allowed to eat). A fourth is that all things are mutually interdependent, so that humans in turn have an inherent dependence on nature.

Yet another misconception is that Genesis 1:28 is the sum total of what Judaism (or, for that matter, Christianity) has to say about the environment. Only if so could the Bible be accused of giving humans unrestricted "dominion" over all animals. Ehrenfeld and Bentley find this accusation superficial. They offer two quick rebuttals. First, there is no evidence that the rabbis ever interpreted the verses as charged. Second, the English translations on which those who make the charge rely are inadequate. According to the medieval commentator Rashi, for example, the Hebrew term for "dominion" connotes "descent" as well. Rashi infers that only when humans act worthily are they superior to the animals. Otherwise, when they act unworthily, they descend to a moral level below the animals. The Hebrew term for "in the beginning" (*bereshith*), moreover, may imply only the relative beginning of our own universe in a much vaster cosmos. In any case, the traditional Jewish prayerbook speaks of creation as an ongoing process, rather than a one-time act, when it praises God for "Daily . . . renew[ing] the work of creation." God is thus understood to invite humans' participation in creation as well, at least when they are morally worthy of it.

Having neutralized the foregoing misconceptions, Ehrenfeld and Bentley point to several rabbinic teachings as, in effect, principles of ecological restraint. One is the teaching of humans' accountability to God, as derived from the Bible's insistence that God alone owns the land (Lev. 25:23). The rabbis understood this to mean that humans live on the land only temporarily, as strangers and sojourners with God. Two further teachings are the prohibitions against wanton destruction (*bal tashchit*) and inhumane treatment of animals (*tza'ar ba'alei chayyim*).[31] *Bal tashchit* is derived from Deuteronomy 20:19–20, as we have already noted. *Tza'ar ba'alei chayyim* is derived from such verses as Deuteronomy 22:6, which forbids killing a mother bird along with her young. Finally, there is the institution of the sabbath as a day of mandatory rest. Obvious extensions of the sabbath in biblical times are the aforementioned sabbatical year, when farms lay fallow, and the jubilee year following every seventh sabbatical, when in addition farms reverted to their original owners (see Lev. 25). The latter practice prevented large-scale land accumulations—and possible large-scale land abuses as well. Ehrenfeld and Bentley cite no rabbinic evidence to confirm the historicity of either of these practices, however. They do mention that Alexander the Great and Julius Caesar forwent collecting Jewish tribute every seven years, and that Tacitus thought the sabbatical showed Jews to be lazy. For the rabbinic evidence about the sabbatical in particular, we must turn to Blidstein's piece, on which Ehrenfeld and Bentley also rely.

Gerald Blidstein: The Environmentalism of the Sabbatical Year

Blidstein shows how rabbinic sources illuminate both the historical practice and the ethical meaning of the sabbatical year. The Bible itself imposes two main restraints: the soil could not be planted that year; and its spontaneous produce was to be left for the taking, for humans and animals alike (Ex. 23:10–11, Lev. 25:4–7). These restraints narrowed the privileges exercised by the land's legal owners, so as to spread its residual abundance to all its ecological dependents. According to Blidstein, rabbinic commentators well understood the law's "leveling" purpose, for which "man's technological ingenuity, his economic activity, in short, his customary potent manipulation of the world about him, are severely restricted." At the same time, in their statutory rulings and discussions, the rabbis tried—unsuccessfully in the long run—to accommodate the law's "radical demands" to the ongoing "social reality" of property ownership.

That the sabbatical law was not meant simply to favor the poor, Blidstein argues, is shown from the rabbinic injunction to dismantle fences that year to allow free access to fields and orchards. Biblical law guaranteed permanent gleaning privileges to the poor anyway. Dismantling a fence therefore meant "pulling down the symbol and reality of private ownership," so as to efface a distinction on which economic life normally depends. Even so, a dissenting school of rabbinic interpreters stipulated that one should refrain from gathering sabbatical produce from any unfenced landowner who deserved special consideration. Blidstein infers that the intrarabbinic dispute here shows how the sabbatical law challenged the right to private property as such. Despite that challenge, or rather because of it, the two institutions—the sabbatical law and private property—could not easily coexist. Sabbatical practices eventually declined in importance, in face of the harsh truths of economic life. Blidstein also connects that historical decline with the theological circumstances of the Exile. Jews could no longer expect God to sustain them by granting overabundant harvests in the sixth year, as formerly when they lived entirely under their own Law (Lev. 25:20–21).

Returning to the sabbatical restrictions themselves, Blidstein details how harvesting practices underwent *shinnui* (or "change" from the normal routine). Sabbatical-year produce could be harvested, but without the usual labor-saving devices (specialized knives, wine presses, large-scale olive processors, etc.); harvested produce could be used only for immediate consumption or barter, not for wholesale or sophisticated commerce; produce harvested but unused that year had to be destroyed or else publicly redistributed; and humans and domesticated animals alike had to stop eating sabbatical produce already harvested and instead consume storage food from the previous year, once there was no longer enough left in the fields for wild animals to eat as well. In short, the sabbatical law scaled down both acquisition and consumption drastically. It forced our ancestors to "relinquish that which [their] human capabilities have achieved, and in [their] use of the growth of the soil be reduced to the lowest of creatures that live off the soil." Temporarily, at least, humans had to adjust their standard of living so as to be guided by their untamed environment, rather than go out of their way to maintain or raise that standard by the work of their own hands.

Blidstein is tempted here to speak of the sabbatical law's "primitivism," but on second thought he doubts the term's adequacy for characterizing the sabbatical practices in full, as well as its clarity or precision quite apart from its possibly hasty application to the Bible. Trying to see how ecological matters as we are given to understand them fit historically into the biblical setting thus finds us once again at an impasse. Before turning to readings that face the resulting ethical and philosophical questions more directly, then, it may be helpful to take a fresh look at the biblical passage at the heart of our controversy, Genesis 1:28, in terms of the first chapter of Genesis as a whole, as Sacks does as part of his larger commentary on that biblical book.

Robert D. Sacks: The Biblical Context of Genesis 1:28

The question of how the Book of Genesis may be said to view humans' relation to nature is a quiet theme of Sacks's commentary.[32] In considering that theme, we shall keep the overtones of our previous discussion in mind. In particular, we want to learn, with Sacks's help, whether the interpretation of Genesis 1:28 as encouraged by White and Toynbee—who think it means that humans are free to exploit nature as they wish—has to be modified, especially given that "nature" itself is not a biblical term. Sacks suggests that Genesis 1 is indeed concerned with human freedom (as White and Toynbee also imply). He prefers to speak, however, of humans' "openness"—their combined awareness of and susceptibility to the things around them (including, of course, God). According to Sacks, Genesis 1's apparent inattention to "nature" in its six-day account of the creation of the world is the counterpart of its focusing on the perplexing character of human openness. By spelling out the six-stage contrast between humans and the various creatures in their nonhuman environment, Sacks's exegesis indicates how Genesis 1 depicts the nonhuman environment above all as the setting for that openness (rather than, say, as the material for subsequent human exploitation, as White and Toynbee think).

Sacks wonders at the outset whether the term "In the beginning" (Gen. 1:1) refers to creation out of nothing, or only to God's creating our own, visible universe as a niche in a larger, pre-existing cosmos (as Ehrenfeld and Bentley also consider in passing). The difficulty, Sacks notes, stems from a grammatical anomaly. Genesis' first word, *bereshith*, normally means "In the beginning of . . ."; but here no word follows to say whether the "beginning" in question is that of an all-embracing cosmos, or merely of a more circumscribed creating process within the larger whole. Creation out of nothing, Sacks reasons, may only be a postbiblical gloss in response to the subsequently confronted claims of "the great rival to biblical thought—Greek philosophy." (The latter entertained alternatives such as the pre-existence of matter and the eternity of the cosmos as a whole.) Like Ehrenfeld and Bentley, Sacks is inclined to understand creation as a circumscribed phenomenon. Still, he cautions, the opening verse by itself does not let us decide. "Cosmos" itself may be a misnomer. Genesis 1:1 speaks instead of "the sky and the earth." These are two things, not one. All the text may be saying for certain, especially in the light of what follows, is that the created world is not a simple unity.

Paradigmatic for God's creative activity, Sacks indicates, is day one of the six-day process: "And God said, Let there be light: and there was light" (Gen. 1:3). By a grammatical peculiarity, the Hebrew words for "let there be light [*yehi or*]" are the same as those for "there was light [*yehi or*]." Assuming that the repetition in the text is not unintended, Sacks comments that it serves to emphasize how God's initial order is fulfilled immediately. That the fulfillment is meant to be not only paradigmatic, but also elusive, becomes clear in retrospect. Day one is the only day where deed follows speech without a hitch. Even so, God at once proceeds to "distinguish" light from dark (1:4), as if to imply that the newly emergent light would otherwise disappear by blurring and mixing with the surrounding dark. God then goes on to seal that distinction by naming the resulting pair "day" and "night" (1:5). Names in Genesis 1, Sacks observes, "are not mere handles but give definite shape to the things around us." Without them, the world would remain a "spectrum," with "nothing solid to grasp." Thus, on the second day too, God divides the chaotic waters above from those below by means of an "expanse" that, given its set boundaries, is then named "sky." Likewise on the third day, the waters below are divided—and so bounded—by the "dry"; and the two separate entities that result are then, and only then, named "sea" and "land." Meanwhile, starting from day one, the created world in turn retains indelible traces of its nameless, shapeless origins. Day one closes with a refrain, soon to be repeated on each of the other five days: "And there was evening, and there was morning" (1:5; cf. 1:8, 13, 19, 23, 31). Evening and morning are regularly recurring mixtures of light and dark. They are repeated reminders of happenings that fall between the boundaries originally established by God's creating, dividing and naming, and therefore cannot be accounted for simply in term of these.

What Sacks has already said about the second day—that God divides the waters above from waters below by an expanse named sky—means that "sky" here functions as a protective film or transparent buffer against the surrounding chaos. Torrential rains from above and angry seas below, Sacks adds, are alike part of that chaos. Genesis 1 suggests that God is able to sustain or withdraw that buffer at will—to loosen the faucets, as it were, as in the case of Noah's flood, or to tighten them, as in the case of the drought that is part of the biblical sanctions for violating the provisions of the sabbatical year.[33] Sacks's comments lend plausibility as well to Schaffer's account of how the four species of *Sukkot* emblemize God's providing seasonal rains as part of his covenant with Israel.

So far, Sacks has said nothing explicit about "nature" or its absence in the Bible. His comments about day three suggest why the term may not quite fit at all. Instead of creating vegetation directly, God now delegates the creating activity to the newly formed earth. Using a grammatical construction known as cognate accusative, which repeats the verbal root in the object of the sentence, God tells the earth, literally, to "grass grass [*tadshe . . . deshe*]" (1:11). The significance of this formulation comes out in that the earth fails to respond exactly as intended: "And the earth sent forth grass [*va-totsey . . . deshe*]" (1:12). The difference between what God tells the earth to do and what it then does is tantamount to that between a unified or self-contained activity—like singing a song or dancing a dance, to use Sacks's comparisons—and an activity that results in a product other than itself—like making a chair, where the artifact is separate from its maker. Evidently God intended to bring about a world that was self-contained, but had to settle for less. Had the earth succeeded in simply "grassing grass," then its vegetating activity would presumably have been self-sufficient and self-perpetuating (or, as we say unbiblically, "natural"). But as things are, the earth is unequal to the task God originally set for it, and improvises instead, so as to produce at the same time an unintended residue that does not fully share in the planned fruitfulness: a tree, for example, is not entirely edible, even though the fruit it bears is. What then accounts for the earth's unplanned splitting up of vegetation into fruit and dross? We are forced to recall the residual chaos that has been clinging to or lurking alongside created things since day one. The chaos does not utterly absorb or destroy the items that are created from it, so long as God continues to sustain them—though it may interfere in their activity. Even so, that created things have an ongoing need for divine support implies that they are inherently precarious, rather than simply viable on their own (or "natural").

Still, the plausible absence of the term "nature" does not mean that Genesis 1 ignores the plainly observable features of things. On the contrary, Sacks emphasizes that the biblical narrator, unlike poets or for that matter scientists, focuses exclusively on such features. He shows how the coming into being of created things follows at least two plainly visible patterns. One pattern is the day-by-day increase in their complexity: the sky of day two is more complicated in its features than the light of day one; the earth and seas of day three are more complicated than the sky; etc. A second pattern becomes evident on day four. The sun, moon, and stars created on that day recall the light already present since day one. Likewise day five will recall day two, and day six will recall day three. In general, things created on each of the last three days inhabit an environment created on the matching day earlier in the week: day four's sun, moon, and stars move in the light established on day one; day five's fish and fowl move in the waters below and sky established on day two; and day six's land animals and humans move in the dry land and vegetation established on day three. Meanwhile the movements of each newly installed set of creatures continue to increase in complexity of design as days four through six progress. Thus, on day four in particular, God delegates to the sun and moon the unprecedentedly complicated tasks of dividing day from night, signaling the set times of days and years, and illuminating the earth (1:14–15). At the same time, God is forced to keep making ad hoc concessions to suit the changed circumstances that result. Here, as an unplanned afterthought, sun and moon are said to "rule" the day and night, respectively (1:16, 18). Rulership, in this case, is little more than God's token acknowledgement of the sun and moon's limited preeminence. It is a consequence of their delegated tasks, rather than of any inherent fitness for ruling on their part. Accordingly, the verb "to rule," as used here, lacks the harsh connotations of the corresponding verb "have dominion" as used of humans in verses 26–28, towards which our analysis of Sacks has been heading.

The term Genesis 1 uses in lieu of "nature," the verb "created," first occurs only on the fifth day, as Sacks notes. Here God once again begins by speaking grammatically in a cognate accusative, along with another, similar construction. The waters are to "swarm swarms" of living souls, and "flying fliers" are to appear in the face of the sky (1:20). But we do not see the waters, etc., immediately complying—just as the earth in verse 11 did not simply "grass grass" earlier. By now aware of their incapacity to comply as intended, God instead "creates" aquine and airborne life himself (1:21). Two novel consequences result. First, like the humans created on day six, the fish receive a blessing: "be fruitful and multiply" (1:22; cf. 1:28). Second, for the first time since day two, the narrator does not add the words "and it was so" (cf. 1:7, 11, 15). To be "so," as Sacks points out, does not mean here to be in deed as was said in speech, but to be "just so" (the Hebrew root means to be prepared, fixed, established, etc.). Fish and birds share motility with the sun, moon, and stars which have preceded them, and which are indeed said to be "so"; but unlike the movements of the latter, those of the fish are neither set in an ecliptic, nor relatively fixed in direction (like the land animals of day six, which do not receive a blessing either); they remain open to the chaos of their watery environment. "Man shares this openness of direction with the fish," Sacks remarks. Because a way is not originally "marked out" for humans, because it "had to develop," and because even then humans could wander from it, like the fish they too "required a blessing."

Coming at last to the sixth day's injunction that humans "have dominion" over all other animals (1:26, 28), Sacks acknowledges that its immediate meaning is not entirely clear. As he has already mentioned, the Hebrew verb has harsh overtones. Sacks might therefore seem to be favoring the position of White and Toynbee, in conceding that the chapter makes humans the unqualified pinnacle and the purpose of creation. But like Ehrenfeld and Bentley, Sacks emphasizes that Genesis 1 gives only a partial view. It is followed by a second view, that of the Garden of Eden in Genesis 2–3, which introduces the need for restrictions on human behavior. So the issue remains unresolved for the moment. Generally, Sacks's comments derive from paying careful attention to the literary context. In context, the dominion humans are to have is part of the blessing they receive from God, following the precedent of the fish. The blessing, as we have already seen, is a sign of their problematic openness: it raises, but does not answer, the question of how far humans themselves are to be held responsible for the bad things that happen to (and around) them, and how far the bad is attributable instead to the surrounding chaos. This question is further addressed thematically in the subsequent chapters of Genesis, and in the narrative and other books of the Bible that ensue—and indeed in the tradition that the Bible sets in motion—as Sacks's larger commentary shows.[34] We shall postpone further consideration of how the Bible itself treats that question, until the selection from Leon R. Kass which concludes our readings.

Meanwhile we shall pick up some of the loose threads that we have left dangling, and turn instead to proposals for applying traditional Jewish teachings to our ecological situation nowadays.

THE ETHICAL QUESTION: HOW SHOULD JEWS FACE THE CRISIS?

The next several readings emphasize what I have called *the ethical question*: What Jewish teachings appropriately address today's environmental crisis? Each reading is conscious of being selective. Bradley Shavit Artson's "Our Covenant With Stones: A Jewish Ecology of Earth" adduces the theological notion that the earth itself is included in the Jewish covenant with God. Lawrence Troster's "Created in the Image of God: Humanity and Divinity in an Age of Environmentalism" assimilates the Jewish view that humans are created in God's image to the contemporary Gaia movement. Eric Rosenblum's "Is Gaia Jewish? Finding a Framework for Radical Ecology in Traditional Judaism" suggests that the biblical institutions of the sabbatical and jubilee years embody ecological and economic principles as sound and as radical as anything proposed today. Jeremy Benstein's "'One, Walking and Studying . . .': Nature vs. Torah" draws ecologically salutary implications from a rabbinic text that seems at first glance to be disparaging the entire notion of a Jewish environmental concern. Eilon Schwartz's "*Bal Tashchit*: A Jewish Environmental Precept" elaborates the rabbinic prohibition against wanton destruction. Finally, Hans Jonas's "Contemporary Problems in Ethics from a Jewish Perspective" shows the need for summoning Jewish teachings counseling restraint, in order to meet our ecological and other crises in an age of nihilism. Let us consider each's argument in turn.

Bradley Shavit Artson: Including the Earth in God's Covenant

Artson complains that Jewish defenses against charges of ecological negligence have been largely "episodic" or piecemeal. Defenders have responded by stressing Judaism's record on this or that issue—ecological awareness, environmental stewardship, the sabbatical year, etc., to cite examples we have already seen. Even so, White, Toynbee, and others who are not sympathetic or well acquainted with Judaism have been allowed to dictate the terms of the Jewish responses. Artson proposes responding instead with "intrinsically Jewish categories." He seeks to "construct a Jewish ecology" that would have the added advantage of "enriching the traditional structure of Judaism."

The basis for Artson's ecologically friendly structural modification of Judaism is the biblical notion of the sanctity of the soil. This notion turns out to be twofold. On the one hand, God is understood to have created all lands, settled as well as uncultivated. "As the source of all places," Artson infers,

"God's sanctity must somehow touch every place." On the other hand, the Land of Israel is said to be holier than any other land. It is the place where the Israelites are to obey the *mitzvot* (commandments), especially those willed by God as proprietor of the land: *peah* (leaving the corners of the field unharvested for the poor to glean), *orlah* (not consuming the fruit of newly planted trees until the fifth year), *kilayim* (not yoking or mating mixed animal species, not sowing mixed grains in the same field, not wearing clothing of mixed fiber), *terumot* (sacrificial and tithe offerings to the priests and Levites), and *bikkurim* (first-fruit offerings).[35] Israel and the other lands are nevertheless connected. God punishes the Israelites' failures to obey the mitzvot with exile. Not just the Land of Israel, then, but the whole earth suffers defilement. All the same, God's covenant obliging the Israelites to obey is not canceled. Exile only alters the conditions under which that covenant is to be kept. "The Earth is not only a witness to the covenant (*brit*)," Artson concludes, "but a participant in the unfolding drama of righteousness, chastisement, and rebuke."

Rabbinic thought, according to Artson's way of construing it, reduces the importance of living in the Land of Israel by elevating the importance of obeying the *mitzvot*. The rabbis thus seek "to align Jewish religion to the reality of Jewish settlement beyond the borders of the Land of Israel." "Whereas the Torah esteems living in Israel as the goal [*sic*] of pious observance," Artson argues, "the Rabbis . . . cherish living on the Land [of Israel] *because* it allows for greater observance." From being the putative purpose of Jewish worship, in other words, settlement on the Land becomes instead a mere means for enhancing it. This shift is said to be confirmed by the wording of the rabbinically instituted blessings over food. Blessings are to be recited whether or not the food is eaten or grown in Israel, though clauses in the blessings after meals also recognize that difference. More important in the wording of the various blessings is whether and how the food to be eaten emerges from the soil—that is to say, whether directly, through a vine, through a tree, or none of the above. In any case, the blessings are the rabbis' newfound way "to recognize the sanctity of the entire planet, to ground that holiness in God's ownership, and at the same time to maintain the special status of the Land of Israel."

Artson's remodeling of biblical and rabbinic thought is not without further difficulties, however. His argument carries the implication that the rabbis care more, or more deeply, about obeying the *mitzvot* than does the Bible itself. Is it adequate to say, as Artson does, that our biblical ancestors were expected to obey simply "in order to merit the Land"? Does the Bible not command the *mitzvot* also for the sake of moral decency as such (Ex. 23:1–9; Lev. 19:13–18; Deut. 15:1–18, 22:6–7), not to mention the possibility of wisdom and self-understanding (Deut. 4:5–8)?[36] Be that as it may, given that Artson reconfigures the connection between biblical morality and rabbinic thought so as to accommodate Judaism as such to modern environmentalism, it is not clear where the large-scale accommodation he suggests is preferable to the "episodic" accommodations by, say, Ehrenfeld and Bentley—who leave the Bible and Jewish tradition more or less intact in moral matters, without thereby minimizing the urgency of the current crisis. Artson's redesign is admittedly intended to mirror in full the claim by White and other contemporary environmentalists to offer a new and improved understanding of human life in the world, despite their one-sided acquaintance, or rather lack of acquaintance, with the biblical view they mean to improve on.[37] But, we may ask, are not the counterarguments of "episodic" apologists like Ehrenfeld and Bentley sufficient to have exposed the one-sidedness of White, Toynbee, et al. for what it is?

Lawrence Troster: Assimilating Judaism to Gaia Worship

Let us examine this question further by looking at Troster, who agrees with Artson in seeing a need to accommodate Judaism fully to twentieth-century environmental thinking—to the contemporary Gaia movement, in Troster's case.

The Gaia movement seeks to replace so-called "anthropocentrism" (or looking at our environmental predicament with a view to the well-being of humans above all) with "biocentrism" (or looking at it instead with a view to the well-being of all living species as such). The movement's premise is that the earth itself is a single, self-sustaining and self-regulating organism. Evidence cited by James Lovelock, the movement's founder, in support of this premise includes the fact that the earth alone among neighboring planets maintains a suitable atmosphere and temperature for the intricate web of plant and animal life found on it. Humans, according to Lovelock, function ecologically as the earth's brain cells, or collective intelligence, able to anticipate and help meet the ongoing survival needs for the planet as a whole. But humans cannot carry out this function so long as they continue to use the earth exclusively as a farm for their own benefit. The biblical notion that humans are to dominate the other species is thus ecologically unwarranted. A "democratic" order is required instead, among human and non-human species alike. Theologically, therefore, it is necessary for Earth—or Gaia—to displace the biblical God as presiding divinity.

All this might seem to go against the Jewish view that humans, unlike other species, are created "in the image of God" (Gen. 1:26–27); but Troster argues that the Jewish and Gaian views are not necessarily incompatible. He avails himself of interpretive possibilities authorized by the rabbinic tradition. Accordingly, a given biblical text admits of homiletical, symbolic, and mystical meanings, alongside its plain or literal meaning. Troster thus offers three glosses—literal, homiletical, and symbolic—from diverse Jewish commentators to suggest that the views of Gaia and of Genesis 1:26–27 may be reconcilable after all.

Even so, he interprets his sources rather freely. In the first place, he argues, when Genesis 1:26–27 speaks of God's "image" (*tzelem*), it means literally a reflection of God's presence, as an official royal statue reflects the extended authority of the king. Here Troster appeals to the overtones of the Babylonian/Akkadian cognate *tzalmu*, as outside support for the putatively plain meaning of the corresponding Hebrew word. The creation of humans in God's image is thus said to imply that "humanity is the physical extension of God's power and presence on earth." In the second place, then, a midrash (or rabbinic homily) speaks of God's creating humans with four "angelic" attributes—upright stance, speech, understanding, and peripheral vision—together with four animal-like ones—ingesting, procreating, excreting, dying. Troster infers that the homily means that humans' divine *tzelem* is inescapably linked to their earthbound character. In other words, having the two sets of characteristics, high and low, "we are aware of our connection to God, and to other living beings, and of our earthly origin and limitations as well." Finally, in the third place, Troster cites Maimonides to the effect that *tzelem* in Genesis 1:26–27 symbolizes intellectual apprehension.[38] He goes beyond what Maimonides himself says, however, in identifying the latter with human consciousness as such, including humans' awareness of moral choices (as embodied beings) and their apprehending the divine (by way of biblical revelation).[39] Accordingly, Troster concludes, "our consciousness provides us with the self-awareness to realize our responsibilities to God and to the earth which we tend."

The "Gaian" component of Troster's three Jewish glosses on the meaning of *tzelem* is thus tantamount to the view that God is not only "transcendent," or separate from nature, but also "panentheistic," or inclusive of nature—and therefore "immanent," or inside nature, as well. "Gaia is part of God," Troster concludes, though "not all of God." All the same, does not Troster thereby break with Judaism's biblically mandated opposition to nature worship, i.e., to divinizing the spirits attributed to created things? (Here we should perhaps recall the Second Commandment, which Troster does not mention; cf. Ex. 20:3–6, Deut. 5:7–10, with Deut. 4:15–19.) What, besides Troster's harmonizing glosses, could possibly invite such a break? We seem obliged to consider the following: Troster, like Artson, sees in contemporary environmentalism more than an "episodic" rival to Judaism, one that would oppose the Bible and Jewish tradition on this or that ecological issue. In its claim, however faulty, to provide a new and improved understanding of the human situation, contemporary environmentalism may be said to be a potential replacement for Judaism. For that reason, Artson and Troster seem correct in supposing that a merely exegetical, homiletical, or rhetorical reply to it is not enough. Deeper theological reflection is needed too. Even so, *pace* Artson and Troster, does openness to the ecological insights supplied or confirmed by movements like Gaia worship necessarily require radical theological reconstruction? Let us turn to Rosenblum's essay with this question in mind.

Eric Rosenblum: Gaia's Jewishness

Rosenblum finds Judaism's main kinship with Gaia worship and the like not in theology, but in the biblical institutions of the sabbatical (*shemittah*) and the jubilee (*yovel*). From Blidstein's account of the rabbinic sources concerning the sabbatical year in particular, we have already seen that ecologically beneficial elements were integral to its postbiblical practice, however short-lived. Rosenblum returns to the biblical provisions themselves to show that, together with their rabbinic refinements, they provide a model for sound environmental legislation which transcends their time and place of origin. "What most ecological activists—and not a few Jews—might find surprising," he observes, "is that the principles of Deep Ecology are fully expressed in traditional Judaism." He therefore examines the sabbatical and jubilee laws in their own terms, with an eye to how they might help us gain our bearings on ecologically related matters nowadays.

As for the sabbatical law, he elaborates the ecological implications of its four main provisions. *Refraining from both planting and harvesting* every seventh year (Lev. 25:1–7) reversed the debilitating effects of steady cultivation: The soil breathed anew; rains flushed salt accumulated through artificial irrigation; organic fertilizer supplied by unharvested "volunteer" vegetation increased tilth and improved soil texture, without the expense and pollution of chemical fertilizers; strains from the surrounding countryside could sprout and cross-pollinate in the fallow fields so as to strengthen future crops by mixing with them genetically; and crops deliberately left in the fields to feed domestic animals were available to wildlife as well, to help ensure its survival. *Remitting debts* every seven years (Deut. 15:1–3) relieved economic pressures on poor farmers to exhaust their land's resources. *Obliging the land to rest* along with its inhabitants (Lev. 25:2) meant viewing the earth as alive—though not self-sustaining. Rosenblum indicates the Bible's theological disagreement with modern Gaia worship on this last point by adducing Sacks's comment on Genesis 1:11 to the effect that the earth remains susceptible to the encumbrances of chaos; viewing the earth, in consequence, as irrepressibly error prone—as "more Groucho Marx than . . . Gaia," in Rosenblum's words—was thus an ecologically beneficial counterweight to Genesis 1:28's directive to humans to subdue the earth and rule its animals, especially since the directive is preceded by a blessing (Gen. 1:26) and "blessings are only given when error is likely and God's help is needed." *Reading the Law in public* during *Sukkot* each sabbatical year (Deut. 31:10–13) emphasized that the sabbatical and other provisions were binding on the community as a whole, not just on individuals.

As for the jubilee law (Lev. 25:8–10), Rosenblum argues that it more than offset any remaining economic obstacles to environmental protection; it positively removed them, every fifty years at least. *Adding an extra year without harvest* (Lev. 25:11–12) and *returning farms to their original land-grant families* (Lev. 25:23–28) after every seventh sabbatical not only hindered disproportionate wealth accumulation by any one family, but also "curb[ed] the environmental abuses that occur when extreme wealth is unconstrained." Besides, the latter provision served as an ecologically favorable restrictive clause on the sale of farmland: since the sale— or, rather, lease—price was calculated by anticipating the worth of what the farm would produce from the date of transfer until the jubilee, the law effectively discouraged practices that might weaken the land's fertility during that time. Furthermore, *freeing all indentured servants* at the start of the fiftieth year (Lev. 25:39–41) included providing one-on-one assistance in the form of zero-interest loans, free room and board, etc., to prevent ex-slaves from relapsing into the hopeless poverty that drove them into servitude to begin with. Impoverished populations are often hard on the environment, Rosenblum remarks, as when the nonavailability or non-affordability of alternative fuels promotes deforestation through over-harvesting of firewood; and they are hard on the social order too, as when the unrestrained exploiting of workers invites the support (or intervention) of tyrannical governments, which "have equally bad records on human rights and environmental protection."

By and large, then, traditional Judaism and contemporary Deep Ecology are allies, not rivals. Where they do differ, Judaism's views turn out to be preferable, as Rosenblum argues by comparing the opinions and arguments of radical environmentalists with the Jewish notions of creation, revelation and redemption as understood by the twentieth-century religious existentialists Martin Buber and Franz Rosenzweig. A brief sketch of his argument must suffice. Both Judaism and Deep Ecologists oppose an anthropocentric view of humans' place vis-à-vis nature; but Judaism avoids going to the extreme of blurring humans' specific difference from other species by holding "nature and humanity equally accountable to a Creator, who assigns them complementary roles and responsibilities." Similarly, both Judaism and Deep Ecology acknowledge a need for overall guidance in arriving at an ecologically sustainable society, and both insist that modern science is not equipped to provide such guidance but must instead "be guided by something that is not strictly science"; here Judaism as a religion offers "a view of reality that includes the possibility of revelation in the form of laws like *shemittah* and *yovel* that emanate from an all-encompassing biocentric principle: 'Choose life.' (Deut. 30:19)." Finally, Deep Ecology's notion of ecological restoration as a step-by-step process that involves clean-up, pollution prevention, and reinstatement of biodiverse ecosystems, is like Judaism's notion of redemption, or atonement with God, which involves making restitution to the wronged and resolving to avoid future error, before seeking forgiveness through prayer and right action; for Judaism, "ecosystem restoration and spiritual redemption are both achieved when the entire community turns toward God and embraces the commandments."

Rosenblum's account of the existing interface between Judaism and Deep Ecology, unlike Artson's and Troster's suggestions for rebuilding that interface from the Jewish side, confirms the view of Ehrenfeld and Bentley that Jewish tradition as it stands ought to satisfy worried outsiders who doubt its ecological credentials. Satisfying worried insiders, like Artson and Troster, may well be another matter, however. Benstein, for one, calls attention to a well-known mishnaic admonition that appears at first glance to discourage an appreciation of nature altogether for Jews as Jews. Let us turn to his insider's account of that admonition.

Jeremy Benstein: The Jewish Appreciation of Nature

Benstein proceeds by way of in an extended meditation on *Pirkei Avot* 3:7:

> One, who while walking along the way, reviewing his studies, breaks off from his study and says, "How beautiful is that tree! How beautiful is that plowed field!" Scripture regards him as if he has forfeited his soul.

The Mishnah's admonition arouses Benstein's concern that "the Torah and its study have often been a wedge, distancing us from a direct relationship with the natural world." He therefore tries to recover the original, unreconstructed meaning of the admonition, so as to determine its ecological bearing here and now.

His preliminary discussion of the difficulties in translating the original Hebrew is instructive in itself. If "one . . . walking on the way" (*ham'haleich baderech*), for example, is an allusion to Deuteronomy 6:7—"you shall repeat them [*sc.*, the Torah's words] . . . while you sit in your house and while you walk along the way and while you lie down and while you arise"—then the admonition's harshness must have to do with the walker's interrupting his performance of that commandment, and so with his possibly forgetting what he is supposed to be repeating. If "plowed field" (*nir*) suggests a farm road rather than a deep woods setting, moreover, then the likely season is springtime just before planting, when budding trees, etc., are particularly attractive, and so distracting. Yet the full difficulties Benstein sees are more than philological. What scriptural authority if any, he wonders, underlies the Mishnah's admonition? And how is merely being distracted here tantamount to a capital offense? Benstein surveys Jewish commentators, traditional and modern, for plausible answers.

He divides traditional commentators into three groups—each ecologically unsatisfying. One group considers nature an unworthy alternative to the Torah as a focus of serious attention (Meiri, Abarbanel, and in effect Duran). A second group acknowledges that appreciating nature as God's handiwork is important, but less important than Torah study (Bertinoro, Magriso; also Bulka). Finally, Joseph Caro, whom Benstein considers at some length, argues that the study of nature would be superior to the study of Torah in lead-

ing humans to God, except for a certain danger. The danger according to Caro
has to do with the need for nature to be interpreted adequately in order to be
understood.[40] Nature is therefore open to misinterpretation, including heretical misinterpretation by those who are intellectually weak and look to nature's novelties, rather than to its orderliness, for miracles that supposedly indicate divine providence.[41] Given this circumstance, the study of nature for
Caro is, as Benstein sees, "less trustworthy [than the Torah as a means for understanding God], and needs to be backed up by, or placed within the framework of, divine truth as revealed in the Torah." The danger to which the Mishnah alerts us is thus that, whereas nature is always available to humans, the
Torah is easily forgotten; hence the Mishnah's warning that anyone so distracted has "forfeited his soul" means that he has, in Caro's words, "left the
Source of Living Waters, our Holy Torah, which comprised his learning according to what human reason is capable of, and to what he is accustomed."
Nevertheless Benstein accuses Caro of self-contradiction for claiming, on the
one hand, that nature is always in front of humans' eyes and so in less danger of being forgotten than the Torah; and, on the other hand, that most humans are unable to appreciate nature for what it is—"certainly," he adds, "a
form of forgetting." One should note, however, that this accusation does not
take into account Caro's crucial premise to which Benstein has already called
attention, namely, that nature in order to be understood needs adequate interpretation, which nature by itself does not supply.[42]

At any rate, unsatisfied with the foregoing, Benstein turns to modern and
Zionist responses to the rabbinic admonition. To Steven Schwarzschild,
whom we shall consider more fully later on, the Mishnah's apparent disdain
for nature study is an uncontroversial and accurate statement of the traditional Jewish view. To the social commentator Eric Hoffer, the Mishnah is an
example of the fanaticism of single- or narrow-minded believers. To the nov-
elist Cynthia Ozick, the Mishnah confirms that the Jewish soul, unlike the
pagan's, is forever repressed by being book-bound. To the political Zionist
Micha Yosef Berdichevski, the Mishnah ought to be reversed so as to rank
nature appreciation above Torah study, in the interest of fostering nationalis-
tic pride in the resettlement of the Land of Israel. And to the religious Zionist
Chaim N. Bialik, who in turn cites the cultural Zionist Ahad Ha'am, the Mishnah must be understood in the context of the wanderings of the Exile, and is
revisable as Jews return to their ancestral Land.

Benstein himself offers yet another suggestion. He proposes supplement-
ing the traditional categories that characterize Jewish teachings as either *bein
adam le-chavero* ("between a human and his companion," i.e., ethical) or
bein adam le-Makom ("between a human and God," i.e., mainly ritual), by
introducing a third: *bein adam le-olamo* ("between a human and his
world"). If the Mishnah's admonition is placed in this new category, he says,
it would amount to a warning against "the dichotomizing of the world and
our own souls" or "the radical rupture between Nature and Torah." That is,

it would forbid insulating the study of nature from the study of Jewish texts, and vice versa. Benstein reiterates that his own gloss is a necessary corrective for the dichotomizing tendencies of all previous commentators. He makes no allowances for that dichotomy, however, in light of the possible tension between the study of nature and the study of Jewish texts as understood, say, by Caro (or, for that matter, Genesis 1 or 1 Kings 5:13ff.).[43]

Eilon Schwartz: Judaism and Wanton Destruction

Schwartz, like Benstein, seeks to enhance Judaism's environmental credentials by elucidating the intra-Jewish discussion of a recognized Jewish teaching. In Schwartz's case, it is the rabbinic prohibition against wanton destruction (*bal tashchit*).

The biblical basis for *bal tashchit* is, as we have already seen, Deuteronomy 20:19–20, restricting the cutting down of trees during wartime. Schwartz indicates how verse 19 contains an ambiguity that divided subsequent exegetes. The clause often translated as "Are [*ki*] the trees of the field human to withdraw before you under siege?" could also be translated "for [*ki*] the tree of the field is man's life to employ them in the siege." The difference turns on whether the Hebrew conjunction *ki* should be read as interrogative or as causative. The interrogative reading, followed notably by Rashi, emphasizes the biblical passage's protecting trees in general on the grounds that, not being parties to the war, they do not deserve to suffer war's devastation, but cannot protect themselves from it. Yet Rashi's reading is grammatically forced, as Schwartz a points out; and, in any case, it does not account for the passage's going on to protect fruit trees in particular. The causative reading, followed notably by Ibn Ezra, emphasizes protecting the fruit trees as a source of human food. Schwartz shows how rabbinic law expands the biblical restriction variously in both directions—concern for the general well-being of created things, as in Rashi's reading, and concern for the specific well-being of humans, as in Ibn Ezra's reading—without seeing any overriding need to arrive at a uniform consistency.

A mishnaic ruling, for example, exempts property owners from liability for cutting down their own plants, although nonowners remain liable (*Baba Kamma* 8:6). Evidently there are misgivings here about cutting down any plant. The Talmud thus adds a restriction to the effect that the plants to be cut down must no longer be economically viable (*Baba Kamma* 91b–92a). Elsewhere, however, it records an incident to the effect that God punishes with death owners who cut down even immature plants, however unprofitable—so as to suggest mysteriously, as Schwartz remarks, something more than a simple cost-benefit analysis (*Baba Batra* 26a). Meanwhile the immediate context of the Mishnah's ruling is a discussion of whether anyone is exempt from harming himself. The Talmud elaborates by asking whether tearing one's clothing, a Jewish mourning practice, is a case of *bal tashchit* when done to excess. It answers yes, by citing the incident of a sage who avoided tearing his clothes by lifting them while walking through scrub brush, and letting his body suffer cuts and bruises instead, since the body could be repaired but the clothes could not (*Baba Kamma* 91b). Yet another talmudic passage implies no, when it puts human welfare first in questions of *bal tashchit* by allowing humans to destroy furniture for firewood if necessary even on the Sabbath (*Shabbat* 129a). "However," Schwartz comments, "the very presence of the question suggests that the answer is not taken for granted." Rather, there is an ongoing "tension" concerning whether created things are merely for human use or whether they have a inherent dignity that must be respected.

Schwartz documents how rabbinic appeals to *bal tashchit*, despite their predominantly utilitarian tendency, accord created things a dignity of their own. He cites the Talmud's wish to discourage conspicuous consumption without thereby insisting on human discomfort or asceticism (*Shabbat* 140b, *Ketubot* 8b, etc.). In elaborating further talmudic applications of *bal tashchit*, the rabbinic tradition's subsequent Responsa literature likewise follows both courses. Its mainstream Schwartz calls "minimalist," for its holding that other creatures exist mainly for the sake of human convenience. A countercurrent, however, he calls "maximalist," for its seeking to fit human convenience with other creatures' needs. Schwartz describes both streams in some detail.

He concludes by indicating where *bal tashchit* as understood by the rabbinic tradition is congenial with contemporary discussions of environmental ethics and where it is not. Given the rabbis' openness to both "minimalist" and "maximalist" arguments, Schwartz counsels against looking for a single Jewish standpoint on environmental questions. The intra-rabbinic controversy over whether created things are merely utilitarian or are ends in themselves, he adds, parallels our own contemporary discussion, as does the aforementioned dominance of the utilitarian view. At the same time, rabbinic thought is said to lack the peculiarly modern notion that humans are somehow part of a larger, scientifically intelligible ecosystem, or that they need to recover a long lost and more salutary connection with their nonhuman environment. According to Schwartz, the chief barrier between rabbinic and contemporary thought, then, is "cultural." The halakhic (or rabbinic legal) setting, with its proliferation of biblical and talmudic prooftexts, seems alien to today's ethical discussions. The latter tend to assume that ethical arguments are either "utilitarian" or "rights-based," and either "anthropocentric" or "biocentric," to appeal to rights rather than duties, to focus on abstract principles rather than particular cases, and to take their bearings by the individual rather than by the community. Be that as it may, we cannot help noticing that the latter-day features Schwartz mentions seem to characterize today's *philosophical* discussions primarily, and the larger culture only secondarily. If so, perhaps it is worthwhile for us to ask, as Jonas does in the following selection: What are those characteristic assumptions bequeathed by contemporary culture in general to philosophical discussions of ethics in particular, which tend to rebuff—or, on reflection, require—a distinctively Jewish response?

Hans Jonas: Judaism and Contemporary Ethical Problems

Jonas's starting point is that contemporary philosophy has, notoriously, had nothing to say in answer to the question of deepest importance to Judaism: How ought human beings to live? Philosophy, he observes, has nowadays become a camp follower of modern science, which disclaims competence about such questions. Three causes contribute indirectly to philosophy's nihilistic disclaimer: the modern concept of nature, the modern concept of man, and the concomitant fact of modern technology. Jonas looks at each in turn. He does not dwell on environmental questions except in passing. But he does clarify, from both a Jewish and a philosophical point of view, why modern life has occasioned an environmental crisis, and why the crisis is one of theory as well as practice.

The *modern concept of nature*, according to Jonas, denies the biblical belief that the world "is not its own ground but proceeds from a will and plan beyond itself." Rather, the world is said to be entirely self-made and continuously self-making. It can therefore be measured by nothing other than itself. Nor then can it be called either "good" or "bad," "perfect" or "imperfect," "noble" or "base," etc. These must be considered merely human attributions. Hence the world cannot contain evidence of God's goodness either. "The modern heavens," Jonas says with an eye to Psalm 19, "no longer tell the glory of God. If anything, they proclaim their own mute, mindless, swirling immensity; and what they inspire is not admiration, but dizziness; not piety, but the rejoinder of analysis." So we cannot, as moderns, speak of nature's purposes, goals, or "values." These originate within humans alone, and have no outside support.

Similarly, the *modern concept of man* implicitly contradicts the corresponding biblical view. Darwinism, for example, denies that humans are made in God's image. They are, in contrast, "the temporal (and possibly temporary) outcome of the chance transactions of the evolutionary mechanics." The reason for their existence is merely that they have survived. In other words, humans are "an accident, sanctioned by success." But success, biologically speaking, means only a high rate of reproduction. Jonas comments that the only biblical commandment Darwinism recognizes, as it were, is "Be fruitful and multiply."

Modern historical relativism, moreover, holds humans to be simply the product of their own history and its man-made creations, or "cultures." Each culture is said to generate "value systems"—moralities that are imposed rather than true, relative rather than absolute, convenient rather than unconditional. But if so, Jonas laments, the biblical claim that God has told humans what is good (Micah 6:8) no longer has standing.

Finally, modern psychology "has proved to be the most effective way of cutting man down to size and stripping him in his own eyes of every vestige of metaphysical dignity." Nietzsche's genealogy of morals, for example, exposes the "higher" features of the human psyche as masks constructed by, and in service to, humans' baser drives; and contemporary psychoanalysis, which Jonas describes as popularized Nietzscheanism with scientific trappings, reduces the voice of God to "the superego which speaks with spurious authority—spurious because dissembling its own questionable origin—and this speaker can be put in its place by *reminding* him of his origin." The origin of the distinctively human is thus low, not high. Modern psychology borrows its reductionist mode from modern science. Its teaching resembles the Christian view of humans after the Fall, except that it lacks any divine standards to which they might return.

Even as humans' stature is reduced in the foregoing ways, however, their power is increased phenomenally by means of modern technology. As a result, technology gives humans a plenitude of "license" in a "vacuum of norms." This result, according to Jonas, is the main challenge that contemporary ethics—including environmental ethics—has to face.

Modern technology, he observes, is the morally indifferent offspring of modern science. By leaving nature with no dignity of its own, science has given technology a free hand to exploit nature as it wills. Besides, the ever-extending reach of technology, the now-and-future prospects for success in "remaking and outwitting" nature according to our own self-initiated projects, and the businesslike routinizing of our methods for doing so all contribute to removing any traces of old-fashioned reverence for a divinely created world which may have survived the purely analytical work of science. We can no longer count on awe or shame to restrain our technologically enhanced will to power over our environment.

But have not humans, as makers of new worlds, "gained in metaphysical status what nature has lost"? Jonas answers soberly. Our inevitable attempts to apply technology to remaking ourselves—as in today's techniques for sociopolitical and psychological manipulation, tomorrow's biological engineering, and (who knows how soon?) genetic reprogramming—are enough to deflate any premature boasting, he warns. For, if all our concepts are ephemeral, how can we be sure that, in redesigning not only how humans will live but what they will be, we benefit the generations to come? And what of unplanned, or irreversible, errors along the way? "Never was so much power coupled with so little guidance for its use," he remarks. "Yet," he adds, "there is a compulsion, once the power is there, to use it anyway."

So Jonas asks, as a Jew, "Can we afford the happy-go-lucky contingency of subjective ends and preferences when (to put it in Jewish language) the whole future of the divine creation, the very survival of the image of God [*sc.*, in human beings] have come to be placed in our fickle hands?" Or, to connect Jonas's question about the threat that modern technology poses with our questions about Judaism and environmental ethics in particular: How might Jewish tradition address the "irreversible consequences that concern the total condition of nature on our globe and the very kind of creatures that shall or shall not populate it"? Jonas adduces three counsels.

First, we need "modesty in estimating our own cleverness in relation to our forebears." We do not know that our technological superiority to past generations means that we are wiser than they in every respect—especially concerning those perplexities that, as we have just seen, go beyond scientific technology.

Second, we need "*reverence* for certain inviolable integrities sanctioned by [the biblical] idea [of creation]." Genesis 1, in other words, mandates humans' "sovereign use" of God's other creatures, not their "biological impoverishment." "Nowhere does the Jewish idea of man's preeminence in the created scheme justify his heedless plundering of this planet," says Jonas, presaging what we have already learned from Cohen, Allen, Kay, Ehrenfeld, and Bentley, and others. The created order does require us to exploit nature, Jonas concedes. But we ought to do so "with respect and piety." "Care for the integrity of creation should restrain our greed."

Lastly, the idea of creation should inspire "reverence for *man*," as created in the image of God. Numerous ethical precepts follow, Jonas suggests, although he limits himself here to two: rejection of genetic reprogramming, and rejection of psychological manipulation (brainwashing, subliminal conditioning, etc.). He admits that these negative precepts do not by themselves provide positive guidance. Nevertheless, he argues, they are a start; they recall the Ten Commandments, which are mostly negative; and they fit "the modern situation, whose problem, as we have seen, is an excess of power to 'do' and thus an excess of offers for doing."

Jonas's argument thus favors, on the whole, the views of Rosenblum, Benstein, and Schwartz, who likewise start from an appreciation of what Jewish tradition forbids before looking to see what it then permits, as against those of Artson and Troster, who seek to refashion Judaism to look like modern thought but in so doing overlook modern thought's ethical departures from Judaism, especially those pointed out so starkly by Jonas. Still, perhaps Jonas has overstated his case against modern thought in general and contemporary philosophical ethics in particular? Perhaps the latter, at least in their Jewish environmental versions, are capable of addressing the otherwise abandoned question about how humans ought to live? To see whether they are up to the task or not, let us turn to our last group of readings, which I have gathered under the heading of *the philosophical question*.

THE PHILOSOPHICAL QUESTION:
DO ECOLOGY, JUDAISM, AND PHILOSOPHY MESH?

In one way, each of our readings so far has given a straightforward, though not always sufficient, answer to the practical question of how humans ought to live in the face of the current environmental crisis, by looking to Judaism for guidance. Just what Judaism itself has to say about the current crisis, however, is not entirely agreed upon by all concerned. At the same time, the deference that our readings pay to Judaism is complicated by an additional fact. Each appeals as well, in various ways, to the authority of modern science. Needless to say, neither the Bible nor Jewish tradition recognizes the authority of modern science—at least, in the case of Jewish tradition, not until modern times. So the question about how Jews ought to face the current crisis is somewhat novel or unprecedented. It involves a larger question: How, if at all, do Judaism and modern science fit together? That this larger question is neither a simply religious one nor a simply scientific one is clear, since it straddles both disciplines. It requires independent reflection, quite apart from our practical commitments to either Judaism or science. In other words, it is a philosophical question. Given the further fact that how philosophy relates to both Judaism and science is also inherently controversial, the larger question turns out to be about the fit, or possible misfit, among all three, as I began by suggesting at the very outset.

Let us therefore look at what each of the following answers to the practical question—How should we live in the face of the current environmental crisis?—suggests about where Judaism, science, and philosophy meet (or perhaps miss) one another. Steven S. Schwarzschild's "The Unnatural Jew" defends what he takes to be the traditional Jewish antipathy toward the appreciation of nature, by assimilating Judaism's ethical teaching to Kant's philosophical teaching about ethics. His essay provokes vigorously dissenting responses by David and Joan G. Ehrenfeld and by Jeanne Kay. Michael Wyschogrod's "Judaism and the Sanctification of Nature" offers a modified version of Schwarzschild's view, while adding that the Bible's failure to give a full hearing to the ancient nature worshipers it opposes is, given our current circumstances, a matter for some regret. Eilon Schwartz's "Judaism and Nature: Theological and Moral Issues to Consider While Negotiating a Jewish Relationship to the Natural World" counters that even if opposition to the appreciation of nature represents something of Judaism's traditional view, the current crisis requires us to reconsider the "ambivalences and ambiguities" of that view as well. Eric Katz's "Nature's Healing Power, the Holocaust, and the Environmental Crisis," recalling both Schwartz's and Benstein's discussions, notes a disturbing kinship between modern "ecocide" and Nazi genocide, and suggests that a corrective for both may be found by looking to nature rather than to Judaism. Ze'ev Levy's "Ethical Issues of Animal Welfare in Jewish Thought" likewise looks to nature in wondering why Judaism does not espouse animals' rights nowadays, given that traditional Jewish sources do not directly address modern environmental–ethical concerns such as the food and drug industry's inhumane treatment of animals. J. David Bleich's "Judaism and Animal Experimentation" and "Vegetarianism and Judaism," on the other hand, analyze and defend the traditional Jewish position on these matters. Finally, Leon R. Kass's "Sanctified Eating: A Memorial of Creation" argues that the biblical laws concerning meat eating foster not only moral (and environmental) responsibility but also philosophical self-understanding.

Steven S. Schwarzschild: Judaism versus Nature

Schwarzschild's defense of Judaism's traditional antipathy toward nature appreciation is, to begin with, anecdotal. He cites his own longstanding dislike for picnic excursions. He goes on to adduce the poet Paul Celan's allegorical short story "Conversation in the Mountains," where two Jewish conversationalists deliberately ignore their scenic surroundings because, in Schwarzschild's words, "God does not communicate with Jews through nature." Afterwards he appeals to Jewish philosophy, contemporary ecological thought, and Jewish texts, respectively, in support of his contention that the disconnectedness between Jews and nature is basic to Judaism.

The distinctively Jewish element in Jewish philosophy, at least in its major trend according to Schwarzschild, is "alienation from and confrontation with nature." Schwarzschild seeks to elucidate that element by way of a contrast with the Christian doctrine of the incarnation, as spelled out in the philosophy of Hegel.[44] According to the latter, God becomes human by taking the form of Christ. As a result, God is said to enter nature; nature is subsequently reshaped by the efforts of Christians and others to make it receptive to Christ's eventual historical return; and the difference between God's activity and nature's is thus gradually narrowed—until there is no difference whatever.

Judaism, in contrast, resists identifying God with nature at all. Judaism's God remains absolutely transcendent. Accordingly, nature merely serves God's purposes. Human beings are indeed "in 'the image of God,'" but only insofar as they are guided by rational or ethical motives when exercising their will over nature. Nature itself, on this view, offers humans no rational or ethical guidance. "In such a rationalistic, volitionalistic, and transcendental context," Schwarzschild insists, "nature possesses no value in itself. Its value lies in its serviceability to man and God, although, to be sure, it must be protected and even improved for precisely this purpose." In short, Jews are "alienated" from nature because, as Jews, they look for guidance from the will of the transcendent God, rather than from nature. Following Hegel, Schwarzschild identifies the Jewish position here with the philosophical position of Kant.[45]

He goes on to suggest that Judaism's "alienation" from nature is perfectly compatible with a sound humanistic ecology. In apparent agreement with White and Toynbee, he calls Genesis 1:28 the "biblical theorem that man is master of nature." To be sure, he denies White's and Toynbee's inference that those verses give humans "license to damage or destroy any part of nature whose immediate human usefulness is not obvious or at least possible." Nor does he see any grounds for linking the biblical notion of mastery of nature, so understood, with the alleged "capitalist domination, exploitation, and alienation of human beings" denounced by philosophical ideologues of the political Left. Nor, finally, does he find merit in ecological arguments for rejecting the biblical view and reasserting the sacredness of nature. Pointing to three such arguments, Schwarzschild suggests why each should be rejected.

1. To argue that nature has inherent purposes that ought to be considered sacred is to imply that nature is analogous to humans in that regard— an implication that Schwarzschild, appealing to the authority of Kant, dismisses as "nonsensical." In any case, he adds, it would mean considering nature's own violence (for example, nature's producing and extinguishing species long before humans even arrived on the scene) as if it were sacred too.
2. To argue that nature ought to be considered sacred inasmuch as humans can construe natural phenomena as objects for aesthetic contemplation, is—if Kant is correct—to ignore the role of art as indicating the difference between "reality" (or what is, as found in natural phenomena) and "ideality" (or what ought to be, as discovered by contemplating natural phenomena in the light of ethical standards that nature itself does not supply).
3. To argue that nature ought to be considered sacred on the grounds that it provides the setting for the evolution of higher organisms, including human beings, is—again, if Kant is correct—to confuse "causality with validity," i.e., to ignore the difference between the material conditions that produce human beings, on the one hand, and the proper object of human worship, on the other.

Finally, Schwarzschild lists a number of Jewish texts in support of his main contention that Judaism and an appreciation of nature are mutually incompatible. Most of these texts we have already seen examined in greater detail by Benstein and Schwartz, whose own pieces may well have been undertaken, at least in part, in response to Schwarzschild's rather peremptory and compressed way of arguing. Schwarzschild unfortunately assumes that his narrower (Kantian) thesis about how Judaism relates—or fails to relate— to nature is adequately explained and defended by showing that it is consistent with his broader (Hegelian) thesis about how Judaism is opposed to

Christianity. Perhaps for this reason, both the Ehrenfelds and Kay, who
claim no familiarity with Kant or Hegel or their twentieth-century epigones,
find Schwarzschild's argument exasperating.[46] Even so, their main objections seem worth noting.

On the one hand, they consider Schwarzschild's anecdotal evidence im-
pertinent. To Schwarzschild's dismissive question, "Who was the last famous
Jewish mountain climber?", for example, the Ehrenfelds respond politely by
offering to provide him with a list of postbiblical figures from all walks of life,
including the first-century legalist Akiva and the twentieth-century Israeli
general Avraham Yoffe, who all have hands-on appreciations for nature. To
Schwarzschild's personal testimony that his urban forebears for generations
disdained nature as well, Kay responds by suggesting that the reasons for
their disdain may not have been "philosophical," as he seems to be claiming,
but "historical," namely, the forced ghettoization of Jewish life in his native
Germany during times past. She gently urges him to leave his office and walk
outdoors a little more often.

On the other hand, the Ehrenfelds and Kay also find Schwarzschild's citations of Jewish sources insufficiently attentive to their original, ecological setting. The Ehrenfelds remind Schwarzschild of texts his argument
overlooks, including various laws prohibiting cruelty to animals, protecting nature during warfare, conserving natural resources, linking the calendar and festival celebrations to the earth and its cycles, and instituting
the sabbath so as to harmonize the ongoing mastery of nature with "stewardship" (as discussed in the Ehrenfeld–Bentley piece we examined earlier). Kay, for her part, faults Schwarzschild's argument for being unrepre-
sentative of how Jews, demographically speaking, understand themselves.
She adds that, inasmuch as the views he claims Judaism opposes for their
purported concern for nature—pantheism, paganism, Christianity—are
"not necessarily ecologically sound," the range of alternatives he mentions
need hardly be considered exhaustive.

While the Ehrenfelds and Kay miss the philosophical dimension of
Schwarzschild's argument, the serious doubts they raise about its practical
implications for Judaism and ecology seem, in general, warranted: Does the
merging of Judaism with, say, Kantianism here do justice to the relevant Jewish texts? Does it also do justice to the pressing ecological demands of today,
or any day? Let us turn to the modified version of Schwarzschild's position as
found in Wyschogrod's essay, which seems to have the latter question in
mind, though not necessarily the former.

Michael Wyschogrod: Judaism and "Upper Ecology"

Wyschogrod takes his bearings less by a direct appeal to philosophical or
theological arguments, than by reflecting on the current state of ecological
thought. He distinguishes between what he calls "lower" and "upper ecology."

By "lower ecology," he means thoughtful warnings about the practical dangers, often hidden and long-term, resulting from the careless use of modern technology. No thoughtful person, according to Wyschogrod, should avoid considering, for example, the pollution risks of malfunctioning nuclear reactors, or the health risks of overuse of X-rays. By "upper ecology," on the other hand, he means belief in the sanctity of nature as an overall preventative for that carelessness. Unlike, say, White and Toynbee, Wyschogrod does not think that "upper ecology" is a mandatory response to the dangers pointed out by "lower ecology." But he does think that the seriousness of those dangers invites us to weigh "upper ecology's" pros and cons.

The main advantage of believing in the sanctity of nature as understood by "upper ecology," he says, is to supply a picture of human beings fully at home in their natural environment and in harmony with it. Still, Wyschogrod notes a difficulty with that picture. It may well fit the way of life of native North and South Americans whose small tribal societies once occupied a vast, untamed continental setting. But does it also fit the way of life of the European settlers who came to displace them and have since urbanized much of that setting? In other words, does nature worship suit our own, citified, and sophisticated way of life? This seems to be Wyschogrod's central question. In effect, he replies in the negative, though with some misgivings, as we shall see. He states his own conviction about the urbanizing effect on America's settlers of the Christianity they brought with them—and so, ultimately, of Christianity's underlying Jewish or biblical roots too. Both Judaism and Christianity, he says, understand themselves in terms of civilizing, historical events, such as the exodus from Egypt, rather than in terms of nature. Both, then, focus "on the actions of human beings rather than on natural cycles." Unlike Schwarzschild, who sees a fundamental opposition between Judaism and Christianity, Wyschogrod sees them in agreement as urban religions with a shared opposition to nature worship.

The remainder of Wyschogrod's argument points to the morally deleterious effects of nature worship, as found nowadays in what he calls "evolutionary thinking." By the latter, he means the Darwinism that dominates much of today's philosophical discussions of human life vis-à-vis our natural environment. "Evolutionary thinking" holds that ethical standards are the mere product of a struggle for existence which humans share with subhuman life. As a chilling example of "evolutionary thinking" in this sense, Wyschogrod points to the Nazi policy of mass murdering the handicapped and, subsequently, the Jews, on the purported rationale that the designated victims were impediments to the evolutionary development of the human race. Nazism is said to be indebted to Nietzsche's evolutionary view of biblical morality as "slave morality"—a survival device by which the powerless "brainwash" the powerful against using their natural strength to destroy the weak, including widows, orphans, the poor, and in general the disadvantaged whom biblical morality seeks to protect. Wyschogrod also criticizes

Plato's *Republic*, which he sees as a pre-Darwinian example of identifying moral standards with biological standards for its allowing infanticide in the interest of a politically salutary eugenics. Such are the dangers, according to Wyschogrod, of recognizing nothing sacrosanct beyond nature. In contrast, the biblical account of creation implies that nature is not the be-all or end-all, and that whatever sanctity it has derives only from the sanctity of its divine creator. Like Schwarzschild, Wyschogrod insists that the biblical account meets the need to treat our nonhuman environment respectfully, without nature-worship's moral callousness as found in the foregoing examples. Wyschogrod's reasoning seems to be as follows: Given that humans are created with bodies that are akin to and dependent on other living bodies in nature, the Bible expects them to consider the welfare of those other bodies as they would their own, in their own self-interest. Yet only because humans are also more than bodies, as the biblical account maintains, are they also capable of ignoring or misconstruing what is in their self-interest—to the point of abusing the rest of nature as well. For just that reason, our current ecological crisis is better understood and corrected in terms of the biblical account, Wyschogrod implies, than in terms of current "evolutionary thinking."

In a curious postscript, Wyschogrod regrets that the biblical writers were not more informative about the nature-worshiping religions they opposed. He wonders whether recorded interviews with priests of Baal and Ashteret (pagan nature gods whose worshipers the biblical prophets excoriate) would have been helpful. He does not speculate further on what such help would amount to nowadays. Presumably he means that their testimony, despite its moral dubiousness in other respects, would provide us with added reasons for moderating our potential for abusing the environment by means of the technological mastery alleged to have been encouraged by the Bible. Still, it is not clear why Wyschogrod would have us turn for help in understanding our present predicament to the ancient nature worshipers mentioned in the Bible, who are possibly inarticulate and in any case no longer available, instead of the highly articulate and readily available writings of Nietzsche and Plato, whom he has also classified as nature worshipers. We are left to wonder whether he has dismissed the latter all too hastily. In any case, Wyschogrod seems to be modifying his earlier stance. Practically speaking, he now appears to be leaning in the direction of those who accuse the biblical view of responsibility for our environmental crisis after all. Despite his earlier argument—or perhaps because of it—Wyschogrod cannot help leaving the final impression that the biblical account of creation is not sufficient, or not sufficiently persuasive, to meet the current crisis as pointed out by the "lower ecology" he endorses, to say nothing of the "upper ecology" he rejects. Wyschogrod's ambivalence is noted by Schwartz, who therefore asks whether Judaism can succeed in accommodating itself to respect for nature in ways Wyschogrod (and Schwarzschild) may have overlooked.

Eilon Schwartz: Judaism's Lack of Environmental Consensus

In "Judaism and Nature," Schwartz argues that the current lack of consensus over the proper Jewish attitude toward environmentalism may be an asset, not a liability. Disagreement invites us to re-examine the basic issues, without having to slur Judaism's "ambiguities and ambivalences." Schwartz therefore seeks to "engage the points of tension" among contemporary Jewish views about environmentalism, with the suggestion that Judaism's longstanding but often overlooked ecological concerns are not peripheral, but central to serious theological and philosophical discussions about Judaism nowadays.

He looks first at how contemporary Jewish theologians differ among themselves in determining where Judaism stands vis-à-vis today's proliferating sanctification-of-nature movements.[47] Aharon Lichtenstein (like Schwarzschild and Wyschogrod) considers the opposition between Judaism and nature worshipers theologically irreconcilable, in the same way as Judaism remained theologically irreconcilable with the Greek and Roman paganism of Hellenistic times. Everett Gendler, on the other hand, points to Judaism's own, longstanding tradition of nature appreciation (e.g., in its harvest festival motifs, New Moon rituals, etc.), dormant since postbiblical times, but recently revived, especially with modern Zionism's reasserting Jews' ancestral connection with the land of Israel. Meanwhile Norman Lamm locates the pertinent theological disagreement—over whether God alone is holy or nature is as well—within Judaism itself, and assimilates it to the controversy between Mitnagdim and Hasidim which arose in the eighteenth century, during the dawn of Jewish modernity. Finally, Ismar Schorsch observes that, whatever separates Judaism and paganism theologically, they share common ground ethically when it comes to ecological issues. Schwartz agrees with Schorsch that the divergence between Judaism and paganism is best explored by starting from their common ethical ground.

Is the ethical concern for the well-being of our natural environment which Judaism shares with paganism, then, better understood, and so promoted, by appealing first and foremost to Judaism's transcendent God or by appealing more directly to nature itself? Taking his bearings by a distinction invoked by Schwarzschild and Wyschogrod, Schwartz reduces the foregoing alternative to two different understandings of human history.[48] That is, is history, as Schwarzschild and Wyschogrod assert, a linear progress toward a final, divinely mandated goal for human beings—like an arrow? Or does it consist rather of an accumulation of purposive acts, each more or less self-contained and without a common linear direction, except that the same kinds of acts tend to be repeated—as if in cycles? In identifying Judaism exclusively with the former, or arrowlike view of history, Schwarzschild and Wyschogrod sever it from the latter, or cyclical view. According to Schwartz, however, either view of history is, by itself, one-sided. It follows that both views ought somehow to be combined. Schwartz wonders whether what prevented Schwarzschild and Wyschogrod from considering this last possibility was their looking at nature, in effect, through narrowly Darwinian eyes.[49]

As Schwartz himself says in his critique of Wyschogrod, "attempting to understand morality as an outgrowth of the natural order does not necessarily demand understanding morality as 'survival of the fittest.'" But if so, then in order to avoid the one-sidedness Schwartz warns us against, must we not raise the deeper philosophical question that he rightly touches on, namely, "whether ethics are learned from the natural order," and, if so, how? Because Schwartz himself does not pursue this question beyond a few passing suggestions, we are left to do so ourselves during the remainder of our readings.

Eric Katz: Genocide and "Ecocide"

Katz's way of raising the question of how we might learn ethics from nature is to recount his recent tour of several former Nazi death camp sites in Eastern Europe. We are invited to ponder the link between genocide ("the planned extermination of European Jewry") and "ecocide" ("the massive destruction of the earth's biosphere"). The link, Katz suggests, is "the concept of domination."

What struck Katz as tourist was the scenic beauty of the once grim, filthy, chimney-smoke shrouded sites. The new and spontaneous vegetation, he surmises in retrospect, "demonstrates the power of Nature to reassert itself in the midst of human destruction and human evil." At the time of his visit, however, the lush scenery distracted him from contemplating the evil the former camps were preserved to commemorate. Indeed (in a manner reminiscent of the Mishnaic text analyzed by Benstein, though not mentioned by Katz), the scene positively "prevent[ed]" him from contemplating that evil. Only after leaving the scene entirely did the evil in question present itself to him again, when he read an historian's account of the role of the camps in the Nazis' East-European agricultural policies. The policies had included not only the redesigning of conquered farms and villages on the German model; the replanting of trees, shrubs, and hedges to protect crops; and the humidifying of the indigenous climate by enhancing local dew and cloud formation; but also the routine "ethnic cleansing" of Jews and others to accommodate the planned importation of German settlers. "The domination of nature and [the domination of] humanity," Katz observes, "are clearly linked." This observation leads him, in the remainder of his essay, to locate the evil he has been seeking in the activity of domination itself.

Katz is impressed by an apparent similarity in the attempts to dominate both nature and humans by Nazism and—as he gathers from the sources cited by Schwartz and Benstein, at any rate—by Judaism. From Schwartz's account of Judaism's rejecting paganism and giving humans the task of improving nature, Katz infers that Judaism's "desacralization of natural processes" is equivalent to its "plac[ing] an ethical order on an amoral natural reality."[50] And from Benstein's emphasis on Caro's argument that the study of nature ought to be guided by the study of Torah, he infers that Judaism says that "Our knowledge of Nature . . . must be organized and modeled by our knowledge of spiritual law."[51] If Schwartz's and Benstein's arguments are correct, he concludes, then Judaism too seeks to "impose human ideas of truth and goodness on our understanding of the natural world." Judaism's aim is thus likened in turn (as White and Toynbee would also have it) to the modern "Enlightenment project" of attempting to "control, manipulate, and modify natural processes" for the sake of our own convenience and comfort. In drawing out the ethically dubious implications of these various efforts at domination, Katz goes so far as to include contemporary environmentalism too. He suggests that even well-meant attempts at ecological restoration nowadays—e.g., reflooding drained wetlands, replanting strip-mined hills, reforesting former farms—amount to imposing our own, convenience-oriented technology in order to redirect nature's once-spontaneous processes and then deceiving ourselves into thinking that we have let nature itself re-emerge, instead of reflecting more soberly on whether we ought to have had enough self-restraint to have left those particular wetlands, hills, and forests alone in the first place.

What then does nature teach us here in the way of a proper environmental ethic? Katz qualifies his answer by saying that it is only preliminary to a more comprehensive teaching needed for how humans ought to relate to themselves and their natural environment. Even so, he recalls how nature is able to heal its own scars, including those we humans have inflicted,[52] if we just let it be. From this initial observation, he infers that we ought to restrain our efforts to dominate nature wherever possible, so as to allow it the same "free and autonomous development" we think desirable in human individuals and communities.

Katz's counsel of restraint resembles that of Jonas, who also recoils at the specter of modern technology's ever-tightening grip over nature. Still, the argument Katz offers remains subject to difficulties that Jonas perhaps avoids. Jonas, finding insufficient guidance within modern thought for the self-restraint needed to loosen technology's grip, turns for ethical support to Judaism, which he recognizes as an ethically sound supplement to modern thought. Katz's argument, however, has the effect of assimilating Judaism to modern thought as he understands it, by viewing both, at bottom, merely as differing ways for humans to exercise domination. But if so, how can we turn to Judaism's ethical teachings for our needed supplement? Philosophically, Katz can only stipulate the desirability of tolerance by humans for nature, as something like the desirability of mutual tolerance among humans themselves. His underlying premise seems to be the similarity between flora-and-fauna on the one hand and humans on the other, as beings collectively worthy of human respect.[53] Yet it is difficult to reconcile this premise with Katz's further assertion, when commenting once again on the lush foliage covering the former death camp site, that nature here is acting "without an intention or design." If subhuman nature acts merely pointlessly, if plants or animals lack any inherent purposiveness besides "domination," why should we accord them the same ethical recognition we are expected to accord our fellow humans, who *seem* at any rate to be led by nobler purposes as well (ethical decency, for example, if we may adduce Katz's evident purpose in offering his argument in the first place)?

Given the ecological stakes here, to say nothing of the Jewish ones, we can only look further for guidance on this question. Let us do so by considering, first, Levy's argument for animals' rights, and then the essays by Bleich and Kass, which address the related issues of animal experimentation and meat eating.

Ze'ev Levy: Judaism and Animal Rights

Levy's plea for Judaism to endorse animal rights seems motivated by two pressing concerns. As a professor of philosophy, he is aware of the nineteenth-century German philosopher Arthur Schopenhauer's dubious charge that Judaism is insensitive to animals. And as a Jew, he has misgivings about the pain inflicted on animals nowadays during experimental research and mass food-processing. His argument for making animal rights part of Judaism is thus both philosophical and religious.

Philosophically, the issue Levy raises is limited to whether or not we have ethical obligations to animals, and if so, whether our obligations are direct or merely indirect. He shows that the philosophical tradition contains arguments for all three possibilities. (1) René Descartes implicitly denied that we have ethical obligations to animals, by suggesting that animals were no different than machines (*automata*). Levy dismisses Descartes's denial, however, by saying that we know animals feel pain. (2) Immanuel Kant attributed consciousness to animals, but not self-consciousness or rationality, the prerequisite for our having any direct obligations toward them. Hence, Kant inferred, our obligations toward them are at best indirect. According to Levy, however, Kant assumed that animals exist merely as a means for our ends, an assumption Levy considers unwarranted, on the grounds that animals may be held responsible for their misdeeds[54] and that humans who do not have or exercise full rational capacities are not considered simply as means for others' ends either.[55] Levy acknowledges Kant's further argument that cruelty to animals is likely to foster cruelty toward humans as well, but considers this "psychological" likelihood "ethically insufficient." (3) Finally, Levy approves of the view shared by the Utilitarians Jeremy Bentham and John Stuart Mill, that animals and humans deserve equal moral respect based on their common capacity to suffer. Yet Levy finds Utilitarianism, too, insufficient, since its basic principle—"the greatest happiness for the greatest number"—justifies the suffering routinely caused by the crowded conditions and forced feeding imposed on animals by today's food industry, and the unanesthetized experiments performed on them by today's drug industry, so long as there is widespread popular approval of mass-produced meat and animal-tested medicines. In any case, neither Bentham nor Mill went as far as Schopenhauer, who insisted (as against what he took to be Genesis 1:28's derogation of animals) that animals are directly worthy of moral respect in their own right. In what follows, Levy tries to show how far Judaism goes in meeting Schopenhauer's standard and why the added endorsement of animal rights would both round out Judaism's ethical teachings and satisfy Schopenhauer.

Religiously, then, Levy argues that the biblical and talmudic sources, with some exceptions, come closest to Kant's position that we have only indirect obligations to animals. Throughout the Bible, he admits, God is said to care for animals as well as humans,[56] often as a direct obligation.[57] Yet the biblical commandments themselves are mostly concerned with the humane treatment of domestic animals—perhaps for their own sake, but perhaps only for the sake of their owners.[58] For example, while the Talmud stipulates that one should not buy an animal before having food for it, or sit down to eat before feeding one's animals,[59] both Saadya and Maimonides in their explanatory comments emphasize only the strictly human benefits of doing so. Besides, while some biblical commentators suggest that humans were originally meant to be vegetarians,[60] and a talmudic story has heaven punish Rabbi Judah the Prince (editor of the Mishnah) with a thirteen-year toothache for failing to take pity on a calf seeking refuge from slaughter,[61] meat eating is nevertheless permitted. Levy himself regrets that neither the Bible nor the Talmud explicitly condemns killing animals for reasons other than food and self-defense,[62] or insists on vegetarianism, which would have been more consistent with Judaism's general opposition to causing animals pain (i.e., to *tza'ar ba'alei chayyim*, as we have already seen it called). In addition, no biblical or talmudic source directly addresses the two aforementioned forms of cruelty to animals about which Levy is most concerned nowadays. The suffering caused by today's factory-like raising and killing of animals for food, he admonishes, is hardly justified by the profit motive behind those methods. Any rationale for the painful and debilitating use of animals in laboratory experiments, he adds, would also justify using human beings in the same way, i.e., without their informed consent. Nor is Levy persuaded by the rationale that such experiments are justified for the limited purpose of advancing human health: Since such limits are in practice hard to define, they are easily overstepped (as Jonas too has observed).

The core of Levy's argument is thus that Judaism does not go far enough in preventing mistreatment of animals, especially if Genesis 1:28 means (as Levy thinks it does) that nature exists simply for the benefit of human beings. Nevertheless, in offering a philosophical argument to the effect that Judaism ought to stipulate that animals have rights of their own against potential human abusers, Levy does not say what, if anything, entitles them to such rights besides their capacity to suffer. As it stands, his argument does not come to terms with the obvious difference between animals, which evidently lack reason, and humans, who are at least capable of it—a difference essential to Judaism's ethical teachings generally speaking.[63] Levy, like Katz, tends to gloss over that difference. Without minimizing the importance of the pressing issue to which Levy alerts us, therefore, in what follows we must question the adequacy of his arguments for meeting that issue. First, then, does the apparent silence of biblical and talmudic sources on such matters as animal experimentation and vegetarianism serve to allow environmental abuse—in this case, abuse of animals—as Levy claims? Second, is Levy simply correct about the meaning of Genesis 1:28? We shall consider each of these questions in turn, by looking at the arguments of Bleich and Kass, respectively.

J. David Bleich: Judaism's Views of Animal Experimentation and Vegetarianism

Bleich's defenses of Judaism on animal experimentation and vegetarianism are particularly à propos here. For one thing, he includes among his extensive biblical and talmudic sources the same ones Levy does, but treats them in much more detail and with thoroughgoing references to latter day rabbinic authorities, whom Levy does not discuss. At the same time, following the rabbinic authorities he cites, Bleich shares Levy's premise that Genesis 1:28 implies that nature exists simply for the benefit of human beings. Bleich thus allows us to rethink Levy's argument without having to ignore Levy's basic worry that Genesis 1:28 somehow authorizes unwarranted animal suffering. Our analysis will therefore concentrate on where Bleich's assessment of Jewish sources differs from Levy's, and why. We shall postpone further consideration of Genesis 1:28 itself till our discussion of Kass.

Since no biblical or talmudic sources explicitly mention animal experimentation, Bleich's essay on "Judaism and Animal Experimentation" aims to discover their implicit position. He adduces pertinent rabbinic arguments in four related areas: concern for animal welfare, slaughter of animals, *tza'ar ba'alei chayyim* for human benefit, and morality beyond the requirements of the law.

To begin with, he cites numerous biblical passages that the rabbis understand to "reflect a concern for animal welfare."[64] Nevertheless he cautions that such passages, separately or together, do not amount to an overall "system of normative duties or responsibilities." Among them, to be sure, are biblical laws "designed to protect and promote animal welfare" in specific instances: Passersby must stop to help unload an overburdened beast of burden (Ex. 23:5); oxen treading grain must be left unmuzzled so that they can eat of it as they wish (Deut. 25:4); flesh must not be torn from a live animal for food (Gen. 9:4 and Deut. 12:23, at least according to talmudic exegesis); and animals must be allowed Sabbath rest (Ex. 23:12, Deut. 5:14) and be fed before humans can eat (Deut. 11:15, again according to talmudic exegesis). Still, Bleich implicitly agrees with Levy that neither the biblical passages themselves, nor the rabbinic inferences drawn from them, necessarily put animals' welfare first, ahead of the welfare of their owners.

One rabbinic discussion Bleich cites does seem to reverse that priority. According to *Baba Metzi'a* 32b, stopping to help unload an overburdened animal, as mandated by Exodus 23:5, is required less for the sake of the animal's owner—who, after all, may be at fault as the cause of the overloading—than for the sake of alleviating the animal's own pain. Yet Bleich adds that the full talmudic passage here goes on to record a dispute over whether *tza'ar ba'alei chayyim*, as a legal principle, is or is not strictly biblical. Among later authorities who hold that it is biblical, only a small minority, including Rashi, derive it from the Exodus verse. Others seeking a biblical basis for *tza'ar ba'alei chayyim* prefer to derive it from the incident of Balaam's ass (Num. 22:27ff.), as does Maimonides, or else from the prohibition against muzzling oxen (Deut. 25:4). Still others can only appeal to less obvious sources, such as Moses' miraculously producing water from a rock to let the Israelites and their cattle drink (Num. 20:8), God's extending his "tender mercies over all his works" including animals (Ps. 145:9), or the Torah's general injunction to "walk in [God's] ways" (Deut. 28:9, with 11:22). In any case, Bleich notes as Levy does that rabbinic law has no concept of animal "rights" as such. Neither animals nor their owners can institute judicial proceedings to prevent their being victimized, for example, even though rabbinic law also stipulates that animals accused of manslaughter are entitled to due process, including the right to be present during their trial.

In short, Bleich does not differ from Levy in conceding that Jewish law is more concerned for the moral welfare of human agents than for the bodily welfare of animals themselves.[65]

Accordingly, Bleich is not surprised that *tza'ar ba'alei chayyim* is "less than absolute." Slaughtering animals, though circumscribed by rabbinic law, is nonetheless permitted. Questions of *tza'ar ba'alei chayyim* concern not so much whether they may be slaughtered, as how and why. Thus various commentators on Genesis 9:4, where meat eating is explicitly permitted to humans for the first time, note that the ritual means for slaughtering animals—namely, carefully slitting the throat so as to induce death by simply letting the blood drain out—is appropriate both for minimizing pain to the victims and for not inculcating cruelty as a human character trait. Only about whether animals may also be slaughtered by other means and for other purposes, do authorities seriously disagree. Some hold that the mere act of slaughtering can never constitute wanton destruction, so long as the animal is caused no further pain. (Accordingly, causing an animal's death by starvation or thirst, for example, would be forbidden.) Others disallow even the putatively painless slaughtering authorized by rabbinic law, except for some overriding human need, such as food.

(Accordingly, destroying an unwanted pet would be forbidden.) Further controversies, as Bleich reports them, concern the permissibility of hunting for the purpose of obtaining food (although or because all rabbinic authorities forbid it as a sport) and of using live animals as dog food (although or because there is general agreement, following Genesis 9:4, that humans may not sever a living limb from an animal for that purpose).

In connection with this last controversy, Bleich suggests that, according to one rabbinic authority at least, the question of imposing suffering on animals merely for the benefit of other animals is parallel to the question of imposing suffering on humans for the benefit of other humans. In the human case, imposing such suffering is justified only if the sufferer has given prior consent. Obviously animals lack the capacity to grant that consent among themselves. A fortiori, Bleich reasons, they also lack the capacity to consent for the sake of humans—a point we have already seen to be decisive for Levy's argument against animal experimentation. Here we see, once again, that Bleich and Levy agree, at least on where rabbinic tradition stands in such matters. The question on which they divide concerns what circumstances, if any, override animals' incapacity to give their consent.

That rabbinic law permits inflicting pain on animals for a variety of legitimate human purposes, Bleich shows by citing two rabbinic rulings. First, ritual slaughterers are allowed to inflict incidental pain while removing neck wool from sheep, or neck feathers from birds, if the removal is necessary to accomplish the prescribed throat-slitting. Second, the tendons of a deceased king's horse may be severed in order to honor the king during his funeral. Generally speaking, then, it is permitted to inflict incidental pain on animals for purposes besides human food—presumably including, as a matter of course, human healing.

But are there legal limits to the range of practices deemed to warrant causing animals incidental pain? Or is rabbinic law, however well-intentioned, unable to prevent the extreme pain inflicted on animals by, say, experimental vivisection or drug testing, as Levy for one suspects? Levy's suspicions are not without plausibility, since, as Bleich indicates, rabbinic authorities frequently consider legitimate financial gain sufficient by itself to outweigh *tza'ar ba'alei chayyim*. For example, although castrating an animal is forbidden (in line with Lev. 22:24), removing a rooster's comb for the supposed purpose of inducing sterility, though painful, is permitted. Similarly, examining a dove bleeding at the neck before slaughter, in order to see whether the trachea and esophagus are sound so as to certify the dove's fitness for human consumption, is permitted even if the examination requires painfully enlarging the original cut. Also, although selling a kosher chicken to an idolater is forbidden lest he offer it as a pagan sacrifice, nevertheless mutilating the chicken during the sale is permitted in order to render it unfit for such a sacrifice.

All the same, Bleich finds that rabbinic authorities recognize instances where painful practices technically allowed by the law—plucking quill feathers from a live bird, for example—should be refrained from on account of their inherent cruelty. He therefore turns to a discussion of the role of morality above and beyond the specific requirements of the law in such matters.

In referring to the Talmudic story of Rabbi Judah the Prince's thirteen-year toothache (*Baba Metzi'a* 85a), cited as well by Levy, Bleich emphasizes that, although the rabbis acknowledge that ultimately laws against insensitivity toward animals cannot be humanly enforced since insensitivity as a private motive is not necessarily publicly discernible, still someone of Rabbi Judah's moral stature is expected to exercise proper sensitivity anyway. That is, as what we would call a role model, he is to be judged by higher standards—by the standards of the heavenly court, as the rabbis say. All the same, Bleich cites a more recent rabbinic authority to the effect that supralegal standards of behavior may well not apply to questions of animal experimentation: whether or not to be bound by standards over and above the law seems to be a personal decision and not one that can be imposed on others; the goal of eliminating human pain by means of the knowledge gained through animal experimentation outweighs the pain caused in the animals themselves;[66] and the resulting knowledge would in any case benefit the community at large and not just a human individual, who could easily consent to his own private suffering rather than cause pain to others but could not take it upon himself to preempt the possibility of relieving others' pain. Nor is that all. According to another recent authority whom Bleich cites, since feeding experimental animals a poisonous substance does not cause them pain directly or immediately, as plucking quill feathers would, therefore such an act cannot constitute *tza'ar ba'alei chayyim*—assuming, at any rate, that it is the cruel intent, rather than the mere animal suffering, which rabbinic law finds objectionable. Indeed, as yet another recent authority insists while defending animal experimentation, quills may be plucked from dead animals as well as living ones, whereas experiments may well require living ones; but *tza'ar ba'alei chayyim* occurs only when the pain being caused is unnecessary, as was the case with Rabbi Judah's gratuitous scolding of the frightened calf.

In sum, whereas Levy argues that rabbinic espousal of animal rights is necessary in order to prevent the infliction of any and all animal suffering that may accompany animal experimentation, Bleich implies that the longstanding tradition of rabbinic moral admonitions against wanton cruelty to animals, when combined with the extant rabbinic legal rulings to the same effect, is sufficient to underwrite the just treatment of animals without depriving the community of the benefits of possible medical advances achieved by means of animal experimentation. Before commenting further on Bleich's defense of Judaism here, let us turn to his discussion of Judaism on meat eating, the other chief human cause of animal suffering which arouses Levy's worry.

Bleich begins his "Vegetarianism and Judaism" by noting that, for Judaism, whether or not an ethical principle is binding depends on whether it is authorized by divine revelation, i.e., ultimately by the written text of the Torah. Thus, he adds, defenders of vegetarianism as a moral ideal within Judaism often appeal to *Sanhedrin* 59b's observation that meat eating was not permitted to Adam in the Garden of Eden, but only to Noah and his descendants after the Flood. Such defenders go on to argue that, because Noah lived in the wake of generations of moral decline subsequent to Adam's banishment, permission was granted only because humans could no longer be routinely expected to live up to the higher moral standards of the Garden, even though those standards, including vegetarianism, remain the ideal to which all humans should aspire. Bleich casts doubt on this argument, however. He points out that the text of the Torah is silent about its reasons for permitting meat eating, and cites two rabbinic authorities to the effect that the change in humans which occasioned the sanctioning of meat eating may only have been biological: Adam did not desire meat at all before eating the forbidden fruit (*Tur Shulkhan Arukh* on Gen. 1:29), and the geographical dispersion of humans outside the Garden may be said to have weakened them physically, not just spiritually (Malbim on Gen. 9:3). In any case, Bleich adds, there is not just one but a plurality of views among rabbinic scholars concerning vegetarianism. He gathers them into three.

A first view is apt to be misconstrued from a talmudic source forbidding meat eating to ignoramuses, i.e., to those insufficiently familiar with the intricacies of Judaism's dietary laws (*Pesachim* 49b). The point here, as Bleich's further sources emphasize, is not to reward scholars with food choices denied to others, but to call attention to the complexity of the meat eating restrictions themselves—which require differentiating kosher from nonkosher animals, removing forbidden fat and veins, soaking and salting meat, etc. The implication of *Pesachim* 49b as far as vegetarianism is concerned, then, is simply that abstaining from meat remains a valid option within the practice of Jewish law. Bleich cites the anecdotal example of pious immigrants to the United States during the early part of the twentieth century who preferred vegetarianism when *kashrut* supervision was lax.

A second view justifies vegetarianism for the sake of avoiding the meanness and cruelty likely to arise in humans who are in the habit of slaughtering animals, rather than for the sake of the welfare of animals as such. Bleich shows that at least one rabbinic authority, Joseph Albo, finds the appeal to animals' welfare as such morally dubious for its characteristic inability to take into account the superiority of humans to animals—an inability we have already met up with in considering both Katz's and Levy's arguments. Albo maintains, for example, that Cain's erroneous assumption that animals and humans are equal led him to sacrifice to God cultivated vegetation rather than a slaughtered animal, and afterwards to misconstrue God's acceptance of Abel's animal sacrifice by slaughtering Abel for that purpose as well.[67] Bleich goes on to suggest that, from the viewpoint of Albo and others, God's permitting meat eating to postflood generations was "required only as a means of explicitly negating the residual notion that animals are somehow endowed with rights and that man's obligations vis-à-vis animals are somehow rooted in such rights rather than in a concern for the possible moral degeneration of man himself."

Finally, a third view endorses vegetarianism as a moral ideal for a future eschatological age, but not for humans here and now. As Bleich shows, its oft-cited twentieth-century proponent, Rabbi Abraham Isaac Kook, actually advances four distinct arguments *against* vegetarianism as a contemporary goal: First, there are more pressing moral priorities nowadays, e.g., eliminating national hatreds and racial discrimination. Second, humans as presently constituted cannot sublimate their desire for meat, and so are likely to eat other humans if animal flesh is denied to them. Third, to grant humans dominion over animals befits humans' higher spiritual capacity and moral obligations, whereas to accord animals equal rights would give humans an excuse to degenerate spiritually and morally to the level of the brutes. Finally, vegetarianism is compatible with human callousness, so that an exaggerated concern for animals' well-being might easily displace proper concern for humans' well-being—a point Bleich illustrates by recalling the specter of Germans during the Nazi years "watching with equanimity while their Jewish neighbors were dispatched to crematoria and immediately thereafter turning their attention to the welfare of the household pets that had been left behind."

In sum, Bleich finds that Jewish tradition neither requires meat eating as such, nor endorses vegetarianism as a moral ideal, but confines such matters to the private discretion of the practicing Jew.

Bleich's finding that Jewish tradition does not require meat eating seems open to the objection that the biblical text explicitly commands celebrating festivals by means of animal sacrifices, i.e., by eating meat. This objection loses some, though not all, of its force, in the light of a rabbinic controversy Bleich reports concerning whether festive meat eating is required nowadays, given that the ancient Temple has been destroyed and animal sacrifices are no longer officially feasible. Bleich concludes his essay by elaborating the controversy in some detail. On the one hand, he cites a number of authorities who consider festive meat eating optional not only now but perhaps even during biblical times, on the grounds that other prescribed forms of rejoicing appear to suffice, notably wine drinking and wearing fine clothes. On the other hand, he notes that Maimonides and others nevertheless insist on festive meat eating, to enhance the joyous mood of the given festival. Bleich himself does not try to decide the controversy, except to add that "it is certain that the Sages [i.e., those rabbinic authorities recorded in the Talmud] encouraged and urged the practice." In the final essay in our readings, Kass takes up anew the question of the merits of Judaism's laws concerning meat eating, albeit from within the biblical setting quite apart from subsequent rabbinic tradition. Let us postpone further direct consideration of the question of meat eating until then.

Meanwhile, a passing claim Bleich makes about ethical arguments indicates our additional need to turn to Kass. Bleich remarks that "Ethicists [meaning professors of philosophy like himself] who do not accept the notion of revelation are left with a problem with regard to the nature of ethical propositions." Bleich has in mind the problem of distinguishing between an assertion of my own private preference (e.g., "I like spinach") and the assertion of a moral norm that ought to be shared by others besides myself (e.g., "Meat eating, or animal experimentation, is a good thing"). Assertions of moral norms, unlike assertions of merely private preferences, amount to double assertions according to Bleich:[68] the private preference ("I approve of meat-eating") plus the appeal to others to share it ("So should you"). The problem as Bleich sees it, then, concerns whether the "So should you" part of the double assertion has any sound basis beyond the "I approve of" part— i.e., whether the assertion of a moral norm is at bottom anything more than the speaker's own subjective preference, or prejudice. When all is said and done, if the "I approve of" part of the moral norm is not based on revelation, so runs Bleich's claim, then it lacks a sound basis.

Bleich's claim contains a deeper philosophical difficulty, however. It has to do with his supposition that revelation as such guarantees the more-than-subjective character of moral norms. Consider that there may well be a variety of revelations—not just the biblical one, or at any rate not just the biblical one as understood by Jewish orthodoxy. At the very least, Bleich would have to restrict "revelation" to the written text of the Torah as interpreted by Jewish orthodoxy, a restriction he may tacitly intend anyway. Even so, the variety of interpretations of revelation remains within orthodoxy itself, as is evident from Bleich's own attempts to resolve the controversies over animal experimentation and meat eating in particular. Characteristic of Judaism's moral norms, then, are not only the controversies they often beget, but also the need to resolve those controversies by means of reason, as Bleich himself illustrates so impressively. The difficulty in Bleich's account of moral norms thus concerns the role of reason in efforts such as his own. Is reason here simply a *means* for resolving controversies that arise in interpreting revelation, or is it in some sense the *measure* or criterion of revelation? On the one hand, to say that reason is simply a means is to say that the controversies Bleich attempts to resolve are, in the end, merely competing glosses on principles incontrovertibly revealed in the written text of the Torah. If so, however, it is hard to say why those incontrovertibly revealed principles should beget controversy in the first place—unless we are to locate the cause in the moral and/or intellectual limitations of the interpreters. But then, for discerning their limitations we would seem to need further principles, say, psychological or philosophical ones; and if these in turn are not incontrovertibly revealed in the written text as well—as they do not appear to be[69]— then the burden of arriving at them falls instead on reason as Bleich seems obliged to construe it here, namely, on reason as little more than a supplier of the means for conflict resolution. Yet what is left to prevent us from saying further that the very notion of the incontrovertibility of revelation is likewise a means that reason supplies for resolving controversies among more or less limited interpreters—by stipulating that they defer in any case to *some* interpretation of the written text—with the unfortunate result that the written text of the Torah could no longer be said to consist of incontrovertibly revealed principles pure and simple. On the other hand, however, perhaps the Torah is the wise product of a wise author after all, i.e., the embodiment of reason which sets forth the most reasonable way of life for Jews as Jews, so that the true interpretation of its moral norms is accessible to those Jews whose reason is most highly developed, and just to that extent. If so, Bleich's claim about the difference between moral norms and subjective prejudices would have to be widened to accommodate the likelihood that the Torah's norms would recommend themselves to reason anyway, although or because they happen to be revealed. Bleich's claim, in short, does not adequately address the necessary, if problematic, role of reason in interpreting the Torah's moral norms.

If I am not mistaken, the foregoing difficulty is intimated by the text of the Torah itself, which speaks of its norms, etc., as "your wisdom and your understanding in the eyes of the nations" (Deut. 4:6). The text seems to leave it open whether the Torah's norms are intelligible only to its pious adherents ("*your* wisdom and *your* understanding"), as Bleich perhaps supposes, or to any properly respectful observer ("in *the eyes of the nations*"). We therefore turn to Kass's essay on the assumption (which Kass also shares with Sacks) that the Torah may be understood to a considerable extent by readers who are observant in the philosophical—not merely the religious—sense of the term.

Leon R. Kass: Eating and Holiness

Kass's essay, as I have already mentioned, is the culminating chapter of his book on eating and human ethics. It takes the form of a broad philosophical commentary on the biblical dietary laws, as spelled out mainly in Leviticus 11. Kass's comments are guided in part by Leviticus 11's own summary of those laws.

> This is the Law (*torah*) of the beast and the fowl and of every living creature that moves in the waters and of every living creature that swarms upon the earth; to make a difference (*lehavdil*) between the unclean and the clean, between the living thing that may be eaten and the living thing that may not be eaten. (Lev. 11:46–47)

This summary prompts the following considerations: Because the laws appeal to the distinctions among animals, as well as between animals and humans, as articulated in Genesis 1, Kass examines the bearing of those distinctions on the question of eating in general. Because the laws also cap a series of diet changes that correlate with the developmental stages of the human race as traced in the subsequent chapters of Genesis, Kass comments on the anthropological significance of those changes. Because the laws expect their adherents to exercise reason in distinguishing between permitted and forbidden foods, Kass elaborates the principles implicit in that distinction. Finally, because the laws occur at the beginning of a ten-chapter sequence of laws about personal, ritual, and moral purity (Lev. 11–20), Kass concludes with some brief remarks about holiness as such.

As a preliminary, Kass admits to some reluctance about inquiring into the philosophical implications of the dietary laws at all. Besides doubting whether it is necessary or even possible to say anything new about them, he has no wish to startle anyone whose pious adherence to the laws rests simply on their being revealed, i.e., to weaken the force of those laws as laws. Insofar as his inquiry is motivated by sympathy for piety rather than by piety per se, Kass must justify his somewhat untraditional defense of the reasonableness of the laws philosophically as well. First, then, given that the Bible is a source of our modern cultural heritage, he sees the importance of clarifying the—literally—central place of the dietary laws in the biblical text.[70] Second, and more important, given that we moderns have an urgent need to understand "the nature of nature and . . . the place of man within the whole," Kass finds implicit in the dietary laws three viable and mutually entailed principles: the dignity of living things in the world order, the threat that humans as consumers of living things pose to that order, and the pious deference owed to the mysterious source of that order in providing food "both for life and for thought."

Kass's account of Genesis 1 stresses its cosmological character. That is, what emerges in the six-day sequence of creation is a hierarchical arrangement of creatures that are said to be good—especially good for humans, who stand at its peak. Mythical beasts and imaginary gods are excluded; the created world has a manifest order. Because the world is set up by its divine creator so as to provide for human life and well-being, its orderly principles not only allow for the distinctive goodness of human life, but support it. Read in this way, Genesis 1 turns out to be an account of the coming to be of the *principles* governing human life in its living and non-living environment, rather than a historical or scientific account as understood by the modern disciplines. So we must judge the validity of Genesis 1's account of creation by understanding it first in its own terms, independently of our commitments to the latter-day disciplines. Here Kass does not differ from Sacks, whose remarks on Genesis 1 we have already looked at in some detail. Kass differs only in maintaining that the resulting distinctions among creatures may fittingly be called "natural," whereas Sacks has indicated why it is problematic from the biblical viewpoint to speak of them as "natural."

For Kass, the Bible is compatible with philosophy or science; for Sacks, it is an—or the—alternative to philosophy or science.

According to Kass, the chief principle governing Genesis 1's creation account—the principle governing the coming into being of its various other principles—is the principle of distinction, or "separation," as such. Recall that the six-day sequence of creatures consists of two parallel three-day sequences: (1) light, (2) heaven, i.e., the space between the waters above and below, and (3) dry land plus vegetation then (4) sun/moon/stars, (5) fish/birds, and (6) land animals plus humans. The last three sets of creatures move, respectively, within regions separated out of the primordial chaos by the creating of the first three sets. The separating process is thus a series of bifurcations, or divisions into two, as Kass shows: what lacks place (light) versus what has place; unoccupied places (heaven, sea, earth) versus occupants of places; nonmotile . . . (plants) versus motile occupants; nonliving . . . (sun, moon, stars) versus living motile occupants; nonterrestrial . . . (fish, birds) versus terrestrial living motile occupants; terrestrial living motile occupants *not* in God's image (land animals) versus . . . in God's image (humans).[71] Yet that is not the whole story, as Kass also shows. God himself adds three blessings—bestowing fecundity on the fish (Gen. 1:22), fecundity and rulership on humans (1:28), and separateness and holiness on the seventh day (2:3). The blessings, like the overall arrangement of creatures, occur in an ascending order: "for life, for rule, and for holiness, or as we scholars might say, the natural, the political, the sacred." How the blessings fit with the six-stage arrangement in general, and with the togetherness of animals and humans within that arrangement in particular, may be said to be the burden of Kass's overall argument.

Besides moving more freely than the heavenly bodies created on day four, the living creatures created on days five and six share the following characteristics, as Kass lists them: Each occupies a distinct place (in the waters, above the earth, or on the earth); each is formed according to distinct kinds; each's distinctive movements fit its proper place (swimming, flying, walking, etc.); each reproduces according to its kind; each is sentient; and each is needy and vulnerable. Humans alone among living creatures are in God's "image" as well. An image, Kass explains, is a likeness to something else; while not the same as its model, the image depends on the model for what it is like. Looking at Genesis 1, Kass finds humans to be like God in the following ways: God speaks, makes freely, looks at the world, and cares about goodness as well as about other living creatures. These "godlike" characteristics obviously belong to humans quite apart from the biblical text. Even so, Kass points out how the text seeks to curb any tendency to exaggerate humans' status. To the blessing bestowing fecundity and dominion on humans, God immediately attaches food instructions:

And God said: "Behold I have provided you with all seed-bearing plants which are on the face of the earth, and every tree which has seed-bearing fruit; to you I have

given it as food. And to every living being of the earth and to everything that creepeth upon the earth which has a living soul in it, I have given every green herb as
food"; and it was so. (Gen. 1:29–30)

Here humans and animals alike are told to be vegetarians. In the ideal case,
a vegetarian diet leaves the created order more or less intact, Kass remarks,
since parent plants suffer no harm when fruits and seeds are eaten, plant re-
generation goes on unimpeded when fruits are eaten and seeds discarded,
and the earth continues to produce edible greenery as its cover (cf. Gen.
1:11–12). That animals and humans need to be told what to eat, however,
suggests that they are also capable of eating other things, specifically other
animals, and that their ungoverned appetites could in principle destroy the
orderly arrangement of things, including themselves. That this threat is real,
that life is environmentally destabilizing and self-threatening, is the problem
faced in Genesis' subsequent chapters as Kass reads them.

In the biblical diet changes that follow, Kass discerns marked anthropological changes too. These are, respectively, the changes from prehuman to
human life (as a result of the Garden of Eden), from prepolitical to political
life (subsequent to Noah's flood), and from political to sanctified life (beginning with the patriarchs after Babel).

Kass connects the change from prehuman to human life with the change
from fruit eating to bread eating. In the Garden, God lets Adam and Eve eat
the fruit of any tree except the tree of the knowledge of good and bad. Since
knowledge does not literally grow on trees, the forbidden tree is only a
metaphor. It symbolizes that Adam and Eve's well-being requires limiting
their desires, even or especially in an ideal environment that perfectly satis-
fies their strictly dietary needs. In forbidding them the knowledge of good
and bad, God acts benevolently on their behalf. He preempts their need to
seek their own good for themselves, i.e., to reason or choose freely. Reason
is tantamount to autonomy, the opposite of the perfect obedience that is the
condition of life in the Garden, as Kass points out. Autonomy, in turn, is the
subversive promise of the serpent—symbolizing the awakening of reason as
it presents itself to Eve's imagination. Eve's desires thereby expand, "partly
enticed by the [serpent's] promise of godlike wisdom, mostly fueled by her
newly empowered imagination." Having acquired a glimmer of knowledge
of good and bad, she and Adam at once grow self-conscious and self-con-
cerned; they begin to be human and are expelled into a new, less hospitable
but ultimately more suitable environment, where they must now cultivate
food on their own. Bread, their new diet, requires not only farming but
milling, baking, etc., and Cain, the first farmer, is both the first founder of a
city and the ancestor of the originators of the civilized arts. Cain is also the
first manslaughterer, however, and within ten generations following him humans and animals alike have become corrupt and violent enough to warrant
destruction, or rather they have succeeded in destroying much of the created

order on their own as a matter of course. "The return through the flood to the watery chaos of the beginning," says Kass, "completes the dissolution into chaos that life itself has wrought."

The change from the largely prepolitical condition of human life before the flood to the political condition afterwards is begun in response to Noah's gratuitous sacrifice of some of the animals God had told him to rescue on the ark. Humans had presumably drifted into meat eating as part of the preflood violence and destruction, Kass reasons, and certainly some animals must have too. Evidently Noah himself has a taste for blood. Instead of another wholesale inundation to eliminate humans' ongoing carnivorousness and the underlying bloodthirst it signals, however, God resorts to governing it by laws. Meat eating is now legitimized. At the same time, God emphasizes humans' difference from animals by making both homicide and blood eating punishable offenses, and requiring humans to enforce them within the conditions of political life, i.e., under laws. While laws by themselves do not eliminate vices like bloodthirst, comments Kass, they can serve to moderate them.

Finally, Kass calls attention to a later incident in Genesis which anticipates the change from living under merely political laws to living under laws aimed as well at sanctifying personal, ritual, and moral behavior. In Genesis 32:25–33, the patriarch Jacob's wrestling match with an angel (as his mysterious opponent is called by later traditions) leads to a further food restriction. During the struggle, Jacob acquires the name Israel. He also acquires a limp, when the angel bruises Jacob's inner thigh by touching its sinew. Jacob's descendants, called the children of Israel from that moment on, are said to recall the double outcome of the incident by refraining from eating the thigh sinew of animals. It is his descendants' first dietary law as a nation. This law, Kass observes, is both a restraint and a reminder. "[The Israelites] remember, negatively, that Jacob was injured in the process of struggling against God; positively, that God was close enough to be encountered and struggled with."

Kass warns that Leviticus' dietary laws are far from being satisfactorily explained in terms of hygiene (since, e.g., pigs are said to be "unclean" only "to you"). Nor are they simply a means for inducing self-discipline (since why forbid some animals and not others?). Nor, finally, is it enough to say that they are a way for the Israelites to separate themselves from the idolatrous practices of their neighbors (since calling neighboring nations' food practices, etc., "abominable" has to do with specifically theological beliefs about what is and is not holy). Rather, the purpose of the dietary laws is holiness, as Kass demonstrates from the biblical context. Laws regulating moral or political relations, and also addressing religious passions by instituting the Tabernacle and animal sacrifices, have already been established in Exodus. The incident of Nadab and Abihu's gratuitously offering "strange fire" before God (Lev. 10:1–11) introduces Leviticus's further dietary restrictions, etc., just

as the incident of Noah's gratuitous sacrifice has introduced the postflood restrictions. The announced theme of the new laws is thus for the Israelites to
"make distinction [*lehavdil*] between the holy [*qodesh*] and the profane
[*chol*]"—between what is kept apart for sacred purposes (the original meaning of *qodesh*) and what is common or has become dissolute or lacks integrity (the root meaning of *chol*)—"and between the unclean and the clean
[*tahor*]" (Lev. 10:10).

The verb *lehavdil*, "to distinguish or separate," appears in Leviticus 10:10
for the first time since Genesis 1, Kass remarks, as a sign that the distinctions
mandated in Leviticus 11 are those of the creation account. Animals are categorized according to their respective places in the created scheme: land
(Lev. 11:2–8, 41–45), water (11:9–12), air (11:13–23). Clean land animals
must have thoroughly cloven hooves and chew a cud; they must not crawl
or swarm. Clean water animals must have fins and scales. Clean birds are not
specified, only contrasted with a list of unclean ones; clean winged insects,
those specified at least, all leap rather than walk. How then does Leviticus
understand "clean" (or "pure," as Kass could also have translated the Hebrew
tahor)? Generalizing, Kass shows that the criteria are Genesis 1's. "Clean" animals must occupy a distinct place, embody a distinct form, move as befits
their distinct place, and eat so as to preserve the overall distinctions of the
created order. Ruled out, for example, are amphibians, which cross the distinct boundaries between land and water. Also ruled out are creatures whose
forms are insufficiently distinct, for their being fluid (e.g., jellyfish or oysters),
deceptive (e.g., eels), or incomplete (e.g., animals with only partly cloven
hooves). Creatures whose movements blur distinctions are ruled out too, as
when they occupy water but move as on land (e.g., lobsters), or occupy land
but move as in water (e.g., crawling insects), or have wings but nevertheless
move on legs (except for two-legged leapers, like grasshoppers), or else
walk on too many legs (e.g., centipedes) or on none at all (viz., belly-
crawlers, such as snakes) or on paws (i.e., on handlike feet). Finally, carnivores are ruled out for violating the original order-preserving vegetarianism
of Genesis 1. "Clean" animals, in general, are those that respect the created
order in their own behavior and thereby remind their human observers of
the need to respect that order as well.

The Levitical dietary laws thus emend the Noachic laws by refitting them
to the sixfold environmental distinctions of Genesis 1, as Kass goes on to
show. In allowing meat eating but prohibiting blood eating as well as homicide, the Noachic laws recognize no more than the superiority of humans
over animals and, at the same time, the inviolability of what humans share
with animals, namely, their lifeblood. The Noachic laws look to what animals
have in common; they treat animals' differences indifferently. By going on to
prohibit the eating of animals whose activities elide the distinctions spelled
out in Genesis 1—namely, animals that occupy multiple regions or display
ill-defined looks or sport incongruous movements or ingest other animals—

the Levitical laws require the Israelites in addition to do their part in preserving the boundary lines indigenous to their primordially created environment. Or, to restate this last point of Kass's in language more congenial with the environmentally oriented readings in this volume: Leviticus's dietary laws, as compared with Noah's, are proof positive that Genesis 1 is environmentally focused and articulate not just incidentally, but deliberately and essentially.

Kass faces the objection implicit in his own observation that Leviticus 11's increased restrictions on meat eating amount to a partial return to pre-Noachic vegetarianism. Would not a complete return to vegetarianism be more consistent and desirable? This question prompts Kass's reconsideration of Noah's gratuitous sacrifice, the religiously ambiguous prelude to the Noachic laws. Perhaps, he suggests, the sacrifice celebrates above all Noah's dawning discovery of his difference from the animals, as a result of his shipboard incarceration with them during the Flood. Kass implies that the Noachic laws' limited licensing of meat eating, joined as it is with the imposition of blood taboos, addresses not just humans' animal-like capacity to destroy life, but also their more-than-animal capacity to see where they stand in the created order. Unlike animals, humans are potential knowers as well as potential destabilizers of the created order. Indeed, humans' animal-like potential for destabilizing is, as the Genesis narrative itself indicates, a developmental precondition of their godlike potential for knowing. Even so, their freedom to destabilize, though regrettable, is perhaps restrainable. "To mark his self-conscious separation from the animals, [Noah] undertakes to eat them; to acknowledge his own godlikeness, [he] accepts the prohibition of homicide (Genesis 9:3–4, 9:6)." Law-abidingness, in short, is the biblically stipulated compensation for human carnivorousness. Is that compensation adequate, one may ask? Is not a less environmentally taxing vegetarian diet, shared with the more peaceable animals, the ethically proper food for humans as such? Meat eating is justified, Kass replies, only as part and parcel of humans' distinctive exercise of their God-given rationality. The Levitical laws, he adds, even more than the Noachic laws, both solicit and warrant that exercise. "Celebrating the principle of rational separation, they celebrate not only man's share in rationality, but also his openness to the mystery of intelligible yet embodied form."

Yet the Levitical laws also draw humans to the mysterious source of that rationality. Kass considers once more the difference between the Levitical and the Noachic laws. The Levitical laws revise the Noachic laws' assumption that blood—the vital fluid common to both humans and animals—is more worthy of respect than the diverse looking and diversely moving animal bodies that house it. Blood aside, all subhuman life remains in principle edible for Noah. But the Levitical laws restrict the edible to the "clean," i.e., the pure. "The legal distinction between clean and unclean is higher than the natural principle of living and nonliving, even as it incorporates and modifies it." While relegating life that is "unclean"[72]—i.e., boundary-crossing, amorphous, dysfunctional, or predatory—to the status of the detestable, the Levitical laws raise the edible to the status of the holy. They sanctify proper eating. Kass therefore concludes by looking briefly at sanctification.

To sanctify something, as Kass points out, is to set it apart either in *obedience* to or else in *imitation* of the divine creator, "the mysterious source of form, separation, and intelligibility." On the one hand, to obey the biblical God's divinely revealed laws—those designed to separate us, for example, from improper food or constant work—is to elevate our otherwise humdrum daily or weekly routines by reminding us regularly of God as the separate source of all separation. On the other hand, to imitate divine reason—by exercising our God-given minds to discern the ever present and varied distinctions inherent in our created environment—is to be godlike without being God, inasmuch as we thereby come to know that we ourselves are not the source of those distinctions, nor of our ability to know them, but owe our share in these things to something both higher than ourselves and mysterious. Kass implies that human reason and the biblical laws alike are divine gifts or, to speak biblically, blessings. It follows from Kass's overall argument that the biblical blessings inserted in or superadded to the environmental distinctions spelled out in Genesis 1 are meant to complement those distinctions, not override them. Here Kass rejoins Sacks, who likewise sees that God blesses humans (Gen. 1:28) in order to enhance their ability to face the created environment rather than to authorize their unrestrained sway over it. If so, then whether in the end there is a smooth fit between the Bible and philosophy or science, as Kass maintains, or a tension since the goodness of human life of which philosophy or science is a part depends on the biblical God's mysteriously keeping his promises of support implicit in his blessings, as Sacks suggests—to judge by the biblical evidence, Genesis 1:28 is by design environmentally friendly.

A SUMMING UP

Where then do we stand concerning the three interrelated questions with which we began? The reader will forgive my not seeking a simple consensus here. I have no wish to blur instructive differences among the various views we have been considering.

As for the historical question about whether Genesis 1:28 or any other authoritative Jewish text gives humans a license for environmental callousness and recklessness as White and Toynbee charge, almost all our readings agree that the charge is undeserved—Katz and (presumably) Leopold being the sole exceptions. Most—including Cohen, Allen, Kay, Schaffer, Ehrenfeld and Bentley, Blidstein, Rosenblum, and Schwartz—proceed by way of the historical record, by adducing biblical and rabbinic teachings that meet modern standards of ecological correctness. Others—notably Artson, Troster,

Benstein, and Levy—may be said to defend Judaism as religious penitents, by arguing that the ethical standards of twentieth-century environmentalism require us to modify Jewish views or practices so as to ensure conformity with an ecologically wholesome interpretation of Genesis 1:28. Still others— Schwarzschild, Wyschogrod, and again Schwartz—undertake a more sophisticated defense, by noting areas of agreement between an ecologically sound understanding of nature and a philosophically congenial understanding of Judaism. Even so, while showing that White and Toynbee overlook the considerable evidence in support of Judaism's ongoing heritage of environmental conscientiousness, the aforementioned readings leave Judaism vulnerable to the lingering charge that Genesis 1:28 may still be responsible—if inadvertently—for originating the specifically modern project to master nature by means of environmentally threatening high-technology. The lingering charge seems implicitly addressed by the remainder of our readings. On the one hand, as Bleich for one suggests, Judaism need not give up any moral high ground here, since even where rabbinic law admits of loopholes allowing possible abuse to, say, animals, pious Jews are expected to exercise proper moral restraint as a matter of course—as Jonas too emphasizes. And on the other hand, as both Sacks and Kass suggest, Judaism need not give up any philosophical high ground either, since a careful look at the biblical text indicates that Genesis 1:28's "fill the earth and master it," far from authorizing us to ignore or destroy the environmental diversity outlined in Genesis 1, means for us to appreciate and preserve it. In any case, the burden here seems to be on White and Toynbee and their admirers to prove that they have not misinterpreted either the biblical text or the references to it by the chief architects of the modern project[73]—i.e., to prove that their own arguments do not rest on abuses of those writings in a manner analogous to the environmental abuses from which they properly recoil.

As for the ethical question about how Jews ought to face the crisis, all except Katz and Levy agree on the appropriateness of Judaism's moral teachings—e.g., God's ownership of the land, the prohibitions of wanton destruction and cruelty to animals, the sabbatical and jubilee years—once these are correctly understood and applied. A further question arises, however, as to whether applying traditional teachings to our unprecedented crisis is helped or hindered by the theological or hermeneutical innovations of, say, Artson, Troster, or Benstein. The test seems to be whether such innovations serve to enhance or to undermine the rest of Judaism's moral teachings. Unfortunately, Artson's reconstruction of how rabbinic teachings supplant biblical ones appears to downsize biblical law itself into rules of expediency for living in a lost homeland; Troster's embrace of Gaia appears to shun the Second Commandment; and Benstein's wish to mend Caro's splitting nature study from Torah study appears to disregard Caro's warning about the dangers of mixing those two competing ways of interpreting things.[74] There is need to clarify the larger moral implications of each of these proposals.

Finally, as for the philosophical question about how ecology, Judaism, and philosophy fit together if at all, much depends on whether we are to understand them as specialized disciplines or as separate ways of life. If each is no more than a specialized discipline as found, say, within the walls of a modern university designed to house and protect them, then there is no compelling reason for any of them to seek mutual consultation; there are only freely chosen mutual interests, mutual borrowings at the discretion of individual specialists, and presumably mutual tolerance. Nevertheless we have already seen that specialists like Leopold, White, Toynbee, and others are apt to overreach and trespass into areas that are foreign to them—and so ought to be called to account, especially where practical issues are at stake. Besides, whatever the ancestry of modern ecology—Leopold has traced it good-humoredly to the biblical prophets—Judaism and philosophy, at least, long antedate the modern university and its administrative structure. Like the more-than-academic environmentalism that has become a visible and audible part of our public life during the past century, then, Judaism and philosophy too seem best described as ways of life. That they do not simply come together but also part company here and there over how we are to face our present crisis, moreover, suggests that our pressing need to compare the larger practical and theoretical implications of what each has to say is more than academic; it is also religious and philosophical. Let the readings in this volume serve as a modest introduction to that threefold task.

NOTES

1. See *Companion to* A Sand County Almanac: *Interpretive and Critical Essays*, ed. J. Baird Callicott (Madison, Wis.: University of Wisconsin Press, 1987); Callicott, *In Defense of the Land Ethic: Essays in Environmental Philosophy* (Albany, N.Y.: SUNY Press, 1989).

2. Aldo Leopold, *A Sand County Almanac* (New York: Oxford University Press, 1949), viii.

3. Leopold does allow that "Individual thinkers since the days of Ezekiel and Isaiah have asserted that the despoliation of land is not only inexpedient but wrong" (*A Sand County Almanac*, 203).

4. Leopold, *A Sand County Almanac*, 204f.

5. See especially the readings by Artson (159–71), Bleich (333–70), and Rosenblum (183–205), respectively, in this volume.

6. Leopold, *A Sand County Almanac*, 201.

7. Leopold, *A Sand County Almanac*, 201f.

8. Consider Jacob Howland, *The* Republic: *The Odyssey of Philosophy* (New York: Twayne, 1993), 51: "Homer's epic poem may be interpreted as a voyage of deepening self-knowledge, in which the hero's homeward journey involves a growing understanding of the whole of human experience and the rejection of ways of life that fail to recognize, and recollectively to internalize, essential elements of that experience. The philosophic suggestiveness of this interpretation is strengthened by

evidence that *noos* or *nous*, the 'mind' or 'intelligence' that distinguishes Odysseus from his forgetful comrades, and *nostos*, the 'homecoming' that intelligence enables and by which it is in turn tested and strengthened, are derived from a common Indo-European root, **nes-*, meaning something like 'return to light and life.'" See also John Alvis, *Divine Purpose and Heroic Response in Homer and Virgil: The Political Plan of Zeus* (Lanham, Md.: Rowman & Littlefield, 1995), 85–136; Seth Benardete, *The Bow and the Lyre: A Platonic Reading of the* Odyssey (Lanham, Md.: Rowman & Littlefield, 1997).

   9. Homer, *Odyssey* II 230–34.

   10. Homer, *Odyssey* XIX 353–55, 372–75, 482–502, XX 6–8; cf. XIII 304–45, XIX 65–95.

   11. Homer, *Odyssey* XXII 417–72.

   12. This is not an entirely idle question, however. Consider that the first mention of the term "nature" (*physis*) in Western literature occurs at *Odyssey* X 313, where Homer ascribes to it an integrity to which both gods like Hermes and humans like Odysseus must defer. Consider also the following description by Leon R. Kass: "Everything in the world is appropriable and appropriate for his voracious, limitless appetites. No natural form or given order elicits his respect or reverence. He lives believing nothing stronger or higher than himself. . . ." (*The Hungry Soul: Eating and the Perfecting of our Nature* [New York: Free Press, 1994], 113). Kass is describing Homer's Cyclops (*Odyssey* IX 105–566); but these same words might also serve to describe something of what Leopold himself has in mind when he says, in criticism of what he takes to be the root of the modern tolerance for environmental abuse, "Land, like Odysseus' slave-girls, is still property. The land-relation is still strictly economic, entailing privileges but not obligations." (*A Sand County Almanac*, 203) Cf. Kass's related critique (*The Hungry Soul*, 114–18) of the vegetarianism of Homer's flower children, the Lotus Eaters (*Odyssey* IX 82–104), with the readings by Levy (321–32), Bleich (371–83), and of course Kass (384–409) in this volume.

   13. Lynn White Jr. "The Historical Roots of our Ecological Crisis," *Science* 155 (10 March 1967): 1203–1207; reprinted in White, *Machina ex Deo: Essays in the Dynamism of Western Culture* (Cambridge, Mass.: MIT Press, 1968), 75–94. Arnold Toynbee, "The Religious Background of the Present Environmental Crisis," *International Journal of Environmental Studies* 3 (1972): 141–46. (White's and Toynbee's essays are also reprinted in *Ecology and Religion in History*, ed. David and Eileen Spring [New York: Harper & Row, 1974], 15–31 and 137–49.) See also Clarence J. Glacken, "Man Against Nature: An Outmoded Concept," in *Man's Struggle to Live with Himself*, ed. Harold W. Helfrich Jr. (New Haven, Conn.: Yale University Press, 1970), 129–30; and Ian A. McHarg, *Design with Nature* (Garden City, N.Y.: Doubleday, 1969), 26. On White in particular, see Jeremy Cohen, "The Bible, Man, and Nature in the History of Western Thought: A Call for Reassessment," *Journal of Religion* 65 (1985): 169–71. See also the bibliography in Cohen, *"Be Fertile and Increase, Fill the Earth and Master It": The Ancient and Medieval Career of a Biblical Text* (Ithaca, N.Y.: Cornell University Press, 1989), 323–57; my citations immediately above recapitulate Cohen's short list in "The Bible, Man and Nature," 156, n. 2.

   14. White, "The Historical Roots," in *Machina ex Deo*, 86.

   15. Toynbee, "The Religious Background," 142.

   16. White, *Machina ex Deo*, 87.

   17. White, *Machina ex Deo*, 84; cf. Cohen, "Bible, Man, and Nature," 170.

18. White, *Machina ex Deo*, 88.

19. White, *Machina ex Deo*, 85; cf. Cohen, "Bible, Man, and Nature," 170.

20. Cohen, "Bible, Man, and Nature," 170f.

21. White, *Machina ex Deo*, 94.

22. White, "The Context of Science," in *Machina ex Deo*, 100; "Natural Science and Naturalistic Art in the Middle Ages," *American Historical Review* 52 (1947): 434; cf. Cohen, "Bible, Man, and Nature," 171.

23. Toynbee, "The Religious Background," 144.

24. "In 1661," says Toynbee in a manner reminiscent of Leopold, "this read like a blessing on the wealth of Abraham in children and livestock" ("The Religious Background," 143).

25. Cohen appeals to Gadamer's notion of "the fusion of horizons"—where "old and new [world outlooks] continually grow together to make something of living value, without either['s] being explicitly distinguished from the other"—as the condition for the possibility of historical periodizing. See Hans-Georg Gadamer, *Truth and Method* (New York: Crossroad, 1982), 273, 337f., 358.

26. See especially, Eilon Schwartz, *"Bal Tashchit"* (230–49, in this volume).

27. In his *"Be Fertile and Increase, Fill the Earth and Master It,"* 11, Cohen dismisses this question as methodologically imprecise: "A historical study of biblical interpretation may not casually presume that at the moment of its composition a scriptural text possessed a clear, indisputable meaning from which all subsequent understanding of that text departed. It is difficult if not impossible to determine whether a text ever had an original, uninterpreted meaning; more often than not, the qualitative distinction between this meaning and later, interpretive expositions is untenable. The extant text of the Bible itself derives from several lengthy processes of transmission, reflection, and revision; it never did have a single, absolute value that the historian can recover." Contrast, e.g., Robert D. Sacks, *A Commentary on the Book of Genesis* (Lewiston, N.Y.: Edwin Mellen Press, 1990), ii: "Of recent times it has become the custom to preface any work of this nature with a discourse concerning Methods of Interpretation, and yet it is difficult to see how that can be done. To do so would presuppose that we already know how to read the book before we begin. Unfortunately that is untrue. Each book has its own way about it, and generally we begin to learn how to read a book by stumbling around in it for a very long time until we find our way. Otherwise we risk the danger of reading the book by a method foreign to the intent of the author."

28. Bacon, e.g., *New Organon*, Part I, Aphorisms 3, 129 (ed. F. H. Anderson [Indianapolis: Bobbs-Merrill, 1960], 39, 117–19); *New Atlantis* (in *New Atlantis and The Great Instauration*, ed. Jerry Weinberger [rev. ed.; Arlington Heights, Ill.: Harlan Davidson, 1989], esp. 71–83).

29. Descartes, *Discourse on Method*, Part 6, paragraph 2 (in *Discours de la méthode/Discourse on the Method*, ed. and trans. George Heffernan [Notre Dame, Ind.: University of Notre Dame Press, 1994], 86–87).

30. See, for the following, 1 Kings 5:14; 9:16, 24–25; 10:1–13; 11:1–12:24.

31. On *bal tashchit*, see Schwartz (230–49); on *tza'ar ba'alei chayyim*, see Levy (321–32) and Bleich (333–70) in this volume.

32. For an account of Sacks's overall approach to the biblical book, see Martin D. Yaffe, "Biblical Religion and Liberal Democracy: Comments on Spinoza's *Theologico-Political Treatise* and Sacks's *Commentary on the Book of Genesis*," *Political Science Reviewer* 23 (1994): 284–341.

33. Consider such biblical expressions as "the floodgates of heaven were opened" (Gen. 7:11) and "I will make [literally, "give"] your heavens as iron" (Lev. 26:19), with our discussion of Schaffer (15–16, in this volume).

34. Consider, e.g., Sacks's comment on Gen. 9:12–17: "During the course of reading Genesis we shall meet a man named Abimelech, from the pre-legal point of view the most decent man in the book. The Bible does not dispute the existence of such men. Natural foundations are available for the decent life of a private man, but these foundations are inadequate on the political level. The origin of the insufficiency of natural political bonds lies within the insufficiency of the natural bonds which hold heaven and earth together. Heaven and earth do not form a single cosmos, and the expanse is not able to protect the world from the waters of chaos by itself. The *foundations of the deep* and the *windows of the sky* can only be secured by a promise." (*Commentary on the Book of Genesis*, 67f.)

35. Artson takes the Hebrew terms from the Tractate titles of the Mishnah's *Seder Zeraim*. See *Mishnayoth*, ed. Philip Blackman (7 vols.; Gateshead, Eng.: Judaica Press, 1977), I, 81–132 (*Peah*), 443—57 (*Orlah*), 181–230 (*Terumoth*), 295–342 (*Kilayim*), 467–86 (*Bikkurim*).

36. Consider Maimonides, *Guide of the Perplexed* II 40, III 27, 28 (trans. Shlomo Pines [Chicago: University of Chicago Press, 1963], 384f., 510–14).

37. "Environmentalism heralds a fresh conception of the individual and society in relation to the natural order, offering a new understanding of what it means to be human." Artson calls the biblical teaching (in contrast?) an "ideology" (163, in this volume).

38. See Maimonides, *Guide of the Perplexed* I 1 (trans. Pines, 22f.).

39. Maimonides himself excludes moral awareness from man's *tzelem* per se, however. See *Guide of the Perplexed* I 2 (trans. Pines, 24f.): "the intellect that God made overflow unto man and that is the latter's ultimate perfection, was that with which Adam had been provided before he disobeyed. It was because of this that it was said of him that he was created *in the image of God and in His likeness*. It was likewise on account of it that he was addressed by God and given commandments, as it says: *And the Lord God commanded, and so on*. For commandments are not given to beasts and beings devoid of intellect. Through the intellect one distinguishes between truth and falsehood, and that was found in [Adam] in its perfection and integrity. Fine and bad, on the other hand, belong to the things generally accepted as known, not to those cognized by the intellect. For one does not say: it is fine that heaven is spherical, and it is bad that earth is flat; rather one says true and false with regard to these assertions. . . . Accordingly when man was in his most perfect and excellent state, in accordance with his inborn disposition and possessed of his intellectual cognitions— because of which it is said of him: *Thou hast made him little lower than Elohim*—he had no faculty that was engaged in any way in the consideration of generally accepted things, and he did not apprehend them." Cf. also II 36 (trans. Pines, 369–73).

40. In the sources Benstein cites, Caro refers in particular to rebellion, stumbling, and falling into transgression, as well as—or as arising from—the danger of misinterpretation.

41. Benstein speaks of "the spiritually shortsighted," where Caro evidently cites the biblical expression "they have eyes but will not see" (Jer. 5:21, Ps. 115:5, 135:16) to mean being unwilling or unable to pay full attention (216, in this volume).

42. Consider the following remarks by Caro: "all the miracles and wonders through which the Holy Blessed One makes known his might and glory, were

created solely for the people who have not reached this spiritual level of knowledge of the Creator, and they are the vast majority, but for *those few whose eyes
are open to see the wonders of Nature, these enlightened ones will observe, and
reflect*, and come to know the wonders of God" (215, in this volume; italics added,
M. Y.); "If people's consciousness were fuller, they should know their Creator from
the wonder of His creatures, and His acts, but in truth, judging from human nature,
this is not the case, for *the people's discernment is insufficient to consider and understand the complete significance of those things to which they have become accustomed*" (216, in this volume; italics added, M. Y.). Cf., in general, Socrates's account of his "second sailing" in Plato, *Phaedo* 96A-100A; and, from the viewpoint
of the distinctively modern investigation of nature, Bacon, *New Organon*, especially Part I, Aphorisms 2, 10, 18–26 (ed. Anderson, 39, 41, 42–45).

43. Consider also our discussions of Kay (12–14) and Sacks (20–23) in this volume.

44. Schwarzschild's clarification proceeds by way of an ongoing critique of Hans
Jonas's "Jewish and Christian Elements in Philosophy: Their Share in the Emergence
of the Modern Mind," in Jonas, *Philosophical Essays: From Ancient Creed to Technological Man* (Englewood Cliffs, N.J.: Prentice-Hall, 1974), 21–44.

45. Schwarzschild further argues that the assimilating of God to nature (which he
calls "immanentism") originated historically as a minor, heretical trend in Jewish
thought. He finds it to have surfaced in Western culture in Paul's Christian theology,
in Spinoza's pantheism, and in Marx's dialectical materialism. He also accuses Jonas's
overall argument of catering too much to immanentism. Schwarzschild identifies his
own position with that of the neo-Kantian Hermann Cohen; see Schwarzschild, "The
Lure of Immanence: The Crisis in Contemporary Religious Thought," in *The Pursuit
of the Ideal: Jewish Writings of Steven Schwarzschild*, ed. Menachem Kellner (Albany,
N.Y.: SUNY Press, 1990), 61–82.

46. Oddly, Schwarzschild may have shared their exasperation about his own argument. In an introductory footnote, he confesses his own inability to reduce his original
article to manageable size, without the "heroic" editing efforts of a sympathetic reader.

47. Schwartz (299, in this volume) mentions the paganism recommended by White
as an alternative to (what White regards as) the biblically authorized exploitation of
nature, the pagan rituals called for by some ecofeminists, the Gaia movement, etc.

48. See Schwarzschild (269–72), and Wyschogrod (292) in this volume. Schwartz
also appeals to Mircea Eliade, *Cosmos and History: The Myth of the Eternal Return*
(New York: Harper and Row, 1959), and Stephen Jay Gould, *Time's Arrows, Time's Cycles: Myth and Metaphor in the Discovery of Geological Time* (London: Penguin, 1988).

49. Cf., in this connection, Schwarzschild's polemic (271f., in this volume)
against Jonas's argument in *The Phenomenon of Life: Toward a Philosophical Biology* (New York: Harper and Row, 1966), where Jonas shows how Darwinism
would have to be modified in order to accommodate an understanding of human
freedom as grounded in animal metabolism.

50. Katz (313, in this volume) evidently identifies Schwartz's view with
Wyschogrod's, which Schwartz happens to be analyzing at the moment (303–304, in
this volume).

51. Katz (313, in this volume) identifies Benstein's view with Caro's, about which
Benstein himself has some doubts (215–217, in this volume).

52. Only on our natural environment, he emphasizes, not on the human beings:
"The natural vegetation that covers the mass grave in the Warsaw cemetery is not the

same as the vegetation that would have grown there if the mass grave had never been dug. . . . The grassy field in the Majdenek parade ground does not cover and heal the mud and desolation of the death camp—it rather grows from the dirt and ashes of the sites' victims" (see 317 in this volume).

53. "We can think of Nature as . . . attempting to dominate—humanity, just as we can think of humanity attempting to dominate Nature" (see 315 in this volume).

54. Levy interprets, e.g., the biblical verses mandating the killing of oxen that gore (Ex. 21:28–29), and of herd animals that are allowed to go up into Mount Sinai or touch its border (Ex. 19:12–13), as imposing punishments on the animals themselves (see 322f. in this volume).

55. At the same time, Levy doubts the adequacy of Peter Singer's argument against "speciesism" as an argument for animal rights (*Animal Liberation: A New Ethics for Our Treatment of Animals* [New York: Random House, 1975]; *Practical Ethics* [Cambridge, Eng.: Cambridge University Press, 1979], ch. 3, 5), since Singer fails to do justice to our obvious need to favor humans over other animals, and also fails logically to come to terms with the possibility of racism and sexism within any given species (notably, of course, the human species).

56. Jon. 3:8, 4:11; Ps. 36:7, 104:14, 145:9,16, 147:9; Job 38:39, 41.

57. Is. 43:20; Ps. 104:21, 27, 147:9; Job 38:41; also Deut. 22:6–7.

58. Ex. 20:10; Ex. 23:5; Lev. 22:28; Num. 20:18; Deut. 5:14, 22:10, 25:4; Prov. 12:10. Cf. also Gen. 24:14, 16–20; Num. 22:32.

59. *Yerushalmi, Yebamot* 15:3; *Gittin* 62a.

60. Cf. Gen. 1:29, with 9:3; etc.

61. The punishment was lifted, as Levy reports, only after he saved a litter of kittens (*Baba Metzi'a* 85a). The passage is also cited and discussed by Bleich (see 350 and 352 in this volume).

62. He does call attention to Maimonides's condemnation of hunting for sport or out of cruelty (*Guide of the Perplexed* III 17, 48; trans. Pines, 473f., 598f.).

63. In citing Spinoza's view (as he construes it) that "all *sentient* beings possess some moral [*sic*] rights," Levy admits that "no defender of animal rights makes the claim that animals and humans have identical rights." However that may be, Levy fails to add that Spinoza, unlike Judaism, identifies right with might, i.e., with what Katz calls "domination"; cf., e.g., Spinoza, *Theologico-Political Treatise*, Chapter 16, and *Political Treatise*, Chapter 1, Section 5 (Spinoza, *Opera* [4 vols.; Heidelberg: Carl Winters Universitätsbuchhandlung, 1925], III, 189–200, 275). Nor does he cite Spinoza's explicit statement on the question of the treatment of animals, in *Ethics Demonstrated in a Geometrical Order*, Pt. IV, Prop. 37, Scholium 1: "it appears that the law about not slaughtering animals is founded on vain superstition and womanly compassion rather than on sound reason. . . . Still, I do not deny that brutes feel; but I deny that it is not permitted on that account to consult our own utility and use them at our discretion and treat them as is more agreeable to us [*prout nobis magis convenit*]—since they do not agree with us by nature [*nobiscum naturâ non conveniunt*] and their emotions are different by nature from human emotions (see Pt. III, Prop. 57, Scholium)" (Spinoza, *Opera*, II, 236f.).

64. Bleich cites Prov. 12:10, Ps. 145:9, 15–16, 147:9, Job 38:41, Jon. 4:11, Ps. 36:7.

65. In this connection, Bleich cites *Sefer ha-Chinukh*, no. 596, and Maimonides's *Guide of the Perplexed* III 17 and 48 (trans. Pines, 473f., 598f.), to the effect that the purpose of sparing animals pain wherever possible is to prevent our acquiring the habit of cruelty and to inculcate habits of kindness and mercy.

66. In order to meet the possible counterargument of Levy (and Jonas) that this particular justification would open the way to using animals for frivolously motivated experiments as well, as in the cosmetics industry, Bleich would seem compelled to return to the need for supralegal standards of morality.

67. Joseph Albo, *Sefer Ha-Ikkarim* III 15 (ed. Isaac Husik [4 vols. in 5; Philadelphia: Jewish Publication Society of America, 1946], vol. III, 131–34.)

68. Here Bleich embraces the "emotive" theory of ethics as found in Charles L. Stevenson, *Ethics and Language* (New Haven: Yale University Press, 1944), 20–26.

69. Possible candidates might be Ex. 23:1–9 or Deut. 1:16–17; but consider, e.g., Rashi on Ex. 23:2: "There are glosses [*midrashei*] of Israel's wise men on this text, but the language of the text does not sit well with them on account of its manner [*ayn l'shon hamikra m'yushav bahen 'al-ofnav*]," and the various unreconciled glosses Rashi adduces for "you shall hear out the small and the great alike" (Deut. 1:17).

70. Lev. 11–20 are the central chapters of Leviticus, the central book of the Five Books of Moses.

71. Kass acknowledges his reliance on Leo Strauss, "On the Interpretation of Genesis," *L'homme: Revue française d'anthropologie* 21.1 (1981): 5–20; reprinted in Strauss, *Jewish Philosophy and the Crisis of Modernity: Essays and Lectures in Modern Jewish Thought*, ed. Kenneth Hart Green (Albany, N.Y.: SUNY Press, 1997), 359–76. Consider, however, Strauss's emphasis that the cosmology implicit in Gen. 1 "is not the theme of the biblical author" but only "the unthematic presupposition of the biblical author" and that there is "a deep opposition between the Bible and cosmology proper and, since all philosophy is cosmology ultimately, between the Bible and philosophy" (*Jewish Philosophy*, 368, 369).

72. Or "contaminated," as Kass could also have translated the Hebrew *tame*.

73. Consider, for example, that the announced practical aim of modern science according to Bacon's *New Atlantis* ("enlarging the bounds of Human Empire, to the effecting of all things possible") and Descartes' *Discourse on Method* ("rendering ourselves as masters and possessors of nature") implies less that God is authorizing humans than that humans are replacing God; see the references in nn. 28 and 29, above. See also, on Bacon, Robert K. Faulkner, *Francis Bacon and the Project of Progress* (Lanham, Md.: Rowman & Littlefield, 1993), 238–39, 244–46; and on Descartes, Michael Davis, *Ancient Tragedy and the Origins of Modern Science* (Carbondale, Ill.: Southern Illinois University Press, 1988), 75–77, 90–91.

74. See nn. 40–42, above.

I

THE HISTORICAL QUESTION

1

On Classical Judaism
and Environmental Crisis

Jeremy Cohen

Twenty years ago this spring, I worked as a high school intern in the national offices of a Jewish youth organization. My job involved the preparation of study material on the subject of Judaism and ecology. As politicians, theologians, students, writers, and others were hastening to identify with environmental concern in general and with the ecology movement in particular, we felt that we too had to take a stand. Judaism, we presumed, had to address the fundamental questions of ecology, and, more importantly, it had to prove compatible with the correct, desired answers (just as it had to guide us properly with regard to the war in Vietnam and the civil rights movement).

We were especially concerned with the harsh and popular indictment of Judaism's biblical foundations, which were blamed for our typically Western exploitative attitude to nature. The biblical God's initial instruction to the first human beings (Genesis 1:28) to "be fertile and increase, fill the earth and master it, and rule the fish of the sea, the birds of the sky, and all the living things that creep on earth" struck many as the guiltiest culprit.

In his frequently reprinted speech to the American Academy for the Advancement of Science on "The Historic Roots of Our Ecologic Crisis," Lynn White Jr. understood this verse to mean that "God planned and fashioned all of the natural world 'explicitly for man's benefit and rule: no item in the physical creation had any purpose save to serve man's purposes.'" Arnold Toynbee agreed that the biblical creation story underlay the Western proclivity for technology. Writing in *The International Journal of Environmental Studies,* he noted that while "in 1661, this [verse] read like a blessing on the wealth of Abraham in children and livestock, in 1971 it reads like a license and an incentive for mechanization and pollution." Cultural geographer Clarence J. Glacken viewed "the idea of man against nature in Western thought" as deriving directly from the Genesis cosmogony. And landscape architect Ian L. McHarg denounced the divine injunction with greater severity still, inasmuch as it provided "the sanction and injunction to conquer nature—the enemy, the threat to Jehovah." Surely, we believed, along with numerous theologians who took up the cause of the Bible, surely Judaism could not have abandoned the environment and its advocates in our hour of collective need. It was inconceivable that biblical and rabbinic literature could have left us disarmed and alienated as the decade of the sixties gave way, at times painfully, to that of the seventies.

Long after the heyday of the ecology movement, my interest in the issues the movement raised has remained. Prolonged research into the "career" of the biblical injunction to "fill the earth and master it" has convinced me that popular condemnation of this text on ecological grounds was grievously in error. Above all else, it proceeded from a flawed methodology. Scholars simply assumed that their own understanding of the verse matched that of its author, that this understanding characterized Jewish and Christian readers of the Bible throughout the intervening centuries, and that one may therefore link the verse directly to specific social and scientific tendencies of our own day and age. Yet these scholars had not investigated the history of the verse's interpretation to determine whether it justified these assumptions. Nor had they grappled with the theoretical question of how one attributes meaning to a text, and to a sacred text in particular.

Must a text that inspires us itself be primarily responsible for such inspiration, or does the inspiration derive from a referential system within which we interpret the text? More simply put, does the meaning that we find in a text originate, ultimately, in the text itself or in the "baggage" that we as readers bring to the text? Perhaps the answer lies somewhere in between. Perhaps the meaning of a text derives from what the German philosopher of hermeneutics Hans-Georg Gadamer termed the "fusion of the horizons" of text and reader—in which case one must measure the cultural impact of a text in terms of its societal function and its interpretation over time.

Approaching the message of Genesis 1:28 from such a perspective, one finds that premodern readers of the verse, Jews and Christians, found in it relatively little bearing on the natural environment and its exploitation. Rather, God's initial words to human beings, especially those words mandating sexual reproduction, repeatedly raised the theological issue of divine covenant. Theologians, jurists, preachers, mystics, and poets—in their respective idioms—focused on this verse as an expression of (1) God's relationship with all of humanity and (2) the tension between that universal commitment and God's election of a single people.

In the first instance, the sexual and ruling functions mandated by our verse struck many readers as paradoxical if not contradictory: humans procreate like animals, but they exercise dominion like God. To reproduce and fill the earth on the one hand, and yet to master it on the other, suggested that humans are situated on a cosmic frontier, between terrestrial and supernal realms of existence. Our verse led exegetes to harp on this puzzling aspect of human nature, which the Bible openly cast as divine blessing: How, they wondered, were humans to confront their sexuality properly, so as to attain divine reward and realize the godliness implicit in their dominion? *Mutatis mutandis,* biblical, talmudic, and medieval Jews all struggled with this problem, to which the midrashic anthology *Genesis Rabbah* (8.11) offered a characteristic solution:

> R. Tifdai said in the name of R. Aba: The creatures of the upper world were created in the divine image and likeness and do not engage in procreation, while the creatures of the lower world engage in procreation and were not created in the divine image and likeness. The holy one, blessed be He, said, "I shall hereby create him [man] in the divine image and likeness like the creatures of the upper world, and as one who engages in procreation like the creatures of the lower world."
>
> R. Tifdai said in the name of R. Aba: The holy one, blessed be He, said, "If I create him like the creatures of the upper world, he will live and never die; and if [I create him] like the creatures of the lower world, he will die and not live. Rather, I shall hereby create him like creatures of the upper world and like creatures of the lower world. If he sins, he will die; and if he does not sin, he will live."

The homilies attributed to the otherwise unknown R. Tifdai follow immediately upon a list of those characteristics—four in each case—that humans share with angels (erect stature, speech, understanding, and sight) and with beasts (the consumption of food and drink, procreation, defecation, and death). For R. Tifdai, however, the dialectic between the angelic and beastly traits of human beings boils down to the tension between human sexuality and the divine image in which God created man and woman. R Tifdai's midrash suggests that the anomalous, sexual, godlike human being defies the apparent logic of this polar opposition.

Tifdai's second homily indicates that unlike the angel and the beast, humans can determine their own destiny; their merits will yield for them the deserts of the upper world or those of the lower, epitomized in life and death, respectively. Within such a framework, sexual reproduction denotes not only an attribute of the lower world, but also—along with the divine image—the essence of that singular perfection which allows humans, and humans only, to choose between life and death. The ensuing discussion in *Genesis Rabbah* (8.12), which plays upon alternative vocalizations of God's proclaimed intention that human beings "shall rule" (*yirdu,* Genesis 1:26) other creatures, reflects similarly upon the second half of the primordial blessing:

> *And rule the fish of the sea.* . . . R. Hanina said: If he has been meritorious, "they will descend (*yer-du*)." R. Jacob of Khar Hanan said: "And rule (*u-r-du*)" [applies] to him who is in our image and likeness; "they will descend (*yer-du*)" [applies] to him who is not in our image and likeness.

Vocalizing the consonants of the verb *yrdw* in Genesis 1:26 to mean "they will descend (*yer-du*)"—or perhaps "they will be ruled (*yeradu*)"—rather than "they shall rule (*yirdu*)" as in Scripture, R. Hanina and R. Jacob both instruct that humans can merit either reward or punishment, embodied in the fulfillment or nonfulfillment of God's primordial blessing. Sexuality and the divine image are the defining characteristics of the human being, and their proper expression leads directly to the reward of dominion.

In the second instance, the universal applicability of our verse continually troubled Jewish and Christian exegetes. The ostensive election of all human beings challenged their notion of a chosen people, prodding them to address the problem exegetically. Rabbinic lawyers, for example, expanded much casuistic effort to exclude gentiles and women from the commandment to "be fertile and increase," the blatant literal meaning of the Bible notwithstanding. (According to Genesis, God had addressed his instructions to both of the first parents, who lived twenty generations before the first of the Hebrew patriarchs.) Medieval Jewish kabbalists deemed the commandment of paramount importance, labeling the Jew who fails to have children "a despoiler of the covenant." Noted church fathers beheld the blessing of "fill the earth and master it" fullfilled in the rapid expansion of Christendom in late antiquity. And a famous monastic preacher of the high Middle Ages claimed that Catholics alone enjoy the blessing of "fill the earth and master it," while Jews, infidels, and heretics inherit the curse of Eve (Genesis 3: 16), "in pain you shall bear children." Overall, the recurring covenantal interpretation of "be fertile and increase" provides a helpful framework for considering what little the rabbis did have to say about God's ensuing instructions to fill, to master, and to rule. In a sole instance, the Talmud attributes quasi-halakhic significance to this call for human dominion over the earth, questioning whether it actually entitled the first humans to consume other animals for food. Elsewhere, classical rabbinic interpreters generally construed dominion to signify human primacy in the natural order, in physical, intellectual, and spiritual terms. According to some, Adam's dominion was reflected in his enormous size. According to others, dominion over the earth involved its development with the tools and fruits of human creativity. A third view linked dominion with the unique intellectual capability to acknowledge God. Yet another interpretation stressed that the blessing of dominion depended on human compliance with God's will, and that God punished and rewarded throughout history with the removal and conferral of this blessing.

Among some medieval commentators, dominion did entail the license to control the environment for one's own advantage, although one never senses a dispensation for noxious exploitation or destruction. In the first half of the tenth century, Saadya Gaon described most graphically how the blessing of "rule" in the Genesis cosmogony

includes the entire range of devices with which man rules over the animals: over some with fetters and bridles, over some with ropes and reins, over some with en-

closures and chains, over some with weapons of the hunt, over some with cages
and towers, and so on. . . .

And the word "the fish" includes the stratagems for catching fish from the bottom of the sea and the rivers, the preparation of the permitted species in cooking
utensils and their consumption, the extraction of pearls from the shells, and the use
of the appropriate portions of skin and bones and everything associated with this.
And [God] added the word "of the sea" to include man's subjugation of the water
as well; for he finds it within the ground and raises it out with pulleys or with con-
tainers or with a machine utilizing force and pressure. And thus he dams rivers to
transfer water from one side to the other, and he uses it to power the mills. . . .

And his word "and the birds" corresponds to the various snares for hunting birds
which fly in the sky, the process of taming some in order to hunt others, the preparation from them of foods for his sustenance and potions for medicines and the
like. And he added "of the sky" to include the ability of man to understand the
heavenly sphere and its composition . . . and to prepare the various instruments
for measuring the hours and their components.

And with the word "the cattle" he gave him the authority to lead and the power
to make use of them all, to eat the flesh of those fit for consumption through various means of cooking and in the different forms of food, to heal from that which
is medicinal, to ride on those suited for riding like mules, and to know all their
diets, that is, how to feed them.

Both in their length and in their elaboration of dominion Saadya's comments are exceptional, but they too speak to the same essential concern that
dominated the classical Jewish understanding of Genesis 1:28. I have quoted
them so extensively precisely because they comprise a glorious ode to *the
cultural achievements of men and women.* Human nature rather than the
physical environment (which is hardly the same as human nature at the expense of the physical environment) dominated rabbinic consideration of the
primordial blessing. Even those Jewish theologians who, like Abraham Ibn
Ezra and Moses Maimonides, denied that God created the world expressly
for the purposes of human beings shared a fundamental Western anthropocentrism that they inherited as much from Hellenistic traditions as from
the Bible. Reconciling this outlook with a life of Torah remained central to
this discussion. Issues ecological were usually absent.

Perhaps this traditional focus on human beings grates in our postpositivist,
pluralistic, global society. Yet I believe that a responsible Jewish approach to
environmental problems cannot afford to deny or neglect its own lineage.
Rather, it must commence from a focus through which one can best appreciate the halakhic principle most pertinent to environmental preservation:
bal tashchit. The rabbis set limits on human interference with the natural
order not in their midrash on the Genesis cosmogony but in their reflection
on Deuteronomy 20:19–20:

When in your war against a city you have to besiege it a long time in order to capture it, you must not destroy *(lo tashchit)* its trees, wielding the ax against them,
You may eat of them, but you must not cut them down. Are trees of the field

human to withdraw before you under siege? Only trees that you know do not yield
food may be destroyed; you may cut them down for constructing siegeworks
against the city that is waging war on you, until it has been reduced.

From the words "you must not destroy," the rabbis derived a general
rule—*bal tashchit*—against the needless destruction of anything. But at the
heart of this principle lies the question of needlessness. The Torah itself does
not prohibit the destruction of all trees, only those which bear fruit. And
while the Bible appeared to justify its injunction with a rhetorical query as to
the powerlessness of the tree—"Are trees of the field human to withdraw before you under siege?"—the rabbinic *Sifre* on Deuteronomy (203) understood the question differently: "Is a human being like a tree of the field?" In
other words, the verse "teaches that human life is dependent upon the tree."
The fundamental human need for food and its priority over the needs of battle underlay the commandment of *lo taschit*, not any sacred inviolability of
the physical environment.

When it abstracted the principle of *bal tashchit* to other situations as well,
rabbinic tradition remained consistent in its evaluation of environmental
concerns. On the one hand, *bal tashchit* applies, in theory, to everything.
One may not destroy buildings or wildlife, waste food or money, or even
squander energy for no good reason. On the other hand, the applicability of
bal tashchit gives way before the legitimate desires of men and women, of
society at large, and of God. One is therefore permitted to chop down even
a fruit-bearing tree for the food, fuel, and enrichment of the individual; to
clear a space for a public building; and to use its wood in the performance
of a divine commandment.

Implicit in this principle of *bal tashchit* is the demand for acute environmental sensitivity. The *halakhah* requires that one carefully weigh the ramifications of all action and behavior, for every interaction with the natural
world involves the setting of priorities, the weighing of conflicting interests,
and the permanent modification of the environment. Humans may have a
singular capacity to control other creatures, even as they too constitute part
of the environment they dominate. The Torah relates (Genesis 2:15) that "the
Lord God took the man and placed him in the Garden of Eden to till it and
to tend it." To till and to tend, or to develop and to preserve—a pair of
human responsibilities to God's creation characterized by complexity and dialectic, if not outright contradiction. Judaism charges its adherents to recognize and balance these responsibilities and, most importantly, to remember
their heavenly source and rationale.

Essential to this lesson of *bal tashchit* is the talmudic comparison (*Shabbat* 105b) of reckless destruction to idolatry:

One who tears his clothes in anger, or one who breaks his tools in anger, or one
who wastes his money in anger you should consider as an idolater. For such is the
craft of the evil inclination. Today it tells a person, "Do this," tomorrow it tells him,
"Do that," until it tells him, "Go, practice idolatry," and so he does.

If the Talmud thus characterizes the wanton exploitation of dominion, it is most instructive that the abuse of the first gift of the primordial blessing—the sexual power of reproduction—merits the only other application (*Niddah* 13b) of this talmudic account of "the craft of the evil inclination." Ultimately, the mandate of Genesis 1:28 and the restrictive principle of *bal tashchit* conveyed an identical message. Responsible interaction with the environment offers men and women the deepest personal and spiritual fulfillment, while environmental irresponsibility will lead to their physical and spiritual demise.

Judaism's environmental consciousness originated long before the ecological *cause célèbre* of our generation and, I should hope, will long outlive it. Like so much else in the rabbinic ethos, it calls upon human beings to be mindful of whence they have come, where they are going, and before whom they will have to account for their actions.

NOTE

From *Tikkun Magazine: A Bimonthly Jewish Critique of Politics, Culture and Society*, 2107 Van Ness Ave., Suite 302, San Francisco, CA 94102.

2

The Hebrew View of Nature

E. L. Allen

Western man today has two conflicting attitudes to nature. Sometimes it is beneath him, to be used without scruple for his purposes; then again it is above him, and he turns to it—or shall we say, to her?—for spiritual healing. In the first instance, as in Kant's famous dictum that "the understanding gives laws to nature," nature is the mere pattern of sensation into which the intellect introduces cohesion, system, and significance. Or, as in the term "natural resources," it is the totality of objects, animate or inanimate, minerals, plants, and animals which are available within a certain area for man's use. His attitude to these resources is aptly expressed by the verb "to exploit," for they have no claim of any kind upon him; their status is that of the thing, and he employs them as he will for his own advantage. The animate and the inanimate are reduced to the same level; the sheep's value lies in the wool it grows and the mutton it becomes, as that of the soil lies in the minerals it contains. So the term "naturalism" comes to be used for a system of thought which does injustice to the spiritual aspects of our experience and makes everything explicable, dull, and devitalized.

On the other hand, there is such a thing as "nature mysticism," and this is by no means absent from our urban civilization. The man who claims that he can worship God better in the open air than in a stuffy building is not thinking of nature as a system of sense-data ordered under the categories of the intellect or as a possible source of dividends. In so far as he is sincere in what he avers, nature is for him what it was for Wordsworth,

> The anchor of his purest thoughts, the nurse,
> The guide, the guardian of his heart, and soul
> Of all his moral being.

80

Nature brings to such a person the sense of an all-encompassing and sustaining Presence. Such an experience is not without its dangers. It may dull moral sensitivity, and entice one to self-forgetfulness by absorption in a great whole rather than summon one thereto by consecration to a worthy task. As one attitude to nature produces the utilitarian type of person, for whom Niagara is of interest only as a source of power, so the other breeds the dilettante and the mere aesthete.

The Hebrew view of nature has a depth which is lacking to the first and a robustness which is sadly needed by the second. For the man of the Bible nature is never seen in abstraction either from God or from the tasks which He has assigned to man in the world. Nature is envisaged as one of the spheres in which God meets man personally and in which he is called upon to exercise responsibility. Man, that is to say, is "before God" in nature as he is in history. Hence the indignation with which the prophets reject the fertility cults taken over from the Canaanites, for which nature is a depositary of magical powers and man seeks to utilize these by ritual acts. They cannot conceive of any sphere of life which is not ethically conditioned. Hence also the absence from Hebrew thought at this stage of anything such as the doctrine of transmigration, which would obliterate the distinction between human and animal life, between what is ordered by conscience and what is not. It is noticeable that it is just those religions which maintain in this way the barrier between man and the animal which inculcate humanity even towards the brute creation.

In the opening chapter of Genesis, man shares with nature its origin from God while at the same time rising above nature because he is designed for a relation to God into which it cannot enter. While he is appointed by God to dominion over the lower creation, this does not place it at his mercy: rather is it a trust which he receives. The statement that plants and animals were made each after its own kind shows that, for the writer, there is an order in nature which man is bound to respect. One is reminded at once of the prohibition in the Law of those mixtures which are held to be contrary to nature. Man has a task assigned to him, he has actually to subject nature to his own purposes; but that again is only permitted to him because he has in his being that which corresponds to God's own wisdom. He rules therefore by a delegated authority and not by his own caprice. When creation is as it were renewed after the Deluge, the same subjection of nature to man is proclaimed, and in still stronger language. "The fear of you and the dread of you shall be upon every beast of the earth." But his authority is modified by the requirement that life be respected even in its lowest forms. "Flesh with the life thereof, which is the blood thereof, shall ye not eat" (Gen. 9:1–7).

So far we have spoken of man. But man, of course, exists only as a concrete being in a particular community and in a particular territory. There is in the Bible a close association between people and land, and only those who can sympathize with this are able to appreciate what exile meant. The land of Israel belongs to Israel in virtue of the covenant with the fathers, and it therefore can only remain Israel's as the children show the same fidelity to God as that for which the fathers were blessed. "If ye be willing and obedient, ye shall eat the good of the land: but if ye refuse and rebel, ye shall be devoured with the sword" (Is. 1:19f). The world of nature is therefore no neutral background to the life of the people; it is one of the means by which the judgment of God upon them is executed. This is the meaning of the so-called dogma of retribution in the Deuteronomic literature. Retribution is no automatic procedure, but a personal response of God to the conduct of the people to whom He has given the land of Israel as their place of responsibility. So, for a later writer, "the world shall go forth with 'God' to fight against His insensate foes" (Wisdom 5:20). If this is a moral universe, how should nature not have a part to play in it?

If the people retain or lose the land according as they do or do not discharge the trust which comes to them with it, equally the land suffers for the people's sins. In the earlier creation story, the earth is cursed for the folly of our first parents. The land may indeed be so aggrieved by the sins of those who dwell on it that it will vomit them out (Lev. 20:22). The fertility of the soil is not to be secured by sacrifice and homeopathic magic but by fidelity to the covenant. That is the theme of Hosea 2. Corn and wine and oil were gifts of Jehovah, and the failure to recognize this will lead to the devastation of the land. Only as the nation, schooled by disaster and sadly reduced in numbers, returns to a right relation with its God, will the covenant be renewed with its animal inhabitants and with the soil itself. Nature will serve the gracious purpose of God as it has served His chastisement. "I will answer the heavens, and they shall answer the earth; and the earth shall answer the corn, and the wine, and the oil" (2:21f).

For "the relation between the earth and its owner is . . . a covenant-relationship, a psychic community, and the owner does not solely prevail in the relation. The earth has its nature, which makes itself felt, and demands respect. The important thing is to deal with it accordingly and not to ill-treat it" (Pedersen, *Israel* I-II, 479). That even the earth has its rights is clearly affirmed in Job's great liturgy of innocence, perhaps the high watermark of ethics in the Hebrew Bible. "If my land cry out against me, and the furrows therefore weep together; if I have eaten the fruits thereof without money, or have caused the owners (perhaps 'the laborers') thereof to lose their life; let thistles grow instead of wheat, and cockle instead of barley" (Job 31:38–40). To quote Pedersen again: "The task of the peasant is to deal kindly with the earth, to uphold its blessing and then take what it yields on its own accord. If he exhausts it, then he attacks its soul and kills it; after that it will only bring forth thorns, thistles and whatever else pertains to the wilderness." There are duties to the soil one tills as to the labour one employs.

The same idea lies behind the institution of the sabbatical year in Lev. 25:1–7. The earth has the same right to a period of rest as man and the animals have, for it must not be exhausted, it must be allowed opportunity for the renewal of its vital forces. In the somewhat utopian account of the year of jubilee which follows, it is promised that the blessing upon the land will be such in the sixth year as to ensure the people against any hardship. Here again the land is regarded as involved in the covenant–relationship between God and the people. Nature is no mere thing. It is alive and all life has in it a certain rhythm. Man must forgo for a while his right to subdue and exploit the environment on which he depends; it must be allowed a period of liberty in which to live as it were its own life. During that time (Ex. 23:10–11) those who ordinarily have no part in the forcible utilization of nature by the peasant—the poor and the wild beasts—come into their rights as well. The seventh year of liberty is theirs also to enjoy.

So far we have spoken mainly of the land and the relation of the peasant thereto. But nature for the Israelite included also the beasts of the field. These can be classified in two quite different ways. There is first the purely religious or cultic distinction between clean and unclean animals, one which is regarded as so basic to life that it occurs even in one version of the Flood story. It belongs to the structure of creation and so must be preserved when that creation is renewed after the episode of destruction. The importance of this classification lies in the fact that it brings God also into the relation between man and nature. The reasons given for the abstentions here required can of course be variously explained: as they are taken up into the religion of Israel they are governed by the same principle as that which inspires the ceremonial law, that acts which in themselves might be regarded as morally indifferent can nevertheless take on a moral quality by being referred in some way to God. They become the sphere of obedience or disobedience. They are therefore to be described as taboos only if it is borne in mind that the taboo is the form under which, at a certain level of development, the sacred is apprehended.

The second classification is that of animals as tame and wild. The domestic animal has a place within the household, as is shown by the fact that it shares in the rest on the seventh day. It is unlike its wild counterpart inasmuch as it has entered into a covenant–relationship with man so as to become his servant in perpetuity (Job 41:4). If this implies man's right to use the animal for his purposes, it implies also that he must respect the life of his beast. There is a personal relationship between man and animal which might well serve as a model for that between Israel and God. (Is. 1:3) Paul only shows how far he is from the mentality of his people in earlier days when he comments on the precept "Thou shalt not muzzle the ox when he treadeth out the corn" (Deut. 25:4). "Is it for the oxen that God careth?" (1 Cor. 9:9). It is one of the characteristics of the righteous man in Proverbs that he is kind towards domestic animals (12:10). Behind all this is the Hebrew conviction that life as such is mysterious, sacred, and from God. Schweitzer's ethic of reverence for life goes farther, to be sure, than the Hebrew conception does.

For the latter is conscious that all living creatures are not on the same level, that it is with the domestic animal only that man is in covenant–relation.

That does not mean, of course, that the wild beast has no place in God's world, that it is there merely to be destroyed by man at his pleasure. That wild animals can be used by the moral government of God is brought out in the story of the lions which prey upon the Assyrian colonists in the North. In the speech from the storm in Job the wild beast symbolizes and expresses that in God's power and wisdom which forever surpasses man's poor understanding. The untamed world beyond the frontiers of human society is fraught with the numinous; it is a constant reminder that man is not master in the world but only a privileged and therefore responsible inhabitant of it. This world also has its relation to God, not mediated through man. The young ravens cry to God for their food, and He supplies them (Job 38:41). The folly of the ostrich is by God's ordinance, yet how can man hope to comprehend a purpose which requires this maladjustment on the part of so noble a creature (Job 39:17)? When Amos looks for a symbol of God's judgment, he finds it in the lion and the bear (3:4, 5:19). The Genesis story makes it evident how uncanny the serpent appeared in the eyes of the Hebrew and how easily it came to symbolize for him the power of evil.

Yet it is not to be forever so. The ideal condition, that which obtained in Eden and that which will return at the consummation of history, is that the distinction between tame and wild creatures should be broken down and both alike be incorporated into the covenant with man. This return to the lost harmony of man and nature is an integral part of the prophetic vision of the future. The daring faith of Second Isaiah sees it beginning already in the return of the exiles, when the desert will be transformed and its wild creatures will come to drink at the oases which have been miraculously opened in the desert. Hosea looks for a covenant "with the beasts of the field, and with the fowls of heaven, and with the creeping things of the ground" (2:18). Yes, even the ancient animosity between man and the serpent will be eliminated. In the restored earthly paradise of Isaiah's hopes, "the cow and the bear shall feed; their young ones shall lie down together; and the lion shall eat straw like the ox. And the sucking child shall play on the hole of the asp, and the weaned child shall put his hand on the basilisk's den" (11:7f). The prophet cannot be content with a purely human ideal. There must be a place in it for the beasts that have served man well and even for those against which he has had to contend.

It has only been possible in this article to touch on a few aspects of the Hebrew conception of nature. But perhaps even so enough has been said to suggest that, however strange it may seem to our urban mentality, there are features in it which we need to learn to recognize again. Has not recent experience taught us, for example, that even the soil has its rhythms which must be respected, that it needs its periods of recuperation, and that to take from it without making any return is to invite disaster? Has not the plight of displaced persons and the fervor with which the proclamation of the State of Israel was greeted reminded us that the connection between a people and its land is integral to a healthy life for that people? It is quite true that to speak of animals, and still more of the earth, as possessing rights would raise many problems. What we can say without hesitation is that the ancient Israelite was not mistaken when he saw that there are restraints, moral in character, upon man's use of his power over nature, even over inanimate nature, that here also he is responsible and is under God.

NOTE

From *Journal of Jewish Studies* 2 (1951): 100–104.

3

Concepts of Nature
in the Hebrew Bible

Jeanne Kay

INTRODUCTION

Fresh analyses of environmental thought in the Hebrew Bible (Christian Old Testament) seem long overdue.[1] Many authors have reiterated the same few verses from Genesis and the Psalms to demonstrate either the Bible's antagonistic attitude toward nature or paradoxically its protective approach toward the environment. Most scholars additionally have studied the Bible as only part of a broader problem, such as Christian or even Western environmental attitudes, and they typically view the problem through the perspectives of the modern environmentalist movement.[2] In this paper I have different purposes: (1) to interpret the Hebrew Bible synchronically,[3] that is, in its entirety as a work of ancient literature and (2) to interpret the Bible geosophically,[4] in terms of its own Iron Age, Near Eastern perspectives. I apply these interpretations to the Bible's depiction of plants and animals as well as to the biota's relationship with humanity, and develop an argument that is very different from either side of the standard despot-stewardship debate. I demonstrate similarities with key elements of ancient pagan religions, with ecological realities of the ancient Middle East, and with the currently unfashionable retribution theology, and in doing so set the Lynn White–initiated debate about the Bible on a different and hopefully more productive footing.

THE "LYNN WHITE DEBATE": PROBLEMS AND PROSPECTS

The argument proposed by Lynn White Jr. that the root of current environmental problems is Judeo-Christian arrogance toward nature,[5] promptly

encouraged two competing groups of scholars to examine religious attitudes toward the environment. These two opposing camps largely shaped
the outlines of discussion about nature, Judaism, and Christianity during
the subsequent 20 years. One group might be termed the despotism school
because it views Gen. 1:26–28 and subsequent Christian writers as mandating tyrannical human control over nature. The competing stewardship
tradition interprets the identical verses and other early Christian writings as
assigning humans a caretaker role.[6]

This lively and long-lived debate has frustrated attempts at reconciliation
between the two camps. The reason may lie in some of the debate's basic assumptions. Three basic challenges have so far criticized the logic of the po-
larized despot/steward debate. First, the assumption that the entity to blame
for the modern environmental crisis is in fact "Judeo-Christian" has been
challenged. Passmore has argued that the tradition in question was not
Judeo-Christian, but rather Greco-Christian.[7] He sees little evidence that the
Hebrew Bible was anti-environment, and additional evidence that the Bible
constrained human use of nature. Ehrenfeld and Bentley as well as Helfand
have pointed out that Judaism and Christianity are two separate religions,
and have examined Jewish beliefs alone in support of a stewardship position.[8] Schwarzschild has also examined Jewish beliefs independently in
order to support the despot model.[9] Second, Tuan and Kay, in contrast, have
questioned the assumption that religious beliefs have such influence over
human environmental impact, arguing that a variety of cultural and ecological factors moderate the impact of beliefs on nature.[10] Third, Glacken and Attfield have argued that the Bible's environmental attitudes should be understood through their own ancient perspectives rather than through the
hindsight and potential ethnocentric bias of the modern environmentalist
movement.[11] Bratton has promoted a historical approach that focuses specifically on the Christian Old Testament rather than on the Bible as interpreted
through related or subsequent traditions.[12]

In addition to questions about the existence of a Judeo-Christian tradition,
the effects of environmental beliefs on environments, and the enormous potential bias in viewing Iron Age beliefs through modern environmentalist
lenses, there are other problems. The first concerns the wisdom of considering any intellectual tradition over several millennia without first ensuring that
each individual period, critical source, and important author are first understood. For example, of the many studies of Western religion and nature, relatively few recent ones look exclusively at the fundamental reference, the Bible,
before moving on to later periods or modern environmentalist concerns.

The second is the problem of identifying biblical beliefs, let alone a "Judeo-
Christian tradition," in studies which at most examine a handful of verses in
Genesis and Psalms and perhaps a few additional verses from the Wisdom
Literature. The rest of the biblical books should be systematically investigated
for environmental messages that perhaps do not refer to White's concerns.

The third concerns the problem of translation. The Jewish Bible *cum* Old Testament was written in the ancient Hebrew language, whereas most English-speaking participants in the despotism/stewardship debate apparently read it only, or at least primarily, in English translation. Students of ancient Middle Eastern languages devote entire careers to debating the meanings of single biblical Hebrew words, an occupation that should give pause to Anglophones who claim to understand the Bible's environmental thought based solely on English translations. Examples of the translation problem for Anglo-American environmentalists abound. The names of many plant and animal species are misidentified in the King James version—and in fact many identifications have been lost since the early centuries C.E.[13] The Hebrew Bible does not even have an equivalent term for the generalized English word *wilderness*, but rather has several terms for specific types of Near Eastern habitats, such as the seasonally arid pastureland (*midbar*). Although much good scholarship has come out of the Lynn White debate, some fundamental concerns remain about its underlying assumptions, regardless of an individual author's side in the matter.

Each of the challenges sketched above could form the basis of an entire paper. In this paper, however, I contribute a more detailed look at the Jewish Bible and its attitudes toward nature through a more literary, synchronic approach to the Bible and a more literal, geosophical interpretation.[14] Although several literary approaches are current in biblical scholarship, I work the rich vein struck by Robert Alter.[15] Of particular relevance to biblical environmental studies are Alter's examination of the modes of biblical communication (e.g., reticence, binary opposition) and of motifs and themes extending within and across narrative cycles. If the Bible's environmentalism seems rather thin to modern environmentalists, the reason may be that standard historical or philosophical approaches are less suitable for the Bible's mode of expression. The geosophical approach attempts to understand a culture's geographical beliefs in its own terms, rather than through an unflattering comparison with the researcher's own ethnocentric biases.[16] Geosophy, rather than blaming the Bible for a harmful environmental stance, might reconstruct the worldview of Israelite society and its environment to determine what conditions made a given attitude a rational response to their environmental relationships.

I specifically examine biblical concepts of plants and animals both as independent entities and as entities whose fate depends on human behavior. The model of nature as God's instrument of divine reward and retribution may be out of favor with theologians and environmentalists today, but it clearly fits better the scope of biblical texts than do the despot or stewardship models, which are more recent innovations. Once nature is understood through the Bible's moral concerns with reward and punishment, ancient Judaism's proscriptions against both arrogance toward nature and nature worship can be better understood.

THE STATUS OF PLANTS AND ANIMALS IN THE HEBREW BIBLE

The Bible's discrete distinctions between God, nature, and humanity form a core of current scholarly thought on biblical attitudes toward nature.[17] Because God is distinct from his creation, nature is effectively secularized. Stewardship proponents would add to this typology their biblical evidence of God's continuing care for and participation in nature. An extreme view within the despotism school, however, holds that since monotheism does not deify nature or equate its deity with nature, monotheism therefore perceives nature as mere matter, devoid of independent integrity and completely subjugated to human will. If whatever is not deified is spiritless matter, however, this logic places humanity itself in a peculiar position.

The Bible actually describes an intermediate level of being somewhere between God and potter's clay, in which both living nature and humanity exist: that of the "living soul" or "living creature" (*nefesh chayyah*). The Bible in fact characterizes animals and sometimes plants in ways very reminiscent of the pantheistic nature religions that Judaism is supposed to disparage. For example, the Carmodys state in their environmentally oriented survey of world religions that Eskimos regard all nature as living; both animals and people have true souls: "The basic image for those souls was either a shadow or a breath."[18] The Hebrew word *nefesh* is used in the Bible both as the human spirit and also for animal spirits. English translations usually call animals living creatures rather than "souls," but compare *nefesh* in Gen. 1:20 ("Let the earth bring forth the living creature") with Ps. 42:2–3 ("My soul thirsteth for God"): the Hebrew word is *nefesh* in both cases.

Ruach, meaning wind, spirit, or breath, is the force through which God animates all life (see Ps. 104:30).[19] Ecclesiastes (3:19, 21) states, "For that which befalleth the sons of men befalleth beasts . . . yea, they have all one *breath*; so that man hath no pre-eminence above a beast; . . . Who knoweth the *spirit* of man whether it goeth upward, and the *spirit* of the beast whether it goeth downward to the earth?" Ecclestastes uses the same Hebrew term, *ruach*, in all three cases. This use of the same terms for both human and animal souls, combined with our joint creation on the sixth day (Gen. 1:24–26), suggests more similarities in biblical human and animal conditions than is generally recognized.

The biblical concept of nature is strongly anthropomorphic. Nature has its own commandments. In Genesis, God commands animals to be fruitful and multiply, along with Adam and Noah (Gen. 1:22, 8:17). God creates plants simultaneously with their reproductive potentials (Gen. 1:11–12, 9:3). Domesticated animals are to observe the Sabbath (Deut. 5:14) and refrain from murder (Gen. 9:7).

Creation has a covenantal relationship with the Creator. Animals share with Noah's family in God's covenant to sustain the earth and its seasonal cycle (Gen. 8:21–22, 9:10–17). Creation enters into the Mosaic covenant in its role as witness to the Israelites' observance of the *mitzvot* (commandments) (see Deut. 30:10). In the millennium, God promises a new covenant with animals, birds, and creeping things so that they will no longer fear destruction and will live amicably with humans and among themselves: carnivory is to be abolished (Isa. 11:6–9, 65:25; Hos. 2:20). Nature, like man, is to praise the Creator and to rejoice:

> Praise ye Him, sun and moon:
> Praise Him, all ye stars of light.
> Praise Him, ye heaven of heavens,
> And ye waters that are above the heavens . . .
> Praise the Lord from the earth.
> Ye sea-monsters, and all deeps;
> Fire and hail, snow and vapor,
> Stormy wind, fulfilling his word;
> Mountains and all hills
> Fruitful trees and all cedars;
> Beasts and all cattle,
> Creeping things and winged fowl. (Ps. 148:3–4, 7–10)

In the Psalms, hills are girdled with joy, valleys shout for joy (65:13–14), floods clap their hands, the whole earth worships God and sings praises to His name (66:1–4, 89:6). In I Chron. 16:23–33, the fields exult and the trees of the wood sing for joy. Like man, nature also fears God (Ps. 68:9) and trembles at His presence. Nature's *mitzvot* (commandments) of worshiping God and rejoicing are to become much easier in the millennium, however, when nature will no longer suffer for human transgressions.

MAN'S DOMINION OVER NATURE, NATURE'S DOMINION OVER MAN

Most of the debate about humanity's dominion over nature has been too simplistic. The despot and stewardship schools actually both agree that Genesis 1:26–28 sets humanity in a separate and superordinate position over nature: they disagree only about whether this dominion is to be arrogant or responsible. The Bible's portrayal of the dominion issue is actually more detailed and complex than most studies have indicated. The Bible indicates a variety of ways in which nature is subservient to man, but also ways in which man is subservient to nature.

To be sure, Genesis 1:26 and 2:19 tell Adam to rule over the biota, but biblical writers of the ancient Middle East probably had no experience of an egalitarian society. The Bible depicts few relationships among equals of any kind. In the biblical world, Adam rules Eve, patriarchs rule their extended families and servants, kings rule their nations. The sun rules the day and the moon rules the night (Gen. 1:16). Leviathan apparently rules the sea (Job 40:25–32, 41:1–26), and Behemoth the world of land animals (Job 40:15–24). God rules the whole. Nor can we rule out the historical possibility that the book that explains the origins of rainbows, place names, and musical instruments merely intended to describe, rather than prescribe, this ranking in explaining the observed activities of hunting, fishing, and plant and animal domestication, presumably all invented in the Neolithic period before the Bible was written.

Although the relationship between man and nature in the Bible is un-equivocally homocentric, the Bible depicts additional relationships within nature in which humans do not figure, and which center upon the needs of other living beings. Man's use of plants and animals for his own comfort is only part of what the Bible has to say about nature. Animals are more than just meat for the table or traction for the plow; plants are more than firewood or bread. Glacken advances the idea that various elements of the environment are created in their respective forms in order to serve one another—a biblical concept of symbiosis (Ps. 104:14–20. See also Gen. 1:30; Ps. 145:16, 147:8–9; Job 38:39–41, 39:1–8, 28). Glacken notes that God's care for nature is without reference to utilitarianism: at times the Bible mocks man's inability to comprehend, let alone to use or dominate the wild nature which exists outside of his own cultural landscape (Job 38:25–27, 39:9–12; Eccles. 11:5).[20]

Where nature is subservient to humanity, its relationship can be helpful and empathetic. Nature sorrows and rejoices with the fortunes of the Is-raelites (Joel 1:12; Amos 1:2; Jonah 3:7–9; Isa. 14:7–8). Fruit trees and vines willingly serve man in his ritual observance by providing oil, fruit, and wine:

> The trees went forth on a time to anoint a king over them; and they said unto the olive-tree: Reign thou over us. But the olive-tree said unto them: Should I leave my fastness, seeing that by me they honor God and man, and go to hold sway over the trees? And the trees said to the fig-tree: Come thou, and reign over us. But the fig-tree said unto them: Should I leave my sweetness, and my good fruitage, and go to hold sway over the trees? And the trees said unto the vine: Come thou, and reign over us. And the vine said unto them: Should I leave my wine, which cheereth God and than, and go to hold sway over the trees? (Judg. 9:8–13)

Although Jotham's parable refers to political maneuverings for the kingship of Shechem, the text clearly shows the idea of the service of trees in religious ritual.[21] For trees, at any rate, to serve man ultimately is to serve God (see Deut. 8:7–10, 26:10–11).

But nature has another, less cheerful relationship with mankind. Plants and animals actually ascend in the Bible's moral landscape and dominate people who misbehave. The Bible describes nature's dominion over man in the straightforward realm of divine punishment: God sends wild beasts to de-stroy people, or strikes agricultural fields with insect pests. Plant and animal dominion over man, however, has other literal meanings. When God delivers the Israelites into the hands of their enemies, who reduce their walled cities to rubble and destroy their agriculture, these devastated sites are invaded by bird and mammal scavengers (see Jer. 15:3, 35:20). "Thorns and thistles," ruderals even today of Israel's derelict lands, invade former habitations as a pioneer stage of ecological succession. In the final humiliation, corpses of the slain are consumed by worms and maggots, and man indeed returns to the dust from which he was taken (Hos. 13:8; Joel 1:4; I Kings 21:23–24; Isa. 13:17–22, 14:11).

Isaiah 34–35 provides a representative example of the themes of nature's dominion over humans and of nature's empathy for them. Because of its peoples' wickedness (in this instance against Israel) God will totally devastate the land of Edom, leaving it as the domain of predators, weeds, and scavengers:[22]

> And the streams thereof shall he turned into pitch,
> And the dust thereof into brimstone,
> And the land thereof shall become burning pitch. (34:9)
>
> . . . the pelican and the bittern shall possess it,
> And the owl and the raven shall dwell therein; (34:11)
>
> And thorns shall come up in her palaces,
> Nettles and thistles in the fortresses thereof; (34:13)
>
> And it shall he a habitation of wild-dogs . . .
> And the wild-cats shall meet with the jackals. (34:14)
>
> Yea, there shall the kites be gathered,
> Everyone with her mate. (34:15)

During Israel's future salvation, however,

> The wilderness and the parched land shall be glad;
> And the desert shall rejoice, and blossom as the rose.
>
> It shall blossom abundantly and rejoice
> Even with joy and singing. (35:1–2)

Springs of water are to break out in the thirsty ground, domesticated animals areto replace the wildlife endemic to war-demolished cities, and predators are to disappear (35:6–10).

Similar patterns echo throughout the other prophets: the environment of sinful countries, both of Israel and of neighboring lands, is to deteriorate and nature is to make a mockery of "man's dominion" over nature. In the future, whether following the Jews' return from exile or in the millennium, a harmonious and joyful nature is to sustain the commonweal of Israel and her allies. Nature is God's tool of reward and punishment, and its beneficence depends on human morality.

In another variation of the theme of animal dominion over humans, a few righteous people gain ascendancy over animals by virtue of their wholeheartedness toward God.[23] The "beasts of the field" are not to multiply against the Israelites under Joshua. The shepherd David overcomes the lion, ravens feed Elijah, King Solomon gains unprecedented knowledge about nature and its ways (I Sam. 17:34–36; I Kings 5:13, 17:6). In contrast, Baalam's ass prevents him from cursing the Israelites, and bears come out of the forest to kill Elisha's tormentors (Num. 22:23–33; II Kings 2:24). The great fish swallows the errant Jonah, but delivers the prophet safely to shore when he repents.

The theme of the negative correlation between human and animal power crystalizes in the book of Daniel. The righteous Daniel is unharmed in the lions' den (Dan. 6:21–23), while his false accusers are torn to bits (Dan. 7:23). Even more striking is Nebuchadnezzar's metamorphosis. God made Nebuchadnezzar great and delivered into his hand "the children of men, the beasts of the field, and the fowls of heaven" (Dan. 2:38). In a dream, the king is compared to a mighty tree in which all the birds and animals find refuge. The king's dream then predicts that the king's glory is near an end: "Let his portion be with the beasts in the grass of the earth; Let his heart be changed from man's, And let a beast's heart be given unto him" (Dan. 4:15–16). Because of the king's hubris, God deprives him of his kingdom, and in his descent from power, Nebuchadnezzar takes on animal characteristics. "He was driven from men, and did eat grass as oxen, and his body was wet with the dew of heaven, till his hair was grown like eagles' feathers, and his nails like birds' claws" (Dan. 4:33). When the king learns to praise God, his animal features disappear, and his royal stature returns to him.

Discussions of animal dominion over people are foreign to most modern commentaries on Genesis, which stress humanity's role as either despot or steward. However, the ideal of nature's ascendancy over erring humans definitely made sense to rabbinical commentators of late Roman times.[24] In the Bible, human kingship over nature is a conditional post, based upon moral fitness. This ascendancy in a few instances applies to surface waters, as in the examples of Moses and the Israelites' crossing of the Red Sea, and Joshua and the Israelites' crossing of the Jordan River (Josh. 3:15–17).

The biblical theme of humans created in the divine image (Gen. 1:26–27: Ps. 8) also relates to humanity's conditional dominion over nature. In Genesis 1:26 the concepts are grammatically conjunctive. Anthropomorphisms aside, what does it mean to be created in the Creator's image? Most environmentalist commentators have explained this theme as mandating either human despotism or stewardship over nature, apparently authorizing man to wield godlike power over human fertility and the environment. Conversely, the rest of the Bible abounds in narratives of ungodly behavior and the ecological punishment it accrues. A geosophical interpretation of man's formulation in the divine image would hold that humans who deliberately sin bestialize their divine image, thus necessarily diminishing their authority over nature and their own fertility. By behaving "worse than animals," the ungodly set into motion animal control over human destiny. In contrast, lordship over nature and progeny result when humans behave according to their divine image. The concept of evil as an affront to man's divine image is most clearly articulated to Noah in Genesis 9:7: "Whosoever sheddeth man's blood, by man shall his blood be shed: for in the image of God made He man." Following this verse is a repetition of the command to multiply, suggesting that, just as murder diminishes the divine image, procreation magnifies the divine image.

Readers familiar with the Bible may at this point argue that the Bible is inconclusive or contradictory: the commandment to subdue nature is followed by many accounts of nature controlling man. The role of nature as reward and punishment is contradicted by Job and Ecclesiastes who assert that reward and punishment do not correlate with moral and immoral behavior. These are but examples, however, of the biblical mode of communication in thesis and antithesis, which Alter describes as one of the Bible's grand themes: divine plan in conflict with human failing.[25] The ability to interpret seemingly contradictory verses as part of a literary theme, rather than as textual flaws, is a strength of the synchronic-literary approach to the Bible.

THE BIBLE ON HUMAN ARROGANCE TOWARD NATURE

Regarding the issue of whether the Bible entitles an arrogant humanity to destroy nature, one should notice that biblical images of God's punitive blighting of the landscape, whether described or predicted, appear far worse than any ecological deterioration which ancient peoples could have expected simply from their technologically unsophisticated mismanagement of resources. The Bible's frequent reminders of the absolute destruction of the landscape surrounding Sodom and Gomorrah are a case in point (see Deut. 29:22; Zeph. 1:9). While the Bible unquestionably develops the belief in God's continuous care for the environment, that theme is also contrasted, in characteristic biblical fashion, to passages of God's destruction of the natural world. However, this dilemma points out what may be the Bible's most relevant position for modern environmentalists. In the Bible, premeditated decimation of nature is not man's prerogative but God's.

God's prerogative is to sustain or to destroy the Bible's most exalted wild species, the cedars of Lebanon:

> The voice of the Lord breaks the cedars;
> Yea, the Lord breaks in pieces the cedars of Lebanon.
> He makes them also to skip like a calf;

Lebanon and Sirion like a young wild ox.
The voice of the Lord makes the hinds to calve
And strips the forests bare. (Ps. 29:5–6, 9; cf. Also Zech 11:1–3; Hab. 3:5–8)

In contrast, proud mortals who usurp God's role in Lebanon's wilderness forests are humiliated. Arrogance against nature is blasphemous arrogance toward God. Isaiah prophesies against King Sennacherib of Assyria:

> By thy messengers thou hast taunted the Lord,
> And hast said: With the multitude of my chariots
> Am I come up to the height of the mountains,
> To the innermost parts of Lebanon;
> And I have cut down the tall cedars thereof,
> And the choice cypresses thereof,
> And I have entered into his farthest lodge,
> The forest of his fruitful field
> I have digged and drunk strange waters.
> And with the sole of my feet have I dried up
> All the rivers of Egypt. (II Kings 19:23–24)

In images evoking man's subjugation of animals, God promises Sennacherib to "put My hook in thy nose, And My bridle in thy lips" (II Kings 19:28; see also Isa. 9:9–10, 10:13–19, 14:24). Thus, the king who boasted of his ascent over nature is to descend to the level of a beast of burden. (Sennacherib is subsequently slain by his own sons.)

In similar examples, Habakkuk (Hab. 2:17) predicts humiliation for wanton destroyers of nature: "For the violence done to Lebanon shall cover you, And the destruction of the beasts, which make them afraid; Because of men's blood and the violence done to the land. . . ." In Judges 6:3–6, the pagan Midianites and Amalekites overpopulate the land of Israel with their livestock and destroy the pasturage, but are beaten by the Israelites under their righteous leader Gideon (cf. also Ezek. 29:3–5, 9; 31:3–14).

Boastful destruction of resources apparently was common testimonial to the might of kings in the ancient Middle East.[26] The biblical condemnation of deforestation for self-aggrandizement may be contrasted with the Mesopotamian Epic of Gilgamesh (third millennium B.C.E.), in which the heroic king destroys a cedar forest to "establish his name."[27] To be sure, Joshua urges the tribe of Joseph to clear hillside forests for their allotment, but it is because of an insufficiency of previously cleared land necessary to secure subsistence, not a demonstration of the tribe's power (Josh. 17:14–18). The Bible credits Solomon and Hiram with a massive joint lumbering project, but whatever the environmental outcome, the two undertake it to glorify God rather than Solomon.

In the Bible, humans indirectly bring about environmental destruction as the outcome of sin, or do so directly through foolish arrogance. These analyses scarcely support the theory that the roots of the modern environmental crisis rest in perspectives intrinsic to the Bible.

THE MORAL LANDSCAPE OF THE BIBLE

The foregoing discussion raises a troublesome question about the Bible's concept of the immoral destruction of nature. Why should innocent nature deteriorate on account of human transgressions in seemingly unrelated areas of life? Regarding nature as victim, the Torah clearly considers that crimes against God or society are simultaneously crimes against the landscape in which they are committed. After Cain murders Abel in the field, God charges, "The blood of your brother cries out to Me from the ground; *Therefore* you are cursed from the ground, which opened her mouth to receive your brother's blood from your hand." (Gen. 4:10) Concerning the Canaanites, Leviticus 18:25 states: "And the land was defiled, *therefore* did I visit the iniquity thereof upon it, and the land vomited out her inhabitants." (cf. also Ezek. 12:19; Hos. 1:1–3). The Bible prescribes not only reward and punishment, but *reciprocal* justice. This concept is crucial for understanding why the Bible threatens to punish misdemeanors in business or interpersonal relations with drought or eviction from the land. In the Bible, all moral and immoral deeds have positive or negative impacts on the land on which they are perpetrated, and the land responds accordingly.

Biblical justice implies enormous injustice for innocent bystanders who happen to be present when the punishment descends. Humans do not commit evil in isolation without repercussions for the community. In the biblical narratives, the people are punished for the sins of the king, the sins of the fathers are visited upon the children, and a landscape suffers for the crimes of its inhabitants (for the antithetical view, see Ezek. 18).

The idea that God punishes evil committed in a given place through ecological deterioration of that place seems to leave nature at a major disadvantage. At times, the Bible itself appears to question this philosophy of nature. ("Is it, O Lord, that against the rivers, Is it that Thine anger is kindled against the rivers, Or Thy wrath against the sea?" Hab. 3:81.) Rabbis in late Roman times were also perplexed as to why the earth should be punished for human transgressions. Some suggested that the earth and its creatures were themselves culpable, such as through carnivory (shedding blood) or otherwise failing to obey God's commandments to them in the beginning. Other sages argued that the "Mother Earth" was chastised for the sins of her human children, for whom she, as parent, was responsible.[28]

The Bible's concept of divine punishment is that the masses may suffer for the crimes of a few. The moral implication is a tremendous burden of responsibility upon each individual. Each must behave uprightly to protect the innocent within one's own nation, as well as to preserve the environment upon which all depend. This responsibility extends far beyond one's direct impact upon specific people or sites and calls for their sustenance through exemplary behavior in all realms of religious and interpersonal life. If these biblical concepts were carried to their logical conclusion, we would have to recognize the entire set of commandments as set forth in the Torah as a comprehensive guidebook for environmental maintenance. (Moses does as much in the last chapters of Deuteronomy.) In a belief system that postulates environmental repercussions for the entire range of human actions, humans indeed "hold nature in jeopardy."[29] The belief that all human offenses potentially imperil nature is the Bible's strongest statement about human dominion over the environment.

WOSHIPING IN NATURE AND WITH NATURE

An additional problem of the Bible in the eyes of some environmentalists is its condemnation of animism and nature worship. Despite the efforts of Tuan and others, many environmentalists still presume that nature-worshiping societies are more ecologically beneficent than either Judaism or Christianity.[30] A further elaboration of biblical attitudes toward plants and animals and of nature as reward and punishment may help to explain the Bible's attitudes toward nature worship, the obverse of human dominion over the environment.

One should first note that the Bible makes few direct attacks against the worship of natural features per se, whether in the context of neighboring polytheistic cultures or within Judaism itself. On occasion, the Bible condemns the worship of celestial bodies, stones, or the Egyptian animal deities (see Deut. 4:16–19; Ezek. 8:16). Biblical scholars currently debate whether sacred trees were worshiped in ancient Israel: for example, backsliding Israelites venerated objects called *asherim* but researchers are uncertain as to whether these were sacred trees, pillars, or carved idols.[31] The literal worship of natural features is not a preoccupation of the Bible, perhaps because of the ancient Middle East's elaborate anthropomorphic pantheons. The Bible does strongly and persistently condemn the veneration of manufactured images of these deities, which have been excavated in great numbers from archaeological sites in the region.

Natural features, nevertheless, provided both Jews and polytheists with milieus in which supernatural visitations were expected. With both kinds of religions, adherents often do not worship the literal natural object itself, but rather deem it sacred because of a spirit which they believe to live within or nearby it. The spirit, rather than its ecological housing, is actually the object of deification.[32] Thus, the prophets typically condemned Israel for worshiping pagan gods "under every leafy tree," not for worshiping the trees themselves. The Bible depicts both Israelites and heathens as sanctifying specific types of environments. The former do so without condemnation when they worship God: the Bible, however, denounces both groups when nature becomes the setting for worship of Baal, Asherah, or other deities (cf. Jer. 2:20–23, 3:13; Ezek. 20:28).

Although Judaism eventually relinquished worship in outdoor settings in favor of worship in the Jerusalem temple, the Bible obliquely depicts an Israelite religion with a strong sense of nature as sacred space. Mountain tops, such as Mount Sinai and Mount Zion, were sites of divine manifestations to both Jews and non-Jews. The Bible mentions terebinths (*Pistacia atlantica*) as identifying sites where God appears to Abram/Abraham (Gen. 12:6–8, 18:1–3), and an angel to Gideon (Judg. 6:11). Joshua sets up a monument under a terebinth (oak in some translations, Josh. 24:26) (cf. also Gen. 35:4. 8; I Chron. 10:12). The Hebrew root *el*, or god, appears in both *elah*, the terebinth, and in *elon* or *alon*, the oak, implying that these trees had divine associations for the ancient Israelites and their neighbors.[33] (The same root is in *Elohim*, the Creator name among Hebrew names for God; and in *El*, the Canaanite father-creator deity.) Hareuveini and Schaffer discuss the role of the plant species essential to the ritual observance of the biblical festivals of *Sukkot* (Tabernacles) and *Shavuot* (Weeks), a role verging on sympathetic magic.[34]

Jewish literature codified in postbiblical times, though probably originating during the late biblical period, suggests that ancient Jews believed in other spirits animating nature, such as angels. The apocryphal I Enoch of the third to first centuries B.C.E. identifies specific angels responsible for governing various types of weather and seasons.[35]

The natural aspects of the biblical God Himself are often overlooked, perhaps because they relate so strongly to the cultural ecology of the ancient Near East. The Bible describes God as living in heaven, today considered an abstract or spiritual state entirely separate from creation. This distinction was not an ancient Mediterranean one: the biblical Hebrew term *shamayim* means both sky and heaven. It is occupied by God, the all-important dispenser of rainfall, upon whom all life depends in Israel's seasonally arid Mediterranean and hot desert environments. Israel's spiritual and agricultural dependency on God as the God of rainfall is explicitly described in the convenanted gift of Israel (Deut. 11:10–17) and in a variety of other situations (see Deut. 28:22–24; Jer. 14:1–6). (Compare with the competing Canaanite rainfall diety Baal.) God as the ruler of heaven was thus not simply a spiritual abstraction for ancient Israelites, but a way of portraying their crucial dependence on precipitation:

> He sends forth His word to the earth:
> His command runs swiftly.
> He lays down snow like fleece,
> scatters frost like ashes.

He tosses down hail like crumbs—
Who can endure His icy cold?
He issues a command—it melts them:
He breathes—the waters flow. (Ps. 147:15–18)

In the context of the biblical God as the sky-dwelling ruler of rainfall, we can also understand the Bible's apparent dislike of arid wildlands like the southern Negev and Sinai deserts. If God rewards with rainfall and punishes with drought, a true desert may be interpreted as cursed. Rain in the desert, one of the Bible's most powerful ecological metaphors, symbolizes both a belief in God's blessing and forgiveness for the landscape, and by extension symbolizes Israel's hoped for transition to a state of harmony with God and nature.

God in the Bible manifests Himself in a variety of natural settings. God is also often described as the God of earthquakes and volcanoes (see Ps. 18:29). In the Bible, Moses fears the God who speaks through the burning bush and its precinct of sacred ground. Jonah senses his need to submit to the God who acts through an ocean storm, a great fish, and a vine, and Job to the God who speaks out of the whirlwind. David praises a God manifested in thunder (Ps. 29). Such natural theophanies, especially considered with God's action through climate, suggest a more nature-oriented Bible than is generally recognized.

LIFE AND DEATH BLESSING AND CURSE: REINTERPRETING GENESIS 1:28

The Bible develops a pervasive theology of nature: it sanctifies certain aspects of the environment and its characters are very concerned about environmental well-being. Yet they do not worship nature. To see why they do not, we need to consider not only the biblical concepts of the ultimate governance of nature, but also Judaism's emphasis on life rather than on death or life after death.

At the conclusion of the giving of the law at Mount Sinai. Moses tells the assembled Israelites:

See, I have set before you this day life and good death and evil, in that I command you this day to love the Lord thy God, to walk in His ways, and to keep His commandments and His statutes and His ordinances; then you shall live and multiply. . . . But if your heart turns away, you shall surely perish. . . . I call heaven and earth to witness against you this day, that I have set before you life and death, the blessing and the curse; therefore choose life, that you may live, you and your seed, to love the Lord your God . . . for that is your life and the length of your days. (Deut. 30:5–20)

The Bible's preoccupation with life versus death is at the heart of the ancient Jews' relationship with nature. What does it mean to choose life? Or to put the question in operational terms, what does one do as one chooses life? The survival instinct is strong in most living souls, presumably even in those Israelites who disobeyed God and invoked the curses upon their compatriots' heads. By "choose life," the Bible must mean something more than mere survival instinct. In this passage from Deuteronomy, choosing life is also held to be synonymous with keeping the *mitzvot.*

Apart from biblical exegesis, what does it mean to choose life? At the most individual level, it means having enough to eat and the ways to produce it, protection from extremes of moisture and temperature, freedom from lifeshortening events like war, murder, or disease. At the level of a population, it means reproduction at numbers sufficient to ensure continuity. To the religious mind, choosing life may also mean aligning oneself with that which provides the means of preparing food and shelter and of escaping from life-threatening events. That which empowers nature, the source of food and shelter, may be envisioned as spiritual forces within plants, animals, and physical features, or as the spiritual force which created them. To choose death must mean the opposite.

The Bible speaks of individual decisions to choose life or death in these terms. For example, despite the negative association of carnivores and scavengers with death as the outcome of sin, the Bible does not actually express dislike for these creatures. The lion and the eagle are also admired as powerful symbols of freedom and strength (Prov. 30:18–19, 30–31; Isa. 40:31). Nor does the Bible actually despise wilderness. In another example of unfortunate English translations, Hebrew terms like *Arava, Negev,* and *Midbar,* which refer to specific places or kinds of habitats, have been translated broadly as "wilderness" or "desert" in English Bibles. When the prophets threaten that the Jews' fruitful landscape will turn into the *Arava,* the prophecy must be understood as meaning a specific portion of the Jordan Rift Valley which receives less than five inches of precipitation per year and has insufficient vegetation for year-round pasturage, not as a blanket dislike of wild places. Compare, after all, the powerfully positive images of the wild mountains of Lebanon (see Hos. 14:6–7). The negative association of lions and deserts in the Bible simply reflects the fact that they were inimical to the "life" of an ancient pastoral-agricultural people. Lions are known to attack humans and livestock. The Arava desert of the Jordan Rift Valley and the neighboring Negev are beautiful but arid and could support few people. The *midbar* apparently means a rugged land of seasonal pasturage unfit for cultivation.[36] For a people absolutely and precariously dependent on crops and livestock for survival, choosing a course of behavior believed to incur lion attacks and desertification would indeed be to choose death.

Part of what is necessary for life also includes the troublesome concepts of Genesis 1:28, to multiply and to subjugate the earth. To produce children and to "live to see [one's] children's children" must indeed have seemed a course toward choosing life in ancient Israel. The Hebrew Bible does not promise people an eternal afterlife of the soul: that concept belongs to postbiblical Judaism and to Christianity. Progeny were the Israelite parents' best hope for immortality. Manipulating the earth, such as the gift of the land of Canaan, may also be seen as choosing life: both land and the ability to utilize it were necessary to provide subsistence for a pastoral-agricultural economy. To lose one's homeland or the right to use it for life's necessities would indeed be to choose death.

The Bible's horror of idolatry and nature worship can be interpreted in terms of the Mosaic concepts of life and death, blessing and curse. The Bible's most extensive passages on idolatry mock idols as insensate, powerless manufactures of wood and stone, incapable of sustaining human life (see Isa. 46).

In ancient times, some idols apparently "demanded" child sacrifice of their worshipers.[37] In this sense, to worship an idol would indeed be to choose death. Even natural features, such as trees or animals could not be venerated according to the Torah's view of life and death. A tree itself is mortal and dependent on the Creator for its life. Animals also are fellow travelers on earth, *nefeshot chayyot.* The physical environment is awesome and powerful, but it too is a dependent variable.

Ancient Judaism differs from pantheism not in any inability to perceive spirits in animals and plants, but because it does not deify the spirits which it sees. Animate nature has a *nefesh* or *ruach* as do people. But just as the Hebrew Bible does not deify human beings, it cannot deify nature. Nature in the Bible may be loved for its beauty, its utility, or its unfathomable ways, but the Bible portrays it as incapable in itself of sustaining life. Like humankind, nature depends upon the Creator for its existence. God may speak through thunder, earthquake, and the burning bush, but His presence within them is never taken for the natural phenomena themselves, nor for their anthropomorphized traits. Judaism's belief in nature dependent upon a single Creator–God is therefore a belief in the fundamental unity of nature rather than in its fragmentation under different powers as depicted by some forms of pantheism.

To "choose life," as the concept probably seemed to ancient Jews, therefore required use of nature for human purposes. Indeed all societies, whether biocentric or homocentric in their worldview, must extensively use nature in order to survive. But there is no textual or archaeological evidence that ancient Jews believed that God commanded humanity to deplete the environment to such an extent that its life-supporting capabilities would deteriorate. In contrast, a life-sustaining environment, with sufficient rainfall and fertile soil, is considered among the most desirable of God's gifts. It is a principal reward for the demands of a Jewish life (Deut. 11:14–17).

CONCLUSIONS

In this paper I present an alternative interpretation to the current stewardship and despot models of the Jewish Bible's environmental ethics.

However, I ultimately side with those who disagree with the idea that the Bible is ecologically arrogant, because the Bible in fact condemns the ruthless despoilation of nature, or any choice of "death" rather than life for humanity, the earth, and its creatures. The Bible upholds as its millennial ideal a symbiosis of animals and people in which all living creatures dwell in peace. However, the Bible views observance of its commandments, rather than specific attitudes toward nature or techniques of resource protection, as the prerequisite of a sound environment.

Because the interpretation of biblical environmental ethics described here is so different from modern environmentalist thought, the Bible may be less relevant to modern environmental issues than the stewardship school has claimed. A society that explains destruction of pasturage as the result of God's anger over idolatry or insincerity in Temple sacrifices rather than as the direct outcome of climatic fluctuations or overgrazing may have little to offer modern resource management. Few environmentalists today believe that environmental deterioration results from oppression of widows and orphans. Moreover, the Bible's environmental imagery, blessings, and curses refer specifically to one small piece of Middle Eastern territory with its own unique ecological geography. Biblical environmental messages may be very difficult to translate to other places where the climate and agricultural economy are quite different.

Yet an environmentalism based upon biblical commandments can discourage coveting one's neighbor's property and exploiting the poor as steppingstones to wealth and power: greed has long been blamed as a root of the current environmental crisis. An environmentalism based in biblical poetry can encourage us to see in nature living souls who praise their Creator and shout for joy. A belief that the entire range of human actions has environmental repercussions can add a new dimension to ecological awareness. A biblically based environmentalism can function compatibly alongside a deeply sensitive care for nature and with modern principles of resource management.

NOTES

From *Environmental Ethics* 10 (1988): 309–27.

Thanks are due to Robin Doughty, Temi Goldwasser, Paul A. Kay, and Aharon Kellerman for their comments on earlier drafts of this essay.

1. Numerous English translations and commentaries on the Masoretic (traditional) text of the Jewish Bible were consulted for this study, most frequently the Jewish Publication Society's standard 1917 translation and the 1945–50 multivolume Soncino edition. In some biblical quotations, the author has emended the English of the standard translation in favor of current English.

2. This literature is now too voluminous to review in full. For some recent overviews, see Robin Doughty, "Environmental Theology: Trends and Prospects in

Christian Thought," *Progress in Human Geography* 5 (1981): 234–48; Richard Hiers, "Ecology, Biblical Theology, and Methodology," *Zygon* 19 (1984): 43–60; and Nigel Pollard, "The Israelites and Their Environment," *The Ecologist* 14 (1984): 125–33. More recent papers and book reviews on the topic are regularly published in *Environmental Ethics* and *Environmental Review.*

3. Robert Alter, *The Art of Biblical Narrative* (New York: Basic Books. 1981); *The Literary Guide to the Bible,* ed. Robert Alter and Frank Kermode (Cambridge: Harvard University Press, 1987).

4. John K. Wright, "*Terrae Incognitae*: The Place of Imagination in Geography." *Animals of the Association of American Geographers* 37 (1945): 1–15.

5. Lynn White Jr., "The Historical Roots of Our Ecologic Crisis," *Science* 155 (1967): 1203–1207. For a critique of this debate, see the editor's Preface to *Religion and Environmental Crisis*, ed. Eugene C. Hargrove (Athens, Ga.: University of Georgia Press, 1986), xv–xvii.

6. Robin Attfield, *The Ethics of Environmental Concern* (New York: Columbia University Press, 1983), 4–20.

7. John Passmore, *Man's Responsibility for Nature: Ecological Problems and Western Traditions* (New York: Scribner, 1974).

8. David Ehrenfeld and Philip J. Bentley, "Judaism and the Practice of Stewardship" [reprinted in this volume, 125–35]; Jonathan Helfand, "The Earth is the Lord's: Judaism and Environmental Ethics," in *Religion and Environmental Crisis*, 38–52.

9. Steven S. Schwarzschild, "The Unnatural Jew," [reprinted in this volume, 265–82].

10. Yi-Fu Tuan, "Treatment of the Environment in Ideal and Actuality," *American Scientist* 58 (1970): 244–49; Jeanne Kay, "Preconditions of Natural Resource Conservation," *Agricultural History* 59 (1985): 124–35.

11. Clarence J. Glacken, *Traces on the Rhodian Shore: Nature and Culture in Western Thought from Ancient Times to the End of the Eighteenth Century* (Berkeley: University of California Press. 1967), 166; see Attfield, *Ethics of Environmental Concern*, 25.

12. Susan Power Bratton, "Christian Ecotheology and the Old Testament," *Environmental Ethics* 6 (1984): 195–209.

13. Fortunately, Israeli botanists and biblical scholars have contributed much research in this direction. Yehuda Feliks, *Nature and Man in the Bible: Chapters in Biblical Ecology* (London: The Soncino Press. 1981); Nogah Haruveini, *Nature in Our Biblical Heritage* (Kiryat Ono, Israel: Neot Kedumim, 1980) and *Tree and Shrub in Our Biblical Heritage* (Kiryat Ono, Israel: Neot Kedumim, 1984); Michael Zohary, *Plants of the Bible* (Cambridge: Cambridge University Press, 1982).

14. Wright, "*Terrae Incognitae*"; Luis J. Stadelmann, *The Hebrew Concept of the World: A Philological and Literary Study* (Rome: Pontifical Biblical Institute, 1980); *Analecta Biblica* 39:8.

15. Alter, *The Art of Biblical Narrative.*

16. Wright, "*Terrae Incognitae.*"

17. Passmore, *Man's Responsibility for Nature*, 10–12.

18. Denise Carmody and John Carmody, *Ways to the Center: An Introduction to World Religions* (2d ed.; Belmont, Calif.: Wadsworth Publishing Co., 1984), 32, 35.

19. Bratton, "Christian Ecotheology."

20. Glacken, *Traces on the Rhodian Shore.*

21. Tuan, "Treatment of the Environment."

22. Feliks (*Nature and Man in the Bible*, 100–104) and others have suggested that these species are incorrectly identified in English translations, based on the species' autecology. He suggests that most of the birds listed in Isa. 34 are various species of owls.

23. This ascendancy in a few instances applies to surface waters, as in the examples of Moses and the Israelites' crossing of the Red Sea, and Joshua and the Israelites' crossing of the Jordan River (Josh. 3:15–17).

24. *Genesis Rabbah* 8:12 (trans. H. Freedman and M. Simon [London: Soncino Press, 1961], 62–63). See also Ehrenfeld and Bentley, "Judaism and the Practice of Stewardship" [reprinted in this volume, 125–35].

25. Alter, *The Art of Biblical Narrative*, 33–34.

26. Marvin W. Mikesell, "The Deforestation of Mount Lebanon," *The Geographical Review* 59 (1969): 1–28.

27. *The Epic of Gilgamesh* ed, trans. N. K. Sanders (Harmondsworth, Eng.: Penguin Books. 1972), 70–84.

28. *Genesis Rabbah* 9 (trans. Freedman and Simon, 39–40).

29. Stadelmann, *The Hebrew Conception of the World*, 8.

30. Tuan, "Treatment of the Environment."

31. Andre Lemaire, "Who or What Was Yahweh's Asherah?" *Biblical Archeology Review* 10, no. 6 (1984): 42–51; William G. Dever, "Asherah, Consort of Yaweh? New Evidence from Kuntillet Ajrud," *Bulletin of the American Schools of Oriental Research* 255 (1984): 21–37.

32. Mircea Eliade, *The Sacred and the Profane: The Nature of Religion* (New York: Harper and Row, 1961), 11–12, 20–28.

33. Zohary, *Plants of the Bible*, 108–11.

34. The olive, fig, and grape are three of the seven species offered at the "first fruits" festival of *Shavuot*. Hareuveini (*Nature in Our Biblical Heritage*, 30–42), and Schaffer "The Agricultural and Ecological Symbolism of the Four Species of *Sukkot*" [reprinted in this volume, 112–24] stress the connection of ritually important plant species with Israel's annual weather cycles. Thus the plants' assistance in ritual has a secondary meaning akin to sympathetic magic.

35. I Enoch, ch. 60, 69, 82 (*The Apocryphal Old Testament*, ed. H. F. D. Sparks [Oxford: Clarendon Press, 1984]).

36. Stadelmann, *The Hebrew Conception of the World*, 133–39.

37. Lawrence E. Stager and Samuel R. Wolff, "Child Sacrifice at Carthage: Religious Rite or Population Control?" *Biblical Archaeology Review* 10 (1984): 30–51.

4

The Forestry of the Prophets

Aldo Leopold

Who discovered forestry? The heretofore accepted claims of the European nations have of late been hotly disputed by the Piutes. I now beg leave to present a prior claim for the children of Israel. I can hardly state that they practiced forestry, but I believe it can be shown that they knew a lot about forests. (Also, if any of them set fires, they knew better than to admit it.) The following notes, gleaned from a purely amateur study of the Books of the Prophets of the Old Testament,[1] may be of interest to other foresters, and may possibly suggest profitable fields of research for competent Hebraists and physiographers.

The most interesting side of forestry was then, as it is now, the human side. There is wide difference in the woodcraft of the individual prophets—the familiarity with which they speak of forests, and especially the frequency with which they use similes based on forest phenomena. It appears that in Judaea, as in Montana, there were woodsmen and dudes.

Isaiah was the Roosevelt of the Holy Land. He knew a whole lot about everything, including forests, and told what he knew in no uncertain terms. He constantly uses the forest to illustrate his teachings, and in doing so calls the trees by their first names. Contrast with him the sophisticated Solomon, who spoke much wisdom, but whose lore was city lore—the nearest he comes to the forest is the fig tree and the cedar of Lebanon, and I think he saw more of the cedars in the ceiling of his palace than he did in the hills. Joel knew more about forests than even Isaiah—he is the preacher of conservation of watersheds, and in a sense the real inventor of "prevent forest fires." David speaks constantly and familiarly about forests and his forest similes are especially accurate and beautiful. Ezekiel was not only a woodsman and an artist, but he knew a good deal about the lumber business, domestic and foreign. Jeremiah had a smattering of woods lore, and so did

Hosea, but neither shows much leaning toward the subject. Daniel shows no interest in forests. Neither does Jesus the son of Sirach, who was a keen businessman, a philosopher, and a master of epigram, but his tastes did not run to the hills. Strange to say, the writer of the Book of Job, the John Muir of Judah, author of the immortal eulogy of the horse and one of the most magnificent essays on the wonders of nature so far produced by the human race, is strangely silent on forests. Probably forests were his background, not his picture, and he took for granted that his audience had a knowledge of them.

FOREST FIRES IN THE HOLY LAND

Every forester who reads the Prophets carefully will, I think, be surprised to see how much they knew about fires. The forest fire appealed strongly to their imagination and is used as the basis for many a simile of striking literary beauty. They understood not only the immediate destructive effects of fires, but possibly also the more far reaching effects on watersheds. Strangely enough, nothing is said about causes of fires or whether any efforts were ever made toward fire suppression.

The book of Joel opens with an allegory in which the judgment of God takes the form of a fire.[2] This is perhaps the most convincing description of fire in the whole Bible. "Alas for the day!" says Joel. "The herds of cattle are perplexed, because they have no pasture; Yea, the flocks of sheep are made desolate. O Lord, to thee do I cry, for a fire hath devoured the pastures of the wilderness, and a flame hath burned all the trees of the field. Yea, the beasts of the field pant unto thee, for the water brooks are dried up. Blow ye the trumpet in Zion, and sound an alarm in my holy mountain; let all the inhabitants in the land tremble! For a fire devoureth before them; and behind them a flame burneth; the land is as a garden of Eden before them, and behind them a desolate wilderness!"

Joel's story of the flames is to my mind one of the most graphic descriptions of fire ever written. It is "a day of clouds and thick darkness," and the fire is "like the dawn spread upon the mountains." The flames are "as a great people, set in battle array," and "the appearance of them is as horses, and as horsemen, so do they run. Like the noise of chariots on the tops of the mountains do they leap, . . . they run like mighty men; they climb the wall like men of war; and they march every one on his way. They break not their ranks: neither doth one thrust another; they march every one in his path. . . . They leap upon the city; they run upon the wall; they climb up into the houses; they enter in at the windows like a thief. The earth quaketh before them; the heavens tremble; the sun and the moon are darkened, and the stars withdraw their shining."

Joel is evidently describing a top fire or brush fire of considerable intensity. Is there at the present time any forest cover in Palestine of sufficient density to support such a fire? I do not know, but I doubt it. If not, it is interesting to speculate whether the reduced forest cover is a cause or an effect of the apparent change in climate.[3] Isaiah (64:1) adds some intensely interesting evidence as to the density of forest cover in Biblical times when he says: "when fire kindleth the brushwood, . . . the fire causeth the waters to boil." Have there been any fires in this country, even in the Northwest or the Lake States, which caused the waters to boil? One writer, who had to take refuge in a creek during one of the big fires in the Northwest in 1918, states that falling brands caused the temperature of the creek to rise "several degrees," which sounds very tame in comparison with Isaiah's statement. In fact, Isaiah's statement seems almost incredible. Was he telling fish stories? Or is there some special explanation, such as a resinous brushwood producing great heat, or drainage from a sudden rain on a hot fire, or a water hole containing bitumen or oil from a mineral seep? I will leave this question for someone personally familiar with the country.

That top fires actually occurred in the Holy Land is abundantly proven by many writers in addition to Joel. Isaiah says (10:19) that a fire "shall consume the glory of his forest, and of his fruitful field . . . and the remnant of the trees of his forest shall be few, that a child may write them." "It kindleth in the thickets of the forest, and they roll upward in thick clouds of smoke." The individual tree at the moment of combustion he likens most effectively to a "standard-bearer that fainteth." Those who have actually seen the "puff" of the dying tree, as the fire rushes up through the foliage, will not miss the force of this simile. Ezekiel says (20:46): "A fire . . . shall devour every green tree . . . and every dry tree: the flaming flame shall not be quenched."

Surprisingly little is said about how fires started. Man-caused fires were no doubt frequent, as were to be expected in a pastoral community. Tobacco fires were of course still unknown. (Samuel Butler says the Lord postponed the discovery of tobacco, being afraid that St. Paul would forbid smoking. This, says Butler, was a little hard on Paul.) Lightning was no doubt the principal natural cause of fire. Very heavy lightning seems to have occurred in the mountains. David, in the "Song of the Thunderstorm" (Psalm 29), says: "The God of glory thundereth, . . . the voice of the Lord breaketh the cedars; Yea, the Lord breaketh in pieces the cedars of Lebanon." His voice "cleaveth the flames of fire . . . and strippeth the forest bare." It is not entirely clear whether this refers to lightning only, or possibly also to subsequent fire.

How much did the prophets really know about the effects of fires? Joel has already been quoted as to the effects on streamflow, but there is a possibility that he meant that his "water-brooks" dried up, not as the ultimate effect of fires, but as the immediate effect of a drouth prevailing at the time of the particular fire which he describes. David (Psalm 107) plainly states that changes in climate occur, but no forest influences or other causes are mentioned. I think it is quite possible that the effect of forests on streamflow was known empirically to a few advanced thinkers like Joel, but it is quite certain that their knowledge went no further or deeper. The habit of thinking of natural phenomena as acts of God instead of as cause and effect prevails to this day with a majority of people, and no doubt prevailed at that time in the minds of all. But even if the prophets were ignorant of science, they were wise in the ways of men. "Seemeth it a small thing unto you to have fed upon the good pasture, but ye must tread down with your feet the residue of your pasture? And to have drunk of the clear waters, but ye must foul the residue with your feet?" (Ezekiel 24:18). Here is the doctrine of conservation, from its subjective side, as aptly put as by any forester of this generation.

FOREST UTILIZATION IN THE HOLY LAND

The old Hebrew used both saws and axes in cutting timber. Isaiah (10:15) says: "Shall the axe boast itself against him that heweth therewith? Shall the saw magnify itself against him that shaketh it?" "Shaking" the saw is a new bit of woods vernacular that leads one to wonder what the instrument looked like. Here is more woods vernacular: "he shall cut down the thickets of the forest with iron, and Lebanon shall fall by a mighty one." While I am not competent to go behind the translation, the word "iron" seems to be used here in much the same way as our modern engineers used the word "steel," that is, to indicate certain manufactured tools or articles made of steel.

Very close utilization of felled timber seems to have been practiced. Solomon (Wisdom 13:11) tells how a woodcutter sawed down a tree, stripped off the bark, carved the good wood into useful vessels, cooked his dinner with the chips, and used the crooked and knotty remainder to fashion a graven image. Expertness in whittling then, as now, seems to have been a trait of the idle, for Solomon says the woodcutter shaped the image "by the diligence of his idleness, and . . . by the skill of his indolence." Isaiah (44:14) also tells how a man plants a fir tree, and after the rain has nourished it, he cuts it down and uses a part to warm himself, a part to bake bread, a part to make utensils, and a part to fashion a graven image. Graven images, if one is to believe the prophets, must have been an important product of the wood-using industries of that day.

Here is an unsolved mystery in woods practice: "The carpenter . . . heweth him down cedars, and taketh the holm tree and the oak, and *strengtheneth for himself* one among the trees of the forest" (Isaiah 44:14). What is meant by "strengtheneth for himself?" Some process of seasoning? Some custom of individual branding such as is practiced on bee trees? Some process of lamination in woodworking to give strength and lightness?

Ezekiel (27:4) records some interesting data on the sources and uses of timber in his satire on the glories of Tyre. "They have made all thy planks of fir trees from Senir: they have taken cedars from Lebanon to make a mast for thee. Of the oaks of Bashan have they made thine oars; they have made thy benches of ivory inlaid in boxwood, from the isles of Kittim." Isaiah (2:18) also mentions "the oaks of Bashan." Oak would seem to be a bit heavy for the long oars used in those days.

Who made the first chest? Ezekiel (27:24) says that "chests of rich apparel, bound with cords and made of cedar" were an article of commerce in the maritime trade of Tyre. The use of cedar chests for fine clothing seems to be nearly as old as the hills. Solomon's palanquin was also made of cedar. Here is his own description of it, as taken from the Song of Songs (3:9): "King Solomon made himself a palanquin of the wood of Lebanon. He made the pillars thereof of silver, the bottom thereof of gold, the seat of it of purple, the midst thereof being inlaid with love from the daughters of Jerusalem." (I doubt whether Solomon "made himself" this palanquin. He does not give the impression of a man handy with tools. No doubt he had it made by the most cunning artificers of his kingdom.)

Cedar construction in Biblical days seems to have been a kind of mark of social distinction, as mahogany is today. (Witness also the marble-topped walnut of our Victorian forbears!) Solomon's bride boasts (Song of Songs 1:16): "Our couch is green. The beams of our house are cedars, and our rafters are firs." Jeremiah (22:14) accuses Jehoiakim of building with ill-gotten gains "a wide house . . . with windows . . . ceiled with cedar, and painted with vermillion." "Shalt thou reign," exclaims Jeremiah, "because thou strivest to *excel in cedar?*"

The cedar seems to have grown to large size. Ezekiel, in a parable (31), says of one tree: "The cedars in the garden of God could not hide him; the fir trees were not like his boughs, and the plane trees were not as his branches." This cedar was Pharaoh, and the Lord "made the nations to shake at the sound of his fall."

The close utilization which seems to have been practiced at least in some localities, the apparently well developed timber trade of the coast cities, and the great number of references to the use and commerce in cedar, would lead to the surmise that the pinch of local timber famine might have been felt in the cedar woods. That this was actually the case is indicated by Isaiah (14:7). After prophesying the fall of Babylon, he tells how all things will rejoice over her demise. "Yea, the fir trees rejoice at thee, and the cedars of Lebanon: 'Since thou art laid down, no feller is come up against us.'" This impersonization of trees is characteristic of the Biblical writers; David (Psalm 96) says, "Then shall all the trees of the wood sing for joy."

The relative durability of woods was of course fairly well known. Isaiah (9:10) says: "The bricks are fallen, but we will build with hewn stone; the sycamores are cut down, but we will change them into cedars." Ecclesiasticus (12:13) likens the permanency and strength of wisdom to "a cedar in Libanus, and . . . a cypress tree on the mountains of Hermon."

Fuel wood was evidently obtained not only from cull material, as already indicated, but by cutting green timber. Ezekiel (39:9) predicts that after the rout of the invading army of Gog, "they that dwell in the cities of Israel shall go forth, and make fires of the weapons and burn them, . . . and they shall make fires of them seven years; so that they shall take no wood out of the field, neither cut down any out of the forests." It would seem that Biblical fuel bills were either pretty light, or else Gog left behind an extraordinary number of weapons.

HEBREW SILVICULTURE

There are many passages in the books of the Prophets showing that some of the rudimentary principles of silviculture were understood, and that artificial planting was practiced to some extent. Solomon (in Ecclesiastes 2:4) says that he planted great vineyards, orchards, gardens, and parks, and also "made me pools of water, to water therefrom the forest where trees were reared." Isaiah (44:14) speaks of a carpenter who planted a fir tree, and later used it for fuel and lumber. The context gives the impression that such instances of planting for wood production were common, but probably on a very small scale. Isaiah (41:9) seems to have had some knowledge of forest types and the ecological relations of species. He quotes Jehovah in this manner: "I will plant in the wilderness the cedar, the acacia tree, and the myrtle, and the oil tree; I will set in the desert the fir tree, the pine, and the box tree together." He also makes the following interesting statement (55:13), which possibly refers to the succession of forest types: "Instead of the thorn shall come up the fir tree, and instead of the brier shall come up the myrtle tree."

Some of the peculiarities of various species in their manner of reproduction are mentioned. Isaiah (44:4) says: "They shall spring up among the grass as willows by the watercourses." He also speaks of the oak and the terebinth reproducing by coppice (6:12). Job (14:7) also mentions coppice, but does not give the species. Ezekiel (17), in his parable of the Eagles and the Cedar, tells about an eagle that cropped off the leader of a big cedar and planted it high on another mountain, and it brought forth boughs, and bore fruit, and was a goodly tree. I do not know the cedar of Lebanon but it sounds highly improbable that any conifer should grow from cuttings. I think this is a case of "poetic license."

Isaiah (65:22) realized the longevity of some species in the following simile: "They shall not build, and another inhabit; they shall not plant, and another eat; for as the day of a tree shall be the day of my people, and my chosen shall long enjoy the work of their hands." Isaiah disappoints us here in not telling the species. Unlike Solomon and Daniel and Ecclesiasticus, he is not given to calling a tree just "a tree."

MISCELLANEOUS

Barnes has written a very interesting article on grazing in the Holy Land, and there is much additional material on this subject which would be of interest to foresters.[4] One matter which some entomologist should look up occurs in Isaiah (7:18). Isaiah says: "And it shall come to pass in that day, that the Lord shall hiss for the fly that is in the uttermost part of the rivers of Egypt, and for the bee that is in the land of Assyria. And they shall come, and shall rest all of them in the desolate valleys, and in the holes of the rocks, and upon all thorns, and upon all pastures." What fly is referred to? The tsetse fly, or the rinderpest?

There is also considerable material on game and fish in the Old Testament, and additional material on forests in the historical books, both of which I hope to cover in future articles.

In closing, it may not be improper to add a word on the intensely interesting reading on a multitude of subjects to be found in the Old Testament. As Stevenson said about one of Hazlitt's essays, "It is so good that there should be a tax levied on all who have not read it."

NOTES

From *The Forester* 18 (1920): 412–19, published by the Society of American Foresters, 5400 Grosvenor Lane, Bethesda, MD 20814-2198. Not for further reproduction.

1. Quotations are from *Moulton's Reader's Bible*, which is based on the Revised English Version.

2. Parts of Joel 1–2 have been used in printed matter issued by the Southwestern District as fire prevention propaganda.

3. Prof. Ellsworth Huntington's book, *The Pulse of Asia*, contains some very readable and convincing material on climatic cycles in Asia Minor.

4. *National Wool Grower*, February 1915.

5

The Agricultural and Ecological Symbolism of the Four Species of *Sukkot*

Arthur Schaffer

Jewish rituals in the Torah are usually presented together with their symbolic meaning. For example, unleavened bread is eaten on *Pesach*, "for thou camest forth out of the land of Egypt in haste" (Deut. 16:3). Similarly, Jews sit in booths during *Sukkot* "so that your generations may know that I made the children of Israel dwell in booths when I brought them out of the land of Egypt" (Lev. 23:42–43). It is peculiarly striking that there is no symbolic explanation accompanying the prescription for the four species of *Sukkot*. The Torah simply and succinctly states:

> And you shall take for yourselves on the first day the fruit of the *hadar* tree, branches of palm trees, and the boughs of thick leaved trees and willows of the brook and you shall rejoice before the Lord your God seven days. (Lev. 23:40)

The Torah offers not a shred of meaning, religious, historical, or agricultural, about a rite so faithfully and carefully performed to this day.

This silence inspired a great deal of creative exegesis to fill the gap and enhance the ritual with symbolism. However, the majority of post-mishnaic Jews lacked an intimate familiarity with the native flora and plant ecology of Israel. Therefore, the most common and well-accepted symbolisms make minimal use of the four species' botanical characteristics. When these qualities are taken into account, they are interpreted allegorically.

Most of the traditional symbolisms of the four species are recounted in the Amoraic midrashic literature. Perhaps the best known is the view that the plants represent, by their shapes, the key parts of the human body.

> R. Mani opened his discourse with the text, "All my bones shall say: Lord, who is like unto Thee" (Ps. 35:10). This verse was said in allusion to nought else than the

lulav. The rib of the *lulav* resembles the spine of a man; the myrtle resembles the eye; the willow resembles the mouth; and the *etrog* resembles the heart. David said: There are none among all the limbs greater than these, for they outweigh in importance the whole body. This explains, "All my bones shall say." [1]

Another popular interpretation compares the four species to different categories of Jews, symbolizing the necessity for unity amidst diversity.

Another exposition: *The Fruit of the Hadar Tree* symbolizes Israel; just as the *etrog* has taste as well as fragrance, so Israel have among them men who possess learning and good deeds. *Branches of Palm Trees,* too, applies to Israel; as the palm tree has taste but not fragrance, so Israel have among them such as possess learning but not good deeds. *And Boughs of Thick Trees* likewise applies to Israel; just as the myrtle has fragrance but no taste, so Israel have among them such as possess good deeds but not learning. *And Willows of the Brook* also applies to Israel; just as the willow has no taste and no fragrance, so Israel have among them people who possess neither learning nor good deeds. What then does the Holy One, blessed be He, do to them? To destroy them is impossible. But, says the Holy One, blessed be He, let them all be tied together in one band and they will atone one for another. If you have done so (says God), then at that instant I am exalted. Hence it is written, "It is He that buildeth His upper chambers in the heaven" (Amos 9:6). When is He exalted? What time they are made into one band; as it says, "When He hath founded His band upon the earth." Accordingly Moses exhorts Israel: *And Ye Shall Take you on the First Day the Fruit.*[2]

According to other interpretations the species personify the four matriarchs,[3] the three patriarchs and Joseph,[4] and even different aspects of God.[5]

HISTORICAL SYMBOLISM

Rituals, particularly festival rituals, often commemorate a significant aspect of Jewish history. Again, the unleavened bread of *Pesach* and the *Sukkot* booths are fine examples. The four species also have historical significance according to Maimonides: "Passover teaches us to remember the miracles which God wrought in Egypt and to perpetuate their memory; the Feast of Tabernacles reminds us of the miracles wrought in the wilderness."[6] Maimonides continues to elaborate on the four species, but not without first remarking on the value of midrashic interpretations.

As regards the four species . . . , our Sages gave a reason for their use by way of aggadic interpretation, the method of which is well known to those who are acquainted with the style of the sages. They use the text of the Bible only as a kind of poetical language (for their own ideas), and do not intend thereby to give an interpretation of the text.

After some examples of aggadic interpretation, Maimonides continues,

> I believe that the four species are a symbolical expression of our rejoicing that the Israelites changed the wilderness, "no place of seed, or of figs, or of vines, or of pomegranates, or of water to drink" (Num. 20:5), for a country full of fruit trees and rivers. In order to remember this we take the fruit which is the most pleasant of the fruit of the land, branches which smell best, most beautiful leaves, and also the best kind of herbs, that is, the willows of the brook.

Sukkot, states Maimonides, commemorates the wanderings in the wilderness *and* the subsequent entry into the land of Israel. The booth symbolizes the former; the four species, the latter. Disappointingly, though, Maimonides does not attribute much significance to these particular four. They are the most pleasant fruit, beautiful leaves, etc., but their selection was, to some degree, merely practical and utilitarian. He continues:

> These four kinds have also these three purposes: First, they were plentiful in those days in Palestine so that everyone could easily get them. Secondly, they have a good appearance, they are green: some of them, namely, the citron and the myrtle, are also excellent as regards their smell, the branches of the palm tree and the willow having neither good nor bad smell. Thirdly, they keep fresh and green for seven days, which is not the case with peaches, pomegranates, asparagus, nuts and the like.

Maimonides, then, believes that the four species were chosen to symbolize the entry into Israel because they were native flora of Israel that excelled in their respective qualities, were easily available, looked or smelled good or both, and could remain fresh throughout the festival. Given that reasoning, an asparagus shoot may have replaced the palm and a sweet smelling peach, the citron, all things being equal.

Nogah Hareuveni, the founder of Israel's botanical garden Neot Kedumim, offers a fascinating commentary on Maimonides' interpretation.[7] He considers the four species as symbols borrowed from the world of nature which reenact the desert wanderings and entry into the Promised Land. The date palm represents life in the desert, its natural habitat. The willows of the brook portray the plants that grew along the Jordan River, the entry point into Israel. Upon entering, the Israelites encountered the forest thickets covering the hill country, symbolized by the myrtle branches whose natural habitat is the hills. After clearing the thickets, the hill country was cultivated and planted with the choicest fruit trees, represented by the citron. The ritual of the four species, according to Hareuveni, is to teach:

> You led us through the wilderness in the days of the exodus from Egypt and sheltered us in booths in the shade of the date palms. You set us under the willows of the Jordan, and finally You led us across the Jordan River dryshod and brought us to "the land flowing with milk and honey" to clear the "leafy trees" in its thick forestland in order to turn that land into fruit-bearing groves.

AGRICULTURAL SYMBOLISM

All the major holidays have agricultural as well as religious and historical significance. *Pesah* celebrates the barley harvest, *Shavuot* the wheat harvest, and *Sukkot* the harvest of summer crops—fruits and vegetables. The holiday rituals strongly reflect these agricultural realities. During *Pesach* the *omer* offering from the newly harvested barley was presented in the Temple and on *Shavuot* two loaves of bread baked from the freshly harvested wheat were offered. The four species of *Sukkot* have been similarly viewed as four representative species of plant material marking the summer harvest.

If this were true, however, the four species would be made up of cultivated, edible plants that were harvested at the "Festival of the Harvest." The ritual would have been far more meaningful if the commandment were to bring a cluster of dates, a bunch of grapes, two fig leaves, and three olive branches. Instead, neither the willow nor the myrtle was used for food (although the myrtle may have served medicinal purposes), the citron was certainly not a major cultivated fruit, and the part of the date palm required for the ritual was neither harvested nor edible. In fact, harvested, cultivated fruits are strikingly absent from the *Sukkot* rituals. Other than the picturesque custom of hanging fruits in the *sukkah* and the possibility that the *sukkah* symbolized the booths built at the time of ingathering, the harvest actually plays a surprisingly small role in the celebration of a festival meant to commemorate the "ingathering of the fruits."

There is an additional significance to the time of *Sukkot* besides the summer harvest. *Sukkot* marks the major climatic changes of the year which delimits the end of one agricultural cycle and the anticipated beginning of the next.

The Israeli climate is characterized by only two seasons, a wet cool "winter" and a dry, practically rainless, warm "summer." From approximately May until September, very little rain falls in most portions of the country. The first rains (*yoreh*) generally arrive sometime in September or October and continue through April, when the late rains (*malkosh*) end the wet winter season. In Jerusalem, for example, twenty inches of rain may fall between October and May, but there may only be one-half of an inch throughout the rest of the year.[8] Similar proportions are the rule throughout most of the country.

Biblical agriculture was determined by this disproportionate climatic pattern. A tenth century B.C.E. agricultural calendar found at Gezer reflects the climate and describes the cycle of sowing and reaping as follows:

> His two months of (olive) harvest;
> His two months are planting (grain);
> His two months are late planting;
> His month of hoeing up of flax;
> His month is harvest of barley;
> His month is harvest and feasting;
> His two months are vine tending;
> His month is summer fruit.[9]

The calendar begins with the seventh month according to the Hebrew year. Throughout this month and the next, the final harvest of olives and their processing took place. During this period, the *yoreh* rains were eagerly awaited to moisten the parched soil after the long dry summer months. Until these first rains fell, the fields could not be plowed and the new cycle of plantings had to be postponed. Too long a delay of the *yoreh* meant agricultural disaster and imminent famine, and precipitated national fasting and repentance.[10]

The *Yoreh* was followed by planting of grains—wheat, spelt, and barley— which was in turn followed by later plantings of vegetables. The *malkosh* came toward the conclusion of the planting season, while the dry remainder of the year was occupied by harvests, first of barley, then wheat, and finally fruits, concluding with olives.

The ancient agrarians appreciated the significance of God's key blessing, repeated at least twice daily in the Hebrew prayers.

> And it shall come to pass, if you hearken diligently to my commandments which I command you this day, to love the Lord your God, and to serve him with all your heart and with all your soul, that I will give you the rain of your land in its due season, the early rain (*yoreh*) and the late rain (*malkosh*) that thou mayest gather in thy corn and thy wine and thy oil. (Deut. 11:13–14)

They were similarly mindful of the frightening outcome of disobedience.

> Take heed to yourselves, that your hearts be not deceived, and you turn aside and serve other gods and worship them; and then the Lord's anger be inflamed against you, and He shut up the heaven that there be no rain and that the land yield not its fruit. (Deut. 11:16–17)

In accordance with this agricultural timetable, God's power to deliver rain is invoked in the prayers beginning on *Shemini Atseret*, at the conclusion of *Sukkot*. Actually, the prayer might just as well begin at the start of *Sukkot* but is delayed until all have left their booths and are back in their homes with their waterproof roofs.[11] Rain while sitting in a *sukkah* would only be a partial blessing. The invocation ceases at the beginning of *Pesach*, since rain that late would fall on the ripening, drying grain in the field, causing ruin and waste.[12]

The onset of the rainy season takes on even more significance, since biblical Israel depended almost entirely on natural precipitation; irrigation was limited to a small portion of the country. Egypt, in contrast, relied mainly on irrigation. The advantages of natural precipitation are pointed out to the generation of Israelites about to enter into the Promised Land.

> For the land which you are about to invade and occupy is not like the land of Egypt from which you have come. There the grain you sowed had to be watered by your own labors (irrigation), like a vegetable garden; but the land you are about to cross into and occupy, a land of hills and valleys, soaks up its water from the rains of heaven. (Deut. 11:10–11)

The near total dependence of Israel on rain allows only limited mastery and dominion over agriculture. The inhabitants of the land are governed not by their "own labors" but by Divine providence—"the rain of heaven." In the holy land the watchful eye of God, His nurturing care and concern, permits agricultural success; man's labors alone are not sufficient. Accordingly, the contrast to Egypt does not merely point out the physical advantages of nonirrigated agriculture. The fact that Israel is a land that "drinks water from the rain of heaven" underlines the special relationship between God and Israel, the land and people, and bears testimony that Israel is "a land which the Lord thy God cares for: the eyes of the Lord thy God are upon it from the beginning of the year until the end of the year" (Deut. 11:12).[13]

RAIN FESTIVAL

Sukkot, then, in addition to celebrating the harvest, marks the climatic transition between summer and winter, drought and rain. It was a time for the biblical Israelites to acknowledge and praise God for the previous year's rain and subsequent abundant harvest of the agricultural year, that was now coming to a close. At the same time, it was a period that evoked their deepest hopes, concerns, and fears regarding the expected and awaited rains so necessary for a successful forthcoming agricultural cycle.

In fact, almost all the rituals of *Sukkot*, including those observed only in the Temple, revolve around rain and water; the harvest is conspicuously ignored. In many respects, water is the dominant theme of the "Festival of the Harvest."

The Mishnah states that "on *Sukkot* judgment is passed in respect to rain."[14] In light of this, it is only fitting that the festival literally overflows with water rituals.

Throughout the year, certain sacrifices in the Temple were accompanied by wine libations. During *Sukkot*, however, water libations (*nissukh hamayim*) were added to the daily morning offering,[15] and both wine and water were ritually poured along the sides of the altar.

The Mishnah describes the occasion as follows:

How was the water libation [performed]? A golden flagon holding three *logs* was filled from the Siloam. When they arrived at the water gate, they sounded a *teki'ah* (long blast), a *teru'ah* (tremulous note) and again a *teki'ah* (long blast). [The priest then] went up the ascent [of the altar] and turned to his left where there were two silver bowls. R. Judah said, they were of plaster [but they looked silver], because their surfaces were darkened from the wine. They had each a hole like a slender snout, one [hole] being wide and the other narrow so that both emptied themselves together. The one on the west was for water and the one on the east for wine.[16]

The significance of the rite is pointed out by Rabbi Akiba.

> Why did the Torah enjoin on us to pour out water on Tabernacles? The Holy One, blessed be He, said Pour out water before Me on Tabernacles so that your rains this year may be blessed.[17]

Related to the water libations was the *simchat bet ha-shoevah*, the celebration of the water drawing, considered the most joyous event of the year. "Whoever has not seen the rejoicing at the place of the water drawing has never seen rejoicing in his life,"[18] is an indicative mishnaic statement. The purpose of the festivity, which took place each entire evening preceding the water libation, was to joyously celebrate the water drawing and libation of the following morning in fulfillment of "And ye shall draw water with joy" (Isaiah 12:3). The celebration began in the evening and continued until the morning, when the water was drawn from the Siloam Pool with much pomp and excitement and returned to the Temple, where it was poured at the morning sacrifice.

In addition to the water libations and their accompanying festivities, there was a ritual of the willows, independent of the willows of the four species.

> How was the precept of the willow branch [carried out]? There was a place below Jerusalem called Moza. They went down there and gathered thence young willow-branches, and then came and fixed them at the sides of the altar so that their tops bent over the altar. They then sounded a *teki'ah:* (long blast), a *teru'ah* (tremulous blast), and again a *teki'ah*. Every day they went round the altar once, saying "we beseech thee, O Lord, save now, we beseech thee. O Lord, make us now to prosper." R. Judah said, [they were saying] "save now," but on that day[19] they went round the altar seven times. When they departed, what did they say? Thine, O altar is the beauty! Thine, O altar, is the beauty! R. Eliezer said, [they were saying] "To the Lord and to thee, O altar, to the Lord and to thee, O altar.[20]

Willow branches, eleven cubits long (*Sukkah* 45a) were used each of the festival days, while on the seventh day *Hoshanah Rabba,* a special detailed ritual was performed.

Willows are the plant world's symbol of water *par excellence*, the "willows of the brook." Their natural habitat is banks of rivers and brooks; they thrive in moist, even flooded, soils. Physiologically they are particularly adapted to life in wet, water abundant areas,[21] and this characteristic naturally made them the floral centerpiece on the Temple altar during *Sukkot.*

The reading from the Prophets for the first day of *Sukkot* also bears evidence that water is a major theme of the festival. "And on that day living water (*mayim chayyim*) shall go out from Jerusalem" (Zech. 14:8). And further on,

> And it shall come to pass that everyone that is left of the nations who came against Jerusalem shall go up from year to year to worship the King, Lord of Hosts, and to

keep the Feast of Booths. And whoever does not come up of all the families of the earth to Jerusalem to worship the King, Lord of Hosts, *upon them shall be no rain.* (Zech. 8: 16–17)

Even the custom of staying awake the night of *Hoshanah Rabba* studying Torah is a reflection of the centrality of water to the holiday. Torah study is a human expression of thanks and gratitude to the Almighty. Therefore, twice during the year appreciation is expressed in this manner: on *Shavuot* for the spiritual gift, the Torah itself, and on *Hoshanah Rabbah* for the primary material gift, water.

The rituals of *Sukkot* all point to water as a major, if not the major, theme of the festival. Water libations, the willows, the start of prayers for rain, all serve to underline the tremendous importance and necessity of rain for the region and help to direct the prayers for the "water of life" to "the giver of life."

THE FOUR SPECIES

Both the Jerusalem and Babylonian Talmuds refer to the four species as symbols of water.

> Said R. Eliezer: Seeing that these four species are intended only to make intercession for water, therefore as these cannot [grow] without water so the world [too] cannot exist without water.[22]

The Jerusalem Talmud begins Tractate *Ta'anit* with the following parallel statement: "The reason of R. Eliezer is that since these four species grow on water therefore they come as intercessors for water."[23]

The Talmuds see, then, the four species as advocates for water at the period that "the world is judged regarding water."[24] But what is unique about the citron, date palm, willow, and myrtle? After all, every plant "grows on water" and "cannot grow without water!"

In truth, the four species uniquely and specifically represent water, in a manner that bears uncontestable evidence to our ancestors' intimate familiarity with the native flora and ecology of Israel.

The willow (*Salix* species), as already mentioned, is one of the plant world's finest symbols of water. Described by the Torah as "willows of the brook," the Talmud even questions whether willows that have not grown along water are permissible for use in the ritual.[25] Post, in his classic, *Flora of Syria, Palestine and Sinai*, describes the *Salix purpurea*, the purple osier willow, as growing "by water." He describes the habitats of the other species of the *Salix* genus as "banks of streams," "near water or in it," and "wet places."[26] Michael Zohary, in the definitive work *Flora Palaestina*, similarly describes the willows of Israel as growing "by water."[27]

The willows, in general, are water-loving plants that can grow in habitats too wet for other species to survive. In the ritual of the four species, they present themselves as advocates for an abundance of rain.

The *lulav* is the as yet unopened date palm frond, or leaf. The palm (*Phoenix dactylifera*) is a sign not merely of the desert but specifically of the oasis in the desert, the island of water in a sea of sand. Where the date is found, water cannot be far away. One of the first stops of the Israelites in the wilderness, after the Exodus, was "Elim, and in Elim were twelve fountains of water and seventy palm trees" (Num. 33:9).

Jericho was known as the "city of palms" (Deut. 34:3)—fitting since it, too, is an oasis. Its annual rainfall characterizes it as desert; but because of its springs, it became one of the earliest cities in history capable of supporting civilization. Josephus describes at length the fountains of Jericho and mentions the characteristic palm trees nourished by them.[28]

> Notwithstanding which, there is a fountain by Jericho, that runs plentifully, and is very fit for watering the ground; it arises near the old city, which Joshua the son of Nun, the general of the Hebrews, took the first of all the cities of Canaan, by right of war. . . . Accordingly, the power of it is so great in watering the ground that, if it but once touch a country, it affords a sweeter nourishment than other waters do, when they lie so long upon them till they are satiated with them. For which reason, the advantage gained from other waters when they flow in great plenty is but small, while that of this water is great when it even flows in little quantities. Accordingly, it waters a larger space of ground than any other waters do, and passes along a plain of seventy furlongs long and twenty broad, wherein it affords nourishment to those most excellent gardens that are thick set with trees.

Josephus then continues,

> There are in it many sorts of palm trees that are watered by it, different from each other in taste and name; the better sort of them, when they are pressed, yield an excellent source of honey, not much inferior in sweetness to other honey.

An old Arab folk saying attests to the date palm's natural habitat. "Its head should be in the sun and its feet in water."[29] The *lulav*, then, functions as the advocate for water even in the driest regions of Israel, the desert wilderness.

The natural habitat of the myrtle (*Myrtus communis*) is the hilly and mountainous areas of Israel in general, but more specifically "the riverine thickets," according to Michael Zohary,[30] and the "slopes of stream banks" on "Israel's mountains and hills," as described by Nogah Hareuveini.[31]

The Bible takes for granted the myrtle's hydrophilic characteristic and utilizes the myrtle as a metaphor for an abundance of water.

Isaiah prophesies (41:17–20):

> The poor and the needy seek water and there is none and their tongue is parched for thirst; I, the Lord will answer them, I the God of Yisrael will not forsake them.

I will open rivers art high places, and fountains in the midst of valleys; I will make the wilderness a pool of water, and the dry land springs of water. I will plant in the wilderness the cedar, the shitta tree, and the myrtle, and the oil tree; I will set in the Arava cypress, maple and box tree together: that they may see and know and consider and understand together that the hand of the Lord has done this, and the holy One of Yisrael has created it.

In response to the cries for water, God will benevolently deliver such an abundance of water that not only will the desert support plant life, but even water-loving plants like the myrtle will flourish.[32]

Similarly, the prophecy that "in place of the thistle will arise the myrtle" (Isaiah 55:13) does not simply mean that attractive plants will replace obnoxious weeds, but rather that God will turn the dry waste from an arid habitat to one with so much water that the myrtle will thrive and naturally replace the thistle.

The myrtle is also mentioned in a complex vision of Zechariah, who saw "a man riding upon a red horse, and he stood among the myrtles that were in the *metzulah*" (1:8). There are numerous definitions and interpretations of *metzulah*,[33] but one cannot ignore its use in the Song of Moses, where the Egyptians are described as drowning in the *metzulot*, the depths of the sea.[34]

Other than the biblical descriptions of the *Sukkot* festival, the sources brought here are the only ones in the Hebrew Bible that mention myrtle.[35] Clearly, this plant whose natural habitat is the riverine areas of hills serves as a biblical metaphor for water. Its role in the four species is thus to represent the hills and mountains in the yearly plea for rain.

The citron (*Citrus medica*), too, is a symbol of water. Although not a native, it was the first tree of the citrus family (which includes lemons, oranges, and grapefruits) introduced into Israel. There has even been some doubt whether it had been introduced as early as the biblical period. Samuel Tolkowsky, a noted expert on the citrus family, suggested that the citron was not used for the *Sukkot* ritual until the Maccabean period, prior to which the "fruit of the goodly tree" was identified as a cedar cone![36] He even pinpoints the introduction of the citron into the ritual to October, 136 B.C.E., on the evidence of Maccabean coins with pictures of citron fruit.

However, there is some archaeological evidence for the presence of the citron in the Middle East in the biblical period,[37] and Tolkowsky's arguments are not completely convincing. Even Harold Moldenke, noted American scholar on the botany of the Bible, who in the text of his *Plants of the Bible* does not discuss the citron, adds in an appendix that he believes the citron to be the "fruit of the goodly tree."[38]

The citrus family as a whole demands heavy irrigation, and the citron, being the first of the citrus in Israel, undoubtedly quickly earned the reputation of being a lover of water. Even today, citron fields in Israel must frequently be irrigated. Rabban Gamliel goes so far as to compare the citron to a vegetable in one respect.[39] The Talmud explains:

> The nature of a citron is like that of vegetables. Just as it is the nature of vegetables to grow by means of all waters (that is, artificial irrigation), and its tithing is determined by the time when it is gathered; so is it the nature of the citron to grow by means of all waters and therefore its tithing is determined by its gathering.[40]

A powerful corroboration is the talmudic play on words of the phrase *pri ets hadar* (the fruit of the goodly tree).[41]

> Ben Azzai said. Read not *hadar* but *hydor*, for in Greek water is called *hydor* (hydro, water). Now what fruit is it that grows by all water? Say, of course, it is the citron.

Accordingly, the citron may be called the "fruit of the water tree"! Although this is obviously not the literal interpretation, the statement is indicative of how the citron was viewed: as a water-loving cultivated fruit tree. It represented the hopes for rain mainly on the cultivated plains.

The four species, then, symbolize water in the diverse ecological habitats of Israel: the desert wilderness, the mountains and hills, the cultivated plains, and the river valleys. They are part of a stimulating and thought-provoking ritual of thanking God for the previous year's rain and, at the same time, serve to direct and concentrate man's prayers for the rains to come.[42]

Needless to say, the de-emphasis of the agricultural and ecological symbolism of the four species of *Sukkot* is in no small part due to the Jewish people's temporary separation from the land of Israel. The native flora in their natural habitats regretfully faded from memory; the palms of Jericho turned from reality to hopeful symbols on prayerbook covers. With the modern-day return to the land and fulfillment of "Arise, walk through the land in the length of it and the breadth of it" (Gen. 13:17), the natural history of the land of the Bible is being relearned. The land that "the eyes of the Lord thy God are upon" no doubt eagerly awaits this continued rediscovery.[43]

NOTES

From *Tradition: A Journal of Orthodox Thought* 20 (1982): 128–40.

I would like to express my thanks to Dr. David Ehrenfeld, Professor in the Department of Horticulture & Forestry, Rutgers University, for critically reading the manuscript and for many stimulating conversations. All errors, though, are my own.

1. *Lev. Rabba* 39:14. Translations from *Midrash Rabba* are taken from the Soncino edition (London, 1939). Biblical translations are generally from the Koren edition (Jerusalem, 1969). Quotations from the Mishnah and Talmud are from the Soncino edition (London, 1938). Other translations, unless indicated, are my own.

2. *Lev. Rabba* 30:12.

3. *Lev. Rabba* 30:10.

4. *Lev. Rabba* 30:10.

5. *Lev. Rabba* 30:9.

6. *Guide for the Perplexed* III 43 (tr. M. Friedlander [2nd ed.; London, 1904]).

7. Nogah Hareuveni, *Nature in our Biblical Heritage* (Israel: Neot Kedumim, 1980), 78.

8. A. Reifenberg, *The Struggle Between the Desert and the Sown* (Israel, 1955), 21.

9. F. W. Aibright, "The Gezer Calendar," *Bulletin of the American Schools of Oriental Research* 92 (1943): 16–26.

10. *Mishnah Ta'anit* 1:4–7. Also see D. Sperber, "Drought, Famine and Pestilence in Amoraic Palestine," *Journal of the Economic and Social History of the Orient* 17 (1974): 272–98.

11. *Mishnah Ta'anit* 1:1

12. *Mishnah Ta'anit* 1:7.

13. Eliezer Schweid, *Moledet ve-Eretz Ye'udah* (Tel Aviv, 1979), especially 25. I would like to thank Rabbi Shalom Carmy for pointing this important philosopher's work out to me.

14. *Mishnah Sukkah* 1:2.

15. B. T. *Yoma* 26b.

16. *Mishnah Sukkah* 4.9.

17. B. T. *Rosh Hashanah* 16b.

18. *Mishnah Sukkah* 5:1.

19. *Hoshanah Rabbah*.

20. *Mishnah Sukkah* 4:5.

21. R. Crawford, "Tolerance of Anoxia and the Regulation of Glycolysis in Tree Roots," in *Tree Physiology and Yield Improvement,* ed. M. G. R. Cannell and F. T. Last (New York, 1976).

22. B. T. *Ta'anit* 2b.

23. B. T. *Ta'anit* 2a.

24. *Invu Bemitzvot,* a *piyyut* for the evening service of the second night of *Sukkot* in the diaspora, also refers to the four species as symbols of water.

25. B. T, *Sukkah* 33b.

26. G. E. Post, *Flora of Syria, Palestine and Sinai,* 2nd ed. (Beirut, 1932), Vol. 2, 531.

27. Michael Zohary, *Flora Palaestina,* Vol. I, Pt. 2 (Jerusalem, 1966), 25.

28. *Wars of the Jews,* tr. W. Whiston (Michigan, 1960), Bk. IV, Ch. 8, par. 3.

29. H. and A. Moldenke, *Plants of the Bible* (New York, 1952), 285.

30. Zohary, *Flora Palaestina,* Vol. II, Pt. 2 (Jerusalem, 1972), 371.

31. Zohary, *Flora Palaestina,* Vol. I, Pt. 2, 84.

32. See commentary of R. Abraham Ibn Ezra to 41:18.

33. F. Brown, F. S. E. Driver, and C. A. Briggs, *A Hebrew and English Lexicon of the Old Testament* (Oxford, 1966), 846–47; L. Koehler, and W. Baumgartner, *Lexicon in Veteris Testamenti Libros* (Leiden, 1958), 556; *The Interpreter's Bible,* Vol. 6, 1061.

34. Ex. 15:5.

35. Lev. 23:40, Neh. 8:15.

36. S. Tolkowsky, "The Meaning of *Pri Ets Hadar,*" *Journal of the Palestine Oriental Society* 8 (1928): 17–23.

37. E. Isaac, "The Influence of Religion on the Spread of Citrus," *Science* 129 (1959): 179–86.

38. H. and A. Moldenke, *Plants of the Bible*, 290.

39. *Mishnah Bikkurim* 2:6.

40. B. T. *Kiddushin* 3a.

41. B. T. *Sukkah* 35a, J. T. *Sukkah* 13b, and *Leviticus Rabba* 30:8 attribute the comment to Aquilas the proselyte. I would like to thank Dr. Norman Bronznick of Rutgers University's Department of Hebraic Studies for pointing out this source to me.

42. Eliyahu Ki-Tov regards, as well, the waving of the four species in the various directions as a sign for the prevention of destructive winds that may accompany the rain. *Sefer Ha-Toda'ah* (Jerusalem, n.d.), 92 (commenting on B. T. *Sukkah* 37b).

43. The Society for the Protection of Nature in Israel is responsible for a good part of this reeducation. See, for example, Azariah Alon's *The Natural History of the Bible* (New York, 1978).

6

Judaism and the Practice of Stewardship

David Ehrenfeld and Philip J. Bentley

During the past millennium or more of Jewish history, the Jews have become, partly by choice but mostly by force, an increasingly urban people. Hedged in by laws restricting land ownership, occupations, and dwelling places, especially in Christian Europe, they often found themselves living in crowded ghettos out of touch with the natural world.[1] The Hasidic Jews, who more than any other group cling to this European Jewish ghetto culture of centuries past, are like the Amish in many respects, yet a people more cut off from nature and the natural world cannot be imagined. When one thinks of Jews one thinks of merchants, financiers, shopkeepers, peddlers, professional people, artists, intellectuals, and craftsmen; one does not usually think of farmers, fishermen, or naturalists, although of course there have been exceptions.

Thus it is not surprising that most people, including most Jews, are unaware that Judaism was one of the first great environmental religions—that it speaks of humanity, land, and nature not in vague generalities but in great depth and detail and with a wisdom that seems to grow more profound with each passing decade.

One volume of the Mishnah is entitled *Seeds*. It describes in exacting detail the Jewish legal strictures about every phase of agricultural practice, documenting the originally intimate relationship between Jews and the land. Many of the early Jewish sages were farmers—indeed by the seventh century, during the first Islamic conquests, it was only their needed agricultural skills that saved some Jews in Arab lands from being put to the sword.[2]

Among the religions that speak profoundly of humanity's need to care for nature, for the rest of God's creation, Judaism stands at one end of a philosophical spectrum—the human-centered end—in which the human role in the world is that of careful steward. At the other end of the spectrum are religions such as Jainism, which emphasize humanity's role in nature as one of absolute nonviolence and noninterference. A Jain monk abstains from eating meat, fasts frequently to avoid hurting plants, walks barefooted so as not to injure the small creatures of the earth, and may even breathe through a mask of seven thickness of gauze to avoid inhaling and killing any of the tiny organisms of the air.[3]

Judaism is not at all like this. Jews commonly believe that every live thing on earth must have some human reference and use, even if it is only to remind us of our place in the scheme of things. And Jains believe that every live thing on earth is, or has a right to be, free of human reference.

Both of these attitudes towards nature have great validity and appeal, yet they are extreme positions. On the one hand, it seems to most of us that it is neither possible nor desirable for billions of humans to live in the world without changing it substantially; therefore, wise stewardship is necessary. On the other hand, stewardship is easily corrupted to the belief that we are lords, not caretakers, and that we are capable of managing and resolving all of the technological and social problems that we may have produced in our complex society.[4]

We cannot speak to the objections to Jainist doctrine. It is clear, however, that restraint, noninterference, and humility were an integral part of the original Jewish concept of stewardship, regardless of corruptions that may have taken place subsequently, and that these restraining virtues may yet prevail. This idea is a quiet corollary of the powerful theme running through Jewish teaching that human beings are not to be defined, that we are not true lords of anything except our free will. In the talmudic tractate *Sanhedrin* we find the statement:

> Our masters taught:
> Man was created on the eve of die Sabbath—and for what reason?
> So that in case his heart grew proud, one might say to him:
> Even the gnat was in creation before you were there.[5]

Nevertheless, it cannot be denied that while it is almost impossible to pervert the Jain philosophy in a way that leads to widespread environmental damage, the same thing cannot be said of the Jewish, or for that matter Christian, ideas of a human-centered world. As Jews and Christians have found, to their sorrow, the practice of stewardship, under the intoxicating influence of the power that comes with science and technology, is easily twisted and distorted so that stewardship becomes subjugation. When this occurs, as it does all around us, the vision of a power higher than humanity, which gave the original sanction and limit to the idea of stewardship, is itself washed away in a flood of collective egomania.

One effect of this humanistic arrogance has been to turn some environmentalists against Judaism and Christianity, the religions of stewardship, as if it were the notion of stewardship rather than its distortion that has caused all of the trouble. Such criticisms are usually supported by the quotation of Genesis 1:26, 28, the familiar injunction to have dominion over the earth and to subdue it, about which we will have more to say.

Christian thought and Christian interpretation of Jewish and Christian Scripture are so pervasive in Western society that even most of the Jews who think about these matters do not realize that the problem of the chasm between humanity and the rest of nature exists more for Christians than for Jews. Christianity has a stronger emphasis on the Other World than on this world, and classical thought has a much stronger hold on Christianity than on Judaism.[6] In the classical view, nature is an entity unto itself and humanity is something apart from it. In Judaism we consider this world of great importance. As for nature, there is not even a Hebrew word for it, at least not in rabbinic Hebrew.

HISTORICAL CONTEXT

Before examining the practice of stewardship in Judaism. we must pause a moment for an important caution. It would be a mistake to pretend that the ancient rabbinic sages had any inkling of the extent, or even the possibility, of the kind of global pollution and massive environmental destruction that we are witnessing today. To the ancients the world was a huge place. No one had seen with his own eyes the physical extent of it, nor could he have imagined a worldwide crisis concerning such basic resources as water or air, particularly a crisis caused by man. If we could not control the elements, we could not destroy them either.

So one cannot ask, "What does traditional Judaism say about our environmental crisis?" It doesn't say anything about it. That does not mean, however, that Judaism offers no guidance on the question of humanity's relationship to the environment. We simply have to search the literature properly, phrasing our questions to suit the context of the times, and interpreting the rabbinic answers in a restrained and literal way, in order not to interject our own ideas.

When this caution is observed, several critically important ecological ideas can be seen occurring in the Jewish tradition, even apart from the ideas of stewardship and the Lord's dominion.

First is the idea that *if man does evil, nature reacts*. This idea, which was brilliantly explored by Faulkner in *Go down Moses*, has yet to be grasped by either the majority of people in the industrial world or their leaders, but it is often encountered in the older Jewish literature, including the Torah itself (e.g., Deut. 11:13–17).

A second ecological concept that is part of the tradition is *that there is a definite order to the world ordained by God as part of creation. Nothing was created for no purpose or in vain*. In our century, the best secular statement of this ancient idea was made by Aldo Leopold, and it has found its way into nearly every conservationist's philosophy—although, frankly, it is easier to defend from a theological than an ecological standpoint.[7]

Third is that most general of ecological principles: *you don't get something for nothing*. This is entrenched in the early Jewish writings, and finds one of its best expressions in the accepted rabbinic belief, based on Scripture and the oral tradition, that Adam was not allowed to eat in the garden of Eden until he had first worked for his food by tilling and keeping the garden.[8]

And fourth, embedded deep within Judaism is the profound ecological idea of *human dependence upon nature*; our work alone does not suffice to keep us alive. In fact, as Richard Hirsch has pointed out, the idea is taken far beyond this. He writes that "our sages formulated a philosophy which could be called 'survival of the sustainers,' succinctly expressed in the [talmudic] saying, 'Not only does man sustain man, but all nature does so. The stars and the planets, and even the angels sustain each other.'"[9]

DOMINION, CREATION, AND THE HEBREW LANGUAGE

The verses of Genesis 1:26, 28, in which man is given "dominion" over all the animals of the earth, are mistakenly believed by many environmentalists to summarize and represent the entirety of the Jewish and Christian teachings on the subject. We will leave the defense of the Christian tradition to others like Wendell Berry; in the case of the Jewish attitude towards the environment, the attack is easily disposed of, regardless of whether one's biblical interpretation is liberal or strictly orthodox, and without doing damage to the historical context in which the biblical verses first appeared.[10]

There are two answers to the "dominion" criticism, each of which would be sufficient to refute the charge. The first is to point out the superficial nature of the interpretation and its lack of content. There is no evidence, that we are aware of, that these verses of Genesis were ever interpreted by the rabbis as a license for environmental exploitation. Indeed, such an interpretation runs contrary to their teachings and to the whole spirit of the oral law. As Berry has said, to put these verses in their proper context, one need go no farther than Genesis 2:15, Adam's instructions to "dress" and "keep" the garden, which have always been assumed to have a bearing on how the dominion was to be exercised. In other words, although the "dominion" phrases of Genesis could have been interpreted in the harsh, exploitative way that some critics suggest, they were never, in fact, interpreted that way within the rabbinic tradition.

A second answer to the dominion criticism is based on the inadequacy of the English translations of the original Hebrew of the Jewish Scriptures. By chance, an excellent example of this inadequacy concerns the word "dominion" itself. A quarter of a century before William the Conqueror invaded England, Rashi had this to say about the "dominion" of Genesis 1:26: "The

Hebrew [*yirdu*] connotes both 'dominion' (derived from *radah*) and 'descent' (derived from *yarad*); when man is worthy, he has dominion over the animal kingdom; when he is not, he descends below their level and the animals rule over him."[11] Here is a whole dimension of meaning which cannot be conveyed by an English translation.

In the prevailing English translation of the Bible, humankind and its world come "in the beginning," an interpretation that lends itself to arrogance and ego-centeredness. In the original, however, the sense of the Hebrew, from the first word of Genesis, is that we and our universe were not here in the beginning, if there was a beginning, a thought conducive to humility and God-centeredness. This is an oriental vision of tiny humanity in a vast universe, like the Chinese paintings of little human figures set against a background of gigantic waves and mountains, which environmentalists are fond of citing.

More important, perhaps, is the accepted Jewish implication of the word *bereshith* ("in the beginning"), that creation is an ongoing process; it is not finished. In the morning religious service we find the words, "Daily He renews the work of creation." Humanity participates in some aspects of this ongoing act of creation, but only when we act in the proper spirit and appreciate the continuing role of the Creator in His creation. This is the background against which we must view the Jewish idea of stewardship and humanity's relationship to the rest of nature.

STEWARDSHIP

What is the traditional Jewish notion of stewardship really like? If we search in the Hebrew Bible, we find a number of familiar verses that stress God as creator and owner, amid humankind as humble caretaker or steward of the earth: "And . . . God . . . put him into the garden of Eden to till it and to keep it." (Gen. 2:15) "The land shall not be sold forever: for the land is Mine; for you are strangers and sojourners with Me." (Lev. 25:23) Many other biblical texts can be construed as being relevant, in a more or less direct way, to the idea of stewardship.[12]

Many modern Jews and Christians interpret these statements as a biblical mandate for stewardship. But how did the Jewish sages, who lived in a different world, treat them? If one looks at the rabbinic commentaries out Psalm 119:19 and I Chronicles 29:15, both of which repeat the idea of our being strangers and sojourners in God's world, we find no mention of the environment. The reference is to the transitory nature of man's life on earth and the necessity of living the good life and keeping the commandments. Moreover, the environmental connotations of Genesis 2:15 are not even alluded to by Rashi in his commentary.

Does this mean that environmental thought and the idea of stewardship are missing from the philosophy of the rabbis who first codified Jewish law and gave form to its tradition? No. Again, we must remember the historical context of the times in which they lived. Then, "the environment" was not viewed as set apart from humankind; there was nothing to comment on. Nor did humans have the power to take actions that would quickly lay waste large parts of the natural world.

We do not find teachings that say "man has a responsibility to the environment"; rather, we discover that the care of the natural world, which we do not own, was an implicit part of time rabbinic image of the good person. In this image, the idea of human accountability to a higher authority, the Owner, is always central.

An excellent illustration of this point is provided by a quotation from the writings of the great eleventh-century Spanish rabbi, Jonah ibn Janach of Saragossa, the pioneering Hebrew philologist:

> A man is held responsible for everything he receives in this world, and his children are responsible too. . . . The fact is that nothing belongs to him, everything is the Lord's, and whatever he received he received only on credit and the Lord will exact payment for it. This may be compared to a person who entered a city and found no one there. He walked into the house and there found a table set with all kinds of food and drink. So he began to eat and drink thinking, "I deserve all of this, all of it is mine, I shall do with it what I please." He didn't even notice that the owners were watching him from the side! He will yet have to pay for everything he ate and drank, for he is in a spot from which he will not be able to escape.[13]

This quotation deals with humanity's responsibility to God, not with our relationships to nature. Yet it includes the first principle of stewardship: the steward is not owner of the property in his care, and will, ultimately, be held accountable for its condition.[14]

Of course, not all early Jewish references to stewardship of the natural world are indirect or obscure. The following *aggadah* is from *Ecclesiastes Rabbah*, which was redacted in approximately the eighth century:

> In the hour when the Holy One Blessed Be He created the first man,
> He took him and let him pass before all of the trees of the garden of Eden,
> And said to him:
> See My works, how fine and excellent they are!
> Now all that I am going to create for you I have already created.
> Think about this and do not corrupt and desolate My world;
> For if you corrupt it, there will be no one to set it right after you.[15]

BAL TASHCHIT AND *TZA'AR BA'ALEI CHAYYIM*

Beyond the general principles of ultimate ownership and accountability, the exercise of stewardship has never been left to the imagination of the stewards. There are, in Judaism, a number of specific rules—together constituting a kind of "Steward's Manual"—setting forth humanity's particular responsibilities for its behavior towards natural resources, animals, and other parts of nature. First among these rules is the commandment of *bal tashchit.*

In Deuteronomy 20:19 we read: "When you besiege a city a long time, in making war against it to take it, you shall not destroy the trees thereof by wielding an axe against them; you may eat of them, but you shall not cut them down; for is the tree of the field man, that it should be besieged of you?"

From this source is derived the notion of *bal tashchit* (do not destroy), an ancient and sweeping series of Jewish environmental regulations that embrace not only the limited case in question, but have been rabbinically extended to a great range of transgressions, including the cutting off of water supplies to trees, the overgrazing of the countryside, the unjustified killing of animals or feeding them harmful foods, the hunting of animals for sport, species extinction and the destruction of cultivated plant varieties, pollution of air and water, overconsumption of anything, and the waste of mineral and other resources.[16]

Samson Raphael Hirsch eloquently summarized the meaning of *bal tashchit* for a religious Jew:

> "Do not destroy anything!" is the first and most general call of God, which comes to you, man, when you realize yourself as master of the earth. . . . God's call proclaims to you . . . , "If you destroy, if you ruin—at that moment you are not a man, you are an animal, and have no right to the things around you. I lent them to you for wise use only; never forget that I lent them to you. As soon as you use them unwisely, be it the greatest or the smallest, you commit treachery against My world, you commit murder and robbery against My property, you sin against Me!" This is what God calls unto you, and with this call does He represent the greatest and smallest against you and grants the smallest, as also the greatest a right against your presumptuousness."[17]

According to Hirsch, even the practice of hoarding property and doing nothing with it, rather than using it wisely and maintaining it, is condemned under *bal tashchit.* This is strikingly similar to contemporary arguments against many current agricultural practices. It is also in accord with the recent ecological awareness that, when people abandon or neglect land that has previously been farmed with care and skill, the number of species of native wild plants and animals suffers a sharp decline.[18]

Inhumane conduct toward animals is also powerfully enjoined in Jewish law. The prohibition against inflicting *tza'ar ba'alei chayyim* ("pain of living things") has multiple biblical sources, including Deuteronomy 22:6, which forbids the killing of a bird with her young. According to Jewish tradition, the prohibition against one form of inhumane conduct toward animals is one of the seven commandments given to the sons of Noah and, therefore, is binding on all humanity, not just upon Jews. Some kinds of work are even permitted to Jews on the Sabbath, if the purpose is to relieve the suffering of an animal. Kindness to animals is one of the few virtues that the Jewish tradition associates with the promise of heavenly reward.

The ultimate extension of *tza'ar ba'alei chayyim* is to abstain from killing animals at all; the result is vegetarianism, a practice that has been institutionalized in Jainism, Hinduism, and other eastern religions. Vegetarianism, although not mandated by Jewish law, is a practice that has long appealed to Jews; the sages believed (based in part on Genesis 1:29) that humans were vegetarian until after the Flood, when the eating of meat was permitted. The Jewish dietary laws are much simpler for vegetarians to observe than for those who eat meat, and some authorities see this as deliberately punitive, with the intention of reducing the number of animals killed for food. Jewish law mandates only humane slaughter of healthy animals for food, and there are those who maintain that the consumption of animals that have been factory raised under inhumane conditions violates the spirit of *kashrut* as well as the letter of other *mitzvot*. Jewish vegetarianism is a small but strong movement with its own magazine.[19] Its best-known modern advocate was the late Chief Rabbi of Palestine, Abraham Isaac Kook.

SABBATH AND STEWARDSHIP

When stewardship is corrupted by power in the absence of restraint, it becomes ecological tyranny and exploitation. This is the central problem of stewardship, a problem that has always existed but has become critical only with the rise of modern technology and its side effects, including overpopulation. With technology, humanity has achieved a power and a presence that is utterly subversive of the practice of stewardship. Modern theorists have despaired of finding noncoercive ways of resolving this tragic dilemma,[20] and many environmentalists have condemned stewardship itself as an inherently unworkable concept.

Nevertheless, within Judaism there still exists a mechanism—the original mechanism—for reconciling stewardship's absolute need for human restraint and forbearance with the mundane exercise of power. *Bal tashchit* and *tza'ar ba'alei chayyim* are not enough. For Jews, it is the Sabbath and the idea of the Sabbath that introduces the necessary restraint into stewardship. It is also the Sabbath alone that can reconcile the Jewish attitude towards nature with the attitude of secular environmentalism, of holistic ecology, or of the nonanthropocentric religions such as Jainism.

An hour past sundown on Saturday, at the conclusion of each Sabbath, we pronounce a blessing that says in part: "Blessed are You, O Lord, who makes a distinction between holy and ordinary, between the seventh day and the six working days." In this blessing there is no implied criticism of either the ordinary or the six working days. The Sabbath needs the six working days, just as they, in turn, need the Sabbath. Stewardship is one function of the six working days, and it shares this complementary relationship with the Sabbath. Just as the recollection of wise stewardship enhances the Sabbath and makes it possible, so is stewardship incomplete and imperfect without the complementary recollection and restraining influence of the Sabbath *during the rest of the week.*

On the Sabbath, the traditionally observant Jew does more than rest, pray, and refrain from ordinary work. There are at least three other elements of Sabbath observance which are relevant to stewardship: we create nothing, we destroy nothing, and we enjoy the bounty of the earth. In this way, the Sabbath becomes a celebration of our tenancy and stewardship in the world.

Nothing is created, and this reminds us of God's supremacy as Creator and our own comparative inadequacy.[21] Nothing is destroyed, and this reminds us that the creations of this world are not ours to ruin. We enjoy the bounty of the earth, and this reminds us that although our work, if properly done, will uncover for us far more of God's bounty than we would otherwise have enjoyed, nevertheless God, and not human invention, is still the ultimate source of that bounty.

Two tangible environmental applications of the idea of the Sabbath are the Sabbatical and Jubilee years, as described in Leviticus 25.[22] Every Sabbatical or seventh year, the land of Israel is to lie fallow; every fiftieth or Jubilee year, not only was the hand left untilled, but it reverted to its original ownership, thus (when observed) preventing the kind of concentration of large blocks of land in a few hands which now characterizes the American agricultural system and which is the cause of many of our most intractable environmental difficulties.

That the Sabbatical and, presumably, Jubilee years were actually observed in ancient Israel is shown by the fact that Alexander the Great and Julius Caesar both remitted tribute to the Jews every seventh year, and that Tacitus cites the Sabbatical year practice as evidence of the inherent laziness of the Jews.[23] Even today, the Sabbatical year receives some form of recognition from religious Jews in Israel.

But there is yet a deeper environmental significance to the Jewish Sabbath. Abraham Joshua Heschel wrote:

Technical civilization is man's conquest of space. It is a triumph frequently achieved by sacrificing an essential ingredient of existence, namely, time. In technical civilization we expend time to gain space. To enhance our power in the world of space is our main objective. . . . The power we attain in the world of space terminates abruptly at the borderline of time. But time is the heart of existence. . . . The more we think, the more we realize: we cannot conquer time through space. We can only master time in time. . . . Our intention here is not to deprecate the world of space. To disparage space and the blessing of things of space, is to disparage the works of creation, the works which God beheld and saw "it was good." . . . Time and space are interrelated. To overlook either of them is to be partially blind.[24]

To Heschel, control of space without mastery of time, which is eternal, is a meaningless achievement. It is the Sabbath that gives access to time realm of time. Or, as he put it, the Sabbath "tries to teach us that man stands not only in relation to nature but in a relation also to the creator of nature." In our work with nature and its laws, we deal largely with space and things. Yet, as many ecologists perceive, it is always the element of time which eludes the engineers, the agribusinessmen, the planners, and the remodelers of the earth. A desert ecosystem that has been destroyed in seconds by the heedless passage of a few motorized vehicles cannot be restored by us, and will take more than 100 years to restore itself.

Without the influence of the Sabbath, stewardship in practice is corruptible and unstable. For Jews, it is the awareness of the Sabbath during time working days that can bring the realm of time and its accompanying sense of restraint and limit to stewardship. It is the Sabbath that defines the relationship between steward and Ruler. It is the Sabbath, ultimately, that completes and confirms the environmental wisdom of Judaism.

NOTES

From *Judaism: A Quarterly Journal* 34 (1985): 301–11.

1. Even the ownership of family pets—dogs and cats—was, until recently, uncommon among both Ashkenazik and Sephardic households.

2. Norman A. Stillman, *The Jews of Arab Lands: A History and Source Book* (Philadelphia: Jewish Publication Society, 1979).

3. Satish Kumar, *No Destination* (Wales: The Black Big Press, 1977).

4. David Ehrenfeld, *The Arrogance of Humanism* (New York: Oxford University Press, 1981).

5. *A Jewish Reader*, ed. Nahum Glatzer (New York: Schocken Books, 1961).

6. Trude Weiss-Rosmarin, *Judaism and Christianity: The Differences* (New York: Jonathan David, 1943).

7. Aldo Leopold, *A Sand County Almanac* (New York: Oxford University Press, 1966). See, especially, the essay on "A Land Ethic."

8. Compare this with E. F. Schumacher's similar statements about the necessity and divinity of work, in his essay on "Buddhist Economics" in *Small is Beautiful* (New York: Harper & Row, 1973).

9. Richard Hirsch, "There Shall be no Poor," in *Judaism and Human Rights,* ed. M. Konvitz (New York: Norton, 1972).

10. Wendell Berry, in his brilliant essay "The Gift of Good Land" (*Sierra Club Bulletin* [Nov.–Dec., 1979]), actually defends both Jewish and Christian traditions against the charge of anti-environmentalism. One of the first and most comprehensive defenses of the Jewish position was by Robert Gordis, in an essay entitled "Judaism and the Spoliation of Nature" (*Congress Bi-weekly* 9.12 [Apr. 2, 1971]). A more recent evaluation of the charge of anti-environmentalism has been given by Nigel Pollard ("The Israelites and Their Environment," *The Ecologist* 14 [1984]: 125–33), who has assembled many sources and, unlike Berry and Gordis, views the subject from an entirely

secular perspective—at least as far as Judaism is concerned. (See also the essay by Lamm, referenced in note 21.)

11. *The Soncino Chumash: The Five Books of Moses with Haphtaroth,* ed. A. Cohen (London: Soncino Press, 1947), 6.

12. Some commonly cited examples are Deut. 10:14, Ps. 24:1–2, Job 39:26–27, 40:15, 19, Isa. 47:10.

13. *The Living Talmud* ed. and trans. Judah Goldin (New York: Mentor, 1957).

14. The antiquity of this theme is demonstrated by its appearance in *Avot* 3:16 (attributed to Rabbi Akiva) a thousand years before Janach's time. That an association between the idea of stewardship and that of accountability to God is not unreasonable, is borne out for example by the talmudic midrash that Moses and David were not fit to be leaders of Israel until they had been shepherds (*Talmud Yerushalmi, Kilayim* 9:3. 32a; *Bava Mezi'a* 85a).

15. *Midrash Rabbah,* Vol. VIII: *Ruth, Ecclesiastes,* trans. H. Freedman and M. Simon (London: Soncino Press. 1939).

16. Eric Freudenstein, "Ecology and the Jewish Tradition," in *Judaism and Human Rights,* 65–74; Jonathan Helfand, "Ecology and the Jewish Tradition: A Postscript," *Judaism* 20 (1971): 330–35.

17. Samson Raphael Hirsch, *Horeb: A Philosophy of Jewish Laws and Observances,* trans. I. Grunfeld (New York: Soncino Press, 1981), 279–80.

18. For example, see the discussion of bird diversity at a farmed oasis and at a nearby "protected" oasis in the Sonoran Desert, in Gary Nabhan's book, *The Desert Smells like Rain* (San Francisco: North Point Press, 1982), 87–97.

19. *Jewish Vegetarian,* quarterly publication of the Jewish Vegetarian Society, London. See also R. Schwartz, *Judaism and Vegetarianism* (Smithtown, N.Y.: Exposition Press, 1982).

20. Garrett Hardin, "The Tragedy of the Commons," *Science* 162 (1968): 1234–38.

21. For the ecological significance of the difference between human and Divine creativity see Norman Lamm, "Ecology in Jewish Law and Theology," in Lamm *Faith and Doubt* (New York: KTAV, 1971). Lamm also discusses the issue of Genesis 1:28, as well as the subject of Hasidic Immanentism.

22. Gerald J. Blidstein, "Man and Nature in the Sabbatical Year" (reprinted in this volume, 136–42).

23. *The Pentateuch and Haftorahs,* ed. Joseph H. Hertz (2nd ed.; London: Soncino Press, 1978), 531.

24. Abraham Joshua Heschel, *The Sabbath: Its Meaning for Modern Man* (New York: Farrar, Straus and Giroux, 1951).

7

Man and Nature
in the Sabbatical Year

Gerald Blidstein

R. Abbahu, when asked the reason for the laws of *shevi'it* (the sabbatical year), replied, "God said to Israel, 'Sow six years and rest on the seventh so that you might know that the land is Mine'" (*Sanhedrin* 39a). This extension of the Biblical "And the land shall not be sold in perpetuity, for the land is Mine" (Lev. 25:23) is the fundamental exegesis of the institution of *shevi'it*. Nevertheless this institution is a complex and rich one, and its study reveals patterns of meaning independent of R. Abbahu's exegesis, though support-ive of it. It is one of these patterns that I propose to explore here.

The two Biblical citations are of importance to us:

1. And six years thou shalt sow thy land and gather in the increase thereof; but the seventh year thou shalt let it rest and lie fallow, that the poor of thy people may eat, and what they leave, the beast of the field shall eat. In like manner thou shalt deal with thy vineyard and with thy oliveyard. (Ex. 23:10–11)
2. In the seventh year shall be a sabbath of solemn rest for the land, a sab-bath unto the Lord; thou shalt neither sow thy field, nor prune thy vine-yard. That which groweth of itself of thy harvest thou shalt not reap, and the grapes of thy undressed vine thou shalt not gather; it shall be a year of solemn rest for the land. And the sabbath-produce of the land shall be for food for you: for thee, and for thy servant and for thy maid, and for thy hired servant and for the settler by thy side who sojourn with thee, and for thy cattle and for the beasts that are in thy land, shall all the increase be for good. (Lev. 25: 4–7)

The social effects of the restrictions here listed are clearly stated: the sab-bath produce shall be for all—for erstwhile owner and slave, for Jew and non-Jew, and even for the cattle and wild beasts. Despite the largesse granted the needy, the Bible's first concern is clearly not with the poor; *all* share in the bounty—landowner and poor man and even animals. This is in marked distinction to the Torah's sole concern with the poor in the laws of *lekket, shikchah, pe'ah,* and *ma'aser ani.* Not an extension of privilege to the poor, *shevi'it* demands the equalization of all who live off the soil.

This problem of equalization is often posed, in indeed broader dimension, in the book of Psalms; so, too, the seemingly absurd yet of course perfectly apt last sentence of God to Jonah: "And shall I not spare the great city of Nineveh, in which there are more than one hundred twenty thousand men who cannot distinguish between their right hand and their left, and much cattle?" But it is in the Oral Law, as reported in rabbinic literature, that the leveling implicit in the passages of the Torah cited above is understood forcefully; it is in the law of *shevi'it* that man's technological ingenuity, his economic activity, in short, his customary potent manipulation of the world about him, are severely restricted.[1]

The *Mekhilta* (Horowitz-Rabin, 330), taking the word *u-netashta* to mean "and you shall abandon it," comments: "This tells us that the owner must break down his fence, but that the sages restrained him from this duty for the benefit of society." Professor Saul Lieberman has gathered the Talmudic evidence corroborating the practice of dismantling the fences during the *shemittah* year.[2] Clearly, this dramatic line of action was not meant to guarantee the poor access to the fields, for access to the fields (or the fruit) was guaranteed in either case. Rather, in destroying the fences one is pulling down the symbol and reality of private ownership. In the one case, one is entering another man's property and enjoying his generosity; in the other, this distinction has ceased to exist. The "benefit" accruing to society by the limitation of this practice is thus quite obvious, for society depends on such distinctions.[3] Yet even after this restriction, Bet Shammai still maintained that one may not gather permitted fruit in an area where one feels beholden to the original owner, thus acknowledging even emotionally an ownership that did not exist in fact.[4]

Indeed, this conflict between the radical demands of *shevi'it,* on the one hand, and the social reality it seeks to undermine, on the other, is a paradigm of the history of the institution. Ironically, the more potent its observance became, the less were its chances of survival. We have here more than the commonplace struggle between a radical religious demand and an unconsenting world. Rather, we have here an institution that in its essence contests the legitimacy of that world, and threatens to become not merely the symbolic repudiation of its normal social and economic patterns, but its real menace and ultimately its victor.

The potency of *shevi'it* has been its historical doom. In the Chumash, *shevi'it* is only a penultimate reality—the radical leveling of the seventh year is fused into an encounter with the divine Sustainer: "If you will say,

'What shall we eat in the seventh year—for we can neither sow nor gather in our crop?', I shall command my blessing upon you in the sixth year, and that crop shall suffice for three years!" (Lev. 25:20–21). Yet in the course of history this idyll was held to be shattered.

The Oral Law understood the Exile as a disruption in the ideal state of Israel's relation to God through the land. The promise of God miraculously to sustain His people was no longer held effective, and with this divine weight gone, the scale was too greatly tipped in favor of the natural course of events. In fact, one aspect of Exile means precisely this—that in some sense Israel was delivered over to history (despite the hidden presence of God). Hence, the Torah no longer expected the Jew to continue as if nothing had changed; God Himself had declared and decreed change. Furthermore, as the entire people was no longer settled upon the land but alienated from it, another significant blow was struck against *shevi'it* as postulated in the Torah: the service of *the people* is no longer a reality. This, I think, is the theological dynamic underlying the dictum: *"Shevi'it* in our time is of Rabbinic origin."[5]

This dictum was not descriptive alone. It was prescriptive as well. It becomes the rationale by which the world seeks to balance the ravages of *shemittah*. Rabbinical *shemittah* can be narrowed, limited, and in effect abolished. For the more effective *shevi'it* became—or was judged to have become—the harder the world fought back. "R. Judah the Prince wished to abolish *shemittah"* (*Y. Demai* 3.1; 22a). This is the dynamic of the centuries-old struggle between those who would maintain the *shemittah* and those who would not. This, too, is the anguish one hears in the writing of Rav Kook on *shevi'it.* Twentieth-century economics granted to this most beloved *mitzvah* a majesty the community of Israel could not sustain; it was the very success of *shevi'it* which, ironically, was its downfall. And so the reality of *shevi'it* must be deferred, hints Rav Kook, until the Messianic age (Introduction, *Shabbat Ha-Aretz*, 35a).

Let us return now to a closer scrutiny of *shevi'it,* and see the logic of its Halakhah. For the tearing down of fences is not an isolated exercise in economic anarchy. It forms part of a broader, more extensive pattern. Once engaged in the actual gathering of permitted fruit, one's mode of harvest is restricted: "'Thou shalt not gather'—do not gather as you were wont to gather; hence it is said, 'Figs of the Sabbatical year may not be cut with a fig-knife, but may be cut with an ordinary knife. Grapes may not be trodden in the wine press but they are trodden in the kneading trough. Olives may not be prepared in an olive press or with an olive-crusher, but they may be crushed and brought into a small olive-press.'"[6] In a word, we find operating here the concept of *shinnui* (change from the usual method).[7] Man may harvest, but the law prevents him from using the full measure of that technology which his human talents have devised. According to the Gaon of Vilna, certain primary types of labor must be done by hand,[8] thus totally denying man his tool-making achievement.

Once harvested, the fruit of the seventh year is assigned an irrevocable status. Its use is forever restricted. "The fruits of *shevi'it* are to be used for eating, drinking, and anointing—eating that which one normally eats, anointing with that which one normally uses for anointing . . . . *Shevi'it* may also be used to kindle a light."[9] The *Sifra* adds dyeing to this list of approved uses.[10] *Shevi'it* may be sold or exchanged only to acquire food or drink or oil for annointing.[11] These stringent regulations naturally eliminate commercial transactions on a large scale, and apply to poor and rich alike. (The poor man cannot sell or exchange what he has gathered to buy clothing, provide shelter, or pay a creditor, any more than a rich man may.) The crop must be used for its "natural" ends; fruit is to be eaten, juices are to be drunk, and oil is to anoint the human body.[12] We shall later explore further the ban on subverting agricultural produce from these "natural" ends, but even this cursory survey clearly indicates the discrimination between what is the "natural" use of goods and what is a sophisticated human utilization of them to satisfy many of his other needs and urges, including the acquisitive. Such utilization of *shemittah* produce is forbidden.

The Talmud (*Sukkah* 40a) derives this hierarchy of uses from an attentive reading of the verse, "And the sabbatical produce of the land shall be food for you"; the general rule is that any permitted use must share that most evident characteristic of eating—its immediate enjoyment and consumption. Here, too, the primitive use is preferred to the more sophisticated.[13]

As we have pointed out, permitted fruit of the *shemittah* year gathered in accordance with the *shemittah* regulations may be sold (if only to buy other foodstuffs). Yet here, too, the mode of acquisition and sale clearly sets off this exchange from any normal commercial transaction: "One may not engage in business with the fruits of *shevi'it*. . . . One may not buy vegetables and sell them in the market, but one may gather vegetables and they may be sold by one's son. If one bought vegetables for one's own use and could not use them, he may sell them. . . . The fruit of the *shemittah* year may not be sold by measure, weight, or number."[14] To be sure, these regulations serve to emphasize the sacred character of the fruit of the seventh year, but the fact that sanctity is underscored precisely by the withdrawal of the produce from the circuit of commercial transaction is most significant.

Even when sold, the condition that the money may be used only as an intermediate step between different foods, or the like, demonstrates that we have here only an advanced type of barter, rather than anything resembling a money economy. For one cannot convert the produce into money to be spent, saved, or invested indiscriminately. Hence we need not be too surprised at reading, "Bet Shammai say one may not sell the fruit of *shevi'it* for money but only [exchange it] for fruit, lest one buy an ax with it, and Bet Hillel permit it."[15] The immediate source of the disagreement is the degree to which the average man is to be trusted in his observance of this particular law (a theme upon which Bet Hillel and Bet

Shammai disagree elsewhere). Both schools agree, however, as to the nature of exchange of *shevi'it* produce: it is barter. This barter is limited even further by its being a function of the restriction that this produce be used only for eating, drinking, and the like, as pointed out above.

The climax of the *shemittah* year is reached, perhaps, with the observance of *bi'ur shevi'it* (the elimination of produce). In their study of the Talmudic sources, the *rishonim* reached varying conclusions as to the nature of this *bi'ur*; for some it meant public redistribution (Ramban and some Tosafists), for others it meant destruction of the produce (Rambam and, apparently, Rashi), and for yet others it meant a sequence of the two (Ra'abad). What concerns us, however, is an aspect of *bi'ur* which remains constant in all these different interpretations: its date.

The Torah, in its opening of the *shemittah* produce to all who live off the soil, had stated, "and for thy cattle and for the beasts that are in thy land, shall all the increase thereof be for food."[16] Upon this the *Sifra* comments: "The statement 'for thy cattle and for the beasts' compares cattle with wild beasts—as long as the beast finds food in the field, feed the domestic animals. When the food for the beast is exhausted in the fields, stop feeding the domestic animals."[17] Elsewhere[18] the *Sifra* makes a similar comment on the verse (Lev. 25:12), "Ye shall eat the increase thereof out of the field": "While you can eat off the field, you may eat what is in the house; when the fruit of the field is exhausted, eliminate the fruit in the house."

Taken together, these passages (for which parallels can be found in both Talmuds) reveal that man may eat of what he has stored only as long as God's natural storage—the open fields—hold their crops.[19] When the wild animals can no longer find food, man must release the grain in his granaries and the wine in his vats (of the *shemittah* produce alone, naturally). Man must relinquish that which his human capabilites have achieved, and in his use of the growth of the soil be reduced to the lowest of creatures that live off the soil. Man must live the rhythms of nature, despite his obvious ability and duty to circumvent them; he must live the rhythms of the countryside despite the city in which he dwells.

Thus we have seen the two basic statements of the Torah (limiting man's planting of the soil, and opening the land to all who live off it) flower in the Oral Law into a regimen in which man's technological and economic manipulation of the earth's products is restrained, if not eliminated. One is tempted to describe some of these phenomena as embodying a type of "primitivism," despite the ambiguities inherent in that term, the fact that it does not accurately describe other phenomena of the *shemittah* year, and one's general disinclination to label complex structures of one culture by a term already ambiguous in another culture. Perhaps more important than the designation we apply to these phenomena is the attempt to enter into the spirit of an institution whose practice has been made remote by history and experience.

NOTES

From *Tradition: A Journal of Orthodox Thought* 8 (1966): 48–55.

1. The parallel to the Sabbath is too obvious to belabor, and is amply suggested by the Torah itself. See *Commentary* of Rabbi Samson Raphael Hirsch to verses cited in text.

2. S. Lieberman, *Tosefta Ki-Pshutah,* vol. II, 583, n. 2.

3. Cf. Ra'abad, *Commentary to Eduyot,* 5:1. I believe that here there is a slightly different reading of the *Mekhilta* than that presented above.

4. Mishnah *Shevi'it* 4:2. I follow here the Rambam, in his *Commentary to the Mishnah,* among others. See S. Safrai, *Tarbitz* 35.4(5726): 314–16.

5. See *Arachin* 32b, and Maimonides, *Shemittah Ve-Yovel* 10:8–9. I am aware that I have not gone into the critical or historical aspects of these sources. I believe that there is a conceptual meaning to these dicta irrespective of the meaning given them by their origins.

6. *Sifra Bahar,* ch. 1, sec. 3, 106a; Mishnah *Shevi'it* 8:6. I followed the Soncino translation in their identification of the various utensils described. In taking this *Mishnah* to refer to fruit that is *hefker,* I follow Ra'abad (in his *Commentary to the Sifra*), Ramban (*Commentary* to Lev. 25:5 and *Yevamot* 122a), among others; the variations found in even these readings are of no concern to us here. Note also the conclusion to *Tosafot, Sukkah* 39b, *s.v. ba-meh.*

7. Note again the similarity to the Sabbath.

8. *Shenot Eliyahu,* 7:2, 8:6.

9. Mishnah *Shevi'it* 8:2.

10. *Bahar* 1:10, 106c.

11. Mishnah *Shevi'it* 8:4–5, 8; 7:1–2. If sold or exchanged, the money or goods received may not be used for kindling a light or dyeing; cf. Tosefta *Shevi'it* 5.4, 6.14. The halakhic discrimination is hard to discern; cf. *Or Same'ach* to Rambam, *Hilkhot Shemittah Ve-Yovel* 5:8. For a different reading of these last *baraitot,* cf. *Pe'at Ha-Shulchan,* ch. 24, sec. ii, n. 26. The omission of dyeing from Mishnah 8:2 is of interest.

12. Obviously, light and dyeing present difficulties here. It should be pointed out, however, that these two uses apparently play less of a role in the approved uses of *shevi'it* than do the other types of direct human consumption; cf. n. 11, *supra.* It should also be pointed out that according to some, one may oil various utensils and clothing; cf. Mishnah *Shevi'it* 8:9 and *Yerush.* Generally, the text of my essay presents the majority opinion.

13. The *sugyah* is a very difficult one. On the face of it, it presents the typology of permitted uses of *shevi'it* produce as the determinant of which produce is included within the law of *shevi'it.* Once again, my essay assumes the majority view, and does not explore the view of R. Yossi, or the various reasons suggested to explain it.

14. Mishnah *Shevi'it* 7:3, 8:3.

15. Tosefta *Shevi'it* 6:19. Cf. Y. Bahar, *Zion* 27: 32 ff.

16. Despite the openness of the Torah with regard to animal consumption, cf. Tosefta *Shevi'it* 5:20; *Sifra Bahar,* ch. 1, sec. 7, 106c. On the problem of the gentile, cf. the reconciliation of *Tosefta Shevi'it* 5:21 and *Sifra,* op. cit., on the one hand, with *Sifra* ch. 1, sec. 6, 106b, in Ra'abad *ad loc.*

17. *Sifra*, ch. 1, sec. 8, 106c.
18. *Sifra*, ch. 3, sec. 4, 107c.
19. Maimonides, *Shemittah Ve-Yovel,* 7:1, directly links human consumption in the house with animal consumption in the field. I have been unable to find such direct equation in the sources; the equations found in the *Sifra* are those of beast and animal, on the hand, and human consumption in the home with human consumption in the field, on the other.

8

Commentary on the Book of Genesis, Chapter 1

Robert D. Sacks

The Book of Genesis, which we are about to read, we have all read many times before. How often the stories it contains were told to us when we were children and could not yet read. And so they became part of us. This familiarity is both a blessing and a curse. Prejudices and ghosts of former thoughts will peer at us from behind every line, thoughts passed down through the ages, thoughts which were not our own. Only with great effort can we learn to treat the familiar as if it were foreign, but such is our task if we hope to rediscover the author's intention.

The name of the book we are about to read is *In the beginning*. The title *Genesis* was a later addition from the Greek. Similarly, the other books of the Torah are all called by the word or words that happen to appear first in the text. Thus they can hardly even be said to have any names at all. Whenever we pick up a book the first things to hit our eyes are the title, the name of the author, and the date of publication. This is not merely a modern convention. The Book of Amos, for instance, begins as follows:

> The Words Of Amos, Who Was Among The Herdsmen Of Tekoah, Which He Saw Concerning Israel In The Days Of Uzziah, And In The Days Of Jeroboam, The Son Of Joash King Of Israel, Two Years Before The Earthquake . . . Thus Saith The Lord. (Amos 1:1ff)

Here, in the Book of Genesis, no author's name is given, there is no date of publication, and it is even a book without a title. The book does not tell us these things, and therefore we do not know them. Are these deletions significant? Again we are not told, and again we do not know. There remains only the book that lies open before us.

The Book of Amos purports to be an account of the words of the Lord. Homer, too, begins by saying, *Sing, oh goddess, the wrath of Achilles.* While Genesis includes many speeches of God, it contains no claim for the divine origin of the book as a whole. Since no such claim is made and yet accounts are given of the lives of men who lived many years before the time of the author, we feel compelled to assume that he relied heavily on older accounts, either written or in the memory of the people. But we no longer have those older accounts, and therefore we cannot study them. Our only alternative, then, is to reread the book of Genesis in order to see whether he fashioned those tales into an integral whole or not and, if so, what that whole means.

1. *In the Beginning God Created the Sky and the Earth.*

It is somewhat embarrassing for a commentator to confess that he does not even understand the first line of the book he has chosen. The syntax is rather difficult because the Hebrew counterpart of the definite article is missing. The Hebrew reads *bereshith* rather than *bareshith.* There does, of course, exist the possibility that the original text was *bareshith,* since the vowels were not included in writing at the time of the author. However, the general excellence of the text would seem to merit strongly against any such unwarranted assumption. The missing article would be permissible in Hebrew, but then the word *bereshith* would have to mean *in the beginning of,* as in the phrase *bereshith ha-tebhu'a* (in the beginning of the harvest). In that case one would have expected another noun to follow, and there is none. The beginning of what? The whole? In Hebrew such a word would have to be stated, and no such word appears. Is it the beginning of the act implied in the verb created? Hebrew syntax would seem to say no. The present author has no solution of his own but will present two generally accepted translations:

> *In the beginning God created the sky and the earth, and the earth was waste and void:* etc.

or:

> *When God began to create the sky and the earth, the earth being unformed and void with darkness over the face of the deep and a wind from God over the water, God said, Let there be light:* etc.

The central problem is whether *creatio ex nihilo* is implied in the first verse. If the first translation is accepted, two possibilities remain open. Either the first verse speaks about the creation of a primordial earth and sky, or it is to be taken as a chapter heading summarizing the contents of the first chapter. In Chapter 2, the author will present us with a second account of creation, which does indeed begin with such a chapter heading. It would therefore not seem unreasonable to assume that the first sentence of Chapter 1 was intended as a chapter heading and that the waste and void existed prior to any act of creation.

The alternative translation, which reflects the thought of medieval Jewish commentators such as Rashi, would of course exclude the notion of *creatio ex nihilo* from the author's intent.

There are grave difficulties in formulating the issue at stake for one overpowering reason. After the Book of Genesis had been written, its readers came into contact with the great rival to Biblical thought—Greek philosophy. This meeting may have forced those readers to make a decision more decisive than any intended by the author. Once the limitations placed on the Creator by the recalcitrance of matter had become subject to common gossip, the tradition may have been forced into an extreme position.

Fortunately, there is no reason for us to feel compelled to reach a decision at this point. We may wait to see which interpretation is more in keeping with the remainder of the text.

God created a *sky* and an *earth*. Had the text been written in Greek perhaps the author would have used the single word *cosmos*. But according to our author the world has two distinct parts, the *sky* and the *earth*, and does not present itself with quite the unity expressed by the word *cosmos*. Perhaps we would do well to bear in mind this dual character of the world.

The word *sky* has been used intentionally because the theological connotations of the word *heaven* seem to play no role in the early stages of the book.

2. *The earth was without form, and void; and darkness was upon the face of the deep. But a wind sent by God moved over the face of the waters.*

Our interest is directed at first to what will eventually become the lower portion, while the notion of *sky* is temporarily dropped.

In the beginning, the world was not this home with which we are all familiar but a fluid and formless mass of confusion characterized by random motion. Something beyond the waters moved. Was it a *wind* sent by God, or was it the *spirit of God*? The Hebrew could mean either. In any case, something apart from the waters began the motion of Creation.

3. *And God said, Let there be light: and there was light.*

Each day of Creation begins with the words *and God said*. This is strong ground for assuming that Verse Three contains the first act of Creation properly speaking, or in other words, that *creatio ex nihilo* was not intended to be implied by the author. In addition, the words *and God said* will be repeated once in the middle of day three and once in the middle of day six. However, this problem will be discussed later.

Verse 3 is, in the highest sense, paradigmatic of God's activity in bringing the world into being. Its force is more readily seen in Hebrew than in English due to a peculiarity in the use of Hebrew tenses. In the original text, the words which precede the *and* are identical to the words which follow it, whereas English requires a change from *let there be* to *there was*. In this paradigmatic example, everything occurs exactly as God has spoken and through his speech alone. Although the Western tradition has accepted this as the general form of Creation, we shall see that on other days things do not go so smoothly. No material was used in the creation of light, but that will never happen again either. The author seems to have intentionally presented us with this paradigm so that we might understand the work of the following days more fully.

4a. *And God saw the light, that it was good:*
At this point, it would be difficult to say with any precision what is meant by the word *good*. For the present, the most that can be said is that it is a quality inherent in the object itself, since God neither decided *that it was good*, nor called it *good*, but *saw . . . that it was good*. Little more can be said until we examine the things that God sees or does not see as being *good*.

4b. *And God distinguished between the light and the darkness.*
Paradigmatic as this act of Creation had been, it was still in need of improvement. The newly created light was confused and mingled with the darkness that was, and God was forced to distinguish them one from the other.

The word *distinguished* is characteristic of the first, second, and fourth days, just as the word *kind* will be characteristic of days three, five, and six. The world which is about to come into being will be primarily a world of distinguishable and therefore recognizable kinds of things. To the extent that the author presents the world as being composed of distinguishable parts, it is knowable and therefore trustworthy.

5a. *And God called the light day, and the darkness He called night.*
In addition to distinguishing between the light and the darkness, He gave them both names. The importance of names can only be seen if we look ahead a bit to compare the names God gives with the things named.

Things named by God	*Names given by God*
light and darkness	day and night (1:5)
expanse	sky (1:8)
water and dry	sea and land (1:10)

Light and darkness, an expanse, water and dry; they are all shapeless and could all be imagined as infinite seas. But the day ends when the night comes, the sea meets the land at the shoreline, and the sky stops at the horizon. According to this account of Creation, words are not mere handles but give definite shape to the things around us.

A world without speech would still contain friendly things and frightening things. There would be love and hate, but the edges of all things would be blurred. Honor would become pride, and pride merge into arrogance. The world would be a spectrum, and there would be nothing solid to grasp.

5b. *And there was evening and there was morning, one day.*

This line will appear six times as a steady drone throughout the chapter. It is a curious line because the distinction between evening and morning is not a Biblical commonplace, and in fact will never occur again in Biblical literature. One would have expected the phrase to read *and there was night and there was day. Evening and morning*—where did they come from? They are the times when the light and the darkness come together again. In spite of creation and division and the giving of names, an in-between land has arisen which was not created but which just happened. And by constant repetition our author will not let us forget that.

6. *And God said, Let there be an expanse in the midst of the water and let it divide between the waters and the waters.*

Since the word *expanse* appears in no other context, our only recourse is to consider its etymology. It comes from a verb referring to the actions of a coppersmith as he beats his copper to make it spread out into a thin sheet of indefinite shape. Like the *light* and the *waters*, the *expanse* can only be endowed with a form by giving it a name. Originally the water had all been of the same kind, but the expanse, in imitation of God's activity in Verse 4, would now divide the water into two parts

7. *And God made the expanse and it divided the water which was under the expanse from the water which was over the expanse: and it was so:*

God is beginning to share the activity of Creation with other things. The expanse was to be responsible for protecting the world about to come into being. Throughout the remainder of the chapter, God will continue to share His role as maker with others, and their attempts to fulfill God's command will form a significant part of the tale.

According to this account, the expanse which God has made protects us from an outside filled with primordial water, the water present as early as Verse 2. However, little emphasis is placed upon the fact that our world is surrounded by water, and it seems to be mentioned in the text not so much as the threats of an angry God to the simple reader, but as a reminder of the situation to the more careful reader.

There is no fundamental distinction between the waters above the expanse and the waters under the expanse. They differ only by virtue of the expanse itself. The angry sea and the torrential rains, part of our everyday experience, are themselves part of that original chaos, in spite of the fact that by giving them the name seas God placed them within bounds.

8. *And God called the expanse sky: and there was evening and there was morning, a second day.*

The first day was called one day rather than the first day because it established the length of time; in other words, there had been no fundamental measure of time prior to the first day.

9. *And God said, Let the waters underneath the sky be gathered together into one place that the dry place may appear: and it was so.*

Even in the primordial state, dry land and solidity existed, but they were hidden underneath the primordial waters. The first account of the beginning appears to present a Heraclitean world in which all is in flux. Nonetheless, solidity did exist but had to be made apparent by the speech of the Maker.

10. *And God called the dry place, earth; and the gathering of the water, he called seas: and God saw that it was good.*

11a. *And God said, Let the earth grass grass, seed-bearing plants, fruit trees bearing fruit according to its kind, having its seed in it upon the land:*

The Hebrew text uses a construction known as the cognate accusative. It says *Let the earth grass grass,* similar to the English construction to sing a song, to dance a dance, or to think a thought. As we shall see in Verse 12, the response is *and the earth sent forth grass.* The two are not identical. Let us consider the differences. If a man makes a chair, he can leave and another come and sit down. The chair has being wholly apart from its maker, but where is the dance when the dancer has ceased his dancing? A certain kind of unity exists in the first formulation, in sharp contrast to the formulation of Verse 12, which emphasizes the otherness of the grass by the use of the words *sent forth.* The sentence *Let the earth grass grass* is as strange in Hebrew as it is in English. The verb is only used once again in the Bible, and the verse even seems to be a direct reference to our passage. With obvious reference to a coming time of peace and tranquility, if not to a Messianic era, Joel says: "Fear not, ye beasts of the field: for the pastures of the wilderness do grass, the tree beareth her fruit, and the fig and the vine do yield their strength" (Joel 2:22).

It is almost as if the unity between the actor and the action implied in the use of the cognate accusative was intended to express the kind of peacefulness described by Joel. Is any man able to tell exactly what God wanted the earth to do, what kind of unity He was looking for? From what follows, it appears as though even the earth did not have a much clearer idea than we do, for it did *not grass grass* but *sent forth grass.* It is hard to say that the earth and not man was the first sinner. Nevertheless, it is true that the earth had to find its own way of obeying God's command. As we shall see later, even God Himself sees that it is good.

God's original plan called for a certain kind of unity which, given the ways of the earth, proved to be impossible. A general pattern is established here which develops throughout the entire book. God begins by requiring the highest, but is satisfied with the highest possible. The book, from a certain point of view, may be said to contain the search for such a mean.

Rabbi Judah ben Sholom in *Bereshith Rabbah* (Verse 9) saw the significance of the change in the verb. "Now why was [the earth] punished [in Verse 17, Chapter 3]? Because she disobeyed [God's] command. For the

Holy One, blessed be He, said thus: *Let the earth grass grass, fruit trees bearing fruit according to its kind, having its seed in it upon the land.* Just as the fruit is edible, so should the tree be edible. She, however, did not do thus but: *and the earth sent forth grass,* etc.: the fruit could be eaten but not the tree." Rabbi Judah takes the original unity expressed in the cognate accusative to mean that the earth should produce nothing but pure fruitfulness. I can think of no better image.

There does, however, seem to be one completely successful attempt to have the made beings share in the activity of making. Trees will continue to make fruits just as God made the expanse, and these fruits themselves are to bear seeds which will again produce other trees. God wishes to see a world capable of maintaining and perpetuating itself, a world differentiated into separate kinds of beings. There seems to be a stress here upon the notion of fruitfulness, both for each plant with respect to itself, and for each with respect to all other living things, insofar as it will produce both seeds and fruits.

11b. *And it was so.*

This phrase appears six times altogether in the first chapter.

In three of these occurrences the phrase *and it was so* unambiguously appears prior to the coming to be of the object to which it refers (Verses 11, 15, 24). In two cases the order is ambiguous or the question does not apply (Verses 9 and 30). In only one case (Verse 7) the phrase unambiguously occurs after the coming to be of the object. These words then cannot mean anything like *and it was in deed as it had been in speech*; they cannot refer to the actual existence of the object. The original meaning of the word translated to *be so* is to arrange or direct. To be so can only mean something like *having a clear and definite way in which to be.* The sense of this expression is perhaps caught in the English expression *he likes everything to be just so.* The word so comes from the Hebrew root *koon,* which means *to be prepared,* or *ready* and *fixed,* or *secure* and *firmly established.*

God has not yet established the existence of the thing but merely the direct path in which it is to go. The words *and it was so* mean that God has established a clearly defined place for the object in this world. Man, however, will not be said to be *so,* for reasons which are related to what medieval theology will call freedom of the will.

12. *And the earth sent forth grass, seed-bearing plants according to its kind, and trees making fruit with its seed in it: and God saw that it was good.*

The phrase *that it was good* occurs on each of the six days, with the exception of day two, and on days three and six it occurs twice. If for the moment we disregard the final occurrence on day six, since it refers to the work of the whole, it appears as though the missing statements from day two were merely deferred to the middle of day three. In order to understand this, we must consider the general plan for Creation as a whole. On day one light was called into being; on day two the sky was made and the water divided. The third day was devoted to the appearance of dry land together with the production of the plants. On day four the sun, moon, and stars will be made, and on the fifth day the denizens of the sky and the water will come to be, while day six is given to the land-dwelling beings, including man. Perhaps this can be better seen in the form of a chart.

day 1	light	day 4	lights
day 2	sky and water	day 5	birds and fish
day 3	dry land including plants	day 6	land animals including man

Each of the last three days is devoted to the manifestly moving beings which inhabit the places made on the corresponding first three days.

In addition to this general plan which relates the first three days to the last three days, there is a general transition from simple motion to motion of a more complicated character. Enough has been seen so far concerning the order of Creation to reach some answer to our original problem of why the words *and it was good* had to be deferred from the second day to the middle of the third day. Simple and elegant as the above plan is, not even God was capable of completing the seas before making the dry land, since the limits of the sea are the same as the limits of the land. Unlike many mythological accounts, the author does not imply any great and tragic necessity against which God must struggle. The difficulty is nothing more than a simple problem of topology. However, it is a problem which even God Himself must face, and the plan cannot be fulfilled in its simple and most immediate sense. But in spite of the momentary disruption when the sea was finally finished, God Himself said that it was good.

Here again we see that God was willing to accept a compromise, but nothing appeared to Him as *good* until it was completed. In this sense, the word *good* does not mean the highest imaginable, but the actual completion of the highest possible.

13. *And there was evening and there was morning, a third day.*

14. *And God said, Let there be lights in the expanse of the sky to divide day from night: they shall serve as signs for the set times, the days and the years.*

15. *Let them be as lights in the expanse of the sky to shine upon the earth: and it was so.*
Obviously the greatest difficulty with this verse is to understand how there could be light on the first day although the sun and the moon had not been made until the fourth day. Part of the reason for this is, of course, revealed in the general plan for Creation indicated in the chart.

Sun and moon are not presented as being the sole sources of light. Since they were created even after the coming to be of the plant world, they are not the source of those great gifts for which they are praised and deified by other nations. The stars, far from being gods whom we serve, are reduced to servants who tell us the seasons of the year.

16. *God made the two great lights, the greater light to rule the day and the lesser light to rule the night and the stars.*

17. *And God set them in the expanse of the sky to give light upon the earth.*

18. *To rule the day and the night and to divide light from darkness: and God saw that it was good.*

19. *And there was evening and there was morning. A fourth day.*

As we remember, in the first verse both sky and earth were mentioned. In the second verse, the author picked up the account of the earth while dropping the notion of sky altogether. If the early chapters of Genesis are compared either with paganism or with later developments in Judaism or Christianity, it can be seen that the sky or heaven played a much less significant role. God is often called the God, or Possessor, of heaven and earth, but there is never any indication that heaven is more particularly His (Gen. 14:17, 22; also 24:3). To be sure, God is often spoken of as *going down*, but the word *heaven* is never used in these passages. The sky is often associated with God in the sense of the place from which He can send destructive rain (Gen. 7:11 and 19:25) as well as the source of necessary moisture (Gen. 27:28, 39).

On the other hand, the heavens are the unambiguous home of the angels (Gen. 21:17, 22:11, 17). As we shall see, the stars of the heavens will form one image of the blessing which God is to give to Abraham. Although it is intended to be a higher blessing than its corollary, the dust of the earth, still there is no indication that it is to be understood as related to the Divine in any particular way. God is never especially associated with heaven until Chapter 28, in which Jacob's dream appears.

This deemphasis of the heavenly bodies seems also to be implied by the fact that they are merely called *the two great lights*, rather than being given their proper names—the sun and the moon. On the other hand, the notion of ruling which arises in Verse 16 seems to be somewhat out of place, for nothing had been mentioned of that in God's original plan as stated in Verses 14 and 15; ruling appears as a kind of afterthought.

Kingship came to man in a similar way. Samuel's sons grew corrupt, and the people, failing to understand that all things were liable to corruption, demanded a king. Samuel was displeased. In his eyes, God was the only king that Israel needed. But the Lord spoke to Samuel: Hearken unto the voice of the people in all they say unto thee: for they have not rejected thee, but have rejected me that I should not reign over them (I Sam. 8:7).

Partly because of this demand, and partly because the occurrences in the Book of Judges proved that Israel was incapable of living without a human king, God was willing to acquiesce to human demand. That is not to say that the people were allowed to follow their own course. God both appointed the king and laid down many stipulations concerning his rule, but, as will prove critical for our understanding of Genesis as a whole, the original notion of kingship was of purely human origin. Kingship, too, was a compromise between divine aspirations and human needs.

This interpretation of the origins of kingship is primarily due to the fifteenth-century commentator, Don Isaac Abrabanel,[1] and it will continue to play a major role in our understanding of the motion of the book of Genesis as a whole.

Neither sun nor moon was originally created as ruler, but their preeminence seems to have forced rule upon them. One need only think of the story of the Garden of Eden to see that law imposed from the outside was not part of God's original plan. The development of an alternative plan will form the major subject of the present commentary, and the plan, as it is developed, will be called *the new way*. In a certain sense, the first eleven chapters of Genesis are a cosmic counterpart to the Book of Judges. Their purpose is to explain the need for law by exploring a world which might have been better if it had been complete, but which did not take into account human needs. This latter reflection, which culminates in the notion of law, is necessarily an afterthought, since human needs can only become intelligible in terms of that which would have been the highest, had those needs not existed.

After the death of Joshua, each tribe went its own way. At that point God envisaged a loosely connected league of tribes. However, the stories recounted in the Book of Judges show the progressive degeneration of that dream. At the end of the book, kingship becomes inevitable. Nonetheless, kingship itself cannot be understood if it is not seen as a necessary replacement for that original dream.

20. *God said, Let the water swarm swarms of living souls, and flying fowl upon the face of the expanse of the sky.*

Here again we note the use of the cognate accusative *swarm swarms*, and again there is a reference to such a construction in the words *flying fowl*, more literally *flying fliers*. This time one can see what is meant. We can almost see the churning waters filling themselves with fish that remain an integral part of the whirlpool. The only other places in the whole of the Bible that the word *swarm* is used as a transitive verb are Exodus 8:28 and Psalms 105:30, both of which concern the plagues in Egypt. In Exodus God says, *And the rivers shall swarm forth frogs*, and the passage from Psalms is a reference to the same incident. Only in that strange land of Egypt, which was noted for its magicians, could such a form of genesis actually occur, but the present account of the beginning is more sober; and though we can imagine such generation, it cannot take place in fact. The very next verse says that *God created*, etc. Water is not the kind of thing which can produce fish. Although God's attempt to share the activity of Creation with other beings failed, He was both willing and able to make up for the deficiency by merely creating them Himself.

21. *God created the great sea monster and all the living souls that creep which the waters (were to have) swarmed forth, and all flying fowl according to its kind: and God saw that it was good.*

In general, this account of the visible universe is distinguished from both pagan mythology and modern science by the fact that it speaks only in terms of objects which all of us can see any day of our lives.

Both myth and science consider everyday experience to be lacking intelligibility in its own terms. Most of us are able to get along in the world by ignoring about fifty percent of it and concentrating on those things which fall into place. Neither the poets nor the scientists can live in such a world.

The poets wish to extend the limits of our understanding of even the commonplace by showing us a world beyond our lives. They take us to Byzantium, and scientists take us into laboratories. In either case a world without giants or magnetic waves is a world which we cannot fully understand. For the author of Genesis, the sufficiency of an account which speaks only about the things we see every day can be maintained by having its source in an intelligent maker. The great sea monster seems to be the one exception. Throughout Eastern mythical traditions, there were stories and reports of monsters, many of which played great roles in their accounts of the origins of the visible universe. While this role is implicitly denied in the present text, their existence is never questioned. If there were stories and reports from sailors that the great ocean was inhabited by monsters, then perhaps they, too, are part of the visible universe, but from the point of view of the author they must be regarded as just another one of God's creations and of no particular significance.

22. *And God blessed them saying, be fruitful and multiply. Fill the waters of the seas and let the fowl multiply upon the land.*

23. *And there was evening and there was morning, a fifth day.*

On the fifth day, a completely new vocabulary was introduced. For the first time a particular being was said to be *created* rather than made (Verse 21). In Verse 22 the denizens of the sea, unlike any other thing thus far brought into being, received a blessing. However, for the first time the words and *it was so* will not appear in the text.

On the first half of the sixth day things will return to normal. The animals will be said to be *so*. They will be made, not created, and they will not receive a blessing. The only other being which will specifically be said to be created will be man. Man will also receive a blessing, and man, too, will not be said to be *so*. How is this kinship to be understood? The denizens of the seas indeed live a kind of watery existence. They neither follow the ecliptic as does the sun nor are they restricted in the direction of their motion as are the other animals, and hence they are not said to be *so*. Man shares this openness of direction with the fish. The way was not marked out for him in the beginning. It had to develop, and even then he was apt to wander from his path. Since man could err, he too required a blessing.

24. *And God said, Let the earth send forth living souls according to its kind, cattle, creeping things, and wild beasts of every kind: and it was so.*
   This is the second time that God has asked the earth to participate in His work. However, this time God does not use the cognate accusative. In fact, He uses the very words *send forth* which were used to describe the earth's response in Verse 12. God has officially recognized that the world is incapable of the original type of unity which was demanded in the beginning. The second plan follows the exact course which the earth itself chose in Verse 12. Since the earth showed itself capable of bringing forth plants, the present plan calls for it to bring forth the animals.

25. *And God made the living things of the earth according to its kind and the beast according to its kind and all the creeping things of the soil according to its kind: and God saw that it was good.*
   This time, the earth is completely incapable of doing anything, and God again obligingly does it Himself. The Bible gives no indication as to how it was done, but apparently there were no grave difficulties. On the other hand, it does not seem to be the case that mere speech was sufficient.
   Up to this point in the text, we have seen a motion from the best to the best possible, and thus far the author has spoken only about the world around us as it had been before man came into it. From now on, we shall see the same search going on for man. That quest will occupy most of our time, but the author turned first to the world to show us that the fundamental difficulties are to be found there as well. The real problem is not whether God is omnipotent or even whether He created the world *ex nihilo*. The real problem is whether all of man's sufferings are due to his own guilt. Many in fact are, and only by his awareness of that can man be encouraged to overcome them. But there are times when it is of even greater importance to know that suffering is part of the world.
   Man's inability to live according to God's original plan may have been no more man's fault than it was the earth's fault that she could *not grass grass or bring forth animals*. While we shall be primarily interested in developing a way for man, it was important to the author to show that man was not the first to depart from the words of God. The earth did its best and cannot be

called a sinner. But these early verses indicate that the most fundamental difficulties lie not in the heart of man, but in the heart of being.

Within rabbinical circles, it was traditional to distinguish between the simple meaning of a text and its deeper sense. In these passages we can see what there was in the text which led them to make such a distinction. In their terms, one would be justified in saying that according to the simple meaning of the text the world was created perfect.

Man was given a pristine world in which to live, and he alone is responsible for its ills. As we have seen, lying not too deep under the surface is another story. Within the context of everyday human life, there is something true about the superficial story. It leads men to take seriously their position and preserves for them the sense of an immediate goal. At the same time, the author felt that it was important to preserve the deeper account and to be as explicit about it as he could, because ofttimes when men suffer the causes are in the world, and nothing is gained by placing upon them the additional burden of guilt.

26. *And God said, Let us make man in our own image after our own likeness; let them have dominion over the fish of the sea, the birds of the sky, the beast and all the creeping things that creepeth upon the earth.*

27. *And God created man in His own image, in the image of God He created him; male and female he created them.*

The question of what is meant by the image of God has been dealt with by so many authors and preachers that further speculation in this commentary would add little. The verse almost seems to be intentionally ambiguous, as if the author did not wish to commit himself finally and ultimately as to the sense in which man is in the image of God. Nonetheless some aspects of the problem can be clarified.

The Hebrew word for *God* is plural from a morphological point of view, even though it is normally accompanied by a verb in the singular. Here, however, the author chose to use a plural verb. A similar difficulty arises in the case of His *image* in the present verse. The object of His creation is first described as *him* and then as *them*. These two difficulties are ultimately identical. The image of God appears in two different forms—a male and a female—though both are said to be in the image of God. And yet, from the first part of Verse 27, it appears as though God created only one thing. Both difficulties would be solved if there were a certain limited kind of duality in God Himself, at least sufficient duality to allow for the possibility of two separate images. What does this mean?

In order to understand this verse, we must consider the alternatives to Biblical thought. When the Bible speaks of paganism it usually treats it as foolish and vain. Men worship sticks and stones. They carry those gods which should by rights be carrying them. However, it would be foolish on our part to assume that this reticence necessarily implies that the author was unaware of the deeper significance of paganism.

He was faced with a grave difficulty. He could not praise paganism, and yet in some sense he had to speak to those who were aware of its deeper significance.

Certainly one of the most forceful arguments opposing the new religion and favoring paganism was the notion that generation requires duality. A god cannot beget a world without a goddess of some form or other. Monotheism in its strictest sense denies what would seem to be a fundamental truth. However, the fact that both male and female are in God's image implies that there is nothing missing in God which would be required for bringing the world into being. On the other hand, the author seems to face the fact that this does imply a limited form of duality.

28. *God blessed them and said to them, be fruitful and multiply; fill the earth and master it; have dominion over the fish of the sea and the fowl of the sky and all the living things that creepeth on the earth.*

The phrase which is translated *have dominion over* is difficult to understand. It often has a harsh meaning and is somewhat different from the word used to describe the relation between the sun and the day in Verse 16. The word is probably meant to emphasize the sense in which man was intended not only as the pinnacle of Creation but also as that for the sake of which Creation took place. As we shall see in Chapter 2, this is understood by the author of Genesis to be only a partial view of man's relation to the universe, and one which is deeply in need of correction.

29. *And God said, Behold I have provided you with all seed-bearing plants which are on the face of all the earth and every tree which has seed-bearing fruit; to you have I given it as food.*

30. *And to every living being of the earth and to everything that creepeth upon the earth which has a living soul in it, I have given every green herb as food: and it was so.*

As in Verse 14, the unity of Creation is again stressed. The plants exist for the sake of providing for man and the animals. But man's domination over the animal world does not extend to the possibility of being carnivorous. Since the animals will be admitted as food later, the full impact of man's relation to the animal kingdom in this early stage must be understood in the light of the conditions under which the eating of meat will become admissible. A further discussion on this subject will be found in the commentary to Gen. 9:4.[2]

31. *And God saw all that He made and behold it was very good. There was evening and there was morning, the sixth day.*

The whole is said to be *very good* in spite of the fact that it is never specifically mentioned that man himself is good. Perhaps it is implied that a whole in which there is one being whose way is open, and to that extent unknown, is better than a world in which all the inhabitants are known to be good.

NOTES

From Robert D. Sacks, *Commentary on the Book of Genesis* (Lewiston, N.Y.: Edwin Mellen, 1990). Originally in *Interpretation: A Journal of Political Philosophy* 8 (1979–80): 31–47.

1. For an English translation of the relevant parts of Abrabanel's commentary, see *Medieval Political Philosophy: A Source Book*, ed. Ralph Lerner and Muhsin Mahdi (Glencoe, Ill.: The Free Press, 1963), 255–57.

2. Sacks, *Commentary on the Book of Genesis*, 66. [Cf. Leon R. Kass, "Sanctified Eating: A Memorial of Creation," reprinted in this volume, 384–409.]

II

THE ETHICAL QUESTION

9

Our Covenant with Stones:
A Jewish Ecology of Earth

Bradley Shavit Artson

> You will have a covenant
> with the rocks in the field.[1]

Environmentalism heralds a fresh conception of the individual and society in relation to the natural order, offering a new understanding of what it means to be human.[2] Such a general reevaluation of the human condition elicits a Jewish response, in this instance evidenced by articles on Judaism and the environment.[3] Rabbis and scholars of various perspectives who grapple with this popular movement strain Jewish writings through the standards of the Green perspective to argue the relevance of Jewish tradition. Consciously written to refute charges that Judaism (or the "Judeo-Christian heritage") is the source of the problem,[4] many of these essays are insightful, but most are episodic.[5]

The preponderance of these efforts assume that judgment ought to reflect the standards of the environmental movement rather than an internal Jewish assessment of how our tradition and our God would have us relate to the world. In fact, such an evaluation should emerge organically from the categories of Jewish civilization and its writings, rather than from any wholesale adoption of contemporary environmentalism's standards. In practical terms, this apologetic effort has compiled a growing list of Jewish quotations which—removed from their original context or perspective—fit the established categories of environmentalism. Ruptured is the organic Jewish relationship between Biblical verses and Rabbinic wisdom. The pillaged loot gathers dust in the storehouse of ecology.[6]

Such an approach may have been a necessary first step toward alerting Jews to the questions and criticisms raised by environmentalists. But the

161

price we pay for that endeavor is a contextless collage of Rabbinic and Biblical sayings, avoiding the more comprehensive consideration of how Jewish tradition might respond to the larger question of living responsibly with nature, not to a specific political agenda.[7] Such a procedure has an additional flaw: it concedes objective truth and universal morality to environmentalism when that movement simply embodies another particular perspective from which to examine the human condition.

We need a second stage, one which explores helpful conceptions of the Earth and humanity from within the context established by Jewish thought and writings. Although our tradition may say little directly about air pollution[8] or about the polar ice caps, it does dwell at great length on how Jews are to live with the soil, on the sanctity of the Earth and its produce, the holiness of one particular place (*Eretz Yisrael*), and on particular times (*Shabbat, Yovel,* and the *Shemittah*). Perhaps if we begin with intrinsically Jewish categories we might construct a Jewish ecology, enriching the traditional structure of Judaism with a consciousness of environmental issues rather than simply tailoring Jewish religion to fit within the procrustean bed of a dismembered ecological Judaism.

TERRITORY WITHOUT MAP: THE SANCTITY OF THE SOIL

Jewish tradition is especially rich in its attention to the sanctity of the Land, of Israel (*kedushat ha-aretz*).[9] Since the topic of human relationships with the Earth is also a central concern of environmental movements, this subject might provide a useful model, allowing us to trace the contours of a central value concept within Jewish religion while subsequently seeking more practical application.

Attention to the earth as a place of religious meaning pervades the Hebrew Bible (*Tanakh*).[10] The Creation narratives focus attention on the importance of the Earth, to the extent that the term itself (*adamah*) lends its name to the ultimate earthling (*Adam*).[11] The theme of creation, emphasizing God's sovereignty over the entire planet, repeats itself in several prophetic passages as well. Isaiah urges his audience to

> Lift high your eyes and see:
> Who created these?
> He who sends out their host by count,
> Who calls them each by name.
> Because of His great might and vast power,
> Not one fails to appear.[12]

Moses, standing before the burning bush on Horeb, receives the command to "remove your sandals from your feet, for the place on which you stand is holy ground."[13] The same ideology which portrays God as Creator of the heavens and the Earth also establishes a link between all lands and God. Perhaps this appreciation of the entire planet as the creation of the loving God also contributes to the venerable Israelite tradition extolling the wilderness as a place of holiness and purity.[14] As the source of all places, God's sanctity must somehow touch every place.

Yet there is a dichotomy at the core of the Biblical understanding of the sanctity of soil. The whole world may be sacred, but one particular part of it boasts a special degree of holiness. While Israelites can observe their laws anywhere,[15] there is an uncleanness which permeates the nations of the world. Thus Hosea speaks of the Israelites who "shall eat unclean food in Assyria"[16] and Amos portrays the "unclean soil" to which Israel will be banished.[17] The Land of Israel is clearly the focus of the Hebrew Bible's passion for land.

Repeatedly, the Torah describes the Land of Israel as "a good land,"[18] one whose bounty reflects God's beneficence, not the result of any merit or labor on Israel's part.[19] The sanctity of *Eretz Yisrael* overrides the sanctity of all other places; it is only in ancient, preconquest times "that a site outside the Promised Land can be described as holy."[20] So sacred is the land that Jews may offer sacrifices only there, and only there is food considered ritually clean. Throughout the Tanakh, the Land represents both promise *and* goal; Israel observes the mitzvot in order to merit the Land.

Paradoxically, God's sovereignty over the Land of Israel emerges from the creation story itself. God made everything. Therefore, all lands, Israel included, belong to God.[21] In the Book of Leviticus, that reasoning provides the base for God's inalienable ownership of the Land:

> The Land must not be sold beyond reclaim, for the land is Mine; you are but strangers resident with Me. Throughout the land that you hold you must provide for the redemption of the Land.[22]

God's ownership of the Earth is total, and the selection of Israel is a Divine prerogative.

The distinction of the Land of Israel is but one consequence of God's role as creator. Obeying or violating God's will entail immediate consequences for continued existence and well-being on the Land. A series of agricultural laws—*peah,*[23] *orlah,*[24] *kilayim,*[25] *terumot,*[26] *and bikkurim*[27]—provides repeated evidence of God's ownership of the Land of Israel. That the human farmer is only a tenant undergirds all of these requirements—of abstention, of Temple donation, or of provision for the poor. The ultimate proprietor is God alone. In the words of the Talmud, "God acquired possession of the world and apportioned it to humanity, but God always remains the master of the world."[28]

The consequences of violating God's will also link *Eretz Yisrael* to the rest of the Earth. Many passages warn that expulsion from the Land is the price of scorning the *mitzvot*.[29] Its soil is no passive piece of property; it is living and responsive, and there is a dynamic between the People Israel and their Land. Acts of hostility toward God result in acts of hostility toward the actors themselves. The Earth is not only a witness to the covenant (*brit*)[30] but a participant in the unfolding drama of righteousness, chastisement, and rebuke. Other nations, as well as the Land of Israel, share that involvement:

> The earth is withered, sear;
> The world languishes, it is sear;
> The most exalted people of the earth languish.
> For the earth was defiled under its inhabitants;
> Because they transgressed teachings,
> Violated laws, broke the ancient covenant.[31]

The biblical view of the world is not distant or objective; it demands immediate involvement and consequence.[32] That

> observance and non-observance of the commandments have geographic, territorial and cosmic consequences points to the truth that ecology is indissoluble from morality, land and law being mutually dependent, and that a people is ultimately responsible for the maintenance of its "place."[33]

In short, the Biblical conception of the relationship between the People Israel (*Am Yisrael*) and the Land of Israel (*Eretz Yisrael*) is one of covenant (*brit*).

Rabbinic law and legend also begin with the centrality of *Eretz Yisrael*. In the words of Mishnah *Kelim*: "The Land of Israel is holier than all [other] lands."[34] Far more than in Scripture, large sections of the Mishnah are devoted to the agricultural laws of tithing,[35] which are obligatory only within the Land (with the exception of *kilayim, orlah,* and, according to Rabbi Eliezer, eating barley before the *omer*).[36] Further, the purity system is fully applicable only within the Land.[37] Consequently, the impurity of the other lands—a notion which has roots in the Hebrew Bible—continues into Rabbinic thought as well.[38]

Often, the Mishnah postulates the overlap of the People (*Am Yisrael*) and the Land (*Eretz Yisrael*), the two primary concentrations of holiness. Even within the Tannaitic period, however, the existence of significant Jewish populations in Syria, Egypt, and Babylonia required some adjustments to the notion of a single holy Land. Although the People Israel in the Land of Israel (*am yisrael be-eretz yisrael*) remains the ideal, a growing number of cases require distinctions previously unnecessary in Biblical thought. For example, Gentiles living in the Land are exempt from the requirements of *shevi'it, challah,* and *terumah*.[39] This adjustment reflects a new reality, that "Mishnah's Rabbis clearly wish to do justice to both principles—both Holy Land and Holy People—without fully embracing the one over the other."[40]

A similar readjustment is reflected in a dispute between two *tannaim* over whether or not produce exported from the Land of Israel requires the taking of *challah*. Rabbi Eliezer insists that it does, implying a single source of holiness emanating from Zion. Rabbi Akiva, however, postulates a conception of multiple holiness by ruling that such produce is exempt. For Rabbi Akiva,

> the entire world potentially is sacred space. Different areas are subject to different standards, different rules. People in the land and outside the land alike have their own special roles to play.
>
> Quite clearly later Rabbinic traditions follow Akiva's lead, enlarging the scope of the investigation of what the individual's roles should be, in different places, but especially outside the Land, and at different times. The goal is perception of everyday life as participation in a sacred realm of ultimate significance.[41]

Reiterating the sanctity of other lands exercises a profound effect on Rabbinic Judaism, reinforcing the portable holiness which Jews take with them wherever they dwell. That recognition of the sanctity of land beyond *Eretz Yisrael* provides for halakhic accommodation of Jewish settlements in Syria[42] as well as one prominent opinion prohibiting aliyah from Babylonia to Israel:

> Whoever goes up from Babylonia to the Land of Israel transgresses an imperative commandment, for it is said in Scriptures, "They shall be carried to Babylonia, and there they shall be, until the day that I remember them, says the Lord."[43]

Rabbi Yehudah even goes so far as to equate living in Babylonia with living in Israel.[44]

These views reflect a specific Rabbinic agenda: to align Jewish religion to the reality of Jewish settlement beyond the borders of the Land of Israel. Without ever abandoning their commitment to the mitzvah of settling the Land (*yishuv ha-aretz*), the Sages transferred their ideal from living on the land to observing the law.[45] Whereas the Torah esteems living in Israel as the goal of pious observance, the Rabbis invert that estimation; they cherish living on the Land *because* it allows for greater observance. Here the Land does not embody the goal; the Land becomes the means:

> Rabbi Simlai expounded, "Why did Moses, our Rabbi, yearn to enter the Land of Israel? Did he want to eat of its fruit or satisfy himself from its bounty? But thus spoke Moses, 'Many commandments were commanded to Israel which can be fulfilled only in the Land of Israel. I wish to enter the Land so they may all be fulfilled by me.'"[46]

The re-estimation of *yishuv* maintains the centrality of the Land (since certain *mitzvot* can be fulfilled only there), but shifts the weight of Jewish piety to the observance of deeds which can be performed anywhere.[47] The liturgy of the seasons reflects this alteration, emphasizing the needs of Babylonia and concentrating the attention of other Jewish communities on their rhythm as a distinctly religious concern.[48] The calendar—long a source of contention between the Sages of Israel and those of Babylonia—presents a similar struggle, with authority ultimately taken by the Ge'onim of Babylonia.[49] Perhaps as early as the canonization of the Torah in the Second Temple Period, but certainly following the destruction of the Temple and the rise of the Synagogue, Rabbinic Judaism adopted an attitude of provisional portability: a willingness to roam the world until the messianic age restores the nexus between Land and People:

> What the Mishnah does by presenting this cult, laying out its measurements, describing its rite, and specifying its rules, is to permit Israel, in the words of the Mishnah, to experience anywhere and anytime that cosmic center of the world described by the Mishnah: cosmic center in words made utopia.[50]

THE EARTH IS THE LORD'S: BLESSINGS FOR FOOD

This dual geography of holiness becomes clear with the example of the blessings recited before eating different types of food (*birkhot ha-nehenin*).[51]

Understanding the significance of specific *berakhot* requires a moment's reflection on the social importance of structure and of categorization. Meaning is not intrinsic; it is conferred by the people involved. A ritual, for example, reveals little about the role that ritual plays in the life of those engaged in it, unless the words and intentions of the participants of the rite are also available. While investigating meaning, "the thing to ask is not what their ontological status is. . . . The thing to ask is what their import is: what it is . . . that in their occurrence and through their agency, is getting said."[52]

One key to ritual, as with other social rites, is what it can reveal about a context of understanding, how the worshipers construe the world around them and their place in it.

Ritual not only reveals structures of perception and purpose. It also helps to shape that purpose: "Ritual did not merely encode ideas that could be expressed otherwise; rather, it created the essential categories of human thought."[53] When a recitation or symbolic action express a value concept, that performance not only articulates a specific way of seeing the world; it also shapes and reinforces that vision. In our case, an examination of Rabbinic blessings for food reveals the effort to recognize the sanctity of the entire planet, to ground that holiness in God's ownership, and to maintain the special status of the Land of Israel.

The Biblical command to praise God for food specifies that this obligation applies only within the Land of Israel: "For the Lord your God is bringing you into a good land . . . a land where you may eat food without stint. . . . When you have eaten your fill, give thanks to the Lord your God for the good land which He has given you."[54] There is no reported Biblical implementation, but the clear assumption behind this instruction is that the Land of Israel is uniquely holy, and that the landedness of the Jews rightly elicits a unique gratitude. Food grown in God's land requires a means to transfer ownership from God to humanity. Blessings, in this understanding, represent a delivery system by which food in its naturally sanctified state of nature is removed from that natural habitat not only physically but conceptually, so that it may be transformed for use by ordinary human beings.[55]

To eat without blessing, according to the Rabbis, is not only theft. It represents a desecration of the Temple-based system of purity and holiness:

> Our Rabbis taught: It is forbidden to enjoy anything of this world without a *berakhah*, and whoever enjoys anything of this world without a *berakhah* commits sacrilege (*ma'al*). Rav Judah said in the name of Samuel: To enjoy anything of this word without a *berakhah* is like making personal use of things consecrated to heaven.[56]

The Rabbis' assumption that blessings are appropriate both in and out of the Land should be noted from the outset. They place no limitation on the location of the meal or the source of the produce to be consumed. The Torah prescribes gratitude to God as Sovereign of Israel; the Rabbis extend that response to the world:

> It is written: "The earth is the Lord's and the fullness thereof" (Psalm 24:1), [yet] "He has given the earth to human beings" (Psalm 115:16). There is no contradiction. The first verse reflects the situation before we say a blessing, whereas the second verse applies after the blessing has been said.[57]

Characteristic of their ability to mediate a complex agenda, the Rabbis also reinforce the notion of the Land's sanctity (*kedushat ha-aretz*) through the insertion of specific *berakhot* in the blessings after meals, including *birkat ha mazon* and *berakhah achat mei-ein shalosh*, both of which distinguish between produce characteristic of the Land and all other produce. Yet the actual source of the grains, fruit, or vegetables is now irrelevant. What counts is that their species grows in *Eretz Yisrael*.

In at least one other significant way, the series of blessings over food sanctifies the entire Earth. The central organizing category which distinguishes which type of *berakhah* to recite is whether (and, if so, how) food emerges from the soil. Once the produce is identified as a type of fruit (*peri*), further distinctions arise: Does the food emerge from the Earth directly or does it grow on a vine or a tree? Other possible categorizations seem not to matter. "Over something which does not grow from the Earth, one says *sheh-hakol*."[58]

There is no necessary or intrinsic reason to worry about the nuances of distinct agricultural products while lumping together fish, meat and poultry. By establishing the categories of *berakhot* the way they did, the Rabbis lent significance to the soil, to what emerges from the ground, and to the sanctity of all ground everywhere. The categories of the *berakhot* themselves valorize the Earth as a sacred and sustaining presence. "[B]lessings achieve the primal function of freeing that produce from its sacred state."[59] They also enforce the insight that a sacred place is anywhere that life can thrive, that a sacred time is anytime Jews gather to eat and to pray.

APPLICATION AND CONCLUSION

Only after such consideration are we in a position to utilize one Jewish category to address the issues raised by the environmental movement. Starting from within Judaism, a religious path becomes both possibility and pathway.

First, the Hebrew Bible asserts that a place is instrinsically holy, constituting the prime reward for good living (in this case, for mitzvah observance). The Rabbis presume that a place is made holy by the righteousness and piety of its inhabitants. The Land, in their view, is a necessary prerequisite for observance. People can soil the Earth.

Second, humanity relates to soil in relationship. Our planet is not a mute "fact," suitable only for measurement, testing, and objectification. Rather, a full human relationship to the world is one in which the Earth is loved and cultivated, a partner with Jews and all other people in the service of God, creation, and human life. There is a dynamism to human-planetary interactions: our behavior allows the Earth to fulfill its covenantal relationship, and our planet, in turn, provides humanity with further grounds for gratitude to God. The Earth is both witness and participant in our sacred covenant (*brit*).

Third, the early Rabbis, perhaps building on the precedent established in Second Temple times, strive to articulate a notion of holiness which includes not only *Eretz Yisrael* but the rest of the world as well. Through focusing the *berakhot* for food on *peirot* and their subcategories, by adding liturgical petitions on behalf of the weather outside the Land of Israel, by providing for multiple models of land-sanctity, the Mishnah and the Talmud maintain a claim for the holiness of the whole earth, without relinquishing a special Jewish estimation for Israel itself. "Israel living in its Land has consequences for the entire world. When Israel lives in its Land, the entire earth can become sacred space."[60]

As Jews, our loyalty begins with *Eretz Yisrael*. But we are not only Jews. As human beings, we also owe fealty and love to the entire planet, as well as to that corner of it which is home. The path of the Bible and early Rabbinic tradition is one of expanding concentric circles, broadening the notion of holiness into a provisional portability that permits a relationship with the sacred anywhere and anytime. That same schema sanctifies all the earth, summoning us, as Jews and as humans, to a relationship of love and piety with our beleaguered planet.

The Earth can either be our partner in the service of God, or our prosecutor, testifying before the Holy One about our pettiness, self-interest, and shortsightedness. We can make of this planet a place where God's presence can comfortably dwell, so that the whole world becomes a sanctuary. Or we can render life on the earth impossible, sundering our relationship with the soil and our covenant with God. As always, we face a choice.

NOTES

From *Conservative Judaism* 44 (1991–92): 25–35.
I want to express my gratitude to Rabbi Elie Spitz for his helpful critique, and to Dr. David Kraemer, Associate Professor of Talmud and Rabbinics at the Jewish Theological Seminary, for his generous gifts of time and insight in discussing this issue with me. My debt to Max Kadushin, ז״ל, is readily apparent throughout this paper. Any errors are exclusively my own.

1. Job 5:23. All Biblical quotations are from *Tanakh: A New Translation of the Holy Scriptures* (Philadelphia: Jewish Publication Society, 1985).

2. For a lovely example of this broad approach, see "The Global Environmental Crisis," by Jeremy Rifkin in *The Green Lifestyle Handbook*, ed. Jeremy Rifkin (New York: Henry Holt & Company, 1990).

3. Many are assembled in *Judaism and Ecology, 1970–1986: A Sourcebook of Readings*, ed. Marc Swetlitz (Wyncote, Pa.: Shomrei Adamah, 1990).

4. For examples, see Ake Hultkrantz, "Ecology," *Encyclopedia of Religion*, vol. 10, 581; and Lynn White, "The Historical Roots of our Ecological Crisis," *Science* 155 (10 March 1967): 1203–1207.

5. The lone exceptions to this sporadic quality are Richard Schwartz, *Judaism and Global Survival* (New York: Atara, 1987), and *Judaism and Vegetarianism* (New York: Micah, 1988).

6. This same phenomenon, of framing external categories into which Jewish quotations or discussions are then made to fit, is the subject of heated debate within the study of religion generally. See, for example, the critique offered by E. P. Sanders, *Paul and Palestinian Judaism: A Comparison of Patterns of Religion* (Philadelphia: Fortress Press, 1977), especially the introduction, "The Holistic Comparison of Patterns of Religion." For a related critique, see also "In Comparison A Magic Dwells," in Jonathan Z. Smith, *Imagining Religion: From Babylon to Jonestown* (Chicago: University of Chicago Press, 1982). While both offer mutually exclusive approaches, they agree that removing an idea, term, or value from its context intrinsically distorts.

7. For a similar critique, applied in another area, see Jakob J. Petuchowski, "The Limits of Self-Sacrifice," in *Modern Jewish Ethics: Theory and Practice*, ed. Marvin Fox (Columbus, Ohio: Ohio State University Press, 1975).

8. Solitary passages from the Babylonian Talmud, such as *Bava Metzia* 101a restricting which types of wood may be burned on the altar to avoid excessive smoke, and *Tamid* 29b stating that smoke and the odor of a toilet are always undesired intrusions, are not sufficient to establish a Rabbinic ethic of air pollution. For an insightful discussion of this jurisprudential issue from the perspective of Jewish ethics

generally, see Daniel H. Gordis, "Significance Through Symbol: Redefining Authority in Jewish Law," *University Papers* (Los Angeles: University of Judaism, 1986).

9. For an extensive discussion of the importance of place and the sanctity of a specific location in Judaism, see Jonathan Z. Smith, *To Take Place: Toward Theory in Ritual* (Chicago: The University of Chicago Press, 1987).

10. See T. H. Gaster, "Earth," *Interpreter's Dictionary of the Bible* [henceforth *IDB*] (Nashville: Abingdon Press, 1962), 2:2–3.

11. Midrash Ha-Gadol *Bereshith*, and E. A. Speiser, *The Anchor Bible: Genesis* (New York: Doubleday & Company, Inc., 1982), 16, n. 5.

12. Isa. 40:26. See also Amos 5:8, Ps. 19:2, 24:1, and 105:44–45.

13. Ex. 3:5.

14. See S. Talmon, "Wilderness," *IDB Supplement* (Nashville: Abingdon Press, 1984), 946–48; and Ex. 4:22f., 33:12, Deut. 27:9, I Kings 19:4–8, Hos. 2:14–15, Jer. 2:1, 31:2f.

15. Ps. 105:44–45.

16. Hos. 9:3. See also Ezek. 4:13

17. Amos 7:17. See also Isa. 52:11.

18. E.g., Deut. 8:7–8.

19. E.g., Josh. 24:13.

20. Harry Orlinsky, "The Biblical Concept of the Land of Israel," in *The Land of Israel: Jewish Perspectives*, ed. Lawrence A. Hoffman (Notre Dame: University of Notre Dame Press, 1986), 53. This observation was made in the Mekhilta *Pischa* 1: "Before the Land had been especially chosen, all lands were suitable for divine revelation; after the Land had been chosen, all other lands were eliminated."

21. Rashi understood this paradox and comments on it. See his first comment to Gen. 1:1, on "*Bereshith.*"

22. Lev. 25 :23–24. This reasoning is made explicit in the Talmud (*Sanhedrin* 39a): "The Holy Blessed One said to the children of Israel, 'Sow for six years and leave the Land at rest for the seventh year, so that you may know the Land is Mine.'"

23. Lev. 19:9, Deut. 24:19–21, and Mishnah *Peah.*

24. Lev. 19:23–25, and Mishnah *Orlah.*

25. Lev. 19:19, Deut. 22:9–11, and Mishnah *Kilayim.*

26. Num. 18:8, 12, 24.26, Deut. 18:4, and Mishnah *Terumot.*

27. Ex. 23:19, Deut. 26:1–11, and Mishnah *Bikkurim.*

28. *Rosh Ha-Shanah* 31a.

29. For a few examples, see Lev. 18:24–30, 20:22.26, Num. 25:34, Deut. 4:40, 21:6–9, Ps. 106:38f.

30. See, e.g., Isa. 1:2, 41:1, 49:1.

31. Isa. 24:4–5.

32. Monford Harris, "Ecology: A Covenantal Approach," *CCAR Journal* 23 (Summer 1976): 101–108.

33. W. D. Davies, *The Territorial Dimension of Judaism* (Berkeley: University of California Press, 1982), 134–35.

34. Mishnah *Kelim* 1:6.

35. Charles Primus, "The Borders of Judaism: The Land of Israel in Early Rabbinic Judaism," in *The Land of Israel*, 102.

36. Mishnah *Orlah* 3:9, Tosefta *Terumah* 2:13, Tosefta *Orlah* 1:8, Tosefta *Kidushin* 1:9–10, 12.

37. See Mishnah *Mikva'ot* 8:1.

38. Mishnah *Oholot* 2:3, 17:5, 18:6–7, Mishnah *Tohorot* 4:5, 5:1, Mishnah *Nazir* 3:6, 7:3, Tosefta *Mikva'ot* 6:1, Tosefta *Oholot* 17:7–18:11.

39. Mishnah *Shev'it* 5:7, Tosefta *Hallah* 2:6; Tosefta *Terumah* 4:13.

40. Richard S. Sarason, "The Significance of the Land of Israel in the Mishnah," in *The Land of Israel*, 123.

41. Primus, 107.

42. Mishnah *Hallah* 4:11.

43. *Ketubbot* 110b–111a.

44. *Ketubbot* 110b.

45. James Sanders argues, in *Torah and Canon*, that this transformation was engineered long before the Rabbis, during the First Babylonian Exile. That argument has merit, but does not effect the substance of my position, which is that Judaism of the Biblical period reflected a region that presupposed living in the Land of Israel, and that later Judaism was made portable.

46. *Sotah* 14a. See also Mishnah *Kelim* 1:6: "There are ten degrees of holiness. The Land of Israel is holier than any other land. Wherein lies its holiness? In that from it they may bring the *omer*, the first fruits, and the two loaves, which they may not bring from any other land." That same exclusive prerogative forms the principal subject of Mishnah *Challah* 4:1–11.

47. Even prophecy, which is linked in fact to the Land of Israel, was a possibility in other lands as well. The Mekhilta, *Pischa* 1, makes note of this at least three times.

48. See Arnold A. Lasker and Daniel J. Lasker, "The Strange Case of December 4: A Liturgical Problem," *Conservative Judaism* 38 (1985): 91–96, and "The Jewish Prayer for Rain in Babylonia," *The Journal for the Study of Judaism* (June 1984): 123–144.

49. For the history of the Ben Meir calendar controversy, see Henry Malter, *Life and Works of Saadia Gaon* (Philadelphia: Jewish Publication Society, 1921).

50. Jacob Neusner, "Map without Territory: Mishnah's System of Sacrifice and Sanctuary," *History of Religions* 19 (1979): 125.

51. The discussion that follows is based on the work of Lawrence Hoffman, particularly his "Introduction: Land of Blessing and Blessings of Land," in *The Land of Israel*, 1–23. Hoffman's interest is primarily what the structure of blessings reveals about Rabbinic attitudes toward the Land of Israel. Our interest in this case is to examine what that same structure reveals about Rabbinic attitudes toward the Earth in general.

52. Clifford Geertz, *The Interpretation of Cultures* (New York: Basic Books, 1970), 10.

53. Wayne Meeks, *The First Urban Christians: The Social World of the Apostle Paul* (New Haven: Yale University Press, 1983), 141.

54. Deut. 8:7–10.

55. Hoffman, loc. cit.

56. *Berakhot* 35a. A series of such quotations continues on the following side (35b), calling such a practice "robbery" against God and the Jewish People. See also Tosafot *Berakhot* 4:1.

57. *Berakhot* 35a.

58. Mishnah *Berakhot* 6:3.

59. Hoffman, 15.

60. Primus, 106.

10

Created in the Image of God: Humanity and Divinity in an Age of Environmentalism

Lawrence Troster

Humanity was created in the image of God. Modern environmentalism poses many challenges to this Biblical concept. Some authorities consider their differences to be irreconcilable. We shall examine a reconciliation of these positions through three interpretations and a synthesis with the Gaia theory, which conceives of the earth as a living, self-sustaining and self-regulating organism.

IN THE IMAGE OF GOD

> And God said, "Let us make humanity in our image, after our likeness. They shall rule the fish of the sea, the birds of the sky, the cattle, the whole earth, and all the creeping things that creep on earth." And God created humanity in His image, in the image of God He created him, male and female He created them. (Genesis 1:26–27)

References to humanity's being created in the image, or likeness, of God (*betzelem Elohim*)[1] have been some of the most influential Biblical verses in the history of both the Jewish and the Christian traditions. From a Jewish perspective, this value concept is the foundation of Jewish ethics and morality. Rabbinic tradition even considered this ethic to be the essence of the Torah.[2] It expresses the enormous value of a human life, and the inherent dignity and respect required in all interpersonal relationships. Modern Jewish writers on ethics have given an expanded meaning to this concept to include all aspects of the moral life. For example:

> The Theological foundation of Jewish ethics is the duty to imitate God, to "go in His ways" (Deuteronomy 28:9). This duty is rooted in the character of man as created in the image of God. Since we are created in His image we have both the responsibility and the capacity to follow Him.[3]

For Seymour Siegel this value expresses our ability to be godlike but not God. Indeed, for both Siegel and David S. Shapiro, the concept of the "image of God" points both to the enormous potential and the inherent limitations of humanity.[4]

AGAINST THE IMAGE OF GOD

Since the sixteenth century, the development of modern secular culture can almost be encapsulated in challenges to the traditional religious status of humanity as derived from the "image of God" metaphor. These challenges began with the shift from the earth-centered worldview, first articulated by Ptolemy, to the heliocentric view of Copernicus. Earth and humanity were no longer viewed as the center of the universe. The Copernican cosmology asserted that the earth and, by extension, humanity do not occupy a privileged positioned in the universe.[5] There followed what might be called the evolutional critique, which, since Darwin, has asserted that humanity also occupies no special place in nature. Humanity is not an intentionally created species but is rather, in the words of biologist Stephen Jay Gould, a "happy accident,"[6] the result of a long series of evolutionary accidents stimulated by random large scale environmental changes. Indeed, Gould has asserted that if one were to "rewind the tape" of evolution and "replay it," it is highly unlikely that a conscious species like humanity would again emerge.

These paradigm shifts in worldview, plus the growing awareness of the damage done to the environment by humanity, have led to a radical environmental critique of humanity's place in nature. This critique seems to put environmental ethics in direct conflict with Judaism's view of the image of God in humanity.

These radical critiques emerge from the "deep ecologists"—those ecologists who assert that humanity has no special status as a species. This is in contrast to the "shallow ecologists," who favor a conservationist approach to environmental problems. Deep ecology is rooted in biocentrism (as opposed to anthropocentrism, or the more awkward and unfortunate term "speciesism," the biological form of racism). Biocentrism asserts that:

1. The needs, desires, interests, and goals of humans are not privileged.
2. The human species should not change the ecology of the planet.
3. The world ecological system is too complex for human beings ever to understand.
4. The ultimate goal, good, and joy of humankind is contemplative understanding of Nature.
5. Nature is a holistic system of parts (in which man is merely one among many equals), all of which are internally interrelated in dynamic, harmonious, ecological equilibrium.[7]

From this perspective, Judaism and Christianity are sources of the anthropocentric idea which asserts that humans have a special God-given status that separates them from nature and allows them to exercise unbridled domination over creation. From this perspective, God, as transcendent Creator, is also seen as separate from nature, thus desacralizing the environment and furthering humanity's alienation from nature.[8] The solution, according to some biocentrists, lies in a return to a pantheistic conception of God, nature, and humanity: "We must learn anew that it is we who belong to earth and not the earth to us."[9]

Philosophers Steven S. Schwarzschild and Richard A. Watson have both subjected the philosophical basis of biocentrism to a thorough "critique."[10] According to this critique, biocentrism displays anthropocentric features by postulating a human moral concern for nature and by sacralizing the environment. As Watson concludes:

> There are anthropocentric foundations in most environmental and ecosophical literature. In particular, ecosophers say outright or openly imply that human individuals and the human species would be better off if we were required to live in ecological balance with nature. Few ecosophers really think that man is just one part of nature among others. Man is privileged—or cursed—at least by having a moral sensibility that as far as we can tell no other entities have. But it is pretty clear . . . that, on this planet at least, only human beings are (so far) full members of a moral community. We ought to be kinder to nonhuman animals, but I do not think that this is because they have any intrinsic rights. As far as that goes, human beings have no intrinsic rights either. We have to earn our rights as cooperating citizens in a moral community.[11]

In other words, by postulating a human moral stance towards nature instead of an unrestrained competition with other species, biocentrism is also asserting a special status for humanity in nature.

The biocentric thesis also erroneously interprets the specific text (Genesis 1:28) used to "prove" Judaism's anti-ecological foundations, as Jeremy Cohen has shown.[12] This thesis also ignores the Jewish doctrine of humanity's responsibilities to the earth.[13] Judaism always has valued the prohibition of the wanton destruction of nature, as concretized in *halakhah*.[14] Nonetheless, the "image of God" concept does assert that human beings have a unique and dominant role in the world,[15] even if it is as stewards and protectors of the earth.

From an environmental perspective, however, there are problematic aspects of Judaism's regarding the relationship of human beings, divinity, and the earth. Indeed, human beings often are called "partners with God in the Work of Creation." In this view, the world is unfinished, and human beings are empowered by God to complete God's work. Jewish tradition asserts that the world was created essentially for human benefit. Judaism does have an anthropocentric view of the world, its relation to humanity and to God.

Nature is identified with the divine, and its chief "value lies in its serviceability to man and God."[16] From this perspective, Jewish concern for the environment is fundamentally utilitarian: human beings must preserve, protect, and not squander the environment, in striving to attain the goal of creating the Kingdom of God upon earth. Nature is precious as a creation of God; it is not sacred in and of itself.

Humanity's relationship to the earth also reflects its primary concern with morality among humans or between humans and God, rather than our "ecological" morality with the earth. One example will serve to illustrate this. In Genesis 4, Cain is cursed for the murder of Abel by being alienated from the earth.

> Therefore you shall be more cursed than the ground which opened its mouth to receive your brother's blood from your hand. If you till the soil, it shall no longer yield its strength to you. (Genesis 4:11–12)

This curse parallels the curse given to Adam when he and Eve were expelled from the Garden (Genesis 3:17). In both instances the earth is cursed for humanity because of their sin. Now that humanity is *human*, not animal, and subject to the divine categories of right and wrong, earth does not "naturally" produce its bounty for them. Earth must now be worked and managed for human needs. There is a separation from nature that can be seen to reflect a change from a "gathering and hunting" state to a settled agricultural society which manipulates the environment.

Indeed, throughout the Bible the earth is often the vehicle for a reflection of human morality. Earth seems to have a moral sensitivity regarding the way humans behave with respect to one another as well as with respect to God. There is no Biblical idea of humanity's relationship to the earth as an independent sacred covenant. Only within the covenant with God are humans bound to the earth. This picture of humanity, God, and the earth is an interesting counterpoint to much of the biocentric spirituality that is current in many environmental and some Jewish circles.

The "image of God" concept is basic for Jewish morality. To eliminate it, as some have proposed,[17] would radically alter Judaism's basis for its moral code. Nonetheless, modern society's alienation from nature and our disregard for the environment is a serious religious concern.

MOTHER GAIA AND (SOME OF) HER CHILDREN

Human alienation from nature has been confronted by the British chemist James Lovelock in his two books describing the Gaia theory,[18] which asserts that the earth is one living self-sustaining and self-regulating organism. This organism he calls Gaia, after the Greek goddess of the earth.

His theory resulted from the attempt to evaluate life-detecting equipment for NASA's Mars probes in the 1970s. Lovelock decided that one possible way of knowing whether there is life on Mars was first to establish what makes it obvious that there is life on Earth. Comparing Earth to Venus and Mars, the other similar planets in our system, Lovelock stated that the obvious difference lies in the makeup of their respective atmospheres.

Venus and Mars have atmospheres in equilibrium, atmospheres made up of a stable combination of mostly carbon dioxide, some nitrogen, and traces of oxygen and argon. Earth, on the other hand, has an unusual and unstable atmosphere in a state of disequilibrium. It is unstable because the combination of gases that make up the earth's atmosphere (79% nitrogen, 21% oxygen, 0.03% carbon dioxide, 1% argon) react with one another to form byproducts which, left to their own devices, would eventually form an atmosphere much like Mars or Venus—one that is in equilibrium. Therefore, said Lovelock, Mars cannot have life, since a living planet is characterized by having an atmosphere in disequilibrium. What sustains this atmosphere of disequilibrium? Something must be regulating the earth's atmosphere to constantly maintain the proper ratios of gases.

This regulation also controls the surface temperature of the planet. Lovelock found that, despite the fluctuation of solar energy over the last three and one-half billion years, the surface temperature of the earth has remained fairly constant. What regulates the atmosphere of earth? Indeed, what created the unlikely atmosphere of earth so amenable for the development of life?

Lovelock's answer is that life itself created and sustained the atmosphere of earth. The earth is not (as traditional science assumed) "just a ball of rock, moistened by the oceans; [with] nothing but a tenuous film of air exclud[ing] the hard vacuum of space; [with] life . . . merely an accident, a quiet passenger that happens to have hitched a ride on this rock ball in a journey through time and space."[19] The earth is one living organism, says Lovelock, in which the various individual species are like the bodily organs of a larger evolving whole. While Lovelock has not definitively "proven" this theory, much current research suggests he is right. His original analysis is being tested, new "Gaian" factors are being discovered, and what was first seen as a crackpot idea is now seriously debated in scientific circles.

What is the status of humanity in this living organism of Gaia? What is our place in this intricate web of life? How much are we part of this system, and how much are we outside of it? Lovelock sees humans as the "brain cells" of Gaia, since humanity is the only species on this planet with cognitive anticipation, the ability to consciously anticipate needs and then to act on them.

> If we are part of Gaia, it becomes interesting to ask: To what extent is our collective intelligence also a part of Gaia? Do we, as a species, constitute a Gaian nervous system, and a brain that can consciously anticipate environmental changes?[20]

Lovelock suggests that human cooperation and consciousness mean that Gaia has extended her perception beyond her own surface into outer space, not only that Gaia has a possible better way of managing her own environment. In other words, "She is now, through us, awake and aware of herself."[21]

Lovelock also states, however, that we must stop viewing Gaia as a farm for human management. "The Gaia hypothesis implies that the stable state of our planet includes man as part of, or partner in, a very democratic entity."[22] If we do not recognize this fact, then humanity, not Gaia, might be doomed to extinction from environmental change. For Gaia, the extinction of humanity as a result of the "greenhouse effect" would be only a temporary bump in the long road of life. Life would adjust to our passing and continue without us. Given the lifespan of Gaia, however, it is highly unlikely that another self-conscious species would evolve if humanity became extinct.

As a result of many religious responses to his first book, Lovelock devotes a chapter of his second book to the theological implications of Gaia and God. While admitting that he is an agnostic, Lovelock feels that Gaia is as close to divinity as we can possibly get. The origin of life and whether or not the universe was created for the purpose of the emergence of Gaia, Lovelock considers to be "ineffable questions," which are interesting but which serve no real purpose. Gaia, on the other hand, is a "religious as well as scientific concept, and in both spheres it is manageable."[23] For Lovelock, both Gaia and God are concepts for ways to view the relationship of the universe, the earth, and humanity with other living things. Since Gaia is one-fourth as old as the universe, "she" (and Lovelock is very much concerned with the return of the feminine element to the nature of the divine) is as close to immortality as we can experience. We are part of her and she is part of God.

Our concepts of God lack the element of Gaia because of our alienation from the environment. Since most of us dwell in cities, we are away from and out of touch with nature. Lovelock claims that this alienation has led to an extremely reductionist view of life in the sciences which prefers to analyze the parts with little or no reference to the whole. This trend also distances us from the earth. According to Lovelock, the Gaia concept, which was known intuitively by humanity through nature worship and earth goddess religions, has been difficult for science to accept. A more holistic approach to all forms of human knowledge is now showing that Gaia is real. A similar approach to the whole cosmos declares that the universe itself may be "living" in the sense that it is a self-organizing structure. In a such a universe, the evolution of life is inevitable.

Can a Gaian, or biocentric, approach be incorporated within a Jewish perspective on the environment? The Gaia concept appears to show a dichotomy between the Biblical concept of stewardship, or benign management of the earth with God, as compared with the Gaian concept of the partnership or "partnership of humanity with the earth which is God. If humans are a part of Gaia, then must we act towards the earth with a kind of moral behavior as we would with another being/creature/ourselves. "Gaian morality" says that we must move beyond the concept of benign utilitarian management of life on earth.

Let us now examine three interpretations[24] of the term "in the image of God" (*betzelem Elohim*), and a synthesis of these interpretations with the Gaia metaphor which will attempt to harmonize both Jewish and ecological positions.

IN THE IMAGE: *PESHAT*

The Hebrew term for "image" (*tzelem*) has a cognate word in Old Akkadian and Old Babylonian that throws significant light upon the original nuance of the term used in Genesis. The cognate word (*tzalmu*) can mean a statue, a bodily shape, a figurine, or a relief drawing. The term sometimes refers to a statue or an image of the king, which is placed in a captured city or else- where in the kingdom as an extension of the king's presence and the king's law. In other words, it is as if the king were present wherever the king's *tzalmu* is placed. The king rules wherever his *tzalmu* stands.[25]

Seen in this light, humanity is the *tzalmu* of God. Wherever humans are, the presence of God is reflected. This cannot be said of any other creature. Indeed, the command to multiply and spread over the earth is none other than a desire to spread the presence of God and to actualize God's power throughout Creation, rather than a desire for mere numerical increase.[26] It is as if God could not function in the world without humanity. "While he (a human being) is not divine, his very existence bears witness to the activity of God in the life of the world."[27] This is certainly in accord with the Rabbinic idea of human beings as "partners of God in the work of Creation,"[28] neces- sary witnesses attesting to God's existence.[29] Heschel uses this idea in his concepts of the Divine Pathos and the interdependence of God and human- ity.[30] Thus the term *tzelem*, in its plain meaning (*peshat*), connects humanity with God as ruler of the earth, and gives humanity the divine mandate to be stewards of creation. The immanence of God in the world is to be found in the physical presence of human beings.[31]

IN THE IMAGE: *DERASH*

He [God] created him with four attributes of the higher beings [i.e., angels] and four attributes of the lower beings [i.e., beasts]. [The four attributes of] the higher beings are: he stands upright, like the ministering angels; he speaks, like the ministering angels; he understands, like the ministering angels; and he sees, like the minister- ing angels. Yet, does not a dumb animal see?! But this one [man] can see from the side [i.e., with peripheral vision]. He has four attributes of the lower beings: he eats and drinks, like an animal, he procreates, like an animal; he excretes, like an ani- mal; and he dies, like an animal.[32]

For the authors of this midrash, human beings "are situated on a cosmic frontier, between supernal and terrestrial realms of existence."[33] The divine characteristics specified are uniquely human, separating humanity from other creatures, while the characteristics shared with the lower beings bind humanity to nature. Speech and understanding are the attributes which produce human culture and, hence, ethical choice. In other Rabbinic texts,[34] human beings are given the choice to actualize their higher or lower attributes, which determines their ability to be the dominant species on earth. But the midrash reflects the dual nature of human beings, composed of both the earthly (*adamah*) and the divine (*tzelem*). Humans may choose not to actualize the divine tzalmu, but they cannot escape being earthly (*adamah*). Possessing the "higher" attributes makes humanity the conscious link between God and nature.

IN THE IMAGE: *REMEZ*

Here is Maimonides on man in the image of God:

> The term *image*, on the other hand, is applied to the natural form, I mean to the notion in virtue of which a thing is constituted as a substance and becomes what it is. It is the true reality of the thing in so far as the latter is that particular being. In man that notion is that from which human apprehension derives. It is on account of this intellectual apprehension that it is said of man: *In the image of God created him* (Genesis 1:27). . . . Now man possesses as his *proprium* something in him that is very strange, as it is not found in anything else that exists under the sphere of the moon, namely, intellectual apprehension. In the exercise of this, no sense, no part of the body, none of the extremities are used; and therefore this apprehension was likened unto the apprehension of the deity, which does not require an instrument, although in reality it is not like the latter apprehension, but only appears so to the first stirrings of opinion. It was because of this something, I mean because of the divine intellect conjoined with man, that it is said of the latter that he is in the image of *God and in His likeness*, and not that God, may He be exalted, is a body and possesses a shape.[35]

For Maimonides, what is unique about human beings is their intellectual apprehension—or, as we might term it, the human consciousness[36] and therefore what follows from human consciousness: moral choice and apprehension of the divine. For him this is the meaning of *tzelem*. Consciousness, which does not depend necessarily on sense perception, is what humanity shares with a noncorporeal God. Maimonides identifies this quality with the soul, and as a link between humanity and the angels.[37] Thus humanity shares with the "higher beings" an immortal element that is not tied to the natural world. In a modern context, we know that consciousness is a function of our brain, but the extent to which it is dependent on the brain is a matter of much debate.[38] Whether or not other animals have a form of consciousness is also a matter of great debate.[39] For Maimonides, however, consciousness is the great divide between humanity and the rest of the natural world. Even with this divide, Maimonides recognizes the strong link between the body and the soul, and knows that the health of one can influence the health of the other.[40] Nonetheless, it is consciousness that is our unique link to God, and the source of our ability to receive prophecy.

IN THE IMAGE: SYNTHESIS

These three interpretations of *tzelem* present a composite portrait of humanity as a nexus between God and the natural world. As the *tzalmu* of God, humanity is the physical extension of God's power and presence on earth. Having characteristics of both "higher" and "lower" creatures, we are aware of our connection to God, and to other living beings, and of our earthly origin and limitations as well. Finally, our consciousness provides us with the self-awareness to realize our responsibilities to God and to the earth which we tend.

This portrait of humanity as the link between God and the earth is not in conflict with the Gaia theory if we continue to reflect on our images of God. If we continue to look at God only as a transcendent deity separate from nature, then we preserve our morality, and our moral obligation not to waste the earth. However, we still may remain insensitive to non-human life and our own creaturely character. If we see God only from the perspective of pantheism, then all is God, and nature is intrinsically sacred; but we cannot have a human ethical system in the usual sense that Judaism has known it.

We should, instead, think of God as both Being and Becoming—what is called a panentheistic deity. Panentheism assumes that the universe and everything in it is part of God, and that God is also more than the universe. "God is all reality but not all reality is God."[41] Gaia is part of God, but not all of God. Therefore, the immanence of God is displayed in nature (through order, cooperation, and relationships) and we are part of and thus part of God. But God is more than nature, and also stands outside of nature as Creator. We are part of this nature and bound to the laws of nature and Gaia, but we are also the "brain cells" of Gaia. And as the *tzelem* (image) of God, we have the mandate for the cognitive anticipation of Gaia's needs, which ultimately are our own needs. The brain is the locus of consciousness and in control of the body, both in the autonomic nervous system and in conscious choices. But the brain is also dependent upon the body for survival, and is significantly influenced by changes in the body.[42]

If the Earth does reflect our morality, then certainly it is humanity's "environmental debt" that is growing each year. Life is poised on a delicate balance. We must end the "war against nature" that governs so many of our attitudes towards the Earth. Perhaps our newfound environmental awareness is the "real" awakening of Gaia, an awakening that will lead us out of our childhood into the divine image that awaits us.[43]

NOTES

From *Conservative Judaism* 44 (1991–92): 14–24.

1. Cf. Gen. 5:1–2, 9:6.

2. Cf. *Sifra* 7, *Kedoshim* 2:12 to Lev. 19:18, Mishnah *Avot* 3:15 and Mishnah *Sanhedrin* for the common origin and infinite worth of life.

3. Seymour Siegel, "Ethics and the Halakhah," in *Conservative Judaism and Jewish Law,* ed. Siegel (New York: The Rabbinical Assembly, 1977), 125.

4. David S. Shapiro, "The Doctrine of the Image of God and Imitatio Dei," in *Contemporary Jewish Ethics,* ed. Menachem Marc Keller, (New York: Sanhedrin Press, 1979).

5. Cf. John D. Barrow and Frank J. Tipler, *The Anthropic Cosmological Principle* (Oxford: Clarendon Press, 1986), 27–122; Ian G. Barbour, *Issues in Science and Religion* (New York: Harper Torchbooks, 1971), 15–22; and George Gale, "The Anthropic Principle," in *Scientific American,* 245.6 (December, 1981): 154–71.

6. Stephen Jay Gould, *The Flamingo's Smile* (New York: Norton, 1985), 13–14, 292–93.

7. Richard A. Watson, "A Critique of Anti-Anthropocentric Biocentrism," *Environmental Ethics* 5 (1983): 251. Cf. also Paul W. Taylor, "In Defense of Biocentrism," *Environmental Ethics* 5 (1983): 237–43.

8. Lynn White, "The Historic Roots of Our Ecological Crisis," *Science* 155 (1967): 1203–1207.

9. Watson, 247.

10. Watson, 247; Steven S. Schwarzschild, "The Unnatural Jew" [reprinted in this volume, 265–82]. Schwarzschild goes a little too far in asserting that any form of immanentism is a form of Jewish heresy, in which he includes Kabbalah, Christianity, Spinoza, Marx, and Zionism.

11. Watson, 256.

12. Jeremy Cohen, *"Be Fruitful and Increase, Fill the Earth and Master It"* (Ithaca: Cornell University Press, 1989).

13. David Ehrenfeld and Phillip J. Bentley, "Judaism and the Practice of Stewardship" [reprinted in this volume, 125–35]; David Ehrenfeld and Joan G. Ehrenfeld, "Some Thoughts on Nature and Judaism" [reprinted in this volume, 283–85].

14. Deut. 20:19–20; Moses Maimonides, *Hilkhot Melakhim* 6:8–10.

15. Cf. Ps. 8:4–9.

16. Schwarzschild [reprinted in this volume, 270].

17. Cf., for example, Judith Plaskow, *Standing Again at Sinai* (New York: Harper and Row, 1990), 144–45, 155.

18. James E. Lovelock, *Gaia: A New Look at Life on Earth* (Oxford: Oxford University Press, 1982); *The Ages of Gaia* (New York: W. W. Norton and Company, 1988).

19. Lovelock, *The Ages of Gaia,* 11–12.

20. Lovelock, *The Ages of Gaia,* 147.

21. Lovelock, *The Ages of Gaia*, 148.

22. Lovelock, *The Ages of Gaia*, 145.

23. Lovelock, *The Ages of Gaia*, 206.

24. This follows the traditional Jewish interpretive system of *PaRDeS*: *Peshat*, the plain meaning; *Remez*, the symbolic meaning; *Derash,* the homiletical meaning; and *Sod*, the mystical meaning.

25. Cf. Ignace J. Gelb, Benno Landsberger, and A. Leo Oppenheim, *The Assyrian Dictionary of the Oriental Institute of the University of Chicago* (Chicago: Oriental Institute, 1962), vol. 16, 78–85, s.v. *Salmu*. I would like to thank Professor Ted Lutz of the Near Eastern Studies Department of the University of Toronto for this interpretation of *tzalmu*.

26. Cf. Cohen, 20–23.

27. Nahum M. Sarna, *The JPS Torah Commentary Genesis* (Philadelphia: Jewish Publication Society of America, 1989), 12.

28. *Shabbat* 119b.

29. *Sifrei Deuteronomy* 346. Cf. Also *Bereishit Rabbah* 17:4 on God's needing Adam to name the animals and Himself.

30. Abraham J. Heschel, *Man is Not Alone* (New York: Octagon Books, 1972), 241–45.

31. Cf. Jon D. Levenson, *Creation and the Persistence of Evil* (San Francisco: Harper and Row, 1988). Levenson views the Biblical covenant as the partnership of humanity and God needed to maintain order over the forces of chaos.

32. *Midrash, Bereishit Rabbah* to Genesis 1:27. Translation adapted from H. Freedman, *Midrash Rabbah*: Genesis (London: Soncino Press, 1983), 61–62.

33. Jeremy Cohen, "On Classical Judaism and Environmental Crisis" [reprinted in this volume, 71–79].

34. E.g., *Bereishit Rabbah* 8:11 (second half) and 8:12.

35. Maimonides, *Guide of the Perplexed* I 2 (trans Shlomo Pines [Chicago: University of Chicago Press, 1963], 22–23).

36. My thanks to Dr. David Bakan for this interpretation of Maimonides's concept of intellectual apprehension. Cf. David Bakan, *Maimonides on Prophecy* (Northvale, N.J.: Jason Aronson, 1991).

37. *Mishneh Torah, Hilkhot Yesodei Ha-Torah* 4:8–9.

38. Cf. Douglas B. Hofstadter and Daniel C. Dennett, *The Mind's Eye* (New York: Bantam Books, 1982); Roger Penrose, *The Emperor's New Mind* (New York: Vintage, 1989), 526–27.

39. Penrose, The Emperor's New Mind, 526–27.

40. Cf. Maimonides, *Eight Chapters*.

41. Moses Cordovero, quoted in Gershom G. Scholem, *Major Trends, in Jewish Mysticism* (New York: Schocken Books, 1954), 252–53.

42. Cf. Maimonides, *Guide of the Perplexed* I 72 (trans. Pines, 184–94), where the universe is compared to a single living organism.

43. Cf. Lawrence Troster, "The Love of God and the Anthropic Principle," *Conservative Judaism*, 40 (1987–88): 45, 49, on John A. Wheeler's version of the Strong Anthropic Principle. Cf. also Karl E. Peters, "Humanity in Nature: Conserving Yet Creating," *Zygon* 24 (1989). This article is a brilliant statement of the relationship between humanity and nature.

11

Is Gaia Jewish?
Finding a Framework for Radical
Ecology in Traditional Judaism

Eric Rosenblum

> It is a tree of life to all who hold fast to it,
> and all its paths are peace. (Prov. 3:17–18)

INTRODUCTION

The twentieth century, delivered in a horse-drawn wagon, is about to be shipped off in a space shuttle. We now provide more products to more people than at any other time in human history. But when we compare the world our grandparents inherited with the one we are prepared to leave our children, it seems this progress has cost us more than we bargained for. Everywhere we look, our natural systems are deteriorating, and by all accounts they will continue to do so unless we learn to reduce our impact on the environment.

According to its most ardent advocates, the environment's decline is a byproduct of our technological society. No less than chainsaws and bulldozers, our current cultural and political institutions are responsible for the environmental problems we face today. So ecologist John McHale concluded more than twenty-five years ago, "Many of our current social, political and ethical attitudes . . . are dangerously obsolete.[1] By this logic, environmental restoration will require new social and political systems, as anarchist critic Murray Bookchin warns: "Our world, it would appear, will either undergo revolutionary changes, so far-reaching in character that humanity will totally transform its social relations and its very conception of life, or it will suffer an apocalypse that may well end humanity's tenure on the planet."[2]

Western religion in particular has been criticized for failing to stem the tide of ecological destruction and even promoting pollution, consumption, and overpopulation. For instance, the Biblical instruction to "subdue the earth" (Gen. 1:28) has been construed to justify unhampered exploitation of natural resources, while the prospect of Judgement Day inspires some believers (like former Interior Secretary James Watt) to abandon conservation as the millennium nears.[3] Faced with such simplistic interpretations, priest and writer Thomas Berry concludes, "We cannot do without the traditional religions, but they cannot presently do what needs to be done. We need a new type of religious orientation."[4]

Radical ecologists call for a total transformation in science and worldviews which "will replace the mechanistic framework of domination with an ecological framework of interconnectedness and reciprocity."[5] As proposed by Norwegian philosopher Arne Naess[6] and summarized by Merchant,[7] deep ecology is comprehended by the following principles that define a new relationship between nature and humanity:

- Rejection of "man-in-environment image" in favor of the relational, total-field image
- Biospherical egalitarianism
- Principles of diversity and of symbiosis
- Anticlass posture
- Fight against pollution and resource depletion
- Complexity, not complication
- Local autonomy and decentralization

Devall and Sessions[8] characterize the first two principles as the "ultimate norms" of deep ecology, viz., *self-realization* and *biocentric equality.* Borrowed from the science of ecology, the term "self-realization" reflects a special appreciation for the interconnectedness of the self and its "intrinsic relation" with its surroundings.[9] "Biospherical egalitarianism" refers to an equal regard for all life forms "that places human beings on an absolutely equal footing with all the other creatures on the planet."[10] These concepts merge in chemist James Lovelock's "Gaia hypothesis." Named for the Greek earth goddess *Gaia,* this theory holds that our planet acts as a self-regulating organism, endowed with hometostatic impulses that give it something akin to intelligence. The myriad events that occur around the world at any moment— atmospheric, lithoshperic, hydrospheric, and biospheric—actually comprise a kind of planetary intention, in which all life strives to perpetuate life."[11]

What most ecological activists—and not a few Jews—might find surprising is that the principles of Deep Ecology are fully expressed in traditional Judaism. The Sabbatical and Jubilee years in particular combine ecosystem management with progressive economic policies in an approach to environmental protection as radical as any proposed by the movement today. What follows is an exploration of the laws of *Shemittah* and *Yovel,* the Sabbatical and Jubilee years, as the keys to a uniquely Jewish framework for environmental philosophy and action.

SHEMITTAH: "THE LAND WILL HAVE ITS REST"

The Sabbatical Year is first promulgated in Exodus, which simply states:

> Six years you shall sow your land and gather its yield, but in the seventh you shall let it rest and lie fallow. Let the needy among your people eat of it, and what they leave let the wild animals eat. Do the same with your vineyards and your olive groves. (Exodus 23:10–11)

The practice is elaborated in Leviticus (25:1–7), which ordains "a sabbath of holy rest to the land" (*shabbat shabbaton la-aretz*), and in Deuteronomy, where lenders are instructed to forgive all loans in the seventh year. In fact the word used to denote remission of debts (*shemittah*) is a nominative form of the word meaning "to lie fallow" (*tishmetenah*), reinforcing the connection between ecology and economics through regulations designed to protect both natural and human resources. A final reference in Deuteronomy establishes a period of public instruction during the Sabbatical Year. Enunciation of the rules four times in three separate books in the Bible underscores the importance of *shemittah* in Judaism, despite the fact that it was observed only within the borders of Israel, and rarely at all after the destruction of the Temple.

The Best Things in Life are *Hefker*

During the Sabbatical year, it is forbidden to plant, cultivate, or harvest grain, fruits, or vegetables, or even to plant in the sixth year in order to harvest during the seventh year. The volunteer crops that grow untended are not to be harvested by the landlord, but are to be left ownerless (*hefker*) for all to share, including poor people and animals.[12] An entire tractate of Mishnah (*Shevi'it*) is devoted to specifying the prohibited agricultural activities and the extent to which produce can be gathered and consumed or bartered (but not sold) during the Sabbatical Year.

Observance of *shemittah* was an important feature of Biblical agriculture, preserving the productivity of the land at a time when the population of ancient Israel may have numbered in the millions.[13] Farming is in many respects a destructive practice, replacing complex natural ecosystems with artificial cultivated fields. Constant plowing breaks down the physical structure of soil and reduces the void spaces necessary to retain air and water, while irrigation increases the buildup of salts in the root zone. Wheat and barley, the primary grain crops of the Biblical era, take from the earth minerals and nutrients which must be replaced if the soil is to remain fertile. Resting the land during the Sabbatical Year and plowing under volunteer vegetation reverses these effects: nutrients are restored, rains flush salt from the soil, and organic matter increases tilth and improves soil texture.[14]

This "passive" approach to soil restoration contrasts markedly with the destructive agricultural practices employed today. Fertilizers and pesticides constitute one of the largest expenses of modern farming and are a primary cause of water pollution. Runoff of excess fertilizer contaminates lakes and rivers, producing algal blooms and fish kills, while high concentrations of nitrate in rural groundwater causes methemgoblemia, a blood disease fatal to infants. Increased use of pesticides to protect crops grown on weakened soils is a major source of toxic pollution now under scrutiny by the U.S. Environmental Protection Agency. The Sabbatical Year was able to provide the benefits of increased fertility without the negative impacts associated with these technological methods.

Shemittah also promoted diversity in plant life and helped maintain vigorous cultivars. Without the pressures of natural selection, over time crops become less hardy than their wild forbears. By regularly allowing strains from the surrounding countryside to sprout in fallow fields and cross-pollinate with volunteer crops, Biblical farmers may have preserved genetic material to counteract the debilitating effect of cultivation. The value of such material is evident to us today, when the last few kernels of our ancestral food crops are carefully guarded in special "seedbanks" and cross-bred to help weakened modern species resist pests and disease.[15]

Sabbatical year customs also increased diversity in the animal kingdom. *Shemittah* produce was intentionally left in the untilled fields for the "wild beasts," who were accorded the same rights to *hefker* crops as domesticated animals.[16] When a fruit or vegetable was no longer found in the field, stored produce was brought to the marketplace for redistribution so peasants dined as well as the wealthy.[17] Even in non-*shemittah* years, passersby were allowed to pick and eat crops on private property, provided they did not harvest them in bulk for storage or sale (Deut. 24:19–22). The net effect of these practices was to ensure the survival of animals and human beings whose existence may have been undervalued by the economic judgement of the day.

These benefits were not obtained without significant risk. It is difficult for us, in our industrialized society, to imagine the impact of these restrictions on an agricultural community. The remarkable faith needed to forgo two full harvests and hope for a third can only be appreciated by those whose livelihood depends on the vagaries of weather and soil. Asked the rabbis, "Who is more heroic than one who looks out on untilled fields and unworried plantations and shares the scanty yield with others?"[18] Or as one modem commentator noted, "The surprising thing is not that the law was sometimes broken—many persons were suspected of trafficking in fruits of the seventh year—but that so many Jews observed it at great cost to themselves."[19]

Please Release Me

The second custom associated with the sabbatical year is the remission of debts (Deut. 15:1–3). Curiously, there is no mention of the resting the land in

Deuteronomy, just as there is no reference to the release of debts in Exodus or Leviticus. But it stands to reason that it would be hard to collect debts when all planting was suspended and "volunteer" crops could not be sold. In the normal course of events, the farmer expects his fields to produce a crop, and the lender expects the debtor to pay his debt. In both cases, *shemittah* provides temporary relief from these obligations, exposing the connection between human economic customs and our actions toward the environment.

This relationship is now gaining currency among activists who explain that our reliance on pesticides and fertilizers is ultimately driven by the economics of modem farming. "The soil's vitality deteriorates because the competitiveness of the market fulls to allow the large-scale owner or tenant farmer to introduce the additional labor or expense needed to maintain its fertility."[20] On a larger scale, from Brazil to Indonesia massive debt inspires much of the ecological destruction in the world today. In 1995, developing countries owed approximately $200 billion in external debt to global investors. To avoid default, these countries are extracting natural resources at unsustainable rates and converting peasant farms from subsistence agriculture to cash crops, ruining ecosystems and driving local populations to the brink of starvation. Periodic debt restructuring only prolongs the problem, and several international environmental organizations are now calling for "a massive global transfer of wealth and the cancellation of third-world debts" to initiate truly sustainable development. A coalition of activists has initiated a worldwide referendum for third world debt relief under the banner of "Jubilee 2000," invoking the model of the Sabbatical Year.

As *shemittah* was observed in Biblical times, loans to foreigners were exempted from remission. The rabbis further distinguished between cash loans that must be forgiven and other obligations that remained in effect, including "shop debts" (i.e., purchase of goods on credit) and wages for contract labor.[21] Thus the requirement to forgive debts was neither universal nor absolute, but was intended to facilitate observance of the Sabbatical year. Fines and legal penalties were also exempt from release, providing the basis for a loophole in the law called the *prozbul*, which ultimately undermined the practice prescribed in the Bible.

The *prozbul* was a written document that assigned the debt to the court prior to the Sabbatical year, with the intention of collecting the debt at a later time. According to the Mishnah, the *prozbul* was instituted by Hillel the Elder "when he observed people refraining from lending to one another, and thus transgressing what is written in the Law, 'Beware lest there be a base thought in thy heart.'"[22] On the other hand, as Michael Lerner asserts, by adopting the *prozbul*, the rabbis "backed away from the radical meaning of the Torah text."

According to Lerner, "The elimination of debt was a way of saying to everyone that the ultimate important thing was not our money but our caring for one another. . . . The *prozbul* is indicative of the 'realistic' accommodation that the rabbis began to make to the world of imperialism and oppression."[23] A similar note is sounded by Blidstein when he observes that "this conflict between the radical demands of *shevi'it*, on the one hand, and the social reality it seeks to undermine on the other, is a paradigm of the history of the institution."[24] However, when Blidstein comments that "the more effective *shevi'it* became, . . . the harder the world fought back," he clearly refers to the "world of human institutions" as distinct from planet earth. For Gaia needs her rest.

Gaia or Groucho?

One remarkable feature of the Sabbatical Year is that the law is binding both on the inhabitants and on the land itself (Lev.25:2). This joint obligation reflects the Jewish belief that humans share a common origin with all of nature, supporting the concept of biospherical equality. Just as *adam* (man) needs his weekly rest, so *adamah* (earth) requires a periodic return to a natural state.

The land's observance, of course, is dependent on the actions of the landowner. However, should the inhabitants hinder the land's observance, a punishment is specifically designed to redress the wrong: "And I will scatter you among the nations . . . and your land will become desolate, and your cities a ruin. . . . Then the land will rest and make up for its sabbath years . . . that it didn't observe during your Sabbaths when you resided on it" (Lev. 26:33–36). This personification echoes an earlier passage in which the land spits out its inhabitants after it had been "defiled" by the lewd practices of the native Canaanites (Lev. 18:25).

Personification of the land in this fashion is no mere metaphor. The idea that the earth is an animate entity with rights and responsibilities has roots deep in Judaism. A prooftext for this viewpoint is found in Genesis 1:11 when, on the third day of creation, God instructs the land to "grass grass." According to Robert Sacks in his erudite *Commentary on the Book of Genesis*, the use of the cognate accusative *dashe deshe* implies a close relationship between being and doing—a unity of purpose that allows the action to flow easily from the actor.[25] But the earth is incapable of such effortless creation and, in verse 12, can only "put forth" grass instead (*totsei deshe*). Acknowledging this limitation, God later commands the earth simply to "put forth" animals. Says Sacks (referencing Rabbi Judah ben Sholom): "This time the earth is completely incapable of doing anything, and God again obligingly does it Himself."

Ironically, the flawed character of an animate earth lays the groundwork for a bond between humans and their habitat. Sacks takes comfort in the fact that *adam* and *adamah* are similarly limited beings, just as unable to express themselves without error:

> The earth did its best and cannot be called a sinner. But these early verses indicate that the most fundamental difficulties lie not in the heart of man, but in the heart

of being. . . . Man's inability to live according to God's original plan may have been no more man's fault than it was the earth's fault that she could not *grass grass* or *bring forth animals.*[26]

In short, Jewish tradition fully supports the concept of an animate Earth, but one whose character is marked more by pretense rather than perfection— more Groucho Marx than Greek goddess Gaia. But the very limitation we share with the natural world as creatures of God validates the concept of "earth rights" as put forth by EarthFirst!ers and others.

There is another side of this story. Instead of embracing our bond with nature and repudiating the human urge to dominate the natural world, Judaism validates that drive through God's direction in Gen. 1:28 to "subdue the earth and rule the animals" (*v'khivshuha u'redu*). This passage is among the most problematic for ecologically minded Jews, who see in it an open invitation to plunder the planet. By way of mitigation, some suggest that the term *v'khivshuha* should be taken to mean not "subdue" but "suppress," in the sense that a desire held in check is not dead. Similarly, the medieval scholar Rashi understood the word *u'redu* as a warning not to become spiritually debased (*yorda*) through abuse of the physical world, and the scope of the commandment is reduced by the following verses, which institute the Sabbath with its weekly rest. Some commentators even hold that this commandment is superseded entirely by the instructions in the following chapter to till and keep (*le-avdah ul-shamrah*) the Garden of Eden.[27] Later rabbis supported the concept of stewardship with a Midrashic tale in which God warns Adam, "See how beautiful and perfect are my works! All that I have created I have created for you. Therefore, be ever mindful: Do not abuse or desolate My world. For if you do, there is no one after you to repair it."[28]

Although these explanations reign in the urge to unbridled exploitation of nature, none is likely to satisfy those who value the preservation of wilderness above all other rights. Ultimately, Judaism views the human drive to "civilize" nature and the competing force of nature to overwhelm human artifice as an essential tension that attests to our common weakness as creatures of God. That is why the commandment "to subdue and to rule" is preceded by a blessing, says Sacks, since blessings are only given when error is likely and God's help is needed.[29] God's aid, in this case, comes in the form of *shemittah*—the commandment that one year in seven *adam* and *adamah,* man and earth, must relax their struggle, accept their mutual limitations, and take their rest.

A Torah Teach-In

The Sabbatical Year is mentioned for the last time at the end of Deuteronomy, in connection with the practice of reading the Law in public:

At the time of the Year of Release, at the Feast of *Sukkot*, all Israel shall come and appear before the Lord your God at the place He will choose, to read this

Law beside all Israel, in their hearing. Assemble the congregation, the men and the women and the little ones and the stranger that is in your gates, that they hear, and that they learn, and fear the Lord your God, and observe to do all the words of this Law. (Deut. 31:10–13)

Since only the community acting as a whole can perform the duties of the Sabbatical Year, the learning must be public. The actions that the learning inspires are social and not private actions; in modern parlance, "the seventh year becomes our joint commitment to working on the ecology of the planet together."[30] This suggestion does not seem so farfetched, nor so removed from Biblical tradition, when one considers that the goal of the Sabbath itself is to create an island of "eternity within time" in which we reaffirm our divine origins.[31] Likewise, the Sabbatical Year reminds us that we inhabit a divinely created environment that is itself in need of rest.

Finally, it is worth considering how, within the context of *shemittah,* both human and natural systems are seen as somewhat fragile and subject to corruption. From the standpoint of the Sabbatical Year, a society can be degraded by endless debt as surely as ceaseless cultivation will ruin a property, and failure to relieve the one will eventually cause the other to occur. Connected in the observance of *shemittah,* Jewish economic policy and environmental protection become fully integrated in the tradition of the Jubilee Year.

YOVEL: PUBLIC POVERTY AND PRIVATE PROPERTY

The concept of the Jubilee Year is introduced in Leviticus immediately following the description of the Sabbatical Year:

You shall count off seven weeks of years—seven times seven years. . . . You shall proclaim release throughout the land for all its inhabitants. It shall be a Jubilee (*yovel*) to you; each of you shall return to his holding and each of you shall return to his family. (Leviticus 2:8–10)

As set forth in the text, *yovel* is observed three ways: an extra year without harvest (Lev. 25:11–12); return of real property (except urban homes) to the original land-grant families (Lev. 25:23–28); and freeing all Hebrew slaves, regardless of when they were acquired (Lev. 25:39–41).

With these simple rules, *yovel* ensures protection of the land by corraling the economy within strict social boundaries. If the Sabbatical Year suggests a radical approach to environmental protection, then the Jubilee Year is downright revolutionary. By suspending cultivation for a year, *shemittah* imposes a temporary restriction on business; by redistributing farmland every fifty years, *yovel* renders business itself temporary. *Shemittah* chills the economy; *yovel* freeze dries it, reconstitutes it, and serves it back up in recycled packaging, labeled with nontoxic soy ink.

"Proclaim Liberty Throughout the Ecosystem"

The experience of *shemittah* is temporary. At the end of the year, the owner replants his fields; he sells his harvest and regains his power and his wealth. Not so *yovel*. When land is redistributed to the tribes, the owners' rights are ceded forever.

In *Studies in Vayikra*, the late Biblical scholar Nehama Leibowitz explains that *yovel* reinforces ownership of the world, recalling "the custom of temporal kings who appropriate from time to time the lands belonging to their barons . . . to assert royal authority." She equates land with the means of production, and redistribution as equivalent to providing all people access to capital:

> The Jubilee year ensured the redivision of the land in accordance with its original equal distribution among all sections of the people, ruling out the possibility of any monopoly. . . . The Torah, according to this view, intended to prevent the evolving of a landless class and the concentration of power and property in the hand of the few.[32]

By limiting private ownership of capital and labor, the Jubilee Year promised those without wealth the opportunity to improve their lives. A similar promise drew immigrants from Europe to the New World, where American revolutionaries cast the Jubilee cry into the iron of the Liberty Bell: "Proclaim liberty throughout the land and to all the inhabitants thereof" (Lev. 25.10).

From an ecological perspective, economic domination and political repression are two sides of the same dark coin, now used to buy up and consume the natural environment. To increase profits, transnational manufacturers with billion-dollar revenues shift jobs from $15 per hour U.S. workers to Mexican maquiladoras making $5 per day.[33] State-sanctioned agricultural companies from Brazil to Indonesia are burning nation-sized rainforests to fuel their cash economies, while in the United States a predatory conglomerate threatens to level the last remnant of old growth redwoods in California. Above the din of this global pillage, the Jubilee horn sounds across the centuries, challenging our cherished notions of private property for the sake of future generations—a change advocated by many deep ecologists today. The ancient practice of *yovel* reduces the likelihood that any one family would thrive out of all proportion to its neighbors, curbing the environmental abuses that occur when extreme wealth is unconstrained.

Amortizing the Redwood

How might the law of *yovel*, applied today, protect the environment? As a case in point, we should consider the recent assault on California's redwoods by Pacific Lumber Company. Since the 1930s, that California logging company had placed long-term health ahead of short-term profits, rejecting the practice of clearcutting in favor of "sustained yield." By July 1985, they had accumulated more than 180,000 acres of timber valued in excess of $800 million, attracting the attention of corporate raider Charles Hurwitz.

As related by David Harris in *The Last Stand*, it was simply a matter of bringing market forces to bear on an oddly isolate industry outpost:

> They [PLC] weren't harvesting their trees at anything remotely resembling the rates that were standard in the rest of the industry. . . . Cranked up to a competitive pace . . . , [the company stock, then trading at $24 per share] was actually worth $95 a share. Plus, it was an ideal candidate for a leveraged buyout. It had virtually no outstanding debt—so it could be hocked to the hilt—and no one owned more than 5 percent of Pacific Lumber's outstanding stock—so control would be easier to buy.[34]

According to Harris, in its first year as a Maxxam subsidiary, PLC filed as many timber harvest plans with the state department of forestry as it had in the previous half-century under family control. Neither the trees nor the intricate network of life they sheltered will ever be replaced. In retrospect, Maxxam's conquest of Pacific's empire and its quick conversion of redwood into cash seems foreordained: because it was permitted, it was required. But suppose for a moment that the Headwaters Forest overlooked not the Pacific but the Mediterranean, and that Hurwitz and Maxxam operated under some ancient version of the SEC which enforced the laws of *yovel*. Could Jubilee have saved the trees?

The answer is a qualified "yes."

First, by requiring the return of land to the tribe every fifty years, Jubilee opens the door to the imposition of other restrictive conditions on the sale of real estate. In our present economic system, the ideal of unconditional ownership ("no strings attached") works against placing any limitations on an owner after conveyance of title. After the company's takeover in 1985, PLC's corporate bylaws that limited logging to sustainable levels were ruled unenforceable. Under the laws of *yovel,* however, such restrictions would be upheld, especially as they preserve the well being of the property for its future owners.

Second, by equating the value of land with its productivity, *yovel* essentially requires an owner to maintain the level of productivity the land had when it was sold. As stated in the text (Lev. 25:16), the sale price of land must equal the value of its productive capacity from the time of sale until the Jubilee. But if the value of the land is tied to its productivity, and the land must be returned to the tribe at a near future date, then any action by a landowner which diminishes the land's long-term fertility violates both the spirit and the letter of Jubilee, and may therefore be forbidden.

This point bears repeating. The Jubilee law preserves the productive capacity of the land for future generations, and by implication protects the integrity of its natural systems. The period of the Jubilee bridges generations.

Fifty years is not so long that even in antiquity a young person might cele-brate a Jubilee and live to see a second with his children's children. *Yovel-lian* economics run counter to the current practice of "discounting" the future value of resources by an annual percentate equal to the current interest rate, effectively minimizing the importance of our descendants' welfare. The prin-ciples of *yovel* are more in line with the concepts of "intergenerational eq-uity" and sustainable use as defined by the World Commission on Environ-ment and Development: "Sustainability is the use of resources to meet the needs of today's generation without inhibiting the ability of future genera-tions to meet their needs."[35] To this extent, ownership of land in the Jewish legal system is more akin to ownership in trust, which places a higher value on preservation of assets than on short-term profitability.

In short, the Jubilee rules would have essentially placed Pacific Lumber land in trust, protecting it from overharvest and thereby reducing its market value to the point that it would have been a much less attractive takeover tar-get. By requiring protection of the property for future generations, the Jubilee message to Maxxam is simple: no clearcutting, no overharvesting, no sale.

Save the Humans!

The third rule of *yovel* requires an Israelite master to free his Jewish ser-vant at the onset of the Jubilee Year (Lev.25:39). Just as a poor man might sell his land as a last resort to pay his debts, so an even poorer man with no land left might sell himself into bondage. As with the return of tribal lands, the freeing of indentured servants levels the economic playing field and protects both society and the environment from the ruin of institutional poverty.

This rule is introduced with instructions to all Jews to help their brethren avoid the conditions that might result in their enslavement. Assistance ranges from zero-interest loans to free room and board—anything to get them on their feet again. If, despite all precautions, a person is forced into servitude to survive, his kin (or the community if the master is a non-Jew) must make every effort to redeem him. Finally, if efforts at redemption fail, even the most destitute slave can still look forward to the Jubilee, when "he will re-turn to his own family, to live on the land of his inheritance" (Lev. 25:41).

The importance of this economic escape clause is emphasized in the strongest terms, related to God's status as "ultimate employer." Just as the Sabbatical and Jubilee years acknowledge God's ownership of property through periodic suspension of farming and return of land, this rule affirms God's ownership of labor by regulating the conduct of the master towards the servant, and freeing all Israelite slaves. A similar passage in Exodus (21:2–6) stipulates that all Hebrew slaves must be freed after six years of service; this apparent contradiction is reconciled by concluding that all ser-vants are released when the Jubilee happens to occurs prior to the end of the sixth year of their bondage.[36]

Laws of servitude may not seem pertinent to any modern concerns, environmental or otherwise. Abraham Lincoln gave a clue to their relevance, however, when he observed during the Lincoln-Douglass debates that "Slavery is founded in the selfishness of man's nature—opposition to it, in his love of justice."[37] Although the selfishness of slavery was abolished in the United States almost 140 years ago, the self-interest that now fuels our economy is just as much in need of regulation today as slavery was in Lincoln's time. By including rules about indentured workers in the *shemitta/yovel* system, the Torah highlights the connection between our use of natural and human "resources." As business writer and ecologist Paul Hawken notes, an economy "oblivious to the environment may be equally insensitive to its workers and managers."[38]

Exploitation of labor is an environmental problem because, for one thing, impoverished people are hard on their environment, and hard pressed to choose a more sustainable way of life. Deforestation due to overharvesting of firewood is tied directly to poverty and the lack of alternative infrastructure (e.g., oil and gas for cooking and heating) in poor communities. More than two billion people are currently believed to use wood for heating and cooking, and that number is only expected to increase. The implications for the world's forests is troubling.[39]

A second reason is that unrestrained exploitation of low-wage populations ultimately requires tyranny to maintain social order, and totalitarian governments have equally bad track records on human rights and environmental protection. So Bookchin warns: "Domination fulfills its destiny in the ubiquitous, all pervasive State: its legacy reaches its denouement in the . . . complete disintegration of a richly organic society into an inorganic one—a terrifying destiny that the natural world shares with the social."[40] What is true of national governments could prove just as true of the growing hegemony of multinational corporations, "the capitalist analogue of the unitary hierarchy that was the Soviet State."[41] As Tom Athinasiou points out, "Today's future is marked by brutal globalism and disoriented localism, by high technology and dismal village poverty. . . . It is a transnational future of nationalist backlash, in which twentieth century institutions and twenty-first century technology combine to yield an almost nineteenth century capitalism."[42]

Is Robin Hood Jewish, Too?

The wisdom of *yovel's* cyclic revolution is that it allows individuals and corporate entities to acquire wealth for half a century, but reigns them in at the point where their size and success would harden into either plutocracy or dictatorship. The need for such limits is even more acute today, since human values have been largely disconnected from the global marketplace. By systematically redistributing the wealth of the community, *yovel* clearly places economic activity within the boundaries of community well-being, siding with activist Roy Morrison when he argues that "ultimately, those pursuing freedom and community must choose between reconciling our lives with industrial society, and trying to limit and transform industrialism."[43]

Here the Jubilee favors the approach of modern institutional economists who hold that humans are more than economic actors and that "institutions, culture and values are . . . the stuff of socioeconomic life." [44] Progressive neoclassical economists include "externalities" like environmental impacts in the price of goods to reflect their true costs to future generations,[45] but they still rely on the market to allocate resources and drive economic growth. Institutional economists reject the idea that a market that responds only to self-interest is capable of providing for the full range of human values, including environmental protection.[46] Like *yovel*, institutional economists support rules and laws that public policy should be "built on ideas of common good and human need."[47]

Far from incidental, these progressive economic principles form the core of Jewish political theory. As Sacks notes, citing the prophet Jeremiah, "the fundamental reason for the fall of the state was the neglect of the Sabbatical Year, and by implication the neglect of the Jubilee Year as well."[48] Without the Jubilee Year to restore economic balance, all the divine laws together were incapable of sustaining a just society. The Jubilee preserved both liberty and the environment in ancient Israel by preventing the growth of two destructive groups—a ruling class that consumes resources for pleasure and an impoverished majority that strips bare their environment to survive.

ECOPROPHECY IN THE NEXT MILLENNIUM

The simplicity of the Sabbatical and Jubilee laws masks the elegant way in which these old laws protect the environment while promoting economic and social stability. Echoing the principles of deep ecology, *shemittah* promotes "earth rights" (biocentrism) and respects the planet's needs for rest and repair (pollution prevention and conservation). *Yovel* limits economic power through redistribution of capital before wealth becomes a law unto itself (opposition to centralized authority and "classism"). Together, they provide a framework for political and economic life that fosters respect for all life through sustainable interaction with the environment (self-realization).

The similarities between traditional Judaism and Deep Ecology are not superficial. They stem from fundamental notions shared by these two systems of thought. Chief among these is an awareness of context: all things are connected. As a result, value does not inhere in things "in themselves" but emerges in relationship with the whole; in Naess's terms, Judaism rejects "man in environment in favor of the relational total field image." The Gaia hypothesis elaborates this relationship with scientific evidence concerning our biochemical interdependence with the planet, but it is this same relationship that serves as the cornerstone of Jewish existentialism as developed by such seminal thinkers as Martin Buber[49] and Franz Rosenzweig.[50]

From a traditional point of view, the proper relationship for Jews in the environment is to care for creation by following the Law (*Torah*) with the goal of perfecting or redeeming the world (*tikkun olam*). It is worth reflecting on how these fundamental ideas of creation, revelation, and redemption, so central to modern Jewish thought, compare with key concepts of deep ecology.

Creation and the Nature of Consciousness

Traditional Jews and radical environmentalists celebrate Gaia on common ground. But where some Deep Ecologists venerate nature, Judaism holds nature and humanity equally accountable to a Creator, who assigns them complementary roles and responsibilities. In this manner, Judaism avoids anthropocentrism without falling into antihumanism, a charge some social activists level at spiritual ecologists today.[51]

Judaism's balanced view stems from its appreciation of both the common and unique aspects of being human. On the one hand, *adam* and *adamah* share a common ancestry, as humanity evolved out of "the dust of the earth." On the other hand, Judaism recognizes that our unique talent for speech and abstract thought gives us a competitive advantage over other species. Our creation "in God's image" (*betzelem elohim*) refers not to our physical form but to our self-awareness, our capacity to create, and the power and freedom that implies.[52]

At first, this difference seems to argue against any notion of biospherical equality. As deconstructionist philosopher Kate Soper writes, the very fact that human beings concocted such an idea as biocentrism "is incompatible with many of the claims that deep ecology is wont to make concerning human kinship with the 'rest of nature.' For we would not expect any other species to prioritize the needs of others over its own." By insisting on the equal value of all life forms, Soper says, deep ecologists "recall us to the absurdity of going to that extreme."[53]

But the fact that human beings are special is not in itself inconsistent with either biocentrism or the Gaia hypothesis. Uniqueness, after all, is not the same as apotheosis; and, being created "in the image of God," we remain creatures nonetheless, inextricably bound within the web of life. As Robert Gordis affirms in his exegesis of the Book of Job, the traditional Jewish view of the universe "is not anthropocentric but theocentric, with purposes known only to God, which man cannot fathom." By way of example, he cites the speech in the whirlwind, in which wild and mythological animals are described to illustrate the point that the world is filled with useless, uncontrollable creatures "positively repulsive, even dangerous to man." From this he concludes that although "the poet was not concerned with presenting a religio-ethical basis for ecology, he has in effect done so. . . . Man takes his place among the other living creatures, who are likewise the handiwork of God. Therefore he has no inherent right to abuse or exploit the living creatures or the natural resources to be found in a world not of his making, nor intended for his exclusive use."[54]

Unlike the more atavistic elements in Deep Ecology, Judaism does not expect us to unstring the bow of consciousness, only to point the arrow of thought in the right direction. We are the risk the Creator was willing to take for the sake of being known by Creation. Or as Rosenzweig writes in his magnum opus *The Star of Redemption*, "What is creation from God's point of view can only mean, from the world's, the bursting forth of the consciousness of its creatureliness, its being created."[55] Similar views have been propounded by others, like the Jesuit paleontologist Teihlard de Chardin, who blended evolutionary theory with Christian teleology to theorize that "the consciousness of each of us is evolution looking at itself and reflecting upon itself."[56]

This view is not without its critics, including ecologist Stephanie Mills, who characterizes it as a kind of anthropocentric arrogance: "Humans want purpose, and our species a meaning, but becoming the biosphere's ego, if that's what we're doing, is costing an inordinate amount of life in tuition."[57] Jewish tradition is also steeped in ambivalence towards humanity, since "the imagery of man's heart is evil from his youth." (Gen. 8:21) Free will is a risky proposition, especially when refracted through the kaleidoscope of human desire. Consciousness gives rise to a sense of isolation and turns into self-consciousness, which breeds fear and anxiety. As Martin Buber writes in *Good and Evil*, humans need to choose but lack divine wisdom: "In the swirling space of image, through which he strays, each and every thing entices him to be made incarnate by him; he grasps at them like a wanton burglar, not with decision, but only in order to overcome the tension of omni-possibility."[58] So we seek first to limit nature, then to exploit it, by consuming its bounty with increasing speed until ultimately, in our confusion, we exhaust its capacity and face ecological collapse.

But according to traditional Judaism the gift of being created in God's image is inseparable from our responsibility to maintain an appropriate relationship with the rest of creation. As Lawrence Troster asserts, if we are "the 'brain cells' of Gaia," then we also "have the mandate for the cognitive anticipation of Gaia's needs, which ultimately are our own needs."[59] How then do we show our love for Gaia and demonstrate our understanding of her needs? Where do we find the guidance to make and maintain an ecologically sustainable society?

Revelation and Natural Law

For answers, Deep Ecology has combed the historical record, clear back to cave paintings, sifting through the relics of Eurasian paganism for clues to a new communitarian ethic. Goddess religions in particular have enjoyed a rebirth, including modern reconstructions of Native American and other earth-based religions like wicca.[60] According to Devall, ecologists seek "not a revival of the Romantic version of primal peoples as 'noble savages' but a basis for philosophy, religion, cosmology and conservation practices that can be applied to our own society."[61]

As a monotheistic contemporary of many ancient practices, Judaism is critical of their primitive animism, but concedes that some kind of transcendental experience is needed to make a success of what we now call "civilization." Judaism may even be uniquely qualified to advise on environmental matters, given its origin around the time of the first agricultural empires in the Middle East. It was during this period, according to ecopsychologists like Paul Shepherd and Chellis Glendinning, that we first began to "dissociate" from nature as our nomadic lifestyles gave way to settled agriculture.[62] But where some seek innocence in the mists of a lost Eden, Judaism strives to achieve a sustainable future by corralling human behavior within the bounds of the written and oral law, on the grounds that they originated in the mind of the Creator of heaven and earth.

However outmoded, a belief in revelation remains at the core of Jewish tradition. As Professor Leo Strauss explains in *Philosophy and Law*, revelation is not necessarily inconsistent with our experience and cannot be disproved as such. Like the concept of creation, it remained for the philosophers of the Enlightenment to try to prove the irrelevance of this idea by demonstrating that science itself is sufficient as a system of knowledge.[63] While many environmentalists are uneasy with its reactionary implications, the idea of revelation has recently found favor among spiritual ecologists in particular who consider it a subversive alternative to authoritarian planetary management in a world ruled solely by reason.

Here Judaism and Deep Ecology square off against a common enemy: the self-centered arrogance of modem science. As Strauss observes, "Finally, the belief is perishing that man can, by pushing back the 'limits of Nature' further and further, advance to even greater 'freedom,' that he can 'subjugate' nature, 'prescribe his own laws' for her, 'generate' her by dint of pure thought."[64] Or as Arne Naess commented in a 1982 interview, "All the sciences are fragmentary and incomplete in relation to basic rules and norms, so it's very shallow to think that science can solve our problems."[65]

Not all Deep Ecologists concede that we need the advice of religion or that rational thought is incapable of leading the way towards sustainability. As Soper argues, "We cannot seek to protect nature by pretending to forms of belief that have been exploded by the march of science and technology, however destructive that may have proved. What is needed, in fact, is not more Green religion, but more Green science."[66] Entomologist E. O. Wilson sides with Soper in this debate, placing himself squarely in the camp of Enlightenment thinkers who, he agrees, "got it mostly right."[67]

But if philosophy has proved anything in the past three hundred years, it is that reason cannot validate itself without sliding into solipsism and tautology. Notwithstanding Hegel's heroic efforts, modern philosophers have by and large abandoned attempts to banish irrationality to the margins of thought, turning instead to the "phenomenon" of existence and the force of individual choice.[68] Even our studies of the physical world have led us to a new appreciation of the role of chaos in the development of natural systems, revealing increased levels of complexity at every scale, from the cosmic to the subatomic.[69] On a practical level, too, the experience of at least a half-century of environmental management has taught us that the solution to most of our ecological problems depends less on science and technology and more on human values as reflected in public policy.

"We can name it whatever we wish," contends farmer/ecologist Wendell Berry, "but we cannot define it except by way of a religious tradition."

> The Great Economy, like the Tao or the Kingdom of God, is both known and unknown, visible and invisible, comprehensible and mysterious. It is, thus, the ultimate condition of our experience and of the practical questions rising from our experience . . . the circumstance of religion, the circumstance that causes religion.[70]

To Berry, the underlying problem is that our secular perspective "is not comprehensive enough. . . . [I]t tends to destroy what it does not comprehend." Berry claims that a religious point of view is necessary because its scope encompasses all actions and impacts, and it inspires humility and restraint. The instructions derived from such a perspective, while not always explicitly ecological, "are always implicitly so, for all of them rest ultimately on the assumptions . . . that we live within order and that this order is both greater and more intricate than we can know."[71] As an example, Berry cites the conservation of soil in the tradition of *shemittah*: "We build soil by knowing what to do but also by knowing what not to do and by knowing when to stop. . . . This, I take it, is the practical significance of the idea of the Sabbath [i.e., the Sabbatical Year]."[72]

Green science of the kind advocated by Soper, if it is truly green, must be guided by something that is not strictly science. From a philosophical perspective, Judaism supports Deep Ecology by offering a view of reality that includes the possibility of revelation in the form of laws like *shemittah* and *yovel* which emanate from an all-encompassing biocentric principle: "Choose life" (Deut. 30:19).

Redemption and the Restoration of Nature

At the Jubilee, God grants redemption (*ge'ulah*) to the land, releasing it from ownership (Lev. 25:24). All indentured servants are released from bondage (Lev. 25:40), and each family redeems any relatives sold into service to a non-Jew (Lev. 25:47). Elsewhere, God redeems Israel from slavery in Egypt (Ex. 6:6), and the prophets foretell that God will redeem Israel from sin (Is. 59:15–20). The mystic Isaac Luria understood redemption as the "mending" of the broken vessels of creation through the restitution of the world (*tikkun olam*). Modem Jewish theologians have developed this idea to emphasize the role of the individual in bringing about redemption.[73] Through redemption, the broken spirit and the shattered world are made whole.

While it is not often suggested as the goal of Deep Ecology, redemption has a close parallel in the concept of environmental restoration. A literal example of *tikkun olam*, ecosystem restoration has been generally defined as the process of direct intervention by humans to restore natural function to human-disturbed ecosystems.[74] "Like a doctor healing a patient, restoration is a process of synthesis in which humans put non-human nature back together again."[75]

The medical analogy links redemption and restoration, both of which are described as a kind of healing. In all cases—physical, spiritual, and ecological—health is not created directly but is attained by first removing the impediments to well-being and then strengthening natural processes. Spiritually, one atones for past sins (*teshuvah*) by making restitution and resolving to avoid future error before seeking redemption through prayer and right action. Ecosystem restoration begins with site remediation which may last for years (depending upon the severity of past abuse) before dikes are breached or topsoil added to establish habitat. Within the last half century, the focus of environmental protection policy in the United States has generally followed this progression, from clean-up to pollution prevention to restoration of biodiverse ecosystems.

Another similarity is that Judaism and Deep Ecology both approach their ultimate goals with measured steps. They differ in their particulars, but each prescribes a steady diet of small, discrete actions designed to realize in miniature its universal purpose. For example, the "Natural Step" program recently proposed by Swedish physician Karl Henrik Robert suggests four simple principles—resource conservation, pollution reduction, biodiversity, and equity—which serve as a yardstick against which all actions affecting the environment might be gauged.[76] The application of these principles to an infinite number of local environmental conditions implies the same sort of intense logic and debate that characterizes Talmudic discourse.

Given the challenges and uncertainties of their enterprise, those who struggle for redemption and restoration also share a high degree of faith in their aims and devotion to their goals. Deep ecologists acknowledge that ingrained political and economic policies are key obstacles to restoration and that, difficult as it may be, we need to reorient our cultural institutions to support ecologically responsible behavior. From a Jewish perspective, ecosystem restoration and spiritual redemption are both achieved when the entire community turns toward God and embraces the commandments. The reward for both is abundant blessing, although for ecologists their optimistic future may be enhanced by the artful integration of natural systems and appropriate technology. At the other end of the spectrum, both face an apocalyptic vision of plagues and deprivation.

On this point, Judaism and Deep Ecology each take the minority position against a society that fails to recognize the underlying sanctity of nature. But for Jewish ecologists the religious portfolio of the next millennium looks strikingly like the message of prophets from Noah (the archetypal conservationist) to Jonah (the Jewish Cousteau). It is a simple declaration: we forget our Creator and neglect our fellow creatures at our own peril. We are the recipients and not the creators of nature's bounty (Deut. 8:12–19), and the environmental decline we experience today is only the manifestation of our materialism—the natural consequence of failing to "give the land her Sabbaths."

Rituals for Radicals

In the conclusion to her book *Radical Ecology*, Carolyn Merchant forecasts that our ecological crisis "could be relieved over the next several decades . . . through a global ecological revolution brought about by changes in production, reproduction and consciousness that leads to ecological sustainability." [77] Her optimism is fueled by her observation that within radical ecology movements "theory and practice are linked, each informing and inseparable from the other."

Such a revolution is more likely to occur with the support of religions that not only link theory and practice but reinforce both with customs and rituals. Judaism, for instance, draws on its theory of creation to justify the ecological practices of *shemittah* and *yovel*, along with laws that prohibit wanton destruction (*bal tashchit*) and regulate sanitation and urban development. [78] More recently, laws regulating diet (*kashruth*) have been reconstructed as "eco-kashruth," extending the definition of clean and unclean specifically to include the origins of food, its method of growth and its environmental impact. [79]

Equally important, Jewish law and practice are encouraged by Jewish song and prayer, and nourished by Jewish food and drink. It is not sufficient for a religious point of view to comprehend global environmental problems; a religious tradition must maintain the discipline and provide the motivation adequate to address them. So the sabbath, welcomed weekly with fresh bread and sweet wine, invites those who observe it to approach their environment in a more receptive manner. (The thirty-nine categories of work prohibited on shabbat include virtually all the activities likely to be covered in any environmental impact report.) The spring and fall festivals are tied to the rhythms of the agricultural year, and the imagery of the psalms evokes the closeness felt by early Jews to their surroundings.

Many ecologists recognize the necessity of this type of learning, and include ritualistic elements in their activist programs. As Dolores LaChapelle observes, "Ritual is essential because it is truly the pattern that connects. . . . Ritual provides us with a tool for learning to think logically, analogically and ecologically as we move toward a sustainable culture."[80] This must be what the original Deep Ecologist Arne Naess had in mind when he suggested, "It is important to note that the traditional cultural beliefs and practices of much of the world are favorable to the norms of the deep ecological movement."[81] As Naess's translator David Rothenberg explains, "The environmental movement will be strongest if it can be shown that its concise set of principles can be derived from a variety of world-views and backgrounds. The more philosophical, religious, and scientific evidence can be found to support the normative values of environmentalism, the more important and universal the movement will be."[82]

Traditional Judaism has much to teach us about developing ecologically sustainable societies. It remains for those closest to the world's religions to find in their traditions the wisdom required to repair the world. And it is perhaps not the least valuable aspect of religions, including Judaism, that they offer hope at times when many are driven to despair. Such faith, and the courage to live by it, we all need now to protect ourselves and our planet from further degradation by our own hand.

NOTES

1. John McHale, *The Ecological Context* (New York: George Braziller, 1970), 22.

2. Murray Bookchin, *The Ecological of Freedom* (Palo Alto, Calif.: Chesshire Books, 1982), 18.

3. Tom Hayden, *The Lost Gospel of the Earth* (San Francisco: Sierra Club Books, 1996), 60.

4. Thomas Berry, *The Dream of the Earth* (San Francisco: Sierra Club Books, 1988), 87.

5. Carolyn Merchant, *Radical Ecology: The Search for a Livable World* (New York: Routledge Press, 1992), 11.

6. Arne Naess, *Ecology, Community and Lifestyle*, trans. David Rothenberg (Cambridge: Cambridge University Press, 1990), 29.

7. Merchant, 87.

8. Bill Devall and George Sessions, *Deep Ecology: Living as if Nature Mattered* (Salt Lake City: Peregrine Smith, 1985), 66.

9. Naess, 29.

10. Stephanie Mills, *Whatever Happened to Ecology?* (San Francisco: Sierra Club Books, 1989), 127.

11. James Lovelock, *Gaia: A New Look at life on Earth* (Oxford: Oxford University Press, 1979), 138.

12. *Chumash with Rashi-Leviticus*, trans. Rabbi A. M. Silbermann (Jerusalem: Silberman, 1985), 114.

13. Yehuda Feliks, *Nature and Man in the Bible: Chapters in Biblical Ecology* (New York: Soncino Press, 1981), xiii.

14. Daniel Hillel, *Out of the Earth: Civilization and the Life of the Soil* (Berkeley: University of California Press, 1991), 130.

15. Al Gore, *Earth in the Balance: Ecology and the Human Spirit* (New York: Plume, 1993), 132.

16. *Chumash with Rashi*, 114.

17. *Mishnah Shevi'it (with commentary by Kehati)*, trans. Rafael Fisch, ed. Avner Tomaschoff (Jerusalem: Eliner Library/Maor Wallach Press, 1994), 115 (on 9:2).

18. *Midrash Rabbah—Leviticus*, trans. J. Slotki (New York: Socino Press, 1983), 2 (on 1:1).

19. *The Torah: A Modern Commentary,* ed. W. Gunther Plaut (New York: UAHC, 1980), 940.

20. Merchant, 140, 239.

21. *Mishnah Shevi'it (with commentary by Kehati)*, 133 (on 10:2).

22. *Mishnah Shevi'it (with commentary by Kehati)*, 133 (on 10:3).

23. Michael Lerner, *Jewish Renewal, A Path to Healing and Transformation* (New York: Addison Wesley, 1994), 333.

24. Gerald Blidstein, "Man and Nature in the Sabbatical Year" [reprinted in this volume, 137].

25. Robert D. Sacks, *A Commentary on the Book of Genesis* (Lewiston, N.Y.: Edwin Mellen Press, 1990), 8 [reprinted in this volume, 148].

26. Sacks, 14 [reprinted in this volume, 154f.].

27. Lerner, 328.

28. *Midrash Rabbah—Ecclesiates*, trans. A. Cohen (New York: Soncino Press, 1983), 195 (on 7:13).

29. Sacks, 13 [reprinted in this volume, 154].

30. Lerner, 330.

31. Abrham J. Heschel, *God In Search of Man* (New York: Harper and Row, 1955), 418.

32. Nehama Leibowitz, *Studies in Vayikra* (Jerusalem: World Zionist Organization, 1980), 260.

33. Tom Athanasiou, *Divided Planet: The Ecology of Rich and Poor* (Athens, Ga: University of Georgia Press, 1998), 220.

34. David Harris, *The Last Stand: The War Between Wall Street and Main Street over California's Ancient Redwoods* (New York: Times Books, 1995), 27.

35. Robert Costanza et al., *Introduction to Ecological Economics* (Boca Raton: St. Lucie Press, 1997), 15.

36. *Chumash with Rashi*, 120.

37. Samuel Morrison, *Oxford History of the American People* (New York: Oxford Press, 1965), 595.

38. Paul Hawken, *The Ecology of Commerce* (New York: HarperBusiness, 1993), 127.

39. Clive Pointing, *A Green History of the World: The Environment and the Collapse of Great Civilizations* (New York: Penguin, 1991), 293.

40. Bookchin, *Freedom*, 139.

41. Roy Morrison, *Ecological Democracy* (Boston: South End Press, 1995), 53.

42. Athinasiou, 220.

43. Morrison, *Democracy*, 65.

44. Geoffrey Hodgson "Economics, Environmental Policy and the Transcendence of Utilitarianism," in *Valuing Nature? Economics, Ethics and Environment.* ed. John Foster (New York: Routledge, 1997), 61.

45. Costanza, 167.

46. Hodgson, 55.

47. Hodgson, 60.

48. Sacks, 110.

49. Martin Buber, *I and Thou*, trans. Walter Kaufman (New York: Scribners, 1970), 57.

50. Franz Rosenzweig, *The Star of Redemption*, trans. William Hallo (Boston: Beacon Press, 1972), 212.

51. Murray Bookchin, *Remaking Society* (Boston: South End Press, 1990), 10.

52. *Torat Hayim* (Jerusalem: Mossad HaRav Kook), 33.

53. Kate Soper, *What is Nature?* (London: Blackwell, 1995), 256.

54. Robert Gordis, "Ecology and the Judaic Tradition," in *Contemporary Jewish Ethics and Morality,* ed. Elliot Dorff and Louis Newmann (New York: Oxford University Press, 1995), 331.

55. Rosenzweig, 120.

56. Pierre Teilhard de Chardin, *The Phenomenon of Man,* trans. Bernard Wall (New York: Harper & Row, 1959), 221.

57. Mills, 222.

58. Martin Buber, *Good and Evil* (New York: Scribners, 1952), 90.

59. Lawrence Troster, "Created in the Image of God: Humanity and Divinity in the Age of Environmentalism" [reprinted in this volume, 172–82].

60. Dolores LaChapelle, "Ritual is Essential," Appendix F, in Bill Devall and George Sessions, *Deep Ecology: Living as if Nature Mattered* (Salt Lake City: Peregrine Smith, 1985), 247.

61. Devall, 96.

62. Chellis Glendinning, *My Name Is Chellis and I'm in Recovery from Western Civilization* (Boston: Shamballa Press, 1997), 70.

63. Leo Strauss, *Philosophy and Law,* trans. Eve Adler (New York: SUNY Press, 1995), 31.

64. Strauss, 31.

65. Devall, 75.

66. Soper, 277.

67. Edward Wilson, *Consilience: The Unity of Knowledge* (New York: Vintage Books, 1999), 8.

68. Rosenzweig, 10.

69. James Gleick, *Chaos: Making a New Science* (New York: Penguin, 1987), 279.

70. Wendell Berry, *Home Economics* (San Francisco: North Point Press, 1987), 57.

71. Berry, *Home*, 55.

72. Berry, *Home*, 66.

73. Michael Graetz, J. D. Leslie, and G. Scholem, "Redemption," in *Encyclopedia Judaica* (Jerusalem: Keter Publishing House, 1972), 6.

74. Dennis H. Yankee et al. *"Ecosystem Management for Sustainability*, ed. John D. Peine (Boca Raton: CRC Press, 1999), 418.

75. Merchant, 216.

76. Robert Erron, "The Natural Step—A Social Invention for the Environment," *Swedish Institute*, No. 401 (December, 1993) reprinted in *The Natural Step Handbook-Participants' Guide* (1995).

77. Merchant, 239.

78. Ellen Bernstein and Dan Flink, *Let the Earth Teach You Torah* (Wyncote, Pa.: Shomrei Adamah, 1992), 7.

79. Arthur Waskow, "Towards and Eco-Kosher Life Path," in *Jews, Money, and Social Responsibility*, ed. Lawrence Bush and Jeffrey Dekro (Philadelphia: The Shefa Fund, 1993), 177.

80. LaChapelle, 250.

81. Naess, 212.

82. Naess, 4.

12

"One, Walking and Studying . . .": Nature vs. Torah

Jeremy Benstein

רַבִּי יַעֲקֹב אוֹמֵר: הַמְהַלֵּךְ בַּדֶּרֶךְ וְשׁוֹנֶה, וּמַפְסִיק מִמִּשְׁנָתוֹ וְאוֹמֵר: 'מַה נָּאֶה אִילָן זֶה, מַה נָּאֶה נִיר זֶה,' מַעֲלֶה עָלָיו הַכָּתוּב כְּאִלּוּ מִתְחַיֵּב בְּנַפְשׁוֹ (פרקי אבות ג:ז)

Rabbi Ya'akov says: One, who is while walking along the way, reviewing his studies, breaks off from his studies and says, "How beautiful is that tree! How beautiful is that plowed field!" Scripture regards him as if he has forfeited his soul.

—Ethics of the Fathers 3:7

The Orthodox scholar Michael Wyschogrod ends his seminal essay "Judaism and the Sanctification of Nature" with the following thought:

> It is difficult to return to the religion of nature. It is difficult and dangerous, particularly for Jews, to worship nature again. At the same time the destruction of nature, which seems to follow to some extent from the desacralization of nature, has reached a stage that cannot continue. So we must try to combine these two themes. To be perfectly honest, I have long felt that the religion against which the prophets expounded so eloquently in the Hebrew Bible did not get a full hearing from them. I wonder whether the prophets gave a really fair representation of the point of view and theology of the worshipers of Baal and Ashteret. . . . Perhaps it would have been better if the prophets had occasionally sat down with them and said, "Tell us how you see the world." Could there be some insights in what they taught which we need to learn? I am convinced there were; and even if we don't agree with much of what they believed, I think we would profit by better understanding their point of view.[1]

While one can point to many profound ethical insights regarding the care and stewardship of the natural world in Judaism in particular, and Western monotheistic traditions in general, the desacralization of Nature that followed the rise of monotheism in ancient Israel is arguably one of the roots of our contemporary environmental crisis.[2] Perhaps for this reason, modern environmentalists are so drawn to Nature-worshiping (i.e., pagan) religious traditions for words of inspiration and guidance. The castigation and subsequent fear of paganism in Judaism goes back to Moses and the classical prophets' inveighing against its dangers upon entry into the Land, and during first Temple times; it is also a dominant theme in the Jewish reactions to Hellenistic culture and Greek philosophy, which affirmed the eternality of nature and denied Divine Creation. Even simple appreciation of God's handiwork in the world could be seen as dangerous, for appreciation could lead to sanctification, and then to deification and worship, which is heresy.

For Jews, the Torah—the revelation of God's will in words—has functioned as the antidote to the risks involved in unmediated experience of Nature. For that reason, the Torah and its study have often been a wedge, distancing us from a direct relationship with the natural world. But while the slippery slope from admiration to deification was understood, the other side of the coin, the danger of desacralization leading to alienation and then to exploitation, and hence devastation, has only become evident in our day.

The proportions of the contemporary environmental crisis should lead us to re-evaluate aspects of our tradition that perhaps have functioned in negative ways, or at least have had unhealthy side effects. This essay is a modest attempt at such re-evaluation.

CONTEXTS

Being a Jew with strong environmental concerns, one is often led to study the Sources with an eye for those particular teachings that are inspirational for—or at least compatible with—one's own predetermined "green" positions, and thus avoid challenging oneself with texts that don't fit current environmental wisdom. All three sides—Judaism, environmentalism, and ourselves—suffer from this sort of superficial understanding of what it means to learn Torah—or to interact with any age-old wisdom tradition. This essay looks at one of those "tough" traditional texts, one that is seemingly antithetical to any sort of sympathetic portrayal of the natural world, along with the ancient and modern commentaries that show how Jews have grappled with it in different generations, in an attempt to understand what it may be saying to us, in our generation.

The passage has frequently been understood to teach a rejection of the (natural) World, and any appreciation of it, in the face of the supreme—and ultimately, exclusive—value of Torah study. As such, it serves as a central prooftext for the claim that Judaism, at its core, is spiritually alienated from Nature; that Jewish tradition stands squarely behind Revelation (Torah) as its central religious category of experience and source of Truth while Creation (Nature) is seen as a potentially dangerous competitor, as an alternative—and therefore heretical—source of inspiration, or Truth(s), or experience of the Divine, whose seductive charms must be contained, or in this case, vehemently censured.

The text is a saying from that part of the Mishnah known as פרקי אבות *Pirkei Avot*, literally "Chapters of the Fathers," often translated as "Ethics of the Fathers." *Avot*, as it is also called, is a collection of ethical maxims and moral teachings of a nonlegally binding nature, ascribed to the *tannaim*, the sages of the Mishnaic period, who lived roughly from around the turn of the era, until c. 200 C.E. The teaching heads this article, together with a suggested translation. The English version is only one possibility among many, since like most significant ancient sources, it cannot be rendered simply or straightforwardly into modern English. Though the text is not particularly complex or sophisticated in style, any single "literal" translation invariably misses allusions and levels of meaning which not only deepen and enrich our understanding of the original, but also occupied the traditional and modern commentators whose interpretations we also wish to study. Therefore, in order to understand this text more fully, rather than work from a given translation, we will work toward an interpretation, via a close reading of the original, which will be "discussed into English," to use Robert Frost's phrase, in an approach inspired by translations of modern poetry.[3] This process will both facilitate the introduction of the commentaries (for while it is well known that every translation is, in fact, an interpretation, it is equally true that every interpretation is a translation of sorts) and open up the range of possibilities in the text for our own readings.

THE TEXT

רַבִּי יַעֲקֹב אוֹמֵר—Rabbi Ya'akov [Jacob] says. The first question we encounter is the attribution of the teaching. Some manuscripts relate this saying in the name of R. Ya'akov, some in the name of R. Shim'on.[4] This issue is not (just) a pedantic, academic one. It is important to understand this saying—which purportedly denigrates this material World, as compared with the Eternal Torah—in the wider context of the worldview of the sage(s) who allegedly uttered it. Rabbi Ya'akov is Ya'akov ben Korshai, a *tanna* (a sage of the mishnaic period) of the fourth generation, who lived in the mid-second century, and was a member of the Sanhedrin at Usha. He was a disciple of Rabbi Meir, a contemporary of Rabban Gamliel II, and was chosen to be the tutor of the young Rabbi Yehuda Hanasi the redactor of the Mishna, and one of the intellectual leaders of the era.[5] More important is Ya'akov ben Korshai's family background: he was the grandson of the (in)famous apostate Elisha ben Abuya, known as *Acher*—"the other." The very scenario[6] which was reputed to have caused Elisha ben Abuya to have lost his belief in God and in Divine justice, did not shake the faith of his grandson, Rabbi Ya'akov, for it was his firm belief that the poor child who died, though fulfilling two *mitzvot* that should have guaranteed him long life, would receive his length of days and just rewards in the World to Come. This emphasis on the next world seems to be a central axis of his thought, which ties into our mishna as well. Further along in *Pirke Avot*, he is quoted as saying the following: "This world is like a vestibule (פרוזדור) to the world to come; prepare yourself in the vestibule that you may enter into the (banqueting-) hall" (4:16). And: "Better is one hour of bliss of spirit (קורת רוח) in the world to come than all the life of this world."[7] It makes sense that our mishnah came from the same mouth that spoke these "anti-this-worldly" teachings.

Were Rabbi Shim'on to have originated this saying, though, that too would be fitting. The Rabbi Shim'on in question is none other than Rabbi Shim'on bar Yochai, a contemporary of Rabbi Ya'akov ben Korshai. He was one of the five remaining students of Rabbi Akiva who survived the failure of the Bar Kochba revolt, and himself had to flee the Romans and eventually hide out in a cave. According to the talmudic account (T. B. *Shabbat* 33b), he secluded himself, together with his son, for thirteen years, studying Torah day and night. When they finally emerged, they saw people going about their daily affairs, plowing and sowing, and not devoting themselves to Torah. They exclaimed: "מניהין חיי עולם ועוסקים בחיי שננה?" meaning, "they forsake eternal life (i.e., Torah study and its rewards), and devote themselves to temporal life?" When their fiery gazes destroyed all they looked upon, God came to the aid of his Creation and, their passionate devotion to divine Revelation notwithstanding, God rebuked them: "Have you emerged only to destroy My World? Return to your cave!"[8] Elsewhere, in a dispute about the value of labor, Rabbi Shim'on said: "If a person ploughs in the ploughing season, and sows in the sowing season, and reaps in the reaping season, and threshes in the threshing season, and winnows in the season of wind, what is to become of the Torah?"[9] For Rabbi Shim'on, Torah is an all-consuming and exclusive passion; any diversion, such as taking care of one's physical needs (here, significantly, represented by agriculture, i.e., work in nature) is a subversion, and must be fought. His "anti-this-worldliness" stems from considerations very different from those of Rabbi Ya'akov's, but our mishna from *Pirke Avot* dovetails with his value system as well.

The above are just the briefest of thumbnail sketches of the sages involved and their beliefs, but hopefully they serve to add some background, or flavor, to the saying under discussion. In the end, we relate to a teaching on the basis of its content, not on the basis of who it was who taught it, but it is important (where possible) to be aware of the larger intellectual context of the "life and times" of the relevant thinker(s), and the interrelationships among their ideas and values. When this is ignored, or de-emphasized, as is all too often the case, it is easy to forget that a given statement or teaching is the single voice of a particular sage, one view among many. A major point of this essay is to argue (by example) for taking voices like the one represented by this mishna seriously because they are *part of* Jewish tradition—but not because they *are* (the whole of) Judaism. One need look no further than sections of the book of Psalms, or Job, to discover other voices that speak about Nature in very different terms from these. Part of the richness of Judaism—and the excitement of Jewish learning—is the ongoing dialogue between the frequently very disparate voices of that tradition, a dialogue which we shall soon see continues through to the present day.

הַמְהַלֵּךְ בַּדֶּרֶךְ—*the walker on the road; he who walks by the way.* Two things are evident here: the mishnah is referring to an individual (not a group), and that person is out of doors and in transit from one place to another. A good example of a talmudic-style question that some commentators ask is: is this choice of phrasing *be-davka?* That is to say, is the mishnah referring specifically to an individual on the road, and therefore excluding a similar occurrence that might happen to someone sitting under a tree, or at home? Or is this just meant to be a general example, and apply in any situation? Several answers are discussed below.

The other important thing to note is the clear allusion to the Biblical verse (Deut. 6:7): ". . . וּבְלֶכְתְּךָ בַדֶּרֶךְ . . . וְשִׁנַּנְתָּם לְבָנֶיךָ וְדִבַּרְתָּ בָּם"—"and you shall repeat them [these words] to your children, and speak of them . . . when you walk along the way. . . ." If this verse directly underlies our mishnah, then the "peripatetic student" is not just engaging in a rather unusual pastime; he is actually fulfilling a mitzvah.

וְשׁוֹנֶה—*and is studying; while reviewing his studies; repeating [his Torah tradition].*[10] This verb is from the same root as שְׁנַיִם, שֵׁנִי—"two, second," that is, to do something a second time, to repeat. It is predicated specifically of oral review or verbal rote learning.[11] The use of this single, particular word gives us a very concrete image, perhaps different from what we imagined at first: our traveling learner is not walking around absentmindedly with his nose in a book, but rather taking advantage of some quiet time alone to go over what he has learnt, what he is trying to memorize—and very possibly fulfilling a mitzva as well. There is some discussion as to what is permissible subject matter for the road, even whether it is advisable to study while traveling at all. The conclusion in B.T. *Ta'anit* 10b is that rote repetition (מִיגְרַס) is acceptable for wayfarers, but "deep thought" or analysis (עִיּוּנֵי) is potentially dangerous. The danger in excessive engrossment in one's studies is not being alert to physical risks (of attack or mishap) or simply losing one's way. The "danger" in being diverted *from one's studies*—by what one sees along the way—well, that's the subject of our mishnah. But this particular word makes it clear that the literal risk is not so much losing one's train of thought, as actually forgetting the Torah that one is trying to learn.

מַפְסִיק מִמִּשְׁנָתוֹ וְאוֹמֵר—*and ceases his repetition; breaks off his study; interrupts his learning and says.* The strong terminology here seems to imply that this interruption is not a momentary lapse of attention, but a complete shift in the activity and mental state of the subject. The late chief rabbi of England, Rabbi J. H. Hertz, who seems rather ill at ease with the mishnah as a whole in his commentary, interprets these words to mean: "What is deprecated here is a willful distraction of the mind from Torah—meditation—by the surrounding scenery."[12]

מֶה נָאֶה אִילוֹן זֶה—"How beautiful or fine, is this tree!" The appreciation expressed here seems to be clearly of an aesthetic nature.[13] Many commentators have pointed out that there is a prescribed blessing that is to be recited at the sight of beautiful creatures (טובות בריות) and beautiful trees (טובות אילנות), from T.B. *Berachot* 58b: בעולמו ברוך שככה לו—"Blessed is the One whose world is thus."[14] Some claim, therefore, that the person who uttered these words was therefore engaging in an essentially praiseworthy activity, of praising God's creation; others point out that since the phrase here is not the מטבע ברכה, the set text of the blessing as prescribed, the subject here is expressing illegitimate (possibly heretical, at least frivolous), aesthetic expression, that is, not divinely oriented. This will be expanded upon below.

מֶה נָאֶה נִיר זֶה—"*How beautiful, or fine, is this furrow; this plowed field.*" While many translations have simply "field," this is inaccurate. As Rashi correctly points out, a ניר is not a שדה, a field, it is a שדה שנחרש, a field that has been plowed, and made ready for cultivation (see Jeremiah 4:3). This pinpoints the scene described in the mishnah once again: the student is not hiking through deep woods, but rather is walking along a country road, through farmland, apparently before the planting. It is reasonable to assume that it is springtime, which would mean the aforementioned tree is probably in bud (making it particularly attractive)—whether wild, or part of someone's orchard, as now seems likely.

It is also important to note that a furrow is a distinctly human creation, in contrast to the tree. Some commentators make much of this point—the divine creation together with the human.[15] Others point out that, while there is a blessing for the tree (even if our wayfarer only alluded to it, but didn't actually recite it), there is none prescribed for seeing a plowed field, no matter how attractive.

מֶעֲלֶה עָלָיו הַכָּתוּב—*Scripture accounts it to him, regards him; [such a person] is considered by the Torah.* This is another problematic part of our text. Invariably a formulation such as this is accompanied by a prooftext, a verse cited to justify the conclusion: "Scripture *regards* him." But no verse is included here. Rashi claims that that is strong enough evidence to doubt the actual phrasing of the mishnah; some versions[16] in fact do omit the word הכתוב—"Scripture," which results in: "this person is regarded as." Commentators have taken differing tacks. Herford wrote: "it is hard to imagine what text would support such a thesis";[17] likewise Hertz: "No text is, or could well be, quoted in support of this teaching."[18] But earlier than either of them, the authors of the Machzor Vitry, a prayer book composed in eleventh to twelfth century France by followers of Rashi, commented that there are a number of likely candidates: Proverbs 6:22, "when you walk, it will lead you"; the verse quoted above, Deut. 6:7, ". . .when you walk along the way . . ."; and also Deut. 4:9, "take utmost care, and watch yourselves scrupulously, so that you do not forget the things that you saw with your own eyes."[19] None of these verses is quite virulent enough, though, to justify the harsh "judgment" that follows.

כְּאִילוּ מִתְחַיֵב בְּנַפְשׁוֹ—*It is as if he* . . . Here we truly run into translation difficulties. A survey of a dozen editions yields more than ten different renderings. The range of possibilities includes: "were mortally guilty,"[20] "sinned against his own soul,"[21] "committed a capital offense,"[22] "were guilty against his own soul,"[23] "were guilty against himself,"[24] "has become liable for his life,"[25] "were 'guilty of death,'"[26] "had incurred guilt [expiable] by his life,"[27] "has forfeited his soul (life),"[28] "were guilty of deadly sin,"[29] "(has) hurt his own being."[30] This listing is somewhat random—there are undoubtedly other permutations and nuances which are possible.

There are two main difficulties in this three-word phrase, and they are related. The first is the significance of the modifier כאילו—"as if." In a previous mishnah (3:5) we are told that one who stays awake (or awakens) at night, or travels alone, or turns his heart to idle matters, that person has [*actually*] מתחיב בנפשו (choose one of the alternatives above). Why the difference? Why is the "punishment" (or judgment) for this apparent sin only "as if"? Is it less serious?[31] Are there mitigating circumstances? The other obvious difficulty is trying to figure out exactly what that judgment is. להתחייב is "to become, or to be found, guilty" (connected to חוב, הייב), and by extension, "to sin (with respect to)." נפש of course is "soul," but in premodern Hebrew it also refers simply to "self." In the rest of the Mishnah (outside of *Pirke Avot*), the phrase occurs in three other places,[32] all of them in a strictly legal context. All have the force of "receive the death penalty," hence also the rendering here "guilty of a capital offense," that is, worthy of death. But interpreting the guilt or the risk (or the damage) involved as physical harm seems excessively literal; perhaps this should be understood on a spiritual plane.[33] The modifying כאילו—"as if" certainly reinforces this (but in 3:5, without the modifier, the implication seems just as clearly metaphoric—nobody has been sentenced to death for insomnia, or for a penchant for solo travel!).[34] Therefore, in order to express the spiritual nature of the statement, but also retain the legalistic sense of punishment (or loss), the translation "has forfeited his soul" will be used.

This, then, is our reconstructed text:

> Rabbi Ya'akov says: One, who while walking along the way, reviewing his studies, breaks off from his study and says, "How beautiful is that tree! How beautiful is that plowed field!" Scripture regards him as if he has forfeited his soul.

Now, what do the commentaries have to say about it?

THE COMMENTARIES

Commentators over the centuries have responded to a wide range of issues connected to our mishnah, many of which are beyond the scope of this essay. The focus in the following selections will be the question of the relationship of Nature and its appreciation to Torah study and religious experience. It is important to note, however, that certain commentators did not see this as the central issue at all. For example, Shim'on ben Tzemach Duran (Spain, 1361–1444) wrote in his commentary *Magen Avot*:

> And although in our passage the Sages speak specifically of the exclamation, "How handsome is this tree, how handsome this field!"—the same is true of any other chatter (שיחה בטולה). But the Sage is referring to something commonplace, for it is customary for those who walk on the highway to talk of what they see along the way.[35]

Of course, the fact that Duran refers to verbal appreciation of nature as "chatter" (lit. useless or wasted speech) is significant to our discussion, and would place him in line with the views of Meiri and Abarbanel described below.

Most, however, did relate specifically to the issue of Torah and Nature. Regarding the question, we can discern three broad approaches in the classical and contemporary traditional commentaries.[36] All in some way "justify" the mishnah, that is to say, interpret the text in such a way so as to extract a message that is acceptable (to them). None rejects or negates the passage (as the Zionist Berdichevski did—see below). The differences appear in how they relate to Nature per se. The first is complete subordination—to the point of denigration—of the value of Nature, and of appreciation for the works of Creation—in the face of the supremacy of Revelation—and the study of Torah. Meiri (Menahem ben Solomon HaMe'iri, France, 1249–1306) considers such appreciation "vain" and "idle":

> The reason for such strong condemnation is this: by [his] nature man is drawn to vanity (הבלים) and idle matters (שיחות בטולות); [if he does not resist his nature] he will be drawn on from such habits to throwing off the yoke of the Torah completely.[37]

And Don Isaac Abarbanel, the great fifteenth-century Spanish commentator, writes in his commentary *Nachalat Avot* that material concerns such as this are "useless":

> When a person who was walking along the way, and reviewing his studies, stopped his studying in order to pay attention to things that are of no use (תועלת אין בהם), then he forfeits his soul, because he ceased his study, and made it secondary, peripheral (טפל) and made the other worldly, material things (הדברים הגשמים) central (עיקר).

A second, more moderate—and more prevalent—approach also sees the acts of Creation as subordinate to the words of Revelation, but recognizes the act of appreciation of those acts, praising God for the divine handiwork,[38] as correct and valuable in itself, but still not as important as Torah study. Representatives of this approach among traditional commentators are Bertinoro (Obadiah ben Abraham Bertinoro, Italy, 1470–1520):

> And there are those who say that this (particular example) teaches us something significant, that despite the fact that he would be brought to recite a blessing— "Blessed is the One who has such [beauty] in His world"—nevertheless, he is accounted as if he forfeited his life, since he ceased his studying.

And Rabbi Yitzchak Magriso, in the *Me'am Loez*, an eighteenth-century Ladino anthology of commentary and stories:

> The case which he is discussing is not that of a person who puts aside his studies merely to engage in useless chatter, but to praise God for the beautiful tree that he saw. Nonetheless, since this person has stopped studying, it is counted as if he were engaging in useless speech, and it is considered a sin. What one should do under the circumstances is complete the subject of his study, and then praise God for the beautiful sight. From this one can see how great is the sin of interrupting one's studies, since even praising God is considered a waste of time. How much greater is the sin of abandoning one's studies without good reason, for a real waste of time.[39]

Modern commentators have also adopted this approach, which seems to afford a comfortable "middle road," by allowing affirmation of the World, without denying the traditional primacy of Torah study. Reuven Bulka develops this point at length:

> If, as has been posited in the previous mishna, all is God's, this would include the heavens and the earth, nature, the trees, the fields. One can see in all of this the greatness and majesty of God. Nevertheless, this should not develop into an equation of sameness. There is profound significance in everything, but not everything is the same. There is a scale of values; there are priorities and levels of importance. One who is walking by the way in study and interrupts the study to admire nature by saying "*How beautiful is this tree!*" or another such statement that affirms the majesty of God in the world, has made a priority substitution that is distorted. This distortion inheres in that such an individual has seen fit to interrupt Torah study to admire nature. Admiring nature is part of appreciating the beauty of the world, but not a priority when juxtaposed with Torah study. Nature is God's work, but the Torah is God's formula for life. Interrupting Torah to admire nature is a value distortion. The mishna ends by saying that the individual who makes the value distortion *is regarded by Scripture as having forfeited one's soul.* It is unclear which verse in Scripture is the proof text for this. In all probability, it would seem that Scripture in general makes this observation. It is in the very nature of the importance of Scripture. One who denies Scripture's importance by placing primacy on nature, by interrupting Torah meditation to admire nature, Scripture itself sees this

as a rejection of the very notion of Scripture's being so vital to life, and being the most crucial of all human pursuits. Placing this pursuit in a subordinate position to admiring nature denies the primary importance of Scripture. It is as if one has forfeited one's soul, because in the process of placing Torah and its values in a secondary position, one has denied its essentiality to life and has thus compromised the value actualization which is so vital for a meaningful life.[40]

A third approach, very different from the first two, can be seen in the commentary of Rabbi Yosef Hayyim Caro (1800–1895, Eastern Europe). Though unswervingly orthodox—he studied under the great halachist Rabbi Akiva Eiger—Caro had some familiarity with German literature, and was also a proponent of Jewish settlement in Palestine. His commentary is strikingly original, and will be presented and discussed in detail.[41] He begins by formulating the questions that strike him as most troubling, and to which he plans to respond:

> The commentators have had great difficulty in interpreting this mishna: why should one forfeit his life in saying "*how fine is . . . etc.*"? If it is because he ceased from his studies, then it should have been phrased simply "he who was studying, and stops his study, it is accounted to him . . . etc." And also—what is the meaning of the [apparently extraneous] *walking by the way*? Is it permissible then to break off one's studies in one's house?

Clearly, the element of being out of doors and the specific remark about trees and fields is not accidental, and requires addressing. He goes on to explain how he feels that one can know God through natural events:

> It seems to me, that Rabbi Jacob's words refer to the following—There are certain people who know the Blessed Creator through His amazing creations, as in "The heavens declare Your Glory, O God" (Ps. 19). And it is not only in the high heavens that one can discern the actions of the Creator, but also in the seed in the ground, and in the fruit of the tree that grows in the field, in the lowly mosses that can be seen growing on walls, all the way to the mighty, lofty cedars of Lebanon, because all these express the might of God and His wonders.

All of Nature—not just the "celestial fireworks"—bears close scrutiny, for it all is indicative of divine action, and instructive regarding God. Caro's next move is far more radical:

> And were it not for the danger of failure, this way would be the superior one. Not only that, but all the miracles and wonders through which the Holy Blessed One makes known His might and glory, were created solely for the people who have not reached this spiritual level of knowledge of the Creator, and they are the vast majority; but for those few whose eyes are open to see the wonders of Nature, these enlightened ones will observe, and reflect, and come to know the wonders of God through the usual order of natural processes. . . . For from these can be seen that everything has been established in wisdom, understanding and knowledge, and they can sense in their souls that this is the work of a wisdom that far

surpasses any idea or concept [of ours], and this is our transcendent Creator; but people are fools, for everything that seems to them the usual course of nature, they will pay no attention to—"they have eyes, but will not see"—unless God creates something totally new upon the earth, then they will hop and skip like a ram, on the hind legs of their reason, saying: "Look! Now surely Hashem is God!" Like at the Red Sea, which was a sign for the rebellious among them, that they should believe in God, whereas the insightful sage will say, aren't these great waters which have been flowing for thousands of years a greater testament to the might of their Maker? As King David wrote (Ps. 93:4): "from the crash of great waters, the mighty breakers of the sea, The Lord on high is awesome." What could the miracle of those waters drying up for a few hours at God's command, possibly add to that?

Those fancy Biblical miracles—they are for the spiritually shortsighted. The vast majority of people considers those extraordinary events to be proof of God's acting in the world—and needs them, to believe that—while all around them, every day, occur miracles of far greater magnitude, to which they are blind! Those miracles are "invisible" to us because they do not stand out against the background of the natural order—they are the natural order. And that order testifies "more faithfully to the power and glory of the Blessed Creator, than all that He did against Pharaoh and his armies." Were it not for a certain (theological) danger, which will be outlined presently, this way, of the study and experience of Nature, would be superior even to Torah study. Caro continues:

> If people's consciousness were fuller, they should know their Creator from the wonder of His creatures and His acts; but in truth, judging from human nature, this is not the case, for the people's discernment is insufficient to consider and understand the complete significance of those things to which they have become accustomed. . . . Even though in truth it were better for us to strive to know God through the wonders of nature, in any event, were the weakness of our understanding not enough, whoever depended solely on this route is in danger of stumbling, and falling into the trap of denying the belief in a Creation at all and other true beliefs; therefore, the remarks of the Torah, which tell of the wonders of the Creator in upsetting the natural order, are necessary and fitting according to our temperament and characteristics, and also safer, and prevent us from [falling into] stumbling and transgression, as we wrote in a previous work for Jewish children: "the words of the Living God are more trustworthy than the testimony of earth and heaven."

Here Caro "retreats" slightly, and begins to lay the groundwork for explaining why our mishnah is not in fact mistaken in warning against the dependence on Nature for religious inspiration. The idea that God created the World is not something that can be deduced from our experience of it, he claims. It is equally reasonable to assume that the World is eternal, and uncreated—a belief held by the ancient Greeks, and considered heinously heretical by the rabbis. In order for us to understand what we are looking at, we need God's Torah as an interpretive guide. That goes for the sage as well, who, unlike the masses of closed-minded people, does discern the wondrous nature of all that goes on in the environment—but the natural order, however much appreciated, does not interpret itself.

Caro now turns to the text of the mishnah itself, and interprets its particular message:

> This, then, is the meaning of the words of R. Jacob in our mishnah, he who walks by the way, that is to say, that he walks the Way of Goodness, to achieve the object of his desire in knowing God, and establishing in his heart the love and fear of God; and *he was learning and he breaks off his learning, and says "how fine is this tree, etc."* i.e., he ceases his Torah study, saying that we have no need for it to achieve this goal, but rather [knowledge and love of God can be achieved through correct observation of the beauty of the natural order and its creation, he, then, *would forfeit his soul*, for what could be easier than that he should succumb to the disease of heresy, as described above, and he himself would be the guilty party, for he left the Source of Living Waters, our Holy Torah, which comprised his learning according to what human reason is capable of, and to what he is accustomed. . . .
>
> And in saying *"Scripture accounts it to* him . . . ," the mishnaic sage was no doubt referring to the verse [Deut 4:9, quoted in the following mishnah] "Take utmost care and watch yourselves scrupulously, so that you do not forget the things that you saw with your own eyes . . .", in which our Holy Torah warns us to remember the day of the receiving of the Torah, such that we worship God from this perspective, and not from the perspective of the structures of nature. For nature is always visibly present, and it is difficult to imagine forgetting it, but the revelation of the Torah at Sinai, it is only too possible for human beings to forget, and so it is about this that we were warned. Understand this. . . .
>
> We were instructed about [the importance of] learning, and the testimony of the Torah, so that we don't rely exclusively on the testimony of Nature alone.

So Nature is neither useless, nor peripheral; it is clearly on a par with Torah, in the potential it has as a means for reaching God, but it is unfortunately less trustworthy, and needs to be backed up by, or placed within the framework of, divine truth as revealed in the Torah. Torah as Revelation, though, can be forgotten—therefore it requires special attention and care. Nature, on the other hand, is always "out there," Caro claims, and is less in need of human focus to avoid being forgotten. This contradicts in part what he wrote previously, for the inability of masses of people to appreciate the significance of what is always in front of their eyes is certainly a type of forgetting. And the fiery Zionist ideologue Micha Yosef Berdichevski, while admiring many of Caro's sentiments, would certainly disagree with his conclusion.

MODERN AND ZIONIST RESPONSES

Before we turn to Berdichevski and other interpretations inspired by Zionist ideals, it is worthwhile to make mention of three other, very different modern opinions. In his essay "The Unnatural Jew," the late Prof. Steven Schwarz-schild claims not only that, yes, Jews have been alienated from Nature over the centuries, but that this is *good*. "The main line of Jewish philosophy (in the exilic age) has paradigmatically defined Jewishness as alienation from and confrontation with nature." Any other approach, such as pagan ontologism or Greek-inspired Christian incarnationism, "results in human and historical sub-mission to what are acclaimed as 'natural forces.'" Anything which smacks of immanentism—from Spinoza and Marx to Kabbala and Zionism—is a "specif-ically Jewish heresy." Zionism in particular is classed as pagan and non-Jew-ish, in what he derisively refers to as the "back-to-nature thrust [which] in-heres in the Zionist enterprise." It is no surprise, therefore, to find that our mishnah is Schwarzschild's "favorite text." For him, Rabbi Ya'akov represents a positive and candid statement of mainstream Jewish dogma.[42]

For the sociologist Eric Hoffer, on the other hand, Rabbi Ya'akov is only one of a long line of fanatics in the history of the human race, who are characterized by dangerously blind, single-minded devotion to a cause. In his classic study of religious and political dogmas and their fanatical ad-herents, *The True Believer*, Hoffer cites our mishnah, along with the ex-ample of the medieval monk and crusader St. Bernard of Clairvaux, who would pace around beautiful Lake Geneva, lost in thought—never seeing the lake. Hoffer writes:

> The fanatic's disdain for the present blinds him to the complexity and uniqueness of life. . . . In *Refinement of the Arts*, David Hume tells of the monk "who, be-cause the windows of his cell opened upon a noble prospect, made a covenant with his eyes never to turn that way." The blindness of the fanatic is a source of strength . . . but it is the cause of intellectual sterility and emotional monotony.[43]

For Hoffer, it is partly the fanatically exclusive allegiance to an ideology which he finds repugnant; but it is also specifically that such devotion alien-ates the "true believer" from the breadth and richness of the world, and it is no coincidence that his examples are drawn from expressions of being cut off from the natural world in particular.

A particularly compelling literary treatment of our text is provided by Cyn-thia Ozick in her short story "The Pagan Rabbi." The mishnaic quote serves as the epigraph, and, as the title alludes, the story revolves around a rabbinic scholar, Isaac Kornfeld, who progressively forsakes his talmudic studies for an ever-deepening fascination with Nature, culminating in a love affair with a nymph. His romantic attachment to this creature leads to the separation of his soul from his body, and after that, his suicide. From the suicide note passed on to the widowed *rebbetzin*, we gather snippets of the source of his heresy. "There is nothing that is Dead. There is no Non-life. Holy life subsists even in the stone, even in the bones of dead dogs and dead men. Hence in God's fecundating Creation there is no possibility of Idolatry, and therefore no possibility of committing this so-called abomination." This is pagan immanentism, by all accounts, and the "abomination," the coupling of his "indwelling" soul with the free-roaming dryad, leads to his soul's being "snatched straight from (his) frame." She then sends him to confront his soul, which appears to him in the form of an ugly old man, trudging down the road bent over under the burden of a dusty bag stuffed with ancient books. He reads as he goes, "he reads the Law and breathes the dust and doesn't see the flowers." He explains: "'I will walk here alone, always, in my garden'—he scratched on his page—'with my precious birds'—he scratched at the letters—'and my darling trees'—he scratched at the tall side-column of commentary."[44] Ozick's treatment, as an expansion and commentary on our mishnah, reinforces the dichotomizing of Jew and pagan, presenting the soul of the Jew as eternally, irredeemably, book-bound. Though thoroughly repulsed by his own soul—and the image is repulsive in its extremity—the rabbi can only break free from it through suicide. A classical Zionist would see in this character description the height of the *galuti* Jew: that repugnant, "exilic" type of Judaism. It is to the Zionist readings that we now turn.

Three approaches—in the form of explicit interpretations of this mishnah—have been expressed in the context of Zionism, the Jewish national return to the Land of Israel. As one might expect, classical Zionist thought, which represented both a secular-political critique of Diaspora religiosity, seen to be desiccated and overly intellectualized, and an affirmation of the renewed connection with the Land, would have a problem with a teaching such as Rabbi Ya'akov's.

The most extreme reaction is undoubtedly that of Micha Yosef Berdichevski who later took the name Bin Gurion. Berdichevski was born in Russia, in 1865, to a family of distinguished rabbinic lineage. He was soon a recognized scholar in all branches of traditional Jewish learning, including Talmud, Kabbala, and Chassidism. But like many of his generation, the *Haskala* (enlightenment) and the world of secular learning beckoned him. In 1890, he moved to Western Europe and deepened his exposure to the intellectual currents of the time. He was deeply influenced by Nietzsche and the latter's call for "a transvaluation of all values" in culture. When it came to the Jewish tradition, he had a love-hate relationship, and in his writings "he saw only tension and affirmed only revolt."[45] He certainly expressed that Nietzschean idea in his writings on Judaism (a radical secular Zionist had a lot to "transvalue" in Jewish Europe at the turn of the century), but the love-hate ambiguity is also very present in his style. Arthur Hertzberg uses King James cadences in his translation in order to capture Berdichevski's luxuriant Biblical language in this paean to nature, which nevertheless does not negate or exclude God:

> The Universe telleth the glory of God, the works of His hand doth Nature relate;
> for Nature is the father of all life and the source of all life; Nature is the fount of all,

the fount and soul of all that live. . . . And then Israel sang the song of the Universe and of Nature, the song of heaven and earth and all their host, the song of the sea and the fullness thereof, the song of the hills and the high places, the song of the trees and the grass, the song of the seas and the streams. Then did the men of Israel sit each under his vine or his fig tree, the fig put forth her buds and the green hills cast their charm from afar. . . . Those days were the days of breadth and beauty. . . . We had thought that God was power, exaltation, the loftiest of the lofty. We had thought that all that walked upon the heights became a vehicle for His presence, but lo! a day came in which we learned otherwise.

That day was the beginning of the otherworldly, Diaspora mentality that prized ethereal spirituality over all else. The value of political sovereignty, a deep relationship with one's natural surroundings, national pride—all these fell by the wayside.

Is it any wonder that there arose among us generation after generation despising Nature, who thought of all God's marvels as superfluous trivialities?

Is it surprising that we became a non-people, a non-nation—non-people indeed?

I recall from the teaching of the sages: Whoever walks by the way and interrupts his study to remark, How fine is that tree, how fine is that field—forfeits his life!

But I assert that then alone will Judah and Israel be saved, when another teaching is given unto us, namely: Whoever walks by the way and sees a fine tree and a fine field and a fine sky and leaves them to think on other thoughts—that man is like one who forfeits his life!

Give us back our fine trees and fine fields! Give us back the Universe.[46]

Like many Zionists, even in his absolute rejection of them, Berdichevski remains tied to the texts, and the categories of their thought, which formed his identity. He is claiming here that Zionism can only be fulfilled when we not only reject the implications of Rabbi Ya'akov's teaching, but when we adopt the exact opposite outlook. If the tradition gives primacy to Torah study over Nature, then we must reverse the priorities, and make our relationship with the World—in all its manifestations—central, and relegate Torah study to the spiritual backseat, if we validate it at all. If we take his reading at face value, he seems to be claiming that the Land can replace the Book as the Jewish people's prime source of sustenance, of identity, and existence. According to Hertzberg, Berdichevski asserted that "nature worship and idolatry, not biblical monotheism, had been the real religion of ancient Israel in its days of glory."[47] Other Zionist thinkers and writers, notably the poet Saul Tchernichovski, were sympathetic to this quasipagan approach.

Another Zionist understanding of our mishnah is provided by Ahad Ha'am and Chayim N. Bialik. They were of the same generation as Berdichevski, but did not call for a radical rejection of all things Jewish.[48] Instead they worked for a secular rejuvenation of Jewish culture, based on the renewed study, and reinterpretation of our age-old Sources. They also believed that a new relationship between Torah and Nature would have to be forged in the rebuilt Jewish society in the Land of Israel. But rather than rejecting, or inverting the teaching of our mishna, as Berdichevski had done, they *contextualized* it, making it a teaching that was crucial for our years wandering in the Diaspora, but now was in need of revision. Bialik wrote the following in his seminal essay "Halakhah and Aggada," attributing the idea to Ahad Ha'am:

> It is not without significance that the people of Israel, or at least the great majority of them, submitted to the iron yoke of Halakhah, and not only that, but actually chose to carry with them into exile a heavy load of laws and ordinances. . . . And here is what the Halakhist himself says: "If a man studies as he walks, and breaks off his study to say 'How lovely is this tree! How lovely is this field!'—Scripture regards him as guilty of deadly sin." Our aestheticists have spent all their ammunition on this unfortunate mishnah: but even here the sympathetic ear will detect, between the lines, the apprehension, the trembling anxiety for the future, of a wandering people which has nothing to call its own but a Book, and for which any attachment of its soul to one of the lands of sojourn means mortal danger.[49]

So long as the Jews were in lands other than their own Land of Israel, "walking the roads of Exile," connected not to a real homeland, but to their "portable homeland," as Heine characterized the relationship of the Jews to Torah, then, yes, rejecting that spiritual inheritance for the sake of a tenuous connection with "one of the lands of their sojourn" is potentially spiritual suicide. So, according to Bialik and Ahad Ha'am, this mishnah is not talking about all of Nature—only Diaspora Nature.[50] Only that sort of diversion presents a spiritual threat. And it follows that once the Jews return to their land, a new balance can be struck, which can validate both sides of the equation, with neither suffering at the hands of the other. The Land—a metonym of all of Creation, but also the special portion of the Jewish people—would take its place alongside the Book.

CONCLUSION: A NEW VISION

What is that new balance, and how is it to come about? A complete answer to that question has yet to be worked out—for as the Jerusalem educator Moti Bar-Or has remarked, the Jewish people may have begun to make *aliyah* to the Land of Israel, but the Torah has not yet made *aliyah*, has not yet resettled in the Land. In Israel, the Abraham Joshua Heschel Center for Nature Studies has been founded to work out the implications of a Jewishly rooted approach to the natural environment, and to do educational work in this area. We believe this to be of particular concern in the Zionist context of the return of the Jewish people to the Land of Israel, our own particular piece of the natural world; but making our relationship to the World an item on the Jewish educational agenda should be a priority in the Diaspora as well.[51] Ecological concerns are thankfully becoming more prevalent among many sectors of the population, especially youth. Exploring in a deep and sophisticated way the relevancy of Jewish learning to students' deepest personal concerns can only help revitalize Jewish education, and on the other side, give environmentalism significant spiritual roots that can help make it an integral part of our worldview, and not relegate it to the status of a passing fad.

A Jewish environmental ethic should be based on the sense of responsibility that flows from our awe at the wonders of Creation. Regarding responsibility, traditional Jewish teaching has focused on מצוות בין אדם לחברו *mitzvot bein adam le-chavero*, the (ethical) commandments concerning our duties to our fellow human beings, and בין אדם למקום, *bein adam le-Makom*, the (primarily ritual) commandments which help express our relationship to God.[52] What is needed today is a new, third category: מצוות בין אדם לעולמו, *mitzvot bein adam le-olamo*,[53] the *mitzvot*, and the concomitant sense of commandedness, which can inform and define our place in the World, and our responsibility towards it. These commandments bridge, and transcend, the traditional categories of ethics and ritual. The *mitzvah* of בל תשחית, *bal tashchit*, the prohibition of inappropriate use and excessive consumption, is not a ritual, but neither is it ethically directed at the welfare of other human beings. Similarly, *shabbat* and *kashrut* are conventionally considered ritual commandments, yet have significant environmental implications. Once we have a name for something, then we can begin to talk about it on, and in, its own terms.

To this end, Jewish teachers need to learn how to integrate interaction with the natural world, and religious thinking about it, into educational experiences which until now have been classroom-bound, and limited to what can be printed between the covers of a book (or with more creativity and funding—on disk or cassette). We need to reinterpret that other potentially antienvironmental Pirkei Avot text, the saying attributed to Ben Bag-Bag (5:24): הפך בה והפך בה דכלא בה—"Study it [the Torah], and review it, for *everything* is contained within it." The prevalence of this perspective has made us blind to all those things which are not contained in the books—as wide and deep and rich as our vast sacred bibliography is. Jewish summer camping has great potential, though too often stunning natural camp settings are treated as no more than static props, or scenery against which the otherwise unaffected drama of camp life takes place. It is not enough just to be "out there," or take those hikes which have become part and parcel of the Jewish summer camp experience: for true interaction and integration to take place, the learning that goes on must relate to the apple trees and not just take place under them. And rabbis, who are accustomed to trying to elicit religious experiences among their congregants in the synagogue sanctuary, and via the *siddur*, the text of the prayer book (clearly often with only limited success), need to be trained to foster spiritual sensitivity out-of-doors as well, in response to Creation—in the forests, deserts, oceans, and even just the front and back yards of the World. There may be some surprises in store.

Three Zionist approaches were announced above, but only two were presented. The third is a *torah she-be'al pe'*, an oral teaching that has defied all efforts to trace it to a written source.[54] This interpretation zeroes in on two words: מפסיק ממשנתו *ceases, breaks off from his study*. The force of our mishnah hinges on there being a dichotomizing, the breaking off of the Torah study in order to experience Nature. All the commentaries cited above assume this dichotomous reading, whether anti-Nature, like the Meiri or Schwarzschild, or moderately or radically affirming of the value of Nature, like Caro or Berdichevski. This assumption results in an either-or, black-and-white world view; it allows only for a pat acceptance of the *peshat* (in this case, the surface, literal meaning) of the mishnah, or a Berdichevskian rejection, leading to the establishment of an opposite, but equally alienating hierarchy of values. As Jews, whether in the Diaspora or in the Land of Israel, we cannot מפסיק ממשנתו, turn our backs on the texts, or cease to define ourselves in terms of them: an *exclusively* nature-based identity is not a Jewish identity. But neither can we afford any longer to accept the dichotomizing of the world and of our own souls. This third interpretation consciously negates that assumption, and proposes a competing version of the *peshat* based on synthesis.

Yes, if in order to relate to the natural environment you have to cease your learning, then your soul is in grave danger. This, then, is the sin that is castigated here: the radical rupture between Torah and Nature, the traditional, Diaspora-Jewish incommensurability of Creation and Revelation. What is called for today is *synthesis*, a supreme effort to mend that gap, to forge a common language for our disparate forms of religious experience. One who perpetuates this dichotomy, this spiritual feud, is in truth risking great spiritual, and physical harm. But one who walks by the way, engaged in Torah thoughts, and who ממשיך במשנתו—*continues* that study, seeing the beautiful tree and the field and our relationship to them, as an extension, as an expansion, of that study, that person will have performed a great act of *tikkun* (repair): *tikkun ha-'olam*, a mending of the World, and *tikkun hanefesh*, of our (previously endangered) souls.

NOTES

From *Judaism: A Quarterly Journal* 44 (1995): 146–68.

I would like to thank Noah Efron and Noam Zion for their helpful critiques of the form and content of this essay; and the participants of the Beit Midrash Elul workshop on "Nature and the Human Spirit: Jewish Perspectives on the Environment" co-led by myself and Eilon Schwartz during 1993–94 in Jerusalem.

All translations of passages from the Babylonian Talmud are taken from the Soncino translation, Rabbi Dr. I. Epstein, editor, Soncino Press, London. The following abbreviations are used in the notes: M. = Mishnah; T. B. = Babylonian Talmud; T. Jer. = Jerusalem (Palestinian) Talmud.

1. See Wyschogrod, "Judaism and the Sanctification of Nature," 7 [reprinted in this volume, 296].

2. It is important to emphasize "*one* of the roots." Much space in environmentalist scholarship is devoted to thrashing out various points of view. On this issue, David Ehrenfeld, for instance, has argued that the rise of humanism and the scientific revolution plays a much more direct and central role. For a review of this debate, see Anna Bramwell, *Ecology in the 20th Century: A History* (New Haven: Yale University Press, 1989), ch. 2.

3. *The Poem Itself: 45 Modern Poets in a New Presentation*, ed. Stanley Burnshaw, Dudley Fitts, Henri Peyre, and John Frederick Nims (New York: Holt, Rinehart and Winston, 1960); and *The Modern Hebrew Poem Itself*, ed. Stanley Burnshaw, T. Carmi, and Ezra Spicehandler (New York: Schocken Books, 1965). The pithiness of mishnaic texts like *Avot* lend them a poetic compactness that invites this sort of treatment.

4. There are even editions with the name of Rabbi Akiva, but this seems particularly implausible. The weight of scholarly opinion seems to support R. Ya'akov. See R. Travers Herford, *The Ethics of the Talmud: The Sayings of the Fathers* (New York: Schocken, 1945/1962); and H. Albeck and H. Yalon, *Shishah Sidre Mishna* (Hebrew) (6 vols.; Jerusalem: Bialik Institute/Tel Aviv: Dvir, 1952–56), in notes at end of tractate, who has R. Shim'on in the body of the text, but writes: נוסח אחר, ונכון-ר. יעקב.— "a different version, which is correct has: Rabbi Ya'akov."

5. See T. Jer., *Shab.* 10:5, 12c–d; *Pes.* 10:1, 37b.

6. Recounted in T. B. *Kiddushin* 39b, and again at the conclusion of *Chullin* (142a). The mishnah (M. *Kid.* 1:10) which that particular gemara is relating to seems to be claiming that there is direct and immediate reward in this world for the performance of *mitzvot*. Rabbi Ya'akov disagrees, saying: "There is no reward for precepts in this world. . . . [T]here is not a single precept in the Torah whose reward is [stated] at its side which is not dependent on the resurrection of the dead" (i.e., the next world). A Rabbi Joseph is quoted as saying there that if Acher had interpreted as did his daughter's son, Rabbi Ya'akov, he would not have come to sin.

7. *Ethics of the Fathers*, 17.

8. It is interesting to note that the conclusion of this tale is that Rabbi Shim'on bar Yochai (or RaShBi, as he is known) is eventually reconciled with the Jewish people, and the world, when, as Shabbat eve is approaching, he sees an old man running with two myrtle branches in his hand. He asks the old man what they are for, and the old man tells him that they are in honor of the Shabbat, one symbolizing *Zachor* ("remember"—the aspect of the Shabbat emphasized in the Ten Commandments in the book of Exodus) and the other representing *Shamor* ("observe"—the aspect of the Shabbat in the Ten Commandments in Deuteronomy). In other words, the (apparently original, unprecedented) ritual use of the branches of a tree in the context of Shabbat helps put his mind at ease about the fate of the world.

9. T. B. *Berachot* 35b. Due in part to his mystical, fiery character, and also to the mysterious isolation in the cave, RaShBi is traditionally considered to be the author of the great mystical masterwork, the *Zohar*.

10. This last is Neusner's rendition, in his *Torah from Our Sages: Pirkei Avot* (Rossel Books, 1984), 679.

11. The Mishnah (same root—משנה) was the first great codification of the Oral Law, and though we are familiar with it in book form, it was originally oral, meaning

that people learned it by heart (hence the need for constant repetition) and taught it solely verbally. Those people were the *tannaim*, which is also from the same root, with an Aramaic transposition of ת ("t") for ש ("sh").

12. Rabbi J. Hertz, *Sayings of the Fathers* (New York: Behrman, 1945), 53.

13. But there are other uses of this interesting word in נאה. For instance, in a well-known passage from Midrash Tanhuma (*Tazria*, sec. 5; Buber ed., sec. 7), the then curate Turnus Rufus asks Rabbi Akiva: "Whose works are more נאים—those of God or those of human beings?" From the rest of the story and the examples bandied back and forth between them, it seems unlikely that they are talking in purely aesthetic categories; specifically, Rabbi Akiva's *coup de grace*—the superiority of cakes and cloth to raw wheat and flax—seems to imply functional value as well. In-depth study of this *aggada* can reveal a great deal about a rabbinic attitudes towards Nature, culture, and the human role in Creation.

14. This is the Talmudic phrasing. As codified in the *Shulchan Aruch* (*O.H.* 225:10), the full standard blessing בא"י אמ"ה, "Blessed are You, Lord our God, Sovereign of the Universe," is required. It is explained there that the blessing is to be recited upon seeing beautiful creatures of all sorts: this includes people (non-Jews, even idolators, as well as Jews) and all sorts of beasts. In T. J. *Berachot* 13b-c, it is related of Rabban Gamliel that he recited this blessing upon seeing a beautiful Roman woman, no less one of God's handiworks.

This is one of the ברכות הנהנין, the blessings of "enjoyment." As opposed to other forms of benedictions, which are to be recited at prescribed times, either during a prayer service, or before the performance of a mitzvah, these *berachot* are essentially a set form for spontaneous reactions of wonder and thanksgiving for experiences of various aspects of Nature. These blessings potentially have the power to cultivate a deeper appreciation of elements of the world around us, but sadly, they are rather underemphasized in contemporary Jewish spiritual education. This particular blessing, in fact, is apparently no longer said at all by Ashkenazim, according to the *Mishnah Berura*, the authoritative Eastern European law code published less than a hundred years ago (though the blessing still appears in most prayer books that include a section on "blessings for various occasions"). In any event, if said at all, it is best recited in an abbreviated form, without mentioning the name of God or God's sovereignty (בלא שם ומלכות). See *Mishnah Berura*, vol. 2, 225:10, note 32; and *Chayyei Adam* (Avraham Danziger, eighteenth C. Lithuania) 63:1. The latter gives the astonishing reason that, since we are only required to make blessings of this sort upon the very first contact with the creature or object in question—"when the enjoyment is still intense, and the difference [from one's usual routine] is great"—it is no longer appropriate to do so, since: רגילין תמיד בזה, ואין לנו שינוי גדול אנו—"we are always accustomed to this, and don't experience any striking contrast." Even if Vilna of 1790 were exceptionally beautiful (all year round) it is hard to fathom this rationale. This sort of blessing is designed precisely to foster a sense of wonder at things we might otherwise take for granted. Danziger, his rabbinic erudition notwithstanding, seems to be precisely the focus of some of the barbs in Caro's commentary (see below).

15. Neusner, 105, presents a particularly interesting *midrash* on the interaction of human and divine here:

This is a stern message. It emphasizes that the beauty of the tree, the beauty of a field one has worked to plow—the creation of God, the creation of humanity—must not take our minds away from the labor of Torah, which belongs both to God and humanity. God created the tree, humanity plowed the field, we as earnest students of Torah take God's creation and make it humanity's.

16. Charles Taylor, *Sayings of the Jewish Fathers* (New York: Ktav, 1969; first published 1897), 48.

17. Herford, 73.

18. Hertz, 53.

19. Used here is the New J. P. S. translation of this verse. This verse is considered particularly apt by many commentators, since it is explicitly quoted directly in the following mishnah.

Rabbi Yosef Ya'avetz (or Jabez, Spain-Italy, fifteenth to sixteenth C.) presents a fascinating alternate understanding of what it might mean for "Scripture" to accuse. To the modern ear, however, it sounds slightly whimsical:

> The Torah gets angry with him: for this reason it does not say simply "forfeits his life" as it does above (3:5), but rather Scripture accounts it to him—because it is the Torah itself that is angry at him [for abandoning it]. (77)

20. *The Living Talmud,* ed. Judah Goldin (New Haven: Yale University Press, 1955), 127.

21. Ibid., in translation of Aknin's commentary, 128. Also S. R. Hirsch, *Chapters of the Fathers,* trans. Gertrude Hirschler (Jerusalem: Feldheim, 1967), 47.

22. Rabbi Max J. Routtenberg, in his translation of Avot in *Siddur Sim Shalom,* ed. Rabbi Jules Harlow (New York: Rabbinical Assembly, 1989), 623. He adds (664, n. 15): "Literally, 'guilty against his own soul.'" However, in a previous mishnah (3:5), where the identical phrase occurs, he translates: "endangers his life."

23. Herbert Danby, *The Mishnah* (Oxford: Clarendon Press, 1933), 451. Also in *Mishnayoth,* ed and trans. Philip Blackman (Gateshead, Eng.: Judaica Press, 1977), vol.4, 523; the latter, however, renders the other occurrence (according to his numbering, 3:4): "such a one is guilty against himself."

24. Herford, 73. Also Hertz, 53. He, too, renders this phrase otherwise in 3:5: "such a one sins against himself" (51).

25. Neusner, *Mishnah,* 679.

26. Taylor, 48 (inner quotation marks in the original).

27. *Soncino Talmud: Aboth* (ed. and trans. J. Israelstam [London: Soncino, 1935]), 31. An alternative is added there in a note: "or incurs guilty responsibility for his life."

28. Reuven Bulka, *As a Tree By the Waters: Pirkey Avoth: Psychological and Philosophical Insights* (Feldheim, 1980), p. 111. Cf. also Hirsch, ad loc., who adds in his comments (p. 47): "it is as if he had sinned against his own soul, or rather, as if he had forfeited his soul." See also Hertzberg's translation of Berdichevski, included below.

29. This appears in Sir Leon Simon's translation of Bialik's essay "Halacha and Aggada," in the *Anthology of Hebrew Essays,* ed. Israel Cohen, B. Y. Michali (Tel Aviv: Massada Publishers, 1966), 378.

30. From the epigraph to Cynthia Ozick's short story "The Pagan Rabbi," in *The Pagan Rabbi* (New York: Alfred A. Knopf, 1971). See below for a discussion of the views presented in her story.

31. Avraham Shtal, *Pirkei Avot* [Hebrew] (Tel Aviv: HaKibbutz HaMe'uchad, 1988) claims that there is a crucial difference: "there he was engaged in acts that are completely unacceptable, whereas here he praises God by glorifying the Creation. Even so, this too is forbidden, because Torah study is more important" (148). See the following section, which presents other commentaries on this issue.

32. M. *Ketubot* 3:2; M. *Bava Kama* 3:10; M. *Hullin* 1:1. In addition, the phrase occurs in B.T. approximately another dozen times, also with the same sense.

33. There are of course commentators who do read this in a physical sense. Rashi (ad loc.) comments: "מתחייב בנפשו—risks his life, for Satan is not able to harm one who is occupied with Torah." Duran makes a similar comment (*Magen Avot*, quoted in Goldin, 128). And Rabbi Yitzthak Magriso, a compiler of the eighteenth-century *Ladino Yalkut Me'am Loez*, translated from the Ladino into Hebrew by Shemuel Yerushalmi (Jerusalem: Wagschel, 1972), says that the danger involved is that the traveler is liable to be hurt by wild animals, "for wild animals can have no power over a human being unless he becomes like an animal; and a person who does not engage in Torah study is likened unto an animal." (Hebrew version, 125).

34. In the *Encyclopedia Judaica* entry on "Law and Morality" (vol. 10, 1484), Saul Berman writes of the "didactic" use of the death penalty threat:

> While the Bible lays down the penalty of death at the hands of the court for a variety of crimes, the *tannaim* had already begun using the ascription of the death penalty to crimes for which clearly no court would prescribe such punishment. This exaggerated penalty was an effective way of communicating rabbinic feelings about the enormity of misbehavior. The *amoraim* made extensive use of this device to indicate their indignation at immoral behavior. Thus, in a passage which makes manifestly clear that it is aimed at emphasis rather than true legal liability, the Talmud says, "A mourner who does not let his hair grow long and does not rend his clothes is liable to death" (T. B. *Mo'ed Katan* 24a). Similarly the rabbis asserted that "Any scholar upon whose garment a [grease] stain is found is liable to death." (T. B. *Shabbat* 114a)

35. Goldin, 128.

36. I am indebted to my friend and colleague Eilon Schwartz for the suggestion of this analysis of the commentaries, as well as many other insights that contributed to the development of the ideas in this essay.

37. Goldin, 128.

38. Of course even this minimal acceptance of the value of the appreciation of Nature is on the condition that it is not for its own sake, but as a means to praising God and acknowledging the greatness of the Creator. Two twentieth-century Orthodox commentators address this point. Aharon Shelomo Katriel Maharil is particularly clear about this, in his *Avot Ha'olam Hakadmonim* (Jerusalem, 1929):

> since he said "how fine is this tree, how fine is this field" and did not include God's name (i.e., did not say an actual blessing), this then is idle talk and constitutes a break from his studies, and he forfeits his life, as it says in the Zohar (*Lech Lecha*, 92): one who leaves the Torah, even for a single hour, is like one who leaves the life of the world.
>
> Another aspect: there is actually no problem in saying "how fine is this tree," for one can claim that his intention was for the sake of the blessing. But as for "how fine is this field"— there is no blessing, and so that (illegitimately) diverted his mind from Torah, and for that he forfeits his life.

And Irving Bunim, in *Ethics from Sinai* (Feldheim, 1964), adds:

The exclamation of rapture, "How beautiful is this tree," etc., comes forth not as part of religious expression but as an interruption of Torah study, in contrast and opposition to it. Basically, Judaism wants us to enjoy life in this world and experience the pleasures which stem from a contemplation of the beauties of nature. But too many of us appreciate nature merely as nature, as something separate and apart, out of any larger context. We fail to see in nature's great beauty, in its wonder and mystery, the hand of a Creator, the Master of the universe (vol. 1, 267).

39. *Yalkut Me'am Lo'ez*, trans. David Barocas, ed. R. Aryeh Kaplan (New York: Moznaim Pub., 1990), 142–43.

40. Bulka, 111–12; cf. Hirsch, ad. loc.

41. Yosef Chayyim ben Yitzchak Caro, *Minchat Shabbat (Solet LeMincha)* [Hebrew], commentary to *Pirke Avot* (Krotoshin, 1847), ad loc.

42. Steven S. Schwarzschild, "The Unnatural Jew," 360 [reprinted in this volume, 275].

43. Eric Hoffer, *The True Believer* (New York: Harper and Brothers, 1951), 141.

44. Ozick, 20–21, 35–36.

45. This characterization is from Hertzberg, *The Zionist Idea* (New York: Atheneum, 1972; Philadelphia: JPS, 1959), 291. He places his selections from Berdichevski in a section entitled "Rebels at their Most Defiant."

46. This translation is from Hertzberg, 296–97. The original essay, called דו-פרצופים ("Two-Faces," or "In Two Directions," according to Hertzberg), written c. 1900–1903, can be found in his collected works, *Essays*, vol. 45 (Tel Aviv: Dvir, 1960).

47. Herzberg, 292.

48. Actually, neither did Berdichevski. He spent the last years of his life working on a massive collection of Jewish aggada and folklore, *Mimekor Yisrael*, not unlike Bialik's *Sefer Aggada*.

49. Trans. Sir Leon Simon; cf. above, n. 29. This passage appears on 378. The Hebrew original, written in the early years of this century, can be found in the collected writings of Ch. N. Bialik (Tel Aviv: Dvir, 1938; reprinted 1971), 219.

50. This need not sound too strange to the contemporary ear. One of the "hottest" topics in environmental thought today is bioregionalism and "a sense of place"—the importance of one's connection to one's immediate area and its environment. As Jews, can we seriously speak of establishing a deep sense of place, of totally integrating with our environment—making it a part of ourselves and ourselves a part of it— in New England or the American Southwest or the pampas of South America, without always having in the backs of our minds that something is not quite right, that we Jews once had a *monumental* "sense of place," and that it has been renewed for some with the reestablishment of the State of Israel in the Land of Israel? This is the (unabashedly Zionist) question for the reader to ponder: can we speak of "Jewish bio-regionalism" anywhere else but there, in what is known in our tradition as *ha-aretz, the* Land?

51. Important pioneering work in this field is being done by the American group Shomrei Adama. Clearly, Jews need to be approached educationally where they are (physically, and otherwise), and, ethically speaking, a universal vision is essential— but see the reservations expressed in the previous note.

52. The literal translation of this epithet for God—*makom*—is "place." A full exploration of the history and implications of this fascinating term are beyond the scope of this essay, but the potential for "green midrash" is clear. It might even be claimed

that the best Hebrew translation for the ecological term discussed above in note 32, "a sense of place," is precisely this: בין אדם למקום, the relationship between humans and their Place—theological ramifications intended. It should be noted, though, that a classic midrash (*Gen. Rabbah* 68:9) explicates this phrase as a negation of pantheism: "God is the place of the World (העולם), but the World is not the Place of God"; i.e., all of creation, the entire universe, does not—cannot—contain Divinity.

53. Literally, "the commandments between people and 'their' world." For some, this would constitute a fourth category of *mitzvot* after the two original types and the third, Chassidic, addition of בין אדם לעצמו *bein adam le'atzmo*, commandments or duties of a human being to his or her self.

Of course, the possessive pronoun, expressed in the Hebrew suffix "-o" (עולמו), should be interpreted as indicating relationship, not possession, as in the phrase בין אדם לחברו between people and their fellows. For the midrashically minded, the theologically suggestive possibility exists of interpreting that little suffix as referring (possessively) to "'His' world," i.e., God's world—*kemo she-katuv*, as it is written, לה' הארץ ומלואה "the Earth is the Lord's" (Ps. 24:1).

54. Many people attribute the following teaching to Rav Kook, the great thinker and spiritual teacher of the early part of this century, and first Chief Rabbi of Israel. Though this is very much in the spirit of his thought, in the only place he relates expressly to our mishna, he says something very similar to Reuven Bulka above. In his *Orot HaTorah* (9:7, 45) he writes:

מעלה עליו הכתוב כאילו מתחייב בנפשו: כי סוף כל סוף מכל העולם אור חיים זורח הוא, אבל מן התורה שופע אור חיים דחיים, ואין נוזבים קדושה חמורה מקוריית ותופסים במקומה קדושה קלה מנותקת

> The Light of Life shines forth from all parts of the world, but the Torah's effluence is the Light of the Life of Life. Torah is the forceful and original holiness, while Nature in comparison is only a "lighter" and secondary source of holiness.

Though I have found no written reference, the aforementioned interpretation may have been an oral teaching of his son, Rabbi Tzvi Yehuda Kook.

13

Bal Tashchit:
A Jewish Environmental Precept

Eilon Schwartz

INTRODUCTION

No single Jewish concept is quoted more often in demonstrating Judaism's environmental credentials than the rabbinic[1] concept of *bal tashchit* ("do not destroy"). It appears in virtually all of the literature that discusses Jewish attitudes toward the environmental crisis. Yet, rarely are any more than a few sentences given to actually explain its history and its meaning. Such a superficial approach has been widespread in contemporary environmental ethics with regard to traditional cultures. Advocates of a particular culture bring prooftexts to show that the culture is part of the solution; critics use it to show that the culture is part of the problem. Neither approach allows a serious investigation of a cultural perspective different from our own, one which is based on different philosophical assumptions debated in a different cultural language.[2]

In keeping with Clifford Geertz's call for thick anthropological descriptions of culture, I have chosen to analyze *bal tashchit* as it unfolds throughout Jewish legal, or halakhic,[3] history. Only by entering the classical world of Jewish texts is it possible to transcend apologetics and get a glimpse of a traditional cultural perspective on its own terms. In the process, I provide a richer understanding of the *content* and the *context* of Jewish cultural views of the natural world.

BAL TASHCHIT

Historically, Jews have been considered "a people of the book," based on the role texts have played in Jewish life. From the Bible, followed by the

Mishnah and the Gemara, known collectively as the Talmud, continuing through medieval commentaries on these texts, and including compilations of questions posed to rabbis with their answers on the practical application of these ancient texts to new situations, Judaism has developed an elaborate interpretive tradition, rooted in the Bible and extending into modern times. Traditional texts beginning with the Bible are the core texts for subsequent halakhic decisions.

Bal tashchit is based on a relatively small collection of sources. The original basis for it is biblical, although it is expanded by the rabbis far beyond the original context of the Bible. *Bal tashchit* is considered to have its roots as a *halakhah* of the Bible, but to largely consist of prohibitions developed by the rabbis. In order to understand the halakhic precept, it is necessary to explore both its biblical roots and its rabbinic interpretation.

The principle of *bal tashchit* originated in the attempt to explicate one specific biblical passage from Deuteronomy, which describes what constitutes proper behavior during time of war. I include two translations of the original Hebrew in order to emphasize the difficulty in understanding the Hebrew verses and the interpretative possibilities that emerge from the ambiguity of the text itself.

THE BIBLICAL SOURCE

When in your war against a city you have to besiege it a long time in order to capture it, you must not destroy its trees, wielding the axe against them. You may eat of them, but you must not cut them down. *Are trees of the field human to withdraw before you under siege?* Only trees which you know do not yield food may be destroyed; you may cut them down for constructing siegeworks against the city that is waging war on you, until it has been reduced. (Deuteronomy 20:19–20, New Jewish Publication Society translation)

  When thou shalt besiege a city a long time, in making war against it to take it, thou shalt not destroy the trees thereof by forcing an axe against them: for thou mayest eat of them, and thou shalt not cut them down, *for the tree of the field is man's life to employ them in the siege.* Only the trees which thou knowest that they be not trees for food, thou shalt destroy and cut them down; and thou shalt build bulwarks against the city that maketh war with thee, until it be subdued. (Deuteronomy 20:19–20, King James translation)

The passage deals with the proper ethical behavior with regard to trees during wartime. Fruit-bearing trees should not be chopped down while a city is under siege. Only non-fruit-bearing trees may be chopped down. The reason behind this prohibition seems to be cryptically supplied by the verse itself. In the King James translation, the reason is that "the tree of the field is man's life," implying some causal relationship between the human being and trees, such that cutting down the tree is, in effect, damaging the human being as well. Yet, the other translation offers a different interpretation of the verse, translating the verse as a question rather than statement: "are trees of the field human to withdraw before you under siege?" It is a rhetorical question, which denies a relationship between human beings and trees, and implies that trees are not human beings and therefore should not be victims of human disputes.

The discrepancy between the translations echoes medieval commentators' varying interpretations of the verse. The J.P.S. translation seems to agree with Rashi's[4] interpretation of the verse. Rashi accentuates the categorical distance between the human being and the tree to create a rationale for why the tree should not be cut:

> The word *ki* is used here in the sense of *perhaps; should.* . . : Should the tree of the field be considered to be (like) a human being, able to run away from you into the besieged town, to suffer there the agonies of thirst and hunger, like the towns-people—if not, why then destroy it? (Rashi' s commentary on Deuteronomy 20:19)

Rashi's interpretation of the verse is based on his understanding of the Hebrew word *ki* as being interrogative, turning the text into a rhetorical question: Is the tree of the field to be part of the same (moral) world as the human being? No. The tree of the field is not the target of the siege; the people of the town are. One has no moral right to destroy the trees because of a dispute among human beings. The trees must not be destroyed because of human disputes.

Rashi in effect has argued for an environmental ethic that views (fruit) trees as having existence independent of human wants and needs. In spite of its strong anthropocentric language, Rashi's position gives ethical consideration to the trees, although it is still not clear why that should be so. The case is accentuated by the setting of the verse itself. In wartime, when human life is so endangered that values are often eclipsed altogether, it is difficult to maintain an ethical outlook on any issue, how much the more so with regard to nature. Indeed, some commentators were aware of, and concerned by, the radically nonanthropocentric nature of such a juxtaposition in which strategic considerations during war, considerations that might save human life, seem to be overruled by consideration for the trees' welfare. Samuel ben Me'ir [Rashbam] (1085–1144), for example, understands the word *ki* as "unless" and therefore interprets the verse as a prohibition against chopping down the fruit tree unless the enemy is using the trees as camouflage ("unless the human being is as a tree of the field"), in which case the trees may be removed.[5] Nachmanides [Ramban] (1194–1270) argues that if chopping trees is necessitated by the conquest, then it is obviously permissible to remove any and all trees.[6] Rashi's interpretation is an anthropocentric reading.

Yet, Rashi seems to have taken the verse out of context, for, if we accept Rashi's interpretation—"is the human being a tree of the field?"—how are we to understand the very next verse, in which permission is given by God to cut down non-fruit bearing trees? What is the distinction between fruit-bearing and non-fruit-bearing trees which protects one and not the other? Rashi's interpretation does not offer a means for making such a distinction. Indeed, the text questions whether a human being is the tree of the field, whereas Rashi asks whether a tree of the field is like a human being. Rashi's reversal of the syntax of the sentence helps to support his interpretation, but is not supported by the original phrasing of the verse.

Ibn Ezra's (1089–1164) interpretation, later echoed by the King James version, attacks Rashi's position on both grammatical and logical grounds, and offers an alternative possibility:

> In my opinion . . . , this is the correct meaning: that from (the trees) you get food; therefore, don't cut them down; "for man is the tree of the field"—that is, our lives as human beings depend on trees. (Ibn Ezra's commentary on Deut. 20:19)

Human responsibility for the tree is based on human dependence upon the tree. Trees are a source of food, and thus cutting them down reduces the food supply available after the siege. Ramban goes on to suggest that such an act is a sign of loss of faith, for the trees are being cut down to help in the siege. The soldiers, not believing that God will lead them to victory, destroy their own future food supply, fearful that the day of victory will never come.[7]

Ibn Ezra's explanation makes sense in the context of the verse. Fruit trees are not to be chopped down, for their importance as food for human beings is clear. Non-fruit-bearing trees, on the other hand, were seen to have no immediate importance for the human being; therefore, it is permissible to chop them down. The prooftext, "because the human being is a tree of the field," shows us our link to the natural world and how our abuses of nature can result in abuse of ourselves.

THE RABBINIC UNDERSTANDING AND EXPANSION OF THE TEXT

The rabbinic discussion of the text, and the rabbis' extrapolation of it into the halakhic precept of *bal tashchit*, although terse, expands the text in several, and often conflicting, directions. Let us begin with the primary prooftext in the Talmud for *bal tashchit*. It is an expansion on the mishnaic text which states: "He who cuts down his own plants, though not acting lawfully, is exempt, yet were others to [do it], they would be liable" (*Baba Kamma* 8:6).[8] Here it is clearly stated that cutting down plants is acting unlawfully, presumably because of *bal tashchit*. One who cuts down another's plants is monetarily liable. One who cuts one's own plants, while not liable, is also a transgressor. In other words, it is not merely a question of destroying another person's property. Even destroying what appears to be one's own property is forbidden, although seeking monetary penalty or compensation is inapplicable.

The Talmud proceeds to define what is permitted to be cut down and what is forbidden:

> Rav said: A palm tree producing even one kab of fruit may not be cut down. An objection was raised [from the following]: What quantity should be on an olive tree so that it should not be permitted to cut it down? A quarter of a kab—Olives are different as they are more important. R. Hanina said: Shibbath my son did not pass away except for having cut down a fig tree before its time. Rabina, however, said: If its value [for other purposes] exceeds that for fruit, it is permitted [to cut it down]. It was also taught to the same effect: "Only the trees which you know" (Deut. 20:20) implies even fruit-bearing trees; "that they are not trees for food" (Deut. 20:20) means a wild tree. But since we ultimately include all things, why then was it stated, "that they are not trees for food"? To give priority to a wild tree over one bearing edible fruits. As you might say that this is so even where the value [for other purposes] exceeds that for fruits, it says "only." (*Baba Kamma* 91b-92a)

The talmudic passage here defines the worth of the tree in terms of its produce. A palm tree may be allowed to be cut down when it is producing less than one *kab* (2.2 liters) of fruit; an olive tree, which is deemed more important, presumably for economic reasons, can be cut down only when it is producing less than a quarter *kab*. Although such amounts might be an evaluation of the point at which a tree is still fulfilling its purpose in the world, it is just as likely that it is an evaluation of the point at which the tree is still economically valuable, as the claim that olives are "more important" suggests. Rabina offers a general rule of thumb: one may cut down a fruit tree whenever the value of the tree cut down is worth more than its production of fruit. The Talmud thus interprets the original biblical passage in the spirit of its economic reading of the law. "Trees for food" are not simply fruit-producing trees. They are trees that are producing enough fruit to be economically worthwhile. Thus, not only may non-fruit-producing trees be chopped down, but fruit-producing trees that are not economically productive ultimately fall into the same category.

As stated in the mishnah above, one who unlawfully chops down another's tree is to be fined. One who chops down one's own trees, "although not acting lawfully, is exempt." In the talmudic commentary cited above, Rabbi Hanina makes a curious aside when he states that his son died because of having cut down a fig tree before its time, even though it was allowed since its economic worth cut down was greater than its worth as a fruit-producing tree. Death as divine punishment for cutting down the tree, even though it is permitted by the *halakhah*, certainly demands that we relate to *bal tashchit* as something far more substantial than simply respecting the economic value of fruit-producing trees for human society. It is a mysterious theme that reappears often in the halakhic literature. For example, the same story is related in another talmudic passage:

> Raba, son of Rabbi Hanan, had some date trees adjoining a vineyard of Rabbi Joseph, and birds used to roost on the date trees [of Raba] and fly down and

damage the vines [of Rabbi Joseph]. So Rabbi Joseph told [Raba:], "Go cut them!" [Raba said:] "But I have kept them four cubits away" [Rabbi Joseph said:] "This applies only to other trees, but for vines we require more." [Raba said:] "But does not our Mishnah say 'this applies to all other trees'? [Rabbi Joseph said:] "This is so where there are other trees or vines on both sides, but where there are trees on one side and vines on the other a greater space is required." Said Raba, "I will not cut them down, because Rav has said that it is forbidden to cut down a date tree which bears a *kab* of dates, and Rabbi Hanina has said, 'My son Shikhath only died because he cut down a date tree before its time.' You, sir, can cut them down if you like." (*Baba Batra* 26a)[9]

Here the date trees of Raba are the nesting ground for birds that are damaging the vineyards of Rabbi Joseph. The trees must be uprooted, for they are not planted the proper distance from the vineyard of Rabbi Joseph. Nevertheless Raba refuses to uproot the trees, *even though it is halakhically required*, because they are still producing the minimum *kab* of fruit, and Rabbi Hanina's son died for uprooting a date tree before its time. It has been suggested that such fear of cutting down trees might indicate the presence of pagan beliefs in the popular culture of the time.[10] They certainly suggest a more complex equation than a simple cost/benefit analysis. Raba does allow, however, Rabbi Joseph to dare to remove the trees.

So far we have examined two talmudic passages regarding *bal tashchit*. Although one deals with the responsibility of one property owner to his neighbor, and the other deals with responsibility independent of others, they both understand the meaning of the halakhah in similar ways. Both deal solely with fruit trees. As is recalled from the original biblical proof-text, it is allowed to chop down non-fruit-bearing trees. Only fruit-bearing trees are forbidden. In the two talmudic passages, the rabbis limit the prohibition and, in the process, offer an interpretation of the reasoning behind *bal tashchit*. No tree is to be destroyed as long as it is economically worthwhile. However, if the value of the tree is greater for having been cut down (Rabina's dictum), or if the tree is causing damage to the value of another's property (Rabbi Joseph's complaint), then it is permissible to chop it down. The tree's worth, and in general the worth of nature, is ultimately evaluated in terms of its economic worth to humans. Notice that the destruction of the bird's nesting place is of no moral concern in the text. Yet, although the cutting down of the tree is permitted, it appears to be problematic. The death of Rabbi Hanina's son offers a disturbing addendum to an otherwise utilitarian interpretation.

Up until now, I have considered a rather narrow understanding of *bal tashchit*, focusing solely on its implications for duties and obligations concerning fruit-producing trees. The rabbis, however, did not understand *bal tashchit* as a precept solely concerned with fruit trees, but rather as a far-reaching principle that defines our responsibilities and obligations to the created world.

The initial discussion as to whether one is prohibited from cutting down trees takes place in a larger talmudic discussion as to whether one may harm oneself. The mishnaic text, which the Talmud then elaborates, parallels the previously quoted mishnah. They are here quoted together in context:

> Where one injures oneself, though forbidden, he is exempt, yet, were others to injure him, they would be liable. He who cuts down his own plants [*koreit*], though not acting lawfully, is exempt, yet were others to [do it], they would be liable. (*Baba Kamma* 8:6)

Once again, there is a distinction between damage inflicted by another party and damage inflicted by oneself. Here one who injures another person is clearly liable. One who injures oneself, although liable, is not punishable in civil courts. But what is the connection between damage to plants and injury to persons? The link is explicated in the talmudic discussion:

> R. Eleazar said: I heard that he who rends [his garments] too much for a dead person transgresses the command *bal tashchit*, and it seems that this should be the more so in the case of injuring his own body. But garments might perhaps be different, as the loss is irretrievable; for R. Johanan used to call garments "my honorers," and R. Hisda whenever he had to walk between thorns and thistles used to lift up his garments, saying that whereas for the body [if injured] nature will produce a healing, for garments [if torn] nature could bring up no cure. (*Baba Kamma* 91b)

The talmudic text seeks to understand how some rabbis came to the conclusion that it was forbidden to injure oneself. Rabbi Eliezer asserts that ripping clothing, a traditional sign of mourning, when done too much transgresses *bal tashchit*. And, if ripping clothing is a transgression of *bal tashchit*, how much the more so is "ripping," or injuring, one's body? Therefore, injury to one's own body must be forbidden according to *bal tashchit*. Still, the Talmud points out, there is a distinction between garments and the body: ripping a garment can be irretrievable, whereas the body may heal. Indeed, Rabbi Hisda, when walking through scrub brush, used to lift up his garments, preventing them from ripping, while allowing his body to be cut and bruised, knowing that it would heal. Thus, injury to one's body is not prevented by *bal tashchit*, although the ripping of clothing is.

Such a conclusion—that is, that *bal tashchit* does not apply to the human being—is contradicted in another talmudic passage:

> Reb Judab said in Samuel's name: We may make a fire for an ill woman on the Sabbath [in the winter]. Now it was understood from him, only for an ill woman, but not for an invalid; only in winter, but not in summer. But that is not so; there is no difference between an ill woman and any [other] invalid, and summer and winter are alike. [This follows] since it was stated, R. Hiyya b. Abin said in Samuel's name: If one lets blood and catches a chill, a fire is made for him even on the Tammuz [summer] solstice. A teak chair was broken up for Samuel; a table of juniper-wood

was broken up for Rav Judah. A footstool was broken up for Rabah, where upon Abaye said to Rabbah, "But you are infringing on *bal tashchit.*" "*Bal tashchit* in respect of my own body is more important to me," he retorted. (*Shabbat* 129a)

Here *bal tashchit* is used in reference to the breaking of furniture for warming an ill person on the Sabbath, and of course in reference to human health. Notice that it has already been decided that one may disregard rules of the Sabbath in order to take care of the ill. The question now is whether the needs of the individual human being override the rules of *bal tashchit*, in this case, a prohibition on destroying furniture. If we interpret *bal tashchit* in utilitarian terms—that is, the economic worth of something to human beings— then there should be no question. The health of the human being obviously takes precedence over the furniture's existence. Indeed, Rabbah argues just that. However, the very presence of the question suggests that the answer is not taken for granted. There is a tension between an interpretation that evaluates all worth in terms of its use to human beings and one that sees worth independent of human wants and even needs.

But what is the connection between the biblical prohibition on cutting down fruit trees and the expanding rabbinic definition which, as we have so far seen, includes clothing, furniture, and even human beings? Maimonides [Rambam] (1135–1204) argues that the rabbinic prohibition of *bal tashchit* includes the destruction of household goods, the demolishing of buildings, the stopping of a spring, and the destruction of articles of food, as well.[11] Maimonides expands *bal tashchit* to include the destruction before its time of anything, natural or artificial. The world of creation includes the creation of the natural world and the world that humans have created from God's creation. There should be no needless destruction of any of the creation.

The central point, then, is how one is to evaluate "needless" or "wanton" destruction. As I have shown, there is some tension as to whether it is to be evaluated according to the effective use of human beings, or if there is an inherent value that exists apart from human use which must be balanced alongside human wants and needs. Although the dominant interpretation seems to be a utilitarian one, there is evidence of a differing interpretation.

CONSPICUOUS CONSUMPTION

R. Hisda also said: when one can eat barley bread but eats wheaten bread, he violates *bal tashchit.* R. Papa said: when one can drink beer but drinks wine, he violates *bal tashchit.* But this is incorrect: *Bal tashchit*, as applied to one's own person, stands higher. (*Shabbat* 140b)

How is one to evaluate what is permissible, and what is excessive, consumption? In this short piece, the rabbinic debate is presented clearly. Rabbi Hisda states that when one can eat barley bread, a poor man's bread, and instead chooses to eat wheaten bread, a more expensive bread, it is a violation of *bal tashchit*. In the same manner, Rabbi Papa claims that if one can drink beer, a poor man's beverage, and instead drinks wine, a more expensive drink, it is a violation of *bal tashchit*. One must provide for human needs. However, one is not permitted to consume beyond what is necessary to live. To do so would be *bal tashchit*—wanton destruction.

Such a view clearly has ascetic overtones. The link between *bal tashchit* and living a simple life certainly suggests that link between demanding less and not cutting down trees. However, motivation for a simple life has often come from social considerations as well. Excessive consumption means that one is using one's wealth on oneself, often flaunting one's wealth, at the expense of helping out those who are less fortunate. A talmudic passage emphasizes the point:

> At first the carrying out of the dead was harder for [the dead's] relatives than his death, so that they left him and ran away, until Rabban Gamaliel came and adopted a simple style and they carried him out in garments of linen, and all the people followed his example and carried out [the dead] in garments of linen. Said Rabbi Papa: And now it is the general practice [to carry out the dead] even in rough cloth worth [only] a *zuz*. (*Ketubot* 8b)

Although the text makes no mention of *bal tashchit*, later commentators use it as a prooftext in applying *bal tashchit* to excessive consumption. Rambam, for example, links the two in his discussion of the laws of mourning.[12] Here the norm for burial had become so cost prohibitive that the poor would abandon their dead, unable to afford such an expense. Rabbi Gamaliel successfully changed the practice from an excessive one to a modest one, which evolved into virtually an ascetic one. It is clear here that the motivation for simplicity is social.

Yet, for all that can be said for simplicity, the text is blunt as to which perspective wins out in the talmudic argument: "but this is incorrect. *Bal tashchit* as applied to one's own person stands higher." The statement is quite powerful. It is considered *bal tashchit* not to drink the wine or eat the wheaten bread. Human comfort and enjoyment are to take precedence. Not according them priority limits human pleasure in the world, which is a form of destruction—destruction of human pleasure. Although there is a tradition of abstinence in Judaism, it is generally frowned upon. Human beings are to enjoy the bounty of creation. Although two traditions are clearly present, the one which places humans as the evaluator of worth is plainly dominant.

Maimonides canonizes this dominant tradition, leaving out the minority view. In three short *halakhot* in his *Mishneh Torah*, he summarizes the talmudic extrapolation of the biblical text.[13] There is no tension in Maimonides' summary. Wanton destruction is clearly defined as the cutting down of fruit trees when there is no economic justification for its removal. Although the rabbinic expansion of the text is presented, in fact the summary limits the text.

Only when something is clearly of benefit and its destruction does not bring about demonstrably more benefit, is its destruction considered *bal tashchit*. Any time there is economic gain from its use, its destruction is justifiable.

THE RESPONSA LITERATURE

Two positions emerge from the rabbinic discussion on *bal tashchit*. The first, which is clearly the dominant position, I describe as the minimalist position. It limits *bal tashchit* as much as possible to only those situations that are clearly proscribed by the biblical injunction in Deuteronomy. Although seemingly expanding *bal tashchit* to encompass human creation and not simply nature, it in fact creates a clear hierarchy in which human utilitarian needs always override any inherent value of the created object. In contrast, the maximalist position does expand *bal tashchit* as a counterweight to human desires. Human needs define usage, although the definition of what constitutes human need is far from clear. Consumption should be limited to what is necessary, and the inherent value of the creation stands as a countermeasure to human usage.

The many interpretations offered in the literature on the human responsibility to the natural world thus cited leaves much latitude for the application of the concept of *bal tashchit* in Jewish law. An anthropocentric reading of the traditions leads to a minimalist application of the principle, with human considerations always determining the conduct toward nature. However, a reading of the tradition that gives a degree of inherent worth to the natural world independent of human use demands a much more complex negotiation between human wants or needs and nature, leading to what I call a maximalist application of the principle. The halakhic process enabled each *Posek*—each halakhic authority—to offer his own interpretation of the concept through his own reading of the meaning of *bal tashchit* as it is expressed in the texts of biblical and rabbinic literature, and interpreted by later generations. Not surprisingly, different *Poskim*[14] chose to understand the *halakhah* in the different ways suggested by the interpretations already cited. What follows is a representative survey of the responsa literature, according to the minimalist and maximalist traditions.

THE MINIMALIST TRADITION

One of the main halakhic questions, once having accepted the idea of *bal tashchit* as relating to wanton destruction, is in what situations is it to be overridden. The Tosafot, for example, commenting on a talmudic passage, argue that *bal tashchit* is overridden by the obligation to honor royalty.[15] In *Sefer ha-Chasidim*, it is argued that rewriting a page of Torah only so that it looks better also overrides the commandment (*mitzvah*) of *bal tashchit*.[16] Ovadiah Yosef (1920–) claims that the fulfillment of a mitzvah, such as the breaking of the glass as part of the wedding ceremony, overrides *bal tashchit*.[17] He, like *Sefer ha-Chasidim*, also argues that *bal tashchit* is overridden in order to show honor to a *mitzvah*, such as by buying a newer, fancier mezuzah.[18]

It is also permissible to destroy property and even plants for educational reasons. Relying on a talmudic passage that allows one to rip clothing or break pottery in order to demonstrate anger as an educational tool (although it is forbidden to do such acts out of anger),[19] Abraham Isaac Kook (1865–1935) argues that one is allowed to destroy when one is teaching that something is forbidden, so that two trees that are forbidden to be planted together under the laws of *kilayim* may be planted together and then uprooted to teach that such a planting is forbidden. The trees are deliberately planted and then uprooted to teach the halakhah.[20]

Maimonides is asked whether a tree may be cut down which is in danger of falling and damaging a mosque which lies underneath. Here it is a question of whether *bal tashchit* applies when social relations between Jews and Moslems might be jeopardized by not removing the tree. Maimonides, in keeping with his radically minimalist position, answers that it is permitted to cut the tree down not only when there is damage inflicted, but also when there is the potential for damage.[21] Elsewhere Maimonides allows for the removal of a tree that threatens to break off in a storm and injure those walking past in the adjacent public area.

Judah Rosannes (1657–1727) holds that the prohibition is only on the chopping down of the entire tree, and there is therefore no problem with *bal tashchit* when chopping down branches from the tree.[22] Baruch Wiesel gives permission in his *Makor Baruch* (1755) to destroy an older house and build a newer one.[23]

Indeed, the anthropocentric view of *bal tashchit*, which sees nature as having been created for the use of human beings, is a central theme in the literature. Naphtali Zvi Berlin (1817–93) states emphatically that the very purpose of a tree and its fruit is for it to be cut down for the use of human beings.[24] In his commentary on the Deuteronomy verse, Yaakov Tzvi from Kalenburg (d. 1865) states:

> It is not virtuous to use anything in a manner different from that which it has been created . . . [including] a tree, which was aimed in its creation to produce fruit as food for human beings to sustain them; it is forbidden to do anything to them which would harm human beings.[25]

Jonah ben Abraham Gerondi (1200–63) holds that the body of a human being is to be considered part of the world of creation, hence part of that to which *bal tashchit* is to be applied. One has no right to cause it harm.[26] Menahem Azariah Da Fano (1548–1620) states that, although in general one should choose to be stringent with oneself, when it comes to financial losses to oneself, one is forbidden to be severe in order not to transgress *bal tashchit*.[27] Here we see once again the theme of human needs as a concern of bal *tashchit*, which takes precedence over other needs. Ephraim Weinberger argues that any deprivation to the body's health is a transgression of *bal tashchit*:

> Even if he doesn't allow himself to eat foods that are good for his health and strengthen his body, although they are expensive, he transgresses the prohibition. Any abuse of bodily health in general is a transgression of *bal tashchit*.[28]

In a responsa about animal experimentation, Jacob Reischer states that even when there is only the possibility of medical or economic benefit, *bal tashchit* applied to human beings always takes precedence.[29] In the *Shulchan Arukh of the Rav*, in the laws of *bal tashchit* revealingly printed under "laws pertaining to the protection of the body and the spirit and laws of *bal tashchit*," Shneur Zalman of Lyady (1745–1813) states: "and also those that destroy anything that it is destined for human beings to enjoy transgress *bal tashchit*."[30]

The application of *bal tashchit* to the human being expresses the minimalist position quite well: although *bal tashchit* demands that nothing be wasted, it applies first and foremost to the human being. Although some have understood *bal tashchit* as applying to the preclusion of human needs, the most minimalist understanding maintains that preventing human pleasure by preventing human use of the world is an act of *bal tashchit*. The seemingly expansionist position that extends the precept of *bal tashchit* to all things, only to be circumvented by any human desire as the ultimate form of bal tashchit, is presented quite forcefully in both respects in *Sefer ha-Chinnukh*:

> The root reason for the precept is known (evident): for it is in order to train our spirits to love what is good and beneficial and to cling to it; and as a result, good fortune will cling to us, and we will move well away from every evil thing and from every matter of destructiveness. This is the way of the kindly men of piety and the conscientiously observant; they love peace and are happy at the good fortune of people, and bring them near the Torah. They will not destroy even a mustard seed in the world, and they are distressed at every ruination and spoilage that they see; and if they are able to do any rescuing, they will save anything from destruction, with all their power. . . . Among the laws of the precept, there is what the Sages of blessed memory said that the Torah did not forbid chopping down fruit trees if any useful benefit will be found in the matter: for instance, if the monetary value of a certain tree is high, and this person wanted to sell it, or to remove a detriment by chopping them down—for instance, if this was harming other trees that were better than it, or because it was causing damage in the fields of others. In all these circumstances, or anything similar, it is permissible.[31]

According to Zevi Ashkenazi (1660–1718), continuing the position alluded to by *Sefer ha-Chinnukh*, the purpose of *bal tashchit* is not to prevent destruction so much as to teach human beings sensitivity.[32] Nature has no inherent value apart from its use by human beings.

THE MAXIMALIST TRADITION

Jacob Reischer is asked whether one may uproot trees from his garden which obstruct the view from his neighbor's house windows. Reischer rules that the trees are to be removed, but not before searching for another solution such as the replanting of the trees in an alternative location.[33] Jair Hayyim Bacharach, (1638–1702) is asked whether one can remove a fruit tree whose branches obscure the view from one's own window. Note that here permission is being asked to remove a tree which is a nuisance to oneself, as opposed to one which is a nuisance to one's neighbor. Bacharach makes two important points. The first is that since the nuisance can be dealt with through the pruning of the branches of the tree, which is not forbidden by *bal tashchit*, it is not permitted to chop the tree down. The second is that chopping down a tree is to be allowed for essential needs, but not for luxuries. Earlier, we saw that Rashba permitted the expansion of a house. Bacharach relies on this responsum to argue that, while there the chopping down of the tree was for an essential need, here it is not and therefore, based on the precedent of Rashba, it is not to be permitted.[34] Jacob Ettlinger is asked whether one may chop down elderly trees in order to build a home on the only piece of property which the individual is allowed to buy in town. Without having a home, he may not get a license to marry. Ettlinger allows for the trees to be chopped down, although he also points out that everything must be done to find an alternative, and that such permission is granted because not to grant it would prevent the man from marrying. Although permission is granted, the tenor is one of limiting the exceptions to *bal tashchit*, rather than extending them.[35] Similarly, Moses Sofer gives permission to uproot a vineyard that is losing money, and to use the land for field crops instead. Nevertheless, he states that although usually it is forbidden to uproot the vineyard, for this particular time, since the economic loss is so great, permission is given.[36] Ovadiah Yosef also gives permission to chop down a fruit-bearing tree, in this example to expand one's home, while limiting the exceptions. Yosef allows the expansion of the house in this case in order to allow room for a family that has been blessed with many children. However, he asserts that it is forbidden to chop down the trees if one is expanding one's home for luxury, or for landscaping or general beautification. Once again, a distinction is made between perceived needs and wants.[37]

Citing the danger involved in chopping down trees, Pinhas Hai Anu (1693–1765) refuses to give permission to cut down a fig tree in order to build a storage shed.[38] Yaakov ben Shmuel from Tzoyemer (end of the seveneenth century) simply states that it is forbidden to chop down trees in order to build a home.[39] Interestingly, the same Naphtali Zevi Judah Berlin who stated that the purpose of a tree is to be cut down for the use of human beings gives the most maximalist of the interpretations of *bal tashchit*. Asked whether a tree may be removed to build a home, his answer is no. Berlin claims that one may cut down a tree only in cases explicitly spelled out by the Talmud: either when it damages other trees, in which case one tree has no precedence over another, or when it damages another's field.[40]

Berlin points out that there is a distinction between the chopping down of a tree and other transgressions of *bal tashchit* in that only the chopping down of a tree is punishable by flogging. Berlin also mentions the talmudic notion of there being danger involved in the chopping down of trees from the story of R. Hanina's son, as reason to be particularly cautious.

The vast majority of examples from the literature with regard to the cutting down of trees refers explicitly to fruit trees or do not mention the kind of tree being discussed. The original distinction between fruit-producing trees and non-fruit-producing trees seems to be maintained. The Tosafot, however, commenting on a passage from the Talmud that "one who cuts down good trees will never see blessing in his life" state—"One who cuts down even a non-fruit-producing tree." In other words, although not strictly forbidden, such an action will prevent the doer from being blessed in his life's deeds.[41] Although Greenwald (twentieth century) in his responsum makes a distinction between non-fruit-producing trees that have a use as trees for human beings, for example in providing shade, beauty, or even a pleasant aroma, and trees that have use only as firewood and should therefore be used for that purpose, the application of *bal tashchit* to non-fruit-producing trees is a direct rejection of Maimonides' holding that *bal tashchit* does not apply to them.[42]

In the discussion of conspicuous consumption, which as an issue is directly linked to the maximalist position, two responsa are of interest. In the first, Joseph Caro (1488–1575) warns against the wasting of public monies on extravagances.[43] In the second, the first chief Ashkenazic Rabbi of Israel, Abraham Yizhak HaCohen Kook, is asked whether there is any prohibition in the Torah to the improvement of the military cemetery. Kook answers that, while it is certainly a mitzvah to fix up the cemetery so that it is in honorable condition, it would be considered a violation of *bal tashchit* to invest large amounts of money in order that it be lavish.[44]

Finally, two different responsa apply *bal tashchit* to "ownerless property," which includes wild animals and vegetation, and abandoned property.[45] Such a view is in keeping with the idea that there is no such thing as ownerless property, since in fact all the world is ultimately the property of God: "Because the earth is Mine."[46] It is a theocentric utilitarianism. So too in the Sabbatical year, although all land becomes ownerless temporarily—that is, returned to God, its original owner—nevertheless *bal tashchit* continues to apply.

Although it is clear that even in those sources that have been attributed to a maximalist position there is a strong sense of a hierarchy in which human needs override other considerations, nevertheless in the maximalist position there are other considerations that need to be weighed against the human. In all cases, human needs outweigh other considerations. However, there is a debate that takes place as to what defines needs. In addition, there seems to be a distinction made between trees, particularly fruit-bearing trees, and other properties. The halakhic principle of *bal tashchit* has been open to different, often contradictory interpretations. From its beginning, tension existed with regard to how to understand the prohibition: whether such a prohibition was to define the world in terms of human use or whether such a prohibition demanded an evaluation of use that took into account more than human wants.

RELEVANCE TO CONTEMPORARY ENVIRONMENTAL ETHICS

Any analysis of the significance of *bal tashchit* must take into account both the content of the discussion—what has been said—and the context of the discussion—the cultural language of the debate. With regard to the content, several points can be made:

1. It is quite obvious from the survey of the literature that there is no one Jewish approach to *bal tashchit* and its application, but rather multiple approaches that are debated from within the tradition. In general, any claim to the Jewish view on an ethical situation should be held as suspect.
2. The discussion in many ways is remarkably similar to our contemporary discussion. Here too we see two poles on the continuum. The minimalist position has human needs and wants taking precedence over the rest of the creation; the maximalist position has human wants counterbalanced with the legitimate claims of the natural world. The tradition documents a debate between the two positions which has continued since rabbinic times.
3. The minimalist position is without question far more dominant within the tradition. This emphasis too parallels the contemporary debate. Those voices that question a utilitarian approach to the natural world are in the minority.
4. There is no hint in the maximal position of a holistic environmental ethic. This situation should not be particularly surprising, in that the holistic environmental position is based on the science of ecology and the concept of species, and on the assumption that human culture is a small part of the larger ecosystem. Premodern Aristotelian science, which is the scientific tradition within which *bal tashchit* developed, saw nature as static and species as eternal. *Bal tashchit* was applied on the level of the individual. Its concern was domesticated nature, nature in contact with day-to-day living.
5. There is also no hint in the halakhic tradition of *bal tashchit* of the romantic idea of reconnecting humans to their natural selves. At least within the halakhic discussion of *bal tashchit*, respect for nature in no way is connected to a desire to reconnect human culture with its

natural, and truer, antecedents. I believe that the absence of such a tendency reveals a strong preference in Jewish ethical philosophy to see morality as transcendent of the natural world and not immanent within it. The pagan-Jewish debate in many significant ways is connected to a debate about whether morality is defined by "what is"— a naturalist perspective—or by "what should be"—an idealistic model of moral philosophy. Although natural metaphors and images are present in the Jewish textual tradition,[47] particularly in the Bible, nature is primarily not considered to be a pristine state of the world, but a temporal reality that needs to be redeemed.

With regard to the context, any comparison of the contemporary discussion on environmental ethics and the traditional Jewish perspective will be limited. We can only understand another cultural prespective through the prism of our own cultural categories, and therefore any attempt to enter another cultural perspective can only be partial.[48] Only those parts of the tradition that can be explicated in contemporary terms can be translated into a contemporary context. The other parts can only be rumored. What I have so far considered is the part of the traditional discussion that appears to translate relatively easily into the contemporary cultural language and thus can be easily compared. The content, therefore, seems to be similar only when understood as emerging from a similar cultural context. However, the Jewish discussion is in many ways a discussion that is different in kind from the contemporary discussion and that defies a simple comparison.

Because the cultural *contexts* involve very different assumptions, comparison of the two languages of discourse can help locate some of the different cultural assumptions and can teach us about the outlooks of both traditional Jewish and contemporary culture. It helps us to glimpse at that which is incapable of being translated into contemporary categories.

1. Although primarily presented here as a moral discussion, the discussion of the *halakhot* often seems legalistic to the modern ear, without regard to any ethical question. Although the discussion at times seems focused on the moral relationship to nature, with the biblical and rabbinic texts used as prooftexts for the ethical position, at other times the discussion seems to be internally focused, allowing the texts to develop apart from any moral discussion. In short, the discussion of *bal tashchit* hints at a different type of moral discourse, neither utilitarian nor rights-based, neither anthropocentric nor biocentric.

2. The legal assumptions of the halakhic tradition also sound strange to the modern individual. Much of the contemporary environmental discourse concerns the concept of rights. It has been pointed out by some legal historians that such an idea seems foreign to the traditional Jewish halakhic tradition. Rather than focusing on rights, the tradition

focuses on duties. Calling the *bal tashchit* system a system based on duties, rather than rights, is also a partial translation of traditional categories, but it suggests the underlying assumption from which the halakhic system works. The halakhah extends beyond that which is forbidden and legislates normative behavior.[49]

3. The strikingly particularistic nature of the halakhic discussion is also suggestive in terms of the demands of an environmental ethic. The halakhic discussion continually focuses on a particular incident about a particular animal or a particular tree in a particular place. The discussion in those cases no longer revolves around the theoretical question of the human relationship to the natural world, but rather the trade-offs between human and other interests in particular situations. Jewish ethical philosophy is embodied in the material world. Although certain general principles are clearly established from the particular discussion, it is the unique situation which forms the basis of the discussion.

4. The particular nature of Jewish halakhic discussion is connected to the centrality of community as a defining category. Mary Midgley points out in the debate about contemporary environmental ethics that traditional societies lived in "mixed communities" that allowed human sympathies to transcend the species boundary.[50] Callicott extends the concept of "mixed community" to the biotic community as well.[51] The halakhic discussions about *bal tashchit* are testimony to a functioning mixed community. The species barrier is clearly transcended, since discussion includes concern for the community's trees (and, even more centrally, animals)[52] in the deliberation. As Callicott suggests, such a model has various concentric circles of interest, from the most immediate connection of family, but extending out in lesser degrees of concern beyond the species to animals and eventually to the biotic community. It is a morality based on relationships that emerge from particular communities in particular places. Such a dynamic of morality—rooted in relationships between human beings, humans and God, humans and animals, humans and nature—will lead to a very different kind of moral discourse.

In this discussion, I have deliberately echoed a larger argument in ethics between rights-based ethics and the communitarian critique of the limits of such an approach. It should be noted, however, that communitarian positions on the environment nevertheless remain within an anthropocentric view of community, which does not transcend the species barrier.[53] A religious culture that can see creation as having value independent of its utilitarian worth to human beings will philosophically find it much easier to view creation as having inherent worth.[54] Whether that potential can be realized is one of the major challenges facing the Jewish environmental community today.

Contemporary environmental ethics has a rich and complex discourse to describe contemporary society's relationships with the natural world. Yet, we have compromised such rigorous research when treating other cultural perspectives. Doing so caricatures traditional cultures and provides no significant insights into other perspectives. If looking at other cultural perspectives is to be a meaningful stepping-stone in the rethinking of our own perspectives, we must recognize the limitations of cultural translation, while at the same time attempting to describe the culture from within its own cultural language. Only then will we be able to peek into a truly other cultural world and glimpse a different way of seeing. The investigation of *bal tashchit* is offered as both an insight into a Jewish perspective and a glance at what nature looks like through different cultural eyes.

NOTES

From *Environmental Ethics* 19 (1997): 355–74.
The author thanks Jeremy Benstein for his feedback and insights, and Michal Smart, with whom he originally began to explore *bal tashchit.*

1. Although the term rabbinic has a more generic usage, in the context of this essay it refers to the individuals who wrote and codified the Mishnah and Talmud. The Mishnah is the name of the earliest major rabbinic works, first appearing toward the turn of the third century C.E. It is the core document of the talmudic tradition, composed in very terse language and arranged topic by topic over a wide range of subjects. The Talmud primarily refers to the Mishnah combined with its later rabbinic commentaries, the Gemara. The earliest one is the Jerusalem, or Palestinian, Talmud, dating from the first half of the fifth century. Some two centuries later, the Babylonian Talmud was compiled. All talmudic references in this paper are to the Babylonian Talmud.

2. For a literature survey of the contemporary debate on the relationship of Judaism to the environment, and a discussion of the theological/moral issues which are at the root of such a relationship, see Eilon Schwartz, "Judaism and Nature: Theological and Moral Issues to Consider While Renegotiating a Jewish Relationship to Nature" [reprinted in this volume, 297–308].

3. The *halakhah* is the set of rules often known as "Jewish law" which governs Jewish life. The *halakhah*, however, contains far more than what is usually suggested by the term law, as is demonstrated in this paper.

4. R. Solomon b. Isaac [RaShI] (1040–1150), perhaps the most influential biblical and talmudic exegete, French.

5. Samuel ben Meir, commentary on Deuteronomy 20:19, in *Torat Chaim* (Jerusalem: Hotzaat Mosad HaRav Kook, 1993). He is Rashi's grandson, one of the Tosafists, halakhic commentators on the Talmud in twelfth- to fourteenth-century France and Germany.

6. Nachmanides, commentary on Deuteronomy 20:19, in *Torat Chaim.*

7. Ibid.

8. All quotes from the Mishnah and the Talmud are taken from the Soncino translation, unless otherwise cited.

9. I have here changed parts of the Soncino translation, translating in a way similar to Adin Steinsaltz in his Hebrew translation of the Talmud.

10. Meir Ayele, "The Fear of Chopping Down Fruit Trees in the Responsa Literature," in *Tura: Studies in Jewish Thought* [Hebrew] (Tel Aviv: Kibbutz HaMeuchad, 1989), 135–40.

11. Moses Maimonides, *Mishneh Torah* [Hebrew] (Jerusalem: Hotzaat Mossad HaRav Kook, 1962), Laws of Kings 6:10, perhaps the most influential Jewish philosopher ever.

12. Maimonides, *Mishneh Torah*, Laws of Mourning 14:24.

13. Maimonides, *Mishneh Torah*, Laws of Kings 6:8–10.

14. Scholars whose efforts were concentrated on determining the halakhah in practice.

15. Tosefot *Baba Metzi'a* 32b.

16. Judah he-Hasid, *Sefer Ha Chasidim* (Jerusalem: Aharon Block, 1992), no. 339.

17. Ovadiah Yosef, *Yabiah Omer* (Jerusalem, 1993), Pt. 4, *Even HaEzer*, no. 9, former Sephardi Chief Rabbi of Israel.

18. Ovadiah Yosef, *Yabiah Omer*, Pt, 3, Yoreh Deah, no. 18. A mezuzah is a parchment scroll containing portions of the Torah, fixed to the doorpost.

19. *Shabbat* 105b.

20. Abraham Isaac HaCohen Kook, *Mishpat Cohen* (Jerusalem: HaAguda L'Hotzaat Sifrei HaRav Kook, 1937), no. 21, Zionist leader, first Ashkenazi Chief Rabbi of Palestine.

21. Maimonides, *Responsa* [Hebrew], trans. Jehoshua Blau (Jerusalem: Mekize Nirdamim, 1958), no. 112.

22. Judah B. Samuel Rosannes, *Mishneh la-Melekh*, commentary on Maimonides, *Mishneh Torah, Isurei Mizbeah* 7:3, as it appears in *"Bal Tashchit," Encyclopedia Talmudit* (Jerusalem: Hotzaat Encyclopedia Talmudit, 1973), Turkish rabbi.

23. Baruch Baandit Wiesel, *Makor Baruch*, as cited in Ayele, "The Fear of Chopping Down Fruit Trees in the Responsa Literature," 138.

24. Naphtali Zevi Judah Berlin, *Meshiv Davar* (Jerusalem, 1993), ch. 2, no. 56.

25. Yaakov Tzvi from Kalenburg, *HaKatuv v'HaKabalah* (Nurenburg, 1924), on Deuteronomy 20:19.

26. Jonah ben Abraham Gerondi, *Sefer Sha'arei Teshuva* (Jerusalem, 1960), ch. 3, no. 82, Spanish rabbi and moralist.

27. Menahem Azariah Da Fano, *Responsa*, 129, as quoted in Meir Zichal, *Environmental Protection in Jewish Sources* [Hebrew] (Ramat Gan: The Responsa Project, 1989), 31, Italian rabbi and kabbalist.

28. Ephraim Weinberger, *Yad Ephraim* (Tel Aviv: HaVaad HaTziburi LiHotzaat Kitvei HaRav Weinberger, 1976), no. 14, former member of Tel Aviv rabbinic council.

29. Jacob Reischer, *Shevut Yaakov* (Jerusalem, 1972), pt. 3, no. 71.

30. Shneur Zalman of Lyady, "Laws of Protecting the Body and the Spirit and *Bal Tashchit,*" *Shulhan Arukh of the Rav* (New York: Kehot Publication Society, 1975), 31b, founder of Habad Hasdism.

31. *Sefer Hachinukh: The Book of Education* (New York: Feldheim Publishers, 1989), no. 529.

32. Zevi Ashkenazi, *Haham Zevi*, as quoted in Zichal, *Environmental Protection in Jewish Sources*, 9.

33. Jacob Reischer, *Shevut Yaakov* (Jerusalem, 1972), Pt. 1, no. 159.

34. Jair Hayyim Bacharach, *Havvot Yair* (Jerusalem, 1968), no. 195, German talmudic scholar.

35. Jacob Ettlinger, *Binyan Zion* (Jerusalem: Davar Jerusalem, 1989), no. 61.

36. Moses Sofer, *Responsa of Chatam Sofer* [Hebrew], (Jerusalem: Hotzaat Hod, 1972), *Yoreh Deah*, no. 102.

37. Ovadia Yosef, *Yabia Omer* (Jerusalem, 1969), vol. 5, *Yoreh De'ah*, no. 12.

38. Pinhas Hai Anu from Ferrara, *Givat Pinhas*, Pt. 8, no. 2, as it appears in Meir Ayele, "*Givat Pinhas*: The Responsa of R. Pinhas Hal ben Menahem Anau of Ferrara," in *Tarbitz,* Northern Italian rabbi.

39. Yaakov ben Rabbi Shmuel from Tzoyemer, *Beit Yaakov* (Diehernport, 1696), no. 140.

40. Naphtali Zevi Judah Berlin, *Meshiv Davar* (Jerusalem, 1993), chap. 2, no. 56.

41. Tosefot on *Pesachim* 50b.

42. Greenwald, *Keren LeDavid* (Satmar, 1928), *Orech Chaim*, no. 30, Hungarian rabbi.

43. Joseph Caro, *Avatak Rochel* (Leipzig, 1859), no. 18, author of the *Shulchan Aruch*, the authoritative code of Jewish law.

44. Abraham Isaac Kook, *Daat Kohen* (Jerusalem: Mossad Harav Kook, 1969), *Yoreh De'ah*, no. 122.

45. Tzvi Pesach Frank, *Har Tzvi* (Jerusalem: Machon Harav Frank, 1973), *Orech Chaim* 2, no. 102; *Noda Yehuda, Yoreh De'ah*, no. 10.

46. Lev. 25:23.

47. It is quite significant that trees are a central metaphor in Judaism. As one example, the Torah, those parts of the Bible traditionally revealed directly to Moses on Mt. Sinai, is called "a tree of life." Trees played a central role in the economic life in the ancient land of Israel, and were thus proper metaphors for bridging between the socioeconomic life and the theological-moral one.

48. Michael Rosenak, *"Roads to the Palace": Jewish Texts and Teaching* (Providence and Oxford: Berghahn Books, 1995), 5.

49. Moshe Silberg, "Laws and Morals in Jewish Jurisprudence," *Harvard Law Review* 75 (1961–62): 306–31.

50. Mary Midgley, "The Mixed Community," in *The Animal Rights/Environmental Ethics Debate*, ed. Eugene C. Hargrove (Albany: SUNY Press, 1992), 211–25.

51. J. Baird Callicott, "Animal Liberation and Environmental Ethics: Back Together Again," in Callicott, *In Defense of the Land Ethic: Essays in Environmental Philosophy* (Albany: SUNY Press, 1989), 49–51.

52. Paralleling the discussion of *bal tashchit* is the rabbinic precept of *tza'ar ba'alei chayyim*, describing duties toward the prevention of animal suffering.

53. See Avner de-Shalit, *Why Posterity Matters: Environmental Policies and Future Generations* (London: Routledge, 1995).

54. This is perhaps the major point of Max Oelschlaeger, *Caring for Creation: An Ecumenical Approach to the Environmental Crisis* (New Haven: Yale University Press, 1994).

14

Contemporary Problems in Ethics from a Jewish Perspective

Hans Jonas

The crisis of modern man—at least one aspect of it—can be put in these terms. Reason triumphant through science has destroyed the faith in revelation, without, however, replacing revelation in the office of guiding our ultimate choices. Reason disqualified *itself* from that office, in which once it vied with religion, precisely when it installed itself, in the form of science, as sole authority in matters of truth. Its abdication in that native province is the corollary of its triumph in other spheres: its success there is predicated upon that redefinition of the possible objects and methods of knowledge that leaves whole ranges of other objects outside its domain. This situation is reflected in the failure of contemporary philosophy to offer an ethical theory, i.e., to validate ethical norms as part of our universe of knowledge.

How are we to explain this vacuum? What, with so different a past, has caused the great Nothing with which philosophy today responds to one of its oldest questions—the question of how we ought to live? Only the fact that philosophy, once the queen of the sciences, has become a camp follower of Science, made the situation possible; and contemporary religions (it would be too flattering to grace them with the name of theologies) are anxious not to fall too far behind among the stragglers. How this concerns ethics and its present condition has to be articulated.

Three interrelated determinants of modern thought have a share in the nihilistic situation, or less dramatically put, in the contemporary impasse of ethical theory—two of them theoretical and the third practical: the modern concept of nature, the modern concept of man, and the fact of modern technology supported by both. All three imply the negation of certain fundamental tenets of the philosophical as well as the religious tradition. Since we

250

are here concerned with gaining a Jewish perspective on the situation, we shall note in particular the biblical propositions that are intrinsically disavowed in those three elements of the modern mind.

I

1. First, then, we have the modern, i.e. scientific, concept of *nature,* which by implication denies a number of things formerly held, and first of these is *creation*, that is, the first sentence of the Bible, "In the beginning God created the heaven and the earth." To say of the world that it is created is to say that it is not its own ground but proceeds from a will and plan beyond itself—in whatever form one conceptualizes the dependence on such a transcendent "cause." In the view of modern science, by contrast, the world has "made" and is continuously making "itself." It is an ongoing process, activated by the forces at work within it, determined by the laws inherent in its matter, each state of it the effect of its own past and none the implementation of a plan or intended order. The world at every moment is the last word about itself and measured by nothing but itself.

2. By the same token, this scientific philosophy denies the further sentence, "And God saw everything which He had made, and, behold, it was very good." Not that physics holds that the world is bad or evil, that is, in any sense the opposite of good: the world of modern physics is neither "good" nor "bad"; it has no reference to either attribute, because it is *indifferent* to that very distinction. It is a world of fact alien to value. Thus such terms as "good" or "bad," "perfect" or "imperfect," "noble" or "base," do not apply to anything in or of nature. They are human measures entirely.

3. A third negation then follows. A nature pronounced "good" by its creator in turn proclaims the goodness of the maker and master. "The heavens tell the glory of God and the firmament proclaims His handiwork." (Psalm 19). That is to say, the glory of God, visible in His works, calls forth in man admiration and piety. The modern heavens no longer tell the glory of God. If anything, they proclaim their own mute, mindless, swirling immensity; and what they inspire is not admiration, but dizziness; not piety, but the rejoinder of analysis.

4. The disenchanted world is a purposeless world. The absence of values from nature means also the absence of goals or ends from it. We said that the noncreated world makes itself blindly and not according to any intention. We must now add that this renders the whole status of intentions and ends in the scheme of things problematical and leaves man as the sole repository of them. How is he qualified for this solitary role, for this ultimate monopoly on intention and goal?

II

With this question we turn to the second theme, from the modern doctrine of nature to the modern doctrine of man, where again we shall look for the negations of biblical views implied in the affirmations of modern theory. We easily discover such negations in the ideas of evolution, of history, and of psychology as they appear in the forms of Darwinism, historicism, and psychoanalysis—three representative aspects of the contemporary concept of man.

1. The cardinal biblical statement on the nature of man, let us remember, is contained in the second great pronouncement of the creation story after that of the creation of the universe—the statement, made with particular solemnity, that "God created man in his own image, in the image of God he created him." This sentence is the second cornerstone of Jewish doctrine, no less important than the first supplied by the all-inclusive, opening sentence of the Bible. And just as the first, concerning nature as a whole, is denied by the modern doctrine of nature, so the second, concerning man, is denied by the naturalistic doctrine of evolution as it applies to the human species.

In the Darwinian view, man bears no eternal "image" but is part of universal, and in particular of biological, "becoming." His "being" as it actually turned out is the unintended (and variable) product of unconcerned forces whose prolonged interplay with circumstances have "evolution" for their joint effect but nothing (not even evolution as such) for their aim. None of the forms arising in the process has any validity other than the factuality of its having "made the grade"; none is terminal either in meaning or in fact. Man, therefore, does not embody an abiding or transcendent "image" by which to mold himself. As the temporal (and possibly temporary) outcome of the chance transactions of the evolutionary mechanics, with the survival premium the only selective principle, his being is legitimized by no valid essence. He is an accident, sanctioned merely by success. Darwinism, in other words, offers an "image-less" image of man. But, it was the image-idea with its transcendent reference by whose logic it could be said "Be ye holy *for* I am holy, the Lord your God." The evolutionary imperative sounds distinctly different: Be successful in the struggle of life. And since biological success is, in Darwinian terms, defined by the mere rate of reproduction, one may say that all imperatives are reduced to "Be fruitful and multiply."

2. Evolution, however, only provides the natural backdrop for another and uniquely human dimension of becoming, *history;* and the modern concept of man is as much determined by historicism as by Darwinism. Here again it clashes with biblical lore. As Darwinism finds man to be a product of nature and its accidents, so historicism finds him to be the continuous product of his own history and its man-made creations, i.e., of the different and changing cultures, each of which generates and imposes its own *values*—as matters of fact, not of truth: as something whose force consists in the actual hold it has on those who happen to be born into the community in

question, not in a claim to ideal validity which might be judged objectively. There *are* only matters of fact for the positivist creed of which historicism is one form. And, as facts are mutable, so are values; and as historical configurations of fact, i.e., cultures are many, so are value systems, i.e., moralities. There is no appeal from the stream of fact to a court of truth.

This historical relativism-and-pluralism obviously negates the biblical tenet of *one* Torah, its transcendent authority, and its being knowable. "He has told you, O man, what is good": this means that there is one valid good for man, and that its knowledge is granted him—be it through revelation, be it through reason. This is now denied. Relativism—cultural, anthropological, historical—is the order of the day, ousting and replacing any absolutism of former times. Instead of the absolute, there is only the relative in ethics; instead of the universal, only the socially particular; instead of the objective, only the subjective; and instead of the unconditional, only the conditional, conventional, and convenient.

3. The finishing touch on all this is put by modern *psychology*—after evolutionism and historicism the third among the forces shaping the modern concept of man which we have chosen to consider. The psychological argument—because it seems to put the matter to the test of everyone's own verification—has proved to be the most effective way of cutting man down to size and stripping him in his own eyes of every vestige of metaphysical dignity. There has been underway in the West, at the latest since Nietzsche's depth-probing into the genealogy of morals, a persistent "unmasking" of man: the exposure of his "higher" aspects as some kind of sham, a "front" and roundabout way of gratification for the most elementary, essentially base drives, out of which the complex, sophisticated psychic system of civilized man is ultimately constructed and by whose energies alone it is moved. The popular success of psychoanalysis, which gave this picture the trappings of a scientific theory, has established it as the most widely accepted view of man's psychical life and thus of the very essence of man. True or not, it has become the common currency of our everyday psychologizing: the higher in man is a disguised form of the lower.

This psychological doctrine denies the authenticity of the spirit, the transcendent accountability of the person. The moral imperative is not the voice of God or the Absolute, but of the superego which speaks with spurious authority—spurious because dissembling its own questionable origin—and this speaker can be put in his place by *reminding* him of his origin. Note here the reversed meaning which the "reminder of origin" takes on with the reversal of origin itself: it is now forever looked for in the depth, where formerly it was sought in the height. The reductionism, borrowed from natural science, that governs the theory of man, results in the final debunking of man, leaving him in the engulfing miserableness which Christian doctrine had attributed to him as a consequence of the Fall, but now no longer opposed by the "image" to which he might rise again.

Now the paradox of the modern condition is that this reduction of man's stature, the utter humbling of his metaphysical pride, goes hand in hand with his promotion to quasi-god-like privilege and power. The emphasis is on *power*. For it is not only that he now holds the monopoly on value in a world barren of values; that as the sole source of meaning he finds himself the sovereign author and judge of his own preferences with no heed to an eternal order: this would be a somewhat abstract privilege if he were still severely hemmed in by necessity. It is the tremendous *power* which modern *technology* puts into his hands to implement that license, a power therefore which has to be exercised in a vacuum of norms, that creates the main problem for contemporary ethics.

III

Herewith we come to the theme of technology which I had named, together with the theories of nature and man, as the third, and practical, determinant of the present situation. It will be my contention in what follows that the dialectical togetherness of these two facts—the profound demotion of man's metaphysical rank by modern science (both natural and human), and the extreme promotion of his power by modern technology (based on this selfsame science)—constitutes the major ethical challenge of our day, and that Judaism cannot and need not be silent in the face of it.

Modern technology is distinguished from previous, often quite ingenious, technology by its scientific basis. It is a child of natural science: it is that science brought to bear on its object, indifferent nature, in terms of action. Science had made nature "fit," cognitively and emotionally, for the kind of treatment that was eventually applied to it. Under its gaze the nature of things, reduced to the aimlessness of their atoms and causes, was left with no dignity of its own. But that which commands no reverence can be commanded, and, released from cosmic sacrosanctity, all things are for unlimited use. If there is nothing terminal in nature, no formation in its productions that fulfills an originative intention, then anything can be *done* with nature without violating its integrity, for there *is* no integrity to be violated in a nature conceived in the terms of natural science alone—a nature neither created nor creative. If nature is mere object, in no sense subject, if it expresses no creative will, either of its own or of its cause, then man remains as the sole subject and the sole will. The world then, after first having become the object of man's knowledge, becomes the object of his will, and his knowledge is put at the service of his will; and the will is, of course, a will for power over things. That will, once the increased power has overtaken necessity, becomes sheer desire, of which there is no limit.

What is the moral significance of technological power? Let us first consider a psychological effect. The liberties which man can take with a nature made metaphysically neutral by science and no longer accorded an inherent integrity that must be respected as inviolable; the actual and ever increasing extent of the mastery exercised over it; the triumphal remaking and outwitting of creation by man according to his projects; the constant demonstration of what we can do plus the unlimited prospects of what we might yet do; and finally the utterly mystery-free, businesslike rationality of the methods employed—this whole power experience, certified by cumulative success, dissipates the last vestiges of that reverence for nature, that sense of dependence, awe, and piety, which it had inspired in man throughout the ages, and some of which could still survive the purely theoretical analysis of nature. Kant, sober Newtonian that he was, could still voice the profound admiration with which the starry sky above filled his heart, and could even place it alongside the admiration for the moral law within. "Which one did we put there?" asked the post-Sputnik boy when his father explained one of the constellations to him. Some ineffable quality has gone out of the shape of things when manipulation invades the very sphere which has always stood as a paradigm for what man cannot interfere with. "How is it done? How could we do the same? How could we do it even better?"—the mere question divests the nature of things of a sublimity which might stay our hands.

If it is true that both religion and morality originally drew sustenance from a sense of piety which cosmic mystery and majesty instilled in the soul—a sense of being excelled in the order of things by something not only physically beyond our reach but also in quality beyond our virtue: if the wonder and humility before nature had something to do with a readiness to pay homage also to norms issued in the name of an eternal order—then there must be some moral implication in the loss of this sense, in the nakedness of things without their noumenal cloak, offered up for our conquering rape. If reverence or shame has any share in the hold which moral laws may have on us, then the experience of technological power, which expunges reverence and shame, cannot be without consequences for our ethical condition.

IV

But, it may be objected, if *nature* has lost man's respect and ceased to be an object of his reverence, one might expect his respect for himself to have risen in proportion. Man must have gained in metaphysical status what nature has lost—even what God has lost: man has stepped into His place as creator, the maker of new worlds, the sovereign refashioner of things. And indeed, admiration for man's achievement after his long ages of helplessness, and for the genius behind it, is profound and surely not unjust. The collective self-congratulation in which it finds voice sometimes takes the form of humanistic deification: the divine is in man—witness what he can *do*. But there we come before the paradox noted before, viz., that with his very triumph man himself has become engulfed in the metaphysical devaluation which was the premise and the consequence of that triumph. For he must see himself as part of that nature which he has found to be manipulable and which he learns how to manipulate more and more. We have seen before how through modern science he lost the attribute of "image-of-God," as he is not only the subject but also the object of his scientific knowledge—of physics, chemistry, biology, psychology, etc. What we must see now is that he is not merely the *theoretical* object of his knowledge and of the consequent revision of the image he entertains of himself: he is also the object of his own technological power. He can remake himself as he can nature. Man today, or very soon, can make man "to specification"—today already through sociopolitical and psychological techniques, tomorrow through biological engineering, eventually perhaps through the juggling of genes.

The last prospect is the most terrifying of all. Against this power of his own, man is as unprotected by an inviolable principle of ultimate, metaphysical integrity as external nature is in its subjection to his desires: those desires themselves he may now undertake to "program" in advance—according to what? According to his desires and expediencies, of course—those of the future according to those of the present. And while the conditioning by today's psychological techniques, odious as it may be, is still reversible, that by tomorrow's biological techniques would be irreversible. For the first time, man may be able to determine, not only *how* he is to *live,* but *what* in his constitution he is to *be.* The accident of his emergence from a blind but age-long dynamic of nature (if accident indeed it was) is to be compounded by what can only be termed accident of the second power: by man's now taking a hand in his further evolution *in the light of his ephemeral concepts.*

For let no one confound the presence of a plan with the absence of accident. Its execution may or may not be proof against the intervention of accident: its very conception, as to motives, end, and means, must in the nature of things human be thoroughly accidental. The more far-reaching the plan, the greater becomes the disproportion between the range of its effects and the chance nature of its origin. The most foolish, the most deluded, the most shortsighted enterprises—let alone the most wicked—have been carefully planned. The most "farsighted" plans—farsighted as to the distance of the intended goal—are children of the concepts of the day, of what at the moment is taken for knowledge and approved as desirable: approved so, we must add, by those who happen to be in control. Be their intentions ever so unblemished by self-interest (a most unlikely event), these intentions are still but an option of the shortsighted moment which is to be imposed on an indefinite future. Thus the slow-working accidents of nature, which by the very patience of their small increments, large numbers, and gradual decisions, may well cease to be "accident" in the outcome, are to be replaced by the fast-working accidents of man's hasty and biased decisions, not exposed to the long test of the ages. His uncertain ideas are to set the goals of generations, with a certainty borrowed from the presumptive certainty of the means. The latter presumption is doubtful enough, but this doubtfulness becomes secondary to the prime question that arises when man indeed undertakes to "make himself": *In what image* of his own devising shall he do so, even granted that he can be sure of the means? In fact, of course, he can be sure of neither, not of the end, nor of the means, once he enters the realm where he plays with the roots of life. Of one thing only he can be sure: of his *power* to move the foundations and to cause incalculable and irreversible consequences. Never was so much power coupled with so little guidance for its use. Yet there is a compulsion, once the power is there, to use it anyway.

V

Modern ethical theory, or philosophical ethics, has notoriously no answer to this quandary of contemporary man. Pragmatism, emotivism, linguistic analysis deal with the facts, meanings, and expressions of man's goal-setting, but not with the principles of it—denying, indeed, that there are such principles. And existentialism even holds that there ought not to be: Man, determining his essence by his free act of existence, must neither be bound nor helped by any once-for-all principles and rules. "At this point," as Brand Blanshard remarks, "the linguistic moralists of Britain make a curious rapprochement with the existentialists of the continent. The ultimate act of choice is, for both alike, an act of will responsible to nothing beyond itself."[1]

To me it is amazing that none of the contemporary schools in ethical theory comes to grips with the awesome problem posed by the combination of this anarchy of human choosing with the apocalyptic power of contemporary man—the combination of near-omnipotence with near-emptiness. The question must be asked: Can we afford the happy-go-lucky contingency of subjective ends and preferences when (to put it in Jewish language) the whole future of the divine creation, the very survival of the image of God have come to be placed in our fickle hands? Surely Judaism must take a stand here, and in taking it must not be afraid to challenge some of the cherished beliefs of modernity. So I will dare a few Jewish comments on the contemporary ethical predicament.

First a word about the alleged theoretical finality of modern immanence and the death of transcendence, or, the ultimate truth of reductionism. This is very much a matter of the "emperor's clothes" in reverse: "But he has nothing on!" exclaimed the child, and with this one flash of innocence dispelled the make-believe, and everybody saw that the emperor was naked. Something of this kind was the feat of the Enlightenment, and it was liberating. But when in the subsequent nihilistic stage—our own—the confirmed reductionist or cynic, no longer the open-eyed child but a dogmatist himself, triumphantly states, "There is nothing there!"—then, lo and behold, once said with the tautological vigor of the positivist dogma behind it, namely that there *is* only that which science can verify, then, indeed, with eyes so conditioned, or through spectacles so tinted, we do see nothing but the nakedness we are meant to see. And there is nothing more to be seen—for certain things are of a kind that they are visible only to a certain kind of vision and, indeed, vanish from sight when looked at with eyes instructed otherwise. Thus, the bold assertion that the emperor has no clothes on may itself be the cause for the clothes not to be seen anymore; it may itself strip them off; but then its negative truth and our verification of it by our induced blindness are merely self-confirmatory and tautological.

This is the fate suffered by the biblical propositions that God created the heaven and the earth, that he saw that his creation was good, that he created man in his image, that it has been made known to man what is good, that the word is written in our heart. These propositions, i.e., what through the symbolism of their literal meaning they suggest about reality, are of course in no way "refuted" by anything science has found out about the world and ourselves. No discovery about the laws and functions of matter *logically* affects the possibility that these very laws and functions may subserve a spiritual, creative will. It is, however, the case, as in the reversed story of Christian Andersen, that the *psychological* atmosphere created by science and reinforced by technology is peculiarly unfavorable to the *visibility* of that transcendent dimension which the biblical propositions claim for the nature of things. Yet some equivalent of their meaning, however remote from the literalness of their statement, must be preserved if we are still to be Jews and, beyond that special concern of ours, if there is still to be an answer to the moral quest of man. Shall we plead for the protection of a sense of mystery? If nothing more, it will put some restraints on the headlong race of reason in the service of an emancipated, fallible will.

VI

Let us just realize how desperately needed in the field of action such biblical restraints have become by that very triumph of technology which in the field of thought has made us so particularly indisposed to recognize their authority. By the mere scale of its effects, modern technological power, to which almost anything has become feasible, forces upon us goals of a type that was formerly the preserve of utopias. To put it differently: technological power has turned what ought to be tentative, perhaps enlightening plays of speculative reason, into competing blueprints for projects, and in choosing between them we have to choose between extremes of remote effects. We live in the era of "enormous consequences" of human action (witness the bomb, but also the impending threat of biological engineering)—irreversible consequences that concern the total condition of nature on our globe and the very kind of creatures that shall or shall not populate it. The face or image of creation itself, including the image of man, is involved in the explosion of technological might. The older and comforting belief that human nature remains the same and that the image of God in it will assert itself against all defacements by man-made conditions, becomes untrue if we "engineer" this nature genetically and be the sorcerers (or sorcerer's apprentices) that make the future race of Golems.

In consequence of the inevitably "utopian" scale of modern technology, the salutary gap between everyday and ultimate issues, between occasions for prudence and common decency and occasions for illuminated wisdom is steadily closing. Living constantly now in the shadow of unwanted, automatic utopianism, we are constantly now confronted with issues that require ultimate wisdom—an impossible situation for man in general, because he does not possess that wisdom, and for contemporary man in particular, because he even denies the existence of its object: transcendent truth and absolute value, beyond the relativities of expediency and subjective preference. We need wisdom most when we believe in it least.

VII

It is not my purpose here to argue the "truth" of Judaism in general, or of those biblical propositions in particular which we found to be repudiated by modern beliefs. Rather I ask: *if* we are Jews—and a corresponding question Christians and Muslims must ask themselves—what counsel can we take from the perennial Jewish stance in the pressing dilemma of our time? The first such counsel, I believe, is one of modesty in estimating our own cleverness in relation to our forebears. It is the modern conviction, nourished by the unprecedented progress in our knowledge of things and our consequent power over things, that *we know better,* not only in this but *in every respect,* than all the ages before us. Yet nothing justifies the belief that science can teach us everything we need to know, nor the belief that what it does teach us makes us wiser than our ancestors were in discerning the proper ends of life and thus the proper *use* of the things we now so abundantly control. The arrogance with which the scientifically emboldened reason looks down on past ignorance and, thus blinded to past wisdom, assumes confident jurisdiction over the ultimate issues of our existence, is not only terrifying in its possible consequences, i.e., objectionable on grounds of prudence, but also impious as an attitude in lacking the humility that must balance any self-confidence of finite man. Such humility, or modesty, would be willing to lend an ear to what tradition has to say about the transempirical, nondemonstrable meaning of things. Attention to our tradition is a Jewish prescription, directing us, not only to the human wisdom we may pick up there, but also to the voice of revelation we may hear through it. At the least, the modesty of thus listening—a modesty amply justified by our helplessness before the fruits and uses of our acquired powers—may guard us from rashly dismissing the seemingly archaic biblical views as mere mythology that belongs to the infancy of man and has been outgrown by our maturity. The simple attentiveness of such a stance may help us realize that we are not completely our own masters, still less those of all posterity, but rather trustees of a heritage. If nothing else, the tempering of our presumed superiority by that injection of humility will make us cautious, and caution is the urgent need for the hour. It will make us go slow on discarding old taboos, on brushing aside in our projects the sacrosanctity of certain domains hitherto surrounded by a sense of mystery, awe, and shame.

VIII

The recovery of that sense, something more positive than the merely negative sense of caution which humility suggests, is the next step. Informed by the idea of creation, it will take the form of *reverence* for certain inviolable integrities sanctioned by that idea. The doctrine of creation teaches reverence toward nature and toward man, with highly topical, practical applications in both directions.

As to nature, it means especially living nature, and the reverence in question is reverence for life. Immediately we see the practical impact of a creationist view on the choices open to modern technology. God, in the Genesis story, set man over all the other creatures and empowered him to their sovereign use: but they are still his creatures, intended to be and to adorn his earth. Subjection, not biological impoverishment, was man's mandate. Nowhere does the Jewish idea of man's preeminence in the created scheme justify his heedless plundering of this planet. On the contrary, his rulership puts him in the position of a responsible caretaker, and doubly so today, when science and technology have really made him master over this globe, with powers to either uphold or undo the work of creation. While biblical piety saw nature's dependence on God's creative and sustaining will, we now also know its *vulnerability* to the interferences of our developed powers. This knowledge should heighten our sense of responsibility. Exploit we must the resources of life, for this is the law of life itself and belongs to the order of creation, but we ought to exploit with respect and piety. Care for the integrity of creation should restrain our greed. Even if it means forgoing some abundance or convenience, we must not reduce the wealth of kinds, must not create blanks in the great spectrum of life, nor needlessly extinguish any species. Even if it hurts the interest of the moment, we must, for instance, stop the murder of the great whales.

I say this is a religious or ethical responsibility derived from the idea of creation which sanctions the whole of nature with an intrinsic claim to integrity. It is, of course, also plain utilitarian common sense, putting the long-range advantage of our earthbound race before the short calculations of present need, greed, or whim. But quite apart from these parallel counsels of prudence (so easily buffeted by the winds of partisan argument, and always conditional upon the conceptions of our advantage and the cogency of our reasoning), it is something absolute, the respect for the manifestation of life on this earth, which should oppose an unconditional "no" to the depletion of the six-day's plentitude—and also, we might add, to its perversion by man-made genetic monstrosities.

IX

With even greater force than for nature does the idea of creation inspire reverence for *man,* for he alone is said to be created "in the image of God." The ethical implications of this mysterious concept are vast and would deserve fuller elaboration, I will here just indicate a few.

Concerning the "shaping" of this image by man himself, the Jewish posture should be, in the briefest formula: education—yes; genetic manipulation—no. The first kind of shaping is our duty, and of necessity mankind has been doing it, badly or well, since the beginnings of civil society. We may grievously err in the ends and the means of education, but our mistakes can still be redeemed, if not by their victims themselves, then by a coming generation: nothing has been irretrievably prejudged, the potential of human freedom is left intact. At its best, education fosters this very freedom; at worst, it does not preclude a new beginning in which the struggling, true form of man may yet be vindicated.

A different thing is the dream of some of our frontiersmen of science: the genetic remaking of man in some image, or assortment of images, of our own choosing, which in fact would be the scientist's according to his lights. The potentially infinite, transcendent "image" would shrink to charts of desired properties, selected by ideology (or will it be expediency? or fad?), turned into blueprints by computer-aided geneticists, authorized by political power—at last inserted with fateful finality into the future evolution of the species by biological technology. From sperm- and ovary-banks there is only one step to synthetic gene-patterning, with a catalogue of samples to suit different tastes or needs.

Here again, quite apart from the terrible danger of error and shortsightedness inherent in our fallibility, quite apart, that is, from considerations of prudence—we simply must not try to fixate man in any image of our own definition and thereby cut off the as yet unrevealed promises of the image of God.

We have not been authorized, so Jewish piety would say, to be makers of a new image, nor can we claim the wisdom and knowledge to arrogate that role. If there is any truth in man's being created in the image of God, then awe and reverence and, yes, utter fear, an ultimate metaphysical shudder, ought to prevent us from meddling with the profound secret of what is man.

Or, to take a less apocalyptic or fanciful and at the moment much more real example, Jewish morality should say: persuasion—yes; but not psychological manipulation such as brainwashing, subliminal conditioning, and what other techniques there are, be they practiced in Peking or New York. I need not elaborate. The reader can easily draw the connection from the idea of the image of God to the principle of respect for the person, his freedom, and his dignity. The protest should always be against turning men into things. My general point is that the idea of creation provides a ground for reverence, and that from this reverence there issue definite ethical precepts in the context of our present situation.

One may object that these precepts, as far as our examples show, are of the restraining or prohibiting kind only, telling us what not to do, but not what to do. True, but it is at least a beginning. Also, we may remember that even the Ten Commandments are mostly don't's and not do's. Moreover, the negative emphasis fits the modern situation, whose problem, as we have seen, is an excess of power to "do" and thus an excess of offers for doing. Overwhelmed by our own possibilities—an unprecedented situation this—we need first of all criteria for rejection. There is reasonable consensus on what decency, honesty, justice, charity *bid* us to do in given circumstances, but great confusion on what we are *permitted* to do of the many things that have become feasible to us, and some of which we must *not* do on any account.

X

Let me conclude with one last instance of such rejection, which may not fall on too willing ears among Jews, who notoriously value length of life. Contemporary biology holds out the promise of indefinite prolongation of individual life. This must seem glad tidings to those who, in accord with an ever sounded theme of mankind, consider mortality an evil, a curse, which may yet be lifted from us, at least be lessened by indefinite delay. But if we abolish death, we must abolish procreation as well, the birth of new life, for the latter is life's answer to the former; and so we would have a world of old age with no youth. But youth is our hope, the eternal promise of life's retaining its spontaneity. With their ever new beginning, with all their foolishness and fumbling, it is the young that ever renew and thus keep alive the sense of wonder, of relevance, of the unconditional, of ultimate commitment, which (let us be frank) goes to sleep in us as we grow older and tired. It is the young, not the old, that are ready to give their life, to die for a cause.

So let us be Jews also in this. With young life pressing after us, we can grow old and sated with days, resign ourselves to death—giving youth and therewith life a new chance. In acknowledging his finitude under god, a Jew, if he is still a Jew, must be able to say with the Psalmist:

> We bring our years to an end as a tale that is told.
> The days of our years are threescore years and ten,
> Or even by reason of strength fourscore years. . . .
> So teach us to number our days,
> That we may get us a heart of wisdom.

(Ps. 90:10–12)

NOTES

From *CCAR Journal* 15 (January 1968): 27–39, with minor modifications by the author.

1. *Reason and Goodness* (New York: Humanities Press, 1967), 254.

III

THE PHILOSOPHICAL QUESTION

15

The Unnatural Jew

Steven S. Schwarzschild

INTRODUCTION

In my philosophy department, the graduate students organize an annual picnic. For some time past, quasi-formal invitations have explicitly excluded me, on the grounds that I am known to be at odds with nature. So I am. My dislike of nature goes deep: nonhuman nature, mountain ranges, wildernesses, tundra, even beautiful but unsettled landscapes strike me as opponents, which, as the Bible commands (Gen. 1:28–30), I am to fill and conquer. I really do not like the world, and I think it foolish to tell me that I had better. Like Dryden, "I condemn the world when I think on it." One explanation of my attitude is historical. My paternal family lived in Frankfurt-on-the-Main, where I was born, since before 1500. We have been urban for well over half a millennium.

Here I want to analyze whether this is only an idiosyncratic or mainly historical attitude or whether more important, even philosophical, factors are significantly involved. Might it be that Judaism and nature are at odds? Richard Popkin once put this Zen problem to me: Who was the last famous Jewish mountain climber? Indeed, most Jews in remembered history are unnatural persons.

JEWISH LITERATURE: CELAN

Paul Celan (1920–70) is among the most important poets of this century, especially *qua* Jew. Among his few narrative works is "Conversation in the Mountains."[1] The story moves on many levels and, despite its typical compactness, carries a lot of freight. In the following summary, I concentrate on one important theme, probably the central one.

The Jew went into the mountains, away from "where he belongs, in the valleys." There he ran into an older cousin. On the narrative level the two are cousins; on another level, both of them are Celan himself—on his way away from Judaism, when he was small, "Mr. Klein," and on his way back, when he was grown, "Mr. Gross."[2] There is never silence very long between Jews, not even in the mountains, "for the Jew and nature, they are two different things, still now, also today, also here." The cousins pay no attention to the natural beauties that surround them. They have veils behind their eyes, so that in their perception any object that strikes the eye becomes a mixture of the image and the veil. "Tongue are they and mouth." They realize that nature, too, has a language, a visual language, but they say that it is "not for you and not for me . . . a language without 'I' or 'you,' all 'he,' all 'it,' all 'sir [*Sie*].'"[3] God does not communicate with Jews through nature. Nature as such does not communicate, "because no one hears it"; it merely speaks.

Let me take up one more aspect of "Conversation in the Mountains," an aspect of its "inter-textuality," in the sense of contemporary literary and philosophical theory. Twice in the six pages of the story, the Jew went *"wie Lenz"* through the mountains. *Lenz* is the old poetic German for "spring" (compare Lent) and also the hero of Georg Buechner's "Lenz" (1835),[4] a quasi-historical story about a German poet who retired into the mountains. Buechner's "Lenz" begins with these words: "On the 20th [of January, 1778] Lenz went into the mountains."[5] Celan wants to "compare" his two Jews, who went into the mountains, with (because they are "like") the Protestant Lenz, whose experiences Buechner, basing himself on historical evidence,[6] powerfully describes.

I can describe Buechner's story of Lenz here only very selectively, with an eye toward the purpose at hand. It contains lengthy romantic descriptions of nature and of extreme psychological states suffused with mysticism, Protestant Germanic theology, and a strong dose of pantheism. This is a relationship to nature completely different from Celan's; yet, there are important features that Lenz and "the Jew" have in common.

As Lenz walked through the mountains, "he was not concerned with the path," and "he found nothing." And as of "the Jew, you know, what does he have that really belongs to him," also of Lenz it is said that "he had nothing." Celan's story begins with the words, "One evening, the sun, and not only the sun, had gone down." Lenz, too, "would have wanted to run after the sun." On the other hand, the Jew "walked in the shadow," whereas "when Lenz descended the mountain, he saw that a rainbow of rays surrounded his shadow." And quoting a church hymn, although Lenz "has no friend in this world, I have my treasure, and he is far." When he learns that a child has died in a neighboring village, Lenz puts on sackcloth and ashes, goes to the village, and tries to resurrect her. He fails. "He had to laugh aloud, and together with the laughter atheism took hold of him. . . . 'I am the Wandering Jew. . . . But, were I omnipotent. I would save.'"

Celan's very Jewish Jews and the two very German Protestants Lenz and Buechner are in general worlds apart, and yet there are some important characteristics they share. It is far from accidental that the Rumanian Jew Celan, whose entire life, work, and death are totally formed by the Nazi experience, became the most important poet of his century in German-language culture. Lenz, too, eventually went insane. There is an aura of unfinishedness, perhaps intentional, about Buechner and his work. Celan's life also was left tragically unfinished when he walked not into the mountains, but into the Seine.

Celan's Jew, too, is then an unnatural Jew. But this could be an accidental result of Jewish history—the explanation routinely given. That is, Celan's Jew is the end product of two thousand years of exile from "the Land." Some Jews contemporary with Celan did return to Zion, and their relationship to nature is very different from that of Jews of the exile, like Celan, whose suicide came right after his only visit to the State of Israel.

What happened to the two cousins/one person in the mountains after the end of Celan's story? We know that the historical Lenz left the mountains and returned to the densely inhabited world; did they/he, too, return to the valleys, or did he/they perhaps die in the wilderness? The exiled Jew is "alienated" from nature, as his historically characteristic "unhealthy" vocational demography illustrates; but the prevailing view has it that this is due not to the fact that he is a Jew, nor to Judaism, but to his exile.

JEWISH PHILOSOPHY

The main line of Jewish philosophy (in the exilic age) has paradigmatically defined Jewishness as alienation from and confrontation with nature. As text I use an essay by Hans Jonas, "Jewish and Christian Elements in Philosophy: Their Share in the Emergence of the Modern Mind," to develop my argument.[7]

Jonas, following Hegel, isolates the Christian component in Western culture as what is not shared with Judaism, the doctrine of the incarnation. According to this doctrine God becomes man, and as such he enters the world, enters nature. I believe Jonas can be shown to be wrong in holding that "it was not before Hegel's theory of the absolute Spirit, its alienation and self-consummation through history, that the theme of incarnation found major expression in philosophy—and then only by the boldest transmutation."[8] This belief can be shown to have played a major role in Western philosophy long before Hegel.[9] The doctrine of the incarnation is, among other things, a repaganization of Biblical religion in the limited but crucial sense that nature is resanctified. God not only is, was, and can be nature, but also nature was and can be God. The closing thought of Jonas's essay is, therefore, the more true: "[T]he ultimate secularization of theology, the idea of history as a self-operative vehicle of redemption is much more of Christian than of Jewish provenance. One may see in it a transmuted form of the Holy Spirit doing his work through man in the interval between incarnation and the second comings,"[10] because, once God has become nature, thereafter he works through and like nature, by natural law, until it is no longer a limited God = nature identity but a total one—that is, the second coming when God will again have become "all in all" (I Cor. 15:28).

Hegel is penetrating but as usual wrongheaded here. For Hegel, Judaism is what is invariably rendered in English as "the religion of sublimity." The German word for "sublimity" *(Erhabenheit)* is a form of *Un-aufgehobenheit,* i.e.,"unsublatedness." The Jewish God is absolutely transcendent to man and the world, "elevated above naturalness."[11] He is the "absolute alien," *der Fremde.*[12] The Jew is, therefore, in turn, totally alienated from God and his world.[13] Hegel contrasts this with the spiritually emancipated Greek and his Christian heirs who have risen to understand that man and the world are God and God is one with them—"sublated."[14]

Hegel is right factually and wrong in his evaluation. The biblical and Jewish God is, indeed, absolutely transcendent. Nature is never in any way identical with him. It can serve him, as it can serve human beings made in the "image of God." What makes humans "images of God" is that they share with him the "will," the rational and the ethical. Jonas here rightly cites Maimonides and Kant,[15] although the vast bulk of Jewish philosophy would serve equally well,[16] and he even cites Kant as in the Jewish current: "In this connection one must also remember Kant's majestic effort to synthesize voluntarism and rationalism. The synthesis appears in the categorical imperative (surely of Hebrew vintage)."[17] In such a rationalistic, volitionalistic, and transcendental context, nature possesses no value in itself. Its value lies in its serviceability to man and God, although, to be sure, it must be protected and even improved for precisely this purpose. "The Lord God took man and placed him in the garden of Eden to work it and to guard it."[18] To quote a quasi-legal, quasi-authoritative, and less exegesis-ridden text, *Sefer ha-Chinnukh* (a popularization of Maimonides' *Book of the Commandments*), "nature is that which works well and effectively for human beings."[19] This is anthropocentrism, or theocentrism, or ratiocentrism long before Kant. "The understanding obtains its laws [a priori] not from nature but prescribes them to it."[20] Helmut Holzhey correctly summarizes the Kantian conception of nature in his essay about Kantian ecology by saying that "nature is the lawfully determined object of cognition, and its legislator is the human understanding."[21]

Jewish philosophers and theologians in the nineteenth century, primarily in Germany, were then torn between Kant and Hegel, but even those strongly attracted to Hegel had to reassert the primacy of freedom and ethics over the innate dialectic of the world and therewith the ultimacy of Judaism. At the end of the century the battle was decisively won in favor of Kant by Hermann Cohen.

In the High Middle Ages, one shoot branched from Jewish thought which was destined to overshadow its mother-tree. Salomon ibn Gabirol (Avicebron), the neo-Platonist philosopher and poet, tried to solve in one fell swoop two fundamental problems: the origin of matter and the derivation of the manifold from the one. His solution was the daring doctrine that *matter* emerges from the *essence* of God and *form* emerges from his *spirit*.[22] Even most specialized scholars have not seen how this doctrine implies at least logically the materiality of God.[23] Gershom Scholem makes no bones about the perennial stream of the pantheistic temptation, to put it mildly, in Kabbalah throughout his classic *Major Trends in Jewish Mysticism*. For example, he relates the twelfth-century German-Jewish pietists to Scotus,[24] and to bring things down to approximately the period of the Renaissance where we left them philosophically above, he speaks of Cordovero's "formula—a century before Spinoza and Malebranche—that 'God is all reality, but not all reality is God.'"[25]

In subsequent European intellectual history, this strange amalgam of scientific rationalism and near-pantheistic mysticism became the scientific revolution of the seventeenth and eighteenth centuries. In Judaism, Chassidism and other quasi-modernizing movements perpetuated and developed these themes. Martin Buber tries too hard in his "Spinoza, Sabbatai Zvi, and the Baal-Shem"[26] to represent Chassidisim and Spinoza as opponents. Even he cannot close his eyes completely to the pantheistic temptation in Chassidism. In any case, when you eliminate the exclusiveness of the rational/ethical connection between God and man, pantheism is only one of several possible results; the temptation of acosmism, that nothing is all there is, also arose in Chassidism.[27] This entire complex was renewed by the Spinoza revival in the age of Hegel and his successors in German "philosophy of nature."

This is, then, in broad outline the history of a Jewish heretical tendency. Scholem puts it this way: "[A]uthoritative Jewish theology like Saadia, Maimonides and Hermann Cohen . . . formulated an antithesis to pantheism."[28] In an earlier analysis, I conclude that "it is, perhaps, worth noting the Jewish origin of the three great 'immanentists' in Western culture, Paul of Tarsus. Spinoza, and Marx. Like Christianity itself, immanentism would seem to be a specifically Jewish heresy."[29]

Hans Jonas is insufficiently sensitive to the heretical character of this development, because he himself is philosophically somewhere between immanentism and transcendentalism. He advocates a partial, but only a partial, "re-Judaization" of Western, naturalistic, Christian, quasi-pantheistic incarnationism. On the one hand, he follows R. Bultmann.[30] On the other hand, he rightly argues that language (*logos*) is "pure signification . . . free from the bonds of likeness" (that is, sensuousness, in Kantian terms), and that, therefore, especially mathematics and ethics are humanly imposed on nature ("some prophets of Israel saw only injustice about them").[31] These two sides are synthesized by Jonas in his philosophy of biology, which results in a doctrine of "emergent evolution." Inorganic nature contains within itself, (as Spinoza and Teilhard de Chardin say) hylozoistically and panpsychically, the potentiality of higher organic and even rational developments.[32] In *The Phenomenon of Life*, Jonas sees the historical connection that I have made here.[33] Dualism killed the vitalism of the Renaissance, but the mechanistic and rationalistic outlook of dualism can now no longer do justice either to the needs of biological science or to the spiritual needs of human society.[34] As a result, Jonas can still speak of "the Jewish-Christian separation of God and world" and of "Western voluntarism."[35]

Jewish philosophy and culture followed a more "unnatural" path. God and man are totally distinct from and superior to nature. The universe is not even *in potentia* structured as it ought to be by spontaneous natural forces, and therefore reason and morality ought to whip things into shape.

ECOSOPHY

I started in a personal vein and then presented some solid evidence using Celan's view as a paradigmatically Jewish contemporary literary source. I have also presented some philosophical underpinnings of that view. I now deal with the question at issue, the Jewish relationship to nature itself.

Nature has in this century become a matter of major concern, partly as a result of the modern naturalization of philosophy. Add to this the recent anxieties of ecologists and of society about shrinking natural resources. No reasonable person will fail to share these concerns. Anthropocentric ethicists will obviously worry about shrinking natural resources. They will want to husband nature as carefully, intelligently, productively, and economically as possible. As Richard A. Watson puts it: "Preserve . . . ecology: human survival depends on it."[36] But note that this argument is based on the view that nature serves man, not man nature. The biblical theorem that man is the master of nature is fully preserved. As Maimonides interprets Genesis 1:26–28: "Act ye according to your will . . . to build and to uproot the planted and to dig out of the mountains copper and so forth." As Descartes put it: "*nous rendre comme maîtres et possesseurs de la nature.*"[37]

"Humanistic ecology" should not be defined in a narrowly utilitarian fashion. It gives no license to damage or destroy any part of nature whose immediate human usefulness is not obvious or at least possible. Human enjoyment is also to be valued past utility and as long as it does not conflict with moral values. Moral values may sometimes be enshrined by analogy in nonhuman nature: for example, we judge suffering to be offensive not only in humans, but also in nonhuman sentient animals.[38] Unabashed anthropocentrist that I am, I gladly admit that my pacifism and vegetarianism comprise an element of ecologism.[39]

There is, on the other hand, a wild-eyed "ecosophy" whose proponents argue that precisely the Western, Jewish-Christian ethos of lordship over nature has produced the ecological crisis. They assert the contrary ethos, that man is part of nature, nature is sacred, and man therefore ought to serve nature rather than vice versa. "We belong to earth and not earth to us."[40] Lynn White Jr. perhaps the most influential ideologist of this sort in this country, even advocates an "advance" into paganism or Far Eastern quasi-pantheistic religion in order to safeguard the sanctity of nature.[41] White alleges that for historic biblical religion, rape is the only form of engagement with nature. (The claim is White's; the words are those of the Protestant "death-of-God" theologian, William Hamilton.)[42]

As part of their political Leftism, the thinkers of "the Frankfurt school" also insist that capitalist domination, exploitation, and alienation of human beings are the result of the attitude of lordship toward an "alienated, thingified" nature. In the wake of Hegel and Heidegger, they propose a "dialectical," rather than a Kantian dualistic, relationship between nature and reason. Man is to be naturalized and nature humanized in the ultimate synthesis. T. W. Adorno complains that Schoenberg (whom he otherwise admires) dominates nature rather than works in and out of it.[43] In his music, therefore, Schoenberg loses "the instinctual life of the sounds."[44]

Ernst Bloch, in his optimistic way, falls into a sort of pantheistic mysticism with a strong dose of Marxism. He holds that *natura naturans* is a "natural Subject," which, like rational men, assures the reconciliation of man and nature.[45] Herbert Marcuse wagers on "erotic desire"[46] and a "naturalistic foundation for reason."[47] Further, the pessimistic Adorno is reduced to hylozoism: his *reductio hominis* is accompanied, as it has to be, by the ascription of anthropomorphic individuality to objects and by "a love of things."[48]

The resacralization of nature can be defended by three philosophical explanations. One is that nature is sacred in, of, and by itself (*an sich*). But surely Kant made mincemeat of such a view. It is only from the human perspective that nature is important or sacred. To ask what nature is according to any nonhuman perspective, or "to itself," is clearly a nonsensical question by definition.[49] But it is not nonsensical enough to keep Christopher Stone from answering the question of his title *Should Trees Have Standing?*[50] in the affirmative. This "standing" is supported by panpsychic, Spinozistic reasons.

Left to her own devices, nature is a fickle mother anyway. She kills many of her own children. Most species were produced and destroyed long before humans arrived. The sentimental notion of nature as omnibenevolent has rightly been ridiculed by philosophers. The Christian Isaac Watt composed a stomach-turning ditty about "the busy little bee" that gives "for everyday some good account at last." Lewis Carroll thought otherwise: "How doth the little crocodile / improve his shining tail, / . . . How cheerfully he seems to grin. / How neatly spreads his claws / and welcomes little fishes in, / With gently smiling jaws!"[51] As Celan's Jew said in the mountains, nature speaks "not for you and not for me." We can, therefore, quite peremptorily dismiss the notion that nature is sacred.

A second defense of the resacralization of nature is to admit, on the one hand, as critics of the Frankfurt School do, that the "sanctity" of nature is not intrinsic but relational. It arises in a "dialectical" relationship to the human spirit. But then, on the other hand, one can assume an absolutely aesthetic, contemplative, posture toward it, a "pure" relation, as distinguished from Kant's "practical" one. The practical view is Habermas's "humanly interested," *logos*-determined, ideally linguistic posture. In the pure relationship, you have "the preponderance of the object."[52] In the aesthetic attitude, nature is regarded not only as noumenal but also as numinous.[53]

This is the quintessence of paganism. Maimonides accordingly defines idolatry as "the love of a form, because it functions so beautifully."[54] Cynthia Ozick calls art "the religion of the Gentile nations."[55] Here nature is man's lord. Greece has triumphed over Jerusalem. Kant's and Hermann Cohen's ethicization of art, in which sublimity is envisioned as rational infinity, beauty as rational and real morality, and humor as the infinite gap between reality and ideality, is here retracted (as though "the Copernican revolution" had not also occurred in aesthetics!). The neo-Kantian Cohen rejected emphatically what he called "the absolute identity of nature and spirit, this pantheistic vehicle of Romantic metaphysics";[56] and when he, too, like Bloch, needed to advance a postulate of the ultimate, infinite reconciliation of nature with ethical reason, he did it in the wake of Kant's infinite, regulative, ethical ideal and in terms of the Jewish/biblical metaphor of the rainbow,[57] that is, in terms of regulatives of universal human, social morality.

The third argument for the resacralization of nature returns us to Jonas, paralleled in the writings of S. Langer and T. de Chardin, who tend here to converge with the original Frankfurt school. Holzhey discusses a current European school of "evolutionary epistemology" (e.g., G. Vollmer, Lorenz, Riedl, et al.): "What Kant differentiated as an accomplishment of the understanding here becomes a function of the organism."[58] Darwinism is interpreted so that human reason is itself a product of nature. What Holzhey refers to as "evolutionary epistemology," Braun calls "naturalistic evolutionism."[59] Adorno then draws the consistent but unacceptable conclusion: "If human identity is totally repressive, then nature must be liberating";[60] and in this he discovers the following lessons: (a) "end the compulsion to have an identity," and (b) "try to live such that you can believe that you were a good animal."[61] The radical critique of this approach by neo-Kantians in the immediate wake of Darwin is still cogent today: "evolutionary epistemology" confuses causality with validity. Hermann Cohen anticipated even Gilbert Ryle's critique of "the ghost in the machine" by mocking "the ghost of a soul."[62] (What is a good animal, anyway—Isaac Watt's "busy little bee" or Lewis Carroll's "little crocodile"?)

JUDAISM

I can finally return to the basic sources of the Jewish relationship to nature. Christians and Jews have so combed the Bible for a proper understanding of nature that I do not need to go into details here. Nature is precious, because God is its *koneh* ("maker"-"owner"). Man is God's perpetual partner in perfecting the world toward and by means of the kingdom of God. He is the steward, the responsible caretaker, and husbandman of nature. Only with this in mind do "the heavens tell of the glory of God and the firmament [bespeak] his handiwork" (Ps. 19), for "when I see your heavens, the work of your fingers, the moon and the stars that you established—what is man? . . . You have set him as ruler of the work of your hands. You have laid all under his feet." (Ps. 8:4f., 7f.) Even what may look like an occasional biblical, quasi-Rousseauite "return to nature," e.g., the Nazirites or Rechabites who live a desert-like existence without houses, wives, wine, or haircuts, is really just a few ethical athletes (at that not favorably countenanced by authoritative Judaism), who want to abstain from material accumulations, concupiscence, mindlessness, and fashion.

My favorite text is the Mishnah's *Pirkei Avot* 3:9: "Rabbi Jacob said: 'One who walks by the road, studying, and interrupts his study and says: 'How lovely is that tree!' or 'How lovely is that furrow!'—Scripture imputes it to him as if he had forfeited his soul!" This classic Jewish text has attracted the usual commentaries. Recently, Cynthia Ozick returned to the ethos of the Mishnah in her title story "The Pagan Rabbi," using this talmudic text as its motto.[63] The hero of the story is a schizophrenic, who, on the one hand, is "a dusty old man trudging [—] he reads as he goes . . . a Tractate of the Mishnah [—] who passes indifferently through the beauty of the field . . . and won't heed the cricket spitting in the field," and, on the other hand, is "the pagan rabbi" himself, who "insisted on picnics" and who proclaims: "there is nothing that is Dead. . . . Great Pan lives."[64]

Susan Handelman[65] makes clear how contemporary "deconstructionist" literary theory (Lacan, Derrida, Harold Bloom)[66] resumes the struggle of Jewish bookishness ("textuality") against pagan/Christian nature and metaphysics—the Book of Books *versus* "the Book of Nature." A quotation from Derrida shows conveniently how deconstructionism drinks from the Jewish sources that I have here traced: "For the Jew—and the poet—the book becomes folded and bound to itself, infinitely self-reflective, its own subject and its own representation. The home of the Jew and the poet is the text: they are wanderers born only of the book. . . . Between the fragments of the Broken Tablets, the poem grows and the right to Speech takes root. Once more begins the adventure of text as weed, as outlaw far from the 'fatherland of the Jews,' which is a 'sacred text surrounded by commentaries.'"[67] This reads like a conflation of Celan's "Conversation in the Mountains" and *Avot* 3:9.

Steven S. Schwarzschild

In Jewish modern, posttraditional literature, our mishnah was treated by Achad Ha'am and Ch. N. Bialik, the founding fathers of the Hebrew Renaissance, in a locus classicus, "Halakhah and Aggadah."[68] On the one hand, the man walking by the road, studying, is "the people 'walking by the road' that possesses nothing but a book and whose spiritual bond to any of the lands in which it dwells is only spiritual."[69] On the other hand, there is condemnation: "[I]t is a pathetic mishnah" and arouses among our "aesthetic and sensitive people" a great desire to break out into the natural world. Micah Joseph Berdichevsky, a pagan, Nietzschean writer of the Hebrew Renaissance, goes further. Commenting on this mishnah, he says: "But I assert that then alone will Judah and Israel be saved when another teaching is given unto us, namely: Whoever walks by the way and sees a fine tree and a fine field and a fine sky and leaves them to think on other thoughts—that man is like one who forfeits his life! Give us back our fine trees and fine fields! Give us back the Universe. . . . We with our thoughts and feelings . . . and all we have and are, are the drippings of the bucket, the dust in the scales, . . . for Nature is the father of all life."[70] Berdichevski draws the Nietzschean, Zionist, programmatically pagan conclusion: "[T]he blade and the bow, by whose force Israel fared so nobly," must be restored in the place of the book in Israel's renaissance.[71] (In his book *Sinai and Gerisim*, Berdichevski advocated a Jewish return to pre-Mosaic paganism, as Oskar Goldberg did in Germany after World War I.)[72]

The connection between such early Zionist ideology and much later "Canaanism" is obvious.[73] But there is more to it than this. The truth is that a back-to-nature thrust inheres in the Zionist enterprise. In the earlier quotation from Bialik/Ahad Ha'am, the back-to-nature push is only less radical than Berdichevski's, and A. Hertzberg rightly recognizes the Nietzschean inspiration even in the founding-father ideologists of Zionism.[74] Also, among the later and genuine saints of Zionism, the resumed love affair with nature appealed to the widest conceivable circles.[75] The workers' prophet A. D. Gordon proclaimed: "And when, oh man, you will return to Nature, . . . you will know that you have returned to yourself; . . . when you hid from nature you hid from yourself," whereas in the past "the Jewish people has been completely cut off from nature and imprisoned within city walls these 2,000 years."[76] "Nature itself has created the people . . . [which] is like a funnel that receives the infinity of the cosmos."[77] Saul Tchernikovsky, another pagan Nietzschean, the Hebrew poet of that generation, raised Berdichevski's conception to even higher literary levels. On the religious end of the Zionist spectrum, Chief-rabbi Kook incorporated nature mysticism into his panentheistic Zionism.[78] Also the quasi-mystic Martin Buber undergirded his utopian-socialist program with a renewed appreciation of the soil and nature. In short, the Jewish philosophical heretical trend, which originated in the Middle Ages, developed in the diaspora and continues in Zionism.

There is nothing "wrong" with trees. To the contrary, God (*Eccl. R.* 7:28) pointed them out to Adam in the garden of Eden, but immediately added the normative purpose for doing so: "Think about this, and do not corrupt or desolate my world; for if you do corrupt it, there will be none to set it aright after you." The Jew is obligated to recite the following benediction when he sees a blooming tree: "Praised be you, oh Lord, our God, king of the world, who has not left a thing lacking in his world and created in it good creatures and good trees, so that human beings can benefit from them."[79] But when a tree is not blooming, that is, when it is not immediately useful to man, the benediction is much more nonchalant: "Praised be you . . . whose world is like this."[80] Even the sun itself was created so as to serve mankind.[81] In short, the rabbis wanted to enthrone "the beauty of Japhet [Greece] in the tents of Shem [Israel]."[82]

The thought of J. B. Soloveitchik is relevant here. In "The Lonely Man of Faith,"[83] he takes the two texts, from Genesis 1 and Genesis 3, which we have had occasion to use a good deal, and develops an entire typology of man: "Adam, the First," who is practical, and "Adam, the Second," who is aesthetic. In many ways Soloveitchik treats the aesthetic Adam as more akin to *homo religiosus*—at least as more akin to the religious man's mystic, God-intoxicated dimension. Despite this, and undoubtedly due to his self-evident commitment to the centrality of *halakhah* ("praxis"), he eventually subordinates the aesthetic Adam to the practical: nature is conceived as existing for halakhic purposes; man is God's partner in making the world; "the man of *halakhah* is a ruler in the kingdom of reason and spirit"[84]—"the subject rules the object, the person the thing."[85] The practical use of nature rules.

In sum, the culture of beauty is prized but subordinated to the culture of morality by Judaism (as Matthew Arnold also understood in *Culture and Anarchy*).

CONCLUSION

I began by calling myself an urban man for more than half a millenium. It turns out, unsurprisingly, that as a Jew I have been an unnatural man much longer. Well before the rise of towns and cities, Jews were not supposed to reside where there are no synagogues, physicians, artisans, toilets, water supplies, schoolteachers, scribes, organized charities, or courts.[86] An "ignoramus" or *'am-ha'aretz* (literally, a "man of the land," "peasant") is frowned upon by "civilized," pious people.[87] Irving Agus, in his historical studies, summarizes: "The Jews were the first self-ruling town-dwellers of Western Europe in the early Middle Ages."[88] Was it only a pun when the Talmudic rabbis warned against the use of the Torah as a spade *(Avot* 4:7)? Or were they warning against subordinating intellectual and moral pursuits to material ends?

NOTES

From *Environmental Ethics* 6 (1984): 347–62.

The author is grateful for advice by his colleagues and friends, Michael Lützeler, Egon Schwarz, and Richard Watson. He also wishes to thank Holmes Rolston III, for a heroic job of cutting the first draft of this paper out of the body of a text (which will appear elsewhere) that exceeds the present one both in length and subject matter.

    1. *Ausgewählte Gedichte*, ed. Klaus Reichert (Frankfurt: Suhrkamp. 1970), 81–86.

    2. Cf. Celan's acceptance speech of the Buechner Prize, "The Meridian," in *Ausgewählte Gedichte*, 142, 146ff., almost all of which deals with this story. Cf. also Jerry Glenn, *Paul Celan* (New York: Twayne. 1973), 43–46, about this story—which is generally an unsatisfactory introduction.

    3. Compare also Martin Buber's *I and Thou*, 2nd ed. (New York: Scribners, 1958) and the famous Yiddish, Chassidic folk song "The Dudele."

    4. G. Buechner, *Wozzek Lenz* (Frankfurt: Insel-Buecherei, n.d.).

    5. Cf. Georg Büchner, *Sämtliche Werke und Briefe*, ed. Werner R. Lehmann (Hamburg: Wegner, 1967), vol. 1, 436.

    6. *Sämtliche Werke und Briefe*, 436–83, for a comparison of Buechner's text with the eyewitness account of Jean Frederic Oberlin (1740–1826), the pastor after whom Oberlin College is named.

    7. In Hans Jonas, *Philosophical Essays: From Ancient Creed to Technological Man* (Englewood Cliffs, N.J.: Prentice-Hall, 1974).

    8. *Philosophical Essays*, 25.

    9. Cf., e.g., H. A. Wolfson, *The Philosophy of the Church Fathers* (Cambridge, Mass.: Harvard University Press, 1964), 223–32: "'Eternal Generation,' 'by Will' and 'by nature,'" and ch. 16/3, "Orthodox Use of the Analogies of Physical Union." All of Susan A. Handelman's *The Slayers of Moses: The Emergence of Rabbinic Interpretation in Modern Literary Theory* (Albany: SUNY, 1982) turns on the classical and modern opposition between Christian incarnationism and Jewish textuality. It is an important, though far from faultless, book (cf. sec. V, below).

    10. *Philosophical Essays*, 44.

    11. G. W. F. Hegel, *Vorlesungen über die Philosophie der Religion* (in *Werke*, ed. Moldenhauer and Michel [Frankfurt: Suhrkamp. 1969], vol. 17), 47, 83.

    12. *Vorlesungen über die Philosophie der Religion*, 92.

    13. *Vorlesungen über die Philosophie der Religion*, 67, 77, 84.

    14. Compare, e.g., the Section On "Judea" in Hegel's *Philosophy of History*, and his early essay "Athens and Judea: Should Judea be the Teutons' Fatherland?" (1795), in *On Christianity*, trans. T. M. Knox (New York: Harper Torchbooks, 1961), 145ff.

    15. *Philosophical Essays*, 29, 31, 33.

    16. Cf. Steven Schwarzschild, "The Lure of Immanence—The Crisis in Contemporary Religious Thought," in *The Pursuit of the Ideal: Jewish Writings of Steven Schwarzschild*, ed. Menachem Kellner (Albany, N.Y.: SUNY Press, 1990), 63–67, and esp. 69f.

    17. *Philosophical Essays*, 43.

    18. Compare *Avot de R. Nathan* 11. In the pursuit of relevance, a good deal of midbrow literature has recently been produced to demonstrate the ecological morality of historic Judaism. The best technical example of such a compilation is *The Protection of the Environment*, ed. N. Rakover [Hebrew], Series of Studies and Analyses in He-

brew Law, no. 26 (Jerusalem: Justice Ministry, 1972). Compare also P. J. Bentley. "Rabbinic Sources on Environmental Issues," Justice and Peace Committee of the Central Conference of American Rabbis (mimeographed, n.d.); and T. Weiss-Rosmarin. "Relevance and the Jewish Heritage," *The Jewish Spectator* (Summer 1980): 3–7.

19. Commandment 62. Compare M. B. Margolies, *Samuel Darid Luzzatto: Traditionalist Scholar* (New York: Ktav, 1979), 108f., for an example of ecological concern for human ends.

20. Kant. *Prolegomena,* sec. 36, last sentence, in italics in the original (compare first *Critique*, B159f., 163f.). It has often been noted that "Copernican revolution" is a paradoxical term for it: Kant put man, or, anyway, reason, back in the center of the universe, from which Copernicus had expelled him. (Cf. N. Hanson, "Copernicus' Role in Kant's Revolution," *Journal of the History of Ideas* 20 [1979]: 274–81.)

21. Helmut Holzhey, "Kritik und Natur," *Neue Zürcher Zeitung* 4–5 (July, 1981): 60. Compare also the same author's more substantive treatment in "Evolutionäre Erkenntnistheorie und ökologische Kritik," in *Schweizer Monatshefte* 63.3 (March, 1983): 215–27. Unfortunately, the conclusions in both articles remain somewhat up in the air (and he misinterprets the biblical view in the latter article, n. 5).

22. Jonas, *Philosophical Essays*, 36, n. 4. Compare also Jacques Schlanger. *La philosophic de Solomon ibn Gabirol: Étude d'un Néoplatonisme* (Leiden: Brill, 1968), 20–22; J. Guttmann, *Die Philosophie des Jüdentums* (Munich: Reinhardt, 1933), 102f.; and J. Bobik, *Aquinas on Being and Essence* (Notre Dame, Ind.: University of Notre Dame Press, 1965), ch. 5.

23. E.g., H. A. Wolfson, *The Philosophy of Spinoza* (New York: Meridan Books, 958), 223.

24. Cf. G. Scholem, *Major Trends in Jewish Mysticism* (New York: Schocken, 1946), 109.

25. *Major Trends in Jewish Mysticism*, 252; compare also 402, n. 64, on Kabbalistic pantheism; and J. ben-Shlomoh, "The Problem of Pantheism in Theistic Mysticism: R. Moses Cordovero and Meister Eckhart," in *Revelation, Faith, Reason: A Collection of Papers* [Hebrew], ed. M. Hallamish and M. Schwarz (Ramat-Gan: Bar-Ilan University, 1976), 71–81.

26. *The Origin and Meaning of Hasidism* (New York: Harper Torchbooks, 1966), 89ff.

27. Cf. Scholem's attack on "M. Buber's Interpretation of Hasidism," in *The Messianic Idea in Judaism* (New York: Schocken, 1971), esp. 240–44, where he summarizes the acosmic aspect of Chassidism in these words: "It is necessary to reduce things to their nothingness in order to restore them to their true nature" (242). This conception emerges especially in the Tanya. Compare the acosmic and, indeed, nihilistic ending of the Spinozist Isaac B. Singer's *The Family Moskat* (New York: Knopf, 1950).

28. *Major Trends in Jewish Mysticism*, 38.

29. "The Lure of Immanence," 274f., n. 12.

30. Cf. Jonas, "The Abyss of the Will: Philosophical Meditations on the Seventh Chapter of Paul's 'Epistle to the Romans,'" in *Philosophical Essays*, loyally dedicated to Bultmann; but see also Jonas, "Heidegger and Theology," in *The Phenomenon of Life: Toward a Philosophical Biology* (New York: Harper and Row, 1966), ch. 10.

31. Jonas, "Sight and Thought: A Review of Visual Thinking," in *Philosophical Essays*, 231, 233, 235.

32. "Sight and Thought," 222.

33. *The Phenomenon of Life*, 12ff.

34. *The Phenomenon of Life*, 61.

35. *Philosophical Essays*, 29, 39; see Emanuel Levinas, *Autrement qu'être, ou au delà de l'essence* (The Hague: Nijhoff, 1974), 34, 123, 140, 145, 168, 199, 214, 223, etc., on Jewish, philosophical, ethicist anti-"occidentalism" (= ontologism).

36. The last sentence of Richard A. Watson's "A Critique of Anti-Anthropocentric Biocentrism," *Environmental Ethics* 5 (1983): 256.

37. Descartes, *Philosophical Works* (New York: Dover Publications, 1955), vol. I, 119. Cf. also Holzhey, "Evolutionäre Erkenntnistheorie," 219; also 217–19, his accurate derivation of Descartes' posture from the Renaissance spirit in Pico della Mirandola's and (his Jewish associate) Leone Hebreo's *De Dignitate Hominis*, (via E. Cassirer).

38. Peter Singer demonstrates how one can make rational decisions in this field by arguing in favor of "animal liberation," on the one hand (in *Moral Problems—A Collection of Philosophical Essays*, ed. James Rachels [New York: Harper and Row. 1979], 83ff.), and yet countenancing "Fetal Research" (197ff.) within proper ethical limits.

39. For a survey of Judaism on animals, cf. Noah J. Cohen, *Tza'ar Ba'aley Chayyim* [English] (Washington: Catholic University of America, 1959).

40. Quoted by Watson, "Critique," 247.

41. Cf. Lynn White Jr., *Machina ex Deo: Essays in the Dynamism of Western Culture* (Cambridge, Mass.: M.I.T. Press, 1968), ch. 5, "The Historical Roots of Our Ecologic Crisis." White apparently knows nothing of the incarnationist abyss between Christianity and Judaism (cf. Jonas), and he contradicts himself in acknowledging, on the one hand, the special "dynamism of Western culture," only to turn around and advocate the elimination of the very factor to which that dynamism is attributed. Wendell Berry's "The Gift of the Good Land," *Sierra* 64.6 (November/December 1979): 20–26, is a moderate, but also modest, reply to White.

42. Cf. Schwarzschild, "The Lure of Immanence," 276, n. 26.

43. T. W. Adorno, *Philosophy of Modern Music* (Frankfurt: Europaische Verlaganstalt, 1958), 61–65.

44. *Philosophy of Modern Music*, 78, 61–65, 106–16.

45. Cf. P. Brenner, "Aspekte und Probleme der neueren Utopiediskussion in der Philosophie," in *Utopie-Forschung: Interdesziplinaere Studien zur neuzeitlichen Utopie,* ed. W. Vosskamp (Stuttgart: Metzler, 1982); see also J. Habermas, *Toward a Rational Society* (Boston: Beacon Press, 1970), 86–90, on Bloch's peculiar "naturism."

46. H. Marcuse, *An Essay on Liberation* (Boston: Beacon Press, 1969), 10.

47. Cf. the Marcuse-Hahermas interview in *Telos* 38 (winter, 1978–79): 136; and compare H. van der Linden's "The Idea of a Repressive vs. a Liberated Domination of Nature in the Work of H. Marcuse" [Dutch], M.A. thesis, Gröningen, 1978.

48. Carl Braun, *Kritsche Theorie versus Kritizismus: Zur Kant-Kritik T. W. Adornos, Kantstudien Erganzungshefte*, 115 (Berlin: de Gruyter, 1983), 53; compare also his discussion, 176, of Adorno's "reason [developed] genetically from instinctual energy."

49. Watson, "Critique," 250ff., crystalizes other logical incoherences in "ecosophy."

50. Christopher D. Stone, *Should Trees Have Standing? Toward Legal Rights for Natural Objects* (Los Altos: William Kaufmann, 1974). Compare Watson's counterarguments: "Self-Consciousness and the Rights of Nonhuman Animals and Nature," *Environmental Ethics* 1 (1979): esp. 120ff. (I am indebted to Hamner Hill for bringing me up to date on this debate.)

51. Lewis Carroll, *The Annotated Alice*, ed. Martin Gardner (New York: New American Library, 1960), 38f. Carroll was even more correct than he, perhaps, knew: Spinoza's famous passage about might = right (*Theologico-Political Treatise*, in *Chief Works of Spinoza*, trans. Elwes [2 vols.; New York: Dover, 1951], vol. 1, 200) and the passage in *Ethics*, Pt. 4, Prop. 37. n. 1, about "the womanish superstition" of worrying about the feelings of animals, are couched precisely in the metaphor of the big and the little fishes. Compare with regard to the fish metaphor, *'Avodah Zarah* 3f., Rashi to *Beitzah* 23b, "and not," and Seneca, *Moral Epistles* 103:3.

52. Cf. Braun, *Kritische Theorie*, 240ff., 284.

53. Cf. Watson, "Critique," on the Heidegger and Huxley "aesthetic" connections.

54. Maimonides, *Mishneh Torah,* Laws of Idolatry 3:6.

55. Cynthia Ozick, "Toward a New Yiddish," in *Art and Ardor: Essays* (New York: A. Knopf, 1983), 157ff.

56. Hermann Cohen, *Kant's Bergründung der Aesthetik,* (Berlin: Kummler, 1889), 339, 348.

57. Cf. Steven S. Schwarzschild, "Introduction," in Hermann Cohen, *Ethik des reinen Willens, Werke*, vol. 7 (Hildesheim/New York: Olms, 1981), xxiiiff.

58. Holzhey, "Evolutionäre Erkenntnistheorie," 222ff. N.b. that Jonas converges with Ried in the former's *Macht oder Ohnmacht der Subjektivität: Das Leib-Seele Problem im Vorfeld des Prinzips Verantwortung* (Frankfurt: Insel, 1981), 116. Compare *Concepts and Approaches in Evolutionary Epistemology*, ed. F. M. Wuketits (Hingham, Mass.: Reidel, 1983).

59. Braun, *Kritische Theorie*, 245.

60. Braun, *Kritische Theorie*, 271.

61. Braun, *Kritische Theorie*, 282.

62. Cf. Steven S. Schwarzschild, "The Tenability of H. Cohen's Construction of the Self," *Journal of the History of Philosophy* 8 (1975): 363.

63. Cynthia Ozick, *The Pagan Rabbi and Other Stories* (New York: A. Knopf. 1971). Handelman, *Slayers of Moses,* 64f., also refers to this mishnah.

64. It is clever and Derridaesque on the part of Ozick to have her hero study the book that invented him. We have by now encountered schizophrenia as the enactment of man's relationship to nature, especially but not exclusively the Jew's, in the mishnaic man. Lenz, Celan, and now Ozick! As Harold Bloom says, *Kabbalah and Mysticism* (New York: Seabury, 1975), 111: "Schizophrenia is disaster in life, and success in poetry."

65. Handelman, *Slayers of Moses.*

66. Compare Steven S. Schwarzschild, "Authority and Revelation," in *Studies in Jewish Philosophy, Vol. II: Reason and Revelation as Authority in Judaism* (Melrose Park, Pa.: Academy for Jewish Philosophy, 1982), 53f. But see Cynthia Ozick, "Judaism and Harold Bloom," *Commentary* 67.1 (January, 1979): 43–51.

67. Handelman, *Slayers of Moses*, 175f.

68. *Kol Kitvei Ch. N. Bialik* [Hebrew] (Tel Aviv: Dvir, 1951), 210.

69. This is reminiscent of Heine's famous description of the Bible as the Jews' portable fatherland. In fact, I could not find this phrase when I looked for it. The closest I could come is "the written fatherland": cf. *Sämtliche Werke*, ed. H. Kaufman (Munich: Aufbau, 1964), vol. 7, 99.

70. *The Zionist Idea: A Historical Analysis and Reader*, ed. Arthur Hertzberg (New York: Meridian, 1960), 296.

71. *The Zionist Idea*, 296. James Diamond and Sam Fishman have helped me track down the details of this essay by Berdichevsky. It was first published in the American Hebrew weekly *HaPishgah*, 19 August 1898, entitled "the Janus-Face": compare *Ma'amarim*, (Tel-Aviv, 1942), 45.

72. *The Reality of the Hebrews: Introduction to the System of the Pentateuch* [German] (Berlin: David. 1925); Erich Unger, *The Problem of Mythic Reality* [German] (Berlin: David, 1926); compare J. Taubes, "From Cult to Culture," *Partisan Review* 21 (1954): 387–400. Thomas Mann was transfixed by these kooky Jews.

73. Cf. Gerson Shaked, "First Person Plural: Literature of the 1948 Generation," *The Jerusalem Quarterly* 22 (1982), and the Caananite journal *Aleph*; B. Kurzweil, "The New 'Canaanites' in Israel," *Judaism* 21.1 (1953): 2–15, and its Hebrew original; and "The New Hebrew Nation (the 'Canaanite' outlook)," in *Unease in Zion*, ed. E. b. Ezer (New York: Quadrangle, 1974), 201–34.

74. *The Zionist Idea*, 55f., 66.

75. *The Zionist Idea*, 118f. On Berdichevsky (= Bin Gorion), compare U. Jacobson, "Fiction and History in the Writings of . . . ," *Prooftexts* 3.2 (May, 1983): 205–10.

76. *The Zionist Idea*, 37 f., 381. Compare S. H. Bergman, *Faith and Reason: An Introduction to Modern Jewish Thought* (Washington, D.C.: B'nai B'rith, 1961): "Men are but organic parts of the comsos" (103). After the (intellectual) Fall, "through religion man begins to feel once again that he is an inseparable and organic part of creation."

77. Bergman, *Faith and Reason*, 113.

78. Bergman, *Faith and Reason*, 124, 128, 137.

79. *Ber.* 43b, *R. H.* 11.

80. *Ber.* 58b. Bialik realized the connection between our mishnah and these benedictions: cf. *Kol Kitvei*.

81. *Lev. R.* 20:2: "Resh Lakish said in the name of R. Simon b. Menasya: 'The first man was created for God's use and the disk of the sun for human use.'"

82. *Meg.* 96 *ad* Gen. 9:27, about the beauty of the Greek language in the Septuagint.

83. J. B. Soloveitchik, "The Lonely Man of Faith," *Tradition* (Summer, 1965): 5–67.

84. "The Man of the Law," in *Ish haHalakhah: Galuy veNisstar* [Hebrew] (Jerusalem: Zionist Organization of America, 1979), 72.

85. "The Man of the Law," 120. Compare also D. Singer and M. Sokol, "Joseph Soloveitchik: Lonely Man of Faith," *Modern Judaism*, 2 (1982): esp. 251f.; and "Man of Faith," 15; and "But if you Search There," 4.

86. *Sanh.* 7; Maimonides, *Mishneh Torah*, Laws of Belief 4:23.

87. *Avot* 2:5; compare Maimonides, *Mishneh Torah*, Laws of Belief 3:14; *Sotah* 22a. Compare Heidegger's Nazi cult of the peasant.

88. Irving Agus. *The Heroic Age of Franco-German Jewry: The Jews of Germany and France of the 10th and 11th Centuries, the Pioneers and Builders of Town-life. Town-government and Institutions* (New York: Yeshiva University Press, 1969), 87; compare also the very title of his *Urban Civilization in Pre-Crusade Europe* (2 vols.; New York: Yeshiva University Press, 1965).

16

Some Thoughts on Nature and Judaism

David Ehrenfeld and Joan G. Ehrenfeld

Steven S. Schwarzschild's "The Unnatural Jew" presents a distorted and utterly inaccurate portrait of the environmental ethics of Judaism, which contains the most detailed and ecologically sensitive environmental code of any religion.

This is not the place to dissect, point by point, the accomplished cultural patter that makes up the bulk of the article. Nor would it be an easy task, since Schwarzschild's erudition is both confused and confusing. It is far more important to examine what Schwarzschild is saying, for his central thesis is not only false, but—in a muddled and unintentional way—anti-Semitic. Non-Jews especially should understand that Schwarzschild's argument is totally outside the pale of accepted Jewish environmental theory and practice, both now and continuously during the past 3,000 years.

Himself the product of 500 years of ghetto living, Schwarzschild informs us that he is alienated from nature. No doubt. Yet what the ghetto did to him, it did not do to all other Jews, or to Judaism itself. All we can infer from his own alienation is that it has made him incapable of observing the place of nature in Judaism.

"Who was the last famous Jewish mountain climber?" Schwarzschild asks. Although it is a clever question, designed to nourish prejudicial stereotypes rather than evoke information, it makes no sense when examined critically. Who was the last famous Nigerian mountain climber? Indonesian? Eskimo? How silly. If Schwarzschild wants examples of famous postbiblical Jews who were in touch with nature, there are thousands from all walks of Judaism. They range from Rabbi Akiva, the great, first-century codifier of Jewish law, who was a shepherd until middle age,[1] to General Avraham Yoffe, tank commander, hero of the Sinai campaigns, and brilliant conservationist,

283

who in the 1967 war used his reserve units to post thousands of hectares of Sinai nature reserves even before the firing had stopped.

If, as Schwarzschild maintains, there is such a gulf between Judaism and nature, it is strange that there is not even a word for *nature* in biblical and early rabbinic Hebrew. If Judaism had perceived nature as an adversary and a thing apart, surely the ancient Hebrews, masters of words, would have given it a name.

Judaism was the first civilization to promulgate detailed laws prohibiting cruelty to animals, and to enforce them. Judaism introduced the idea of stewardship into a disinterested world and made its practice binding upon Jews. Judaism formulated the first (and only?) laws mandating the protection of nature during warfare. Judaism, via the rabbinic "oral law," set forth one of the earliest and certainly the most detailed set of legal instructions concerning agricultural practice and the conservation of natural resources. Judaism. through its festivals and unique lunisolar calendar, is intimately and completely bound to the earth and its cycles. And Judaism, with its magnificent contribution of the Sabbath, a time when Jews acknowledge the sovereignty of the Creator by refraining from any voluntary acts of creation or destruction, offers what may be the only theological and practical rationale and methodology for the ultimate reconciliation of the idea of stewardship with the idea of technological progress.

These statements cannot be elaborated and detailed in a brief comment; nor is it necessary. They have been well-discussed in the Jewish literature[2]— unfortunately a literature which few writers on environmental ethics have bothered to read, even in English.

In his conclusion, Schwarzschild states that "Jews were not supposed to reside where there are no synagogues, physicians, artisans, toilets, water supplies, schoolteachers, scribes, organized charities, or courts." Exactly. And is not the self-contained and limited community living in harmony with its environment the goal of a host of contemporary ecoprophets—Leopold Kohr, E. F. Schumacher, Wendell Berry, René Dubos, and many more? This confusion is symptomatic of Schwarzschild's entire piece.

Perhaps his central problem stems from the fact that his whole concept of nature is absurd. How can one write about something one admittedly does not understand? How can one who has no conception of the workings of the natural world evaluate its place in Judaism or any system? Paralleling a theme of Richard Watson's comment in his "A Note on Deep Ecology,"[3] we have a right to object to any wholly theoretical approach to environmental issues, one that does not confront, as Judaism has always advocated, the reality of people, plants, and animals living together on the solid earth.

If this were just an isolated piece of Jewish *narishkeit* about the "anti-environmental bias" of the Hebrew scriptures and of rabbinic Judaism, it would not have been worth a comment. However, since the publication of Lynn White Jr.'s well-known paper, environmental journals have used

Judaism as the traditional whipping boy (or "sacred executioner," to use Hyam Maccoby's phrase)[4] to satisfy an ill-defined malaise about the "Judeo-Christian tradition's" attitude toward the environment. Any environmental article, by Jew or Christian, that attacks the Hebrew scriptures or the rabbinic heritage of Judaism is eagerly printed. The Judeo-Christian tradition, nevertheless, is a fiction, and nowhere is this more clear than in the case of the widely divergent Jewish and Christian views of nature. We submit that there is indeed a problem, but that environmentalists of both faiths have been looking in the wrong place. Where are the articles about Christianity and the environment? About the environmental implications and impact of the entirely Christian emphasis given to miracles instead of the natural order, to original sin, to the corruption inherent in "the things in the world," to the supremacy of the afterlife, and to apocalypse?[5]

Is it not time that we all turned our attention from that mistranslated and misrepresented verse of Genesis 1:28 to the utterly un-Jewish New Testament story of Jesus and the fig tree (Matthew 21:18–20; Mark 11:13–14)? If the problem is faced squarely and an honest inquiry is made, satisfactory ways of reconciling Christianity and nature will probably be found. Only when this necessary task has been accomplished will it be reasonable for us to turn to the larger issue of harmonizing the varying effects of all religions upon the living communities of our planet. In the meantime, we can but hope that we have heard the last of the "unnatural Jew."

NOTES

From *Environmental Ethics* 7 (1985): 93–95.

1. The Talmud comments that Moses and David were not fit to be leaders of Israel until they had first been shepherds (Talmud Yerushalmi, *Kilayim* 9:3, 32a; *Bava Mezia* 85a).

2. A selected sample of this literature is as follows: "Ecology in Jewish Law and Theology," in Norman Lamm, *Faith and Doubt* (New York: Ktav, 1971); "The Earth is the Lord's," in *Judaism and Human Rights*, ed. Milton R. Konvitz (New York: Norton. 1972); Gerald J. Blidstein, "Man and Nature in the Sabbatical Year" [reprinted in this volume, 136–42]; Robert Gordis, "Judaism and the Spoliation of Nature," *Congress Bi-Weekly* (2 April 1971); Jonathan Helfand, "Ecology and the Jewish Tradition: A Postscript," *Judaism* 20 (1971): 330–35; Arthur Schaffer, "The Agricultural and Ecological Symbolism of the Four Species of *Sukkot*" [reprinted in this volume, 112–24]; David Ehrenfeld and Philip J. Bentley, "Judaism and the Practice of Stewardship" [reprinted in this volume, 125–35].

3. *Environmental Ethics* 6 (1984): 377–79.

4. Hyam Maccoby, *The Sacred Executioner* (New York: Thames and Hudson, 1982).

5. Trude Weiss-Rosmarin, *Judaism and Christianity: The Differences* (New York: Jonathan David, 1943).

17

Comments on the Unnatural Jew

Jeanne Kay

A serious study of Jewish environmental attitudes is long overdue. Works on the environmental ethics of the so-called Judeo-Christian tradition are generally critiques from a Christian perspective of a few verses in the Old Testament. Critical analyses of the environmental message of the Jewish Bible viewed from a Jewish perspective seldom appear in the environmental literature. Mainstream environmental journals even less frequently publish work on environmental ethics expressed in other significant Jewish texts like Talmud and Midrash. As a Jew, environmental researcher, and wilderness enthusiast, I therefore approached Steven S. Schwarzschild's "The Unnatural Jew" with great interest. Unfortunately, however, I found many examples of biased scholarship in his paper, and a disturbing tendency to stereotype the highly diverse Jewish people in a narrow and demeaning way. The author appears to have substituted for breadth of perspective a self-centered focus in which numerous examples which oppose his claims are trivialized or ignored.

Schwarzschild bases his case for the "unnatural Jew" on the opinions of a few poets, philosophers, and rabbis who depicted Jews as alienated from the environment. He subsequently cites several Jewish writers appreciative of nature, but he describes them as heretics. This is a neat trick arbitrarily to define Judaism as "unnatural," and then to dispatch as pagan or heretical the numerous examples in opposition. Schwarzschild's pairing of a normative Judaism unappreciative of nature with heretical minority opinions is certainly one way to interpret Jewish environmental beliefs; however, one could just as well and perhaps more profitably view the variety of Jewish environmental perspectives as different threads in the rich fabric of Jewish thought, for the Jewish love of debate, and the many different ways of life within Jewish cultures around the world contradict simplistic interpretations of Jewish beliefs.

Even modern Orthodox Judaism does not delimit its attitudes toward nature as strictly as Schwarzschild's dichotomization of Jewish environmentalism. For example, the back-to-the-land aspects of Zionism today are considered heretical among only small numbers of Jews on the extreme left and right. Radicals don't oppose the principle of Jews as farmers, but perceive the settlers as usurping Arab lands. Religious extremists are merely waiting for the Messiah to initiate the ultimate back-to-the-land movement.

Schwarzschild's references appear equally one-sided. It is difficult to imagine that his sources are sufficient to depict Judaism as an unnatural religion. Additional examples that conflict with his claims include the evocative nature writing in the Psalms, Job, and the prophets; the Talmud's conservation legislation proscribing deforestation and overgrazing: and out-of-door holidays like *Sukkot, Lag Ba-Omer*, and *Tu Bi-Shevat*.

Schwarzschild seems to assume that the environmental message of the Bible is restricted to the few overworked verses in Genesis. In fact, the Torah contains an explicit Jewish environmental ethic, repeated throughout the Jewish Bible: it is that ethical and appropriate human behavior, as defined by the 613 commandments, will ensure a favorable environment; breaking the Mosaic covenant will bring about ecological deterioration (cf. Deut. 8, 28). To be sure, this is not a Sierra Club or even a Christian notion of a sound environmental ethic, but it is nevertheless an ancient Jewish one which defines human responsibility for nature.

Even more surprising are Schwarzschild's implied components of "natural" thinking. He argues that Judaism is "unnatural" because it holds that God transcends nature and nature itself is profane, and because "natural" thinking is most appropriately grounded in the worldviews of pantheism, paganism, and Christianity, to which Judaism is opposed. However, religions or philosophies which view deities as part of nature, which consider nature to be sacred, and which fall into pantheistic, pagan, or Christian categories are not necessarily ecologically sound. One would hope for a broader-based discussion of the components of ecologically beneficent thinking. Religions are typically complex and syncretistic bodies of beliefs. Christianity, for example, may have incarnated its deity, but it also proposed that nature and this world are merely painful or tempting preliminaries to the afterlife. Christianity, not Judaism, abolished ritual blessings over nature and the out-of-door holidays. The number of pagan and pantheistic cultures which have caused major ecological damage is too great to cite, though one could begin with the ancient Greeks.

To the extent that Jews have been divorced from nature, historical rather than philosophical factors may be most critical. Schwarzschild does not mention that Jews, in many times and many lands, were forced to live in urban ghettos, were legally excluded from land ownership and even from most outdoor occupations. Western European feudal society had little place other than towns for foreigners outside the closed medieval social system. Jews did not immigrate in large numbers to this country until after the frontier was largely past, and when urban factory employment attracted most immigrants to the United States.

The author's concluding remarks about ancient Jews living close to urban services ignore the realities of agricultural life throughout most of the world until modem times. Most agricultural peoples throughout history typically lived in villages and walked to their fields. These villages were small and nature was close at hand. A few of the rabbis may have disparaged Jewish farmers. The fact remains, however, that Jews through late ancient times were primarily an agricultural or even pastoral people, living close to their environment.

I urge Schwarzschild to leave his office a little more often, to form a more accurate opinion of Jews in nature. Frankly, I don't know a "famous Jewish mountain climber," but I've known some very good ones, as well as many other Jews with environmental vocations and avocations. (I hardly need mention that most environmental professionals in Israel are Jewish.) I especially urge him to consider the implications of stereotyping the highly diverse Jewish people as "unnatural." After all, such a demeaning stereotype could have been what forced his ancestors into urban life 500 years ago.

NOTE

From *Environmental Ethics* 7 (1985): 189–91.

18

Judaism and the Sanctification of Nature

Michael Wyschogrod

The serious condition in which the natural world finds itself is of worldwide interest and concerns all human beings. The more specific question of Judaism and its view of the natural world is also of great importance, and it has had a deep impact on our thinking in the past several decades.

First, some personal remarks. I was born in Europe and return there frequently, so I am very much aware of the fact that the issue of environmental pollution is probably more acute in Europe than it is in the United States, and ecological consciousness is probably more developed there than it is in the United States. Europe is a far more densely settled part of the world, and its problems there are generally much more serious than they are in this country. The death of forests is a visible phenomenon almost all over the continent. It is really frightening to travel through France, Germany, Holland, or Eastern Europe and to observe, without really going out of your way, the enormous environmental damage that has been done.

Nuclear energy in Europe is produced close to highly populated areas. Everyone knows of the Chernobyl disaster, which was of a gigantic magnitude. I have no personal experience with the situation in the Soviet Union near the Chernobyl site, but the impact on Western Europe has been profound. The radiation levels in Switzerland, Germany, France, and other locations are intolerable; clearly the Chernobyl disaster is anything but behind us. It continues to be a significant problem, and it will be decades before we are finished paying the price. The cancer rate among children in Eastern and Western Europe is rising, and in the Soviet Union it is reaching alarming proportions, particularly in the area around Kiev. That Chernobyl is an old Jewish settlement where once there was a Chasidic dynasty is an irony worth noting.

THE UPPER AND LOWER ECOLOGY

Let me begin my presentation with two concepts which I call the *lower* and the *upper ecologies. Lower ecology* is the attitude which claims that the development of technology in our culture has had consequences which are no longer acceptable. Technology has had a profound impact on our planet. Some of its effects are still not known about or even suspected. However, the record is clear. Problems we have not known about in the past have often later turned into severe dilemmas. Let me give you just one example. I remember as a child in Berlin being taken by my mother to buy shoes. The best shoe stores had x-ray machines. The child would try on the shoe and then step into the x-ray machine while the mother and the sales person would look into it and see whether the shoes fit properly. The salesperson and the mother would chat away for two, three, four, five minutes debating the fit of the shoes. Meanwhile the child was having a grand time wiggling his toes on the screen. Everybody thought that this was the greatest invention since the wheel. Nobody suspected at that time how harmful x-rays could be, as they did not seem to have any immediate negative effect. It was thought that x-rays were no more harmful than photographs, yet we know today that the dosage of x-rays to which children were exposed in these stores was clearly dangerous. Technological innovations that we might think are harmless will through experience show themselves to be far from harmless. When effects are harmful, decent intelligent human beings want something to be done to improve the situation. And this, of course, is not always easy.

THE "LOWER ECOLOGY" AND THE
UNINTENDED CONSEQUENCES OF TECHNOLOGY

Ecological damage is often long-range. It is not always immediate. Very often this damage can be caused by many people, such as the case of automobiles. Mostly, the problem is one of balancing advantages against disadvantages. Our culture is simply not prepared to dispense with the automobile. Given that fact, we must weigh the advantages of the easy mobility that the automobile offers us against the damage that it does to the environment. This, unfortunately, cannot be solved strictly by the workings of the market. It requires state action and legislation that involves the political process, jobs, and a delicate balancing act. When jobs are involved, it is difficult to tell people that a plant in a given location must be closed and two or three thousand jobs must be given up because of ecological damage. Still the fact is these things must be done; that is one of the purposes of the political process.

This is what I call the *lower ecology*, because it involves protecting human beings against the damage of technology. This lower ecology, interestingly enough, is already clearly found in the Bible, as in the famous biblical passage, "When in you wage war against a city and you have to besiege it a long time in order to capture it, you must not destroy its trees, wielding the axe against them. You may eat of them, but you must not cut them down. Are trees of the field human to withdraw before you into the besieged city" (Deut. 20:19). The reason given by the Bible for this injunction is that man lives from the trees and it is thus not within man's rights, even in the context of war, to destroy them. This is the famous biblical commandment *bal tashchit*, which was later expanded by the rabbis to include all wasteful destruction of useful things, whether natural or man-made. Thus the purposeless destruction of objects which are potentially useful to man is made into a sin. However, what must be understood in this context is that it is the welfare of human beings that is the main concern. We must not do things that hurt human beings. Any action that will directly or indirectly hurt them is forbidden. This is the lower ecology, which is centered on human beings. It is clearly not being sufficiently cultivated, with the net result that human beings all over the world suffer needlessly.

THE "UPPER ECOLOGY" AND THE RELIGION OF NATURE

The essence of *upper ecology* is a conviction about the holiness of nature. *Upper ecology* takes the human being out of the center of nature and puts nature itself there instead. Human beings are part of nature and, therefore, their attitude toward nature must be appropriate to that which is holy.

There is also an area in which both *lower* and *upper ecology* overlap. In that sense, *upper ecology* cooperates with *lower ecology*. There is also the conviction among followers of *upper ecology* that an attitude of nonsanctity towards nature is harmful to man. But this overlap ought not to be exaggerated, because for *lower ecology*, nature per se is not sacred. What *is* sacred, if anything, is the human being. And it is only when the violation of nature hurts human beings that action is called for. As such, for *lower ecology* nature is a means towards human welfare.

For *upper ecology*, it is nature that is holy. *Upper ecology* is "nature religion," primarily a religious altitude toward nature. The difference between *lower* and *upper ecology* emerges in its most dramatic form when the interests of nature and of human beings are in conflict. In relationship to the divine, *upper ecology* usually expresses itself as polytheism, the theological view that there are many gods. These gods dwell within the forces of nature and are symbols of these forces. Greek or Hindu polytheism is animated by experiencing the powers of nature as sacred and then personifying them in the form of gods. However, this personification should not be of ultimate seriousness, because, from the point of view of polytheistic religion, it is really the natural forces themselves that are divine.

What are the dangers and opportunities in the religion of nature? The deepest spiritual advantage of natural religion is that humans are at home in the cosmos. The cosmos, a sacred setting, becomes the home of human beings, and they fit perfectly into it. They both are part of and interact with nature. Humans emerge from nature and return to it. They are in perfect harmony with it, synchronized to its natural rhythms. Of course humans are born and die, but birth and death are all part of the natural process, and in that respect humans are not at war with the environment in which they have been placed. The divinity ascribed to nature also pertains to human beings because they are essential parts of nature. This harmonious picture usually expresses itself most successfully in situations where small numbers of people live in vast natural settings. For example, the number of Native Americans who inhabited the North and South American continent before the European penetration was, from the point of view of density, relatively small. That very spatial magnitude gave human beings a sense of the vastness of the universe. Yet even under these circumstances, natural religions do not fare well with urbanization. In cities, human beings are concentrated into relatively small spaces and interact intensively with each other. Yet even under these circumstances, natural religion does not disappear overnight.

URBANIZATION AND THE DESACRALIZATION OF THE WORLD

One of the great mysteries of history was the conquest of Greek and Roman religions by Christianity. Within a couple of centuries, Christianity was able to overwhelm those other religions and conquered Europe. I am quite convinced that urbanization had a great deal to do with this. The urban civilization of Rome was ready for the end of natural religions and for the beginning of Christianity, which, in the context of the Roman world, was a form of Judaism. With the urban epoch of history begins the death of natural history. History then focuses on the actions of human beings rather than on natural cycles. History exists in Greece, it develops in Rome, but far more fundamentally it is born in Israel, because the major salvational events of Israel are historic events, specifically the exodus from Egypt. The conflict between history and nature is fundamental to the development of Judaism, and it is essential to examine the mechanisms that bring about this conflict.

As I think about the recent past, specifically about the Nazi period and Adolph Hitler, I am very impressed by how deeply his thinking was influenced by evolutionary concepts. Hitler saw himself as the representative, the spokesperson, the spiritual leader, not so much of Germany (that of course, also), but even more fundamentally, of evolution. His basic insight, if you want to call it that, was that nature has no pity. Animals destroy each other and live from the death of other animals. Carnivorous animals must kill. The stronger kills the weaker, and it is through this process that nature moves ahead. Hitler, of course, did not invent this theory. It has deep roots in Nietzsche.

For Nietzsche—for whom Christianity was just a form of Judaism, perhaps even a degenerate one—Jewish morality was a slave morality and thus anti-evolutionary. Evolutionary morality is the right of the stronger to destroy the weaker. Nature wants the weak to perish. The weak contribute to the march of evolution by perishing; and when they refuse to perish, then the weaker have triumphed over the stronger. This is the reversal of evolution, and it occurs through slave morality, which is the brainwashing of the strong by the weak in order to inhibit them from exercising their strength. The strong have the power to destroy the weak; that is what nature desires because it wants the weak out of the way. The weak invent biblical prophetic morality, which speaks about protecting the widow and the orphan, the poor, the disadvantaged, all those who cannot care for themselves. Evolution is thus stopped in its tracks, and the weak proliferate. Those whose lives are worthless are preserved, and their very presence drags down the masses of the strong who were meant to evolve to a higher state of being. That is why Nazi policy began with the murder of the handicapped, a process that was in the works well before the murder of the Jews. In fact, the techniques of murder that were experimented with and the lessons learned were put to good use in the destruction of Jews and of many others. All in the name of this form of evolutionary thinking.

THE PERILS OF EVOLUTIONARY THINKING AND MODERN NATURE RELIGION

Evolutionary thinking, I would maintain, is a form of modern nature religion, because the basic conflict between nature and history is the conflict between the moral and the natural. It is important to recognize that when we use the word "moral," we must distinguish between Judeo-Christian morality and Greek morality. In Greek thought, the theme of protection of the weak is almost absent. Let us take the *Republic* of Plato, for example, in which the protection of the weak does not find any kind of justification. In fact, Plato very clearly preaches the exposing of imperfectly shaped infants. They ought to be permitted to perish because they do not contribute to the welfare of the society. Plato sees the state as an organism. His model is biological, and in a biological entity there is, above all, a division of labor. Different parts of the body perform different functions. The state that Plato envisions is a state in which the ruling is done by the small, self-elected elite, and the rest of mankind follows the commands of the rulers. This view of the state corresponds exactly to an animal body, where the ruling is done by the brain, which is particularly suited to that task, while all the other parts of the body obey its commands. So, organismic thinking is biological thinking. And biological thinking has the potential of being at war with the ethical.

Now let us look at the other side. Is nature holy? This is the most difficult question, since it is the desacralization of nature that makes science possible. This is best exemplified in the field of medicine. It was really only in the seventeenth and eighteenth centuries that the dissection of human beings began. Prior to that the human body, the dead body, was considered too sacred to investigate. Therefore, knowledge about the organs of the human body was very limited. But it is not only the human body that is at stake here, but all of nature. In order for science to gain control of nature, the gods dwelling in nature too have to be expelled. And when the gods were expelled, nature became an object of study rather than of worship. Thus, when you no longer worship something, you can put it under the knife, or under the microscope, and obtain objective knowledge about it. You do not do that to the sacred.

Notice how, even in our own day, that which remains sacred, namely the human body, is still handled with a great deal of deference; and when the potential for conflict exists between the demands of knowledge and the demands of the holy, as long as you are dealing with the living human body, the holy generally, though not always, wins. At times when the needs of medical experimentation prevail, you can see how the experimenter's urge to know pushes the sanctity of the human body out of the way. This happens even more so with the animal body, because the animal body has less of that sanctity. Thus, we have large scale animal experimentation, with all the violations committed in that context. One is caught in a very difficult dilemma: the tension between the sanctity of nature and the human right to rule over and manipulate nature.

I think that the root of this conflict is in the doctrine of creation. It makes a tremendous difference whether the paradigm of the holy is God, and the sanctity of nature is a reflection of nature's having been created by God, or whether the paradigm of the holy is nature itself as an uncreated entity. Uncreated nature is the deepest source of the sanctity of nature. The moment the doctrine of creation emerges, nature is no longer self-sufficient, no longer eternal, no longer perpetual, no longer all-engulfing. Nature is derived from an act of creation, and this act of creation confers upon it some of the sanctity of the Creator, but it does not confer upon nature an independent sanctity. Thus, the Creator can dispose of nature and destroy it. In my opinion, that is the symbolism of the flood. The very fact that there is a Master over nature undermines its essential and independent sanctity.

THE DISCONTINUITY OF HUMAN BEINGS AND NATURE

It is through the misuse of this notion that western technology went crazy. Nature, in *this* sense, is seen merely as a tool in the hands of human beings, a tool which has no integrity of its own; and to some extent this attitude also pertains to the human being. The human being is an ambivalent and ambiguous creation because she is placed in nature by God and yet is not of nature. It is, after all, possible for God to create human beings with almost no ties to nature. God could have created a natural order and then He could have created human beings. Instead, God created a being who is very deeply rooted in nature, in some ways inseparable from it. From a purely physiological viewpoint, there is no mechanism in the human body that does not have its counterpart in animal mechanisms, from nutrition to reproduction and from respiration to a thousand other biological systems that operate throughout the human organism. The tie between the human being and nature seems to be emphasized by God, and the ultimate tie is, of course, death. The fate of human beings is the same fate of animals. A dead human being is not unlike a dead animal, as they are both absorbed into the soil and become part of the earth.

However, human beings also have dimensions and characteristics that are deeply discontinuous with nature. The very fact that the human being knows about her death, that she anticipates her death, constitutes a profound break with nature. Perhaps even more important, however, is the relationship of the human being to the moral dimension. Human beings do not follow their natural needs. An animal, when hungry and when there is food available, eats. An animal, when sexually aroused and a partner is available, copulates. But a human being has many reasons to do these things or not to do them. The human being can resist every natural force. There is no instinct to which a human being cannot say no, be it hunger, sex, or life itself. Only the human being can commit suicide. Only the human being conducts hunger strikes. Only the human being, for whatever reason, can declare celibacy superior to the married state. There is no natural drive to which the human being cannot say, has not said, and will not say no. Indeed, this is the greatest glory of the human being and his greatest danger, because people can put dignity or self-respect or whatever other idea above life and in the process bring about the end of human existence on this planet. This is something animals cannot and will not do, because the urge to live is rooted in the nature of life, rooted in the nature of the biological; to that extent, the human being can totally reject the biological.

A PARADOXICAL POSTSCRIPT:
LEARNING FROM THE RELIGION OF NATURE

I close on this profoundly ambivalent note. It is difficult to return to the religion of nature. It is difficult and dangerous, particularly for Jews, to worship nature again. At the same time the destruction of nature, which seems to follow to some extent from the desacralization of nature, has reached a stage that cannot continue. So we must try to combine these two themes. To be perfectly honest, I have long felt that the religion against which the prophets expounded so eloquently in the Hebrew Bible did not get a full hearing from them. I wonder whether the prophets gave a really fair presentation of the point of view and theology of the worshipers of Baal and Ashteret. Maybe it is because I have been involved in too much dialogue in recent years, not with the priests of Baal and Ashteret, but, some might say, with priests who are not so different from the priests from Baal and Ashteret. Perhaps it would have been better if the prophets had occasionally sat down with them and said, "Tell us how you see the world." Could there be some insights in what they taught which we need to learn? I am convinced there were; and even if we don't agree with much of what they believed, I think we would profit by better understanding their point of view.

NOTE

From *The Melton Journal* 24 (spring, 1991): 5–7.

19

Judaism and Nature: Theological and Moral Issues to Consider While Renegotiating a Jewish Relationship to the Natural World

Eilon Schwartz

Since the advent of the modern environmental movement some thirty years ago,[1] dozens of articles have been written exploring the relationship of Judaism and the environment, attempting to articulate a Jewish response to the environmental crisis.[2] Many of the articles came in the wake of the environmental movement's attack on the Judeo-Christian ethic, whose biblical injunction to "fill the earth and master it" was seen by many in the environmental movement to be the theological and ethical source for an anthropocentric and ultimately exploitative relationship to the natural world.[3]

Articles were also written to defend tradition, often by presenting Judaism's environmental credentials. Although translations of Jewish culture into terms acceptable to the larger cultural milieu have often sacrificed authentic Jewish perspectives at the altar of cultural relevance, in the case of Judaism and the environment it seemed as though no trade-off was necessary.[4] Finding "green" traditions within Jewish sources is not difficult. Such traditions are strongly anchored in normative Judaism. *Bal taschchit*, *tza'ar ba'alei chayyim*, *shnat shemittah*, *yishuv ha-aretz*, to name a few of the Jewish value concepts most often quoted by environmentally concerned Jews,[5] are all pointed to as representing authentic Jewish environmental perspectives.[6] As they are.

Still, the need to validate a Jewish environmental ethic, to show Judaism's credentials, as it were, stifled a true airing of Jewish positions.[7] Judaism's relationship with the natural world is far more ambivalent than that with which many Jewishly committed environmentalists would feel comfortable. Too few have delved into the complex and intricate relationship between Judaism and the natural world, a relationship which, while containing the "green" traditions often quoted, also contains the admonition in *Pirkei Avot* that

> One, who while walking along the way, reviewing his studies, breaks off from his study and says, "How beautiful is that tree! How beautiful is that plowed field!" Scripture regards him as if he had forfeited his soul. (*Ethics of the Fathers* 3:7)[8]

For Jews to confront the environmental crisis as part of a rich and complex Jewish tradition, it is necessary to come to terms with both sides of the tradition and to understand the interrelationship between them. Only by understanding the theological, philosophical, and moral concerns which are an integral part of the Jewish relationship with nature can Jews offer a voice that will not simply mimic already articulated perspectives, but will offer unique attitudes to help guide the task of *tikkun olam* while confronting issues too long avoided by Jewish thought.

By surveying the literature previously written on Judaism and the environment, I hope to influence the direction of future writing by pointing to places that need exploration. My not-so-hidden agenda is to reassert the *Jewish* perspective in the encounter between Judaism and the environment, with the conviction that a Jewish contribution to the growing debate on environmental ethics can only come from a response strongly rooted in all the ambivalence and ambiguities of the Jewish relationship to the natural world. Perhaps even more importantly, I believe that the reevaluation by the environmental movement of our modern cultural relationship to the natural world, which challenges some of the basic values of our modern culture, deeply confronts ingrained trends in Jewish thought, as well. To engage the points of tension, and not only the points of confluence, will facilitate a dialogue from within the tradition that can lead to a reawakening of the natural world as a central category in our Jewish understanding of what we mean by both the human and the Divine.

PAGANISM AND JUDAISM

Any serious confrontation of the Jewish relationship with the natural world must confront the Jewish relationship with paganism. The conventional wisdom of modern Jewish thought maintains that Judaism came about as a radical distancing of the Holy from immanence within the world.[9] In this account, idolatry is defined theologically as viewing God as being contained within the material world, whereas Judaism came to assert the transcendental, wholly other nature of the Holy. Paganism, both in its biblical and Hellenistic manifestations, understood God as being contained within Nature. Jewish monotheism distanced the Holy from paganism and its concept of nature.

Such a presentation of the Jewish relationship to nature by way of its polemic against pagan idolatry suggests an antagonism to nature, and the theological affinity between paganism and Nature. Indeed, the modern environmental movement is filled with writings that have picked up on such a reading, calling for a rejection of monotheistic approaches to the world, and a rebirth of paganism. Lynn White sees paganism as the alter ego to the Judeo-Christian theologically sanctioned exploitation of nature;[10] some ecofeminists have called for a renewal of pagan customs of May Day, celebrations of the moon, and witchcraft;[11] one of the more radical biological theories of our day holds that the earth is a living organism, and has named her Gaia, the name of the Greek earth goddess.[12] This reassertion of pagan theologies, customs, and language understands paganism as a worldview which sees Nature as Holy. Eastern religions are often included in the list of religions of Nature as well, with the many significant theological and cultural differences between the various historical cultures glossed over. These are juxtaposed to an archetypical monotheism which sees God as transcending nature. The operative conclusions are clear: paganism, seeing Nature as sacred, respects the natural world; monotheism, desanctifying nature, abuses it. The rebirth of paganism is a call for the assertion of the natural over the supernatural, Mother Earth over Father King, holistic Nature over the hierarchical dichotomy of Heaven and earth.

Aharon Lichtenstein, writing about Judaism's approach to nature, accepts the typology as well.[13] While not reaching the operative conclusion that Judaism abuses nature while paganism respects it, he certainly accepts the theological distinction of a monotheism that sets God apart from by contrast with the linking of paganism with present environmentalism. Lichtenstein indeed holds much of the environmental movement, which views nature as Holy, to be idolatrous. And while there might be some practical commonality in action conceivable for a time between the two in order to respond to the immediate manifestations of the environmental crisis, the theological (and what may be assumed, moral) gulf between them is no different than that between Judaism and Greco-Roman paganism.

Everett L. Gendler can be seen as representing the other end of the continuum of modern Jewish responses to the "pagan" critique by the environmental movement.[14] Gendler holds that there is a latent nature tradition within Judaism, a tradition suppressed due to the ancient polemic with paganism, exile from the land of Israel, and subsequent historical forces. Gendler sees this tradition expressing itself in the nature motifs of Jewish festivals, in female rituals surrounding the blessing of the new moon, and in the reassertion of connection to nature in the Zionist movement. Judaism has suffered due to its exile from the natural world; it is time to reassert the role of nature in our understanding of the human spirit.

Gendler is, in effect, asserting a place for an immanently religious tradition within Judaism. Both he and Lichtenstein accept the idea that a relationship with the natural world has tremendous implications for the life of the spirit: Lichtenstein holds Jewish religious life to be transcendental and apart from the natural world, while Gendler believes Jewish religious life has always had a place or a complementary model[15] of spirituality contained within the relationship of the Jew to the natural world.[16]

Lamm elaborates on the content of our continuum by presenting a range of authentic Jewish relationships to nature whose poles he defines by the Hasidic/Mitnagdim controversy.[17] Hasidut, while "utterly different" from pagan thought, nevertheless also had manifestations that affirmed the holiness of nature. Such views, most pronounced in Beshtian Hasidism but present throughout the Kabbalistic tradition, held that the spirit of the Creator is immanent in the Creation, and thus God can be approached through the natural world. While this is different from saying that God is the natural world, a pantheistic/paganistic approach, it does suggest eliminating the hierarchical differences between sacred and profane, and recognizing the theological possibility of the sacred in the profane. From here it is a short distance to antinomian beliefs and behavior, and to seeing Holiness in the most profane of actions. Nevertheless, Hasidut remained safely within the halakhic structure, perhaps partially because of realizing the dangerous antinomian tendencies inherent in such belief.

The Mitnagdic school of the Vilna Gaon, also rooted in the Kabbalist tradition, believed that Hasidut had indeed begun to cross the normative halakhic framework. The Mitnagdim re-emphasized the transcendence of God from the point of view of the human being, and separated holiness from the world, "allowing for the exploitation of nature by science and technology."[18] *Halakhah*, on this side of the pole, acts to prevent ecological abuse in a philosophical system that otherwise legitimizes it. In short, the Hasidic tradition came dangerously close to turning the world into the sacred, the Mitnagdim dangerously close to removing Divine presence from the world.

For Lamm, there is a dynamic tension between the two approaches: created in God's image, the human being is part of the natural world but also transcends it. Living with the paradox of the two approaches, without compromising either, is what it means to be human. Extrapolating from such a view, paganism and its environmental supporters err on the side of the natural in the human; modern Western culture on the side of the transcendent. Judaism has traditionally offered a plurality of approaches, each moving dangerously close to the extremes, but with safeguards to insure remaining within acceptable boundaries. Gendler, using Lamm's terminology, represents the Hasidic tradition; Lichtenstein, the Mitnagdic tradition.

Lamm never addresses the question of where Judaism's modern variations stand on his continuum, perhaps suggesting that such a creative tension continues to exist among various modern Jewish approaches. Schorsch contends that, in response to intellectual currents in the larger cultural setting, modern Judaism was pushed beyond Lamm's Mitnagdic pole:

> We must dare to reexamine our longstanding preference for history over nature. The celebration of "historical monotheism" is a legacy of nineteenth century Christian-Jewish polemics, a fierce attempt by Jewish thinkers to distance Judaism from the world of paganism. But the disclaimer has its downside by casting Judaism into an adversarial relationship with the natural world. Nature is faulted for the primitiveness and decadence of pagan religion, and the modern Jew is saddled with a reading of his tradition that is one-dimensional. Judaism has been made to dull our sensitivity to the awe inspiring power of nature. Preoccupied with the ghost of paganism, it appears indifferent and unresponsive to the supreme challen of our age: man's degradation of the environment. Our planet is under siege and we as Jews are transfixed in silence.[19]

For Schorsch, modern Jewish historians projected a distance between Judaism and the pagan world that is overstated. This modern version of a "one dimensional" Judaism is a distortion of the reality of premodern Jewish thought and life.

If Schorsh is correct that the pagan taboo has contributed significantly to the lack of a healthy Jewish relationship with nature, in which I concur, then only by coming to terms with the content of the conflict can we avoid "throwing out the baby with the bath water." In order to rethink our relationship to nature, or to re-search our traditional relationship with nature, without committing the same transgression of interpreting Judaism solely according to the cultural milieu of the day—historical monotheism then, the emerging environmental movement now—the Jewish relationship with paganism needs to be reexplored.[20] The taboo against paganism in Jewish thought is so deep, and the linkage between paganism and nature is so taken for granted, that to seek to distance ourselves from paganism has meant distancing ourselves from nature, and conversely, an attempt to reconcile Judaism with nature appears to flirt with paganism. Only by exploring the content of the antipagan Jewish polemic can we hope to understand what is truly at stake.[21]

Living in fear of paganism has not only exacted a heavy price on the Jewish relationship with nature. Feminists have argued that the cultural linking of nature with female has meant that a distancing of culture from nature is linked to a distancing of culture from its feminine components.[22] Judaism's fear of paganism, therefore, has potentially led to a distancing of Judaism from its feminine components. The dominance of male God-imagery and masculine formulations of theology over the centuries can be viewed as one outcome of the fear of paganism. Loss of humility through the loss of our ability to wonder and experience awe at the beauty and vastness of the natural world is another. And losing our sense of place, of being a part of the

world, is still another. To confront the byproducts, it is essential that the root
of the debate between pagan and Jewish culture be confronted. And that debate has much to do with how we understand morality.

TIME'S ARROWS, TIME'S CYCLES

The Jewish polemic against paganism was not only theological but primarily
moral. The theological conflict had deep moral implications. Nature worship
was seen not simply as a theological/philosophical mistake, but a worldview with deep immoral consequences. Schorsch's caution that we not
blame nature for pagan excesses notwithstanding, it seems essential to explore what the moral conflict was while we are renegotiating our relationship with the natural world.

Mircea Eliade offers a helpful distinction between the different notions of
time of historical religions and nature religions.[23] Eliade maintains that religions focusing on history have a linear view of time, those focusing on nature, a cyclical view—what Stephen Jay Gould calls time's arrows and cycles.[24] Eliade holds that Judaism was responsible for contributing a linear
sense of history to the world, that is, a progressive sense of history.[25] While
positing history as change, in fact, while creating the very possibility for history, such a perspective, when not counterbalanced with a sense of cyclic
time, can lead to history without a sense of purpose. So Eliade sees our modern period.[26] Linear history, with its beginning and end, needs to be understood in terms of cyclical history, with its transcendent and repeating truths.
Or in Jewish terms, the march forward from Egypt to Sinai to Zion must be
understood in terms of our continual return to Egypt, Sinai, and Zion in each
generation. Time has both its arrows and cycles.

While Eliade believes that the modern period lives in the moral danger
of losing sight of the purpose of history through losing a sense of time's
cycles, the moral critique works in the other direction as well. An overem-
phasis on time's cycles can lead to a history without change. Time is understood only in terms of the natural cycles of the world. Seasons come and go,
the sun rises and sets, and change is illusory. Time stands still. A sense of history demands that human beings break out of the cycle, and accept the responsibility of a history which can move forward and backward. Time's
cycle is connected with what is, time's arrows, with what can be. Focusing
on a religion of nature, one focuses on the cyclical nature of time. A religion
of history offers the moral responsibility that is the meaning of its arrows.
While Eliade holds that arrows without cycles leads to a history without
meaning, an emphasis on arrows has often been understood to mean an emphasis on human responsibility.

Schwarzschild understands the pagan-Jewish debate as exactly one of
differing views of nature coupled with different views of morality.[27] Nature

represents what is. Morality is born in the question of what ought to be. Judaism is profoundly at odds with the natural world, which functions according to certain laws to which history is then subject. Judaism sees the human being as transcending those laws of nature, with the power to impose a moral order on an otherwise amoral natural reality. Through human judgment between "good" and "evil," that which makes the human "in the image of God," moral thought can impose its order on the natural disorder, completing the process of creation.[28] Schwarzschild recognizes that the tradition is not monolithic in this regard. The "heretical, quasi-pantheistic tendency" found expression in medieval Kabbalah, Hasidut, and modern Zionism.[29] However, this view remained a tangential idea, contrary to the traditional Jewish perspective on nature.

Wyschogrod follows Schwarzschild's argument.[30] The heart of the pagan Jewish controversy is the moral question of whether what is, should be. And Wyschogrod, like Schwarzschild, sees the modern environmental movement as resurrecting the pagan notion of morality as equated with the world as it is. While there are certainly many environmentalists who understand the need for change in anthropocentric terms—the need to protect our health and the earth's resources for future generations— "deep" environmentalists subscribe to what Wyschogrod calls "the higher ecology," an environmentalism which attempts to shift our culture from an anthropocentric to a geo/biocentric world view.

Wyschogrod contends that Adolph Hitler and the Nazi movement were deeply influenced by such a perspective.[31] Borrowing heavily from Nietzsche, Hitler believed that nature teaches us the basic laws of morality: that the strong kill the weak, and through such a process nature moves forward. Wyschogrod notes that "Evolutionary morality is the right of the stronger to destroy the weaker. Nature wants the weak to perish. The weak contribute to the march of evolution by perishing; and when they refuse to perish, then the weaker have triumphed over the stronger."[32]

However, Judaism (and Christianity) interfere with the natural order by letting the weak survive.[33] A morality which changes the natural order prevents nature from taking its rightful course. Such a perspective on morality Wyschogrod also locates in Plato. In his ideal state, modeled after an organism, there is no place for protection of the weak. Imperfectly born infants are to be disposed of.

Of course, attempting to understand morality as an outgrowth of the natural order does not necessarily demand understanding morality as "survival of the fittest." Nature's lessons were interpreted in radically different ways by its Social Darwinist interpreters.[34] But, regardless of the particular interpretation of nature's morality, there is a categorical difference between a morality based on the natural order, however that "natural order" is understood, and a morality based on values whose source is outside of materialist understandings of the world. And in the confrontation between the morality of "the world as it is" and "the world as I should be," both Wyschogrod and Schwarzschild understand Judaism as the flagship of a morality that imposes itself on the natural order.

Yet, in spite of his antagonism to a "higher ecology," Wyschogrod acknowledges that the moral philosophy of Judaism, which demanded the desacralization of nature, has contributed to the destruction of nature. Returning to a religion of nature is profoundly dangerous, yet, given that, a reconsideration of the human interconnection with the natural is demanded by the ecological crisis.

Wyschogrod's articulation of the link between a religion of nature and an ethics in which what "is" is defined as what "ought" to be, finds expression in the environmental movement. Indeed, the burgeoning field of environmental ethics continue to confront the question of whether ethics are learned from the natural order. In the debate between animal protectionists and deep ecologists, one of the main points of conflict is whether the interests of the individual should take precedence over the needs of the community. For example, should a herd of deer that overpopulate an area due to the extinction of its local predators be hunted in order to protect the flora that they eat, which, as the primary producers in the energy chain, maintain the health of the ecosystem as a whole? Animal protectionists abhor the idea of hunting as the unnecessary suffering of sentient beings. Some environmentalists have supported hunting at least potentially as part of the laws of nature which maintain the health and well-being of the ecosystem. Some have tended to idealize hunting as a return to the primal state of the human being, a return to the natural world, and have criticized what is popularly called "the Bambi syndrome"—the projection of a human code of morality onto the workings of the natural world.[35] Aldo Leopold, a forerunner of biocentric environmental ethicists, taught the need to learn to "think like a mountain," to think like nature.[36]

The implications for all of this in terms of human existence has been one of the most sensitive subjects of environmental ethics. Parts of the "deep" ecology movement, notably the Earth First! movement, have expressed what Schwarzschild and Wyschogrod's interpretation would suggest: "Some Earth First!ers, who are supposedly motivated by deep ecological ideals, proposed Draconian birth control measures, spoke approvingly of AIDS as a self-protective reaction of Gaia against an overpopulating humanity, used Social Darwinist metaphors, and displayed apparent racist attitudes. Earth First! cofounder Dave Foreman even stated that humans 'are a cancer on nature.'"[37]

The ideas expressed by a particular part of a movement should in no way be chosen to reflect the thoughts of the movement as a whole. Nevertheless, the predictive ability of Schwarzschild and Wyschogrod's thesis forces us to recognize the danger inherent in philosophies currently prevalent in the environmental movement, which foreground moral questions that have been part of the internal environmental debate for over a decade.[38]

The response to such a morality of nature need not be a denial of the place of the natural within Jewish worldviews. Ehrenfeld and Bentley,[39] for example, while understanding Judaism as having a strong anthropocentric component, maintain that "the great chain of being"[40] does not place man at the pinnacle, but rather God. The human place in the God-given scheme of things is caring for God's creation, the role of steward. It is the secularization of the world, the removal of God from the hierarchy and placing the human being at its pinnacle, which results in what Ehrenfeld calls "the arrogance of humanism."[41] The stewardship argument is heard often in the environmental ethic debate, changing the perspective from anthropocentric to theocentric.[42] It is but one attempt to deal with the tension between a hierarchical model of creation and an egalitarian model. The former sees the human being as primarily a spiritual being standing apart from the natural world, while the latter sees the human being as a material being existing as part of her. Reducing our understanding of human purpose to a material, deterministic view of the world has been shown to be a problematic option. But the environmental movement has suggested that a view of human purpose which ignores the material base of human existence is equally problematic. Boyarin claims that such a spiritual/material dichotomy was never part of normative Rabbinic Jewish thought.[43] The Jewish emphasis on the body as a category of spiritual existence suggests the need for a far more complex understanding of the interrelationship of the material and spiritual. Any reassessment of the Jewish relation to nature demands a reevaluation of the spiritual and the material, including the possibility of foregoing such a dichotomy altogether.[44] In answering Disraeli's question whether the human being is ape or angel, emphasizing our affinity to the world of the ape need not by definition distance us from the spiritual. It might even bring us closer.

The environmental crisis offers both a challenge and an opportunity to modern Judaism. All cultures will be judged in future generations by the depth of their response. A Judaism that refuses to respond through its unique language to modernity's spiritual bankrupt relationship to God's world will be judged for its silence. This is also an opportunity, because far too often Judaism has been forced to speak within the narrow confines offered. The environmental crisis challenges modern culture, and offers the opportunity for other voices, long delegitimized, to reassert themselves within the larger culture. Speaking from within the tradition, and confronting the manifold challenges that a reappraisal of Judaism and nature demands, means a renewal of our relationship with our world. It means evaluating how we relate to the world around us, but no less importantly, how that world around us touches our lives. The environmental crisis is not only a crisis of technology, nor a crisis of human values, but most assuredly also a crisis of the human spirit. How we respond to the challenge and opportunity that the environmental crisis presents has implications not only for how we deal with our world, but also for how we deal with ourselves, our fellow human beings, and our God. This is the context in which a Jewish articulation of an environmental ethic must be considered.

NOTES

From *Judaism: A Quarterly Journal* 44 (1995): 437–47.

1. Traditionally understood as 1960, the year of the initial publication of Rachel Carson's *The Silent Spring* in *The New Yorker*.

2. *Judaism and Ecology 1970–1986: A Sourcebook of Readings*, ed. Marc Swetlitz (Wyncote, Pa.: Shomrei Adamah, 1990).

3. Lynn White Jr., "The Historical Roots of our Ecologic Crisis" (*Science* 155 [March 10, 1967]: 1203–1207) remains the classic presentation of this position. See Jeremy Cohen, "On Classical Judaism and Environmental Crisis" [reprinted for this volume, 71–79] for a review of the early environmental movement's polemic against the Judeo-Christian ethic.

4. Scholem's resurrection of the field of Kabbalah as a legitimate part of Jewish tradition is not simply a rediscovery of historically prominent trends within Judaism, but marks a change in the larger culture's mood, as well as a change in the relationship between Judaism and the larger culture.

5. On the justification for extrapolating universal values from particular discussions in Rabbinic thought, see Max Kadushin, *The Rabbinic Mind* (3rd ed., New York: Bloch, 1972), 1–58.

6. On *bal tashchit*, see David Ehrenfeld and Philip J. Bentley, "Judaism and the Practice of Stewardship" [reprinted in this volume, 125–35]; Eric Freudenstein, "Ecology and the Jewish Tradition," *Judaism* 19 (1970): 406–14; Robert Gordis, "Judaism and the Spoliation of Nature," *Congress Bi-Weekly* (April 2, 1971); Jonathan Z. Helfand, "Ecology and the Jewish Tradition: A Postscript," *Judaism* 20 (1971): 330–35; Norman Lamm, "Ecology and Jewish Law," in *Faith and Doubt* (New York: Ktav, 1971). On *tza'ar ba'alei chayyim*, see Ehrenfeld and Bentley; Gordis. On *yishuv ha-aretz*, see Helfand. On *shnat shemittah*, see Gerald J. Blidstein, "Man and Nature in the Sabbatical Year" [reprinted in this volume, 136–42]; Ehrenfeld and Bentley; *The Sabbatical Year: Holiness or Social Welfare?* [Hebrew] (Jerusalem: The Hartman Institute for Jewish Studies, n.d.).

7. A similar argument is made by Bradley Shavit Artson, "Our Covenant with Stones: A Jewish Ecology of Earth," [reprinted in this volume, 159–71].

8. See Jeremy Benstein, "'One, Walking and Studying . . .': Nature vs. Torah" [reprinted in this volume, 206–29].

9. Yehezkiel Kaufmann, *The Religion of Israel* (Chicago: University of Chicago Press, 1960), 1–148.

10. White, "The Historical Roots," 1205.

11. Starhawk, "Power, Authority, and Mystery: Ecofeminism and Earth-based Spirituality," in *Reweaving the World: The Emergence of Ecofeminism*, ed. Irene Diamond and Gloria Feman Orenstein (San Francisco: Sierra Club Books, 1990).

12. James Lovelock, *The Ages of Gaia: A Biography of Our Living Earth* (New York: Bantam Books, 1990).

13. Aharon Lichtenstein, "Man and Nature: Social Aspects," in *Judaism in Our Modern Society* [Hebrew] (Jerusalem: Israeli Ministry of Education, The Branch for Religious Culture, n.d.).

14. Everett L. Gendler, "On the Judaism of Nature," in *The New Jews*, ed. James A. Sleeper and Alan T. Mintz (New York: Random House, 1971). See also "The

Earth's Covenant" (*The Reconstructionist* [November–December 1989]) for a re-statement of his views.

15. The idea of complementary models, mutually exclusive models which describe parts of the same reality, was originally presented by Niels Bohr. For a discussion of Bohr's theory and its implications for religious thought, see Ian Barbour, *Myths, Models and Paradigms: A Comparative Study in Science and Religion* (San Francisco: Harper & Row, 1974), 71–92.

16. Michael Rosenak, "On Ways and Visions: The Theological and Educational Thought of Irving Greenberg," *Melton Journal* (Spring, 1992). The environmental movement is, among other agendas, a call for the reassertion of the Rosenzweigian category of creation in theological discussion. Such a model is helpful in understanding some of the subtle ways environmentalism is in tension with traditional Jewish categories. I believe that the environmental crisis offers an opportunity for a re-asserting of Creation theologies, while having no effect on the larger culture's openness to theologies of Revelation. Arthur Green's recently published elegant presentation of his own theology is an excellent example of such a tendency. I hold it to be largely a theology of creation, strongly influenced by environmental themes. Arthur Green, *Seek My Face, Speak My Name: A Contemporary Jewish Theology* (Northvale, N.J.: Jason Aronson, 1992).

17. Lamm, "Ecology and Jewish Law," 173–77.

18. Lamm, "Ecology and Jewish Law," 177.

19. Ismar Schorsch, "Tending to our Cosmic Oasis, *Melton Journal* (Spring, 1991).

20. See Carolyn Merchant, "Epilogue: The Global Ecological Revolution," in her *Ecological Revolutions* (Chapel Hill, N.C.: University of North Carolina Press, 1989).

21. See Levenson's challenge to Yehezkiel Kaufmann's antimythical portrayal of ancient Israel, in his "Yehezkiel Kaufmann and Mythology," *Conservative Judaism* 36 (1982).

22. For the classic anthropological presentation, see Sherry B. Orner, "Is Female to Male as Nature is to Culture?" in *Woman, Culture, and Society* (Palo Alto, Calif.: Stanford University Press, 1974). For a variety of perspectives in the environmental movement, see *Reweaving the World* (note 10, above). Also, Carolyn Merchant, *The Death of Nature* (San Francisco: Harper & Row, 1980).

23. Mircea Eliade, *Cosmos and History: The Myth of Eternal Return* (New York: Harper & Row, 1959).

24. Stephen Jay Gould, *Time's Arrow, Time's Cycle: Myth and Metaphor in the Discovery of Geological Time* (Baltimore: Penguin, 1988).

25. Eliade, 104.

26. Eliade, 151.

27. Steven S. Schwarzschild, "The Unnatural Jew" [reprinted in this volume, 265–82].

28. In Midrash Tanhuma, *Parshat Tizroah*, there is, for example, the exchange between the Roman General Turnusrufus and Rabbi Akiva. When asked whether God's creation or human creation is superior, Akiva anticipates the challenge to the Jewish practice of circumcision and argues for the superiority of human actions, in that they complete the unfinished work of creation. Thus even the human body, perfect in Greek-Roman aesthetic perception, is born imperfect, so that the Jew through *mitzvot* can participate in acts of creation.

29. No one articulated the pagan sympathies of some Zionist thought better than Saul Tschernichovsky. See Tschernichovsky, "Before a Statue of Apollo," in *Saul*

Tschernichovsky (Ithaca, N.Y.: Cornell University Press, 1968), 97–98; see also "Proto-Judaism," 36–41, and "Fusion of Judaism and Hellenism," 41–52, in the same volume.

30. Michael Wyschogrod, "Judaism and the Sanctification of Nature" [reprinted in this volume, 289–96].

31. For an elaboration of the connection between Nazism and nature, see Robert A. Pois, *National Socialism and the Religion of Nature* (London: Croon Helm, 1986). Pois sees a direct connection between Nazi ideology's pagan beliefs and Nazi Germany's policies.

32. Wyschogrod [reprinted in this volume, 293].

33. Wyschogrod and Schwarzschild differ in their evaluation of Christianity's position on morality and nature. Wyschogrod sees Christianity as a partner in the Jewish polemic against a nature morality. Schwarzschild believes that Christianity is to be found on the pagan end of the moral divide.

34. Antonello LaVerta, "Images of Darwin: A Historiographic Overview," in *The Darwinian Heritage*, ed. David Kohn (Princeton: Princeton University Press, 1985), 958–62. Robert M. Young, "Darwinism Is Social," in the same volume.

35. The "Bambi syndrome" is named for the Disney movie *Bambi*, in which the natural world is pictured as an idyllic Eden save for the encroachment of human beings. It refers to the human misconception of nature as peaceful and nonviolent as a result of viewing nature as *Bambi* portrays her, and thus the misplaced repulsion of many people to hunting. See Matt Cartmill, *A View to a Death in the Morning: Hunting and Nature through History* (Cambridge, Mass.: Harvard University Press, 1993).

36. Aldo Leopold, *A Sand County Almanac* (New York: Oxford University Press, 1949), 129.

37. Michael E. Zimmerman explores the link between Heidegger, his Nazi sympathies, and the deep ecology movement. Heidegger has been portrayed as a forerunner of deep ecology. Zimmerman, by acknowledging the philosophical link between Heidegger and National Socialism, confronts the need to dissociate deep ecology from those philosophical assumptions of Heidegger's thought which lead to sympathy for Nazism. See Zimmerman, "Rethinking the Heidegger-Deep Ecology Relationship," *Environmental Ethics* 13 (1993): 205.

38. The debate between social ecology and deep ecology essentially centers on this moral question. For the social ecology position, see Murray Bookchin, "Why This Book Was Written," in *Remaking Society: Pathways to a Green Future* (Boston: South End Press, 1990).

39. David Ehrenfeld and Philip J. Bentley, "Judaism and the Practice of Stewardship" [reprinted in this volume, 125–35].

40. Arthur O. Lovejoy, *The Great Chain of Being* (Cambridge, Mass.: Harvard University Press, 1964).

41. David Ehrenfeld, *The Arrogance of Humanism* (New York: Oxford University Press, 1981).

42. Wendell Berry, "The Gift of Good Land," in his collection of essays, *The Gift of Good Land* (San Francisco: North Point Press, 1981), 267–81. Berry's poetic piece, defending the Judeo-Christian land ethic from White's frontal attack, is a classic of environmental theology.

43. Daniel Boyarin, *Carnal Israel: Reading Sex in Talmudic Culture* (Berkeley: University of California Press, 1993).

44. Mary Midgely, *Beast and Man: The Roots of Human Nature* (Ithaca, N.Y.: Cornell University Press, 1978).

20

Nature's Healing Power, the Holocaust, and the Environmental Crisis

Eric Katz

Two recent articles have raised fundamental questions about the relationship of Jewish thought to the world of Nature. In "Nature vs. Torah" by Jeremy Benstein, and "Judaism and Nature" by Eilon Schwartz, the authors go well beyond the usual tactic of showing that Jewish law and tradition support environmentalist views.[1] Rather than merely "presenting Judaism's environmental credentials,"[2] or searching traditional sources for passages that support environmental positions,[3] each writer grapples with difficult texts and problematic traditions in the Jewish relationship with Nature. Is Judaism a belief system that is fundamentally transcendent, placing supreme value on a spiritual world totally separate from the material realm of Nature? Or is the natural world, as part of divine creation, sacred? Is the study of Torah so important that a study of the natural world must be avoided? Can we develop an appropriate response to the environmental crisis without returning to a form of paganism? Can we discover an authentic *Jewish* response to the natural environment? As Benstein notes, there is no *one* Jewish tradition concerning Nature, environmentalist or otherwise: "Part of the richness of Judaism . . . is the ongoing dialogue between the frequently very disparate voices of that tradition."[4]

As a secular environmental philosopher who has had some experience with Jewish texts concerning environmental policy,[5] I request permission to enter into this debate. I begin from an unusual and perhaps idiosyncratic starting point. For almost twenty years I have worked in the realm of academic philosophy on questions concerning the moral status of the nonhuman natural world, questions that can be applied to the ethical foundations of environmental policy. More recently, I have become interested in the philosophy of the Holocaust. Does my work as an environmental philosopher have any relevance to an understanding of the evil of human genocide? Can the study of genocide teach us anything about the human-induced destruction of the natural world, what is sometimes called the process of "ecocide"? Schwartz, for example, discusses the dangers of paganism by tying it to Nazi ideology.[6] I believe that there are connections between the massive destruction of the earth's biosphere and the planned extermination of European Jewry. In my view, genocide and ecocide may be linked together by an analysis of the concept of domination. A comparative study of these two evils may point us in the direction of developing a harmonious relationship with both the natural world and our fellow human beings.

This essay is also the result of a visit to several Holocaust sites in Poland and the Czech Republic in October 1995. It is both more and less than a philosophical argument. I could not have developed these ideas through the philosophical method of argument and analysis. The lived experience of these places not only colors my thoughts but to some extent informs them. The essay is my attempt to come to terms with the physical experience of these places, and to place these experiences into the context of philosophical ideas about the meaning of the environmental crisis, the practice of human domination, and the significance of Jewish life in the modern world. It is my hope that these reflections will contribute to the development of a Jewish philosophy of nature appropriate to the environmental crisis which surrounds us.

PLACES

The trees are like a forest. Although I can hear the sounds of traffic on Okopowa Street on the other side of the wall, inside the Jewish Cemetery of Warsaw all is quiet. Light rain and fog, mist and shadows, the grayness of this day, prevent my eyes from seeing deep into the cemetery. There are trees and underbrush, lush and green, growing up and over the scattered and crooked gravestones. One main walkway and a few paths have been cleared, so that tourists can view several hundred of the tombstones. Another path leads to a clearing not of trees, but tombstones. This is the mass grave of the Jews who died in the Warsaw Ghetto before the deportations to Treblinka began in July 1942. The mass grave appears as a meadow under a canopy of tree branches. The area is ringed by gravestones, but the center of the clearing is covered with grass. Dozens of *yahrzeit* candles flicker, remaining lit despite the dampness and the light rain. The beauty of this mass grave surprises and shocks me. Here is the reification of irony. This cemetery, a monument to the destructive hatred of the Nazi Holocaust, is extraordinarily beautiful. Filled with a vibrant, unchecked growth of trees and other vegetation, the cemetery demonstrates the power of Nature to reassert itself in the midst of human destruction and human evil.

The next day I travel to Lublin, near the Ukrainian border—a two-hour drive from Warsaw, through endless flat farmland where Polish farmers still use horses to plow the fields. It is harvest season, and the car slows occasionally to pass a truck filled with sugar beets. Our destination is Majdanek, the death camp lying three kilometers from the center of Lublin. Majdanek fills a treeless meadow stretching as far as the eye can see. Standing at the entrance gate one can see in the distance, a mile off, the chimney of the crematorium.

Unlike Treblinka or Auschwitz-Birkenau, the camp at Majdenek was built near a major urban center that would supply its victims. It was not hidden in the countryside. It is easy to imagine the smoke from the crematorium drifting into the heart of downtown Lublin. Majdenek was first established as a slave labor camp in 1940, but its gas chambers began operating in November 1942. In one day alone, November 3, 1943, 18,000 prisoners were killed by shooting, the bodies piled high in open ditches near the crematorium. Over 800,000 shoes were found at Majdenek when it was liberated in July 1944 by the advancing Russian army. This was the first of the camps to be liberated, the first to be seen by the Allied forces and the Western media. Unlike the camps further west, Majdenek was not destroyed by the retreating German forces. Although many of the wooden barracks have deteriorated through natural decay, the camp as a whole remains relatively intact today as it did in 1944.[7]

I stand in the small open courtyard a few dozen yards beyond the entrance gate. On this spot the selections of arriving prisoners were made—who would live and work in the camp, who would be killed immediately. To my right is the gas chamber. On my left is a row of barracks, used as storerooms and work areas when the camp was in operation. These unheated and dimly lit barracks now house museum exhibits. Beyond the first row of barracks is the main camp, now divided into several sections. Each section consists of two rows of barracks facing a wide open parade ground. I enter the gate and walk through the parade ground and on to the road leading to the crematorium and the site of the November 1943 mass shooting. The camp is virtually empty of visitors. As in Warsaw the day before, there is a light rain and mist, and the autumn air is cold, a harbinger of winter.

The Majdenek camp is too beautiful—the green grass of the parade ground suggests a college campus, not a site of slave labor and mass executions. Can we stand here in this lush grassy meadow and imagine the mud, the dirt, the smell—the unrelenting gray horror of the thousands of prisoners in their ill-fitting striped suits at roll calls? Can we imagine the perpetually gray sky, filled with smoke from the crematorium just down the road? Perhaps it would be better to see the camp in the middle of winter when one is not overwhelmed by the color of the grass.

Throughout my pilgrimage to these Holocaust sites, I continually encounter odd juxtapositions—museums of horror amidst great natural beauty, signs of hope and optimism amidst remnants of death and evil. In

Theresienstadt, I walk along the road to the crematorium at the outskirts
of town. The road is beautiful, a country lane overgrown with trees. Since
it is the end of the tourist season, my party is alone, until we come around
a bend in the road and discover a throng of Israeli high school children,
singing and carrying large Israeli flags. They are at once filled with joy and
awe. They stop at a burial site, remain quiet for a moment, then begin
snapping pictures with their cameras. Everyone is photographed in front
of the monument. They march on down the road. Here the irony brings
me to tears. Whatever horrors the Holocaust inflicted on the Jewish people, there remain survivors, and many more generations of Jews. They
come here to remember and to exult in their people's survival. They come
here to take home snapshots of the ruins of the Nazi death machine.

  I came to Eastern Europe to experience directly the places of the Nazi
evil. Like the Israeli schoolchildren, I make this journey, in part, to assert
my joy in being a survivor, however indirectly, of the plan to make Europe
judenrein. But I also come to try to understand the scope of the evil perpetrated on the Jewish people. I want to see and touch and walk on the
ground of the camps, as if their physical presence alone will convince me
of the horror of history. But the sites are too beautiful—Nature prevents
me from seeing, understanding, and feeling the true dimensions of the
traces of the evil confronting me.

DOMINATION

Why think about the environmental crisis and the Holocaust in each other's
terms? Is there a relationship between ideas of the natural world and the concepts of domination and genocide? The Nazis thought so. As Robert-Jan Van
Pelt recounts in his historical investigation of the development of Auschwitz,
the reconstruction and development of Polish farmland under scientific principles of management was one of the major goals of German settlement in the
conquered lands east of Germany. Van Pelt describes a trip through Poland in
1940 undertaken by Heinrich Himmler, the Reichskommissar for the resettlement of the German people. Himmler and his friend Henns Johst stand in a
Polish field, holding the soil in their hands, and dream of the great agricultural
and architectural projects to come: the re-creation of German farms and villages, the replanting of trees, shrubs, and hedgerows to protect the crops, and
even the alteration of the climate by increasing dew and the formation of
clouds.[8] As part of this plan, of course, there would have to be an "ethnic
cleansing" of the region—the Poles, both Gentile and Jewish, would have to
be moved elsewhere or otherwise eliminated so that a German agricultural
utopia could be developed. Thus we see that the control of nature—the management of agriculture so as to affect even the climate—was part of the Nazi
plan. The domination of nature and humanity are clearly linked.

The control or domination of nature is also, to a certain extent, the central theme underlying the essays by Benstein and Schwartz. Both essays investigate the Jewish perspective of the proper relationship between humanity and nature. Schwartz's argument focuses on the moral significance of Judaism's rejection of paganism—the desacralization of natural processes. As a moral philosophy, Judaism attempts to place an ethical order on an amoral natural reality. To be human, to be a Jew, means to transcend natural laws in one's actions, to improve and repair the world—indeed, to complete the process of creation.[9] Similarly, Benstein's analysis of the conflict between the study of Torah and the study of nature leads him to conclude that the primary flaw in this context is the radical rupture between Nature and Torah. True wisdom is based on a synthesis, the understanding that the study of nature is a continuation of the study of Torah.[10] Benstein thus emphasizes the argument by Rabbi Yosef Hayyim Caro that an appreciation of Nature should not be rejected, but that the study of Torah is a more trustworthy and clear means of reaching God than the study of Nature alone. Our knowledge of Nature, in brief, must be organized and modeled by our knowledge of spiritual law.[11]

Both Benstein and Schwartz thus reveal the extent to which Jewish thought seeks to impose human ideas of truth and goodness on our understanding of the natural world. The imposition of a moral order on the material world of nature is required by the belief in Jewish law—the spiritual imperative for humans to act towards the natural world as God has commanded us through Torah. Although both Benstein and Schwartz leave open the specifics of the human-nature relationship, they clearly establish the framework for any possible synthesis. Human action regarding nature will be guided by the transcendent spiritual principles of Jewish law. We will respond to Nature according to the laws of God.

Modern Judaism thus finds itself squarely in the Western tradition of the domination of nature. As I have argued elsewhere, the primary goal of the Enlightenment project of the scientific understanding of the natural world is to control, manipulate, and modify natural processes for the increased satisfaction of human interests.[12] Humans want to live in a world that is comfortable—or at least, a world that is not hostile to human happiness and survival. This purpose is easy to understand when we view technological and industrial projects that use nature as a resource for economic development—but the irony is that the same purpose, human control, motivates much of environmentalist policy and practice.

Consider briefly those popular examples of an enlightened environmental policy: pollution control and abatement, the clean-up of hazardous waste sites, habitat and species preservation, saving the rainforest, and the reduction of greenhouse gases. All of the policies are based on the beneficial consequences that will result for human beings and human society. Although natural entities, such as endangered species and individual animals and plants, will also be helped by environmentalist practices, we, the human community, are the chief beneficiary of our policies. Indeed, we generally only preserve those natural habitats and species that provide us with some direct good—whether it be economic, aesthetic, or spiritual.

What ties together environmental policies such as these is their thorough-going anthropocentrism—human interests, satisfaction, goods, and happiness are the central goals of public policy and human action. This anthropocentrism is, of course, too surprising. Humanity is in the business of creating and maximizing the human good.

Anthropocentrism as a worldview quite easily leads to the practices of domination, even when such domination is not articulated. In the formation of environmental policy, nature is seen as a nonhuman "other" to be controlled, manipulated, modified, or destroyed in the pursuit of human good. As a nonhuman other, nature can be understood as merely a resource for the development of human interests; as a nonhuman other, nature has no valid interests or good of its own. Even the practice of ecological restoration, in which degraded ecosystems are restored to a semblance of their original states, is permeated with this anthropocentric ideology. Natural ecosystems that have been harmed by human activity are restored to a state that is more pleasing to the current human population. A marsh that had been landfilled is reflooded to restore wetland acreage; strip-mined hills are replanted to create flowering meadows; acres of farmland are subjected to a controlled burn and a replanting with wildflowers and shrubs to recreate the oak savanna of pre-European America. We humans thus achieve two simultaneous goals: we relieve our guilt for the earlier destruction of natural systems, and we demonstrate our power—the power of science and technology—over the natural world.[13]

But the domination of nonhuman nature is not the only result of an anthropocentric worldview—the ideology of anthropocentric domination also extends to the oppression of other human beings, conceived as a philosophical "other," as nonhuman or as subhuman. As C. S. Lewis wrote fifty years ago in *The Abolition of Man*, "what we call man's power over nature turns out to be a power exercised by some men over other men with nature as its instrument." The reason that this exercise of power is justifiable is that the subordinate people are not considered human beings: "they are not men at all; they are artefacts."[14] Anthropocentrism does not convert into a thoroughgoing humanism, wherein all humans are treated as equally worthwhile. Historically, the idea of human slavery has been justified from the time of the ancient Greeks onward by designating the slave class as less than human. In this century, the evaluation of other people as subhuman finds its clearest expression in the Nazi propaganda concerning the Jews, but we also find its echoes in the ethnic civil war in the former Yugoslavia. From the starting point of anthropocentrism, domination and oppression are easily justified. The oppressed class—be it a specific race or religious group, or even animals or natural entities—is simply denied admittance to the elite center of value-laden beings.[15] From within anthropocentrism, only humans have value and only human interests and goods need to be pursued. But who or what counts as a human is a question that cannot be answered from within anthropocentrism—and the answer to this question will determine the extent of the practice of domination.

Thus the ideas of anthropocentrism and domination tie together a study of the Holocaust, the current environmental crisis, and the Jewish conception of the proper relationship to Nature. Schwartz reminds us that the danger in Judaism's desacralization of Nature is that it may lead to the destruction of Nature.[16] Genocide and ecocide are similar in that we conceive of our victims as less than human, as outside the primary circle of value.

HEALING

The resurgence of trees in the Warsaw cemetery and the lush green grass of the meadow at Majdanek serve as a catalyst for rethinking the relationships among nature, humanity, and the practice of domination. In these places, one can only describe the processes of nature as a kind of healing, a soothing of the wounds of evil of the Holocaust. Does Nature make everything better? Can we say that dominated and oppressed entities are saved—redeemed—by the ordinary processes of the natural world? Does nature have this power? And if it does, what are are the implications for the way in which humanity acts in the natural world?

First, we should note that Nature acts upon human beings and the products of human culture in powerful ways. So-called natural disasters, such as earthquakes and floods, are the prime examples of events in which natural forces impact on humanity. But ordinary weather, climate, and even the rotation of the earth are also activities of Nature—natural processes—that affect human life. If we broaden the range of our discourse, we can call this type of activity Nature's imperialism over humanity, for it has a parallel structure to the basic kind of human control over other humans, as well as to the human domination over Nature. Imperialism is a form of domination, in which one entity uses, takes advantage of, controls, exerts force over another. If we consider Nature as both a possible subject and object of imperialism, then we can think of Nature as exerting its power—attempting to dominate—humanity, just as we can think of humanity attempting to dominate Nature.[17]

But my experiences in the Warsaw cemetery and at Majdanek suggest mination in these places is benign; it is the healing of human atrocites, not the oppression of an imperialist. Nature provides the balm to restore the health and goodness of a world wounded by human evil, in this case the oppression and genocide of Eastern European Jewry. Is this an appropriate way to interpret the experiences of these places?

Probably not. Consider the reverse process, the human attempt to heal nature, as in the process of ecological restoration that I mentioned above. We often tend to clean up natural areas polluted or damaged by human activity, such as the Alaskan coast harmed by the Exxon *Valdez* oil spill. But we also attempt to improve natural areas dramatically altered by natural events such as a forest damaged by a massive brush fire, or a beach suffering severe natural erosion. In most of these kinds of cases, human science is capable of making a significant change in the appearance and processes of the natural area. Forests can be replanted; oil is removed from the surface of bays and estuaries; sand and dune vegetation replenish a beach. But are these activities the healing of nature? Has human activity—science and technology—restored Nature to a healthy state?

No: When humans modify a natural area they create an artifact, a product and human design.[18] This restored natural area may resemble a wild and unmodified natural system, but it is, in actuality, a product of human thought, the result of human desires and interests. All humanly created artifacts are manifestations of human interests—from computer screens to rice pudding. An ecosystem restored by human activity may appear to be in a different category—it may appear to be an autonomous living system uncontrolled by human thought—but it nonetheless exhibits characteristics of human design and intentionality: it is created to meet human interests, to satisfy human desires, and to maximize human good.

Consider again my example of beach restoration. The eroded beach is replenished—with sand pumped from the ocean floor several miles offshore—because the human community does not want to maintain the natural status of the beach. The eroded beach threatens oceanfront homes and recreational beaches. Humanity prefers to restore the human benefits of a fully protected beach. The restored beach will resemble the original, but it will be the product of human technology, a humanly designed artifact for the promotion of human interests.

After human restoration and modification, what emerges is a Nature with a different character than the original. This is an ontological difference, a difference in the fundamental qualities of the restored area. A beach that is replenished by human technology is different from a beach created by natural forces such as wind and tides. A savanna replanted from wildflower seeds and weeds collected by human hands is different from grassland that develops on its own. The source of these new areas is different—man-made, technological, artificial. The restored Nature is not really Nature at all.

A Nature healed by human action is thus not Nature. As an artifact, it is designed to meet human purposes and needs—perhaps even the need for areas that look like a pristine, untouched Nature. In using our scientific and technological knowledge to restore natural areas, we actually practice another form of domination. We use our power to mold the natural world into a shape that is more amenable to our desires. We oppress the natural processes that function independently of human power, we prevent the autonomous development of the natural world. To believe that we heal or restore the natural world by the exercise of our technological power is, at best, a self-deception, and at worst a rationalization for the continued degradation of Nature—for if we can heal the damage we inflict we will face no limits to our activities.

This conclusion has serious implications for the idea that Nature can repair human destruction, that Nature can somehow heal the evil that humans perpetuate on the earth. Just as a restored human landscape has a different causal history than the original natural system, the reemergence of Nature in a place of human genocide and destruction is based on a series of human events that cannot be erased. The natural vegetation that covers the mass grave in the Warsaw cemetery is not the same as the vegetation that would have grown there if the mass grave had never been dug. The grass and trees in the cemetery have a different cause, a different history, which is inextricably linked to the history of the Holocaust. The grassy field in the Majdanek parade ground does not cover and heal the mud and desolation of the death camp—it rather grows from the dirt and ashes of the site's victims. For anyone who has an understanding of the Holocaust, of the innumerable evils heaped upon an oppressed people by the Nazi regime, the richness of Nature cannot obliterate nor heal the horror.

MEANINGS

When we look at the processes of Nature at Holocaust sites, what we see is another example of Nature's imperialism over humanity—the mirror image of the human destruction of the natural environment. Nature here acts—without an intention or design—to erase the remnants of human evil. To speak in metaphor, Nature imposes its vision of the world on its human interpreters. But Nature's vision is not our vision, and in this case it does not express the meaning of the places we experience. Although the beauty of the trees in the cemetery cannot be denied, the meaning and value of the cemetery lies not in the trees but in the historical significance of the Nazi plan to kill the Jews of Eastern Europe.

Nature's reemergence at these Holocaust sites is a form of domination: the domination of meaning. Nature slowly exerts its power over the free development of human ideas, human history, and human memory. Now it may seem strange to think of the healing power of Nature—the healing power of anything—as a form of domination. But in *The Reawakening* Primo Levi describes his liberation from Auschwitz in terms that suggest this relationship. He recounts the series of baths that he and the other prisoners were given by the Allies: "It was easy to perceive behind the concrete and literal aspect a great symbolic shadow, the unconscious desire of the new authorities, who absorbed us in turn within their own sphere, to strip us of the vestiges of our former life, to make of us new men consistent with their own models, to impose their brand upon us."[19]

But Levi also compares these baths of liberation with the "devilish-sacral" or "black-mass" bath given by the Nazis as he entered the universe of the concentration camps. Although there are clearly differences between the baths of the liberators and the baths of the Nazis, for Levi at least, all of the baths served as symbols of domination—the molding of human beings into creatures appropriate to their current situations. The cleansing of liberation is thus comparable to the oppression of imprisonment, for both actions deny the autonomy of the free human subject. Healing thus can be an expression of domination, if it modifies or destroys the meaning and the freedom of the original entity.[20]

To understand the multiplicity of the forms of domination, however, is the first step toward developing a comprehensive ethic for evaluating human activity in relationship to both the natural environment and the human community. We must resist the practice of domination in all of its forms. We must act so as to preserve the free and autonomous development of human individuals, communities, and natural systems. We must understand the moral limits of our power to control Nature and our fellow human beings.

Yitzchak Rabin was assassinated shortly after my return from Poland. My thoughts reached back to that day in September 1993 when he shook hands with his enemy, Yasir Arafat, and spoke the lines from the *kaddish* as a call for the healing power of peace. *O-seh sha-lom bim-ro-mov hu ya-a-se sha-lom / A-lay-nu v'al kol yis-ra-eyl v'im-ru a-mayn.* "May he who establishes peace in the heavens, grant peace unto us and to all Israel." In viewing the Warsaw cemetary and the Majdenek death camp, I was moved by the hope that Nature could be the agent that establishes peace. But Nature alone cannot establish this. Nature's relationship to humanity is too complex. And thus I recall the group of Israeli school children on the road in Theresienstadt. The Jewish people survived the Holocaust, and they continue to survive today because they remember the Holocaust. The Jewish people persist because they pass these on to their children, one generation at a time. Now we live in an age in which we must include the preservation of nature in the bundle of ideas we pass on. If there is a God, he works through human knowledge and human will. Only humans can understand the meaning and history of evil. Only humans who understand the need to control our power can halt the practice of domination, can halt the destruction of people and the natural environment. It is only through human action that peace can be restored to our planet and our civilization.[21]

NOTES

From *Judaism: A Quarterly Journal* 46 (1997), 79–89.

1. Jeremy Benstein, "'One, Walking and Studying . . .': Nature vs. Torah" [reprinted in this volume, 206–29]; and Eilon Schwartz, "Judaism and Nature: Theological and Moral Issues to Consider While Renegotiating a Jewish Relationship to the Natural World" [reprinted in this volume, 297–308].

2. Schwartz [reprinted in this volume, 297].

3. Benstein [reprinted in this volume, 207–208].

4. Benstein [reprinted in this volume, 210].

5. Eric Katz, "Judaism and the Ecological Crisis," in *Worldviews and Ecology: Religion, Philosophy, and the Environment* (Maryknoll, N.Y.: Orbis Books, 1994).

6. Schwartz [reprinted in this volume, 303].

7. For a general discussion of Majdenak and the overall history of the Holocaust, see Leni Yahil, *The Holocaust: The Fate of European Jewry*, trans. Ina Friedman and Haya Galai (New York: Oxford University Press, 1990), esp. 362–63; Ronnie S. Landau, *The Nazi Holocaust* (Chicago: Ivan S. Dee, 1994); and Martin Gilbert, *The Holocaust: A History of the Jews of Europe During the Second World War* (New York: Henry Holt, 1985). The death statistics cited in these recent works differ by an order of magnitude from Dawidowicz's classic work, which claims that 1.3 million Jews died at Majdanek. See Lucy S. Dawidowicz, *The War Against the Jews 1933–1945* (New York: Holt, Rinehart and Winston, 1975), 149. Gilbert reports that Hitler was enraged that German SS forces did not destroy the camp before the Russian advance (711).

8. Robert-Jan Van Pelt, "A Site in Search of a Mission," in *Anatomy of the Auschwitz Death Camp*, ed. Yisrael Gui and Michael Berenbaum (Bloomington, Ind.: Indiana University Press, 1994), 101–103.

9. Schwartz [reprinted in this volume, 302–304].

10. Benstein [reprinted in this volume, 223].

11. Benstein [reprinted in this volume, 215–17].

12. See Eric Katz, "The Call of the Wild: The Struggle Against Domination and the 'Technological Fix' of Nature," *Environmental Values* 2 (1993): 223–32; "Imperialism and Environmentalism," *Social Theory and Practice* 21 (1995): 271–85.

13. See Eric Katz, "The Big Lie: Human Restoration of Nature," *Research in Philosophy anbd Technology* 12 (1992): 231–41; "Restoration and Redesign: The Ethical Significance of Human Invention in Nature," *Restoration Management Notes* 9 (1991): 90–96.

14. C. S. Lewis, "The Abolition of Man," reprinted in *Philosophy and Technology: Readings in the Philosophical Problems of Technology*, ed. Carl Mitcham and Robert Mackey (New York: Free Press, 1983), 143–50, quotations from 143 and 146; Lewis's *The Abolition of Man* was originally published in 1947.

15. Thus the power of Peter Singer's argument that animal liberation is necessary to correct speciesism, a prejudice akin to racism or sexism. See Singer, *Animal Liberation: A New Ethics for Our Treatment of Animals* (New York: Avon, 1975), 1–23. Also see Ze'ev Levy. "Ethical Issues of Animal Welfare in Jewish Thought" [reprinted in this volume, 321–32].

16. Schwartz [reprinted in this volume, 304].

17. See Katz, "Imperialism and Environmentalism," 273–74. Holmes Rolston III presents a sustained account of the idea of nature as the subject of an ongoing history. See Rolston, *Environmental Ethics: Duties to and Values in the Natural World* (Philadelphia: Temple University Press, 1988), esp. 342–54.

18. The argument in this setion is based on Katz, "The Big Lie," "Call of the Wild," and "Artefacts and Functions."

19. Primo Levi, *The Reawakening,* trans. Stuart Woolf (New York: Collier Books, 1987), 8.

20. Although it may appear paradoxical to think of the act of healing as a form of domination, consider the long-standing issue of Paternalism in the field of medical ethics. The use of medical procedures against the wishes of a fully rational patient is a violation of individual autonomy, even when these medical procedures are clearly in the best interests (i.e., the health) of the patient.

21. Parts of this essay appear in "Nature's Presence: Reflections on Healing and Domination," *Philosophy and Geography* 1 (1966); other sections were presented at the Society for Philosophy and Technology meeting on Technology and the Holocaust, in conjunction with the Central Division of the American Philosophical Association, Chicago, Ill., April 25, 1996. I thank Rabbi Steven Shaw and David Szonyi of the Jewish Theological Seminary of America, as well as Andrew Light and Avner de Shalit, for helpful comments. The trip to Eastern Europe was made possible by a sabbatical study leave from the New Jersey Institute of Technology.

21

Ethical Issues of Animal Welfare in Jewish Thought

Ze'ev Levy

Ethics until not so long ago was concerned exclusively with humans. No philosopher or theologian deliberated, from the ethical of view, on the status of animals in their own right. Recent years have seen steadily growing interest in animals and their welfare, as well as in ecological and ethological problems in general on the part of philosophers, but this has not yet changed the approach to these matters in a substantial manner. There are relatively few philosophers, and almost no religious thinkers, who challenge the traditional outlook that man is the crown of creation. According to the Jewish sources, the Bible and the Talmud, man was destined to be master over all animals; they were designed to serve man. But they at the same time emphasized that true mastery implies taking care of those who are dependent upon you, and to defend the rights of the weak and the vulnerable. Animals ought not to be treated just any way we like; otherwise the master turns into a despot. God not only gave man dominion over all animals (Gen. 1:26, 28), but on many occasions the Bible elucidates how to carry out this dominion in an appropriate and humane way.

In medieval and early modern thought, the view that animals are living and sentient creatures was pushed aside. Descartes called animal consciousness a "prejudice to which we are accustomed from our earliest years."[1] Unlike humans who are endowed with a soul, animals, he claimed, are no more than *automata*, and incapable of any sort of conscious state, including the feeling of pain. This is obviously ridiculous. We know that animals, especially mammals and birds, feel pain no less than humans. They simply cannot tell us about it, although we can easily infer it from their behavior.

Spinoza, however, in the *Ethics*, contested Descartes's view. From the point of view of Spinoza's ethics, it follows that all *sentient* beings possess some moral rights, especially the higher animals (mammals, birds, fish). This perspective does not award animals full and equal rights with human persons; no defender of animal rights makes the claim that animals and humans have identical rights. The prevalent current distinction is that animals particularly possess consciousness while humans possess self-consciousness. According to this last distinction, only self-consciousness forms the basis for moral concern. Kant, among others, asserted that animals lack the decisive quality of rationality, and are therefore not subject to moral considerations. Only man is an end in itself. "But so far as animals are concerned, we have no direct duties. Animals are not self-conscious, and are there merely as a means to an end. That end is man. . . . Our duties towards animals are merely indirect duties towards humanity."[2]

It is important to observe how prejudices with regard to animal behavior are embedded in common language. Words such as "brutality" and "bestiality" are projected onto animals although what they express is human cruelty and aggression, which are characteristics of humans, not of animals. Worth noting is that Kant recommended kind behavior to animals, because cruelty to animals might foster similar cruelty in man's dealings with his fellow men.

> Thus, if a dog has served his master long and faithfully, his service, on the analogy of human service, deserves reward, and when the dog has grown too old to serve, his master ought to keep him until he dies. Such action helps to support us in our duties towards human beings. . . . We have duties towards the animals because thus we cultivate the corresponding duties towards human beings. . . . [Man] must practise kindness towards animals, for he who is cruel to animals becomes hard also in his dealings with men.[3]

There certainly is some psychological truth in Kant's argument that kind treatment of animals is likely to cultivate this virtue, though it is ethically insufficient. The main weakness of Kant's argument, however, consists in the impossibility of proving the assertion that animals merely exist as a means to an end. In the Bible, by contrast, there are many statements that attribute to God's direct concern for the welfare of animals.

The opinion that animals are devoid of consciousness (Descartes) or self-consciousness (Kant) clashed with the traditional view, still prevalent in the Middle Ages and in the beginning of the modern era. Animals who killed people were brought before the court, condemned to death, and executed. All this was in line with the biblical command that a goring ox should be put to death (Ex. 21:28, 29; perhaps this was also done to prevent blood vengeance on its owner). These practices, so strange to us now, were abandoned only in the eighteenth century. Acts such as hanging an animal in public appear even more disgusting to us than hanging a man, since we do not consider animals to be responsible for their acts. However, in the Bible animals were sometimes considered to be accountable for their deeds, just as men are. "If an ox gore a man or a woman, that they die: then the ox shall surely be stoned" (Ex. 21:28). The next verse adds that if the ox was known to be dangerous, the responsibility includes also his negligent owner, and both should be put to death. Also, both men and animals were not allowed to go up into Mount Sinai or touch its border; for doing so, both should be put to death (Ex. 19:12–13). This means that both were assumed to be responsible for their acts.

There are human beings who, regrettably, are human only because they belong to the species of *homo sapiens*, but lack the faculties that are characteristic of the human species (e.g., mentally debilitated infants, persistently comatose persons, etc.). They are not truly human from the ethical point of view, although our treatment of them must be guided by ethical principles. On the other hand, there are animals who possess certain characteristics distinctive of our species (chimpanzees, gorillas, dolphins, and to a lesser extent dogs, cats, horses, etc.), which these unfortunate humans lack. Should these animals rank higher than, for example, mentally handicapped infants? The issue is also linked to the notion of "sanctity of life." But why is this principle usually limited only to human life? To reformulate it as the principle of "sanctity of human life" would be fallacious, because it might then lead to speciesism, which is morally no more defensible than racism or sexism. So the crucial question is: In what does the *moral* distinction between human and animal life consist? This remains a controversial issue. As noted, humans possess faculties and characteristics which animals lack, but can they serve as an ethical ground for denying certain moral rights to animals?

Although we acknowledge that humans and animals are not equal, neither in the biological nor in the ethical sense, we nevertheless feel uneasy with the argument of speciesism. (The term was coined by Peter Singer.)[4] The term recalls S. D. Luzzatto's argument for the different treatment to be given a Hebrew and a Canaanite slave; the interests of the Hebrews take precedence over those of others because one cares more for one's own family and for one's own kind than for others. So why not extend this plea also to our species? If one prefers the interests of one's family to other people, of one's nation to other nations, why not of one's species to others? Is it not self-evident, or even a platitude, that one should care more for humans than for animals? But the Damocles-sword of this argument is unavoidable. It could also serve to vindicate racism, namely the claim that whites are superior to blacks, Aryans to non-Aryans, and that the interests of the former outweigh those of the latter; it might support sexism (i.e., that men are intellectually and otherwise superior to women). Yet most people who are sincerely opposed to racism and sexism do not extend this ethical outlook of equality to animals. Opposition to racism and sexism does not necessarily entail rejection of speciesism, but it is not the same the other way around.

From the species distinction there is only a relatively small step to race distinctions. The nineteenth-century racists indeed founded their theories on inferences from animals to humans. As there are different races of dogs

Ze'ev Levy

with different characteristics, they claimed, there are distinct human races with allegedly distinct mental capacities. The Achilles heel of the argument obviously is not the fact that there exist different human races, but the assertion that they represent different grades of humanness. Even Kant was convinced that skin color indicates different degrees of human perfection, and believed whites to be superior to black, yellow, and red people.[5] Therefore, the species argument, notwithstanding the best of intentions, is liable, like any other slippery-slope argument, though perhaps inadvertently, to justify racial discrimination.

Thus it follows from all this that it would be simply wrong to disregard the interests of animals because they do not belong to our species. Where animals and humans display common characteristics—for example, suffering and pain—they ought to be treated similarly. The same reason, namely that tormenting *hurts*, applies equally to humans and to animals. On the other hand, where animals differ from humans, they ought to be treated accordingly. But what is most important, if animals are capable of feeling pain like humans, if they also can suffer, then it is ethically no less wrong to inilict pain and suffering on animals than on humans. In that case it is morally irrelevant whether the suffering creature is human or nonhuman. Already, Jeremy Bentham, Kant's contemporary, was aware of this and wrote in a famous passage:

The day *may* come when the rest of the animal creation may acquire those rights which never could have been withholden from them but by the hand of tyranny. The French have already discovered that the blackness of the skin is no reason why a human being should be abandoned without redress to the caprice of a tormentor. It may one day come to be recognized that the number of legs, the villosity of the skin, or the termination of the *os sacrum,* are reasons equally insufficient for abandoning a sensitive being to the same fate. What else is it that should trace the insuperable line? Is it the faculty of reason, or perhaps the faculty of discourse? But a full grown horse or dog is beyond comparison a more rational, as well as more conversable animal, than an infant of a day or a week, or even a month, old. But suppose they were otherwise, what would it avail? The question is not, Can they reason? nor Can they talk? but, *Can they suffer?*[6]

Among the major philosophers, Schopenhauer alone expressly extended ethical norms to animals; this reflected his predilection for Indian religions, which he preferred to Christianity. Regrettably, however, his view included unjustified accusations against Judaism. Since man, according to Genesis, was awarded dominion over animals, Schopenhauer accused Judaism of being the origin of the derogation of animals in Europe. "The alleged lack of rights of animals, the illusion that their treatment by us has no moral significance . . ., that there are no duties to animals, is a disgusting crudeness and barbarity of the occident, the source of which is in Judaism."[7]

He writes still more venomously elsewhere,[8] and exclaims: "It is time to put an end to the Jewish conception of nature, at least with regard to animals, and to acknowledge, defend and respect the eternal essence which exists, as in us, in all animals."[9] Schopenhauer's defense of animals is certainly laudable in itself, and the movement for prevention of cruelty to animals indeed drew much inspiration from him; but together with the ethical elements of his philosophical views on animals, it also absorbed, *nolens-volens,* many of his anti-Jewish prejudices. For this reason, Jews, while on the whole supporting the aims of these movements, manifested a certain amount of suspicion toward them. With Schopenhauer we have, as in a nutshell, the controversy which divides contemporary philosophers in regard to man's relationship to animals, namely, whether we owe them direct duties (Schopenhauer) or merely indirect duties (Kant). We shall encounter this division also in the Jewish literature on man's relationship to animals.

Bentham's disciple John Stuart Mill emphasized the common moral category of suffering humans and nonhumans. To cause suffering is therefore morally wrong with regard to both. Although this seems to be self-evident, most of us nonetheless take it for granted that we can use animals for experimentation and other purposes as we deem fit, despite the suffering involved.

Utilitarianism challenged this deep-seated outlook, that only human beings are worthy of moral considerations, and extended the realm of morality to all sentient beings. Bentham's relentless appeals induced the British parliament, in 1824, to pass a law to prevent cruelty towards animals. From the Jewish aspect, it is noteworthy that, besides Bentham, it was a Jew, Lewis Gompertz, who strongly furthered this cause by his *Moral Enquiries on the Situation of Men and Brutes* (1824). He also was, in 1826, one of the cofounders of the British Society for the Prevention of Cruelty to Animals. Gompertz served as its first secretary; but when it adopted Christian sectarian views in 1832, he was dismissed. He then founded the Animals' Friend Society and published the influential periodical *The Animals' Friend* until 1846.[10] He considered it ethically wrong to use animals for human needs; he was a vegetarian and did not even ride in horse-drawn carriages. This English society was soon followed by the founding of similar associations in other countries. In Israel such groups first sprang up during the British mandate. Unfortunately, in the nineteenth century some of these groups displayed certain anti-Semitic tendencies. They tried to prohibit *shechita,* Jewish ritual slaughter, which they depicted, wrongly, as a cruel form of killing animals. Although the claim was scientifically unfounded, *shechita* was outlawed in Switzerland in 1892, in Norway in 1930, and of course in Nazi Germany.

The Hebrew term for prevention of cruelty to animals—צער בעלי חיים (literally, "grief of living beings")—appears in *Baba Metzi'a* (31a) and other talmudic passages. However, the prohibition of cruelty to animals and the duty to provide for the needs of domestic animals are emphasized in the Bible. God says to Jonah: "And should not I spare Nineveh . . . , wherein there are more than six score thousand persons . . . and also much cattle?" (Jon. 4:11). By the way, the animals, according to the story, repented like the human inhabitants of the city: "But let man and beast be covered with sackcloth, and cry mightily unto God" (Jon. 3:8). Likewise, in the story of the Deluge God punished all animals together with all men, only saving one pair of each kind as he saved one human family. In a similar vein, the psalmist declares: "O Lord, thou preservest man and beast" (Ps. 36:7). God takes care of all his creatures (Psalm 145:9), and provides food for all (Ps. 147:9, Job 38:39, 41), for man and beast alike (Psalms 104:14, 145:16).

Much of God's care of animals belongs to the category of direct duties. He cares for wild goats, rabbits (Ps. 104:18), young lions, ravens and so on, which do not serve man's interests. Because God takes care of animals, they also appeal to him in times of distress (Ps. 104:21, 27; 147:9, Job 38:41). God also expects the "beast of the field, the dragons and the owls" to "honor me . . . because I give waters in the wilderness and rivers in the desert" (Isa. 43:20). These verses, and many kindred ones, emphasize God's care of all animals; similarly, the injunction not to take the bird sitting on its young or on its eggs, together with them, but to let it go first (Deut. 22:6–7) is a clear admonition of *tza'ar ba'alei chayyim*.

Yet most of the biblical commandments to assure fair treatment of animals refer to domestic animals They can be interpreted either as direct or indirect duties. They derive from the assumption that man knows the needs of his household animals. "A righteous man regards the life of his beast" (נפש בהמתו יודע צדיק, Prov. 12:10). There are numerous commands of this kind in the Bible and the Talmud, as well as in later Jewish writings. The Bible uses the word "beasts" (בהמות) to denote wild animals as well as domesticated ones, whereas the Talmud distinguishes linguistically between the two, reserving *behemot* for domestic animals and *chayyot* (חיות) for the others. The distinction appears to have been for the halakhic ritual; the first were considered *kasher* (i.e., allowed to be eaten), while the latter (except the deer and the ibex) were *tareff* (i.e., forbidden to be eaten).

The obligations of humans to animals is a thread that runs through the Bible. On the Shabbat, everybody of the household shall rest, including animals (בהמתך, Ex. 20:10; the translation "cattle" is inaccurate). This is repeated in Deuteronomy where it is explicitly specified that this includes "your ox, your ass and all your beasts" (Deut. 5:14). Likewise, the sabbatical year is designed also for the welfare of "thy cattle, and for the beasts that are in the land" (Lev. 25:7). This verse expresses again a direct duty towards animals ("the beast in the land"). Moses obtained water from the rock, so that "the congregation and their beasts drink" (Num. 20:8).

The Talmud underscores the duty to take care of (domestic) animals. One ought to buy an animal only after having provided food for it (Yerushalmi,

Yebamot 15:3). One should not sit down to eat before having given food to one's animals (*Gittin* 62a). This, of course, brings to mind the story about Rebecca who gave Eliezer drink from her pitcher, and volunteered to water his camels (Gen. 24:16–20). Whatever her motives, this act proved her good character to Eliezer (Gen. 24:14). Moses and David were praised for the devoted care of their flocks. There is the famous story about Moses looking for a stray lamb. Therefore, according to the Midrash, he was deemed fit, by a voice from heaven, to be the shepherd of the People of Israel. Balaam, on the other hand, was rebuked for smiting his ass (Num. 22:32). Fred Rosner rightly describes this as "a classical text for the teaching of humane treatment of animals."[11] The most striking example against cruelty to animals is undoubtedly the commandment to unload an animal, staggering under its burden, even if it belongs to one's enemy (Ex. 23:5). When Maimonides included this commandment in the *Mishneh Torah*, he added that it also applies to the animal of a heathen.[12]

These verses illustrate the obligation to take care of one's household animals arid to treat them well. But there are also many more verses that condemn cruelty to animals. It is forbidden to muzzle an ox when it is threshing (Deut. 25:4), to slaughter an animal and its young on the same day (Lev. 22:28), to plough together with an ox and an ass (Deut. 22:10), and so on. All these laws were emphasized in the Midrashim, and Maimonides elaborated many of them in the *Guide of the Perplexed* and in the *Mishneh Torah*.[13] Kind and careful treatment of animals even justifies the desecration of Shabbat and holidays, in order to relieve them from suffering.[14]

While some of these laws clearly express direct duties to the animal themselves—driving away the mother bird before taking her young, not slaughtering an animal and its young on the same day, and so forth—most of them stressed direct duties in the Kantian sense and have as part of their purpose the education of human beings and the development of decent and humane relationship to animals: they are a training in how not to succumb to cruelty. In this spirit, Maimonides interpreted the biblical and talmudic recommendations with regard to animals as aiming at "perfecting us so that we shall not acquire moral habits of cruelty."[15] Similarly, Saadya pointed out that showing pity toward animals gets a reward in this world.[16]

Although there have been Jewish vegetarian sects, mainstream Judaism was not opposed to eating meat (evidently of kosher animals only). Maimonides, for example, approved of meat eating but condemned the killing of animals out of cruelty of or for sport.[17] This, of course, does not apply to killing dangerous beasts (lions, panthers, snakes, scorpions, etc.), which is an obvious act of self-defense. Some biblical commentators claim that both men and animals were originally vegetarians, and the eating of meat was granted by God only after the Deluge. According to this argument, although God gave humanity dominion over all animals in the Garden of Eden, God, as it were, did not give us their meat to eat: the relevant prooftext cited is

Genesis 1:29: "Behold, I have given you every herb bearing seed which is
upon the face of the earth and every tree in which is the fruit of a tree yielding seed; to you it shall be for meat." This view holds that the antagonism
between man and beast, symbolized by the enmity between Eve and the
serpent, arose only after the expulsion from Eden. Mythological elements of
the story of the Flood aside, it appears improbable that beasts of prey
changed their nature and habits. Unlike human beings, meat-eating animals
cannot choose to become vegetarians. Some commentators tried to explain
the postdeluge permission to eat meat—Every moving thing that lives shall
be meat for you" (Gen. 9:3)—by making the claim that after the flood humanity was weaker and needed additional food. In any event, the Bible
mentions animal sacrifices beginning with the story of Cain and Abel. Was
the meat of these sacrificed animals not consumed?[18] Without entering into
a discussion on the diverse aspects of animal (and human) sacrifices in antiquity, it should be noted that when the prophets condemned sacrifices,
they were not concerned with the suffering of innocent creatures but were
criticizing the prevalent view of their times that human beings can atone by
such sacrifices for their evil deeds (Isa. 1:11ff., Jer. 6:20, Am. 5:22–24, Hos.
8:13, Mic. 6:6–8, Prov. 21:27). They were not motivated by *tza'ar ba'alei
chayyim.*

The most famous Talmudic example emphasizing the ethical aspect of
tza'ar ba'alei chayyim is the story about Rabbi Yehuda ha-Nassi (the editor
of the Mishnah). When a calf, escaping slaughter, sought shelter with him, he
said to it: "Go, for this wast thou created." For this indifference to the calf's
suffering, he was punished from heaven. "Since he has no pity, let us bring
suffering upon him." According to the story, he was afflicted with a
toothache lasting for thirteen years; it was lifted only after he saved a litter of
kittens *(Baba Metzi'a* 85a). This story is quoted often to corroborate the ethical significance of *tza'ar ba'alei chayyim.* The Bible denounces hunting.
Only two hunters, Nimrod and Esau, are mentioned in it. Although the Bible
does not ascribe to them any moral evil—Nimrod, who was a Babylonian,
was only reproached for his idol worship and his pursuit of Abraham—they
have become in some ways a prototype of evil. This holds in particular for
the name of "Esau," which in the Middle Ages acquired a defamatory connotation, as designating Israel's enemies.[19]

There is obviously an essential distinction between shearing sheep to obtain their wool, which does neither hurt nor harm to them, and killing animals for the express purpose of using their skin, fur, plumes, and so on. One
need not be a vegetarian in order to condemn the killing of birds for their
plumes, or mammals (fox, minks, baby seals, and others) for their fur, ele-
phants for ivory, or hunting as a pastime; all of these are ethically repulsive
and objectionable activities.

A fully consistent ethical view regards killing animals for meat as producing harm to them because one deprives them of their life. Untimely death of

animals, even if it is performed painlessly, causes harm. The messianic vision of Isaiah, that

> The wolf shall dwell with the lamb
> and the leopard shall lie down with the kid,
> and the calf and the young lion and the fatling together,
> And the cow and the bear shall feed;
> their young ones shall lie down together,
> and the lion shall eat straw like the ox. (Isa. 11:6–7)

is, of course, no more than a poetical allegory of striving for peace. In nature, there are animals that feed on other animals, human beings among them. There is, however, a distinction that all radical defenders of animal rights emphasize. A lion will never become a vegetarian like an ox, despite Isaiah's wishful dream; lions, wolves, leopards, and bears are beasts of prey that by their very nature depend on meat. Humans, however, need not be meat-eaters; they can also live healthily on vegetarian food. On the other hand, if the theory of evolution links man to animals, his habit of meat eating is not unnatural but a normal part of his nature. One may decide, for ethical (and other) reasons, to become a vegetarian; but it would be wrong to describe those people who continue to consume meat as exhibiting unethical behavior. That would be simply exaggerated and inaccurate. The issue of killing animals for food is not a matter of all or nothing. There is justified killing for food. Although the life of animals is not valueless, the value of human life and animal life is not the same.

The chief ethical issue with regard to animal welfare is not so much the killing of animals for food, but the horrible factory-like methods that achieve this purpose by the most profitable means. Fattening and force-feeding (of geese, calves, turkeys, etc.) are in flagrant contradiction to the nature and way of life of these animals and cause them suffering while still alive. There is no need to enter into details; there exists a vast literature on these matters.

Although the classical utilliarians (Bentham, Mill) called out for animal welfare, the philosophy of Utilitarianism cannot and does not provide any convincing argument against these disgusting forms of animal raising. According to the criteria of utility, such treatment of animals ensures not only the best profitable results for the producers, but also increases happiness among meat-eaters, who form the majority of humankind. Therefore, with all due respect to the personal ethical feelings of the founders of Utilitarianism toward animals, the principles of Utilitarianism—and first of all the principle of assuring the greatest happiness for the greatest number—if it takes into account humans only, does not refute these practices. To fight against these repelling forms of animal raising may look quixotic, but it certainly is an *ethical* question of the first degree.

The same principles that govern animal research and experimentation have existed since antiquity. Animals are not asked whether they assent to experimentation, and—what is of the essence—the experiments performed on them are usually hurtful and in the majority of cases entail debilitation and death. Many modern laboratory experiments on animals are extremely painful, physically as well as mentally (e.g., with Rhesus monkeys). Also, animals, unlike humans who participate in experiments, are kept in small cages, that is, in totally unnatural and unpleasant surroundings. Furthermore, all of us consider it repulsive to conduct experiments on human imbeciles (i.e., mentally retarded people), but most of us have no compunctions about their performance on self-conscious and intelligent animals such as primates. What *ethically relevant difference* is there to account for opposing using humans in a dangerous experiment, involving risk of life without informed consent, which also does not hold say for chimpanzees? Does their different *legal status* entail a *morally* relevant difference?[20] Rabbi M. Isserles had even extended this opinion to other, not only medical purposes. According to his ruling, it is allowable to pluck feathers from living geese in order to obtain quills, but he at the same time recommended refraining from it "because it is an act of cruelty."[21] This corresponds to the Talmudic rule of *Patur aval assur.*

The majority of contemporary rabbinic opinions permit animal experimentation for medical research because animals were, assumedly, created to serve mast *(Kiddushin* 82a–b). They even approve of vivisection, but solely for the advancement of human health. But then one may ask once again, if animals are there to serve man, why restrict their experimental use to health, and not to other needs? It is indeed very difficult to draw the exact line of demarcation. To justify animal experimentation by the biblical view that man was awarded dominion over all animals is ethically untenable, but that man's life and health take precedence over animal welfare can be ethically corroborated and recommended. This view implies, however, that it should be limited solely to medical ends, and that wherever it is possible to obtain the same research results by other means, the latter should be given priority.

Finally, to recapitulate the philosophical problems, raised in this essay: There are perhaps more people now who recognize our duties—whether direct or indirect—to animals, but there are still relatively few who accept the notion of animal rights. To acknowledge the latter is mandatory not only ethically but ecologically as well. Although the concept of animal rights raises questions about the biblical view of humanity's dominion over animals, it perhaps even reinforces humanity's preeminence over the beast-world, because we alone are capable of creating an ethics. Is it not incumbent upon us to extend this ethics to other living beings as well, and thus to contribute to a better and more harmonious relationship with our surroundings?

NOTES

From *Judaism: A Quarterly Journal* 45 (1996): 47–57.

1. From a letter to Henry More, February 5, 1649. R. Descartes, *Philosophical Letters* (Oxford: Oxford University Press, 1970), 65.

2. Immanuel Kant, *Lectures on Ethics* (New York: Century, 1930), 239.

3. *Lectures on Ethics*, 239–40.

4. Peter Singer, *Animal Liberation: A New Ethics for Our Treatment of Animals* (New York: Random House, 1975); *Practical Ethics* (Cambridge, Eng.: Cambridge University Press, 1979), ch. 3, 5.

5. Kant, "Von den verschiedenen Rassen der Menschen," "Bestimmung des Begriffs einer Menschenrasse," *Kants Sämtliche Werke* (Leipzig: Insel Verlag, 1922), vol. 2, 579–618. Only quite recently, the press recorded the "sensational discovery" of an American scientist that Blacks have an I.Q. of 85 in comparison with 100 of the whites. (By the way, he accorded an I.Q. of 115 to the Chinese and Japanese, and still more to Ashkenazi Jews.)

6. Jeremy Bentham, *The Principles of Morals and Legislation* (1789), ch. XVII, sec. 1 ([New York: Hafner, 1948], 311, n.).

7. Arthur Schopenhauer, "Begründung der Ethik," #19, *Schopenhauers Sämtliche-Werke* (Leipzig: Insel Verlag, 1910), vol. 3, 634.

8. Schopenhauer, *Parerga und Paralipomena*, Part 2, ch. XV, "Über Religion," *Schopenhauers Sämtliche Werke*, vol. 5, 403–404.

9. "Über Religion," 409.

10. *Encyclopedia Judaica*, vol. 7, 773.

11. Fred Rosner, *Modern Medicine and Jewish Ethics* (Hoboken, N.J.: Ktav, 1986), 324.

12. Maimonides, *Mishneh Torah, Hilkhot Rotzeach* 13:1, 13:8, 13:9; see also Rosner, 324–25.

13. Maimonides, *Guide of the Perplexed* III 48; Rosner, 323.

14. Rosner quotes the Talmudic tractate *Shabbat* 117b, in order to assert that "to save animals from suffering is regarded as a stronger reason for desecrating the Shabbat than to save oneself from personal loss" (327). It seems difficult, however, to separate the two reasons, because the main example, also brought forward by Maimonides, is the injunction to unload an animal even after the beginning of the Shabbat, in order to relieve it from its burden and suffering (*Mishneh Torah, Hilkhot Shabbat* 21:9–10). One also must milk an animal in order to alleviate its pain; in this case, there is obviously also the reason that otherwise the animal might suffer irreversible harm; that would be also a loss for its owner. The milk, however, should not be used, and the milking ought to be performed by a non-Jew. But in this case, from the halakhic point of view, no desecration of the Shabbat is involved anyway. Employing a "Shabbos-Goy" has become a longstanding practice in Jewish history. But why is it then *not* stipulated that a pack animal should also be unloaded by a Gentile? It therefore seems more plausible that these talmudic injunctions were meant to underscore the ethical importance of considerate treatment of animals as such.

15. Maimonides, *Guide of the Perplexed* III 17; see also Rosner, 325.

16. Saadya Gaon, *Emunot ve-Deot* 5.

17. Maimonides, *Guide of the Perplexed* III 17, 20. Compare with the relevant verses, quoted by Rosner.

18. Compare with the relevant verses, quoted by Rosner, and his rather questionable inferences.

19. The opposition to killing animals is sometimes couched in terms of "reverence for life." Albert Schweitzer wanted to apply it to all living beings. It is noteworthy that similar views were not alien to Jewish thought. Rabbi Isaac Luria

("Ha-Ari"), the great Kabbalist, exhorted his pupils not to kill irritating insects. He thus anticipated Schweitzer, who recommended keeping windows closed at night, even to the extent of breathing stifling air, so that insects would not he attracted by lamplight, singed, and killed.

20. Tom Regan: "Ill-gotten Gains," in *Health Care Ethics,* ed. Donald van de Veer and Tom Regan (Philadelphia: Temple University Press, 1987), 244. See also Immanuel Jakobovitz *Jewish Law Faces Modern Problems* (New York: Yeshiva University Press, 1965), 89.

21. Rosner, 329.

22

Judaism and Animal Experimentation

J. David Bleich

> While our teacher Moses was tending the sheep of Jethro in the wilderness, a kid ran away from him. He ran after it until it reached Hasuah. Upon reaching Hasuah, it came upon a pool of water, [whereupon] the kid stopped to drink. When Moses reached it he said, "I did not know that you were running because [you were] thirsty. You must be tired." He placed it on his shoulder and began to walk. The Holy One, blessed be He, said, "You are compassionate in leading flocks belonging to mortals; I swear you will similarly shepherd my flock, Israel."
>
> —Midrash Rabbah, *Shemot* 2:2

CONCERN FOR WELFARE OF ANIMALS

In a provocative comment, the German philosopher Arthur Schopenhauer remarked that the denial of rights to animals is a doctrine peculiar to Western civilization and reflects a barbarianism which has its roots in Judaism: "*Die vermeintliche Rechtlösigkeit der Tiere . . . ist geradezu eine empörende Rohheit und Barberei des Okzidents, deren Quelle im Judenturn liegt* [The supposed lack of rights of animals . . . is just a disgusting crudeness and barbarity of the Occident, whose source lies in Judaism]."[1]

Whether denial of rights to animals is, or is not, barbaric is a value judgment regarding which reasonable men may differ. Whether or not Judaism actually denies such rights to animals is a factual matter which is readily discernible. The Bible abounds in passages which reflect concern for animal welfare. Concern for the welfare of animals is clearly regarded as the trait of a righteous person: "A righteous man regardeth the life of his beast; but the tender mercies of the wicked are cruel" (Prov. 12:10). Divine concern

for the welfare of animals is reflected in numerous passages: "And His tender mercies are over all His works" (Ps. 145:9); "The eyes of all wait for
Thee, and Thou givest them their food in due season. Thou openest Thy
hand and satisfiest every living thing with favor" (Ps. 145: 15–16); "He
giveth to the beast his food, and to the young ravens which cry" (Ps. 147:9);
"Who provides for the raven his prey, when his young ones cry unto God
and wander for lack of food?" (Job 38:41); "and should not I have pity on
Nineveh, the that great city, wherein are more than six score thousand persons and also much cattle?" (Jon. 4:11); and "Man and beast thou preservest, O Lord" (Ps. 36:7). *De minimis,* these verses serve to establish the theological proposition that divine mercy extends, not only to man, but to
members of the animal kingdom as well.

It further follows that, as a religion in which *imitatio Dei* serves as a governing moral principle,[2] Judaism must perforce view compassion towards
animals as a moral imperative. It is told variously of one or another of the
leading exponents of the *Musar* movement that he kept a cat as a pet and insisted upon feeding the cat personally. That individual is reported to have remarked to his disciples that his motivation was simply to emulate divine conduct. Since God extends "His tender mercies over all His works" (Ps. 145:9),
man should eagerly seek opportunities to do likewise. The story is perhaps
apocryphal in nature but remarkable nonetheless because of its wide currency in rabbinic circles.[3]

These sources, however, serve only to demonstrate that animal-directed
conduct which is compassionate in nature constitutes a "good deed," but do
not serve to establish a system of normative duties or responsibilities. Particularly in light of the strong nomistic element present in Judaism, the absence
of normative regulations might well be regarded as indicative of the absence
of serious ethical concern for the welfare of members of the animal kingdom. But this is demonstrably not the case, for, in Jewish teaching, there is
no dearth of *nomoi* designed to protect and promote animal welfare. The
most obvious example of a regulation having such an effect, and one which
is clearly biblical in origin, is contained in the verse "If thou seest the ass of
him that hateth thee lying under its burden, thou shalt forebear to pass by
him; thou shalt surely release it with him" (Ex. 23:5). The selfsame concern
is manifest in the prohibition against muzzling an ox while it threshes, in
order that the animal be free to eat of the produce while working (Deut.
25:4). Similarly, Scripture provides that both domestic animals and wild
beasts must be permitted to share in produce of the land which grows without cultivation during the sabbatical year.[4] Although the literal meaning of
the biblical text may be somewhat obscure, talmudic exegesis understands
Genesis 9:4 and Deuteronomy 12:23 as forbidding the eating of a limb severed from a living animal. Jewish law teaches that this prohibition, unlike
most other commandments, is universally binding upon all peoples as one
of the Seven Commandments of the Sons of Noah. Sabbath laws contained

in both formulations of the Decalogue reflect a concern which goes beyond the mere elimination of pain and discomfort, and serve to promote the welfare of animals in a positive in manner by providing for their rest on the Sabbath day: "But the seventh day is a Sabbath unto the Lord thy God, on it thou shalt not do any manner of work . . . nor thine ox, nor thine ass, nor any of thy cattle." (Deut. 5:14). Even more explicit in expressing concern for the welfare of animals is the verse "but on the seventh day thou shalt rest, that thine ox and thine ass may have rest" (Ex. 23:12).[5]

Judaism posits yet another regulation regarding the welfare of animals which is regarded as biblical in nature even though the law is not reflected in a literal reading of Scripture. The biblical statement "I will give grass in thy fields for thy cattle, and thou shall eat and be satisfied" (Deut. 11:15) is understood in rabbinic exegesis as forbidding a person to partake of any food unless he has first fed his animals.[6] This regulation is derived from the order in which the two clauses comprising the verse are recorded. The passage speaks first of providing for animals and only subsequently of satisfying human needs.[7] Amplifying this rule, the Palestinian Talmud, *Yevamot* 15:3 and *Ketubot* 4:8, declares that a person is forbidden to purchase an animal unless he can assure an adequate supply of food on its behalf.

Nevertheless, it does not necessarily follow that a general obligation to be kind to animals or, minimally, a duty to refrain from cruelty to animals, can be inferred from any of these biblical regulations or even from all of them collectively. These regulations have been understood by some Sages of the Talmud as establishing particular duties, not as expressions of a more general duty. Nor is it demonstrably certain that even these limited and particular duties are designed primarily for the purpose of promoting the welfare of animals. Even with regard to the particular duty concerning removing the burden borne by a beast, the commandment does not necessarily reflect concern for the welfare of the animal. The obligation to release the ass from its burden (Ex. 23:5), i.e., to assist the owner in unloading merchandise or materials carried by a beast of burden, and the similar obligation to come to the assistance of a fallen animal (Deut. 22:4) are understood by many classical commentators as duties rooted in a concern for the financial loss which would be suffered by the animal's master were the animal to collapse under the weight of the burden. Thus, in formulating the rationale underlying this commandment, R. Aaron ha-Levi of Barcelona, *Sefer ha-Chinnukh*, no. 80, declares:

> The root purpose of the precept is to educate our spirit in the trait of compassion, which is laudable. It is unnecessary to state that a duty lies on us to take pity on a person suffering physical pain; however, it is incumbent upon us to pity and rescue even a person who is in distress because of the loss of his money.[8]

Yet, Judaism most certainly *does* posit an unequivocal prohibition against causing cruelty to animals. The Gemara, *Baba Metzi'a* 32b, carefully defines the limits of the obligation to assist in "unloading" the burden carried by an animal but hastens to add that assistance not encompassed within the ambit of the commandment concerning "unloading" (*perikah*) is required by virtue of a general biblical principle prohibiting cruelty to animals and requiring that measures be taken to alleviate "*tza'ar ba'alei chayyim*—the pain of living creatures." Thus, for example, the commandment concerning "unloading" imposes no obligation in a situation in which an inordinate burden has been placed upon the animal. This exclusion may readily be understood in light of the earlier-cited analysis of *Sefer ha-Chinnukh*. Since the master has brought the impending loss upon himself by reason of his own imprudence, there is no obligation to come to his aid. However, assistance is nevertheless required by virtue of the obligation owed to the animal. The Gemara proceeds to indicate that proper categorization of the nature of the obligation is not of mere theoretical interest but yields a practical distinction. No fee may be demanded for assisting in unloading an animal when such assistance is required by the commandment concerning "unloading," i.e., when the concern is conservation of property; however, compensation may be required if the sole consideration is for the welfare of the animal.[9]

The source of the obligation concerning *tza'ar ba'alei chayyim* which imposes a general concern for the welfare of animals is far from clear. Indeed, the Gemara, *Baba Metzi'a* 32b, cites a dispute with regard to whether the obligation with regard to *tza'ar ba'alei chayyim* is biblical or rabbinic in nature.[10] As has been indicated, if biblical in nature,[11] according to most authorities this duty is not directly derived from the obligation of "unloading." One notable exception is Rashi, *Shabbat* 128b. Rashi states that, according to those Sages of the Talmud who maintain that binding regulations may be inferred from the rationale underlying precepts, obligations concerning *tza'ar ba'alei chayyim* are directly derived from the verse "thou shalt surely release it with him" (Ex. 23:5).[12] Rambam, *Guide of the Perplexed* III 17, and R. Judah he-Chasid, *Sefer Chasidim* (ed. Reuben Margulies), No. 666, regard the biblical prohibition concerning Balaam and his ass as the source of the biblical prohibition against cruelty toward animals. These authorities indicate that the verse "And the angel of the Lord said unto him: 'Wherefore hast thou smitten thine ass these three times?'" (Num. 22:32) serves to establish a prohibition against conduct of that nature.[13] Me'iri, *Baba Metzi'a* 32b, is of the opinion that obligations concerning *tza'ar ba'alei chayyim* are derived from the prohibition against muzzling an ox while it is engaged in threshing (Deut. 25:4). *Shitah Mekubetzet, Baba Metzi'a* 32b, suggests that these obligations may either be derived from the prohibition against muzzling an ox engaged in threshing or, alternatively, *tza'ar ba'alei chayyim* may simply be the subject of *halakhah le-Mosheh mi-Sinai*, i.e., an oral teaching transmitted to Moses at Mount Sinai with no accompanying written record in the Pentateuch.[14]

Other scholars advance less obvious sources as constituting the scriptural basis for obligations concerning *tza'ar ba'alei chayyim*. R. Moses ibn Chabib,

Yom Teru'ah, Rosh ha-Shanah 27a, finds a source for such obligations in the verse "and thou shalt bring forth to them water out of the rock; so thou shalt give the congregation and their cattle drink" (Num. 20:8). Water was miraculously produced from the rock for the benefit of animals as well as of humans. Water was produced for the animals, states R. Moses ibn Chabib, in order to obviate *tza'ar ba'alei chayyim.* In the opinion of this authority, Scripture specifically records that the miracle was performed on behalf of animals as an admonition to man directing him likewise to alleviate the suffering of brute creatures. R. Moses Sofer, *Hagahot Chatam Sofer, Baba Mezi'a* 32b, similarly regards obligations with regard to animal welfare as predicated upon emulation of divine conduct. Thus *Chatam Sofer* cites the verse "And His tender mercies are over all His works" (Ps. 145:9) as imposing an obligation upon man to exercise compassion toward animals. Earlier, *Sefer Charedim,* ch. 4, expressed the opinion that compassion toward animals is mandated by the commandment "and you shall walk in His ways" (Deut. 28:9). Rambam, *Hilkhot De'ot* 1:6, apparently basing himself upon *Sifre,* Deuteronomy 11:22, renders the verse as meaning, "just as He is merciful so also shall you be merciful."

It is nevertheless probably incorrect to conclude that concern for *tza'ar ba'alei chayyim* is predicated upon a legal or moral concept of animal "rights." Certainly, in Jewish law no less than in other systems of law, neither the animal nor its guardian is granted *persona standi in judicio;* i.e., the animal lacks capacity to institute judicial proceedings to prevent others from engaging in acts of cruelty of which it may be the victim. This is so despite the unique provision in Jewish law to the effect that an animal that has committed an act of manslaughter is subject to criminal penalty but is entitled to due process of law, including a right analogous to the Sixth Amendment right of confrontation, viz., the requirement that the proceedings take place only in the presence of the accused animal.

In all likelihood, the rationale governing strictures against *tza'ar ba'alei chayyim* is concern for the moral welfare of the human agent rather than concern for the physical welfare of the animals; i.e., the underlying concern is the need to purge inclinations of cruelty and to develop compassion in human beings.[15] This is certainly the position taken by many early authorities in their discussion of the rationale underlying specific commandments dealing with comportment vis-à-vis animals. Thus, in discussing the prohibition against muzzling an animal while it is engaged in threshing, *Sefer ha-Chinnukh,* no. 596, writes:

> The root purpose of the precept is to teach ourselves that our soul be beautiful, choosing fairness and cleaving to it, and that [our soul] pursue loving kindness and mercy. In habituating [our soul] to this even with regard to animals, which were not created other than to serve us, to be mindful of them in granting them a portion of the travail of their flesh, the soul acquires a propensity for this habit to do

good to human beings and to watch over them lest he cross the boundary with regard to anything which is proper with regard to them and to compensate them for
any good they perform and to satiate them with whatever they travail. This is the
path which is proper for the holy, chosen people.

In a similar vein, Rambam, *Guide of the Perplexed* III 48, declares, "The reason for the prohibition against eating a limb [cut from] a living animal is because this would make one acquire the habit of cruelty." Rambam, *Guide* III
17, makes the same observation with regard to the general obligation with
regard to *tza'ar ba'alei chayyim* in stating that that duty "is set down with a
view to perfecting us that we should not acquire moral habits of cruelty and
should not inflict pain gratuitously, but that we should intend to be kind and
merciful even with a chance animal individual except in case of need."[16]

The concern expressed in these sources is that cruelty to animals con-
sequentially engenders an indiscriminately cruel disposition. Acts of cruelty mold character in a manner which leads to spontaneously cruel behavior. *Tza'ar ba'alei chayyim* is forbidden because cruelty is a character
trait which is to be eschewed. Practicing kindness vis-à-vis animals has the
opposite effect and serves to instill character traits of kindness and compassion. Development of such traits results in spontaneous acts of kindness, compassion, and mercy.

SLAUGHTER OF ANIMALS

Since the concern is for the moral and spiritual health of the human agent
rather than for the protection of brute creatures, it is not at all surprising
that concern for *tza'ar ba'alei chayyim* is less than absolute.

The most obvious exception is the slaughtering of animals for meat, which
is specifically permitted by Scripture to Noah and his progeny: "Every moving thing that liveth shall be food for you" (Gen. 9:3). Rambam, followed by
Sefer ha-Chinnukh, regards this exception as circumscribed by the provisions surrounding the requirement for ritual slaughter in order to eliminate
pain.[17] According to Rambam, those provisions are designed to limit the pain
insofar as possible. Thus in the *Guide* III 26, Rambam states:

> As necessity occasions the eating of animals, the commandment was intended to
> bring about the easiest death in an easy manner. . . . In order that death should
> come about more easily, the condition was imposed that the knife should be sharp.

The same concept is reiterated by Rambam with even greater clarity in III 48
of the *Guide*.

> For the natural food of man consists only of the plants deriving from the seeds
> growing in the earth and of the flesh of animals. . . . Now was since the necessity

to have good food requires that animals be killed, the aim was to kill them in the easiest manner, and it was forbidden to torment them through killing them in a reprehensible manner by piercing the lower part of their throat or by cutting off one of their members, just as we have explained.

Sefer ha-Chinnukh, no. 451, similarly states:

> It has also been said with regard to the reason for slaughter at the throat with an examined knife that it is in order that we not cause pain to animals more than is necessary, for the Torah has permitted them to man by virtue of his stature to sustain himself and for all his needs, but not to inflict pain upon them purposelessly.

Rambam, *Guide* III 26, makes it clear that the concern evidenced in the prescription of the mode of slaughter is identical with the consideration underlying the admonition concerning *tza'ar ba'alei chayyim*. Both the prescriptions concerning ritual slaughter and the prohibition against *tza'ar ba'alei chayyim* are regarded by Rambam as having been imposed "with a view to purifying the people," i.e., in order to prevent internalization of cruelty as a character trait and to promote the tested development of compassion.[18]

Although Jewish law permits consumption of meat only if the animal has been slaughtered in the prescribed manner, there is not to be found an explicit statement in the various codes or in the writings of early authorities prohibiting other forms of slaughter in situations in which the animal is killed for other purposes. If, as Rambam explicitly states, ritual slaughter is ordained to obviate *tza'ar ba'alei chayyim*, it might well be presumed that other forms of slaughter are entirely excluded. Yet, as is well known, the ramifications and applications of Jewish law in fulfilling any specific commandment frequently are not coextensive with the rationale underlying the precept.[19] Thus it cannot be assumed that other modes of killing animals are proscribed by Jewish law, particularly if the method utilized is painless.[20]

In point of fact, there is some controversy among latter-day rabbinic decisors with regard to the permissibility of putting animals to death other than by means of ritual slaughter. Some authorities maintain that the very act of killing an animal constitutes *tza'ar ba'alei chayyim*; others maintain that considerations of *tza'ar ba'alei chayyim* pertain only to the treatment of animals while they are yet alive, but do not preclude the killing of animals by any available method. Stated somewhat differently, the latter authorities maintain that the act of putting an animal to death is excluded from the prohibition against *tza'ar ba'alei chayyim*. The authorities who forbid putting an animal to death (other than for the satisfaction of a legitimate human need, as will be shown later) apparently forbid even "painless" methods, since the act of killing the animal *ipso facto* constitutes *tza'ar ba'alei chayyim*. Thus, according to those authorities, the destruction of an unwanted pet, for example, would be forbidden.

The most prominent latter-day authority to address this question directly is the preeminent eighteenth-century rabbinic decisor, R. Ezekiel Landau, *Teshuvot Noda bi-Yehudah, Mahadura Kamma, Yoreh De'ah*, no. 83. *Noda bi-Yehudah* declares emphatically that the mere killing of an animal does not involve transgression of the prohibition against *tza'ar ba'alei chayyim*, a prohibition which he regards as applicable "only if he causes [the animal] pain while alive."[21] In support of this ruling, *Noda bi Yehudah* cites a narrative reported in the Gemara, *Chullin* 7b. The narrative, in part, illustrates Gemara's assumption that a wound inflicted by a certain type of mule may be particularly dangerous in nature. It is reported that R. Judah the Prince invited R. Phinehas to dine with him. The Gemara relates:

> When R. Phinehas ben Yair arrived at the home of R. Judah, he happened to enter by a gate near which were some mules. He [R. Phinehas] exclaimed, "The angel of death is in this house! Shall I dine with him?" Rabbi [Judah] heard and went out to meet him. He said to him [R. Phinehas], "I will sell them." He [R. Phinehas] said to him [R. Judah], "Thou shalt not put a stumbling block before the blind" (Lev. 19:14). "I shall abandon them." "You would be spreading danger." "I shall hamstring them." "That would cause suffering to animals." "I shall kill them." "There is a prohibition against wanton destruction." (Deut. 20:19)

Since R. Judah suggested killing the animals after already having been apprised that mutilating them is forbidden, argues *Noda bi-Yehudah*, it may be deduced that putting an animal to death does not constitute a proscribed form of *tza'ar ba'alei chayyim*. Moreover, R. Phinehas objected to this proposal only because it would involve "wanton destruction," but not on the basis of considerations of *tza'ar ba'alei chayyim*. An argument based upon the narrative recorded in *Chullin* 7b identical to that of *Noda bi-Yehudah* was earlier advanced by R. Gershon Ashkenazi, *Teshuvot Avodat ha-Gershuni*, no. 13.[22]

It is nevertheless clear from the discussion of *Noda bi-Yehudah* that it is forbidden to put an animal to death in a manner which involves pain prior to its demise. For that reason, *Noda bi-Yehudah* declines to sanction withholding of food and water from an animal in order to cause its death. The method employed must be relatively swift in order to avoid pain to the animal while it is yet alive.

The argument advanced by *Noda bi-Yehudah* in support of his contention that the killing of an animal is not a prohibited form of *tza'ar ba'alei chayyim* is, however, rebutted by the nineteenth-century scholar, R. Joseph Saul Nathanson, *Teshuvot Sho'el u-Meshiv, Mahadura Tinyana*, III, no. 65. *Sho'el u-Meshiv* notes that the white mules in the home of R. Judah the Prince were regarded as posing a threat to human life. Ostensibly, all prohibitions, including both the prohibition against *tza'ar ba'alei chayyim* as well as "thou shalt not wantonly destroy" may be ignored in order to eliminate danger to life. However, observes *Sho'el u-Meshiv*, the danger could not have been of a significant magnitude since Rabbi Judah had already kept the mules in his custody for a significant period of time without the animals having manifested any sign of aggressive behavior. Hence, since no actual danger threatened, "wanton destruction" could not be sanctioned. However, argues *Sho'el u-Meshiv*, pain may be inflicted upon animals in order to alleviate human suffering of a comparable magnitude. Therefore, the transitory pain attendant upon the swift death of an animal would have been justified in order to eliminate even an improbable threat to human life. Hamstringing the mules would, however, have resulted in ongoing suffering on the part of the animals and could not be sanctioned since the suffering caused to the animal would have been disproportionate to the human anguish alleviated thereby.[23] Accordingly, concludes *Sho'el u-Meshiv*, it may be inferred that causing the death of an animal is justifiable only if necessary to alleviate human pain, even if such pain is minor in nature, provided that no "wanton destruction" is involved. However, it cannot be inferred that causing the death of an animal is excluded from categorization as *tza'ar ba'alei chayyim.* According to *Sho'el u-Meshiv*, the exchange between R. Phinehas and R. Judah serves only to support the conclusion that animals may be killed when necessary for human welfare but does not yield the conclusion that killing animals is excluded from the prohibition against *tza'ar ba'alei chayyim.*

A twentieth-century scholar, R. Yechiel Ya'akov Weinberg, *Seridei Esh*, III, no. 7,[24] cites a statement of the Gemara, *Avodah Zarah* 13b, in support of the position that putting an animal to death does not constitute a forbidden form of *tza'ar ba'alei chayyim.* The Gemara's discussion centers upon the problem presented by an animal that has been sanctified during the period following the destruction of the Temple. Since the animal cannot be used for its intended purpose and it is also forbidden to derive benefit from such an animal or to make use of it in any way, the animal can only serve as a vehicle for transgression. Its elimination, if halakhically permitted, would clearly be desirable. The Gemara queries, "Why can it not be made a *gistera*?", i.e., why can it not simply be killed by cutting it in half? It is evident from the question, argues *Seridei Esh*, that destroying an animal does not involve the prohibition of *tza'ar ba'alei chayyim* This argument, however, is not as compelling as it might appear. As will be shown, according to almost all authorities *tza'ar ba'alei chayyim* is permitted when designed to serve a human need. *Noda bi-Yehudah, Mahadura Kamma, Yoreh De'ah*, nos. 82–83, contends that elimination of a potential source of transgression constitutes such a need. Hence rendering the animal a *gistera* might be sanctioned, not because causing the death of an animal is uniformly permitted as not involving an infraction of strictures against *tza'ar ba'alei chayyim*, but because even though it does involve a form of *tza'ar ba'alei chayyim*, causing pain to an animal is permitted when designed to serve a human need. The query "Why can it not be made a *gistera*?" serves to establish that one of two principles is correct: Either the killing of an animal is excluded from the prohibition against *tza'ar ba'alei chayyim*, or *tza'ar ba'alei chayyim* is permitted when designed to serve a human need. Accordingly, this source does serve to establish the principle that killing an animal for a purpose designed to serve a human need does not entail transgression of strictures against *tza'ar ba'alei chayyim*.[25]

Both *Seridei Esh* and R. Judah Leib Graubart, *Teshuvot Chavalim ba-Ne'imim*, I, no. 43, sec. 4, demonstrate that *Tosafot* maintains that killing per se does not constitute an act of *tza'ar ba'alei chayyim*. The Gemara, *Baba Batra* 20a, indicates that considerations of *tza'ar ba'alei chayyim* prohibit the severing of a limb from a living animal in order that the limb may be used to feed dogs. Yet *Tosafot* states that the entire living animal may indeed be cast before dogs, which will then prey upon the animal. Thus, *Tosafot* apparently maintains that although a limb may not be torn from a living animal, nevertheless, causing the death of the animal in much the same manner does not involve transgression of the prohibition against *tza'ar ba'alei chayyim*.[26] *Teshuvot Avodat ha-Gershuni*, R. Meir Fischels, quoted by *Teshuvot Noda bi-Yehuda, Mahadura Kamma, Yoreh De'ah*, no. 82, and *Chavalim ba-Ne'imim* also cite the comment of *Tosafot, Sanhedrin* 80a, in which *Tosafot* remarks that withholding food and drink from an animal constitutes *tza'ar ba'alei chayyim* but that causing its death by use of a hatchet does not.[27]

However, the exclusion of killing animals from the prohibition of *tza'ar ba'alei chayyim* is not recognized by all authorities. Although his comments are not cited in this context by latter-day authorities, Rambam apparently maintains that the killing of an animal, in and of itself, constitutes a form of *tza'ar ba'alei chayyim*. Rambam, *Guide of the Perplexed* III 17, states:

> Divine Providence extends to every man individually. But the condition of the individual beings of other living creatures is undoubtedly the same as has been stated by Aristotle. On that account it is allowed, even commanded, to kill animals; we are permitted to use them according to our pleasure. . . . There is a rule laid down by our Sages that it is directly prohibited in the Torah to cause pain to an animal based on the words: "Wherefore hast thou smitten thine ass?" (Num. 22:32). But the object of this rule is to make us perfect; that we should not assume cruel habits; and that we should not uselessly cause pain to others; that, on the contrary, we should be prepared to show pity and mercy to all living creatures, except when necessity demands the contrary: "When thy soul longeth to eat flesh" (Deut. 12:20).[28] We should not kill animals for the purpose of practicing cruelty or for the purpose of sport.[29]

Rambam's comments regarding unnecessary killing of animals, especially as they single out for censure the killing of animals for sport, stand in sharp contrast to the position of *Noda bi-Yehudah* particularly as formulated in *Mahadura Tinyana, Yoreh De'ah*, no. 10, in which *Noda bi-Yehudah* addresses the question of the permissibility of engaging in hunting as a pastime.[30] Although *Noda bi-Yehudah* is severely critical of those who engage

in this activity, on the grounds that hunting is both frivolous and dangerous, he explicitly states that it cannot be proscribed as a form of *tza'ar
ba'alei chayyim* since, in his opinion, putting animals to death is not
encompassed within the ambit of that prohibition. A similar statement attributed to R. Joseph ibn Migas (known as Ri Migash) is quoted in *Shitah
Mekubetzet, Baba Batra* 20a. In contrast to the earlier cited comments of
Tosafot, Ri Migash states that the slaughter of a domestic animal in order to
feed its flesh to dogs constitutes no less a form of *tza'ar ba'alei chayyim*
than does the tearing of a limb from an animal while it is yet alive. Ri Migash apparently maintains that, although animals may be utilized in a usual
and customary manner in order to satisfy human needs, they may not be
subjected to pain and discomfort in conjunction with a use which is not
usual. Ri Migash contends that, since it is not customary to slaughter animals for dog food, such slaughter even if performed in the ritual manner "is
also *tza'ar ba'alei chayyim*, for it is killing and not ritual slaughter."[31]

In a similar vein, *Sefer ha-Chinnukh*, no. 451, explains that the rationale
underlying the commandment concerning ritual slaughter is the consideration of *tza'ar ba'alei chayyim* and, for that reason, it is forbidden to slaughter
an animal "even with a knife which is notched." Thus, *Sefer ha-Chinnukh*
clearly maintains that killing animals other than in the ritually prescribed
manner is a form of *tza'ar ba'alei chayyim*. Similarly, Rabbenu Nissim,
Chullin 18b, states that killing an animal by crushing its vertebrae rather than
by severing the trachea and esophagus constitutes *tza'ar ba'alei chayyim*.[32]

Latter-day authorities who maintain that putting an animal to death con-
stitutes a form of *tza'ar ba'alei chayyim* include R. Joel Sirkes, *Bayit
Chadash, Yoreh De'ah* 116, *s.v. mashkin*; R. Jacob Emden, *She'elat Ya'avetz*,
I, no. 110; R. Jacob Reischer, *Teshuvot Shevut Ya'akov*, III, no. 71; R. Eliyahu
Klatzkin, *Teshuvot Imrei Shefer*, no. 34; and R. Moshe Yonah Zweig, *Ohel
Mosheh,* I, no. 32.

She'elat Ya'avetz questions whether *tza'ar ba'alei chayyim* applies to all
living creatures, including insects and the like, or is limited to beasts of burden and domestic animals.[33] Presumably, if lower animals are excluded, it is
on the basis of the rationale that they lack highly developed nervous systems
and hence do not experience pain in a manner compararable to mammals
and vertebrates. *She'elat Ya'avetz* concludes that it is permissible to kill
harmless insects because insects are excluded from the prohibition concerning *tza'ar ba'alei chayyim* The clear inference to be drawn from these comments is that, with regard to vertebrates, *She'elat Ya'avetz* maintains that
killing per se constitutes a prohibited form of *tza'ar ba'alei chayyim*.

Echoing the earlier cited statements of Ri Migash, *Imrei Shefer* forbids the
slaughter of animals for purposes of feeding their meat to dogs and adds
the explanatory comment that it is forbidden to cause pain to an animal for the
benefit of another animal. In this regard, the constraint vis-à-vis imposition of
pain upon animals is identical with that concerning causing human suffering.

No pain may be imposed upon a human, even for the benefit of a fellow man, other than upon the consent of the person who suffers the pain. Since animals lack capacity to grant consent, pain may not be imposed upon an animal for the benefit of another member of the animal kingdom.

TZA'AR BA'ALEI CHAYYIM FOR HUMAN BENEFIT

Jewish law, at least in its normative formulation, sanctions the infliction of pain upon animals when the act which causes pain is designed to further a legitimate human purpose. This is evident from two rulings recorded in *Shulchan Arukh*. Rema, *Shulchan Arukh, Yoreh De'ah* 24:8, rules that, prior to slaughtering sheep, the wool covering the area where the neck is to be slit should be removed in order to enable the act of slaughter to be performed in the prescribed manner. *Shakh, Yoreh De'ah* 24:8, extends the same requirement to the slaughter of fowl and requires that feathers be plucked from the throat of fowl prior to slaughter. Rema, *Shulchan Arukh, Even ha-Ezer* 5:14, states even more explicitly:

> Anything which is necessary in order to effect a cure or for other matters does not entail [a violation] of the prohibition against *tza'ar ba'alei chayyim*. Therefore, it is permitted to pluck feathers from geese, and there is no concern on account of *tza'ar ba'alei chayyim*. But nevertheless people refrain [from doing so], because it constitutes cruelty.

This ruling, cited in the name of *Issur ve-Heter* 59:36, is supported by the comments of *Tosafot, Baba Mezi'a* 32b.[34] *Tosafot* poses the following question: The Gemara, *Avodah Zarah* 11a, declares that, in conjunction with the funeral rites of a monarch, it is permitted to sever the tendons of the horse upon which the king rode. This practice is permitted despite its source in pagan rituals because it is intended as an act of homage to the deceased king. If *tza'ar ba'alei chayyim* involves a biblical infraction, queries *Tosafot,* why may the animal be mutilated in this manner? *Tosafot* answers that such a practice is permitted "in honor of king[s] and prince[s] just as 'thou shalt not wantonly destroy' (Deut. 20:19) is abrogated for the sake of their honor." Insofar as the prohibition of concerning "wanton destruction" is concerned, *Tosafot*'s comment is clear. The prohibition against "wanton destruction" is not suspended or abrogated for the sake of royal honor; rather, Scripture forbids only wanton destruction of fruit trees and, by extension, of other objects of value as well. Scripture does not forbid enjoyment of consumables, since such use does not constitute "destruction." Similarly, "destruction" which serves a legitimate purpose is not proscribed, since it is not wanton or "destructive" in nature. "Destruction" for purposes of rendering homage to a deceased monarch is a legitimate use of property and hence is not forbidden. *Tosafot* apparently regards *tza'ar ba'alei chayyim* in a similar light, i.e., as forbidden only when wanton in nature,[35] but permissible when de-signed to achieve a legitimate goal.[36] Hence, declares *Tosafot*, mutilation of the royal steed in conjunction with the funeral of a monarch is permitted even though the animal experiences pain, because mutilation of the animal serves to fulfill a legitimate purpose. In accordance with this position, Rema rules that *tza'ar ba'alei chayyim* is permissible for purposes of healing or for any other legitimate purpose.[37]

Among early authorities, the permissibility of *tza'ar ba'alei chayyim* for human benefit is explicitly accepted by Ramban, *Avodah Zarah* 13b, who states that the "slaughter and causing of pain to animals is permissible for the need of man." A similar view can be inferred from the comments of Rabbenu Nissim of Gerondi, cited by *Nimukei Yosef, Baba Metzi'a* 32b; the Gemara explicitly exempts scholars and others for whom such activity would be un-seemly and undignified from the obligation of assisting in the unloading of a burden from an overladen animal. *Nimukei Yosef* questions why it is that considerations of human dignity are permitted to supersede biblical obliga-tions regarding the welfare of animals. In resolving this difficulty, *Nimukei Yosef* quotes the comments of Rabbenu Nissim, who states that "since *tza'ar ba'alei chayyim* is permitted for the use of humans,[38] *a fortiori* [it is permit-ted] for their honor."[39] Yet another early authority, Ritva, *Shabbat* 154b, main-tains that *tza'ar ba'alei chayyim* is permitted even for financial reasons, as is evident from his statement that "for the purpose of [man's] service and preservation of his money *tza'ar ba'alei chayyim* is certainly permitted."

Terumat ha-Deshen, Pesakim u-Ketavim, no. 105, regards the permissi-bility of causing suffering to animals for the benefit of mankind to be inher-ent in the biblical dispensation granting man the right to use animals for his needs.[40] R. Moses Sofer, *Hagahot Chatam Sofer, Baba Mezi'a* 32b,[41] cites the divine declaration to Adam and Eve, "and have dominion over the fish of the sea, and over the fowl of the air, and over every living thing that creepeth upon the earth" (Gen. 1:28),[42] establishing man's absolute and unlimited mastery over the animal kingdom.[43] R. Judah Leib Graubart, *Chavalim ba-Ne'imim*, I, no. 43, sec. 3, advances an identical argument on the basis of Genesis 9:1–2: "And God blessed Noah and his sons. . . . 'And the fear of you and the dread of you shall be upon every beast of the earth, and upon every fowl of the air, and upon all wherewith the ground teemeth, and upon all the fishes of the sea: into your hand are they delivered.'"

Terumat ha-Deshen, Pesakim u-Ketavim, no. 105, and R. Elijah of Vilna, *Bi'ur ha-Gra, Even ha-Ezer* 5:40, cite a number of talmudic sources as the basis of Rema's ruling. Leviticus 22:24 serves to establish a prohibition against the emasculation of animals. Although the phenomenon is unknown to modern science, the Gemara, *Shabbat* 110b, regards removal of a rooster's comb as causing the rooster to become sterile, but nevertheless permits the practice because it does not involve excision of a sexual organ.[44] This pro-cedure is permissible despite the fact that it is obviously accompanied by

pain. The attendant pain, argues *Bi'ur ha-Gra*, does not render the procedure impermissible, because it is designed to promote a human benefit.
Moreover, the Gemara, *Chagigah* 14b, tentatively considers the possibility
that Scripture forbids only the emasculation of members of those species of
animals which may be offered as sacrifices, an inference that might be drawn
from the context of Leviticus 22:24. Since castration is necessarily accompanied by pain, this possibility could be entertained only if it is accepted as an
antecedent premise that *tza'ar ba'alei chayyim* is not forbidden when necessary to achieve a beneficial result. Furthermore, these scholars indicate that
placing a heavy load upon a beast of burden, an act that is clearly sanctioned
by the Gemara, *Baba Metzi'a* 32b, is in itself a form of *tza'ar ba'alei
chayyim* and is permitted only because the prohibition does not apply in situations in which the act is undertaken for human benefit.[45]

A twentieth-century halakhist, R. Ya'akov Breisch, *Chelkat Ya'akov*, I,
no. 30, sec. 6, seeks to find further support for this position in *Taz's* understanding of a discussion recorded in the Gemara, *Chullin* 28a. In the household of Rava, the skin on the throat of a dove was found to have been
pierced and bleeding. The question confronting Rava was whether or not the
dove might yet be slaughtered and eaten. A perforation or anomaly of either
the trachea or the esophagus would have rendered the bird unfit. Since the
outer skin had been pierced, there was reason to suspect that the trachea
and/or the esophagus might have been damaged as well. Those organs
could not be examined satisfactorily subsequent to the slaughter, since a perforation or anomaly might well have been present at the site of the incision
made by the slaughterer's knife and would not be discernible subsequent to
slaughter. Moreover, since the esophagus is pink in color, it is not possible to
examine any part of the esophagus prior to slaughter because a drop of
blood might possibly be lodged at the site of the perforation and cover a
miniscule hole, or (according to *Tosafot*) the reddish color of the esophagus
itself might render a perforation or an anomaly indiscernible. Rava's son Rav
Yosef counseled that the trachea, which is white, be examined prior to
slaughter and, since fowl (as distinct from four-legged animals) require the
severance of either the trachea or the esophagus but not necessarily of both,
care be taken not to pierce the esophogus. Rav Yosef further directed that,
subsequent to slaughtering the bird, the esophagus be removed and examined along its inner surface, which is white.

This narrative serves as the basis of the normative rule to be applied in
similar situations in which an animal has experienced a trauma in the area
to be incised in the act of slaughter. The problem which arises in such instances is that the site at which the trachea is to be severed must be examined prior to slaughter. If, as must be presumed to be the case, the tear in
the skin covering the trachea is small, such an examination is impossible.
Taz, Yoreh De'ah 33:11, indicates that the tear in the skin of the throat must
be enlarged in order to examine the trachea. Clearly, enlarging the hole in

the skin covering the trachea causes pain to the animal. It must be presumed that this procedure is sanctioned despite the accompanying pain only because the procedure is necessary in order to render the bird permissible for consumption. Accordingly, this ruling would support the thesis that *tza'ar ba'alei chayyim* is permissible when necessary for human welfare. *Chelkat Ya'akov* agrees that subsequent to Rema's ruling there is no question that the procedure described by *Taz* is permissible. However, he points out that the talmudic discussion cited by *Taz* cannot be adduced as the basis of this ruling concerning *tza'ar ba'alei chayyim*. That discussion could well be understood as permitting a procedure of this nature in the rare circumstances in which the requisite visual examination of the trachea can be undertaken without further elongation of the already existing cut.

Teshuvot Shevut Ya'akov, III, no. 71,[46] and *Teshuvot Rav Pe'alim*, I, *Yoreh De'ah*, no. 1, find support for Rema's ruling in the Mishnah, *Avodah Zarah* 13b. It is forbidden to sell a solitary white chicken to an idolator for fear that he may intend to offer the bird as a pagan sacrifice. However, since a mutilated bird would not be used for idolatrous purposes, the Mishnah permits the seller to render the chicken unfit for sacrificial use by removing a digit from the chicken's foot prior to sale. Here, too, such a procedure necessarily entails pain to the chicken. Accordingly, argue *Shevut Ya'akov* and *Rav Pe'alim*, such a practice could be permitted only because it is prompted by legitimate commercial need. The procedure sanctioned by the Mishnah serves as a paradigm establishing the general principle that *tza'ar ba'alei chayyim* is permissible when necessary to satisfy a human need.[47]

Although Rema's ruling is accepted by virtually all latter-day authorities, it appears that his position is rejected by at least one early authority. The authors of the commentary of *Tosafot* on *Avodah Zarah* 11a pose the selfsame question with regard to the mutilation of the royal steed as raised in the commentary of *Tosafot* on *Baba Metzi'a* 32b. However, in their commentary on *Avodah Zarah*, the authors of *Tosafot* resolve the problem in an entirely different manner.[48] But, since the problem is completely dispelled on the premise that *tza'ar ba'alei chayyim* is permissible for human benefit, *Tosafot's* failure to resolve the problem in that manner in the commentary on *Avodah Zarah* presumably reflects the fact that the authors of the *Tosafot* on that tractate (in disagreement with the view of the authors of *Tosafot* on *Baba Mezi'a*) regard *tza'ar ba'alei chayyim* as not permissible even when designed to promote human benefit.[49]

A somewhat modified position is espoused by R. Joseph Teumim, *Pri Megadim*, *Orach Chayyim*, *Mishbetzot Zahav* 468:2. *Pri Megadim* reports that his advice was sought by an individual who maintained exotic birds in his garden and was fearful that they might take flight. The interlocutor sought a ruling with regard to the propriety of breaking "a small bone in their wings" in order to render them incapable of flight and prevent financial loss to their keeper. *Pri Megadim's* response was negative, for, in his opinion, "*tza'ar ba'alei chayyim*, other than in case of great need, is forbidden." Apparently, *Pri Megadim* distinguishes between ordinary "need" or "benefit" and "great need," and sanctions *tza'ar ba'alei chayyim* only in the latter situation. In a similar vein, *Teshuvot Avodat ha-Gershuni*, no. 13, quotes a certain R. Tevel the Physician as declaring that *tza'ar ba'alei chayyim* cannot be sanctioned for purposes of realizing "a small profit."

There is also some controversy with regard to the nature of the need or benefit which is deemed to warrant causing pain to animals. *Issur ve-Heter he-Arukh* 59:36, cites a version of *Tosafot* which differs from the published texts. *Issur ve-Heter he-Arukh* states that, in declaring that *tza'ar ba'alei chayyim*, "if it is efficacious for some matter," is permissible, *Tosafot* intends to permit *tza'ar ba'alei chayyim* only for therapeutic purposes, including procedures necessary for the treatment of even non-life-threatening maladies.[50] Thus, *Issur ve-Heter* apparently regards *tza'ar ba'alei chayyim* which is designed to serve other needs, e.g., financial profit, as improper and forbidden.[51]

Among latter-day authorities, R. Yitzchak Dov Bamberger is quoted by R. Jacob Ettlinger, *Teshuvot Binyan Tsion*, no. 108, as asserting that Rema permits *tza'ar ba'alei chayyim* "only when there is need for medical purposes even for a patient who is not dangerously ill, but we have not found that he permitted *tza'ar ba'alei chayyim* for financial profit."[52] This interpretation of Rema is difficult to sustain for two reasons: (1) Rema, *Shulchan Arukh, Even ha-Ezer* 5:14, rules that "anything which is necessary in order to effect a cure *or for other matters* does not entail [a violation] of the prohibition against *tza'ar ba'alei chayyim*." (2) Rema, *Shulchan Arukh, Yoreh De'ah* 24:8, indicates that plucking feathers from a live bird is permissible as a matter of normative law. The feathers plucked in this manner are designed for use as quills. No one has suggested that the procedure is permitted only if the quill is needed by that physician in order to write a prescription; indeed, such an interpretation could not be sustained, since Rema's caveat regarding the nonacceptability of such practices does not apply to procedures required by reason of medical need.[53] Nevertheless, R. Moshe Yonah Zweig, *Ohel Mosheh*, I no. 32, sec. 11, cites Rabbi Bamberger's position as meriting serious consideration.[54] Rabbi Ettlinger himself, however, distinguishes between "great pain" and "minor pain," and permits minor pain for other "definite" benefits as well.[55] R. Eliyahu Klatzkin, *Teshuvot Imrei Shefer*, no. 34, sec. 1, adopts an intermediate position in stating that Rema intended to permit *tza'ar ba'alei chayyim* for medical purposes or for purposes of similar importance and necessity, but not simply for the purpose of similar, financial gain. *Imrei Shefer* does not indicate what these purposes of similar necessity might be. In support of the position that *tza'ar ba'alei chayyim* may not be sanctioned for financial gain, *Teshuvot Imrei Shefer*, no. 34, sec. 1, cites the statement of the Gemara, *Baba Batra* 20a. The Gemara forbids the severing of a limb from a live animal in order to feed it to dogs because of considerations of *tza'ar ba'alei chayyim*. *Imrei Shefer* notes that were the limb to be fed to the dogs, their master would benefit financially in not having to provide other food on their behalf. Moreover, notes *Imrei Shefer*, in the case under discussion, the limb had already been severed but remained attached to the body. The removal of such a "hanging" limb, asserts *Imrei Shefer*, would not significantly increase the animal's pain. Evidently, then, concludes *Imrei Shefer*, monetary gain is not sufficient to obviate the prohibition concerning *tza'ar ba'alei chayyim*.[56]

However, the majority of rabbinic authorities regard financial gain as a legitimate "need" or "benefit" which, at least as a matter of law, may be fostered even at the expense of *tza'ar ba'alei chayyim*. The comments of a number of authorities who espouse this view have been cited earlier. Other authorities who permit *tza'ar ba'alei chayyim* for monetary advantage include R. Moses Sofer, *Hagahot Chatam Sofer, Baba Metzi'a* 32b,[57] who remarks that the prohibition does not apply when the act is performed "for the benefit of human beings, their honor[58] or financial benefit."[59] An identical position is adopted by *Teshuvot Avodat ha-Gershuni*, no. 13; *Teshuvot Noda bi-Yehudah, Mahadura Tinyana, Yoreh De'ah*, no. 10, *s.v. ve-omnam*;[60] *Teshuvot Panim Me'irot*, I, no. 75; *Teshuvot Pri Yitzchak*, I, no. 24; and *Teshuvot Yad Eliyahu, Ketavim* 3:5.[61] *Pri Chadash, Yoreh De'ah* 53:7, permits the severing of a broken wing from a bird so that the jagged edge will not perforate an internal organ and thereby render the bird nonkosher and hence unfit for consumption. According to *Pri Chadash, tza'ar ba'alei chayyim* is warranted under such circumstances because of potential financial loss. Among contemporary authorities, a similar view is expressed by R. Yitzchak Ya'akov Weisz, *Teshuvot Minchat Yitzchak*, VI, no. 145.

MORALITY BEYOND THE REQUIREMENTS OF THE LAW

Despite his ruling that plucking feathers from a live bird for use as quills is permitted as a matter of law, Rema adds the comment that people refrain from doing so because of the inherent cruelty involved in this practice.[62] The immediate source both of this caveat and of the normative ruling regarding the plucking of feathers is the fifteenth-century rabbinic decisor R. Israel Isserlein, *Terumat ha-Deshen, Pesakim u-Ketavim*, no. 105. *Terumat ha-Deshen*, however, elaborates somewhat and presents a talmudic source for the popular renunciation of this practice. *Terumat ha-Deshen* states, "and perhaps the reason is that people do not wish to act with the trait of cruelty vis-à-vis creatures, for they fear lest they receive punishment for that, as we find in chapter *Ha-Po'alim* with regard to our holy teacher."[63] It is particularly noteworthy that *Terumat ha Deshen* suggests the possibility of divine punishment for cruelty toward animals even in a situation in which no infraction of normative law is involved.[64]

The talmudic source cited by *Terumat ha-Deshen* is an anecdote concerning R. Judah the Prince related by the Gemara, *Baba Metzi'a* 85a.[65] R. Judah suffered excruciating pain for many years until the pain subsided suddenly. In the following narrative, the Gemara explains both why R. Judah experienced suffering and why the suffering was ultimately alleviated:

> A calf, when it was being to taken to slaughter, went and hung its head under Rabbi [Judah]'s cloak and cried. He said to it, "Go, for this wast thou created." [In heaven] they said, "Since he has no mercy, let suffering come upon him." . . . One day, Rabbi [Judah]'s maidservant was sweeping the house; some young weasels were lying there, and she was sweeping them away. Rabbi [Judah] said to her, "Let them be; it is written, 'And His tender mercies are over all His works.' (Ps. 145:9)" [In heaven] they said, "Since he is compassionate, let us be compassionate to him."

Reflected in this account, and in the halakhic principle derived therefrom, is the distinction between normative law and ethical conduct above and beyond the requirements of law (*lifnim mi-shurat ha-din*).[66] In its normative law, Judaism codifies standards applicable to everyone and makes no demands that are beyond the capacity of the common man; but, at the same time, Jewish teaching recognizes that, ideally, man must aspire to a higher level of conduct. That higher standard is posited as a moral desideratum, albeit a norm which is not enforceable by human courts. Not every person succeeds in reaching a degree of moral excellence such that he perceives the need and obligation to conduct himself in accordance with that higher standard. Those who do attain such a level of moral perfection are obliged, at least in the eyes of Heaven, to conduct themselves in accordance with that higher standard. No human court can inquire into the degree of moral perfection attained by a particular individual and, hence, such a court cannot apply varying standards to different persons. The heavenly court, however, *is* in a position to do so and, accordingly, will punish a person who does not comport himself in accordance with the degree of moral perfection which he has attained. Thus, the Gemara, *Baba Kamma* 50a, cites the verse "And it shall be very tempestuous about Him" (Ps. 50:3) and, in a play on the Hebrew word *se'arah*, which connotes both "tempestuous" and "hair," declares that "the Holy One, blessed be He, is particular with those around Him, even with regard to matters as light as a single hair."

R. Yechiel Ya'akov Weinberg, *Seridei Esh*, III, no. 7, hastens to point out that Rema's cautionary statement with regard to normatively permitted forms of *tza'ar ba'alei chayyim* should not be construed as applicable to medical experimentation. In a short comment, *Seridei Esh* rejects the application of Rema's remarks to medical experimentation for what really are three distinct reasons: (1) Moral stringencies beyond the requirements of law are personal in nature; a person may accept stringencies of piety for himself but may not impose them upon others. (2) Elimination of pain and suffering of human beings takes precedence over considerations of animal pain. (3) The concern for avoiding pain to animals, even when it is halakhically permitted to cause such pain, is germane only at the cost of forgoing benefit to an individual, but not when benefit may accrue to the public at large. The last point is supported by the fact that no hesitation is expressed with regard to inflicting pain upon animals for the sake of "the honor of kings," which is tantamount to the honor of the entire community, as evidenced by the earlier cited statement of the Gemara, *Avodah Zarah* 11a, which sanctions hamstringing the steed of the deceased monarch.

Seridei Esh's comments are in opposition to the view expressed by *Chelkat Ya'akov*, I, no. 30, sec. 6, to the effect that, although medical experimentation upon animals is certainly permissible as a matter of law,[67] nevertheless, in accordance with Rema's caveat, it is proper to refrain from inflicting pain upon animals even for such purposes "as a matter of piety to preserve [oneself] from the trait of cruelty." More recently, a member of the Supreme Rabbinical Court of Israel, R. Eliezer Waldenberg, *Tzitz Eli'ezer*, XIV, no. 68, found no difficulty in supporting medical experimentation upon animals, but urged that pain be minimized insofar as possible.

In one of the earliest responses which specifically address the question of the permissibility of animal experimentation, *Shevut Ya'akov*, III, no. 71, draws yet another distinction between plucking feathers, which is eschewed as a form of cruelty, and certain types of medical experimentation. *Shevut Ya'akov* was asked whether the toxicity of certain medications might be tested by feeding them to dogs or cats. *Shevut Ya'akov* replies in the affirmative and states that feeding a possibly poisonous substance to an animal is not comparable to plucking the feathers of a goose. In the latter case, the pain is caused directly and is immediately perceived with the plucking of each feather. On the other hand, the pain caused to an animal as a result of imbibing a poisonous substance is neither direct nor immediate; and hence, rules *Shevut Ya'akov*, there is no reason to refrain from such experimentation, "even as an act of piety." The cogency of this distinction lies in the recognition that, according to Rema, the concern with regard to *tza'ar ba'alei chayyim* in cases in which a human need exists is not with regard to the welfare of the animal but with regard to the possible moral degeneration of the human agent, who may acquire traits of cruelty as a result of performing acts which are objectively cruel even when such acts are warranted under the attendant circumstances. Apparently, *Shevut Ya'akov* feels that concern for developing a cruel disposition exists only when the human act is the immediate and proximate cause of perceivable pain, but not when the act is not immediately associated with the pain experienced by the animal. Quite obviously, *Shevut Ya'akov*'s distinction does not apply to forms of medical experimentation in which the pain is immediately attendant upon the procedure performed, e.g., unanesthetized vivisection, while the criteria formulated by *Seridei Esh* apply to such situations as well.

It should, however, be noted that the foregoing analysis of the consideration underlying the practice of refraining from plucking feathers from a live
animal is not at all obvious. As has been noted earlier, *Terumat ha-Deshen,*
who is the source of Rema's remarks, declares that this practice is eschewed
because of fear of punishment for causing pain to animals even when the
practice is entirely permissible, as is evidenced in the narrative concerning
R. Judah and the calf recorded in the Gemara, *Baba Metzi'a* 85a. Ostensibly,
the concern reflected in that report is for the welfare of the animal. However,
R. Judah Leib Zirelson, *Ma'arkhei Lev,* no. 110, interprets that narrative in a
manner entirely compatible with what appears to be the premise underlying
the distinction formulated by *Shevut Ya'akov. Ma'arkhei Lev* asserts that it is
inconceivable that R. Judah was punished for allowing the calf to be slaughtered for its meat. Rather, declares *Ma'arkhei Lev,* he was punished for his
outburst, "Go, for this wast thou created." That sharp remark betrayed a lack
of sensitivity which was inappropriate for a person of R. Judah's moral
stature. Thus it was for his own lack of sensitivity that R. Judah was punished, rather than for the suffering caused to the calf.[68]

Ma'arkhei Lev himself draws a much broader distinction between the
conduct frowned upon by Rema and other uses to which animals may be
put without breach of even the "trait of piety" commended by Rema. According to *Ma'arkhei Lev,* the crucial factor is the element of necessity.
Quills may be removed from dead fowl as readily as from live ones. Hence,
plucking feathers from a live bird is an entirely unnecessary act of cruelty,
even though the act itself serves a human purpose. According to *Ma'arkhei
Lev,* in any situation in which there exists a need which cannot otherwise
be satisfied, it is not improper to cause discomfort to animals, and refraining from doing so does not even constitute an act of piety. R. Judah was
punished, asserts *Ma'arkhei Lev,* because his sharp and impulsive remark
was entirely gratuitous. In support of this thesis, *Ma'arkhei Lev* cites a ruling recorded in *Shulchan Arukh, Orah Chayyim,* 362:5. On the Sabbath, it
is permissible to carry objects only within an enclosed area. *Shulchan
Arukh* rules that an enclosure may be formed by stationing animals in a
manner such that they constitute a "wall," but only on the condition that
the animals are bound so that they remain immobile. Animals forced to remain in a stationary position for the duration of an entire Sabbath day certainly experience discomfort. Nevertheless, none of the commentaries on
Shulchan Arukh indicate that, in light of Rema's caveat regarding plucking
feathers from a live fowl, the practice of utilizing animals for fashioning a
"wall" should be eschewed.[69] The reason that they fail to do so, argues
Ma'arkhei Lev, lies in the distinction which must be drawn between a use
of animals which is essential for achieving a purpose pertaining to human
welfare and one which, while it serves a purpose, is nevertheless not absolutely necessary in order to achieve the desired end.[70]

CONCLUSIONS

Jewish law clearly forbids any act which causes pain or discomfort to an animal unless such act is designed to satisfy a legitimate human need. All authorities agree that hunting as a sport is forbidden. Although many authorities maintain that it is not forbidden to engage in activities which cause pain to animals in situations in which such practices yield financial benefits, there is significant authority for the position that animal pain may be sanctioned only for medical purposes, including direct therapeutic benefit, medical experimentation of potential therapeutic value, and the training of medical personnel.[71] *A fortiori*, those who eschew the latter position, would not sanction painful procedures for the purpose of testing or perfecting cosmetics. An even larger body of authority refuses to sanction the infliction of pain upon animals when the desired benefit can be acquired in an alternative manner,[72] when the procedure involves "great pain,"[73] when the benefit does not serve to satisfy a "great need,"[74] when the same profit can be obtained in another manner,[75] or when the benefit derived is not commensurate with the measure of pain to which the animal is subjected.[76] Even when the undertaking is designed to promote human welfare, there is greater justification for causing the swift and painless death of an animal than for subjecting it to procedures which cause suffering to a live animal.

Judaism recognizes moral imperatives which establish standards more stringent than the standard of conduct imposed by law. According to the view of most authorities, those moral imperatives should prompt man to renounce cruelty to animals even when the contemplated procedure would serve to promote human welfare.

Medical experimentation designed to produce therapeutic benefit to mankind constitutes an exception to this principle[77] and is endorsed by virtually all rabbinic authorities. Nevertheless, as stated by R. Eliezer Waldenberg, *Tzitz Eli'ezer*, XIV, no. 68, sec. 7, it is no more than proper that, whenever possible, such experimentation be conducted in a manner such that any unnecessary pain is avoided and, when appropriate, the animal subject should be anesthetized.

NOTES

From J. David Bleich, *Contemporary Halakhic Problems, Volume III* (New York: Ktav Publishing House and Yeshiva University Press, 1989), 194–236.

1. *Die Beiden Grundprobleme der Ethik* (Frankfurt A.M., 1841), 243–44; trans. Arthur B. Bullock as *The Basis of Morality* (London, 1915), 218. See also Arthur Schopenhauer, *The World as Will and Representation*, trans. E. F. J. Payne (New York, 1957), II, 645.

2. The obligation of *imitatio Dei* is derived from the verse "and thou shalt walk in His ways" (Deut. 28:9). See Rambam, *Hilkhot De'ot* 1:5–6.

3. See also narratives concerning R. Eliyahu Lapian recounted by Aaron Soraski. *Marbitzei Torah u-Musar* (Brooklyn, 5737), IV, 165, and concerning *Chazon Ish* by R. Shlomoh Cohen, *Pe'er ha-Dor* (Bnei Brak, 5726), I, 175. It is told of the Chasidic master R. Zusya of Anapole that, saddened by the sight of caged birds, he would purchase them from their owner in order to set them free. He informed his disciples that he regarded this to be a form of "ransoming Prisoners," which constitutes a moral imperative.

4. See Me'iri, *Baba Metzi'a* 33a, and *Sefer ha-Chinnukh*, no. 596. The purpose of other biblical laws pertaining to animals is less clear-cut. The prohibition against plowing with animals of different species, recorded in Deut. 22:10, is understood by *Sefer ha-Chinnukh*, no. 550, as well as by *Da'at Zekenim mi-Ba'alei ha-Tosafot* and *Ba'al ha-Turim* in their respective commentaries on Deut. 22:10, as rooted in considerations of prevention of cruelty to animals, but is understood in an entirely different manner by Rambam, *Guide of the Perplexed* III 49, as well as by Ramban in his commentary on Deut. 22:10. However, Rambam, *Guide* III 48, regards the prohibition against slaughtering an animal and its young on the same day, recorded in Lev. 22:28, as a precautionary measure designed to prevent the slaughter of the offspring in the presence of its parent. The underlying concern is to spare the mother the anguish of seeing her young killed before her eyes, "for in these cases animals feel very great pain, there being no difference regarding this pain between man and the other animals. For the love and the tenderness of a mother for her child is not consequent upon reason, but upon the activity of the imaginative faculty, which is found in most animals just as it is found in man." Here, Rambam speaks of concern for the welfare of the animal rather than for the moral character of the human agent; see below, notes 14–15 and accompanying text. This interpretation is reflected in the comments of R. Bahya ben Asher, Lev. 22:28, and, in part, in *Sefer ha-Chinnukh*, no. 294. *Sefer ha-Chinnukh* regards the commandment prohibiting the slaughter of an animal and its young on the same day as designed both to spare the parent from anguish and as a conservation measure as well. See also Abarbanel's *Commentary on the Bible*, ad loc. Rambam's analysis of the rationale underlying this precept is rejected by Ramban in his *Commentary on the Bible*, Deut. 22:6. According to Ramban, the concern is not to avoid pain to the animal but to purge man of callousness, cruelty, and savagery.

Although the Gemara, *Baba Metzi'a* 32a, declares that assistance in unloading a burden from an animal is mandated by reason of *tza'ar ba'alei chayyim* but that the obligation to assist in loading the burden upon the animal is not independently mandated by reason of *tza'ar ba'alei chayyim*, Ritva, cited by *Shitah Mekubezet*, *Baba Metzi'a* 3 1a, s.v. *aval te'inah*, asserts that the commandment requiring a person to render assistance to another who is engaged in loading an animal is predicated upon considerations of *tza'ar ba'alei chayyim*. According to Ritva, a single person engaged in this task is likely to cause additional discomfort to the animal by applying the full force of his body weight whereas, when he is assisted by another, there is no need to apply similar pressure.

Sefer ha-Chinnukh, no. 186, is of the opinion that the prohibition against the slaughter of sanctified animals outside the Temple precincts is rooted in considerations of *tza'ar ba'alei chayyim*. According to *Sefer ha-Chinnukh*, such slaughter is forbidden because no purpose is served thereby and hence constitutes *tza'ar ba'alei chayyim*. See below, note 29.

Neither the prohibition against mating animals of different species, Lev. 19:19, nor the prohibition against emasculation of animals, Lev. 22:24, is understood by classical rabbinic scholars as rooted in considerations of animal welfare. For a discussion of animal welfare as a possible rationale associated with other commandments, see R. Joel Schwartz, *Ve-Rachamav al Kol Ma'asav* (Jerusalem, 5744), 11–16.

5. The requirement that the parent bird be released before the young are taken and the concomitant prohibition against taking both the parent and the young, recorded in Deuteronomy 22:6–7, quite obviously have the effect of sparing the parent from anguish. The Mishnah, *Berakhot* 33b, however, does not view this desideratum, laudable as it may be, as the underlying purpose of the commandment. Cf., however, Rambam, *Guide* III 48; Ramban, *Commentary on the Bible*, Deut. 22:6; and *Sefer ha-Chinnukh*, no. 545.

6. See *Berakhot* 41a and *Gittin* 62a. See also Rambam, *Hilkhot Avadim* 9:8; R. Meir Rothenberg, *Teshuvot Maharam ben Barukh he-Chadashhot*, no. 302; R. Jacob Reisher, *Teshuvot Shevut Ya'akov*, II, no. 13; *Magen Avraham, Orach Chayyim* 167:18 and 271:12; *Chayyei Adam* 45:1; and R. Joel Schwartz, *Ve-Rachamav al Kol Ma'asav*, 59–62. R. Jacob Emden, *She'elat Ya'avetz*, 1, no. 17, rules that there is no absolute requirement to feed a dog or a cat before eating oneself, since those animals sustain themselves on table scraps and forage for foods; but that it is nevertheless proper to feed them first in order "to acquire the trait of compassion." *Magen Avraham, Orach Chayyim* 324:7, declares that providing food for any animal, including animals belonging to other persons and ownerless animals, constitutes a *mitzvah*. See also R. Simeon ben Tzemach Duran, *Teshuvot Tashbaz*, III, no. 293; R. Jacob Ettlinger, *Teshuvot Binyan Tzion*, no. 103; and R. Eliyahu Klatzkin, *Teshuvot Imrei Shefer*, no. 34, sec. 1. Cf. R. Moses Sofer, *Teshuvot Chatam Sofer, Yoreh De'ah*, no. 314, *s.v. ve-la'asot*, and no. 318, *s.v. ve-hinneh*.

7. Similarly, Scripture records that Laban gave straw to the camels, and only afterwards did he provide food for Abraham's servant. See Gen. 24:32–33 and *Sefer Chasidim* (ed. Reuben Margulies), no. 531. Cf., R. Joel Schwartz, *Ve-Rachamav al Kol Ma'asav*, 60, n. 4.

8. The same authority, *Sefer ha-Chinnukh*, no. 540, asserts that the obligation to come to the assistance of an animal that has fallen applies equally with regard to assisting a person who is overladen. See also Rambam, *Sefer ha-Mitzvot, mitzvot aseh*, no. 203, and *mitzvot lo ta'aseh*, no. 270. This is also the position of R. Solomon ben Adret, *Teshuvot ha-Rashba*, 1, nos. 252, 256, 257. Cf., however, R. David ibn Zimra, *Teshuvot ha-Radbaz*, 1, no. 728, and R. Ya'ir Chaim Bacharach, *Teshuvot Chavot Ya'ir*, no. 191.

9. For a full analysis, see commentary of Rabbenu Nissim, *ad loc.*, and R. Joseph Babad, *Minchat Chinnukh*, no. 80

10. Whether *tza'ar ba'alei chayyim* is prohibited by virtue of biblical or of rabbinic law is of no significance whatsoever insofar as the normative regulations prohibiting overt acts of cruelty vis-à-vis animals are concerned. There are, however, a number of distinctions, albeit most of them are currently of relatively minor impact, with regard to the duty to intervene in order to relieve or prevent animal suffering. The most obvious distinctions are those posited by the Gemara, *Baba Metzi'a* 33a: "[If thou seest the ass of him that hateth thee lying under its burden] 'lying' [just now],

but not an animal which habitually lies down [under its burden]; 'lying,' but not stand-ing." The Gemara then queries, "If you say that [relieving the suffering of an animal] is biblically [enjoined], what does it matter whether it was lying [this once only], ha-bitually lay down, or was standing?" It concludes that such distinctions are cogent only if *tza'ar ba'alei chayyim.* is the subject of rabbinic enactment, but that such ex-clusions from the duty to relieve animals from pain cannot be entertained if *tza'ar ba'alei chayyim.* is a matter of biblical law. Indeed, it is Rambam's failure to make such distinctions which, in part, prompts *Kesef Mishneh, Hilkhot Rotzeach* 13:9, to conclude that Rambam maintains that *tza'ar ba'alei chayyim* is biblically enjoined. On the basis of the discussion recorded in *Baba Metzi'a* 33a, *Minchat Chinnukh*, no. 80, concludes that intervention to rescue an animal from pain is mandated only if *tza'ar ba'alei chayyim.* is mandated by biblical law, whereas, if *tza'ar ba'alei chayyim* is the subject of rabbinic decree, such legislation only prohibits acts of cru-elty but does not command intervention. See below, note 11. See also Mahari Perla, Commentary on *Sefer ha-Mitzvot* of R. Sa'adia Ga'on, *aseh* 24, *s.v. ve-adayin tzarikh*. [Cf., however, R. Moses Sofer, *Teshuvot Chatam Sofer, Yoreh De'ah*, no. 314, *s.v. ve-la'asot*, and no. 318, *s.v. ve-hinneh*, who apparently maintains that the obligation to rescue an animal from pain is limited to one's own animals. See also *Teshuvot Chatam Sofer, Choshen Mishpat*, no. 185, *s.v. ma she-katavta me-Rabad*. Thus, *Chatam Sofer* maintains that, although an overt act of cruelty toward any animal is forbidden, one may allow an ownerless animal to starve. See, however, R. Ezekiel Landau, *Teshuvot Noda bi-Yehudah, Mahadura Kamma, Yoreh De'ah*, nos. 81–83, who fails to draw a distinction of this nature. See also *Kitzur Shulchan Arukh* 191:1 and sources cited by R. Eliyahu Klatzkin, *Teshuvot Imrei Shefer*, no. 34, sec. 1.] An-other distinction is found in the application of certain Sabbath restrictions. If it is ac-cepted that obligations with regard to *tza'ar ba'alei chayyim.* are biblical in origin, a non-Jew may be requested to perform acts of labor on the Sabbath, e.g., milking a cow, in order to relieve the animal's discomfort, and certain specific rabbinically pro-scribed acts may also be performed even by a Jew in order to alleviate the animal's pain; but no suspension of Sabbath restrictions is countenanced if duties with regard to *tza'ar ba'alei chayyim.* are the product of rabbinic enactment. See Ritva, *Baba Metzi'a* 32b, as well as Rosh, *Baba Metzi'a* 2:29 and *Shabbat* 18:3; see also *Magen Avraham, Orach Chayyim* 305:11, and *Korban Netanel, Shabbat* 18:3, sec. 50. [Cf., however, *Teshuvot Rav Pe'alim*, 1, *Yoreh De'ah*, no. 1, who maintains that such ac-tions are permitted only when the life of the animal is endangered. Failure to milk a cow, he asserts, endangers the animal.] There is some controversy with regard to whether a non-Jew may be directed to perform a rabbinically proscribed act; see *En-cyclopedia Talmudit*, II, 45. According to the authorities who adopt a permissive po-sition with regard to this question, such a procedure would be permissible with re-gard to *tza'ar ba'alei chayyim.* as well, were it accepted that regulations concerning *tza'ar ba'alei chayyim.* are rabbinic in nature. [The citation of *Pilpula Charifta, Baba Metzi'a* 2:29, in this context by R. Ze'ev Metzger in his useful survey, "Nisuyim Re-fu'iyim be-Ba'alei Chayyim," *Ha-Refu'ah le-Or ha-Halakhah*, vol. II, pt. 3 (Jerusalem, 5743), 11, appears to be inaccurate.] See also below, n. 52.

11. It is the virtually unanimous opinion of rabbinic decisors that obligations with regard to *tza'ar ba'alei chayyim.* are biblical in nature. See Rif, *Shabbat* 128b; *Sefer ha-Chinnukh*, nos. 450–51; Rosh, *Baba Metzi'a* 2:29 and *Shabbat* hat 3:18; *Nim-mukei Yosef, Baba Metzi'a* 32b; Me'iri, *Baba Metzi'a* 32b; *Shitah Mekubetzet, Baba*

Metzi'a 33a; *Sefer Yere'im*, no. 267; *Sefer Chasidim* (ed. Reuben Margulies), no. 666; Rema, *Choshen Mishpat* 272:9; *Levush, Orach Chayyim* 305:18; and *Magen Avraham, Orach Chayyim* 305:11.

Rambam, both in his *Commentary on the Mishnah*, *Beitzah* 3:4, and in the *Guide*, III 17, affirms that the prohibition against *tza'ar ba'alei chayyim* is biblical in origin. There is some dispute regarding the proper understanding of the position adopted by Rambam in his *Mishneh Torah*. Although in *Hilkhot Shabbat* 25:26 Rambam appears to adopt the identical position, the language employed in *Hilkhot Rotzeach* 13:9 is somewhat ambiguous. Nevertheless, *Kesef Mishneh*, ad loc., understands even the latter source as consistent with the view that the prohibition against *tza'ar ba'alei chayyim.* is biblical in nature. However, *Pnei Yehoshu'a*, *Baba Metzi'a* 32b, and R. Elijah of Vilna, both in his *Hagahot ha-Gra al ha-Rosh*, *Baba Metzi'a* ch. 2, sec. 29:1, and in his *Bi'ur ha-Gra*, *Choshen Mishpat* 272:11, understand Rambam's ruling in *Hilkhot Rotzeach* as reflecting the view that these strictures are rabbinic in nature. See also *Minchat im Chinnukh*, no. 80.

Pri Megadim, Orach Chayyim, Eshel Avraham 308:68, and R. Meir Simchah ha-Kohen of Dvinsk, *Or Sameach*, *Hilkhot Shabbat* 25:26, both resolve any apparent contradiction in Rambam's rulings by asserting that in *Hilkhot Shabbat* Rambam's intention is only to affirm the biblical nature of the obligation concerning the requirement that animals be permitted to rest on the Sabbath and that it is that biblical law which prompted suspension of certain rabbinic restrictions regarding Sabbath regulations in order to prevent suffering by animals on the Sabbath. In comments which are at variance with his own heretofore cited thesis, *Or Sameach*, *Hilkhot Rotzeach*, 13:9, offers a novel analysis of Rambam's position. Or Sameach here asserts that Rambam affirms the biblical nature of strictures against *tza'ar ba'alei chayyim.*, but that Rambam distinguishes between practicing cruelty toward animals, which is forbidden, and intervention in an overt manner to spare the animal from discomfort. According to these comments of *Or Sameach*, there is no requirement that a person discomfit himself in order to promote the welfare of an animal. See also R. Jacob Kamenetsky, *Iyyunim be-Mikra* (New York, 5744), Num. 22:32.

Mordekhai, Baba Metzi'a 2:263, rules that *tza'ar ba'alei chayyim.* is biblically enjoined, but, in his work on *Avodah Zarah* 1:799, the same authority rules that such strictures are rabbinic in nature. *Chiddushei Anshei Shem*, *Baba Metzi'a*, sec. 20, endeavors to resolve the contradiction by asserting that, according to *Mordekhai*, "grave pain" (*tza'ar gadol*) involves a biblical prohibition whereas "minor pain" (*tza'ar mu'at*) involves only a rabbinic injunction. It is noteworthy that, according to the *Chiddushei Anshei Shem*, causing an animal to die of starvation involves only "minor pain," whereas killing an animal in an overt manner is categorized as entailing "grave pain." [See, however, R. Jacob Ettlinger, *Teshuvot Binyan Tzion*, no. 108, who states that "perhaps" causing an animal to die of starvation entails "grave pain."] *Nimukei Yosef, Baba Metzi'a* 32b, quite independently draws a similar distinction between "grave pain" and "minor pain" without in any way referring to Rambam's statements. According to *Nimukei Yosef*, "minor pain" is the subject of rabbinic injunction, while "grave pain" is biblically proscribed. See also Ritva, *Avodah Zarah* 11a.

As will be shown later, a latter-day authority, R. Jacob Ettlinger, *Teshuvot Binyan Tzion*, no. 108, permits causing an animal "grave pain" only for purposes of medical needs but permits "minor pain" even for lesser reasons, at least insofar as normative law is concerned.

12. See also Rabad, quoted in *Shitah Mekubetzet, Baba Metzi'a* 32b, s.v. *teda*, and *Levush, Orach Chayyim* 305:18. If obligations concerning *tza'ar ba'alei chayyim* are derived from the commandment concerning "unloading," it would certainly seem to follow that this obligation is not limited to a prohibition against cruelty but includes a positive obligation to intervene in order to rescue from pain. See R. Joel Schwartz, *Ve-Rachamav al Kol Ma'asav*, 43, n. 3, and cf. above, n. 10.

13. See below, note 43.

14. See also *Minchat Chinnukh*, no. 80.

15. It must, however, be noted that, even with regard to rights enjoyed by humans, the emphasis in Jewish law is upon the notion of "duty" rather than "right." Thus, satisfaction of a debt is actionable, not primarily as enforcement of the creditor's right, but as a means of compelling fulfillment of the religio-moral obligation of the debtor. In all matters of jurisprudence, the emphasis is upon prevention of moral degeneration attendant upon the misappropriation of property belonging to another, rather than upon satisfaction of the claim of the rightful owner. In adjudicating claims between litigants, the *Bet Din* acts, as is its duty, primarily to compel fulfillment of a religio-moral duty rather than to redress a wrong. See Moshe Silberg, "Law and Morals in Jewish Jurisprudence," *Harvard Law Review* 75 (1961–62): 306–31. Proper comportment vis-à-vis animals would similarly be compelled by the court as the fulfillment of a religious obligation.

16. See also Ramban's comments in his *Commentary on the Bible*, Deut. 22:6.

17. Indeed, *shechitah* is the most humane method of slaughter known to man. The procedure involves a transverse cut in the throat of the animal with an extremely sharp and smooth knife. Due to the sharpness of the knife and the paucity of sensory cutaneous nerve endings in the skin covering the throat, the incision itself causes no pain. The incision severs the carotid arteries as well as the jugular veins. The resultant massive loss of blood causes the animal to become unconscious in a matter of seconds. There is ample clinical evidence confirming the total absence of pain to the animal as a result of *shechitah*. This has long been recognized by scientists of international repute. In view of recurring misinformed attacks upon *shechitah*, it is instructive to cite at length a portion of a detailed, clarificatory statement authored by Dr. Leonard Hill, Professor of Physiology, University of London, and Director of Applied Physiology, National Institute for Medical Research, which appeared in *Lancet* 205 (1923): 1382 [reprinted in Solomon David Sassoon, *A Critical Study of Electrical Stunning and The Jewish Method of Slaughter (Shechita)* (3rd. ed; Letchworth, 1955), 4–6]. Dr. Hill writes:

It is generally assumed by laymen that the shooting is much more humane than the older methods. They suppose that the cutting of the throat is a most painful operation, and that struggling movements are necessarily a sign of pain. Educated in the false ideas and statements of writers of romance, they are easily led astray by agitators having no knowledge of physiological science, nor surgical experience. Now the surgeon knows that sudden big injuries are not felt at the time of their infliction. He knows, moreover, that structures beneath the skin, apart from sensory nerves, are sensitive to the knife. It is well known that men injured in battle—severely and perhaps fatally—often fight on unaware that they are wounded until they see the blood or become exhausted. At most the wounded feel a dull sensation of a blow and numbness in the injured part. Pain comes later when a wound becomes septic and inflamed. The merciful insensitiveness of man to severe injury was impressed upon me, when I was a young house surgeon, by two cases—one of a man with his pelvis crushed between the buffers of a train. Conscious, although collapsed, he was able to tell me that he had felt no pain; shortly afterwards he died of shock. A similar case was that of a man impaled by the shaft of an iron railing through falling out of a window.

In defending the Jewish method of slaughter from unjust attack, the distinguished surgeon Mr. T. H. Openshaw stated that several cases of throat-cutting, which surviving from their injury had come under his care at the London Hospital, were questioned by him. Not one of these had felt the cut when it was made. When a very sharp knife is used to cut the healthy (not inflamed) skin, very little pain is felt—even by a man who is expecting the cut—particularly so in parts, such as the back, which are not so trained to delicate sensibility as the finger-tips. Horses standing loose in a stall are bled from the jugular vein for the obtaining of anti-diphtheritic serum; they continue during the operation to eat placidly at the manger. Sensitive as the horse is to the sting of a fly, or whip, or prick of a spur, it takes no notice of the cut of a sharp knife. The skin has been evolved sensitive only to those things which concern it in the natural struggle for existence, and deep structures, apart from sensory nerves, protected as they are by the skin, are wholly insensitive to touch. The touch of whip or spur is like the sting of a fly, and is therefore felt by the horse, which must protect himself against a natural enemy; on the other hand, the cut of a sharp knife is not a natural stimulus and is unfelt.

Of these facts laymen are, as a rule, wholly ignorant. As to the duration of consciousness after the cutting of the throat, I can cite an experiment made by myself some years ago when, together with Mr. Openshaw, I defended the Jewish method of slaughter. I anesthetized a calf and inserted a tube in the peripheral end of the carotid artery—that is, in the end connected with the arteries supplying the brain. It must be borne in mind that the vertebral arteries do not supply the brain of cattle but end in the muscles of the head. The tube placed in the artery was filled with a strong saline solution to prevent clotting of the blood, and connected with a mercurial manometer arranged so as to record (on a revolving drum) the blood pressure. The animal's neck was then cut with a sharp knife so as to divide the great blood-vessels at one stroke. The manometer recorded an instant fall of blood pressure which reached zero in a second or two, showing that the circulation in the great brain has ceased. Now we know by human experience that such sudden cessation of the circulation by depriving the brain of oxygen instantly abolishes consciousness, whether produced by pressure on the brain or by heart failure, or by occlusion of the great blood-vessels of the neck. An old medical writer tells of a beggar in Paris who had a large hole in his skull covered with skin. He sat in the street and for a coin allowed a person to press upon his brain, when he fell asleep. The moment the pressure was withdrawn he became conscious again. The very word carotid betokens sleep. Mountebanks used to compress these arteries in a goat and make the animal fall down unconscious or spring up again at their will. The garroter by compressing these arteries by a grip from behind rendered his victim unconscious while he robbed him of his watch and money. A schoolboy playing at hanging has lost consciousness through the sudden compression of these arteries and has died in consequence. This unhappy accident has been repeated through a general ignorance of the danger.

Two facts are, then, indisputably established: (1) that a big injury, such as throat cutting, is not felt at the moment of infliction; (2) that the cutting of the big arteries in the throat instantly arrests the circulation in the great brain and abolishes consciousness.

See also Leonard Hill, "The Jewish Method of Slaughter: A Rejoinder to the Duchess of Hamilton," *The English Review* (June 1923): 604–607; reprinted in Sassoon, 36–38. Further statements confirming the painless nature of *shechitah* by Lord Horder, F.A.C.P., and Sir C. P Lovatt Eveans, Emeritus Professor of Physiology, London University, are included in Sassoon, 38–39. See also Solomon David Sassoon, *Supplement to the Booklet Entitled: A Critical Study of Electrical Stunning and The Jewish Method of Slaughter (Shechita)* (Letchworth, 1956).

Both the absence of pain as a result of the incision and the almost instantaneous loss of consciousness subsequent to *shechitah* are confirmed in a report prepared in 1963 by L. I. Nangeroni and P. D. Kennett of the Department of Physiology, New York State Veterinary College, Cornell University, Ithaca, N.Y., titled "An Electroencephalographic Study of the Effect of *Shechita* Slaughter on Cortical Function in Ruminants." The primary significance of this study lies in the clinical investigation of changes in function which occur in the cerebral cortex following the act of *shechitah*. The investigators utilized an electroencephalograph in order to determine the precise moment at which the slaughtered animal ceases consciously to perceive pain and other environmental stimuli. Recordings were taken with sheep, calves and goats as subjects. It was determined that in the rams tested, the time which elapsed subsequent to the making of the incision until the cerebral cortex lapsed into a state of complete unconsciousness ranged from 3.3 to 6.2 seconds. In calves, it was found that consciousness appeared to be poor by the time that four seconds had elapsed after the cut; and complete unconsciousness, in which condition the animal could not perceive stimuli of any kind, became manifest between 4.4 and 6.9 seconds after the cut. Of two goats tested, one became unconscious 5 seconds after slaughter; in the case of the second goat, the electroencephalogram was obscured, and hence it was impossible to determine the exact time at which unconsciousness was reached. Electroencephalographic evidence serves to determine the precise moment at which the animal becomes unconscious and conclusively establishes the time beyond which it is manifestly impossible for the animal to experience pain. In the animals examined, this ranged between 3.3 and 6.9 seconds subsequent to slaughter. However, this does not mean that the animals experienced pain during the few seconds prior to becoming unconscious. Indeed, there is no way of interpreting an electroencephalogram to determine whether or not pain is actually being experienced by a conscious animal. The electroencephalogram can only serve to establish that the animal is, in fact, unconscious and hence no longer capable of experiencing pain. With regard to the possibility of pain in conjunction with the actual incision before the animal loses consciousness, the report, p. 17, states:

> As anyone who has slit a finger on a page of a magazine knows, the pain from such a cut comes not during the actual cutting, but afterwards when the edges of the cut are rubbed or pressed together and the nerve endings in the skin are stimulated. The edges of the cut neck cannot be thus brought together after *Shechita* simply because of the animal's hanging position.

The absence of pain in association with a sharp incision is confirmed by a report of a bizarre incident recorded by H. Sporri, *Schächten und Tierschutz* (Report, University of Zurich, 1965), who describes the case of a man who cut his throat, including the trachea and esophagus but not the carotids. This person survived to report that the pain had not been severe.

These findings were confirmed by W. Schuize et al., "Versuche zur Objektivierung von Schmerz und Bewusstsein bei der konventionellen (Bolzenschussbetäubung) sowie religionsgesetzlichen (Schächtschnitt) Schlachtung von Schaf und Kalb," *Deutsche Tierärztliche Wochenschrift* 85 (February 5, 1978), 62–66. These researchers found it highly probable that in sheep a state of unconsciousness is reached within 4 to 6 seconds and in cattle within 10 seconds. A completely flat electroencephalogram was reached after no more than 13 seconds in sheep and after no more than 23 seconds in calves. During the few seconds in which consciousness might exist, a thermic pain stimulation caused no change in the EEG. The same authors conducted similar investigations upon animals subjected to electrical stunning and found that it took longer to reach a flat EEG and, moreover, that thermal pain stimulation as well as a subsequent incision produced a change in the EEG. Similar differences between *shechitah* and stunning were found by R. Gross, "Elektroencephalegraphische und elektrocardiographische Verlaufsuntersuchungen nach Bolzenschussbetäubung und nach Töten durch Entbluten in der Form des rituellen Schlachtens," Thesis, University of Hannover, 1976.

See also I. M. Levinger, "Jewish Method of Slaughtering Animals for Food and its Influence on the Blood Supply to the Brain and on the Normal Functioning of the Nervous System," *Animal Regulation Studies* 11 (1979): 111–26, and the studies concerning physiological aspects of *shechitah* cited in the extensive bibliography appended to that article.

18. See also Ramban, *Commentary on the Bible*, Deut. 22:6, and R. Joseph Albo, *Book of Principles* III 15, as well as Ramban,*Commentary on the Bible*, Gen. 1:29, and *Teshuvot Chatam Sofer, Orach Chayyim*, no. 54, *s.v. u-mah.* An identical view is expressed by Philo, *De Virtutibus*, 141.

19. This point is made by *Pri Megadim* with regard to ritual slaughter in particular. See the concluding section of *Pri Megadim*'s introduction to *Hilkhot Shechitah*.

20. See *Taz, Yoreh De'ah* 116:6 and *Taz, Yoreh De'ah* 117:4. See below, note 61.

21. The identical position is reiterated by the same author in *Noda bi-Yehudah, Mahadura Tinyana, Yoreh De'ah*, nos. 10, 13. In the latter responsum *Noda bi-Yehudah* rules that, although *tza'ar ba'alei chayyim* is permitted when necessary to serve a human need, nevertheless, when the option is available, it is preferable to sacrifice the animal rather than to perform a painful procedure upon a living animal. *Noda bi-Yehudah* presumably reasons that, since killing an animal involves no transgression of *tza'ar ba'alei chayyim*, there is no dispensation to cause pain when the same need can be met by killing the animal.

22. A similar position is also espoused by *Sefer ha-Eshkol*, III, *Hilkhot Shechitah*, no. 10; *Teshuvot Bet Ya'akov*, no. 42; R. Yonatan Eibeschutz, *Kereti u-feleti* 57:9; and *Gilyon Maharsha, Yoreh De'ah* 117:4. Cf. R. Eliezer Waldenberg, *Tzitz Eli'ezer*, XIV, no. 68, sec. 4.

23. A similar analysis of the considerations underlying the exchange between R. Phinehas and R. Judah was earlier advanced by *Terumat ha-Deshen, Pesakim u-Ketavim*, no. 105. See also R. Yitzchak Blaser, *Teshuvot Pri Yizchak*, I, no. 24, who offers an even more comprehensive analysis in a similar vein.

24. This responsum was addressed to R. Ya'akov Breisch and was first published in the latter's responsa collection, *Chelkat Ya'akov*, 1, no. 31.

25. Similarly, the Gemara, *Chullin* 27b and 85b, permits the putting of an animal to death by means other than ritual slaughter when the intent is not to use the animal's meat for consumption but to conserve its blood when the blood is required for some other purpose. That source also serves to establish either that *tza'ar ba'alei chayyim* is permitted when designed for human welfare or that putting an animal to death is excluded from the prohibition against *tza'ar ba'alei chayyim*. See below, nn. 28, 61.

R. Moses Sofer, *Teshuvot Chatam Sofer, Yoreh De'ah*, no. 103, citing *Avodah Zarah* 13b, permits the killing of a sickly animal other than by means of ritual slaughter. It is, however, not possible to determine whether *Chatam Sofer* sanctions this practice because he espouses the position that putting an animal to death is excluded from strictures prohibiting *tza'ar ba'alei chayyim* or because the pain inflicted is designed to serve a human need, viz., to prevent the loss that would accrue to the animal's owner were it to become carrion and its meat no longer be salable. This point seems to have been missed by R. Ze'ev Metzger, "Nisuyim Refu'iyim be-Ba'alei Chayyim," *Ha-Refu'ah le-Or ha-Halakhah*, vol. LI, pt. 3, 31. See also below, nn. 57, 61.

26. See also *Tosafot, Chullin* 2a, *s.v. shema*. *Tosafot* apparently permits the killing of an animal by means of ritual slaughter in order to feed its meat to dogs. Cf. above, n. 25 and below, n. 56 and accompanying text.

27. Cf., however, *Sho'el u-Meshiv, Mahadura Tinyana*, III, no. 65, who refutes this evidence, claiming that *Tosafot* merely asserts that when *tza'ar ba'alei chayyim* is warranted it must be minimized insofar as possible.

28. The immediately following verse, "then thou shalt kill of thy herd and of thy flock . . . and thou shalt eat within thy gates" (Deut. 12:21), serves to sanction ritual slaughter for purposes of food. Since, in context, the reference in Deut. 12:20 is to ritual slaughter, it is clear that Rambam regards even the painless mode of ritual slaughter, when undertaken other than for purposes of food, as forbidden by reason of *tza'ar ba'alei chayyim*. However, Rambam would certainly regard ritual slaughter undertaken in order to satisfy other legitimate human needs as tantamount to slaughter for purposes of food. Ritual slaughter other than for purposes of food is clearly permitted as evidenced by the statement of the Gemara, *Chullin* 85b, to the effect that R. Chiyya slaughtered a bird in the prescribed manner because he sought to use its blood to destroy worms which had infested his flax. See *Sefer Chasidim* (ed. Reuben Margulies), no. 667. Moreover, when the blood of an animal is necessary for some beneficial purpose, the Gemara, *Chullin* 27b and 85b, permits putting an animal to death even by means other than ritual slaughter in order to conserve its blood. The comments of Rashi, *Shabbat* 75a, *s.v. shochet*, serve to indicate that, under any circumstances, when an animal is killed for human benefit other than for food, it is not necessary to put it to death by means of ritual slaughter. Cf. Rashi, *Chullin* 27b, *s.v. chayyav le-khasot*.

29. See also *Sefer ha-Chinnukh*, no. 186, who explains that the slaughter of sanctified animals outside of the Temple precincts, even though the act is performed in the ritually prescribed manner, is forbidden because no purpose is served by such slaughter. *Sefer ha-Chinnukh* comments that wanton killing of animals is tantamount to "shedding blood."

30. For other sources prohibiting hunting, see *Va-Yikra Rabbah* 13:3; Rashi, *Avodah Zarah* 18b, *s.v. kenigyon; Teshuvot Mahari Brona*, no. 71; *Teshuvot Maharam Rothenberg*, no. 27; Rema, *Shulchan Arukh, Orach Chayyim* 316:2; *Teshuvot Shemesh Tzedakah, Yoreh De'ah*, nos. 18 and 57; *Giv'at Sha'ul, Parshat Va-Yeshev*, 87–88; *Pachad Yitzchak, s.v. Zeidah; Teshuvot Toldot Ya'akov, Yoreh De'ah*, no. 33; and *Darkei Teshuvah, Yoreh De'ah* 117:44.

31. See also *Teshuvot Imrei Shefer*, no. 34, sec. I; R. Yechiel Ya'akov Weinberg, *Seridei Esh*, III, no. 7, and *Teshuvot Chelkat Ya'akov*, I, no. 31, sec. 4; and R. Moshe Yonah Zweig, *Ohel Mosheh*, I, no. 32. See also R. Jacob Reisher, *Teshuvot Shevut Ya'akov*, II, no. 110, who declares that an "unusual" practice involving pain is prohibited, particularly when designed for only "a minor benefit." Cf. *Teshuvot Rav Pe'alim*, I, *Yoreh De'ah*, no. 1.

32. See *Chavalim ba-Ne'imim*, I, no. 43, sec. 4. This also appears to be the position of *Teshuvot ha-Ge'onim* (ed. Abraham E. Harkavi), no. 375.

33. *Chavalim ba-Ne'imim*, I, no. 43, sec. 6, quotes *She'elat Ya'avetz*'s comments as cited by a secondary source, *Bet Ephrayim, Yoreh De'ah* 117. That source quotes *She'elat Ya'avetz* as stating that *tza'ar ba'alei chayyim* applies only to "work animals." *Chavalim ba-Ne'imim* cites a ruling of *Sefer Chasidim* (ed. Margulies), no. 44, forbidding pulling the ears of a cat and states that this position contradicts the view of *She'elat Ya'avetz*. In point of fact, *She'elat Ya'avetz* explicitly states, "and perhaps even dog[s] and cat[s] are included [in the prohibition] since they also are domesticated and perform work." A more significant contradiction to the position of *She'elat Ya'avetz* is found by *Chavalim ba-Ne'imim* in the comments of *Shevut Ya'akov*, III, no. 71. *Shevut Ya'akov* demonstrates that *tza'ar ba'alei chayyim* is permitted for the benefit of human beings on the basis and of the Gemara, *Shabbat* 77b. The Gemara observes that God did not create a single thing without purpose. The Gemara gives specific examples of the utility of seemingly useless creatures. The fly is crushed and applied to the site of a hornet's sting; the mosquito is crushed and used as a remedy for a serpent's bite; a crushed spider is used as a remedy for a scorpion's bite; and various serpents are boiled to a pulp and rubbed in at the site of an eruption. *Shevut Ya'akov* adduces that dictum as proof that *tza'ar ba'alei chayyim* is permissible for human welfare. *Chavalim ba-Ne'imim* points out that *Shevut Ya'akov*'s argument is cogent only if, in contradiction to *She'ilat Ya'avetz*'s position, he assumes that considerations of *tza'ar ba'alei chayyim* apply to all creatures, including serpents and insects. See also below, n. 46.

34. Cf., however, R. Elijah of Vilna, *Bi'ur ha-Gra, Even ha-Ezer* 5:40, and the comments of R. Jacob Breisch, *Teshuvot Chelkat Ya'akov*, I, no. 30, secs. 2–3, as well as Shmuel, Moshe Mordecai and Eleazar Shulsinger, *Mishmar ha-Leviyim* (Zikhron Me'ir, 5740), no. 20. See also R. Yechiel Ya'akov Weinberg, *Seridei Esh*, III, no. 7, and *Chelkat Ya'akov*, I, no. 31, secs. 1–3.

R. Judah Leib Zirelson, *Ma'arkhei Lev*, no. 110, finds a biblical source for this ruling: "And Samson went and caught three hundred foxes and took torches and turned tail to tail and put a torch in the midst between every two tails. And when he had set the torches on fire, he let them go into the standing corn of the Philistines and burn up both the shucks and the standing corn and also the olive-yards." (Jud. 15:4–5) *Ma'arkhei Lev* argues that inflicting severe pain on the foxes was sanctionable only because it served a human need, and hence the general principle can be traced to these verses. R. Jacob Breisch, *Teshuvot Chelkat Ya'akov*, I, no. 30, sec. 5, cogently rebuts this argument on the grounds that Samson was involved in a defensive war against the Philistines and, in fact, his own life was endangered. Hence Jud. 15:4–5 serves only to establish that *tza'ar ba'alei chayyim* is permitted when human life is endangered, but not necessarily for the sake of a lesser purpose.

35. Cf. *Teshuvot Mareh Yechezkel*, no. 59, who expresses amazement at Rema's ruling, querying, "Whence is it derived that violation of the biblical prohibition of *tza'ar ba'alei chayyim* may be sanctioned to effect a cure or for human benefit?" In light of *Tosafot*'s comments to the effect that the prohibition does not the encompass such contingencies, *Mareh Yechezkel*'s incredulity is misplaced.

36. See below, n. 50.

37. See R. Abraham Hafuta, *No'am*, IV (5721): 223f. *Piskei Tosafot, Avodah Zarah* 1:11, in what is apparently a precis of *Tosafot, Baba Metzi'a* 32b (or the precis of a different manuscript of *Tosafot* on *Avodah Zarah*), states that *tza'ar ba'alei chayyim* is forbidden only when the pain caused to the animal yields "no profit" (*beli revach*).

38. Cf., however, *Teshuvot Imrei Shefer*, no. 34, sec. 11, who endeavors to ascribe a different import to the words of Rabbenu Nissim.

39. *Nimukei Yosef* cites Ramban as resolving this difficulty in an entirely different manner. Ramban asserts that the "commandment concerning honor of the Torah takes precedence over considerations of *tza'ar ba'alei chayyim*." The readily apparent explanation of Ramban's failure to advance an explanation similar to that offered by Rabbenu Nissim is that Ramban does not sanction *tza'ar ba'alei chayyim* for the purpose of satisfying a human need. That position is however rejected by Ramban's own remarks in his commentary on *Avodah Zarah* 13b.

40. This concept is echoed in Ps. 8:7–9, which says of man: "Thou hast made him to have dominion over the works of Thy hands; Thou hast put all things under his feet. Sheep and oxen, all of them, yea, and the beasts of the field. The fowl of the air, and the fish of the sea; whatsoever passeth through the paths of the seas."

As evidenced by numerous biblical verses, it is clear that man is granted license to utilize animals as beasts of burden, for agricultural purposes, as a means of transportation, and the like. Judaism also accepts the view that animals were created for the benefit of mankind. Thus, the Gemara, *Berakhot* 6b, reports: "R. Eleazar said, 'The Holy One, blessed be He, declared, "The whole world in its entirety was not created other than on behalf of this [human species].'" Even more explicit is the statement of R. Simeon ben Eleazar, *Kiddushin* 82b, declaring, "they [animals] were not created other than to serve me." This view is not contradicted by the position espoused by Rambam in a celebrated dispute with Sa'adia Ga'on in which Rambam denies the homocentric nature of the universe. The *Book of Beliefs and Opinions* IV, Intro., asserts that man is the intended and ultimate purpose of creation; Rambam, *Guide* III 13, challenges this view, pointing out that the human species has no need for a great part of the cosmos. Rambam maintains that all parts of the world are equally intended by the divine will but acknowledges that certain beings were created for the service of others. Thus, in Rambam's view, there is no contradiction in acknowledging that service to other species is the instrumental purpose of some creatures while yet affirming their own existence as the final cause of those creatures.

41. See also *Teshuvot Chatam Sofer, Hoshen Mishpat*, no. 185, *s.v. ma she-katavata me-Rabad*; cf., however, *Teshuvot Chatam Sofer, Yoreh De'ah*, no. 314 *s.v. omnam*; and *Teshuvot Imrei Shefer*, no. 34, sec. 2.

42. *Terumat ha-Deshen* rules that, as a matter of law, it is permissible to cause pain to animals even for the esthetic pleasure of man, and, accordingly, permits clipping the ears and tail of a dog "in order to beautify it." Cf., however, *Sefer Chasidim* (ed. *Mekitzei Nirdamim*), no. 589, who forbids any attempt to effect a "change" in correcting a congenital anomaly in a limb or organ of an animal on the grounds that such a procedure constitutes a violation of the prohibition against *tza'ar ba'alei chayyim*. In an even more general statement, *Da'at Kedoshim, Yoreh De'ah* 24:12, declares that acts which cause discomfort to animals are permissible in order to satisfy "any desire of man even if his desire in this regard is not in accordance with the weighing of need or benefit but only a desire without a proper reason." The same authority permits such procedures even if there is only the mere possibility that the need or desire may be satisfied thereby. See also *Da'at Kedoshim, Yoreh De'ah* 23:28. A similar view is expressed by *Ezer mi-Kodesh, Even ha-Ezer* 5:14. Cf., however, below, n. 67.

43. Cf., however, *Sefer Chasidim* (ed. Margulies), no. 666, which applies Gen. 1:28 in a radically different manner. *Sefer Chasidim* remarks that Adam was forbidden to

eat the flesh of animals but was granted dominion over them, whereas the sons of Noah were permitted to eat the flesh of animals but were not were granted dominion over them. According to *Sefer Chasidim*, it is because the sons of Noah were not granted dominion over animals that the angel chastised Balaam in its in demanding, "Wherefore has thou smitten thine ass these three times?" (Num. 22:32) As pointed out by R. Reuben Margulies in his commentary on *Sefer Chasidim, Mekor Chesed* 666:7, *Sefer Chasidim* obviously maintains that Noachides are forbidden to engage in acts involving *tza'ar ba'alei chayyim*. As indicated earlier, Rambam also cites Num. 22:32 as the source of the prohibition against *tza'ar ba'alei chayyim*. Hence there is some reason to assume that Rambam also maintains that *tza'ar ba'alei chayyim* is prohibited to Noachides. *Teshuvot Imrei Shefer*, no. 34, sec. 2 and sec. 8, also suggests that Noachides may be bound by strictures concerning *tza'ar ba'alei chayyim* which, in his opinion, may be encompassed in the prohibition contained in the Noachide Code concerning the eating of a limb torn from a living animal. See, however, *Pri Megadim, Orach Chayyim, Mishbetzot Zahav* 467:2 and R. Shalom Mordecai Schwadron, *Teshuvot Maharsham*, II, no. 364, who apparently maintain that non-Jews are not bound by strictures concerning *tza'ar ba'alei chayyim*. See also *Toldot Ya'akov, Yoreh De'ah*, no. 33.

44. See Rema, *Even ha-Ezer* 5:13. Cf. *Bi'ur ha-Gra, Even ha-Ezer* 5:31; and R. Jacob Emden, *She'elat Ya'avetz*, I, no. 111.

45. For a rebuttal of the evidence yielded by these sources, see R. Yitzchak Dov Bamberger, *Teshuvot Yad ha-Levi*, I, *Yoreh De'ah*, no. 196, and *Teshuvot Imrei Shefer*, no. 34, sec. 10.

46. *Shevut Ya'akov* also adduces proof that *tza'ar ba'alei chayyim* is permitted, at least for medical purposes, on the basis of the statement of the Gemara, *Shabbat* 77b, to the effect that various insects were created so that, when crushed, they might be used as remedies for various bites and that serpents were created so that they might be boiled and used as a cure for eruptions; see above, n. 33. As additional evidence, he cites the statement of the Gemara, *Shabbat* 109b, advising that if one is bitten by a snake "he should procure an embryo of a white ass, tear it open, and be made to sit upon it." A further source which may be cited is the statement of the Gemara, *Shabbat* 110b, dealing with the treatment of jaundice, which advises, inter alia, "let him take a speckled swine, tear it open and apply it to his heart." However, these sources fail to demonstrate that *tza'ar ba'alei chayyim* is permitted for medical purposes if the killing of animals is excluded from the prohibition; see above, nn. 21–25 and accompanying text.

47. See, however, R. Yechiel Ya'akov Weinberg, *Seridei Esh*, III, no. 7, and *Chelkat Ya'akov*, III, no. 31, sec. 4. Rabbi Weinberg argues that this source cannot serve as a basis for Rema's ruling, since "perhaps" such practices are condoned only for the purpose of preventing idolatrous activities. Cf. Ramban, *Avodah Zarah* 13b. In his analysis of the Gemara's citation of the verse "and their horses shall you hough (*et suseihem te'aker*)" (Josh. 11:6), Ramban equates abrogation of idolatrous practices with other human needs. See also *Teshuvot Imrei Shefer*, no. 34, sec. 9, who endeavors to show that *tza'ar ba'alei chayyim* was permitted in the case of the white chicken sold to an idolator only to spare the animal from even greater pain. The same authority, loc. cit., no. 34, sec. 14, also suggests that this procedure was permitted only when performed in a manner which does not entail pain; see below, n. 52. A similar explanation is advanced by *Chavalim ba-Ne'imim*, I, no. 43, sec. 3.

48. *Tosafot, Avodah Zarah* 11a, states that *tza'ar ba'alei chayyim* is permitted "in honor of the king which is the honor of all of Israel, and the honor of the multitude takes precedence over *tza'ar ba'alei chayyim.*" See also *Teshuvot Noda bi-Yehuda, Mahadura Tinyana, Yoreh De'ah,* no. 10.

49. See also the comments of Ramban, cited above, n. 39. *Teshuvot Rema Panu,* no. 102, forbids placing a bird upon eggs of another species in order to hatch them because of concern for *tza'ar ba'alei chayyim.* This ruling is also recorded in *Kitzur Shulchan Arukh* 191:4. Ostensibly, this authority maintains that *tza'ar ba'alei chayyim* is prohibited even when designed for general human benefit or, minimally, when undertaken for financial profit; however, see below, n. 59. Cf. R. Shimon ben Zemah Duran, *Tashbatz,* II, no. 59, cited by *Pitchei Teshuvah, Yoreh De'ah* 297:1, who maintains that this procedure causes no discomfort to the bird.

50. See commentary of *Zev Zakhar,* sec. 17, on *Issur ve-Heter,* ad loc. *Zev Zakhar* points out that an entirely different inference should be drawn from the published text of *Tosafot, Avodah Zarah* 11a; viz., that *tza'ar ba'alei chayyim* is permissible only for the sake of "the king's honor, which is the honor of the multitude." Cf. also *Teshuvot Imrei Shefer,* no. 34, sec. 9. [It should be noted, however, that experimentation designed to benefit the public at large is to be regarded as undertaken for the sake of "the honor of the multitude"; see R. Abraham Hafuta, *No'am* 4 (5721): 224.] *Noda bi-Yehudah, Mahadura Tinyana, Yoreh De'ah,* no. 10, assumes that *Issur ve-Heter* cites *Piskei Tosafot* rather than *Tosafot.* The phraseology employed by *Piskei Tosafot* is "there is no prohibition of *tza'ar ba'alei chayyim* other than if he derives no *revah.*" The term *revah* is somewhat ambiguous and has the connotation of either "profit" or "benefit."

51. See *Or Gadol, Shabbat* 24:1, which endeavors to demonstrate that the permissibility of *tza'ar ba'alei chayyim* in order to prevent financial loss is the subject of dispute among early authorities. According to *Or Gadol,* Rashi permits *tza'ar ba'alei chayyim* in such circumstances, while Ramban and Rashba maintain that *tza'ar ba'alei chayyim* for avoidance of financial loss is forbidden.

52. Evidence in support of the position that *tza'ar ba'alei chayyim* is permitted for financial gain adduced from the statement of the Mishnah, *Avodah Zarah* 13b, permitting removal of a digit from the foot of a chicken, is dismissed by *Binyan Zion. Binyan Zion* argues that, in declaring this practice to be permissible, the Mishnah adopts the position that *tza'ar ba'alei chayyim* is prohibited only by virtue of rabbinic decree, but that, in accordance with the accepted opinion that *tza'ar ba'alei chayyim* is biblically proscribed, dispensation for such acts does not exist. *Chavalim ba-Ne'imim,* I, no. 43, sec. 3, offers the explanation that the Mishnah intends to permit the removal of a digit "only by utilization of a drug which does not entail pain to the chicken." See also *Teshuvot Imrei Shefer,* no. 34, sec. 14, and *Nachal Eshkol, Hilkhot Avodah Zarah* 45:6. Painless amputation by means of a drug was known in the days of the Talmud; see *Baba Kamma* 85a and Rashi, ad loc., *s.v. bein sam le-sayif.* Presumably, reference is to use of a local anesthetic which was known in the days of the Talmud; see *Teshuvot Imrei Shefer,* no. 34, sec. 15.

53. Rabbi Bamberger's letter to *Binyan Tzion* has now been published in *Teshuvot Yad ha-Levi,* I, *Yoreh De'ah,* no. 196. Upon examination of his comments, it is evident that Rabbi Bamberger does not attempt to interpret Rema's comments but rather expresses disagreement with *Terumat ha-Deshen.*

54. See also *Teshuvot Tohdot Ya'akov, Yoreh De'ah,* no. 33, and *Apei Zutrei, Even ha-Ezer* 5:25. Cf., however, R. Eliezer Waldenberg, *Tzitz Eli'ezer,* XIV, no. 68, sec. 5.

55. See above, n. 11. In support of his position, *Binyan Tzion* cites the statement of the Gemara, *Bekhorot* 36b, countenancing infliction of a blemish upon an entire flock of animals in order to circumvent the requirement that every tenth animal be offered as a sacrifice. For a rebuttal of that argument, see *Teshuvot Imrei Shefer*, no. 34, sec. 2.

56. The identical source was earlier adduced by R. Yitzchak Dov Bamberger, *Teshuvot Yad ha-Levi*, I, *Yoreh De'ah*, no. 196, as evidence that *tza'ar ba'alei chayyim* is not permitted for the sake of financial gain.

57. See also *Teshuvot Chatam Sofer, Choshen Mishpat*, no. 185, *s.v. ma she-katavta me-Rabad*. Cf., however, *Teshuvot Chatam Sofer, Yoreh De'ah*, no 314, *s.v. omnam*; and *Teshuvot Imrei Shefer*, no. 34, sec. 2.

58. R. Moses Feinstein, *Iggerot Mosheh, Choshen Mishpat*, II, no. 47, sec. 1, citing Ran. *Baba Metzi'a* 32a, similarly rules that *tza'ar ba'alei chayyim* is permissible only for purposes of human "honor."

59. *Teshuvot Rav Pe'alim*, I, *Yoreh De'ah*, no. 1, rules that *tza'ar ba'alei chayyim* is permitted when designed for human benefit, but only if the desired benefit cannot be achieved in another manner. *Rav Pe'alim* cites *Teshuvot Rema Panu*, no. 102, who forbids placing a bird upon eggs of another species in order to hatch them. Since *Rav Pe'alim* assumes that *tza'ar ba'alei chayyim* is permitted even for the purpose of financial profit, he declares that the ruling of *Teshuvot Rema Panu* applies only in situations in which a bird of the same species is available. See also *Kitzur Shulchan Arukh* 191:4 and *Pitchei Teshuvah, Yoreh De'ah* 293:1.

60. Cf. *Teshuvot Noda bi-Yehudah, Mahadura Kamma, Yoreh De'ah*, no. 83.

61. There are also a number of authorities whose comments yield the conclusion that either *tza'ar ba'alei chayyim* is permissible for purposes of financial gain or that putting an animal to death involves no infraction of the prohibition against *tza'ar ba'alei chayyim*. *Taz, Yoreh De'ah* 117:4, reports that he was asked by a person engaged in the sale of hides whether it is permissible to kill an animal by means other than ritual slaughter, because the hide of an animal slaughtered in the ritual manner commanded a lower price. The Gemara, *Chullin* 27b and 85b, indicates that, when the blood of an animal is required for a beneficial purpose, the animal may be put to death by means other than ritual slaughter. See *Shulchan Arukh, Yoreh De'ah* 28:18, and *Derishah, Yoreh De'ah* 28:6. Similarly, *Taz, Yoreh De'ah* 116:6, quotes *Yam shel Shlomoh, Baba Kamma* 10:37, to the effect that one who owns a dog that causes damage or destroys food may poison the dog even though it presents no danger to human beings, and that the destruction of the animal involves no prohibition of *tza'ar ba'alei chayyim*. See also *Teshuvot Chatam Sofer, Yoreh De'ah*, no. 103, cited above, n. 25.

62. See R. Jacob Emden, *She'elat Ya'avetz*, I, no. 110, who reports that the renowned kabbalist R. Isaac Luria, known as the *Ari ha-Kadosh*, directed his disciples not to kill "even a louse." *She'elat Ya'avetz* states that this directive was based upon "the trait of piety and upon [kabbalistic] mystery." An opposing view is adopted by *Sefer Chasidim* (ed. Margulies), no. 831:

There were two people. One did not want to burn the flies. His friend said to him, "'Be not righteous overmuch' (Eccl. 7:16). Better to burn the flies so that they shall not fall into the food and drink. [Then] one who swallows them will sin. Therefore it is written, 'Be not righteous overmuch.'"

63. Cf., however, *She'elat Ya'avetz*, I, no. 110, who asserts that "perhaps" the calf was the incarnation of a human soul and that this fact was known to R. Judah.

64. Cf., however, *Teshuvot Imrei Shefer*, no. 34, sec. 10, who asserts that *Terumat ha-Deshen* seeks to establish a normative halakhic principle, "for if the matter were permitted there would be no suspicion of punishment."

65. R. Nathan Zevi Friedman, *No'am* 5 (5722): 190, seeks another talmudic source for Rema's comment and, in doing so, apparently overlooks the fact that *Terumat ha-Deshen* himself cites *Baba Metz'ia* 85a as his source.

66. A somewhat parallel, although less clearly developed, concept may be found in Aristotle's notion of "superhuman virtue," which he defines as "a kind of heroic and divine excellence." See *Nicomachean Ethics* VII, 1145a. The concepts are, however, dissimilar in that Aristotle's superhuman virtue appears to be essentially unobtainable and, indeed, Aristotle presents no imperative for seeking its attainment, whereas in Jewish teaching all persons may, and indeed should, aspire to act *lifnim mi-shurat ha-din*. Also, for Aristotle, superhuman virtue is a quality of character from which certain modes of conduct flow. There is no indication that Aristotle ascribes any moral value to an act which merely mimics the conduct of one who has acquired this quality of character. In Jewish teaching, the act itself is deemed meritorious.

67. The sole rabbinic authority to express reservations with regard to the permissibility of animal experimentation as a matter of normative law is *Teshuvot Imrei Shefer*, no. 34, sec. 16. *Imrei Shefer* declares that "it is not clear" that *tza'ar ba'alei chayyim* is permitted "for the purpose of tests and experiments." *Imrei Shefer* readily acknowledges that *tza'ar ba'alei chayyim* is clearly permitted for therapeutic purposes, but distinguishes between therapeutic procedures of demonstrated value and experimentation which is undertaken on the mere possibility that "perhaps there will emerge from this benefit through medical science." [It may be noted that *Teshuvot Noda bi-Yehudah, Mahadura Kamma, Yoreh De'ah*, no. 83, similarly suggests that *tza'ar ba'alei chayyim* may not be permissible when undertaken to avoid possible, but uncertain, transgression. *Noda bi-Yehudah* himself, however, concludes that, at least in some circumstances, *tza'ar ba'alei chayyim* is permissible in order to eliminate the potential for transgression.] *Imrei Shefer* concludes that "we cannot conclusively determine whether, in accordance with the precepts of our holy Torah, license is granted to Jewish physicians to engage in those tests on the bodies of living creatures." As has been noted earlier, *Da'at Kedoshim, Yoreh De'ah* 24:12, explicitly affirms that the concept of benefit to man includes even "possible benefit." See above, n. 42.

The distinction drawn by *Imrei Shefer* between *tza'ar ba'alei chayyim* designed for direct therapeutic benefit and experimentation for the general advancement of medical knowledge is, in effect, an application of a principle of Jewish law first enunciated by *Noda bi-Yehudah, Mahadura Tinyana, Yoreh De'ah*, no. 210, in a classic responsum regarding postmortem examinations. *Noda bi-Yehudah* states definitively that the suspension of virtually any prohibition is warranted in face of an already present danger, or, in rabbinic terminology, in the case of a *choleh le-faneinu* (lit., "a patient in front of us"). The concept of a *choleh le-faneinu* is, roughly speaking, the halakhic equivalent of "a clear and *present* danger." Prohibitions are suspended for the purpose of saving an endangered life, but not in anticipation of a purely hypothetical eventuality. Accordingly, *Noda bi-Yehudah* rules that performance of an autopsy is warranted in order to obtain specific information of value in the treatment of another similarly afflicted patient, but not in the vague hope that some potentially life-saving knowledge may be gained in the process of the postmortem examination. *Imrei Shefer* appears to apply the same principle to experimentation upon animals.

68. Cf. Maharsha, *Baba Metzi'a* 85a, and *Teshuvot Imrei Shefer*, no. 34, secs. 10 and 12, who offer explanations for the censure of R. Judah which differ from the explanation advanced by *Ma'arkhei Lev* but which are entirely consistent with the conclusion reached by *Ma'arkhei Lev*.

69. See, however, R. Chaim Pelaggi, *Ruach Chayyim*, no. 630, who cites this ruling as evidence that *tza'ar ba'alei chayyim* is permitted "for the purpose of a *mitzvah*." A similar view was earlier expressed by *Shiltei Gibborim, Avodah Zarah* 1:21, and *Knesset ha-Gedolah, Choshen Mishpat* 240:6. See also *Sedei Chemed, Ma'arekhet ha-Tzadi*, no. 1, who maintains that the treatment of the scapegoat sent into the wilderness and destroyed in conjunction with the ritual of *Yom Kippur* serves as a paradigm permitting *tza'ar ba'alei chayyim* for the purpose of fulfilling any *mitzvah*. The difficulty raised by *Ma'arkhei Lev* is readily resolved if, as may be assumed, it is recognized that Rema's caveat does not apply to *tza'ar ba'alei chayyim* in a matter pertaining to a *mitzvah*.

70. The analysis of Rema's position as presented by *Ma'arkhei Lev* seems to be at variance with that of *Taz, Even ha-Ezer* 5:11. *Taz* remarks that, in accordance with Rema's caveat, it is improper to remove the comb of a rooster. However, since the presumed sterilization does serve a need which cannot be achieved in another manner, according to *Ma'arkhei Lev's* analysis, removal of the comb should be sanctioned even according to Rema.

71. This does not apply to painful procedures performed on living animals by the students enrolled in laboratory courses as part of their general education. See R. Joel Schwartz, *Ve-Rahamav al Kol Ma'asav*, 56. It should be stressed that even those authorities who sanction the infliction of pain upon animals for the benefit of human beings do so only when the benefit is practical in nature, but not merely for the satisfaction of intellectual curiosity. Thus, even according to those authorities, only experiments directly related to the development of a specific skill necessary for fulfillment of the student's professional or vocational goal may be sanctioned. Nevertheless, in this writer's opinion, students directed to perform such procedures as part of the course requirements for purposes of earning an academic degree may perform such acts according to the opinion of those authorities who sanction *tza'ar ba'alei chayyim* for financial gain or for the fulfillment of a human need, since the earning of a degree leads directly to economic gain. However, since acquisition of theoretical knowledge for its own sake and perfection of skills which are not intended for applied use do not constitute such a need, it is improper for educators to impose such requirements the upon students for general educational purposes. Castration, spaying, and sterilization of living animals is forbidden by biblical law. Accordingly, Jewish students and practitioners may not perform such acts even in situations in which considerations of *tza'ar ba'alei chayyim* do not pertain. Whether such acts are also prohibited to Noachides is the subject of some controversy both among the Tanna'im and among rabbinic decisors; see *Encyclopedia Talmudit*, III, 356.

72. *Ma'arkhei Lev*, no. 110.

73. *Teshuvot Binyan Tzion*, no. 108.

74. *Pri Megadim, Orach Chayyim, Mishbetzot Zahav* 468:2.

75. *Teshuvot Rav Pe'alim*, I, *Yoreh De'ah*, no. 1.

76. *Teshuvot Sho'el u-Meshiv, Mahadura Tinyana*, III, no. 65; and R. Tevel the Physician, quoted by *Teshuvot Avodat ha-Gershuni*, no. 13.

77. Israel-Michael Rabbinowicz, *La médecine du Thalmud* (Paris, 1880), 56, n. 1, and 57, n. 1, cites therapeutic procedures performed upon animals which are reported by the Gemara, *Chullin* 57b, as evidence that vivisection was performed by the Sages of the Mishnah. See, however, *Teshuvot Imrei Shefer*, no. 34, sec. 16, who refutes this contention, arguing that those procedures were undertaken to correct injuries sustained in accidents or the like.

23

Vegetarianism and Judaism

J. David Bleich

> Man will be called to account with regard to everything that his eye beheld but of which he did not eat.
>
> —Palestinian Talmud, *Kiddushin* 4:12

THE IDEOLOGICAL PERSPECTIVE

In Jewish teaching, not only are normative laws regarded as binding solely upon the authority of divine revelation, but ethical principles as well are regarded as endowed with validity and commended as goals of human aspiration only if they, too, are divinely revealed. In his comments upon the introductory section of *Ethics of the Fathers*, R. Ovadiah of Bartenura questions the import of the initial statement of that tractate, "Moses received the Torah from Sinai and transmitted it to Joshua." That statement would have been appropriate as an introduction to the Mishnah as a whole and, as such, would have served as an affirmation of the divine nature of the Oral Law in its entirety, but it seems rather incongruous *in medias res*. Bartenura explains the incorporation of this statement at the beginning of *Ethics of the Fathers* by remarking that, unlike other tractates, *Ethics of the Fathers* is not devoted to an explication of any particular commandment but is composed in its entirety of ethical maxims. "The wise men of the nations of the world," declares Bartenura, "authored ethical treatises in accordance with the inclination of their hearts." Therefore, this tractate, devoted as it is exclusively to matters of ethical conduct, begins with this prefatory statement in order to indicate that "even these [ethical principles] were stated at Sinai." Accordingly, even though Judaism certainly does not posit vegetarianism as a normative lifestyle, its value as a moral *desideratum* can be acknowledged only if support is found within the corpus of the Written or Oral Law.

A prooftext often cited in support of vegetarianism as an ideal to which man should aspire is a statement recorded in *Sanhedrin* 59b:

> Rav Judah stated in the name of Rav, "Adam was not permitted meat for purposes of eating as it is written, 'for you shall it be for food and to all beasts of the earth' (Gen. 1:29), but not beasts of the earth for you. But when the sons of Noah came [He] permitted them [the beasts of the earth], as it is said, 'as the green grass have I given to you everything' (Gen. 9:3)."

Some writers have regarded this statement as reflecting the notion that primeval man was denied the flesh of animals because of his enhanced moral status. Permission to eat the flesh of animals was granted only to Noah because, subsequent to Adam's sin, his banishment from the Garden of Eden and the degeneration of subsequent generations, man could no longer be held to such lofty moral standards. Nevertheless, they argue, man ought to aspire to the highest levels of moral conduct and, consistent with such a value system, man should eschew the flesh of animals.

In point of fact, this talmudic dictum is simply a terse statement of the relevant law prior to the time of Noah but is silent with regard to any validating rationale. While the statement in question may well be compatible with a vegetarian ideal, it may quite readily be comprehended as reflecting entirely different considerations. Indeed, the classic biblical commentators found entirely different explanations for the change which occurred with regard to dietary regulations. Thus, for example, R. Jacob ben Asher, renowned as the author of the *Tur Shulchan Arukh,* in his commentary on Genesis 1:29, explains that, prior to partaking of the fruit of the Tree of Knowledge, Adam lacked any desire for meat; only subsequent to eating of the forbidden fruit did man acquire a carnivorous nature. Hence the dispensation granted to Noah to eat the flesh of animals simply reflects man's transformed biological needs. R. Meir Leibush Malbim, in his commentary on Genesis 9:3, remarks that Adam was endowed with a "strong" constitution and that the produce available in the Garden of Eden was nutritionally optimal in nature. Under such circumstances, Adam's dietary needs could be satisfied without recourse to meat. Only as mankind degenerated physically as well as spiritually, became geographically dispersed and hence subject to the vagaries of climate, and as the quality of available produce became nutritionally inferior, did it become necessary for man, in his "weakened" state, to supplement his diet with animal products in order to assure the availability of the nutrients required for his biological needs.

An examination of the writings of rabbinic scholars[1] reveals three distinct attitudes with regard to vegetarianism:

(1) The Gemara, *Pesachim* 49b, declares that an ignoramus ought not to partake of meat: "'This is the law of the animal . . . and the fowl' (Lev. 11:46): whoever engages in [the study of] the Law is permitted to eat the flesh of animals and fowl, but whoever does not engage in [the study of] the Law may not eat the flesh of animals and fowl." This text should certainly not be construed as declaring that meat is permitted only to the scholar as a reward for his erudition or diligence.[2] Maharsha indicates that this text simply reflects a concern for scrupulous observance of the minutiae of the dietary code. The ignoramus is not proficient in the myriad rules and regulations governing the eating of meat, including the differentiation between kosher and nonkosher species, the porging of forbidden fat and veins, the soaking and salting of meat, etc. Only the scholar who has mastered those rules and regulations can eat meat with a clear conscience. Indeed, an earlier authority, Rabbenu Nissim, citing R. Sherira Ga'on, explains that an ignoramus is advised to refrain from eating meat because he is ignorant of the proper method of performing ritual slaughter and of examining the internal organs. A similar interpretation is advanced by R. Moses Isserles, *Teshuvot Rema,* no. 65, who remarks that the ignoramus is not proficient in the laws of ritual slaughter. Maharsha notes that this stricture applies only to the eating of the flesh of land-animals but places no restriction upon the eating of fish, even though reference to fish is also made in the very same biblical verse. The reason for this distinction is that the dietary code pertaining to consumption of fish is relatively simple and can be mastered by everyone, while preparation of animal meat is governed by complex regulations requiring diligent study. Historically, there certainly have been individuals who, depending upon circumstances of time and place, did deny themselves meat, not because of the ethical implications of a carnivorous diet, but because of their concern for inadvertent transgression of provisions of the dietary code. For example, during the early part of the twentieth century, many pious immigrants to the United States declined to eat meat because of the lax standards of *kashrut* supervision then prevalent in this country. Such individuals adopted vegetarianism as a lifestyle, but did so because of concern for observance of the technicalities of religious law rather than because of moral considerations.

(2) A number of medieval scholars, including R. Isaac Abarbanel in his commentary on Genesis 9:3 and Isaiah 11:7, and R. Joseph Albo, *Sefer ha-Ikkarim,* Book III, chapter 15, regard vegetarianism as a moral ideal, not because of a concern for the welfare of animals, but because of the fact that the slaughter of animals might cause the individual who performs such acts to develop negative character traits, viz., meanness and cruelty. Their concern was with regard to possible untoward effect upon human character rather than with animal welfare.[3]

Indeed, R. Joseph Albo maintains that renunciation of the consumption of meat for reasons of concern for animal welfare is not only morally erroneous but even repugnant. Albo asserts that this was the intellectual error committed by Cain and that it was this error that was the root cause of Cain's act of fratricide. Scripture reports that Cain brought a sacrifice of the produce of the land while Abel offered a sacrifice from the animals of his flock. Albo opines that Cain did not offer an animal sacrifice because he regarded men and animals as equals[4] and, accordingly, felt that he had no right to take the life of an animal, even as an act of divine worship. Abel shared the basic conviction of his brother but nevertheless maintained that man was superior to animals in that he possessed reason as demonstrated in his ability to use his intellect in cultivating fields and in shepherding flocks. This, Abel believed, gave man limited rights over animals, including the right to use animals in the service of God, but did not confer upon him the right to kill animals for his own needs. Abel's error was not as profound as that of Cain, but it was an error nonetheless. And, declares Albo, because Abel shared the error of his brother, at least to the degree of not recognizing the superiority of man over members of the animal kingdom, he was punished by being permitted to die at the hands of Cain. Albo further explains God's acceptance of Abel's sacrifice and His rejection of that of Cain as being directly related to their respective views regarding the relative moral status of men and animals. Cain's error was egregious in the extreme. Hence he was so lacking in favor in the eyes of God that his sacrifice was rejected. Although he was also guilty of error, Abel's sacrifice was accepted by God because his error was not as serious as that of his brother. According to Albo, Cain failed to understand the reason for the rejection of his sacrifice and continued to assume that his own value system was correct but that, in the eyes of God, animal sacrifice was intrinsically superior to the offering of produce. Since Cain remained confirmed in his opinion that man and animals are inherently equal, he was led to the even more grievous conclusion that just as man is entitled to take the life of an animal so also is he entitled to take the life of his fellow man. This position, Albo asserts, was adopted by succeeding generations as well, and it was precisely the notion that men and animals are equal that led, not to the renunciation of causing harm to animals and to concern for their welfare, but rather to the notion that violence against one's fellow man was equally acceptable. The inevitable result was a total breakdown of the social order, which ultimately culminated in punishment by means of the flood. Subsequent to the flood, meat was permitted to Noah, Albo asserts, in order to impress upon mankind the superiority of man over members of the animal kingdom.

Albo does not explain why the generations after the flood drew the correct conclusion and were not prone again to commit the error of Cain. Rather than recognizing the inherent superiority of man that is reflected in the dispensation granted them to partake of the flesh of animals, they might have concluded that violence against man is similarly justified because men and animals are coequal. It was precisely this conclusion that Cain drew from God's acceptance of animal sacrifice. It may, however, be possible that, at that juncture of human history, the possibility of drawing such a conclusion was effectively obviated. Genesis 7:23 declares that during the period of the flood God destroyed not only man but also every living creature. The Gemara, *Sanhedrin* 108a, queries, "if man sinned, what was the sin of the animals? Rabbi Joshua the son of Korchah answered the question with a parable: A man made a nuptial canopy for his son and prepared elaborate foods for the wedding feast. In the interim his son died. The father arose and took apart the nuptial canopy declaring, 'I did nothing other than on behalf of my son. Now that he has died for what purpose do I need the nuptial canopy?' Similarly, the Holy One, blessed be He, said, 'I did not create animals and beasts other than for man. Now that man has sinned, for what purpose do I need animals and beasts?'" Those comments serve to indicate that the extermination of innocent animals in the course of the Deluge must be regarded as proof positive of the superiority of man over members of the animal kingdom. Animals could be destroyed by a righteous God only because the sole purpose of those creatures was to serve man. Hence, if man is to be destroyed, the continued existence of animal species is purposeless. Thus the basic principle, i.e., the superiority of man over members of the animal kingdom, was amply demonstrated by the destruction of animals during the course of the flood. No further demonstration of the relative status of man and beasts was necessary. Permission to eat the flesh of animals was then required only as a means of explicitly negating the residual notion that animals are somehow endowed with rights and that man's obligations vis-à-vis animals are rooted in such rights rather than in a concern for the possible moral degeneration of man himself.[5]

Albo's basic position is reflected in a comment of *Bereshit Rabbah* 22:26 which indicates that Cain did not understand the enormity of his misdeed:

> And the Lord said unto him, "Therefore whosoever slayeth Cain, vengence shall be taken on him sevenfold." (Gen. 4:15) R. Nehemiah said, "The punishment of Cain is not as the punishment of other murderers. Cain killed, but he had none from whom to learn [the enormity of his crime]. [But] henceforth whosoever slayeth Cain shall be slain."

The implication of this statement is that Cain was not aware of the heinous nature of his crime. According to Albo, Cain lapsed into grievous moral error because, having accepted the equality of man and members of the animal kingdom, he regarded divine acceptance of animal sacrifice as license to take the life of others.

(3) One modern-day scholar who is often cited as looking upon vegetarianism with extreme favor is the late Rabbi Abraham Isaac Kook. It is indeed the case that in his writings Rabbi Kook speaks of vegetarianism as an ideal and points to the fact that Adam did not partake of the flesh of animals. In context, however, Rabbi Kook makes those comments in his portrayal of the eschatological era.[6] He regards man's moral state in that period as being akin to that of Adam before his sin and does indeed view renunciation of enjoyment

of animal flesh as part of the heightened moral awareness which will be manifest at that time.[7] But Rabbi Kook is emphatic, nay, vehement, in admonish-
ing that vegetarianism dare not be adopted as a norm of human conduct prior
to the advent of the eschatological era. Rabbi Kook advances what are, in effect, four distinct arguments in renunciation of vegetarianism as a goal toward
which contemporary man ought to aspire:

(i) Addressing himself to members of the vegetarian movement, Rabbi
Kook remarks almost facetiously that one might surmise that all problems of
human welfare have been resolved and the sole remaining area of concern is
animal welfare. In effect, his argument is that there ought to be a proper or-
dering of priorities. Rabbi Kook is quite explicit in stating that enmity between
nations and racial discrimination should be of greater moral concern to
mankind than the well-being of animals and that only when such matters have
been rectified should attention be turned to questions of animal welfare.[8]

(ii) Given the present nature of the human condition, maintains Rabbi
Kook, it is impossible for man to sublimate his desire for meat. The inevitable
result of promoting vegetarianism as a normative standard of human conduct,
argues Rabbi Kook, will be that man will violate this norm in seeking self-
gratification. Once taking the life of animals is regarded as being equal in ab-
horrence to taking the life of man, it will transpire, contends Rabbi Kook, that
in his pursuit of meat, man will regard cannibalism as no more heinous than
the consumption of the flesh of animals.[9] The result will be, not enhanced respect for the life of animals, but rather debasement of human life."[10]

(iii) Man was granted dominion over animals, including the right to take
their lives for man's own benefit, in order to impress upon him his spiritual
superiority and heightened moral obligations. Were man to accord animals
the same rights he accords fellow human beings, he would rapidly degenerate to the level of animals in assuming that he is bound by standards of
morality no different from those espoused by brute animals.[11]

(iv) In an insightful psychological observation, Rabbi Kook remarks that
even individuals who are morally degenerate seek to channel their natural
moral instincts in some direction. Frequently, they seek to give expression to
moral drives by becoming particularly scrupulous with regard to some specific aspect of moral behavior. With almost prescient knowledge of future
events, Rabbi Kook argues that, were vegetarianism to become the norm,
people might become quite callous with regard to human welfare and
human life and express their instinctive moral feelings in an exaggerated
concern for animal welfare.[12] These comments summon to mind the specta-
cle of Germans watching with equanimity while their Jewish neighbors were
dispatched to crematoria and immediately thereafter turning their attention
to the welfare of the household pets that had been left behind.[13]

Despite the foregoing, vegetarianism is not rejected by Judaism as a valid
lifestyle for at least some individuals. There are, to be sure, individuals who
are repulsed by the prospect of consuming the flesh of a living creature. It is

not the case that an individual who declines to partake of meat is *ipso facto* guilty of a violation of the moral code. On the contrary, Scripture states, "and you will say: 'I will eat meat,' because your soul desires to eat meat; with all the desire of your soul may you eat meat" (Deut. 12:20). The implication is that meat may be consumed when there is desire and appetite for it as food, but may be eschewed when there is no desire and, *a fortiori,* when it is found to be repugnant.[14] The question is one of perspective. Concern arises only when such conduct is elevated to the level of a moral norm.

Ethicists who do not accept the notion of revelation are left with a problem with regard to the nature of ethical propositions. Ethical statements are clearly more than an expression of subjective likes or dislikes since man has no difficulty in distinguishing between the expression of a mere preference and the expression of what he regards as a moral norm. C. L. Stevenson drew the distinction in essentially the following manner: The statement "I like spinach" is a reflection of subjective feeling and nothing more. The proposition "X is good" resolves into two statements, viz., "I approve of X. You do so as well." The proposition "X is good" goes beyond the proposition "I like spinach" in that it is addressed to others and seeks to have them adopt the attitude of the speaker.[15] An individual's subjective repugnance at the prospect of consuming the flesh of an animal is an aesthetic response rather than a moral reaction. It becomes a moral position only when expressed in advocating the adoption of such norms of conduct by others as well. Jewish tradition does not command carnivorous behavior; it rejects the notion that, at least during the current historical epoch, renunciation of the eating of meat should be posited as a moral ideal for mankind. Thus although "moral vegetarianism" finds no support in Jewish ethics, "aesthetic vegetarianism" is not incompatible with Jewish teaching.[16]

MEAT ON *YOM TOV*

One halakhic consideration standing in the way of adherence to a strict vegetarian regimen is the obligation of *simchat Yom Tov,* i.e., rejoicing in the festivals. According to most authorities, throughout the period during which the Temple stood, there was an absolute obligation, at least on the part of males, to partake of the flesh of the festival offering. The Gemara, *Pesachim* 109a, records:

> R. Judah ben Beteira declared, "During the time that the Temple existed there was no 'rejoicing' other than with meat, as it is said, 'and you shall slaughter peace-offerings and you shall eat there; and you shall rejoice before the Lord your God' (Deut. 27:7)."

The juxtaposition in a single verse of the commandments concerning the peace offering and the obligation regarding rejoicing is regarded by the

Gemara as establishing the principle that the "rejoicing" in the festival that is explicitly commanded (Deut. 16:14) is that of partaking of the meat of the sacrifice.[17]

Subsequent to the destruction of the Temple and the consequent lapse of the sacrificial order, whether or not there exists an obligation to partake of ordinary meat on the festivals is a matter of some dispute. There would appear to be no basis for assuming that such an obligation exists, since the obligation posited by the Gemara explicitly specifies that meat of the festival offering must be used for this purpose. Indeed the statement of R. Judah ben Beteira concluded with the remark, "but now that the Temple does not exist there is no rejoicing other than with wine, as it is written 'And wine [that] gladdens the heart of man' (Ps. 104:15)." The ostensive implication of this statement is that, subsequent to the destruction of the Temple, the commandment concerning rejoicing on the festival is fulfilled only by drinking wine and not by eating meat. Similarly, the Gemara, *Pesachim* 71a, indicates that, even while the Temple stood, when the sacrificial animal could not be cooked, i.e., on the Sabbath, the obligation of rejoicing was satisfied by donning clean raiment and drinking "old wine" rather than by eating ordinary meat prepared in advance of the Sabbath. This is indeed the position of Ritva, *Kiddushin* 3b, and of *Teshuvot Rashbash*, no. 176, who maintain that there no longer exists an obligation to partake of meat on the festivals. Moreover, *Tosafot, Yoma* 3a, and Rabbenu Nissim, *Sukkah* 42b, citing the earlier-mentioned statement recorded in *Pesachim* 71a and the statement of the Gemara, *Chagigah* 8a, which speaks of "all forms of rejoicing," assert that, even during the Temple period, the eating of meat was not an absolute requirement. Rabbenu Nissim characterizes the requirement to eat the meat of the festival offering as a *mitzvah min ha-muvchar*, i.e., the optimal manner of fulfilling the obligation, but not an absolute requirement.

However, Rambam, *Sefer ha-Mitzvot, mizvot aseh*, no. 54, adopts an entirely different position: "Included in His statement 'and you shall rejoice in your festivals' (Deut. 16:14) is that which [the Sages] said to rejoice in them with [various] forms of rejoicing and [because] of this to eat meat, to drink wine, to don new clothes and to distribute fruits and sweets to children and women." Even more explicit is Rambam's statement in *Hilkhot Yom Tov* 6:18. After codifying the requirement of eating the meat of the festival-offering during the days of the Temple, Rambam turns to an explication of other ramifications of the commandment to rejoice in the festival: "How [is the commandment fulfilled]? Children are given parched corn, nuts and sweets; for women one buys beautiful clothes and ornaments in accordance with one's financial ability; and men eat meat and drink wine, for there is no rejoicing other than with meat and there is no rejoicing other than with wine." This view is also adopted by *Tur Shulchan Arukh, Orach Chayyim* 529.

Bet Yosef, Orach Chayyim 529, questions the requirement posited by Rambam and *Tur* regarding eating meat on the festival since the Gemara seems to indicate that, in our day, the commandment is satisfied by merely drinking wine.[18] The statement of *Chagigah* 8a, "'and you shall rejoice in your festivals' (Deut. 16:14): to include all forms of rejoicing," is apparently understood by Rambam as creating a normative obligation beyond that posited in *Pesachim* 109a with regard to partaking of the meat of the festival offering. Therefore, maintains Rambam, when meat of sacrificial animals is not available, ordinary meat must be eaten for purposes of fulfilling the commandment of rejoicing.[19] It is quite evident that the Sages maintained that the consumption of ordinary meat gives rise to joy since the Gemara, *Sanhedrin* 70a, declares that it is forbidden to eat meat or to drink wine on the day preceding the ninth of Ab.[20] This prohibition was later extended to prohibit the eating of meat beginning with the first day of Ab. However, if all appropriate forms of rejoicing are mandatory, why does the Gemara, *Pesachim* 109a, speak of wine as obligatory only in our day, but not when the meat of the festival offerings was eaten? *Yam shel Shelomoh, Beitzah* 2:5, suggests that, when the Temple stood, rejoicing was possible without the inebriating effect of wine; only in exile is wine necessary to dispel melancholy and to generate joyousness in order to restore faith that God has not forsaken us. *Yam shel Shelomoh* fails to explain why *Pesachim* 71a speaks of an obligation with regard to drinking "old wine" prior to the destruction of the Temple.

Among latter-day authorities, *Magen Avraham, Orach Chayyim* 696:15, states that, subsequent to the destruction of the Temple, there is no obligation to eat meat on festivals. This statement is, however, contradicted by another comment of *Magen Avraham* himself. *Magen Avraham, Orach Chayyim* 249:6, cites a similar statement in the name of *Levush* declaring the eating of meat on the festivals not to be obligatory in our day and, pointing to *Sanhedrin* 70a, declares *Levush* to be in error. In yet another comment, *Magen Avraham, Orach Chayyim* 529:3, declares it to be a *"mitzvah"* to eat meat on *Yom Tov.*[21]

One ramification of the view that the eating of meat on the festivals is an absolute requirement is found in *Teshuvot Chavot Ya'ir*, no. 178. The sole ritual slaughterer in a small village fell ill prior to Passover with the result that the townspeople were faced with the prospect of being without meat for the holiday. One of the members of the community was proficient in the laws of slaughtering but did not possess formal *kabbalah*, i.e., rabbinic license to serve as a ritual slaughterer. *Chavot Ya'ir* ruled that, were there no question with regard to the actual *kashrut* of the slaughtered animal, the requirement for *kabbalah* must be waived in order to make it possible to fulfill the commandment of rejoicing in the festival. R. Shalom Mordecai Schwadron, *Da'at Torah, Yoreh De'ah* 1:10, contested this ruling on the grounds that, according to many authorities, subsequent to the destruction of the Temple, the eating of meat on *Yom Tov* is not an absolute requirement. This latter view is also the position of *Shenei Luchot ha-Berit* 74b, cited by *Pitchei Teshuvah, Yoreh De'ah* 18:9.

Another matter that is directly contingent upon the resolution of this question is addressed by R. Moshe ha-Levi Steinberg, *Chukkat ha-Ger, Kuntres ha-Teshuvot*, no 1. The question concerns the conversion of a proselyte who is a vegetarian and hence will not assume the obligation of eating meat on *Yom Tov*. If such consumption of meat is an absolute obligation, the conversion is invalid. This conclusion follows from the principle formulated in *Bekhorot* 30b and the *Mekhilta, Parshat Kedoshim* 19:34, which provides that the candidate's failure to accept any provision of Jewish law invalidates a conversion.[22] If, on the other hand, the eating of meat on *Yom Tov* is not a normative requirement, the conversion is entirely valid.

Regardless of whether or not there exists a normative obligation to eat meat on *Yom Tov*, it is certain that the Sages encouraged and urged such practice. Even practices that are not mandated by the obligation concerning rejoicing nevertheless constitute a fulfillment of the commandment when they result in feelings of gladness and joy.[23] In forbidding the eating of meat on the day preceding the ninth of Av because consumption of meat gives rise to joy, the Gemara forbids only the eating of types of meat comparable to that of sacrificial animals. Thus, fowl and preserved meats are not included in this prohibition. It then follows that according to Rambam, who requires the eating of meat on *Yom Tov*, it is the meat of animals rather than of fowl which must be eaten. Nevertheless, the Gemara, *Beitzah* 10b, explains that doves slaughtered on *Yom Tov* must be designated for that purpose in advance, lest, if the doves have not been previously examined, they may be found on *Yom Tov* to be insufficiently fattened, with the result that a person relying upon them for the *Yom Tov* meal will be lacking in "the joy of the festival." Since, even according to Rambam, the obligatory commandment of rejoicing cannot be fulfilled by eating doves, it is clear that, even absent a normative obligation, the Sages sought to promote the eating of tasty meat on *Yom Tov* because the consumption of such food enhances the joyfulness and festivity of the day. Thus, even if there is no normative obligation to partake of meat on *Yom Tov*, abstaining from meat on *Yom Tov* because of considerations of vegetarianism would not have been looked upon with favor by the Sages.

NOTES

From J. David Bleich, *Contemporary Halakhic Problems, Volume III* (New York: Ktav Publishing House and Yeshiva University Press, 1989), 237–50b.

1. Abstinence from the flesh of animals is also the subject of scattered comments in kabbalistic writings. R. Moses Cordovero, *Shi'ur Komah* (Warsaw, 5643), 84b, advises that a person seeking spiritual perfection should "distance" himself from eating meat. Accepting the principle of transmigration of souls, R. Moses Cordovero expresses the concern that the soul of a wicked man may be present in a slaughtered animal and exert a deleterious influence over the person who consumes its flesh.

In a footnote appended to that text, the editor remarks that, according to this thesis, one who is imbued with the Divine Spirit, and hence is capable of determining that no such soul is incarnated in the animal he is about to eat, has no reason to refrain from eating meat.

A similar position is attributed to *Reishit Chokhmah* by *Sedei Chemed, Asifat Dinim, ma'arekhet akhilah,* sec. 1. *Reishit Chokhmah* 129b, is cited as stating that one should not eat the flesh of any living creature. The reference appears to be to the Amsterdam, 5668 edition *of Reishit Chokhmah.* However, an examination of 129b–130a of that edition reveals that, rather than advising total abstinence from the flesh of living creatures, *Reishit Chokhmah* offers counsel with regard to the time of day most suitable for partaking of meat.

Opposition to consumption of meat appears to be a narrowly held view even within the kabbalistic tradition. A number of kabbalistic sources indicate that, quite to the contrary, the doctrine of transmigration yields a positive view regarding the eating of meat. According to these sources, transmigrated souls present in the flesh of animals may secure their release only when the meat of the animal has been consumed by man. The *mitzvot* performed in preparation and partaking of the meat and the blessings pronounced upon its consumption serve to "perfect" the transmigrated soul so that it may be released to enjoy eternal reward. See, for example *Shevet Mussar,* ch. 36, and R. Zevi Elimelech of Dinov, *Bnei Yissaskhar, Ma'amarei ha-Shabbatot, ma'amar* 10, sec. 4, and *Sivan, ma'amar* 5, sec. 18. Righteous individuals who must undergo transmigration in expiation of minor infractions are incarnated in fish in order to spare them the pain of slaughter. Scripture speaks of fish as "gathered" rather than as slaughtered and similarly speaks of the righteous as being "gathered" to their forebears rather than as experiencing the throes of death. See also R. Moshe Teitelbaum, *Yismach Mosheh, Parshat Va-Yeira, s.v. va-yikach chemah ve-chalav.* R. Yechiel Michal ha-Levi Epstein, *Kitzur Shelah* (Jerusalem, 5720), 161, advises that particular effort be made to eat fish on *Shabbat* so that the souls of the righteous which may be incarnated in the fish be "perfected" through consumption of the fish by a righteous and observant Jew. R. Menachem Mendel Schneerson is quoted as having expressed opposition to vegetarians, at least tentatively, on kabbalistic grounds. He is reported to have voiced the concern that refraining from consumption of meat will prevent the "elevation of sparks," a goal that is central to the kabbalists' view of man's purpose in life. See the comments of R. Shear-Yashuv Cohen, published as the introduction to R. Menachem Slae, *Min ha-Chai* (Jerusalem, 5748).

2. This text has also been understood homiletically as underscoring the lesson that man was created to study Torah and that, should he fail to do so, he remains in a spiritual state analogous to that of lower animals. Since such a person has not developed his unique spiritual potential as a human being, he should not regard himself as endowed with superiority vis-à-vis members of the animal kingdom. See R. Isaac Arama, *Akeidat Yitzchak, Parshat Bashalach, sha'ar* 41, and R. Moses Feinstein, *Iggerot Mosheh, Choshen Mishpat* II, no. 47, sec. 1. Cf. Maharal of Prague, *Netivot Olam,* ch. 15. *Shevet Mussar,* ch. 36, adduces this text in support of his contention that only the pious are superior to animals and hence only the pious are entitled to partake of the flesh of animals.

3. See also R. Abraham I. Kook, *Iggerot Re'iyah* (Jerusalem, 5722), II, 230.

4. In contemporary times some advocates of animal rights have adopted precisely this position in arguing that all sentient creatures have equal moral standing.

According to this view, there is no moral difference between a man and a dog; hence the pain suffered by dogs must be weighed no differently from the pain suffered by humans. The most influential exposition of the moral equality of species is that of Peter Singer, *Animal Liberation* (New York, 1977).

5. See R. Ben-Zion Firrer, *Panim Chadashot ba-Torah* (Jerusalem, 5735), I, 45.

6. It should be noted that Rabbi Kook espouses the kabbalistic view that in the eschatological era the so-called lower animals will be endowed with intelligence similar to that of man in the present era. See R. Abraham I. Kook, *"Afikim ba-Negev," Ha-Peles* 3.12 (Elul 5663): 718.

7. Yet it must be noted that it is in that era that the Gemara, *Baba Batra* 75a, declares that God will prepare a feast for the righteous consisting of the flesh of the leviathan. Similarly, *Va-Yikra Rabbah* 13:3 speaks of a meal consisting of the meat of animals to be served to those who presently observe the restrictions concerning carrion and forms of prohibited meat.

8. See *Ha-Peles* 3.11 (Ab 5663): 658, excerpted in *"Chazon ha-Tzimchonut ve-ha-Shalom," Mishnat ha-Rav*, ed. Abraham Rieger and Yochanan Fried (Jerusalem, 5721), 211–12.

9. A recent writer presents a strikingly similar argument in decrying attempts to ban animal experimentation. He argues that prohibiting the use of live animals in biomedical research may well result in replacement of animal subjects with humans. See Carl Cohen, "The Case for the Use of Animals in Biomedical Research," *The New England Journal of Medicine* 315.14 (October 2, 1986): 868.

10. See *Ha-Peles*, 658; *Mishnat ha-Rav*, 212.

11. See *Ha-Peles*, 659; *Mishnat ha-Rav*, 214–16.

12. See *Ha-Peles*, 659–60; *Mishnat ha-Rav*, 217.

A related, but different, concept is the Freudian notion of reaction formation; i.e., when faced with an unacceptable impulse, the ego may try to sidetrack the offensive impulse by transforming its conscious representation into its opposite. Thus an unconscious aggressive or destructive instinct may be masked and hidden from awareness by manifestations of excessive felicity. In terms of this theory, the concern with regard to the development of character traits based upon reaction formation is that a breakthrough of the original impulse is a continuous danger. See Sigmund Freud, "Notes upon a Case of Obsessional Neurosis," trans. A. Strachey and J. Strachey, in *The Standard Edition of The Complete Psychological Works of Sigmund Freud*, Vol. X, ed. J. Strachey (London, 1955), 249; "Psychoanalytic Notes upon an Autobiographical Account of a Case of Paranoia (Dementia Paranoides)," trans. Strachey and Strachey, in Vol. XII (London, 1958), 3–82; and "Inhibition, Symptoms and Anxiety," trans. Strachey and Strachey, in Vol. XX (London, 1959), 75–174.

13. Note should also be taken of Hitler's proclaimed abstinence from meat as well as from coffee, alcohol, and sexual activity. In the words of one author, "Hitler thus proved his moral right to free the Germans from their post-war masochism and to convince them that they, in turn, have a right to hate, to torture, to kill." See Erik Erikson, *Childhood and Society* (New York, 1963), 342. However, reports of Hitler's alleged vegetarianism are contradicted by a number of other sources. Perhaps the most significant of these is Robert Payne, *The Life and Death of Adolf Hitler* (London, 1973), 346, who relates that Hitler particularly enjoyed Bavarian sausages. Other biographers note that ham, liver, and game were included in his diet. See John Toland,

Adolf Hitler (New York, 1976), 30, 54, 107 and 256; and Albert Speer, *Inside the Third Reich* (New York, 1981), 89.

14. See *Ha-Peles*, 657; *Mishnat ha-Rav*, 209.

15. See Charles L. Stevenson, *Ethics and Language* (New Haven, 1944), 20–26.

16. By the same token, adoption of a vegetarian lifestyle because of a sincere conviction that consumption of meat is deleterious to health is not incompatible with Jewish teaching.

In a similar manner, some scholars advocate abstemiousness or complete abjuration of meat and wine, health permitting, as a form of self-mortification for the purpose of expiation of sin. See *Sedei Chemed, Asifat Dinim, ma'arekhet akhilah*, sec. 1.

17. According to most authorities, the parallel obligation on *Shabbat* is *oneg* or "delight" and does not mandate the eating of meat as an absolute obligation. See sources cited by R. Shalom Mordecai Schwadron, *Da'at Torah, Yoreh De'ah* 1:10, and *Sedei Chemed, Asifat Dinim, ma'arekhet dinim*, sec. 1.

18. Cf., R. Moshe Sternbuch, *Mo'adim u-Zemanim*, I, no. 29, and VII, no. 111, notes 1, 2.

19. Cf., also, *Bach, Orach Chayyim* 529.

20. It is certainly arguable that, even according to Rambam, a man who genuinely finds meat repulsive is not required to eat meat on *Yom Tov*. The obligation to eat meat subsequent to the destruction of the Temple is based upon the derivation "to include all forms of rejoicing" formulated in *Chagigah* 8a. The specific forms of rejoicing are not uniform to all people as evidenced by the fact that women are not obligated to eat meat but to rejoice with new clothes and jewelry. This halakhic provision reflects the judgment of the Sages that women do not derive the same pleasure from eating meat as is experienced by men. A male who does not derive pleasure from eating meat, arguably, must seek other forms of rejoicing. Cf. R. Moshe ha-Levi Steinberg, *Chukkat ha-Ger* (Jerusalem, 5741), *Kuntres ha-Teshuvot*, no. 1.

21. One latter-day authority, R. Shlomoh Haas, *Kerem Shlomoh, Yoreh De'ah* 1:1, declares the obligation to eat meat on *Yom Tov* to be rabbinic in nature. A contradictory statement attributed to that author by some contemporary writers is patently incorrect. See Richard Schwartz, *Judaism and Vegetarianism* (Pompano Beach, Fla., 1982), 148, n. 3. This source is, in turn, cited by Elijah Judah Schochet, *Animal Life in Jewish Tradition* (New York, 1984), 342, n. 12. The similarly cited *Yakhel Shlomoh, Orach Chayyim* 59:2, attributed to R. Shlomoh Haas appears to be a non-existent work. The reference is presumably to *Kerem Shlomoh, Orach Chayyim* 529:2, which speaks only of "other forms of rejoicing" in lieu of partaking of the meat of sacrificial animals.

22. Even were such conversions valid, assistance in such a conversion may yet involve a transgression of *lifnei iver*. R. Shlomoh Zalman Auerbach, *Minchat Shlomoh*, no. 35, sec. 3, questions the validity of conversions in which it is known that the proselyte does not intend to observe the commandments of the Torah and adds that were such conversions to be regarded as valid, "all who assist" in such procedures would be guilty of "placing a stumbling block before the blind" since, were the proselyte not to have become a Jew, such actions would be entirely permissible.

23. Cf. *Sha'agat Aryeh*, no. 65.

24

Sanctified Eating

Leon R. Kass

The upright being may stand tall above the animals, but he remains dwarfed by the larger whole of which he is a part, albeit special part. As he gazes, thanks to upright posture, on the distant horizon and on the lofty heavens, as he comes to know the many-splendored forms that share with him the earth and help him to survive, and as he comes to reflect on both his neediness and his capacities, he is moved to recognize his dependence on powers and possibilities not of his own making. He is moved by awe, fear, wonder, and gratitude to try to understand his place and meaning in the larger whole. He is moved to discover just how it stands between human beings and the divine. Such concerns and outlooks, too, are incorporated into the customs of eating, in innumerable religious practices and mores throughout the world. Thus the meaning of eating not only reflects human self-understanding, it also embodies the intimations we have regarding our relation to divinity.

I make no attempt here to survey past or present religious practices regarding eating or to attempt, empirically, to gather up their common and divergent strands. Rather, I propose to consider as illustrative a particular set of religious dietary laws that show how the activity of eating can be not only ennobled but even sanctified. For if the argument of this book is sound, one would expect to find exemplary culminating customs regarding eating that manifest a more or less true understanding of the world, including the place of man within the whole. Such an understanding, I submit, is embodied in the dietary laws of the Israelites, first established in biblical times and still practiced by religiously observant Jews down to the present day.

The laws of interest are enunciated primarily in the eleventh chapter of the Book of Leviticus, which sums up its contents as follows: "This is the Law (*torah*) of the beast and of the fowl and of every living creature that moves in the waters and of every creature that swarms upon the earth; to make a difference (*lehavdil*) between the unclean and the clean, and between the living thing that may be eaten and the living thing that may not be eaten." (vv. 46–47) Distinctions elaborated in this chapter define the central dietary laws of the Children of Israel, just as these dietary laws are themselves central to defining Israel as a separate people. But they intend not just a separate people but a *holy* people. God concludes his speech to Moses and Aaron, detailing these laws about eating (and touching),[1] by connecting their observance with holiness. For the first time in the entire Torah, God enjoins the pursuit of holiness in imitation of His own holiness: The exhortation, "Be ye holy, for I am holy," occurs *twice* at the end of the eleventh chapter (vv. 44–45), and offers the apparent purpose for the preceding dietary laws.

Why *these* dietary laws? What have they to do with holiness? These are questions I consider in this chapter. They are not new questions—they have been raised, by friend and foe alike, for centuries[2]—and the many answers that have been proposed indicate how unlikely we are either to say anything new or to say anything definitively true. Moreover, from the point of view of the tradition whose laws these are, it is a questionable practice to raise questions about the why of the dietary laws. The first and also the last thing to be said about them is that they are laws, to be obeyed; that they are commanded by God is the sole and sufficient reason for obeying them. Like law in general, the dietary laws are to be kept, not interrogated. To inquire about the reason or meaning of law—any law—threatens to weaken its force, given that its binding power lies mainly in its *being* law, rather than in the reasonableness of its content—all the more so in this case, its being a divine commandment. True, if the content of the law, on examination, turns out also to seem reasonable or if it points clearly to the source or principle of law—in this case, to the holy—obedience will not become irksome or less acceptable for this discovery; on the contrary, it might even prove psychically helpful to obedience if the laws, once thought about, can be shown to be not utterly unintelligible and founded not only on the lawgiver's arbitrary will. True, Joshua was commanded to meditate on the Torah day and night (Joshua 1:8), admittedly as a preparation for obedience, but to meditate nonetheless, and the First Psalm calls blessed the man whose delight is in the law of the Lord and who mediates in it day and night. Still, one risks misunderstanding, not to mention disrespect, by treating the dietary laws as a subject of philosophical inquiry even when the approach is sympathetic.

Nevertheless, I am willing to run these risks, for two reasons. The lesser reason is for cultural self-understanding. Everyone acknowledges that the West is what it is largely because of biblical religion; Jerusalem is one of the sources of our civilization. A central document of Western civilization, the Torah, or Pentateuch, has at its center a set of dietary regulations. Though these now strike even many believers as quaint, and though the tradition (especially among Christians) now regards them as much less important than the so-called ethical teachings of the Bible (for example, the Decalogue), the Bible itself makes no such distinction. At the very least we risk ignorance of our own Judeo-Christian tradition if we do not try to understand even these seemingly irrational rules of eating and their place in the way of life set forth by the Bible. To gain such understanding, there is no alternative but to scrutinize the text. One must therefore put aside both one's fear that such scrutiny constitutes an act of impiety and one's suspicion that only the religiously observant have access to the text's meaning. There is even biblical warrant for this venture: According to Deuteronomy 4:6, the law is Israel's wisdom and understanding *in the eyes of the nations.* Thus, even though the law had to be revealed, once revealed anyone ought to be able to recognize it as wise.

The search for wisdom is, in fact, the second and more important reason, and clearly the one most pertinent to the present volume, which is one long philosophical (that is, wisdom-seeking) inquiry and argument about the nature and conduct of eating. Previous chapters have explored customs of eating in relation to notions of the just and the noble; the account would be incomplete without an exploration of customs of eating related to notions of the sacred and divine. In this way the end of the inquiry returns to the beginning, as custom returns to seek contact with that which lies beneath custom and beyond convention—the natural order, the cosmic whole. For, as this chapter will suggest, the Jewish dietary laws reflect—and mirror—a comprehensive anthropological and cosmological teaching, one that can still command assent. They embody and reflect a more-or-less true understanding, first, of the problematic character of eating, but, more significantly, of the nature of nature and of the place of man within the whole. They (a) implicitly pay homage to the articulated order of the world and the dignity of life and living form; (b) incorporate into the act of eating an acknowledgment of the problematic character of eating as a threat to order, life, and form; and (c) celebrate, in gratitude and reverence, the mysterious source of the articulated world and its generous hospitality in providing food, both for life and for thought. These remarkable customs not only restrain and thwart the bad, they also commemorate the true and beckon to the good. As I shall now try to show, the dietary laws of Leviticus commemorate the Creation and the Creator and beckon us toward holiness.

GENESIS I: THE CREATED ORDER

Perhaps the preferable way to proceed would be inductively—that is, to begin with the dietary laws themselves and to try to elicit from them certain intimations of the Creation. But in the interests of brevity I shall speak first and directly about the Creation itself. If the dietary laws are to remind us of the Creation, we need first to learn or remember some things about it so that we can then be reminded of them. By "the Creation" I mean the "world" as presented in the first chapter of Genesis; this account gives us a complete cosmology, a full articulation of all the parts of the whole and of their relation to one another.[3]

It seems reasonable to suggest that the two most important assertions or claims of the so-called first creation story are, first, that the heaven and earth and everything therein are creatures (that is, creations) and creations of God—that is, they are not themselves eternal or divine; the sun and the stars are not gods; second, that the whole as created was seen and proclaimed by its maker to be very good—and, it seems, also very good for man—man, who stands divinelike at the peak of the creatures, at home in the world, addressed and cared for by God, blessed with fruitfulness and dominion, and well provided with food.[4] There are, needless to say, deep mysteries in the account—most especially about the very beginning (the first two verses) and also about the meaning of "the image of God." But for the most part—and for my purposes this is most important—we are presented an articulation of the created world as we know it and as human beings have always known it, free of mythical beasts and imaginary generations of gods and goddesses. We are given, through a sequential unfolding, *our* world, hierarchically arranged, in an account that, carefully read, can be made to reveal also the rational principles embodied in the articulated world. God is mysterious, but not entirely so. Much in the text is accessible to human reason and, I think, still affirmable by human reason, even today.

Such a claim will, no doubt, surprise many a modern reader who thinks that modern science, especially in its discoveries of evolution or of multiple solar systems and in its current theories of the origin of the universe, has rendered simply "unbelievable" the entire account of Genesis 1. But if we take care to separate questions about either the origin and coming-into-being of the universe (cosmogony) or of the ultimate cause(s) or source(s) of this process from questions about the character or nature of that universe *once it is present* (cosmology), we can see that certain things long ago thought true about our world might remain true, even in the face of changing explanations of how they got to be that way. As we argued in Chapter 1, a science of how things work and of where they came from has only limited power (and, often, less interest) to understand *what* things are and how they might be relatively ranked, either in power or dignity. Or, to put it another way, scientific (or historical) evidence and argument can refute (or confirm) only that which is itself presented as science or history; and it is my contention that Genesis 1 is neither. Certainly the categories "science" and "history" (and also "religion," "politics," and "philosophy") are foreign to the text. Since we do not know from the text what kind of text we have, we have no better choice than to try to read it without categorical or disciplinary prejudice, and see if what it says is intelligible and reasonable.[5]

Let us first remember the order of creation (see table 1): day one, light and the separation of light and dark; day two, heaven, a dividing vault that

separates the waters above from the waters below, opening up room before heaven, beneath which life can move; day three, *first*, the gathering
of the waters to reveal the dry land—that is, the separation of earth and
seas; and *second*, the earth's putting forth of vegetation, after its kind. The
second three days bring creatures that all have locomotion, beginning
with the creation of the heavenly lights on day four; day five brings the
fish and fowl, each after their kind; day six, *first,* the land animals, after
their kind; *second*, man, created in the image of God. Table 24.1 shows at
a glance how the second three days closely parallel the first, bringing (respectively) motion, life, and the possibility of freedom and creativity to the
realm of light, to sea and sky, and finally to the earth (twice the focus of a
day that brought two creative acts). The creatures of the second three days
each depend upon and exploit the corresponding creatures of the first
three days, as, for example, the land animals and man depend upon the
earth and its fruitful vegetation.

Table 24.1   The "Creatures," Day by Day

1. Light	4. Lights (heavenly)
2. Heaven[a] (waters and sky)	5. Fish and fowl
3. a. Earth (dry land)	6. a. Land animals
b. including plants (makers of fruit)	b. including man[a]

[a]Not said to be "Good."

We must not forget that there is, either completing or transcending the creation a seventh day on which God desisted from creating. We also note that
three blessings were given: the fish and fowl for fecundity ("Be fruitful and
multiply"; 1:22); man for fecundity and rule over other living things ("Have
dominion"; 1:28); and the seventh day, not only blessed but separated, hallowed—that is, made holy (2:3).[6] Three blessings: for life, for rule, and for
holiness, or as we scholars might say, the natural, the political, the sacred—
an ascending order that, as we shall see, is imitated in the Torah's unfolding
account of human life.[7]

The main principles at work in the creation are *place, separation, motion,* and *life,* but especially *separation* and *motion;* places are necessary
regions for the placement of separated kinds, and backgrounds for the de-
tection of their motion, while life may be looked at—at least at a first
glance, which I must later correct—as a higher and more independent
kind of motion.[8] Further, if one then treats locomotion as a more advanced
kind of separation, in which a distinct being already separated from others also separates itself from place, we could say that *the* fundamental
principle through which the world is created is *separation.* Creation is the
bringing of order out of chaos largely through acts of separation, division,

distinction. This view is encouraged by the language of the text: the word "divide" or "separate" (*badal*) occurs explicitly five times in the first chapter, and the idea is implicitly present ten more times in the expression "after its kind," which implies the separation of plants and animals into distinct and separable kinds.[9]

We cannot here attempt a thorough line-by-line analysis of the chapter, but here is how Leo Strauss summarizes the sequence of creation in the first chapter, showing the principle of separation at work:

> From the principle of separation, light [which allows discernment and distinction]; via something which separates, heaven; to something which is separated, earth and sea; to things which are productive of separated things, trees, for example; then things which can separate themselves from their places, heavenly bodies; then things which can separate themselves from their courses, brutes; and finally a being which can separate itself from its way, the right way. . . . The clue to the first chapter seems to be the fact that the account of creation consists of two main parts [days 1–3, days 4–6]. This implies that the created world is conceived to be characterized by a fundamental dualism: things which are different from each other without having the capacity of local motion and things which in addition to being different from each other do have the capacity of local motion. This means the first chapter seems to be based on the assumption that the fundamental dualism is that of distinctness, otherness, as Plato would say, and of local motion. . . . The dualism chosen by the Bible, the dualism as distinguished from the dualism of male and female, is not sensual but intellectual, noetic, and this may help to explain the paradox that plants precede the sun.[10]

The creation of the world, in accordance with these intelligible principles, proceeds through acts of intelligible speech. Creation through speech fits creation by separation, for speech implies the making and recognition of distinctions. To name something is to see it distinctly, both as the same with itself and as other than everything else. To predicate or combine words in speech is to put together what mind has first seen as separate. Separation, otherness, distinction—or, if you prefer, the principle of contradiction, that A is other than not-A—is the very foundation of the possibility both of speech and of an articulated world. With this in mind, we look again at the order of creation, as it is called into being through acts of speech. I again quote Strauss (see figure 24.1):

> The first thing created is light, something which does not have a place. All later creatures have a place. The things which have a place either do not consist of heterogeneous parts—heaven, earth, seas; or they do consist of heterogeneous parts, namely, of species or individuals. Or as we might prefer to say, the things which have a place either do not have a definite place but rather fill a whole region, or [are] something to be filled—heaven, earth, seas; or else . . . they do not fill a whole region but [fill] a place within a region, within the sea, within heaven, on earth. The things which fill a place within a region either lack local motion—the plants; or

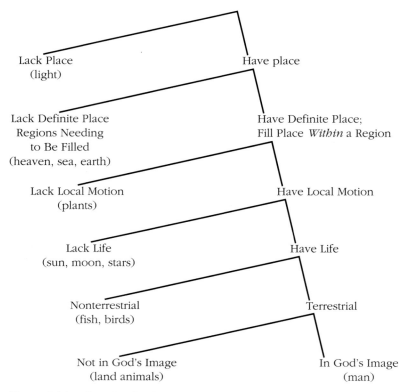

Figure 24.1   Creation by Division

they possess local motion. Those which possess local motion either lack life, the heavenly bodies; or they possess life. The living beings are either non-terrestrial, water animals and birds, or they are terrestrial. The terrestrial living beings are either not created in the image of God, brutes; or in the image of God—man. In brief, the first chapter of Genesis is based on a division by two, or what Plato calls *diaresis* (division by two).[11]

It has not escaped our notice that this account of the world, though presented in a religious text, is in substantial agreement with the world as we experience it and as we reflect on it. Our world is indeed an articulated world, with distinctly different kinds of beings occupying different kinds of places, and moving with varying degrees of freedom—some in fixed courses, some in fixed ways, and, with human beings, in ways partly of their own devising. A formed world is necessarily a world of distinction, a world of forms ordered along intelligible lines. In our world and in the world according to Genesis, the most interesting and lively forms are the various forms of animal life.

The work of creation is completed by living things, created on days five and six. Living things are higher than the heavenly bodies, by virtue of having greater freedom of motion, man most of all. They are characterized also (1) by having a *proper place*—in the waters, above the earth before the firmament, or on the earth; (2) by being *formed* according to their *kinds*; (3) by having *motion appropriate* to their *place* (freer on land); and (4) by reproducing themselves, according to their *kinds*. Unlike the heavenly lights, they also have (5) powers of awareness—especially hearing—which are implied in the receipt of God's blessing; they can recognize the distinctions that are manifest in the world, and ultimately, at least one of them—man—can understand those conveyed in speech. Finally they are characterized also (6) by neediness and vulnerability, which may be what makes them in need of God's blessing.[12]

Though brought into being in company with the land animals (both on the sixth day), man also stands clearly at the peak of the creatures. Blessed with dominion or rule over the other animals, man is the most godlike or godly of the animals: Man alone is said to be in the image of God. Understanding what this means is no small task, but it is probably safest to begin with the term *image* itself and to consider its meaning in the local context provided by the text.

The Hebrew word translated "image" is *tzelem,* from a root meaning "to cut off," "to chisel"; *tzelem,* something cut or chiseled out—in the first instance a statue—becomes, derivatively, any image or likeness or resemblance, something which both *is* and *is not* what it resembles. Although being merely a likeness, an image not only resembles but also points to, and is dependent for its very being on, that of which it is an image.

To see how man is godlike, we look at the text to see what God is like. In the course of recounting His creation, Genesis 1 introduces us to God's activities and powers: (1) God speaks, commands, names, blesses, and hallows; (2) God makes and makes freely; (3) God looks at and beholds the world; (4) God is concerned with the goodness of perfection of things; (5) God addresses solicitously other living-creatures. In short: God exercises speech and reason, freedom in doing and making, and the powers of contemplation, judgment, and care.

Doubters may wonder whether this is truly the case about God—after all, it is only on biblical authority that we regard God as possessing these powers and activities. But it is certain that we human beings have them, and that—as we argued on quite independent grounds in Chapter 2[13]—they lift us above the plane of a merely animal existence. Human beings, alone among the creatures, speak, plan, create, contemplate, and judge. Human beings, alone among the creatures, can articulate a future goal and use that articulation to guide them in bringing it into being by their own purposive conduct. Human beings, alone among the creatures, can think about the whole, marvel at its many splendored forms and articulated order, wonder about its beginning, and feel awe in beholding its grandeur and in pondering the mystery of its source.

These demonstrable truths do *not* rest on biblical authority. Rather, our reading of the text, addressable only to us, and our responses to it, possible only for us, provide all the proof we need to confirm the text's assertion of our special being. *Reading* Genesis 1 demonstrates the truth of its claims about the superior ontological standing of the human. This is not anthropocentric prejudice but cosmological truth. And nothing we shall ever learn about *how* we came to be this way will ever make it false.

But the text does not exaggerate our standing. Man may have powers that resemble divinity, but he is also at most merely an image; man, who, quite on his own, is prone to think of himself as a god on earth (*Omnivorosus erectus*, the potential tyrant) and to lord it over the animals, is reminded by the biblical text that he is, like the other creatures, not divine. He, like the animals, shares in the precariousness and neediness of life.

The vulnerability and neediness of life, not a prominent theme, is in fact not forgotten. The very last subject of the first chapter, before God's pronouncement that everything was very good, is the matter of food. After blessing man to be fruitful and multiply (as He also did the fish and fowl) and to have dominion over all life, God teaches man that dominion over the animals does not mean appropriation or exploitation, at least not as food:

> And God said: "Behold I have provided you with all seed-bearing plants which are on the face of all the earth, and every tree which has seed-bearing fruit; to you I have given it as food. And to every living being of the earth and to everything that creepeth upon the earth which has a living soul in it, I have given every green herb as food"; and it was so. (vv. 29–30)

The only instruction given to man, the ruler, created in the image of God, is about necessity, about food—his and that of his subjects. Though they are to eat different things—seeds and fruit for man; green herbs for all other animals (yes, including the lion and the tiger)—they are all to be what we call vegetarian. Keeping to this diet would disturb almost not at all the order of creation: Eating seeds and fruits does not harm the parent plants; eating fruit and discarding the seeds does not even interfere with the next generation. And the green herbs to be eaten by the animals are constantly produced by the earth, almost as a head produces hair. (The plants, from the Bible's point of view, are not alive: They lack sentience and motion—that is, liveliness; they more or less belong to the earth in which they are rooted and from which they originate. Indeed, in the "command" to the earth to produce vegetation, God uses the cognate accusative construction—"Let the earth grass grass"—as if grass were (to be) the surface display of the earth's native activity.)[14] The disruptions caused by meeting necessity through eating would, in the idealized case, be negligible.

We must, however, imagine that man and the animals as created *were capable* of eating meat. True, they were encouraged not to do so, especially as the fruits of the earth were said to be bountiful. But that they needed to be told what to eat is perhaps a sign that, left to their own devices, their appetites might have extended to incorporate one another. In this very subtle way the text hints that the harmonious and ordered whole contains within it a principle—life, or if you will, appetite, and eventually omnivorousness and freedom—that threatens its preservation as an ordered whole. Once again the biblical account speaks truly: Life is destabilizing and threatens itself; man does so in spades. Despite (because of?) being created in the image of God, man alone among the creatures—except for heaven—is not said to be good.[15] The sequel indicates that life's destructive power is not an idle concern, especially regarding man but even also with the animals. Perhaps this is even the reason that the animals are in need of a ruler.

BIBLICAL ANTHROPOLOGY: THE PROBLEM OF EATING

We leave behind the majestic first chapter, with its timeless presentation of the hierarchic order of creation, and move to the account of human life. In this account, beginning in the Garden of Eden, the problem of eating and its regulation—barely hinted at in Genesis 1—receives prominent attention. The Bible seems to agree with Aristotle that the *first* reason for dietary laws is the need to restrain, moderate, and define the naturally unrestrained, immoderate, and boundless appetites of human beings—appetites that are by no means restricted to the desires for food but for which the problem of eating is somehow emblematic. The need for dietary laws is, to begin with, identical to the need for law in general, and the acquisition of laws to regulate conduct is very often heralded by or presented in terms of regulations of eating. Indeed the Torah presents us with a series of stages in the development of the human race—leading up to the formation of the people of Israel—each of which is marked by a change in the diet, usually involving restriction. For example, at the beginning, in the bountiful Garden of Eden, the man was a fruit eater, allowed to eat of every tree of the garden save one. Though the tree of knowledge of good and bad is only metaphorically a tree—knowledge does not grow on trees—the image suggests an explicit connection between human autonomy and human omnivorousness, by representing the limit on the former in the form of a limit on the latter.

Though we learn from the sequel that he was even in his origins a being potentially possessed of reason, and hence of open appetite and choice, man was, to begin with, guided by nature, instinctively seeking only the things needful for life, which—his needs (food, water, and rest) being simple—nature adequately provided. A prescient and benevolent God, solicitous of the man's well-being sought to preserve him in this condition; He sought to keep him from trying to guide his life by his own lights, exercised on the things of his experience, from which he would form for himself autonomous—that is, self-prescribed, freely chosen—knowledge of good and bad, which is to say, knowledge of how to live. Or, to put the same point in terms of appetite, God sought to protect man from the expansion of his desires beyond the naturally necessary or from the replacement of desire given by nature with desires given by his own mind and imagination. These tempting but dangerous prospects—of autonomy, choice, independence, and the aspiration to full self-command, and of emancipated and open-ended desire—lay always at the center of human life; for to reason is to choose, and to choose for oneself (even to choose to obey) is not-to-obey, neither God nor instinct nor anything else. The rational animal is, in principle, the autonomous and hence disobedient animal.

When the voice of reason awoke, and simple obedience was questioned (and hence no longer possible), the desires of the man began to grow. Though he did not know what he meant exactly, he imagined that his eyes would be opened and he would be as a god—that is, self-sufficient, autonomous, independent, knowing, perhaps immortal, and free at last. Such did the serpent promise—the smooth voice that asked the world's first question and so disturbed its peace of mind forever: "Ye shall *not* surely die; for God doth know that in the day ye eat thereof, then your eyes shall be opened, and *ye shall be as gods* [or *God*] knowing good and bad" (3:5; italics added). The human imagination is liberated by the rational assertion of opposites, of negation, of the possibility of "not": Things may not be what they seem; even better, things need not be as they are. With alternatives now freely before her, the woman's desire grows on its own, partly enticed by the promise of god-like wisdom, mostly fueled by her newly empowered imagination.

The biblical narrator connects this imagining of godliness with new imaginings about the forbidden food: "And when the woman *saw* that the tree *was good for food,* and that it *was a delight to the eyes,* and that the tree *was to be desired to make one wise,* she took of the fruit thereof and did eat; and she gave also unto her husband with her, and he did eat" (3:6; italics added). The tree was looked upon with fresh eyes—perhaps, in fact, *really* looked at here for the very first time—under the sway of new desires tied to new imaginings.[16] We have here the momentous and transforming act of free choice, based on new judgment about what is good (and bad).[17] The result, as we know, is the beginning of concerned self-consciousness—shame and vanity, modesty and love, and all higher human aspirations: in short, the first stages of humanization.

The expulsion from the garden is coupled with a shift from fruit to bread,[18] *the* distinctly human food, and marks the next major step toward humanization through civilization. Men turn from gathering naturally available food (fruits) to toilsome cultivation of grain, itself in need of artful transformation before it becomes edible as bread. Cain, the first man born of woman and the first man who never knew the garden (that is, *the* human prototype), is a tiller of the ground and presumably, therefore, an eater of bread. He is also the founder of the first city (4:17) and his descendants are the originators of the arts (4:20–22). But civilization here proceeds in the absence of law. Men are left to their own devices and, beginning with the fratricide of Cain, the whole earth soon becomes corrupt and violent—including also the animals (6:12), by which we may understand that they have become carnivorous. By the tenth generation men are disordering and dissolving the created order, with no respect for life and limb. The return through the flood to the watery chaos of the beginning completes the dissolution into chaos that life itself has wrought.

The next and crucial stage, just after the flood, is marked by the first law for all mankind and the first covenant between God and man, through Noah. To use nonbiblical language, man here emerges from what Rousseau would later call the state of nature and becomes civilized or political, in "the moment when, right taking the place of violence, nature was subjected to law."[19] The first law of the first law sanctions for the first time man's eating of all animal flesh,[20] but, at the same time, prohibits the eating of blood, which is the life.

Why does this move to law come about? An answer is suggested by the episode that immediately precedes the covenant. Noah, immediately on leaving the ark, builds an altar and (presumably in an act of thanksgiving, but without command or instruction) sacrifices some of the animals God had him rescue from the antediluvian world of violence and bloodshed. God, in reaction to Noah's sacrifice, remarks, one imagines sadly, "The imagination of man's heart is evil from his youth" (8:21).[21] Even Noah, righteous and simple Noah, is not pure at heart and has a taste for blood. God decides against blotting out and starting over; it would not do any good to begin again. Instead God chooses the way of law. The covenant with Noah makes a concession to man's violence and carnivorousness,[22] but only by bringing it somewhat under law. In becoming a creature under law, quasi "political," man is decisively separated from his animal friends and relations, in the interests of elementary decency and justice in human life. For the Noachic law also for the first time prohibits murder and compels human beings to execute its punishment. We surmise that God was willing to tolerate meat-eating in the hope that man's ferocity would thereby be sated, that murder might become less likely if human bloodlust could be satisfied by meat.

We skip lightly over the transition to the next stage, in which man becomes fully political—that is, divided into *separate* nations. The Noachic covenant had separated mankind, homogeneously considered, from *all* other animals, homogeneously considered (as nonhuman),[23] but as yet there were no separate polities. Of the division of mankind (as with the Creation), two accounts are given, the second connected with the audacious project toward self-sufficiency that is the city and tower of Babel, the first connected with the descendants of the sons of Noah. Once again men show themselves prone to chaos and the effacing of distinctions: Noah, drunk on wine, lies prostrate and undignified in his tent; Ham ratifies his father's unfathering of himself by looking on him naked; and (in the other account) the builders of Babel defy God's order to disperse by seeking to close the gap between the human and the divine.[24] The remedy for these distinction-denying tendencies is, in both accounts, the emergence of distictions among nations: politics (and war) come into being, and presumably also distinct customs, including distinctive dietary practices.

Laws governing diet do more than restrain human omnivorousness and ferocity. Well before Leviticus, Genesis already hints that dietary laws are not merely ethical or, in the broad sense, political, designed to moderate human appetites so that men may live more justly with one another. It shows us that dietary laws are also meant to help distinguish one people from another. Peoples are distinguished from one another most decisively by what it is they look up to and revere—by their gods. And their view of the divine and their experience of the divine is often reflected or embedded in their customs and laws. As practiced, the laws bind a people to particular and distinctive way. But as objects also of reflection, they may serve as symbols and reminders—in the highest instance, of the divine and our relation to it. Genesis gives us a dietary model.

The specifically Jewish dietary laws are anticipated in the story of Jacob's wrestling with the mysterious being that later traditions call an angel (Genesis 32:25–33). As a result of this striving with God, Jacob acquires the name that becomes the name of his people, Israel, but he is also marked with a limp in his thigh. The narrator interrupts his story of the wrestling to announce the first specifically Jewish dietary law: "Therefore the children of Israel—[this, by the way, is the Torah's first mention of the name of the future people "children of Israel"; they get their name in the same verse that announces their first dietary law]—eat not the sinew of the thigh which is upon the hollow of the thigh, unto this day: because He touched the hollow of Jacob's thigh, even in the sinew of the thigh" (v. 33). The children of Israel *remember* by a dietary practice that ambiguous and mysterious encounter of their father Jacob with the divine. They are restrained in eating, as was Jacob by the limp; but they are touched in this denial with a memorial of a divine encounter. They remember, negatively, that Jacob was injured in the process of struggling against God; positively, that God was close enough to be encountered and struggled with.

The basic anthropological sequence, as taught in Genesis, is this:

1. A prehuman condition   Men eat fruit
   (Garden of Eden)

2. A prepolitical condition,   Men eat bread, but they
   before law   lapse naturally also into
   (Cain to the Flood)   eating meat

3. A political condition,
   (a) beginning with   (a) Men eat meat, but
   elementary justice   under law, respecting
   (Noah)   the blood as life

(b) continuing to the
formation of separate
peoples
(Descendants of
Noah; after Babel)

(b) (Presumably) Different
peoples have different
dietary practices,
based on differing
conventions

4. A more-than-political
condition, in which one
people is brought beyond
the just into some relation
with the holy, finally
to aspire to holiness itself

Further restrictions of
diet, connected with purity
and holiness, eventually
to be built on the
distinction between
clean and unclean

After this much-too-hasty review of the pre-Levitical dietary restrictions,[25] we are ready to approach Leviticus 11 and ask about the particular laws governing the eating of other living things. The thesis is that these particular and parochial laws build into the fabric of the daily life of the people of Israel a reminder of the nonparochial and universal beginning and source of all form and life.

THE DIETARY LAWS OF LEVITICUS: METAPHYSICAL SEASONING

Why *these* dietary laws? Many people now seek to explain or rationalize the dietary laws of Leviticus in terms of concrete practical benefits that observance would yield to the Israelites, say, for example, in improved health. But attempts to explain the laws in terms of hygiene and public health cannot be supported by the text. Only a benighted Enlightenment reason, which holds cleanliness to be more important than godliness, could confidently imagine God as the forerunner of Louis Pasteur, threatening to cut men off from their people in order to keep them from trichinosis. In fact the law does not say that the pig or the eagle is unclean simply; it says it is unclean *to you*—though we shall see in a moment in what sense the pig is in fact itself a defiler. Perhaps more plausible is the thesis that the laws intend to provide a discipline good for the soul, partly by the mere acts of self-denial, but mainly by the need to attend scrupulously to details of diet. But this explanation (or any other that alleges a different concrete benefit) cannot suffice, for it fails to account for the *particularities* of the prohibitions: Why rule out the camel, the lobster, or the raven? Why permit the locust but not the ant?

There is much to be said for the view (favored by Maimonides and others) that the laws are meant solely to separate the children of Israel from other peoples, most especially from the Egyptians behind and the Canaanites before, peoples whose practices (especially in sexual matters) and pagan beliefs are from God's point of view abominable: whatever the

Egyptians eat, let that be unclean to you—lest you stray easily into their ways. But left at this point, this explanation does not go far enough. For, as I have argued, the ways of the Egyptians and the Canaanites—indeed, the practices of any people—embody their beliefs about the world and especially about the divine, in this case a belief in nature gods. The avoidance of the abominable turns out to be the start of the turn toward holiness. The true concern of the dietary laws is holiness.[26]

The context in which the dietary laws of Leviticus are given demonstrates that the concern is with purity and sanctity. Most of the laws governing the moral or political relations between man and man had already been given in Exodus. These were followed by laws addressing the religious passions, laws for the building of the Tabernacle, and laws regarding sacrifices.[27] In fact, the immediate antecedent to the giving of the laws about the clean and unclean beasts is the problematic sacrifice of Nadab and Abihu, who "offered strange fire before the Lord, which He had not commanded them" (Leviticus 10:1), just as the immediate antecedent to the Noachic law was the problematic, uninstructed massive sacrifice of animals by Noah, immediately on taking them from the ark. It is in the sequel to this wild, "Dionysiac" episode that God makes known both the importance of and the connection between distinguishing the clean from the unclean and distinguishing the holy (*qodesh*, "apart as sacred or holy," possessing an original idea of *separation)* from the profane (*chol*, "common"; from a root meaning "to bore, to wound, to dissolve, to break"—in short, "to destroy wholeness and form").

God's first speech after this episode of the strange fire gives something of a dietary law to Aaron and the priests—no wine or strong drink before entering the sanctuary—and introduces us for the first time to the all-important and related distinctions, holy and common, unclean and clean, using the same verb, *lehavdil* (the root is *badal)*, "to separate or distinguish," that was so prominent in the first chapter of Genesis and *which has not been used in this way since*: "And that ye may make distinction between the holy and the common and between the unclean and the clean, and that ye may teach the children of Israel all the statutes which the Lord has spoken unto them by the hand of Moses" (Leviticus 10:10–11). This is the context for the laws of purity which follow.

Chapter 11 is, in fact, only the first of several chapters that articulate the distinction between the clean and the unclean, the holy and the common. Each deals with what might be described as "transgressions" of the natural boundaries between the human being and his surroundings: Chapter 11, food—that is, that which crosses the boundary coming from the outside in; Chapter 12, childbirth, and Chapter 15, bodily issues, things that cross the boundary going from the inside out, and, in the first and very special case, with the bodily separation of one life coming out from within another; in between, Chapters 13 and 14 deal with a disease that translators have called

leprosy (but that experts now believe to be a different disease, as yet uniden-
tified); as described in the text, it is a disease of the living boundary itself,
one that effaces the surfaces separating the inside from the outside and that
erodes and alters the human form. The laws that especially separate the Israelites from other nations, and that legislate the separation of clean and unclean, concern themselves with regulating "threats" to the embodiments of
the principle of separation. The principle for separating clean and unclean is
none other than separation itself. We cannot but think of the Creation.

The principles important to Genesis 1—place, form or kind, motion, and
life—are all at work in Leviticus 11.[28] The animals discussed are presented
according to their place: first the land animals (vv. 2–8; also vv. 41–45), then
those of the waters (vv. 9–12), finally the fliers, birds and insects (vv. 13–23).
To be clean, land animals must have completely cloven hoofs and must
chew the cud; animals that go upon the belly or upon all fours, that have
many feet, that swarm upon the earth, or that do not chew the cud are unclean. To be clean, water animals need fins and scales. Among the fliers, we
are given only a list of named unclean birds; but among the winged swarmers—that is, insects—those that leap on jointed legs are clean; those that,
though winged, walk on all fours are unclean. Though I cannot account for
all the details, I observe that the criteria used to identify the clean and the unclean refer to their form, their *means of motion*, and how they *sustain* life—
that is, what they eat to live—specifically, whether they eat other animals or
not. Ruled out are creatures that violate any of the principles of Creation:
place, form, motion, and especially the original dietary code, the one that
would least disturb the created order. Ruled out are:

1. Creatures that have no proper or unambiguous place; for example the
   amphibians.
2. Creatures that have no proper form, especially the watery ones,
   (a) by having *indefinite* form, with fluid shapes, lacking a firm bound-
       ary defined, say, by scales—that is, jellyfish or oysters;
   (b) by having *deceptive* form, like eels (fish that do not look like fish); or
   (c) by having *incomplete* form—like the incompletely cloven-footed
       animals.
3. Creatures that violate proper *locomotion*, such as those animals that
   live in the water but walk as on land (lobsters); those that live on land
   but swarm as in water ("all the swarmers that swarm on the earth"; in
   Genesis 1, the swarmers belonged in the waters); those insects that
   have wings for flying but that nevertheless go on all fours—that is, walk
   (the insect leapers, though they have legs, are treated as more akin to
   the true fliers, and are clean); also, those with too many legs (centipedes) or no legs at all (that go on their belly, for example, snakes,
   worms); and those that go on all fours—that is, on their paws (and thus
   use their hands as feet).

4. Creatures that violate the *original dietary code*, showing no respect for life—that is, the carnivorous ones; this consideration is especially evident (a) in the unclean birds, those we can identify being mainly birds of prey; and (b) in the requirement of chewing the cud, the mark of the ruminant animals that eat what God originally gave all animals to eat, the green herb of the earth.

Let us consider more closely a few of the particular requirements. The clean and unclean land animals are distinguished according to their feet (parting the hoof) and according to their diet (chewing the cud)—that is, according to motion and eating. The fish are distinguished by their form (fins and scales) and their mode of locomotion (fins);[29] the birds presumably by what they eat; the winged hoppers by how they move. *How* an animal *moves* reveals its relation to its *place* in the whole. *What* an animal *eats* reveals its relation to other parts of the whole, If they have fitting relations, they are clean.

Hoofed animals are grazing animals: Their feet are fit only for walking and moving, not for grabbing and clawing; they are footed to stand in the world (and generally poised well above the ground, more erect than the carnivores), not to tear at it. Cud chewers are so far from eating other animals that they finally chew and swallow only the homogenized stuff they have already once swallowed and raised: When the pig, a notorious omnivore, is declared unclean, the Torah says it is because "he does not chew the chew," using the cognate accusative construction (*vehu gerah lo yiggar;* 11:17), presenting by implication, as it were, the ideal of the perfect fit of activity and object. The pig is a would-be ruminant gone bad: One should chew not life but chew— that is, that which is fit for chewing. The chew chewers are poles apart from that first accursed and most unclean animal, the belly-crawling serpent, which is in fact a moving digestive tract and which "voraciously" swallows its prey whole and live.

By attending to these natural differences of animal form, the dietary laws of Leviticus refine and improve on Noachic law. At first, in the covenant with Noah, all animals were given to all men as food, as a concession, save only not the blood. Avoiding the eating of blood does indeed show some respect for the life that one is nevertheless violating. But the common principle of vitality—blood—itself ignores and homogenizes the distinctions among the *kinds* of animals. It shows respect for life but not for separate living form. Focusing only on blood ignores especially the distinction between those animals that do and those that do not honor in their eating the original separations of the world. The Levitical laws of purity reintroduce those early distinctions: The Children of Israel are not to incorporate animals that kill and incorporate other animals.[30] The restricted carnivorousness of Israel tacitly acknowledges the problem of carnivorousness. The Children of Israel are also not to incorporate or have contact with beings that do not honor in their motion the original separations of the world. These restrictions on their freedom, which rule out animals that take "illegitimate"—that is, order-destroying—liberties, tacitly acknowledge the problem of freedom. In all these ways the dietary laws build into daily life constant concrete and incarnate reminders of the created order and its principles and of the dangers that life—and especially man—pose to its preservation. In these restrictions on deformation and destruction, there is celebration of Creation—and of its mysterious source.

In a certain sense the dietary laws push the Children of Israel back in the direction of the "original" "vegetarianism" of the pristine and innocent Garden of Eden. Although not all flesh is forbidden, everything that is forbidden is flesh. Thus any strict vegetarian, one could say, never violates the Jewish dietary laws. Yet though he does not violate them, he could not be said to follow them. For only unknowingly does he not violate them, and, more to the point, he refrains *indiscriminately,* that is, without regard to the distinctions among the kinds of living things that might and might not be edible. In this sense the strict vegetarian, though he rejects the Noachic permission to eat meat, shares exactly the indiscriminate Noachic grouping-together of all the animals and its concentration only on the blood, which is the life.

But why, one might still ask, does not the Torah institute other dietary laws that push back all the way to vegetarianism, reversing altogether the Noachic permission to eat meat? Is not vegetarianism the biblical ideal if the restricted meat diet of Leviticus is really nothing more than a compromise, a recognition that it is too much to expect these stiff-necked human beings to go back to nuts and berries? Perhaps we were wrong to see the Noachic dispensation as merely concessive, a yielding to Noah's (and mankind's) prideful bloody-mindedness. Perhaps, looked at again, we can see here also something elevating. Noah, the incipiently civilized man, having spent time in close quarters with the animals, figured out as a result his human difference; he learned that he was more than just king of the animals. He learned that he was the ambiguous-because-godlike animal, both capable of and in need of self-restraint through the rule of law, and also open to the intelligible order of the multiform world. The result is the new world order after the flood: To mark his self-conscious separation from the animals, man undertakes to eat them; to acknowledge his own godlikeness, man accepts the prohibition of homicide (Genesis 9:3–4, 9:6). Eating meat may indeed be part and parcel—albeit a worrisome one—of our humanization. The recognized humanization of the human animal, it seems, can only be achieved at some cost to the harmony of the whole. This price is noted with regret, but it also must be paid. And it may be worth paying in order to keep the human being ever-mindful of the forms and distinctions that are the foundation of the world. It may be superhuman, and (as some will argue) more godlike, but it may also be less than human—and it surely is paradoxical—for human beings to renounce on the basis of reason their rational difference from the animals (to renounce also their participation in the transcendent

yearnings of Dionysus) and to affirm by an act of choice the pre-human, instinctive diet of fruit and seeds. The Levitical dietary laws fit the human animal in his distinctive uprightness: Celebrating the principle of rational separation, they celebrate not only man's share in rationality but also his
openness to the mystery of intelligible yet embodied form.

But there is more to the dietary laws than the celebration of rational order.
There is motion also toward the source of that order, toward that which is
highest over all. The Noachic covenant with all flesh had denied in a way the
dignity of flesh as variously formed and active, reserving it only for blood.
Whether as a concession to unavoidable necessity or as a mark of human superiority, the lower, flesh, was permitted, but the higher, life, was not. "Do
not eat the high," says the Noachic law on meat. The Levitical permissions
and prohibitions say the reverse: "Do not eat the detestable." Only the clean
is to be incorporated. The legal distinction between clean and unclean is
higher than the natural principle of living and nonliving, even as it incorporates and modifies it. There is elevation in these restrictions. The clean and
the holy, once far removed, are incorporated into daily life: Eating the clean,
under laws given by the Holy One, symbolizes the sanctification of eating.
We conclude with a brief look at sanctification.

SEPARATION AND HOLINESS

At the end of Leviticus 20, in an exhortation that concludes a long ten-
chapter section on personal, ritual, and moral purity God speaks together of
separation and holiness. He first calls on the Children of Israel to keep and
do the laws, in order to avoid becoming abominations to the land and ab-
horrent to God, like the Canaanites whom He is casting out before them.[31]
He concludes as follows:

> I am the Lord your God, who have *separated (hivdalti)* you from the peoples. You
> shall therefore *separate (vehivdaltem)* between the clean beasts and the unclean
> and between the unclean fowl and the clean; and you shall not make your souls
> detestable by beast or by fowl or by anything wherewith the ground teemeth,
> which I *separated (hivdalti)* for you to hold unclean. And you shall be *holy (qa-
> doshim)* unto Me; for I the Lord am *holy (qadosh),* and have *separated (va'avdil)*
> you from the peoples, that you should be Mine. (vv. 24–26; italics added; the verb
> *badal,* "to separate," the verb of the creation, occurs four times)

How does making and observing separations between the clean and the
unclean conduce to holiness? What does it mean, "Be ye holy, for I am holy"?
I do not know. But I offer one observation and two suggestions.

The dietary laws should remind us not only of the created *order* but of
the order as *created*, not only of the intelligible separations and forms but
of the mysterious source of form, separation, and intelligibility. The prac-

tice of the dietary laws reflects and achieves the separation of the people, around the rule of separation, to celebrate through obedience the holiness and separateness of the holy *source* of separation itself—and, by the way, also of the bounty of food.

And how might one become holier through observing these separations? Two suggestions. On the one hand, through obedience: One reduces the distance between the holy and the profane by sanctifying the latter through obedience to the former. The low is made high—or at least higher—through acknowledgment of its dependence on the high; the high is "brought down," "democratized," and given concrete expression in the forms that govern ordinary daily life. The humdrum of existence and the passage of time are sanctified when the hallowed separateness of the Seventh Day is brought into human life when it is commemorated as the Sabbath. Likewise the commonness of eating is sanctified through observance of divine commandments, whose main principles remind the mindful eaters of the supreme rule of the Holy One.

On the other hand, through imitation: God seems to say to the creature made in His image, "You should make distinctions because I make distinctions. Because I made the separations that created the world, because I also separated you from the peoples that know Me not that you should be Mine in holiness, so you must make and honor these separations in pursuit of holiness, of more perfect God-like-ness." This suggests that it is also in the fullest rational activity that man imitates and comes closer to God—but with these most important qualifications:

We can discern the distinctions in things, but *we* have not made them separate.

Neither have we made that power of mind that registers the articulations of the world and permits us to recognize distinctions.

The rational man is therefore only an image—and knows it. Brought by his mindful appreciation of forms before the mystery of form and mind, he must bow his head—as he alone can—to powers greater than human reason. The upright animal, his gaze uplifted and his heart filled with wonder and awe, in fact stands tallest when he freely bows his head.

In order that we not forget these qualifications, the dietary laws, like the Creation they memorialize and the world we inhabit, will never be wholly transparent to reason.

NOTES

From Leon R. Kass, *The Hungry Soul: Eating and the Perfecting of Our Nature* (New York: Free Press, 1994), 195–225.

1. This discussion will not treat the laws regarding touching. The text connects but also distinguishes between becoming defiled through contact with *unclean* (*tame*) things and becoming detestable through eating *detestable* (*sheqetz*) things.

The former pollution, harder to avoid but less serious, lasts only until the evening, whereas the duration of the latter, though not stated, is presumably permanent. The eater becomes akin to what he eats, because it comes to be part of him. The defilement of touching is more superficial; the boundary between the toucher and the outside is soiled but not penetrated. Though one can show in this way the resemblance between eating and touching—with eating producing, one might say, a "permanent contact"—it is possible that the prohibitions of certain touchings function (also? rather?) as a fence around the law regarding eating; what cannot even be touched is much less likely to get eaten. (See, in this connection, Genesis 3:3, where the woman enlarges the divine prohibition to include not *touching* the tree of knowledge of good and bad.

2. See, for example, Matthew 15:11: "Not that which goeth into the mouth defileth a man; but that which cometh out of the mouth, this defileth a man." See also Mark 7:18–20.

3. In offering comment on the beginning, I lean heavily on U. Cassuto, *A Commentary on the Book of Genesis* and especially on a remarkable essay, posthumously published, by Leo Strauss, "On the Interpretation of Genesis." See U. Cassuto, *A Commentary on the Book of Genesis* (Jerusalem: Magnes Press/Hebrew University, 1961). Also see Leo Strauss, "On the Interpretation of Genesis," in Strauss, *Jewish Philosophy and the Crisis of Modernity: Essays and Lectures in Modern Jewish Thought*, ed. Kenneth Hart Green (Albany: SUNY Press, 1997), 359–76.

4. The text tacitly implies that the evils in the world that afflict human beings are mainly of human origins—a thesis explicitly, even loudly, proclaimed by the Garden of Eden story related in Genesis 2–3.

5. For an extensive discussion of the ability of the biblical cosmology to withstand the challenge of modern science, see my essay, "Evolution and the Bible: Genesis 1 Revisited," *Commentary* (November, 1988), 29–39. This article offers a more complete exegesis of Genesis 1 than is possible here.

6. The blessing of the fish and fowl is directly quoted (v. 22); the blessings of the man and woman are not only directly quoted, but God's speech is explicitly said to be addressed to them (v. 28). In contrast, we have only the narrator's report of the blessing of the seventh day, not the actual words. The seventh day and its holiness are, to begin with, beyond the human realm altogether. A major concern of the subsequent biblical teaching is to bring the human into relation with the holy. This is accomplished, as I will argue, largely through the sanctification of everyday life, beginning with eating.

7. This ascending order is imitated also in the movement of this book—from nature, to human nature, to laws and customs (of justice and nobility), to holiness.

8. Actually the correction has already been given in Chapter 1, where we saw that life entails not only local motion but also self-forming and other-transforming motions (or activities), and (especially) desire and awareness. The heavenly movers lack appetite, awareness, and receptivity.

9. If one considers further that the separations actually made were all *makeable*, one might even come to think that the creatures—or at least the broadly possible *kinds* of creatures—were present *potentially* in the world, well before they were called forth into being (that is, "created"). With this addition, one begins to see how one might attempt a doctrine of *evolving* or unfolding creation or, in other words, how even certain evolutionary accounts of the emergence of living forms are compatible with the Bible's presentation of a graded and sequential unfolding of the cos-

mos through progressive acts of separating out implicit or latent possibilities. "Creation" and "evolution" might be perfectly compatible, at least in principle; everything depends on what is meant by each notion. Such speculations, however, are beside the present point, which is the primacy of separation in both the activity of creating and the "world" created: Creation is creation by separation.

10. Strauss, "On the Interpretation of Genesis," 366–67.

11. Strauss, "On the Interpretation of Genesis," 367.

12. This biblical account of living things squares perfectly with the account I have given in Chapter 1 (Kass, *The Hungry Soul*, 19–56). Notice the intimations of the three great powers—action, awareness, and appetite—based on neediness.

13. Kass, *The Hungry Soul*, 59–93.

14. Curiously the earth in "complying" is said to "put forth" grass, not to "grass" it. The desired harmony or unity of activity and product sought in speech was not attained (not possible?) in deed. This observation has led some to suggest that the earth was first in disobedience. (For these observations I am indebted to Robert Sacks's remarkable commentary on Genesis.) Robert Sacks, *Commentary on the Book of Genesis* (Lewiston, N.Y.: Edwin Mellen Press, 1991). This book was first published in serialized form in *Interpretation: A Journal of Political Philosophy*, beginning in May 1980 (vol. 8, no. 2/3) and ending in May-September 1984 (vol. 12, no. 2/3).

15. On what understanding of "good" might it be simply true that man, as created, cannot yet be said to be good?

"Good" as used throughout Genesis 1 cannot mean *morally* good; when "God saw the light that it was good," He could not have seen that the light was honest or just or law abiding. The meaning of "good" seems rather to embrace notions such as the following: (1) fit to the intention; (2) fit to itself and its work—that is, able to function for itself and in relation to the unfolding whole; and, especially, (3) complete, perfect, fully formed, clear and distinct and fully what it is. A being is good insofar as it is fully formed and fully fit to do its proper work.

As we showed in Chapter 2 (Kass, *The Hungry Soul*, 91–93), man as he comes into the world is not yet good. Precisely because he is the free being, he is also the incomplete or indeterminate being. More pointedly, precisely in the sense that man is in the image of God, man is not good—not determinate, finished, complete, or perfect. It remains to be seen whether man will *become* good, whether he will be able to complete himself (or to be completed).

Man's lack of obvious goodness, metaphysically identical with his freedom, is, of course, the basis of man's moral ambiguity. As the being with the greatest freedom of motion, able to change not only his path but also his way, man is capable of deviating widely from the way for which he is most suited or through which he—and the world around him—will most flourish. The rest of the biblical narrative elaborates man's moral ambiguity and God's efforts to address it, in the service of making man "good"—complete, whole, holy.

16. However mistaken the woman may have been in these imaginings about the tree, their announced sequence shows a progressive, ever-more-humanizing direction: first, "good for food," second, "delight to the eyes," third, desire for wisdom. First comes animal necessity; second, aesthetic pleasure; third, intellectual enlightenment and/or prudent insight and judgment. The hungry human soul, quite on its own, aspires to climb a ladder of human ascent, roughly similar to the one imitated in the structure of this book. (I owe this observation to Michael Fishbane.)

17. Compare the marvelous discussion of these biblical passages given by Kant in his "Conjectural Beginning of Human History":

> So long as inexperienced man obeyed this call of nature all was well with him. But soon reason began to stir. A sense different from that to which instinct was tied—the sense, say, of sight—presented other food than that normally consumed as similar to it; and reason, instituting a comparison, sought to enlarge its knowledge of foodstuffs beyond the bounds of instinctual knowledge (3:6). This experiment might, with good luck, have ended well, even though instinct did not advise it, so long as it was at least not contrary to instinct. But reason has this peculiarity that, sided by the imagination, it can create artificial desires which are not only unsupported by natural instinct but actually contrary to it. These desires, in the beginning called concupiscence, gradually generate a whole host of unnecessary and indeed unnatural inclinations called luxuriousness. The original occasion for deserting natural instinct may have been trifling. But this was man's first attempt to become conscious of his reason as a power which can extend itself beyond the limits to which all animals are confined. As such its effect was very important and indeed decisive for his future way of life. Thus the occasion may have been merely the external appearance of a fruit which tempted because of its similarity to tasty fruits of which man had already partaken. In addition there may have been the example of an animal which consumed it because, for it, it was naturally fit for consumption, while on the contrary being harmful for man, it was consequently resisted by man's instinct. Even so, this was a sufficient occasion for reason to do violence to the voice of nature (3:1) and its protest notwithstanding, to make the first attempt at a free choice; an attempt which, being the first, probably did not have the expected result. But however insignificant the damage done, it sufficed to open man's eyes (3:7). He discovered in himself a power of choosing for himself a way of life, of not being bound without alternative to a single way like the animals. Perhaps the discovery of this advantage created a moment of delight. But of necessity, anxiety and alarm as to how he was to deal with this newly discovered power quickly followed; for man was a being who did not yet know either the secret properties or the remote effects of anything. He stood, as it were, at the brink of an abyss. Until that moment instinct had directed him toward specific objects of desire. But from these there now opened up an infinity of such objects, and he did not yet know how to choose between them. On the other hand, it was impossible for him to return to the state of servitude (i.e., subjection to instinct) from the state of freedom, once he had tasted the latter. (Immanuel Kant, "Conjectural Beginning of Human History," trans. Emil Fackenheim, in *Kant on History*, ed. Lewis White Beck [Indianapolis: Bobbs-Merrill, 1963], 55–56.)

One further remark about eating and autonomy. To have reached for the tree already implied possession of the knowledge that, allegedly, was to be acquired only by eating, autonomous knowledge of good and bad; in fact, eating merely ratified (or symbolized) the autonomous (that is, nonobedient and, hence, disobedient) act of *choosing* to eat, which was based on the self-generated belief that the eating would be *good*. Only a being who already distinguishes good and bad and who has opinions about which is which can make such a choice.

18. Genesis 3:19 announces the shift prospectively. The first explicit mention of agriculture comes with Cain, after the expulsion from the garden.

19. Jean-Jacques Rousseau, "Discourse on the Origin and Foundations of Inequality Among Men," trans. Roger D. Masters and Judith R. Masters, in *The First and Second Discourses*, ed. Roger Masters (New York: St. Martin's Press, 1964), 102.

20. The institution of law, which permanently distinguishes man from all other animals, has as its first instance this permanent separation of man from all other animals—viz., the permission to eat (use) them. The Bible, despite its clear mis-

givings about this step (see below), hints in this way that meat eating (but with re-strictions: not raw) is, in some sense, *the* specifically human way of nourishing. To this extent, then, the Bible shares the view of Plato's *Republic* (discussed in Chap-ter 3 [Kass, *The Hungry Soul*, 120]) in which the full humanization of the city built in speech occurs with the eruption of the spirited element in the human soul, made evident when Glaucon faults the first or healthy (vegetarian) city, declaring it a "city of pigs," and insists on his desire for meat. As in the *Republic*, the bibli-cal account seeks to tame the spirited element and, as we shall see, leads the Is-raelites back toward a thoughtful or pious (a more-than-human?) vegetarianism, but meat would seem to be the food of man as man.

21. Noah's sacrifice is certainly ambiguous. The narrator's opening remark, "And the Lord smelled the sweet savour" (8:21), is generally taken to be evidence that God was pleased with the sacrifice. But in view of the negative judgment later in the same verse, one might interpret the beginning to mean that God discerned that the smell of roast meat was sweet *to Noah*. Noah, not having been told how to express thanksgiving, gave God a gift on the assumption that God would like what he, Noah, liked. To give of what one treasures most is praiseworthy; to kill the animals (his former roommates on the ark) and to relish their flesh is not. Nei-ther is the presumptuous assumption that "God likes what I like"—that is, that "I am like God." (I was first made aware of the ambiguity of Noah's sacrifice by Robert Sacks, St. John's College, Santa Fe, New Mexico. See his *Commentary on the Book of Genesis*, cited earlier in this chapter.)

22. That it is a concession to something fundamentally questionable is indicated by the fact that the eating of blood is prohibited. Bloodlust may have to be tolerated, but it is not simply approved.

23. This abstraction from the distinctions among the animals, i.e., from the princi-ple of "kinds" and "forms," reflects the form-homogenizing tendency of eating as such, qualified here only in excluding human beings from the realm of the edible (or killable and usable). Attention to distinctive forms returns with the dietary laws of Leviticus (see below).

24. Kass, "Seeing the Nakedness of His Father," *Commentary* (June, 1992): 41–47.

25. There are additional dietary regulations between Genesis and Leviticus 11. Some clearly serve as memorials of the deliverance from Egypt; that is, those institut-ing and governing the feast of unleavened bread (Exodus 21:14–20). Also in Exodus (23:19) is the prohibition against seething a kid in his mother's milk, the textual basis for the Jewish refusal to mix meat and dairy products in the same meal; explanations for this proscription vary but include the suggestion that the death-dealing activity of cooking ought not to be mixed with life-giving milk, or, similarly, that the cruel ne-cessity of eating meat not be compounded by the cruelty of slaughtering the animal in the presence of its mother or with the participation of her life-giving juices. In addi-tion, early in Leviticus (3:17, 7:22–27), a new prohibition against the eating of fat is added to the Noachic prohibition of blood. The reason for this prohibition is not given.

26. Accordingly, we expect that considerations having to do with holiness—with the being and ways of God—will help to explain the particularities and peculiarities of the dietary regulations.

27. The institution of animal sacrifice, not only divinely commanded but conducted in the holy sanctuary, raises a difficulty for part of the explanation I shall offer below for the designated "uncleanness" of some animals, namely, their carnivorousness. If

life is to be respected, why animal sacrifices, and on such a large scale? But what if the crucial fact about the law of sacrifices is not that God desires or enjoys sacrifice but that He restricts and regulates the ambiguous human impulse to sacrifice under the strictest laws and confines it to a single and special place? The passions for sacrificing have been present almost from the beginning, and the moral ambiguity of the practice—like that of eating—has been subtly indicated throughout, beginning with the sacrifices made by Cain (the initiator of sacrifices) and Noah. Because we simply assume that the human disposition to sacrifice is good, we fail to see its questionable character: Sacrificing rests on certain assumptions one has no right to make, at least not before the divine reveals itself and makes its wishes known. Uninstructed sacrifice is always a manifestation of pride in the guise of submission. To bring animal sacrifice uninstructed, one would presumptuously have to assume at least the following: (1) God would like to hear from me; (2) God is the kind of god that likes presents; (3) God; being an eating god, likes presents of food—just like me—and especially animal flesh: God is a carnivore. The biblical account does not support these assumptions, and there is no evidence that God *for His part* wants sacrifices. On the contrary, the one sacrifice He requests—Isaac, from Abraham—He makes clear He does not want; it is as if He were trying to purge Abraham of such bloody notions about the divine. What God wants, rather, is man's wholehearted devotion to uprightness and man's acknowledgment of his dependence on God.

When animal sacrifice is finally commanded, the context suggests the rationale. The laws regarding the Tabernacle and the institution of sacrifices were given in the immediate aftermath of two disquieting episodes, reported at the end of Exodus 24: (1) a rather wild animal sacrifice, initiated by Moses without God's instruction, with much strewing and sprinkling of blood; and (2) the encounter of the elders with the divine, which they experienced only sensually and in whose presence they did eat and drink. The impulses to animal sacrifice, the desire for sensual religious experience, and other enthusiasms and forms of zealousness cannot, it seems, be eliminated from the human soul; they can only be delimited, by bringing them under law. Indeed it is the giving of regulations for these ineradicable Dionysiac passions that the Torah presents to be coincident with Moses' forty days and forty nights on the mountain; these same passions erupted in Moses' absence, in the episode of the golden calf. Animal sacrifice, like meat eating, would seem to be a concession to human weakness or wildness.

28. The observations that follow agree largely with those of Mary Douglas and Jean Soler though they were arrived at independently and are made in a completely different spirit. These scholars are content to discover the patterns and logic of what Soler calls "the Hebrew mind." They do not consider the possibility that those patterns and that logic might reflect truly the intelligible patterns of the world, or that the insights of and about this people might have universal anthropological meaning. See Mary Douglas, "The Abominations of Leviticus," in Douglas, *Purity and Danger* (London: Routledge & Kegan Paul, 1966). Also see Jean Soler, "The Dietary Prohibitions of the Hebrews," *New York Review of Books* (June 14, 1979).

29. The omission of a dietary criterion for the water creatures may be related to a fact perhaps embarrassing to my suggestion that carnivorous animals are, ipso facto, not to be eaten: Fish eat other fish. Yet this may really pose no great difficulty. Many cultures do not regard fish as animals—some peoples of the Far East call fish "the *vegetable* of the sea"—and this judgment is somehow also reflected in the fact that

some vegetarians will eat fish. In the creation of fish in Genesis 1, God bade the waters "to swarm swarms," as if fish were a certain exuberant manifestation of the being of the seas themselves. Fish are certainly less separable from and independent of the waters than are the land animals regarding earth. The easier procedures of Koshering fish are another sign that they are not regarded as full-blooded animals.

30. The reader might wonder why, if my explanation is correct, the Israelites are not enjoined to eat only the defilers rather than the animals that are clean. After all, why should man's hunger be set against those creatures whose ways are least offensive, while the guilty are allowed to cavort, humanly unmolested? The following rejoinders can be offered. First, eating and being eaten are not punishment; therefore the clean animals are not being dealt with unjustly, nor are the carnivores getting away with murder. Second, and more important, eating is incorporation; one eats only those whose qualities one wants to share, but one rigorously abstains from those whose qualities one finds abominable. To incorporate a defiler is to defile oneself. This conclusion need not require a belief in the material transfer of psychic properties through ingestion; symbolically, one dirties and pollutes oneself by pursuing, by contact with, and especially by taking in the unclean. It is instructive to compare this logic focused on purity with that of the utilitarian Benjamin Franklin, who asserts that he gave up vegetarianism when he remembered that fish eat other fish: "Then thought I; if you eat one another, I don't see why we mayn't eat you. So I din'd upon Cod very heartily and continu'd to eat with other People, returning only now and then occasionally to a vegetable Diet. So convenient a thing it is to be a reasonable Creature, since it enables one to find or make a Reason for every thing one has a mind to do." (See *The Autobiography of Benjamin Franklin*, ed. R. Jackson Wilson (New York: Modern Library, 1981), 41–42. See also R. Jackson Wilson's discussion of this episode, and of other passages about eating, in his Introduction, xix–xxvii.)

31. "Ye shall therefore keep all My statutes, and all Mine ordinances and do them, that the land whither I bring you therein, vomit you not out. And ye shall not walk in the customs of the nation, which I am casting out before you; for they did all these things, and therefore I abhorred them. But I have said unto you: 'Ye shall inherit their land, and I will give it to you to possess it, a land flowing with milk and honey" (20:22–24). Among the abominable practices that defile the land, emphasis is placed especially on those surrounding sexuality and generation—failure to observe the crucial distinctions between those with whom one may and those with whom one may not have sexual relations ("uncover nakedness"); failure to honor father and mother; giving one's seed to Molech. These practices specially make a people nauseating, even to the earth which "vomits" them out. To dwell in the land of milk and honey, both sexual and dietary uprightness are required. Leviticus 20 thus revisits and addresses the pre-Abrahamic (that is, uninstructed) excesses of the polymorphously perverse animal—regarding food, drink, and sex—that were presented in the story of Noah: Noah's unwelcome sacrifice of animals, his drunkenness, his son Ham's trafficking in the uncovered nakedness of his father, and Noah's curse on his son ("giving his seed to Molech"). See my essay "Seeing the Nakedness of His Father" (Kass, 41–47).

Bibliography

Baker, John Austin. "Biblical Attitudes to Nature." In *Man and Nature*, edited by Hugh Montefiore. London: Collins, 1975.

Barr, James. "Man and Nature: The Ecological Controversy in the Old Testament." *Bulletin of the John Rylands Library* 55 (1972): 9–32. Reprinted in *Ecology and Religion in History*, edited by David and Eileen Spring, New York: Harper & Row, 1974, 48–75.

Belkin, Samuel. "Man as Temporary Tenant." In *Judaism and Human Rights*, edited by Milton R. Konvitz. New York: Norton, 1972. Taken from Belkin, *In His Image*, New York: Abelard-Schuman, n.d.; also reprinted in *Judaism and Ecology: A Sourcebook of Readings*, edited by Marc Swetlitz, Wyncote, Pa.: Shomrei Adamah, 1986, 24–28.

Benstein, Jeremy. "At Home: The Importance of 'A Sense of Place.'" *Judaism Today* 7 (spring 1997): 16–19.

Bernstein, Ellen, and Dan Fink. *Let the Earth Teach You Torah*. Wyncote, Pa.: Shomrei Adamah, 1992.

Berry, Wendell. "The Gift of the Good Land." *Sierra* 64, no. 6 (November–December 1979): 20–26.

Carmell, Aryeh. "Judaism and the Quality of the Environment." In *Challenge: Torah Views on Science and its Problems*, edited by Aryeh Carmell and Cyril Domb. New York: Feldheim, 1976. Reprinted in *Judaism and Ecology: A Sourcebook of Readings*, edited by Marc Swetlitz, Wyncote, Pa.: Shomrei Adamah, 1986, 34–46.

Cohen, Jeremy. *"Be Fertile and Increase, Fill the Earth and Master It": The Ancient and Medieval Career of a Biblical Text*. Ithaca, N.Y.: Cornell University Press, 1989.

———. "The Bible, Man, and Nature in the History of Western Thought: A Call for Reassessent." *Journal of Religion* (1985): 155–82.

Cohen, Noah J. *Tza'ar Ba'aley Chayyim*. Washington, D.C.: Catholic University of America Press, 1959.

Dresner, Samuel, and Byron L. Sherwin. "To Take Care of God's World: Judaism and Ecology." In *Judaism: The Way of Sanctification*. New York: United Synagogue of America Press, 1978. Reprinted in *Judaism and Ecology: A Sourcebook of Readings*, edited by Marc Swetlitz, Wyncote, Pa.: Shomrei Adamah, 1986, 97–102.

410

Ehrenfeld, David. *The Arrogance of Humanism.* New York: Oxford University Press, 1981.

Eisenberg, Evan. *The Ecology of Eden.* New York: Random House, 1998.

Feliks, Yehuda. *Nature and Man in the Bible: Chapters in Biblical Ecology.* London: Soncino Press, 1981.

Fortin, Ernest L. "The Bible Made Me Do It: Christianity, Science, and the Environment." *Review of Politics* 57 (1995): 197–223. Reprinted in, *Human Rights, Virtue, and the Common Good: Untimely Meditations on Religion and Politics,* edited by J. Brian Benestad, Lanham, Md.: Rowman & Littlefield, 1996, 111–33.

Freudenstein, Eric. "Ecology and the Jewish Tradition." *Judaism* 19 (1970): 406–14. Reprinted, without complete footnotes, in *Judaism and Human Rights,* edited by Milton Konvitz, New York: Norton, 1972; reprinted in *Judaism and Ecology: A Sourcebook of Readings,* edited by Marc Swetlitz, Wyncote, Pa.: Shomrei Adamah, 1986, 29–33.

Freundel, Barry. "Judaism's Environmental Laws." In *Ecology and the Jewish Spirit: Where Nature and the Sacred Meet,* edited by Ellen Bernstein. Woodstock, Vt.: Jewish Lights, 1997.

Gendler, Everett. "On the Judaism of Nature." In *The New Jews,* edited by James A. Sleeper and Alan L. Mintz. New York: Random House, 1971. Reprinted in *Judaism and Ecology: A Sourcebook of Readings,* edited by Marc Swetlitz, Wyncote, Pa.: Shomrei Adamah, 1986, 53–58

———. "The Earth's Covenant." *Reconstructionist* (November-December, 1989). Restatement of "On the Judaism of Nature."

Gerstenfeld, Manfred. *Judaism, Environmentalism, and the Environment: Mapping and Analysis.* Jerusalem: Jerusalem Institute for Israel Studies/Rubin Mass, 1998.

Gordis, Robert. "Ecology and the Jewish Tradition." In *Judaic Ethics for a Lawless World.* New York: Jewish Theological Seminary of America Press, 1986. Reprinted in *Judaism and Ecology: A Sourcebook of Readings,* edited by Marc Swetlitz, Wyncote, Pa.: Shomei Adamah, 1986, 47–52.

———. "Ecology and the Judaic Tradition." In *Contemporary Jewish Ethics and Morality,* edited by Elliot Dorff and Louis Newman. New York: Oxford University Press, 1995.

———. "Job and Ecology (and the Significance of Job 40:15)." *Hebrew Annual Review* 9 (1985): 189–202.

———. "Judaism and the Spoliation of Nature." *Congress Bi-Weekly* (April 1971): 9–12.

Green, Arthur. "God, World, Person: A Jewish Theology of Creation." *Melton Journal* 24 (spring 1991): 4, 6–7; 25 (spring 1992): 4–5. Excerpted from Arthur Green, *Seek My Face, Speak My Name: A Contemporary Jewish Theology,* Northvale, N.J.: Jason Aronson.

Harris, Monford. "Ecology: A Covenental Approach." *CCAR Journal* 23 (1976): 101–108. Reprinted in *Judaism and Ecology: A Sourcebook of Readings,* edited by Marc Swetlitz, Wyncote, Pa.: Shomrei Adamah, 1986, 59–63.

Haruveini, Nogah. *Nature in Our Biblical Heritage.* Kiriat Ono, Israel: Neot Kedumim, 1980.

———. *Tree and Shrub in Our Biblical Heritage.* Kiriat Ono, Israel: Neot Kedumim, 1984.

Helfand, Jonathan. "Ecology and the Jewish Tradition: A Postscript." *Judaism* 20 (1971): 330–35.

———. "The Earth Is the Lord's: Judaism and the Environmental Crisis." In *Religion and the Environmental Crisis,* edited by Eugene C. Hargrove. Athens, Ga.: University of Georgia Press, 1986. Reprinted in *Judaism and Ecology: A Sourcebook of Readings,* edited by Marc Swetlitz, Wyncote, Pa.: Shomrei Adama, 1986, 16–23.

Heschel, Abraham Joshua. *The Sabbath.* New York: Farrar, Straus and Giroux, 1951.

Hillel, Dan. *Out of the Earth: Civilization and the Life of the Soil.* Berkeley: University of California Press, 1991.

Hirsch, Samson Raphael. "Do Not Destroy!" In *Judaism and Human Rights,* edited by Milton R. Konvitz. New York: Norton, 1972. Taken from Hirsch's Pentateauch Commentary, *ad* Deuteronomy 20: 19–20.

Hughes, J. Donald. "Ancient Israel and the Natural Environment." In *Ecology in Ancient Civilizations.* Albuquerque, N.M.: University of New Mexico Press, 1975.

Hüttermann, Aloys. *The Ecological Message of the Torah: Knowledge, Concepts, and Laws Which Made Survival in a Land of "Milk and Honey" Possible.* Atlanta: Scholars Press, 1999.

Isaac, Eric. "God's Acre." In *The Subversive Science: Essays Towards an Ecology of Man,* edited by P. Shepherd and D. McKinkley. New York: Houghton Mifflin, 1969.

———. *The Jewish Sourcebook on the Environment and Ecology.* Northvale, N.J.: Jason Aronson, 1998.

Jacobs, Louis. *What Does Judaism Say About . . . ?* Jerusalem: Keter, 1973.

Jonas, Hans. "Responsibility Today: The Ethics of an Endangered Future" and "The Concept of Responsibility: An Inquiry into the Foundations of an Ethics for Our Age." In *On Faith, Reason and Responsibility.* Claremont, Calif.: Institute for Antiquity and Christianity, 1981.

Judaism and Ecology. Edited by Aubrey Rose. London: Cassell, 1992.

Judaism and Ecology. Edited by Moshe Sokol. Cambridge, Mass.: Harvard University Center for the Study of World Religions, forthcoming.

Judaism and Ecology: A Sourcebook of Readings. Edited by Marc Swetlitz. Wyncote, Pa.: Shomrei Adamah, 1986.

Katz, Eric. "Are We the World's Keepers? Toward An Ecological Ethic for Our Home Planet." *Melton Journal* 24 (spring 1991): 3, 11–2.

———. "Judaism and the Ecological Crisis." In *Worldviews and Ecology,* edited by Mary Evelyn Tucker and John A. Grim. Lewisburg, Pa.: Bucknell University Press, 1993. Reprinted from *Bucknell Review* 37 (1993): 55–79; reprinted in *Nature as Subject,* edited by Eric Katz, Lanham, Md.: Rowman & Littlefield, 1997, 205–20.

Kaufman, Gordon. "A Problem for Theology: The Concept of Nature." *Harvard Theological Review* (1972): 337–66.

Lamm, Norman. "Ecology in Jewish Law and Theology." *Faith and Doubt.* New York: Ktav, 1971. Reprinted in *Judaism and Ecology: A Sourcebook of Readings,* edited by Marc Swetlitz, Wyncote, Pa.: Shomrei Adamah, 1986, 76–87.

Lasker, Arnold A., and Daniel J. Lasker. "The Jewish Prayer for Rain in Babylonia." *Journal for the Study of Judaism* (June 1984): 123-44.

Leibowitz, Nehama. *Studies in Beresit.* Jerusalem: World Zionist Organization, 1972.

Lerner, Michael. "The Ecological Religion." In *Jewish Renewal: A Path to Healing and Transformation.* New York: Grosset and Putnam, 1994.

Levi, Leo. "Torah and the Protection of the Environment." In *Torah and Science: Their Interplay in the World Scheme.* Jerusalem: Feldheim, 1983.

Levine, Aaron. "External Costs" and "External Benefits." In *Free Enterprise and Jewish Law*. New York: Ktav/Yeshiva University Press, 1980.

Kalechofsky, Roberta. *Vegetarian Judaism: A Guide for Everyone*. Marblehead, Mass.: Micah Publications, 1998.

Kay, Jeanne. "Human Dominion over Nature in the Hebrew Bible." *Annals of the Association of American Geographers* 79 (1989): 214–32.

Lichtenstein, Aharon. "Man and Nature: Social Aspects." In *Judaism in Our Modern Society* [Hebrew]. Jerusalem: Ministry of Education, The Branch for Religious Culture, 1971.

Loevenger, Neal Joseph. "(Mis)reading Genesis: A Response to Environmentalist Critiques of Judaism." In *Ecology and the Jewish Spirit: Where Nature and the Sacred Meet*, edited by Ellen Bernstein. Woodstock, Vt.: Jewish Lights, 1997.

Novak, David. "Nuclear War and the Prohibition of Wanton Destruction" and "Technology and Its Ultimate Threat." In *Jewish Social Ethics*. New York: Oxford University Press, 1992.

Pelcovitz, Ralph. "Ecology and Jewish Theology." *Jewish Life* 37 (1970): 23-32.

Pollard, Nigel. "The Israelites and their Environment." *The Ecologist* 14 (1984): 125–33.

Raboy, Victor. "Jewish Agricultural Law: Ethical First Principles and Environmental Justice." In *Ecology and the Jewish Spirit*, edited by Ellen Bernstein. Woodstock, Vt.: Jewish Lights, 1997.

Ravitzky, Aviezer. *The Shemittah Year: Collection of Sources and Articles*. Translated by Mordell Klein. Jerusalem: World Zionist Organization, 1979.

Schochet, Elijah Judah "Kinship and Compassion" and "The Delicate Tool." In *Animal Life in Jewish Tradition: Attitiudes and Relationships*. New York: Ktav, 1984. See also review by Robin Aronson, "Animal Life in the Light of Jewish and Christian Traditions," *Melton Journal* 24 (spring 1991): 8, 10.

Schorsch, Ismar. "Tending to Our Cosmic Oasis." *Melton Journal* (spring 1991).

Schwartz, H. Richard. "Ecology." In *Judaism and Global Survival*. New York: Vantage Press, 1984.

———. "*Tsa'ar Ba'aley Chayyim*—Judaism and Compassion for Animals." In *Judaism and Vegetarianism*. Smithtown, N.Y.: Exposition Press, 1982.

Schwartz, Joel. "The Rights of Nature and the Death of God." *The Public Interest* (fall, 1989): 3-14.

Schwarz, H. "The Eschatological Dimensions of Ecology." *Zygon* 9 (1974): 323-28.

Shapiro, David. "God, Man and Creation." *Tradition* 15 (1975): 25–47. Reprinted in *Judaism and Ecology: A Sourcebook of Readings,* edited by Marc Swetlitz, Wyncote, Pa.: Shomrei Adamah, 1986, 64–75.

Snoeyenbos, Milton H. "A Critique of Ehrenfeld's Views on Humanism and the Environment." *Environmental Ethics* 3 (1981): 231–35.

Solomon, Norman. "Judaism and Conservation." *Christian-Jewish Relations* 22.2 (1989): 7–25.

Tamari, Meir. "The Challenge of Wealth" and "Environmental Issues and the Public Good." In *With All Your Possessions: Jewish Ethics and Economic Life*. New York: Free Press, 1987.

The Land of Israel: Jewish Perspectives. Edited by Lawrence A. Hoffman. Notre Dame, Ind.: University of Notre Dame Press, 1986.

Torah of the Earth: Exploring 4,000 Years of Ecology in Jewish Thought. 2 vols. Edited by Arthur Waskow. Woodstock, Vt.: Jewish Lights, 2000.

Toynbee, Arnold. "The Religious Background of the Present Environmental Crisis." *International Journal of Environmental Studies* 3 (1972): 141–46. Reprinted in *Ecology and Religion in History*, edited by David and Eileen Spring, New York: Harper & Row, 1974, 137–49.

Trees, Earth, and Torah: A Tu B'Shvat Anthology. Edited by Ari Elon, Naomi Mara Hyman, and Arthur Waskow. Philadelphia: Jewish Publication Society of America, 1999.

Troster, Lawrence. "'In Your Goodness, You Renew Creation': The Creation Cycles of the Jewish Liturgy." In *Ecology and the Jewish Spirit: Where Nature and the Sacred Meet*, edited by Ellen Bernstein. Woodstock, Vt.: Jewish Lights, 1997.

———. "Journey to the Center of the Earth: *Birkat Ha-Mazon* and the Quest for Holiness." *Conservative Judaism* 47, no. 2 (winter 1995): 3-16.

———. "*Kedushah* as a Form of Environmental Awareness." *Proceedings of the Rabbinical Assembly* 54 (1992): 86–93.

Vorspan, Albert. "The Crisis of Ecology: Judaism and the Environment." In *Jewish Values and Social Crisis*. Rev. ed. New York: Union of American Hebrew Congregations, 1974. Reprinted in *Judaism and Ecology: A Sourcebook of Readings*, edited by Marc Swetlitz, Wyncote, Pa.: Shomrei Adamah, 1986, 103–108.

Waskow, Arthur. *Down-to-Earth Judaism*. New York: William Morrow, 1996.

Welbourne, F. B. "Man's Dominion." *Theology* 87 (1975): 561–68.

White, Lynn, Jr. "The Historical Roots of Our Ecological Crisis." *Science* 155 (March 10, 1967): 1203–207. Reprinted in *Machina ex Deo: Essays in the Dynamism of Western Culture*, edited by Lynn White, Cambridge, Mass.: MIT Press, 1968, ch. 5; also reprinted in *Ecology and Religion in History*, edited by David and Eileen Spring, New York: Harper & Row, 1974, 15–31.

———. "Continuing the Conversation." In *Western Man and Environmental Ethics: Attitudes Toward Nature and Technology*, edited by Ian Barbour. Reading, Mass.: Addison-Wesley, 1973.

Zohary, Michael. *Plants of the Bible*. Cambridge, Eng.: Cambridge University Press, 1982.

Index

Note: Entries for individual rabbinic authorities are, by and large, limited to those mentioned extensively or thematically in the text. The rest are included in the general entry: rabbinic authorities. Complete indices to the Bleich chapters may be found in his *Contemporary Halakhic Problems*, vol. 3 (New York: Ktav Publishing House and Yeshiva University Press, 1989), 391–415.

About the Contributors

The late Rev. E. L. Allen was head of the Department of Divinity at University of Newcastle, England. Among his books are *Kierkegaard: His Life and Thought; Christianity and Society: A Guide to the Thought of Reinhold Niebuhr; The Self and Its Hazards: A Guide to the Thought of Karl Jaspers; Christian Humanism: A Guide to the Thought of Jacques Maritain; Freedom in God: A Guide to the Thought of Nichaolas Berdyaev; Existentialism from Within; Christianity among the Religions;* and *From Plato to Nietzsche.*

Bradley Shavit Artson is dean of the Ziegler School of Rabbinic Studies at University of Judaism, Los Angeles. He is author of *It's a Mitzvah! Step by Step to Jewish Living.*

Jeremy Benstein is associate director of the Abraham Joshua Heschel Center for Environmental Learning and Leadership in Tel Aviv, Israel.

Philip J. Bentley is rabbi at Temple Sholom in Floral Park, New York.

J. David Bleich is a *Rosh Yeshiva* and the *Rosh Kollel Le-Hora'ah* at the Rabbi Isaac Elchanan Theological Seminary, professor of Law at the Benjamin N. Cordozo School of Law, and Herbert and Florence Tenzer Professor of Law and Ethics at Yeshiva University. He is author of *Contemporary Halakhic Problems* (five volumes); *Judaism and Healing; Providence in the Philosophy of Gersonides; Bircas ha-Chammah* (Hebrew); *Time of Death in Jewish Law; Bioethical Dilemmas: A Jewish Perspective;* and *Be-Nitivot ha-Halakhah* (Hebrew, three volumes). He is also editor of *With Perfect Faith* and coeditor of *Jewish Bioethics.*

Gerald Blidstein is professor of Jewish Thought at Ben Gurion University, Israel. He is author of *Honor Thy Father and Mother: Filial Responsibility in Jewish Law; Ekronot Mediniyim be-Mishnat ha-Rambam: Iyyunim be-Mishnato ha-Hilkhatit* (Hebrew); *"God Overturned the Mountain Like a Cask": A Homily and its Problematics; Ha-Tefilah be-Mishnato ha Hilkhit shel ha-Rambam* (Hebrew); and *In the Rabbis' Garden: Adam and Eve in the Midrash.*

Jeremy Cohen is professor of Jewish History at Tel Aviv University, Israel. He is author of *The Friars and the Jews: The Evolution of Medieval Anti-Judaism; "Be Fertile and Increase, Fill the Earth and Master it": The Ancient and Medieval Career of a Biblical Text;* and *Living Letters of the Law: Ideas of the Jew in Medieval Christianity.*

David Ehrenfeld is professor in the Department of Environmental Resources, Cook College, Rutgers University. He is author of *Biological Conservation; The Arrogance of Humanism; Beginning Again: People and Nature in the New Millennium;* and *Conserving Life on Earth.* He is also founding editor of the journal *Conservation Biology.*

Joan G. Ehrenfeld teaches in the Center for Coastal and Environmental Studies, Rutgers University.

The late Hans Jonas was the Alvin Johnson Professor of Philosophy at the New School for Social Research. His books include *Augustin und das paulinische Freiheitsproblem: Eine philosophische Studie zum pelagischen Streit; The Gnostic Religion: The Message of the Alien God and the Beginnings of Christianity; The Phenomenon of Life: Toward a Philosophical Biology; Philosophical Essays: From Ancient Creed to Technological Man;* and *The Imperative of Responsibility: In Search of an Ethics for the Technological Age.*

Leon R. Kass, M.D., is the Addie Clark Harding Professor in the Committee on Social Thought and the College of the University of Chicago. He is author of *Toward a More Natural Science: Biology and Human Affairs* and *The Hungry Soul: Eating and the Perfecting of Our Nature* and coauthor of *The Ethics of Human Cloning.*

Eric Katz is associate professor of Philosophy at New Jersey Institute of Technology. He is author of *Nature as Subject: Human Obligation and Natural Community* and coeditor of *Beneath the Surface: Critical Essays in the Philosophy of Deep Ecology* and *Environmental Pragmatism.*

Jeanne Kay Guelke is professor of Geography and former dean of the Faculty of Environmental Studies, University of Waterloo, Canada.

Aldo Leopold (1886–1948) was a member of the National Wildlife Federation's Conservation Hall of Fame. He was posthumously honored in 1978 with the John Burroughs Medal for his lifelong achievements in conservation, including authorship of *A Sand County Almanac*.

Ze'ev Levy is professor of Philosophy Emeritus at Haifa University, Israel. He is author of *Mevaser Eksistentsialism Yehudi: Mishnato shel Franz Rosenzweig ve-Yahasah le-Shitat Hegel* (Hebrew); *Between Yafeth and Shem: On the Relation between Jewish and General Philosophy; Baruch or Benedict: On Some Jewish Aspects of Spinoza's Philosophy; David Baumgardt and Ethical Hedonism;* and *Ha-Acher veha-Acharayut: Iyyunim be-Filosofyah shel Immanuel Kant* (Hebrew).

Eric Rosenblum is an environmental engineer in San Jose, California.

Robert D. Sacks is a tutor at St. John's College, Santa Fe, New Mexico. He is author of *A Commentary on the Book of Genesis*.

Arthur Schaffer is an environmental biologist living in Israel.

Eilon Schwartz is director of the Abraham Joshua Heschel Center for Environmental Learning and Leadership in Tel Aviv, Israel.

The late Steven S. Schwarzschild was professor of Philosophy at Washington University, St. Louis, Missouri. His books include *Franz Rosenzweig: Guide for Reversioners* and *The Pursuit of the Ideal: Jewish Writings of Steven Schwarzschild*.

Lawrence Troster is rabbi at Congregation Beth Israel, Bergenfield, New Jersey.

Michael Wyschogrod is professor of Philosophy at University of Houston. He is author of *Kierkegaard and Heidegger: The Ontology of Existence* and *The Body of Faith: Judaism as Corporeal Election*.

Martin D. Yaffe is professor of Philosophy and Religion Studies and a member of the Center for Environmental Philosophy at University of North Texas. He is author of *Shylock and the Jewish Question* and coauthor of *Thomas Aquinas: The Literal Exposition on Job, A Scriptural Commentary Concerning Providence*.